PRAISE FOR

ZINN & THE ART OF ROAD BIKE MAINTENANCE

"Lennard Zinn's book is packed with in-depth explanations and useful diagrams."

—*Velo* magazine

"Lennard Zinn is a veritable cycling Einstein, and as a naturally gifted teacher he has the unique ability to explain even the most difficult mechanical task. So unless you currently ride on a high-profile pro team with your own mechanic (and maybe even then), *Zinn & the Art of Road Bike Maintenance* is an absolute 'must-have' book."

—Davis Phinney, Olympic medalist, U.S. Pro champion, and Tour de France stage winner

"Lennard Zinn is an institution in the bicycle world—a legend. Legions of cyclists have learned to repair bikes from him, ridden bicycles he's built, or used his advice as guidance on how to better enjoy the world on two wheels."

—*Bicycle Times* magazine

"Zinn is very good at taking you incrementally through the learning process—whether you are a beginner or expert mechanic."

—*Out There Monthly* magazine

"*Zinn & the Art of Road Bike Maintenance* has instructions on anything an aspiring wrench would want to know. What impresses most is Lennard's overall approach of simplifying a task and reminding us how rewarding it is to perform our own service."

—PodiumCafe.com

"There really is no other bicycle repair manual like this. *Zinn & the Art of Road Bike Maintenance* is very up-to-date, very clear—thanks to the profuse illustrations—and accurate and comprehensive. . . . And it's all in a very enjoyable format intended to be encouraging and confidence-building."

—USCyclingReport.com

"Simple to read and follow, the illustrated, large-format paperback manual features everything from replacing a flat to repairing components. It's a great addition to any new biker's library but offers invaluable advice for experts, too."

—*Sports Guide* magazine

"If ever there was a classic text on bike maintenance, this has to be it. . . . Like its predecessors, it goes from super simple right through to complete re-builds. All are explained by a combination of Zinn's unique humour-filled, insightful and clear text, with Todd Telander's brilliant illustrations."

—220Triathlon.com

ZINN & THE ART OF
ROAD BIKE
MAINTENANCE

The World's Best-Selling Bicycle Repair and Maintenance Guide

ZINN & THE ART OF
ROAD BIKE
MAINTENANCE

The World's Best-Selling Bicycle Repair and Maintenance Guide

4TH
EDITION

LENNARD ZINN

Illustrated by Todd Telander and Mike Reisel

VELO press

BOULDER, COLORADO

Zinn & the Art of Road Bike Maintenance, 4th Edition
Text copyright © 2013 by Lennard Zinn
Illustrations copyright © 2013 by VeloPress

▼velopress®

3002 Sterling Circle, Suite 100
Boulder, Colorado 80301–2338 USA
(303) 440-0601; Fax (303) 444-6788; E-mail velopress@competitorgroup.com

Distributed in the United States and Canada by Ingram Publisher Services

Library of Congress Cataloging-in-Publication Data
Zinn, Lennard.
Zinn & the art of road bike maintenance / Lennard Zinn; illustrated by Todd Telander and Mike Reisel.
—Fourth edition.
          pages cm
Includes bibliographical references and index.
ISBN 978-1-934030-98-1 (pbk.: alk. paper)
1. Bicycles—Maintenance and repair. 2. Road bicycles—Maintenance and repair. I. Title. II. Title: Zinn and the art of road bike maintenance.
TL430.Z557 20113
629.28'772—dc23
                                        2012047821

For information on purchasing VeloPress books, please call (800) 811-4210, ext. 2138, or visit www.velopress.com.

Illustrations by Todd Telander and Mike Reisel
Cover and interior design by Erin Farrell/Factor E Creative
Cover photo by Brad Kaminski; bike built by Lennard Zinn
Title font Ciutadella; body text Deca Serif

This paper meets the requirements of ANSI/NISO Z39.48-1992 (Permanence of Paper).

14   15   /   10   9   8   7   6

CONTENTS

A TIP OF THE HELMET TO . . .

Mike Reisel. A picture is worth a thousand words, adding up to many thousands that Mike has added in this edition to the hundreds of thousands of illustrative "words" from Todd Telander's capable hand over the years. Mike's and Todd's drawings make my written words more intelligible and this book more useful and beautiful.

My everlasting appreciation goes to the late Bill Woodul for teaching me much of what I know about working on road bikes. I have also learned tricks from thousands of other people too numerous to count, every one of whom I greatly appreciate. I have incorporated suggestions from Scott Adlfinger, Paul Ahart, Sheldon Brown, Peter Chisholm, Saul Danoff, Skip Howat, Paul Kantor, Calvin Jones, Dan Large, Paul Morningstar, Tom Ritchcy, Dag Selander, Wayne Stelina, Stu Thorne, and many others, including innumerable readers of my Q&A column on velonews.com who have written to me with great tips. Thanks!

Many thanks to Ted Costantino for his gentle nudging of me toward completion and his fine editing, to Kara Mannix for her editing as well and for keeping this book moving smoothly through the editorial process, and to Charles Pelkey for his editing contributions and content suggestions. My appreciation to Dave Trendler and Renee Jardine for keeping the fires burning under this book and for their contributions to making VeloPress such a fine organization to work for.

And thanks to Felix Magowan and John Wilcockson for creating VeloPress in the first place, and to Competitor Group for keeping it going.

And, last, thanks to my family for providing endless support and a nice environment at home for me to work in, as well as the freedom to work away from it.

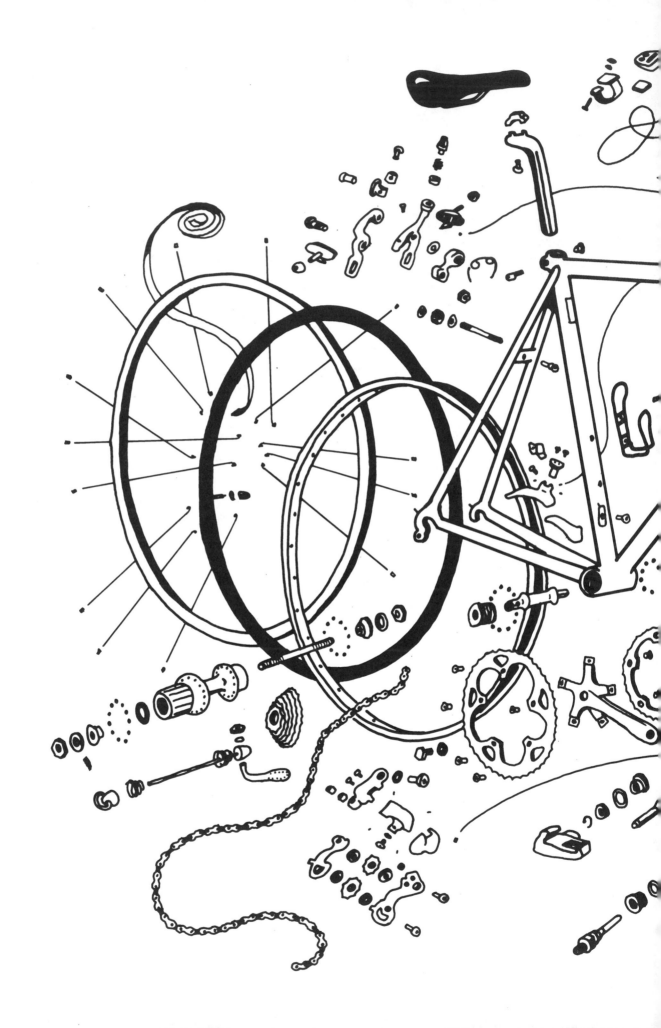

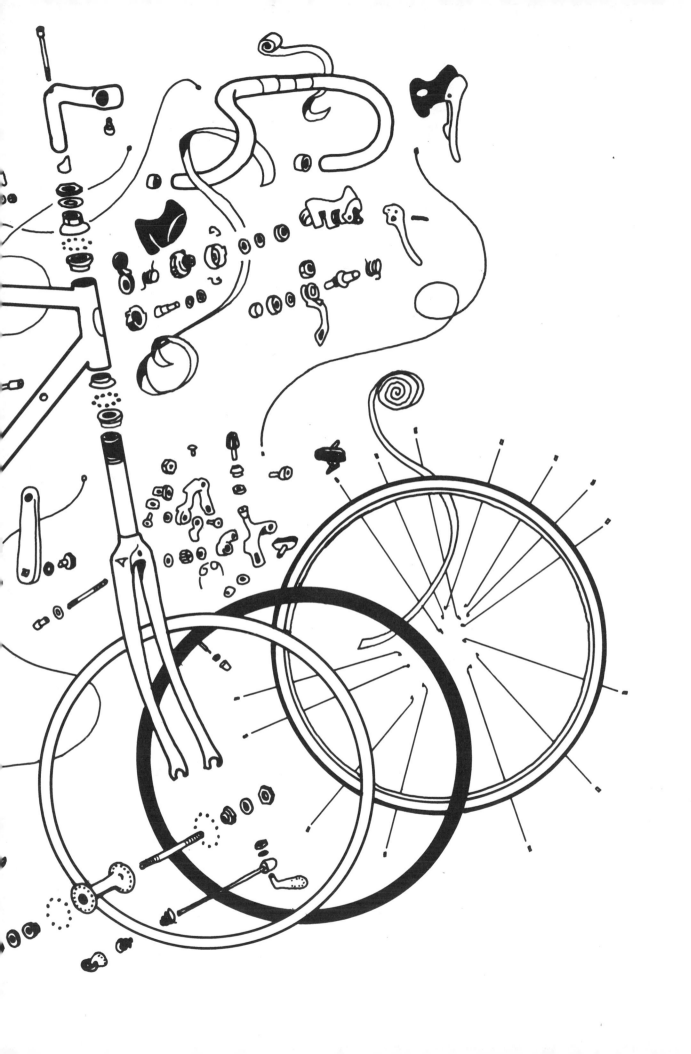

INTRODUCTION

First things first, but not necessarily
in that order.
—Doctor Who

ABOUT THIS BOOK

So, you want to maintain your road bike? Congratulations. You will be glad you took this step. Although it is nice to learn about your bike from friends or shop employees who know more about bicycles than you do, you don't want to depend on them for routine maintenance or fixing basic mechanical problems. And the exhilaration of riding with the wind in your hair will be enhanced by understanding the structure of the mechanical system on which you are sitting and to which you are trusting your life.

Even the purest romantic can follow the simple step-by-step procedures and exploded diagrams in this book and discover a passion for spreading new grease on old parts. And, I hope, everyone will develop an appreciation for how infusing love into the work will guarantee success at bike maintenance. If not, frustration will take over, you will use less care, and your riding enjoyment will be compromised.

Zinn & the Art of Road Bike Maintenance allows you to pick maintenance tasks appropriate for your level of skill and confidence. However, I firmly believe—and my experience with the repair classes I have taught confirms this—that anyone can perform the repairs illustrated on these pages. It takes only a willingness to learn and the appropriate tools.

This book is intended for everyone from shop mechanics to those who only want to know about the most minimal maintenance their bike requires. Chapter 2 is for those whose interest is limited to the latter; the rest of the book is for those who choose to go to greater lengths to make everything work optimally and look clean and beautiful. Even for those who wish to focus on Chapter 2, the information in Appendix C on fitting your bike to y ou instead of the other way around will increase your riding pleasure and safety.

WHY DO IT YOURSELF?

There are a number of reasons for learning to maintain your bike. Obviously it is a lot cheaper to fix a bike yourself than to pay someone else to do it. Once you have some skill and experience, it is also faster. And home-based maintenance is a necessity for most racers and others who live to ride and have no visible means of support.

As your income increases, economic necessity ceases to be a significant issue. However, you may find that you enjoy working on your bike for reasons other than just saving money. Unless you have a trusted mechanic who services your bike regularly, you are not likely to find anyone who cares as much about your bicycle's smooth operation and cleanliness as you, or who will make your bike a priority when you need to have it the next day or in the next few hours. Furthermore, if you love to ride, you need to be able to fix mechanical breakdowns that occur on the road, especially if you ride alone.

If time is your biggest issue, having someone else work on your bike might seem like a no-brainer. But in reality, even finding the time to drop off your bike and pick it up from the shop, while coordinating with the shop's schedule, can be hard. You may be able to perform a simple repair faster or more conveniently than you can make a trip to the bike shop during working hours. And you won't like missing a ride during beautiful weather while your bike sits in a shop that is backed up with repairs. Finding out that you can't just drop off your ailing bike during high season and expect anything faster than a three-week turnaround on a minor repair can ruin your day. Even arranging and adhering to a repair appointment with a shop can be a hassle. Finally, a shop slammed with summer work may return your bike in less than optimal condition because too little time was devoted to the repair or the mechanic was inexperienced. Ultimately, you may decide that having someone else work on your bike creates more aggravation than it alleviates.

Working on your bike can be fun. Bicycles are the manifestation of elegant simplicity. Bicycle parts, particularly high-end components, are a fantastic value. They are made to work well and last a long time. With the proper attention, they can shine in appearance and performance for many years. Satisfaction can be found in dismantling and cleaning a filthy, barely functional part, lubricating it with fresh grease, and reassembling it so that it works like new. Knowing that you made those parts work so smoothly—and that you can do it again when they next need it—is rewarding. You will be eager to ride hard and long to see how your work holds up, rather than being reluctant to get far from home for fear of breaking down.

It is liberating to go on a long ride confident that you can fix just about anything that may go wrong. Armed with this confidence and the tools to put it into action, you will have the freedom to explore new roads and go farther than you may otherwise have gone. You may also find yourself more willing to share your love of the sport with riders who are less experienced. You will enjoy riding with them more if you know that you can fix their questionably maintained bikes, and you can bask in their appreciation after you have eliminated an annoying squeak or skipping chain.

HOW TO USE THIS BOOK

Skim through the entire book. Look at the table of contents and the exploded diagrams, and get the general flavor of the book and what's inside. When it's time to perform a particular task, you will know where to find it, and you will have a general idea of how to approach it.

Illustrators Mike Reisel and Todd Telander and I have done our best to make these pages as understandable as possible. The exploded diagrams show precisely how each part goes together. Nevertheless, the first time you go through a procedure, you may find it easier to have a friend read the instructions out loud as you perform the steps.

Obviously, some maintenance tasks are more complicated than others. I am convinced that anyone with an opposable thumb can perform any repair on a bike. Still, it pays to spend some time getting familiar with the really simple tasks, such as fixing a flat, before throwing yourself into a complex job, such as building a wheel.

LEVEL 1

LEVEL 2

LEVEL 3

Tasks and the tools required to accomplish them are divided into three levels indicating their complexity or your proficiency. Performing level 1 tasks demands level 1 tools and requires of you only an eagerness to learn. Level 2 and level 3 tasks also have corresponding tool sets and are progressively more difficult. All suggested tools are shown in Chapter 1. At the end of Chapter 2 is the must-read section "A General Guide to Performing Mechanical Work" (§ii-19); it states general policies and approaches that apply to all mechanical work. Note that the symbol § and the lowercase Roman numeral following it (§i) denote the chapter in the book; the number after the hyphen refers to the section in a chapter (e.g., §ii-19 indicates material found in section 19 of Chapter 2).

Each chapter starts with a list of suggested tools in the page margin. If a section demands more than basic experience and tools, there will be an icon designating the difficulty. Tasks and illustrations are numbered for easy reference.

If you're wondering what to do first, a routine maintenance schedule is included at the end of Chapter 2 (§ii-20). A troubleshooting section is included at the end of some chapters. This is the place to go to identify the source of a certain noise or particular malfunction in the bike. There is also a comprehensive troubleshooting index in Appendix A.

For those into cyclocross, almost every chapter includes a specific cyclocross maintenance section.

Many tasks will be simplified or improved by using the information presented in the appendixes. Appendix B is a complete gear chart and includes instructions on how to calculate your gear if you're using nonstandard-size wheels or tires. Appendix C is an extensive section on selecting the proper-size bike and positioning it to fit you. It includes information about setting up your bike for time trials or triathlons, as well as road and cyclocross. Appendix D, the glossary, is an inclusive dictionary of bicycle technical terminology. Appendix E lists the tightening (torque) specifications of almost every bolt on the bike. I can't emphasize enough how useful it is to use a torque wrench to tighten bolts as tightly as the component manufacturer intended, but no tighter. Flag Appendix E so you can flip to it easily whenever you work on your bike.

The Internet can be a useful supplement to this book. For instance, bikeschool.com, dtswiss.com, and other sites have spoke-length calculators to use when you are building wheels. And exploded views of some parts can be found on component company websites, such as bocabearing.com, campagnolo.com, realworldcycling.com, shimano.com, sram.com, and mavic.com.

i.1 The object of our attention (and affection), racing version

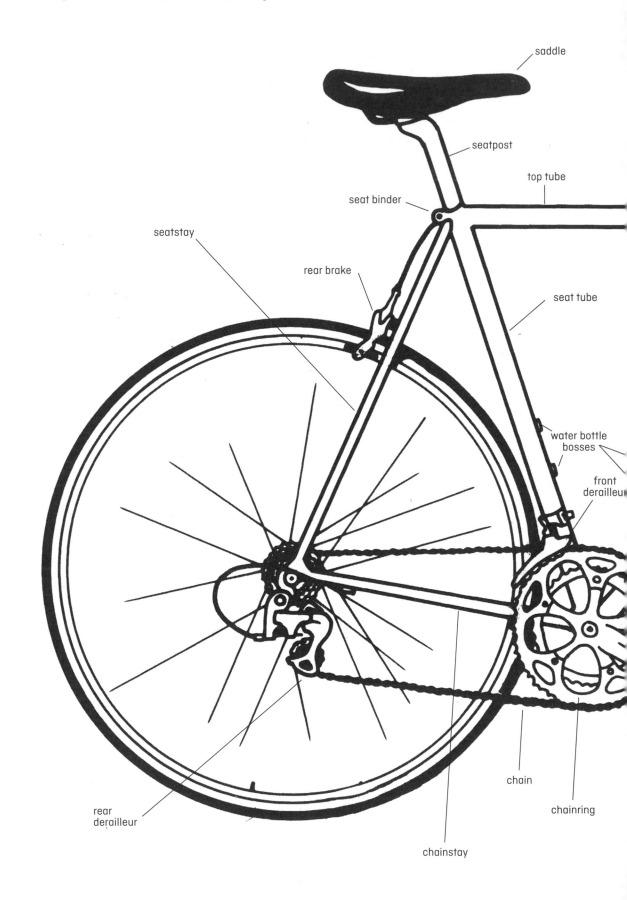

saddle

seatpost

top tube

seat binder

seatstay

rear brake

seat tube

water bottle bosses

front derailleur

rear derailleur

chainstay

chain

chainring

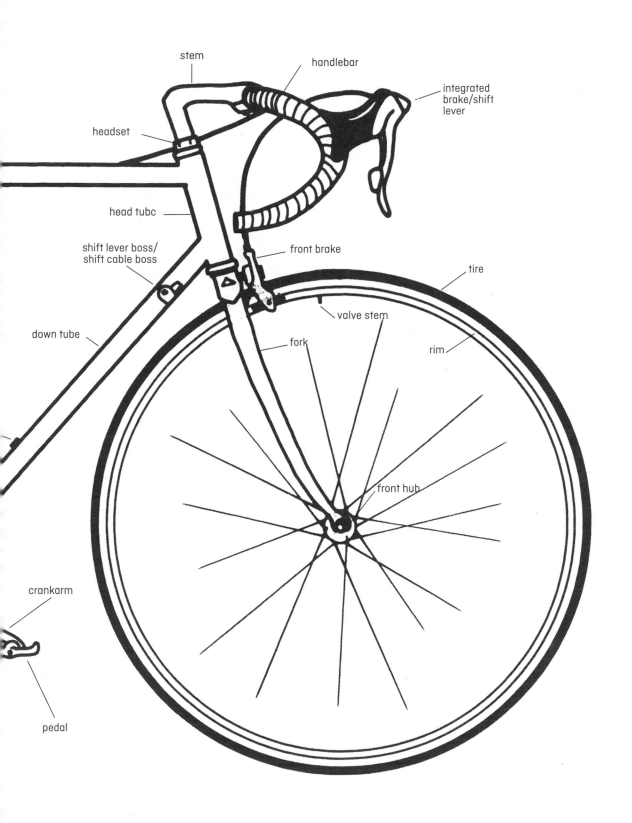

stem

handlebar

integrated
brake/shift
lever

headset

head tubc

shift lever boss/
shift cable boss

front brake

tire

valve stem

down tube

fork

rim

front hub

crankarm

pedal

THE ROAD BIKE

This is the creature (Fig. i.1) to which this book is devoted. All of its parts are illustrated and labeled. Take a minute to familiarize yourself with these parts now, and then refer back to this diagram whenever necessary.

The road bike comes in a variety of forms, from road racing (Fig. i.1) to time trial or triathlon (Fig. i.2), to longer-wheelbase touring models, which are rigged for carrying luggage (Fig. i.3), to models with front—and even rear—suspension. Some cousins are the track bike (Fig. i.4) and the cyclocross bike (Fig. i.5).

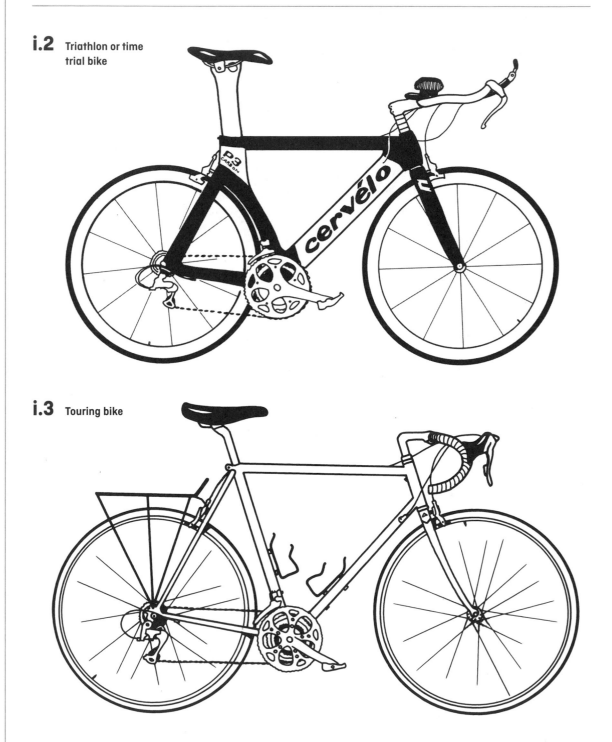

i.2 Triathlon or time trial bike

i.3 Touring bike

i.4 Track bike

i.5 Cyclocross bike

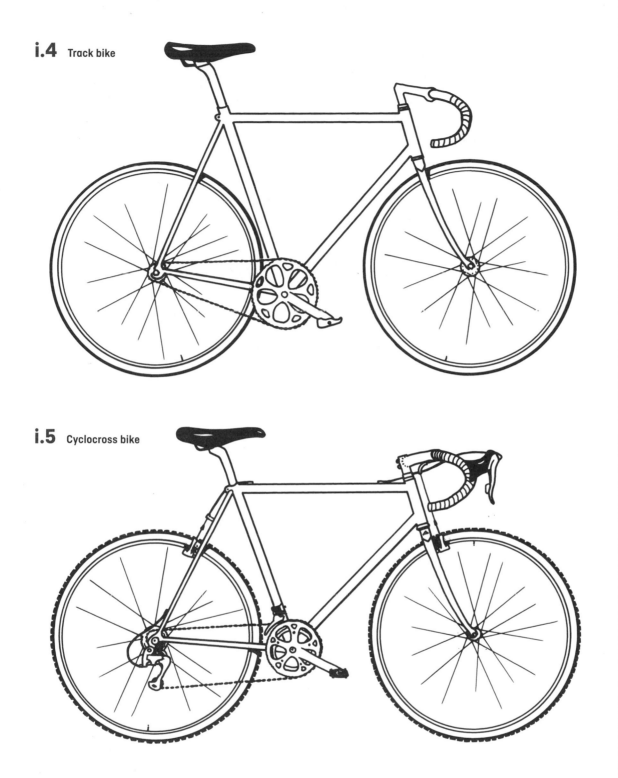

THIS MEANS YOU!

Because this book clearly spells out the steps necessary to properly maintain and repair a road bike, even those who see themselves as having no mechanical skills will be able to tackle problems as they arise. With a willingness to learn and a little practice, you will find that your bicycle will become transformed from a mysterious contraption too complicated to tamper with to a simple, understandable machine that is a delight to work on. Just allow yourself the opportunity and the dignity to follow the instructions, take your time, and trust yourself.

So, if you think you are not mechanically inclined, set that opinion aside, along with any other factors that may stand in the way of rolling up your sleeves to improve your bike's performance. The bicycle is one of our greatest inventions. Another is the book. Here is a chance to use them both. See you on the road!

If the only tool you have is a hammer,
you tend to see every problem as a nail.
                          —Abraham Maslow

You can't do much work on a bike without a basic tool assortment. Bicycles—like other evolved machines such as automobiles and watches—have specific fasteners and threads that require specific tools to fit them. This chapter will clarify which tools you should consider owning, based on your level of mechanical experience and interest.

As I mentioned in the introduction, the maintenance and repair procedures described in this book are classified by degree of difficulty. Nearly all repairs are classified as level 1, because most bicycle repair jobs are pretty easy to complete once you understand the principles involved. The tools for levels 1, 2, and 3 are pictured in Figures 1.1A, 1.2, and 1.3, respectively, and described on the following pages. In addition, the tools you may need for a specific repair are listed in the margin at the beginning of each chapter.

For the novice, there is no need to rush out and buy a large number of bike-specific tools. The Level 1 Tool Kit (Fig. 1.1A) consists of standard metric tools, many of which you may already own. This is the same collection of tools, in a more compact and lightweight form, that I recommend for carrying on long rides (Fig. 1.6).

The Level 2 Tool Kit (Fig. 1.2) contains several bike-specific tools, allowing you to do more complex work on the bike. Level 3 tools (Figs. 1.3, 1.4) are extensive (and sometimes expensive) and ensure that your riding buddies will show up not only to ask your sage advice but also to borrow your tools. If you are willing to lend tools, you may consider marking your collection and keeping a list of who borrowed what, to help recover items that may otherwise take a long time finding their way back to your workshop.

i-1

LEVEL 1 TOOL KIT

Level 1 repairs are the simplest and do not require a workshop, although a well-lit, comfortable workspace is nice to have. For easy repairs, you will need the following tools (Fig. 1.1A):

- **Tire pump with a gauge** and a valve head to match your tubes (either Presta or Schrader valves; see Fig. 1.1B).
- **Standard slot-head screwdrivers**: small, medium, and large.
- **Phillips-head screwdrivers**: one small and one medium.
- Set of three plastic **tire levers**.
- At least two **spare tubes**—or **tubulars**—of the same size and valve type as those on your bike.
- Container of regular **talcum powder** for coating tubes and the inner casings of tires.

NOTE: *Do not inhale this stuff; it is bad for your lungs.*

- **Patch kit**. Choose one that comes with sandpaper instead of a metal scratcher. Every year, check that the glue has not dried out.
- One 6-inch **adjustable wrench** (also called a "Crescent" wrench, which is a brand name).
- **Pliers**: regular and needle-nose.
- Set of **metric hex keys** (or Allen wrenches) that includes 2.5mm, 3mm, 4mm, 5mm, 6mm, and 8mm sizes. Folding sets are available and keep wrenches organized. I also recommend buying extras of the 4mm, 5mm, and 6mm sizes, and a long-handled 8mm hex key for removing and installing some pedals and crankarms.
- Set of **metric open-end wrenches** that includes 7mm, 8mm, 9mm, 10mm, 13mm, 14mm, 15mm, and 17mm sizes.
- A 15mm **pedal wrench**. This wrench is thinner and longer than a standard 15mm wrench and thicker and longer than a cone wrench, to fit into the space between the pedal and crank (Fig. 9.3). A pedal wrench is not necessary for pedals with only a hex-key hole and no wrench flats on the spindle (Fig. 9.4).
- **Chain tool** for breaking (opening) and reassembling chains. If you have a 9-, 10-, or 11-speed

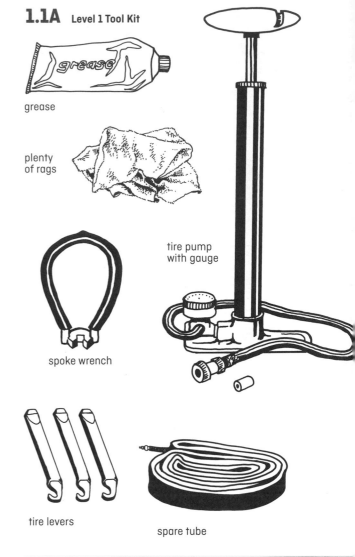

1.1A Level 1 Tool Kit

grease

plenty of rags

spoke wrench

tire pump with gauge

tire levers

spare tube

system, you may need a narrower chain tool to avoid bending the center prongs of the tool. Shimano's TL-CN23 and TL-CN32 (Figs. 4.18, 4.19) work for 7-, 8-, 9-, and 10-speed chains. Many other chain tools work as well (Figs. 4.20–4.23); you can ask your bike shop for the brand of tool that matches the brand and size of the chain on your bike.

- **Chain-elongation gauge**. This handy little plastic item helps you determine whether a chain needs to be replaced (Figs. 4.5, 4.6). An accurate 12-inch ruler will substitute adequately.
- **Spoke wrench** to match the size of the spoke nipples on your bike's wheels.

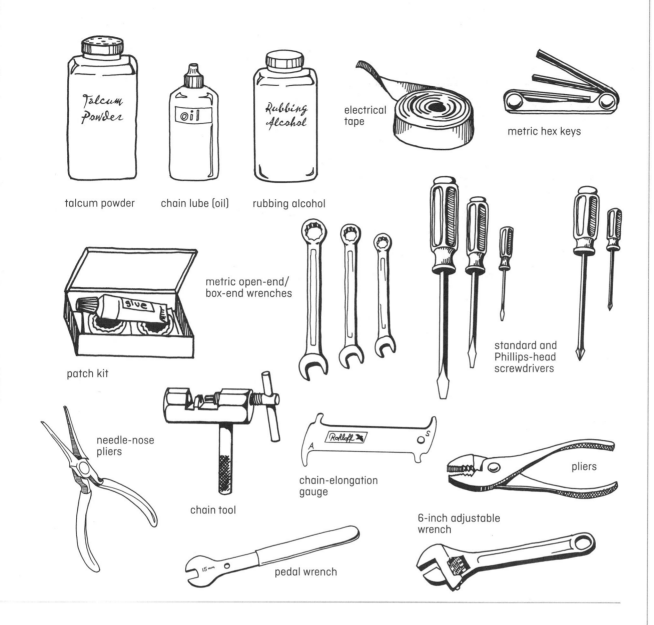

talcum powder · chain lube (oil) · rubbing alcohol

electrical tape

metric hex keys

patch kit

metric open-end/ box-end wrenches

standard and Phillips-head screwdrivers

needle-nose pliers

chain tool

chain-elongation gauge

pliers

6-inch adjustable wrench

pedal wrench

- Tube or jar of **grease**. I recommend using grease designed specifically for bicycles, but standard automotive grease is okay.
- Drip bottle or can of **chain lubricant**. Choose a nonaerosol; it is easier to control, uses less packaging, and wastes less in overspray.
- **Rubbing alcohol** for cleaning brake tracks on rims, doing other light cleaning, and removing and installing handlebar grips, if you have them instead of handlebar tape.
- **Electrical tape** for taping off the end of the handlebar tape and for marking your seat height.
- A lot of **rags**! Old T-shirts work fine.
- **Safety glasses**.

1.1B Valve types

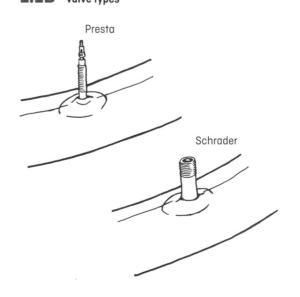

Presta

Schrader

- **Rubber gloves** or a box of cheap latex gloves.
- A **bucket**, **dish soap**, **large brushes**, and **sponges** (Fig. 1.7). These will serve you well for cleaning a dirty machine rapidly.

i-2

LEVEL 2 TOOL KIT

LEVEL 2

Level 2 repairs are a bit more complex, and I recommend that you attack them with specific tools and a well-organized workspace with a shop bench. Keeping your workspace well organized is probably the best way to make maintenance and repair easy and quick. You will need the entire Level 1 Tool Kit (Fig. 1.1A) plus the following Level 2 Tool Kit tools (Fig. 1.2):

- **Portable bike stand**. The stand must be sturdy enough to remain stable when you're really cranking on the wrenches. If you have a time trial/triathlon bike or other bike with an aero seatpost, you won't be able to clamp it in a standard bike stand, which is designed to clamp around round tubes. In that case, you will need a bike stand that holds the bike by the bottom bracket and the front or rear end with one wheel out. It will have a cradle for the bottom bracket to sit in and a sliding clamp on a long horizontal arm with a quick-release mount to clamp either the fork ends or rear dropouts (see the "race mechanic's bike stand" in Fig. 1.4).
- **Shop apron** to keep your nice duds nice.
- **Hacksaw** with a fine-toothed blade or a sintered blade for hard materials and composites.
- Set of **razor blades** or a sharp **shop knife**.
- **Files**: one round and one flat, with medium-fine teeth.
- **Cable cutter** for cutting brake and shift cables without fraying the ends.

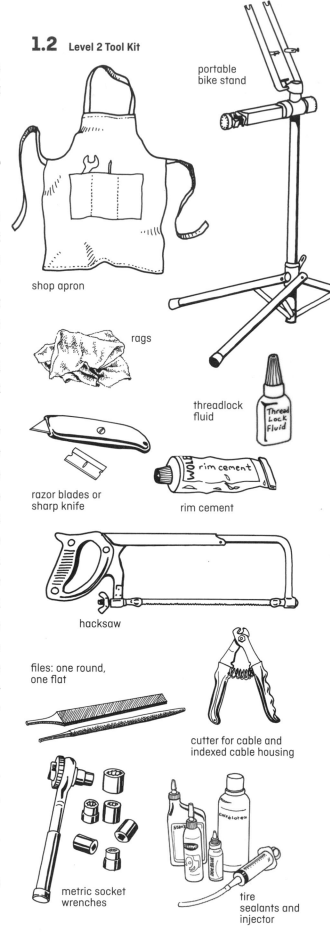

1.2 Level 2 Tool Kit

portable bike stand

shop apron

rags

threadlock fluid

razor blades or sharp knife

rim cement

hacksaw

files: one round, one flat

cutter for cable and indexed cable housing

metric socket wrenches

tire sealants and injector

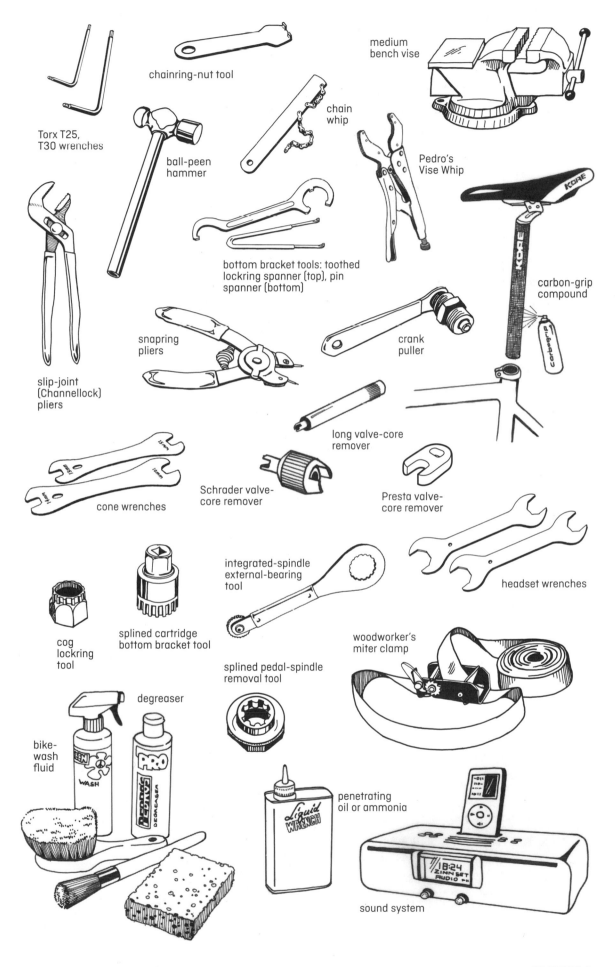

Torx T25, T30 wrenches

chainring-nut tool

medium bench vise

ball-peen hammer

chain whip

Pedro's Vise Whip

bottom bracket tools: toothed lockring spanner (top), pin spanner (bottom)

slip-joint (Channellock) pliers

snapring pliers

crank puller

carbon-grip compound

long valve-core remover

cone wrenches

Schrader valve-core remover

Presta valve-core remover

cog lockring tool

splined cartridge bottom bracket tool

integrated-spindle external-bearing tool

headset wrenches

woodworker's miter clamp

splined pedal-spindle removal tool

degreaser

bike-wash fluid

penetrating oil or ammonia

sound system

- **Cable-housing cutter** for cutting coaxial-indexed cable housing. If you purchase a SRAM, Shimano, Park, Pedro's, or Jagwire housing cutter, you won't need to buy a separate cable cutter, because all of these cut cables as well as housings.
- Set of **metric socket wrenches** that includes 7mm, 8mm, 9mm, 10mm, 13mm, 14mm, and 15mm sizes. This assumes you have a ratchet handle; if not, get one.
- **Torx wrenches**, which look like hex keys with star-shaped tips; they fit some brake bolts and chainring bolts. Torx T25 and T30 are common sizes on road bikes.
- **Chainring-nut tool** for holding the nut while you tighten or loosen a chainring bolt.
- Medium **ball-peen hammer**.
- Medium-size **bench vise** (bolted to a sturdy bench).
- **Cog lockring tool** for removing cogs from the rear hub (Figs. 6.39, 6.40). Note that Campagnolo lockrings require a different tool than do Shimano, SRAM, or Mavic.
- **Chain whip** for holding cogs while loosening the cassette lockring (Fig. 6.39). In place of a chain whip, a **Pedro's Vise Whip** will hold the cog firmly (Fig. 6.40).
- **Bottom bracket tools**. For external-bearing cranks (Figs. 8.2, 8.8, 8.19), you'll need an oversized splined wrench to remove the cups and, in some cases, a little splined tool to tighten the left crank's adjustment cap. For Campagnolo Ultra-Torque integrated-spindle cranks (Fig. 8.8), you'll also need a long, 10mm hex key to tighten the bolt in the middle of the axle. For BB30 cranks (Fig. 8.17), you'll need only snapring pliers. For sealed cartridge bottom brackets (Figs. 8.23, 8.25), you'll need the splined cartridge bottom bracket tool (Fig. 8.33). Note that if you have an ISIS or OctaLink splined-spindle bottom bracket, you need a splined tool with a bore large enough to swal-

low the fatter spindle (Fig. 8.25). And for cup-and-cone bottom brackets (Fig. 8.22), you'll need a lockring spanner and a pin spanner to fit your bottom bracket (Fig. 8.36).
- **Snapring pliers** for BB30 cranks (Fig. 8.17) and other unthreaded bottom brackets with snapring grooves. Also useful for removing snaprings from pedals and other parts.
- **Crank puller** for removing crankarms (Fig. 8.7). This tool is only necessary for older cranks; it is not needed for most integrated-spindle cranks (Figs. 8.2, 8.8, 8.17–8.19) or for cranks with self-extracting crank bolts. The pushrod of this tool is sized for either square-taper spindles (Figs. 8.21–8.23) or ISIS/OctaLink spindles (Figs. 8.24, 8.25) but not both, so get the right one for your crankset.
- **Cone wrenches**, if the wheel hubs have loose bearings (Figs. 6.30–6.37). The standard sizes are 13mm and 14mm, but check the size before buying.
- **Slip-joint pliers** (also called "Channellock" pliers, which is a brand name).
- **Splined pedal-spindle removal tool**. Note that Shimano's plastic tool (Fig. 9.13) is different from Look's, although high-end Shimano and Look pedals no longer require either (they take standard 20mm and 19mm wrenches).
- Two **headset wrenches** (only needed for older bikes with threaded headsets; Figs. 11.1, 11.8, 11.11, 11.23). Check the size of the headset on your bike before buying.
- **Rim cement** for tubular tires, if you have them. Use Continental clear glue or Vittoria Mastik'One for aluminum rims, but stick to Mastik'One for carbon-fiber rims.
- **Valve-core remover** for Presta valves (tools shown include a Schrader valve-core remover on the other end).
- **Carbon-grip compound** for clamping carbon seatposts and handlebars.

- **Tire sealants** and **sealant injector syringe** to prevent small punctures and to set up tubeless tires.
- **Woodworker's miter clamp** for gluing tubulars (optional).
- Stereo, iPod, or other **sound system**, if you plan on spending a lot of time working on your bike.
- **Threadlock fluid**, **specialty bike-wash fluid**, **degreaser**, **penetrating oil** (or **ammonia** for breaking free stuck parts), and **antiseize grease** for titanium bolts will all come in handy.

<hr>

i-3

LEVEL 3 TOOL KIT

LEVEL 3

If you are an accomplished level 3 mechanic, you are completely independent of your local bike shop's service department. You can even build a complete bike from a bare frame. By now, you have a well-organized, separate space intended solely for working on your bike. Some elements of the Level 3 Tool Kit (Fig. 1.3) are heavy-duty replacements or substitutions for parts of the Level 2 Tool Kit.

- **Parts washing tank**. Use an environmentally safe degreaser. Dispose of used solvent responsibly; check with your local environmental safety office.
- **Fixed bike stand** (optional). Be sure it comes with a clamp designed to fit any size of frame tube.
- **Master-link pliers** (Fig. 4.25).
- A **tire pressure gauge** separate from the one on a floor pump is more accurate at low pressures and can save time.
- A **telescoping** or **articulating magnet** for picking up dropped parts or small tools.
- Large **ball-peen hammer**.
- **Soft mallet**. Choose a leather, rubber, plastic, or wooden one to prevent damage to parts.

- **Headset press** used to install headset bearing cups (Fig. 11.44) and bearings and bearing cups into threadless bottom bracket shells (Fig. 8.29). The press should not push on the bearing's inner race; if it does, get the appropriate insert to adapt your headset press to the particular headset and bottom bracket bearings and cups you will be installing.
- **Headset-cup and PF30 bottom bracket remover.** Called a "rocket" tool due to its shape, this tool expands inside the head tube (Figs. 11.37, 11.38) or bottom bracket shell behind the bottom bracket or headset cup.
- **Small press-fit PF24 (BB86) bottom bracket remover**. Identical to a headset remover rocket but smaller for the press-fit bottom brackets for cranksets with 24mm integrated spindles.
- **Fork-crown-race punch** (slide hammer) for installing the fork-crown headset race (Fig. 11.43). Thin Shimano or Chris King crown races require a second support tool to protect the crown race during installation.
- **Star nut installation tool** for threadless headsets.
- **Freewheel removers**. If you will be working on retro stuff, you'll need these for unscrewing freewheels from threaded hubs.
- **Torque wrenches** for checking proper bolt tightness. Most component manufacturers provide torque specs to prevent parts from stripping, breaking, creaking, or falling off while riding. There is a complete torque specification list in Appendix E of this book. You need a long torque wrench that goes to high torque for big items like crank bolts, bottom bracket cups, and pedals, and a short torque wrench accurate at low torque settings for small items like stem bolts, shoe cleat bolts and cable-clamp bolts. Also get a set of **metric hex-key and Torx bits** to fit the wrenches.
- Set of **metric thread taps** that includes 5mm × 0.8, 6mm × 1, and 10mm × 1. These will thread

1.3 Level 3 Tool Kit

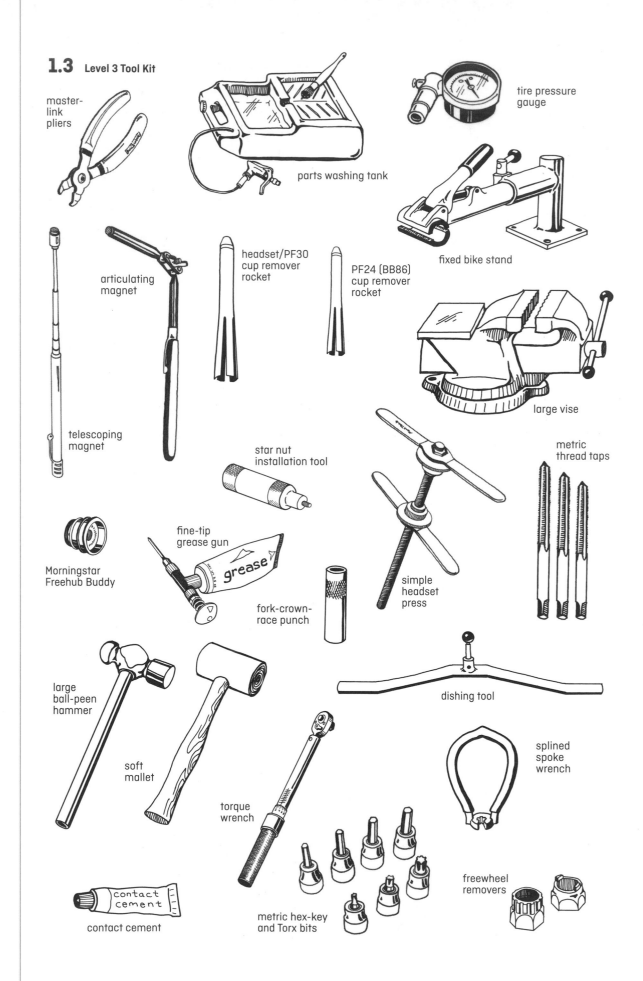

master-link pliers

parts washing tank

tire pressure gauge

fixed bike stand

articulating magnet

headset/PF30 cup remover rocket

PF24 (BB86) cup remover rocket

large vise

telescoping magnet

star nut installation tool

metric thread taps

Morningstar Freehub Buddy

fine-tip grease gun

grease

simple headset press

fork-crown-race punch

large ball-peen hammer

soft mallet

torque wrench

dishing tool

splined spoke wrench

contact cement

metric hex-key and Torx bits

freewheel removers

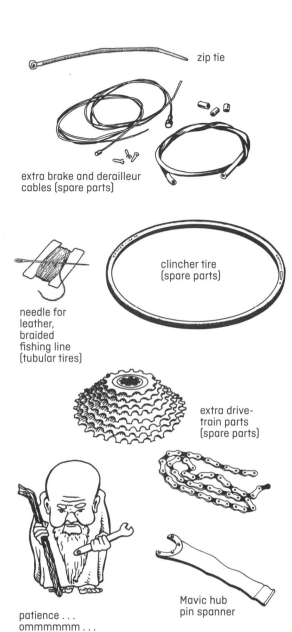

extra brake and derailleur
cables (spare parts)

needle for
leather,
braided
fishing line
(tubular tires)

clincher tire
(spare parts)

extra drive-
train parts
(spare parts)

patience . . .
ommmmmm . . .

Mavic hub
pin spanner

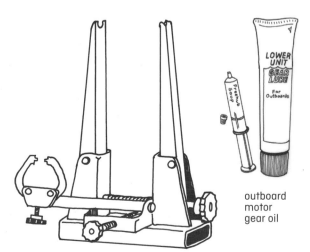

truing stand

Freehub Soup

outboard
motor
gear oil

bottle bosses, seat binder clamps, derailleur hangers, and cantilever bosses (on touring or cyclocross frames).

- **Fine-tip grease gun** for parts with grease fittings and for Campagnolo headsets with grease holes.
- **Morningstar Freehub Buddy** for lubricating Shimano freehubs (Figs. 6.42, 6.44).
- **Outboard motor gear oil** or **Morningstar Freehub Soup** for lubricating freehubs.
- **Truing stand** for truing and building wheels.
- **Dishing tool** for checking whether wheels are properly centered.
- A full range of **spoke wrenches**, including splined ones and other nonstandard spoke wrenches for certain wheels.
- **Pin spanner** for adjusting Mavic hubs.
- **Needle** for leather, braided **fishing line**, and **contact cement** for patching tubular tires.
- One healthy dose of **patience** and an equal willingness to work and rework jobs until they have been properly finished.

Other Stuff

- **Spare parts** to save you from having to make a lot of last-minute runs to the bike shop for commonly used parts. Any well-equipped shop really requires several sizes of ball bearings, bolts, spare cables, cable housing, housing ferrules (cylindrical housing end caps), cable-end caps, valve extenders, and zip ties. You should also have a good supply of spare tires, tubes, chains, and cogsets.

i-4

NOW, IF YOU REALLY WANT A WELL-STOCKED SHOP . . .

The following tools (Fig. 1.4) are not included in the Level 3 Tool Kit and are rarely needed for bike repairs. That said, they sure do come in handy when you need them.

1.4 **Tools for the well-stocked shop**

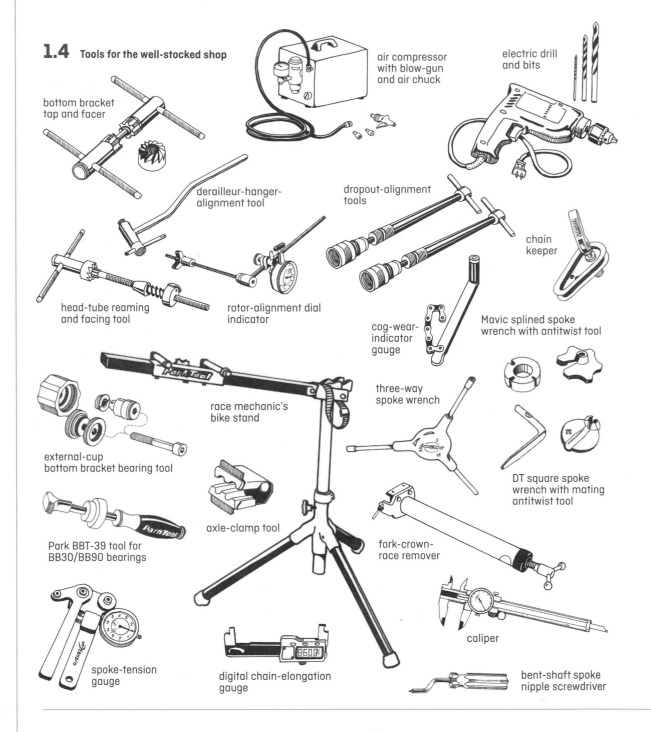

air compressor
with blow-gun
and air chuck

electric drill
and bits

bottom bracket
tap and facer

derailleur-hanger-
alignment tool

dropout-alignment
tools

chain
keeper

head-tube reaming
and facing tool

rotor-alignment dial
indicator

cog-wear-
indicator
gauge

Mavic splined spoke
wrench with antitwist tool

race mechanic's
bike stand

three-way
spoke wrench

external-cup
bottom bracket bearing tool

DT square spoke
wrench with mating
antitwist tool

Park BBT-39 tool for
BB30/BB90 bearings

axle-clamp tool

fork-crown-
race remover

caliper

spoke-tension
gauge

digital chain-elongation
gauge

bent-shaft spoke
nipple screwdriver

- **Bottom bracket tap set**. This tool cuts threads in both ends of the bottom bracket while keeping the threads in proper alignment. English-threaded taps are required for most modern road bike frames. Most Italian frames, however, have Italian threads and will require appropriate taps. French threading and Swiss threading are separate standards, but these threads are rare in modern road bikes. (If you run into these latter threads and the repair will be a onetime thing, it may be best to take the frame to a competent shop with the correct taps and have the shop do the work, rather than hunting down these tools.)

- **Bottom bracket facer**. Like a bottom bracket tap, this tool cuts the faces of the bottom bracket shell so that they are parallel to each other.

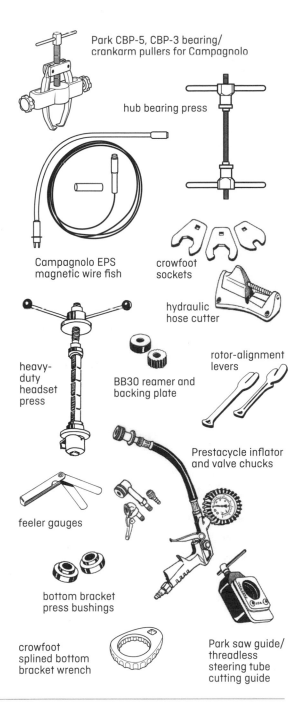

Park CBP-5, CBP-3 bearing/
crankarm pullers for Campagnolo

hub bearing press

Campagnolo EPS
magnetic wire fish

crowfoot
sockets

hydraulic
hose cutter

heavy-
duty
headset
press

BB30 reamer and
backing plate

rotor-alignment
levers

Prestacycle inflator
and valve chucks

feeler gauges

bottom bracket
press bushings

crowfoot
splined bottom
bracket wrench

Park saw guide/
threadless
steering tube
cutting guide

- **BB30 reaming cutter and base plate** that fit on bottom bracket tap handles.
- **Bearing press/remover** for popping cartridge bearings in and out of external bottom bracket cups.
- **Park BBT-39 bearing remover** for BB30 and BB90 bottom brackets.
- **Bushings** for pressing in bottom bracket bearings and cups.

- **Park CBP-5 and CBP-3 bearing puller** for Campagnolo/Fulcrum Ultra-Torque bottom brackets, arm puller, plug and pads for Campagnolo Power Torque cranks, and bearing puller extension for removing Campagnolo Power Torque drive-side bearing.
- **Hub bearing press**. This tool has bushings for all bearing sizes and ensures that the bearings press in parallel to each other.
- **Electric drill** with drill bit set for customizing.
- **Dropout-alignment tools** (tip adjusters).
- **Derailleur-hanger-alignment tool** to straighten the derailleur hanger after you shift the derailleur into the spokes or crash on it. If your bike has a replaceable derailleur hanger, you may want to get an extra one of these too.
- **Chain keeper** (attaches to dropout to hold chain while cleaning drivetrain with wheel off).
- **Cog-wear-indicator gauge** determines whether cogs are worn out.
- **Three-way spoke wrench** with square-drive, 5mm, and 5.5mm sockets for the purpose of tightening spoke nipples internal to a deep rim, or a specialty wrench for a specific type of internal nipple.
- **Spoke nipple screwdriver** with bent, freespinning shaft (for quicker wheel building).
- **Antitwist tool** for preventing twisting bladed (aero) spokes during truing with a spoke wrench.
- **Spoke-tension gauge**. Brings spoke tension up to precise specs for long-lasting, stable wheels.
- **Campagnolo EPS wire guide tool**. The magnet on the end of the cable pulls EPS wires through by means of a mating magnet that snaps onto the wire's connector.
- **Head-tube reaming and facing tool**. This tool keeps both ends of the head tube perfectly parallel and bored out to the right size.
- **Park universal fork-crown-race remover**. This hefty tool can remove a fork-crown race from

any shape of fork without using a hammer and screwdriver and suffering consequent collateral damage to the fork.

- **Heavy-duty headset press** installs headset bearing cups (Fig. 11.44) and bottom bracket bearings and bearing cups into threadless bottom bracket shells (Fig. 8.29) more quickly and accurately than a simple threaded headset press can. The press should not push on the bearing's inner race; if it does, get the appropriate insert to adapt your headset press to the particular headset and bottom bracket bearings and cups you will be installing.
- **Cutting guide for threadless steering tubes**. The guide slot keeps the hacksaw blade lined up perpendicular to the steerer.
- **Digital chain-elongation gauge**. Precise monitoring of the gradual increase in chain length allows timely chain replacement without overdoing it.
- **Hydraulic hose cutter**. Hydraulic disc-brake hoses that are cut off cleanly and straight are less likely to leak.
- **Rotor-alignment dial indicator**. Finds out rapidly exactly where a disc brake's rotor is out of true.
- **Rotor-bending tools**. Use in conjunction with dial indicator to precisely bend the rotor into alignment.
- **Crowfoot sockets**. Turn big nuts and bottom bracket cups to precise torque settings. Have the crowfoot at 90 degrees to the torque wrench handle to achieve torque setting shown on the wrench handle (i.e., if the crowfoot is extended straight out or back, it multiplies or reduces the torque setting shown on the wrench handle).
- **Feeler gauges**. Measures precision of disc-brake pad spacing from the rotor.
- Measuring **caliper** with a vernier, dial, or electronic gauge to precisely measure parts.

- **Axle-clamp tool**; clamped in a vise, it will hold the end of a hub axle.
- An **air compressor** makes quick work of mounting tires.
- **Prestacycle tire inflator**. Hook this baby up to your air compressor to inflate to exact pressure quickly.
- **Prestacycle valve chucks**. Inflate accurately regardless of the type or geometry of access of tire valves.
- A European-style **race mechanic's bike stand**, which supports the bottom bracket and has a long arm with a quick-release clamp to hold the fork ends or the rear dropouts, can be the only way to work efficiently on a bike with an integrated seat mast or an aero seatpost, as there is no way to clamp such a bike in a conventional work stand.

i-5

SETTING UP YOUR HOME SHOP

Make your shop clean, well organized, and comfortable, and you'll find that the speed and quality of your work will improve. Hanging tools on pegboard or slatboard or placing them in bins or trays helps maintain an organized work area. Being able to lay your hand on the tool you need will increase the enjoyment of working on a bike. It is hard to do a job with loving care when you can't find the cable cutter. Placing small parts in a bench-top organizer, one with several rows of little drawers, is another good way to keep chaos at bay.

i-6

TOOLS TO CARRY ON A RIDE

a. For everyday rides

You can keep everything you need for light repairs (Fig. 1.5) in a **small bag** under your seat.

Some people may prefer a fanny pack. As you stock this bag, look for tools and parts that are light and serviceable. Many tools are available in combination and sold as "multitools." Test all tools at home before taking them on the road.

- **Spare inner tube** or **tubular**. Always carry one. Make sure the valve matches the ones on your bike and is sufficiently long for your rim depth. If rarely needed, keep it in a plastic bag to prevent deterioration.
- **Tire pump** or **air cartridge**. Longer is better for pumping but heavier for carrying. Road bike pumps need to be thin to attain high pressures. Minipumps are okay, but they're slow. Make sure the pump head matches the tire valves (Presta or Schrader). If you prefer air cartridges, get the correct volume for the spare tube or tubular (probably 12g [grams], unless you are filling a huge touring tire, in which case you may need a 16g cartridge).
- At least two plastic **tire levers**, preferably three (for clincher and tubeless tires only).
- **Patch kit**. You'll need this if you puncture your spare tube. Check it at least once a year to make sure the glue has not dried out. You can also carry glueless patches.
- **Small screwdriver** for adjusting derailleurs and other parts; ideally on a multitool.
- Compact set of **hex keys** that includes 2.5mm, 3mm, 4mm, 5mm, 6mm, and 8mm sizes; a folding set or multitool is a good investment.
- **Torx T25 wrench**, ideally on a multitool, if the chainring bolts and brake bolts have Torx heads.
- For pre-1980s bikes, bring **8mm and 10mm open-end wrenches**. These are often included on some older multitools, eliminating the need to bring separate wrenches.
- Small clip-on **taillight**.
- Warm **outerwear**. Arm warmers, knee warmers, nylon vest or jacket, and a cap for a ride in the mountains or on any cool day. In the

1.5 Tools to take on all rides

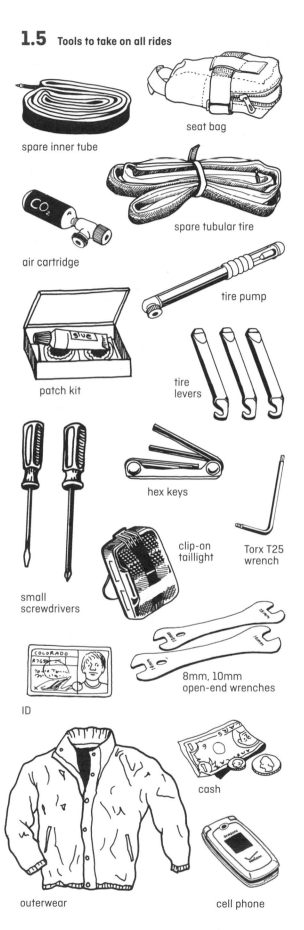

spare inner tube

seat bag

air cartridge

spare tubular tire

patch kit

tire pump

tire levers

hex keys

clip-on taillight

Torx T25 wrench

small screwdrivers

ID

8mm, 10mm open-end wrenches

outerwear

cash

cell phone

mountains and in questionable weather, thin gloves and shoe covers are also a good idea.

- **Identification**.
- **Cash** for food, phone calls, and to boot sidewall cuts in tires.
- A **cell phone** can come in handy, but it can also interrupt your rides.

b. For long or multiday trips

Carry the items in Figure 1.6, as well as all of the items in Figure 1.5.

- **Spare folding clincher tire** and a second **spare inner tube**; if you ride tubulars, bring two spares.
- **Rain gear**.
- Properly sized **spoke wrench** (can be on a multi-tool).
- **Combination wrench and chain tool** in case you break the chain. Chain tools (or "chain breakers") are often included in compact multitools, eliminating the need to bring a separate chain tool (as well as arate screwdrivers, hex keys, and even box-end or open-end wrenches). Try the chain tool at home to make sure that you can repair the chain 100 percent of the time. This testing is important insurance on long solo rides that include extended stretches away from civilization or cell phone coverage.
- **Spare chain links** from your chain. If you are using a Shimano 8- or 9-speed chain, bring at least two subpin rivets or master links of that width. For 10- or 11-speed chains, bring master links for that width chain (you may have to use a 10-speed master link on an 11-speed chain to get home).
- **Spare spokes**. Innovations in Cycling and FiberFix sell a really cool folding spoke made from Kevlar. It's worth getting one for emergency repairs on a long ride.
- Small plastic bottle of **chain lube**.
- **Sealant-filled compressed-air tire inflaters**. Especially if you're using tubulars (which you

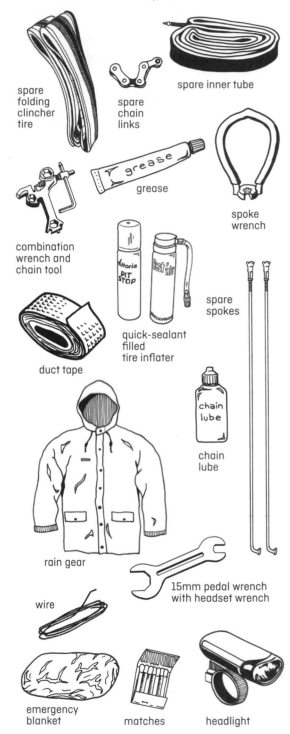

1.6 Tools for extended trips on the road

spare folding clincher tire

spare chain links

spare inner tube

grease

spoke wrench

combination wrench and chain tool

quick-sealant filled tire inflater

spare spokes

duct tape

chain lube

rain gear

15mm pedal wrench with headset wrench

wire

emergency blanket

matches

headlight

can't patch on the road), this can get you home if you've ridden through thorns or over a tack.

- Small tube of **grease**.
- Small amount of **duct tape**.
- Small amount of **wire** and/or zip ties (Fig. 1.3).

- Compact **15mm pedal wrench** if your bike requires it. Be sure to get one with a headset wrench on the other end, if your bike requires that as well.
- **Headlight**. This can be a lightweight unit to clip onto the handlebar or a headlamp with a strap that will fit over your helmet.
- **Matches**.
- A lightweight, aluminized, folding **emergency blanket**.

NOTE: *Read Chapter 3 on emergency repairs before embarking on a lengthy trip. If you are planning a bike-centered vacation, be sure to take along a Level 1 Tool Kit in your car, some headset wrenches (if your bike has a threaded headset), and incidentals like duct tape and sandpaper.*

i-7

TOOLS FOR CYCLOCROSS RACING

Cyclocross races always have a "pit" where riders exchange their dirty bike for a clean one. Often the pit is set up so that riders pass it in two directions, meaning that they can pick up a clean bike every half lap. If you are performing mechanic service for a fast friend (maybe you are switching off, each doing service for the other if you race in different categories), you may have only five minutes to clean the bike (and fix anything that your buddy yelled wasn't working right when dropping it off) before he or she is back expecting a clean bike again. In a muddy race, you have to be efficient, which means having the correct tools (Fig. 1.7) as well as the right clothing and a calm demeanor.

- **Digital tire pressure gauge**. Accuracy is critical at low pressures with low-volume cyclocross tires.
- **Waterproof pants**.
- **Rubber gloves**.
- **Rubber boots**.

- Warm and/or waterproof **jacket and hat**, as conditions mandate.
- **Spare bike** set up the same as the bike the rider starts on (i.e., same pedals, same saddle and handlebar position, same type and number of cogs).
- **Spare wheels** with the same type cogs (i.e., same or compatible brand, same number of speeds, ideally same gear range) as the bikes have.
- **Spare shift and brake cables**, **chain links**, and **master links**.
- **Spare saddle**, **seatpost**, and **seat binder clamp**. You'd be amazed how often these parts break in cyclocross.
- Two or three large, stable, reusable **buckets**, ideally that nest together.
- Large **sponge**(s).
- Large **brush**.
- Small, stiff **cylindrical brush** and/or **narrow brush** with long, thin bristles.
- Curved plastic **cog pick**.
- Environmentally friendly **bike cleaner** or dish soap.
- Environmentally friendly **degreaser**.
- **Chain lube**.
- 3mm, 4mm, 5mm, 6mm, 8mm, and 10mm **hex keys** and a **Torx T25 key**, two of each in case you lose some in the mud. Don't waste precious minutes searching for lost tools; find them after the race.
- **Long, thin screwdriver** for derailleur adjustment and cleaning mud out of tight spaces.
- **Large screwdriver**.
- **Scissors**.
- **Pliers**.
- **Cable cutter**.
- **Floor pump**.
- **Chain keeper** (attaches to dropout to hold chain while cleaning drivetrain with wheel off).
- **Crank puller**, if the bike requires more than a hex key to remove the crank.

1.7 **Tools for cyclocross racing**

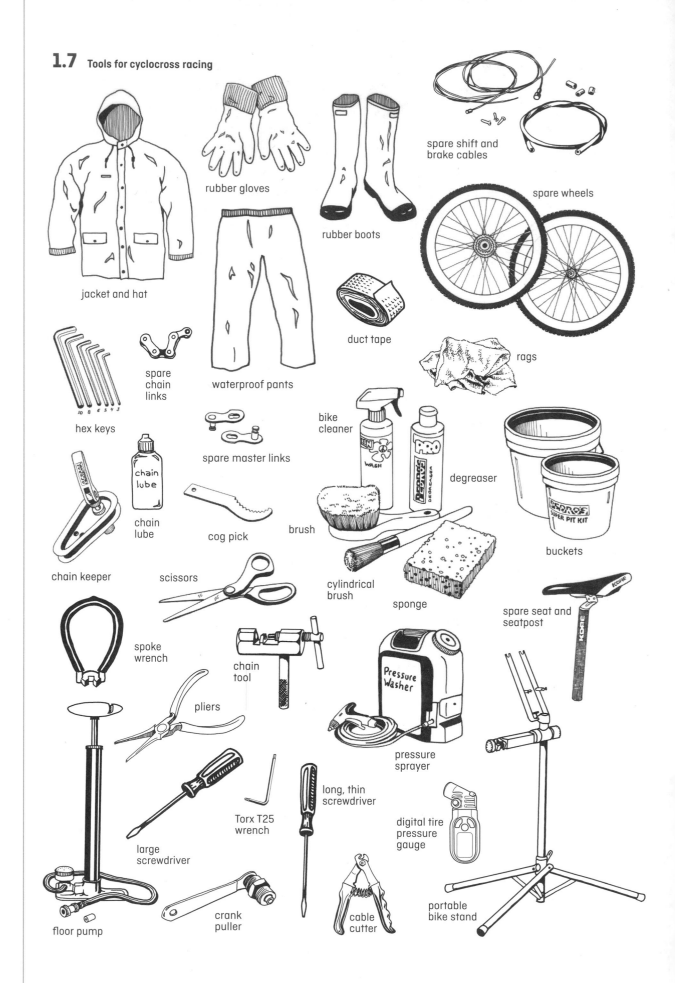

jacket and hat

rubber gloves

rubber boots

spare shift and
brake cables

spare wheels

spare
chain
links

waterproof pants

duct tape

rags

hex keys

spare master links

bike
cleaner

degreaser

chain
lube

chain
lube

cog pick

brush

buckets

chain keeper

scissors

cylindrical
brush

sponge

spare seat and
seatpost

spoke
wrench

chain
tool

pliers

Pressure
Washer

pressure
sprayer

long, thin
screwdriver

Torx T25
wrench

digital tire
pressure
gauge

large
screwdriver

floor pump

crank
puller

cable
cutter

portable
bike stand

- **Spoke wrench**.
- **Duct tape**.
- **Chain tool**.
- Fresh water. Lots, if it's a muddy race.
- **Rags**. Lots.

One quick way to equip yourself for the task is with Pedro's Super Pit Kit 2.0 bucket, which contains a sponge, brushes, bike cleaners, degreasers, lubricant, and polish. Its screw-on lid allows you to toss other tools in it and keep everything together in the car and when walking to the pit. The 2.0 version is upgraded to be more Earth-friendly; after all, you are generally doing this in a public park, an open field, or some generous institution's lawn, and you don't want to despoil it with diesel fuel or other toxic solvents.

- If the race supplies a hose or a pressure washer, bring a **portable bike stand**.
- If you expect a muddy race and your buddy is a superstar, you can bring a portable **pressure washer**, either a rechargeable battery-powered one like the pictured Nomad unit, or a gas-powered one (Karcher and Honda are good brands). Make sure you have enough water (if there's no pond or lake to pull from at the race site, you'll need a large rain barrel with a hose fitting at the bottom, available at garden stores) and enough battery power or gas to run the compressor through the race. Some races provide a pressure washer, so check with the organizer before buying your own.

BASIC STUFF

PRERIDE INSPECTION, WHEEL REMOVAL, GENERAL
CLEANING, AND MECHANICAL METHODS GUIDE

*Basic research is what I am doing when I
don't know what I am doing.*
—Werner von Braun

TOOLS

Chain lubricant

Rags

Optional

Solvent (citrus-based)

Chain-cleaning tool

Old water bottle

Bucket(s)

Large sponge

Large and small
brushes

Dish soap

Cyclocross pit kit
(see §i-7)

Always check your bike before heading out on a ride. This inspection can help you avoid getting stranded far from home due to parts failure. You should know how to remove and reinstall a wheel so that you can deal with minor annoyances like flat tires or jammed chains. And even if you do nothing else to your bike, keeping its chain clean and properly lubricated, as outlined in this chapter, will make every ride smoother and quieter.

LEVEL 1

All of the tasks in this chapter are straightforward and require minimal tools, so I have designated the work as level 1 throughout.

ii-1

PRERIDE INSPECTION

1. **Check that the wheel quick-release levers or axle nuts (which secure the hub axle to the dropouts) are tight.**

2. **Check the brake pads for excessive or uneven wear.**

3. **Grab and twist the brake pads and brake arms to make sure that the bolts are tight.**

4. **Squeeze the brake levers.** A good squeeze should bring the pads flat against the rims (or slightly toed in) without hitting the tires. Make certain that you cannot squeeze the levers all the way to the handlebar. For details, see Chapter 7 (§vii-2) on brake adjustment.

5. **Spin the wheels while eyeing the rims, not the tires.** Check for wobbles. Make sure that the rims do not rub on the brake pads.

6. **Spin the wheels again, this time eyeing the tires.** Check for wobbles. If a tire wobbles excessively on a straight rim, it may not be fully seated in the rim. There is usually a mold line or an edge of a tape strip on the tire that should be parallel to the rim edge all the way around. Look for areas where the tire bulges and/or the mold line or tape edge is higher above the rim or deeper into the rim than the rest of the way around the tire. To fix an improperly

seated tire, you need to completely deflate the tire and carefully seat it uniformly all the way around before reinflating.

7. **Check the tire pressure.** On most road bike tires, the proper pressure is between 80 and 120 pounds per square inch (psi). Look to see that there are no foreign objects sticking in the tire. If there are, you may have to pull the tube out and repair or replace it. If you have an aversion to fixing flats, turn to the section on tire sealants (i.e., goop inside the tube that fills small holes) in Chapter 6 (§vi-14).

8. **Check the tires for excessive wear, cracking, bulges, or gashes.**

9. **Make certain that the handlebar and stem are tight and that the stem is lined up with the front tire.**

10. **Check that the gears shift smoothly and the chain does not skip or shift by itself.** Ensure that each indexed (click) shift moves the chain one cog, starting with the first click. Make sure that the chain does not overshift the smallest or biggest rear cog or the inner or outer front chainring, which would throw the chain off to one side or the other.

11. **Check the chain for rust, dirt, stiff links, or noticeable signs of wear.** It should be clean and lubricated (but not overlubricated; gooey chains pick up lots of dirt). The chain should be replaced on a road bike about every 1,500 to 3,500 miles of paved riding. See §iv-6 to accurately evaluate chain wear.

12. **Apply the front brake and push the bike forward and back.** The headset (fork bearings; see Fig. 11.1) should be tight and not make clunking noises or allow the fork any fore-aft play.

13. **Grasp one crankarm and push and pull it laterally, toward and away from the frame, to ensure that the crank bearings or crankarms are not loose.**

14. **Grasp each wheel and push and pull it laterally, perpendicular to the plane of the wheel, to ensure that the hub bearings are not loose.**

15. **If all this checks out, go ride your bike!** If not, check the table of contents, go to the appropriate chapter, and fix the problems before you go out and ride.

ii-2

REMOVING THE FRONT WHEEL

You can't fix a flat if you can't remove the wheel. Front wheel removal is also generally required for placing a bike on a roof rack or in a car. As outlined in the following sections, wheel removal involves releasing the brake (in most cases) and opening the hub quick-release or bolt-on skewer, or the axle nuts on inexpensive bicycles.

ii-3

RELEASING THE BRAKE

Most brakes have a quick-release (QR) mechanism to open the brake arms so that they spring away from the rim, allowing the tire to pass between the pads. Most road bike sidepull brake calipers have a lever that you flip up to open the brake (Fig. 2.1). Alternatively, Campagnolo Ergopower systems have a pin near the top of the brake lever that you push outward to allow the lever (and consequently the caliper) to open wider (Fig. 2.2). Cheap sidepull brakes on cheap bikes—as well as early sidepull brakes on classic racing bikes from the late 1960s and early 1970s—don't have a quick-release for the brake. The same is often true with time trial bikes and triathlon bikes, as well as bikes with Campagnolo brake calipers coupled with non-Campagnolo aerodynamic brake levers on the ends of bullhorn bars (see Fig. i.2).

2.1 Releasing the brake

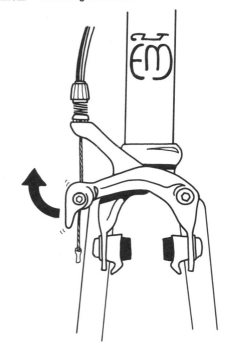

2.2 Releasing a Campagnolo brake

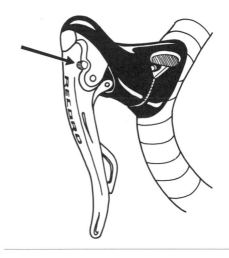

If the brake has no quick-release and the tire is not skinny enough to slip past the brake pads as the wheel is removed, you need to deflate the tire to avoid damaging it and perhaps even dislodging the brake pads when pulling the wheel out.

Center-pull brakes (rare now, but common on pre-1975 bikes; see Fig. 7.3) have a cable-hanger yoke that must be pulled down to release from the straddle cable while the pads are held against the rim.

Cyclocross bikes and some touring bikes have cantilever-type brakes (Figs. 7.19–7.38) that mount on pivots attached to fork legs or seatstays. Most standard cantilever brakes are released by pulling the enlarged head of the straddle cable out of a notch in the top of the brake arm while holding the pads against the rim with the other hand. Really old cantilever brakes are released like the center-pull brakes mentioned in the previous paragraph.

Another type of cantilever brake, less common on road and cyclocross bikes because of incompatibility with the brake levers on drop bars, is commonly called a "V-brake" (Fig. 7.42), after a popular Shimano design. V-brakes are incompatible with drop-bar brake levers because more cable pull is required to move the long brake arms than they can provide unless a shortie V-brake is used or a cam is installed along the brake cable to multiply the lever's cable pull. A V-brake is released by pulling the end of the curved cable-guide tube (the "noodle") out of the horizontal link atop one of the brake arms while squeezing the pads against the rim with the other hand.

Disc brakes (Figs. 7.43–7.53) require no release of the pads; the rotor should simply drop straight down out of the slot in the caliper.

ii-4

DETACHING A FRONT WHEEL WITH A QUICK-RELEASE SKEWER

You don't need a tool for this task.

1. **Pull the lever outward to open it (Fig. 2.3).**
2. **After you open the hub quick-release lever, the wheel is ready to fall out on most bikes with forks built before 2003 or so.** If it will not fall out, the fork ends most likely have wheel-retention tabs, which are designed to keep the wheel in place even if the quick-release inadvertently opens (or, most likely,

2.3 Opening a quick-release skewer

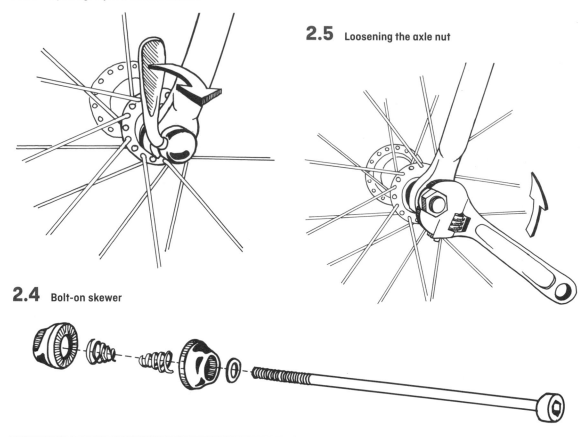

2.5 Loosening the axle nut

2.4 Bolt-on skewer

is left open by mistake). In this case, unscrew the nut on the opposite end of the quick-release skewer's shaft until it clears the fork's wheel-retention tabs.

3. **Lift the bike so the wheel drops out.**

ii-5

DETACHING A WHEEL WITH AXLE NUTS

NOTE: *Some bikes—usually those of lightweight fanatics or track bikes with hollow axles—have bolt-on skewers (Fig. 2.4), often made of titanium to save weight. The wheel is removed by unscrewing the skewer with a 5mm hex key.*

1. **Unscrew the nuts on the axle ends (usually with a 15mm wrench) until they allow the wheel to fall out (Fig. 2.5).** Really old road bikes may have wing nuts for finger tightening instead.

2. **Loosen the nuts enough to clear the retention tabs on the fork ends.** Your bike may have some type of wheel retention system consisting of nubs or bent tabs on the fork ends, or an axle washer with a bent tooth hooked into a hole in the fork end. These systems prevent the wheel from falling out if the axle nuts loosen. Removing the nuts completely from the axle is not usually necessary.

3. **Pull the wheel out.**

ii-6

INSTALLING THE FRONT WHEEL

Leaving the brake open (or the tire deflated, if there is no brake quick-release and the tire won't fit through the brake while inflated) and sliding the tire past the brake pads, lower the fork onto the wheel so that the bike's weight pushes the top of the dropout slots down onto the hub axle. This action will seat the axle fully into the fork and center the rim between the brake pads. If the fork or wheel is misaligned, you will need to hold the rim centered between the brake pads when securing the hub (and as soon as you can, true the untrue wheel—see §vi-16—or get the bent fork fixed or replaced). To secure the wheel, continue with the steps given in the section that is appropriate for your bike's configuration (§ii-7, §ii-8, or §ii-9).

With a disc brake, ensure that the rotor is lined up with the slot in the brake caliper and that it slides up between the pads as the fork is lowered onto the wheel.

---

ii-7

TIGHTENING THE QUICK-RELEASE SKEWER

The quick-release skewer is not a glorified wing nut and should not be treated as such.

1. **Hold the quick-release lever in the "open" position.**

2. **Tighten the opposite end nut until it snugs up against the face of the dropout.** (If there are no wheel-retention tabs on the fork and you did not unscrew the skewer nut, this step is unnecessary because the skewer will still be in adjustment.)

3. **Push the lever over (Fig. 2.6) to the "closed" position (it should now be at a 90-degree angle to the axle).** It should take a good amount of hand pressure to close the quick-release lever properly; the lever should leave its imprint on your palm for a few seconds.

4. **If the quick-release lever does not close tightly, open the lever again, tighten the end nut a quarter turn, and close the lever again.** Repeat until tight.

5. **If, on the other hand, the lever cannot be pushed down flat, then the nut is too tight.** Open the quick-release lever, unscrew the end nut a quarter turn or so, and try closing the lever again. Repeat this procedure until the quick-release lever is fully closed and snug. The lever should leave an imprint on the palm of your hand for a few seconds. When you are done, it is important to have

---

2.6 Tightening the quick-release skewer

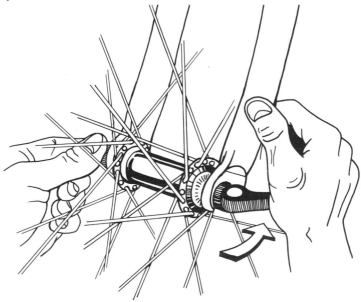

the lever pointing straight up or toward the back of the bike so that it cannot hook on obstacles and be accidentally opened.

6. **Hit the top of the tire with your open palm to check that the wheel is not loose and you cannot bang it out.**

ii-8
TIGHTENING BOLT-ON SKEWERS

Hold the end nut with one hand and tighten the bolt-on skewer (Fig. 2.4) with a 5mm hex key. Control Tech, a maker of these skewers, recommends 65 inch-pounds (in-lbs) of tightening torque for steel bolt-on skewers and 85 in-lbs for titanium ones. You can approximate the accurate tightening torque by using a short hex key and tightening as tightly as you can with your fingers. These skewers can be overtightened; avoid that problem by being conscious of how much pressure a quick-release skewer applies and do not go higher than that. But make sure it is tight enough to securely hold the wheel and not loosen on its own.

ii-9
TIGHTENING AXLE NUTS

Snug up the nuts clockwise (opposite direction in Fig. 2.5) with a wrench (usually 15mm) a little from each side until they are quite tight. In the case of wing nuts, the procedure is the same: The tools are your fingers.

ii-10
CLOSING THE BRAKES

The steps required to close the brakes are always the reverse of what you did to release them.

1. **For sidepull brakes:** With most road bikes, closing the brake caliper is simply a matter of flipping closed the quick-release lever on the sidepull brake caliper (Fig. 2.1 in reverse). With Campagnolo Ergopower, pull the brake lever and push the pin inward to engage the shallower notch in the lever body (Fig. 2.2).

2. **For cantilever, center-pull, V-, and disc brakes:** With many cantilever brakes (cyclocross and some touring bikes; Figs. 7.19–7.38), hold the brake pads against the rim with one hand and hook the enlarged end of the straddle cable back into the end of the brake arm with your other hand. On older bikes with center-pull brakes (Fig. 7.3), as well as with some cantilevers, hook the straddle cable yoke under the straddle cable. With V-brakes (Fig. 7.42), pop the end of the curved cable-guide tube (the "noodle") back into the horizontal link atop one of the brake arms while squeezing the pads against the rim with the other hand. There is no quick-release to close on a disc brake (Figs. 7.42–7.53); simply slide the rotor up between the pads. Make sure with hydraulic disc brakes that you don't squeeze the lever when there is no rotor or spacer between the pads, because it will push the pads out too far to allow the rotor to fit in between them. You will need to push the pistons back in their bores (§vii-15) before you can install the wheel.

3. **Check that the brake cables are connected securely by squeezing the levers.** Lift the front end of the bike and spin the front wheel, gently applying the brakes several times. Check that the pads are not dragging. If they are, center the wheel (or adjust the brakes as described in Chapter 7). If every-

thing is reconnected and centered properly, you're done. Go ride your bike.

ii-11

REMOVING THE REAR WHEEL

Removing the rear wheel is just like removing the front, with the added complication of the chain and cogs.

1. **Open the brake (or deflate the tire), as outlined in §ii-3.**
2. **Shift the chain onto the smallest rear cog:** Lift the rear wheel off the ground, turn the cranks, and shift.
3. **To release the wheel from the rear dropouts and the brakes, follow the same procedure as for the front wheel.** When you push the wheel out, you will need to move the chain out of the way. Unless you have rear-entry dropouts (see below), this maneuver is usually a matter of grabbing the rear derailleur and pulling it back so that its jockey wheels

(pulley wheels that guide the chain onto the cogs) move out of the way, while you push forward on the quick-release or axle nuts with your thumbs and let the wheel fall as you hold the bike up (Fig. 2.7). If the bottom half of the chain catches the wheel as it falls, lift the wheel and jiggle it upward to free it.

ii-12

REMOVING THE REAR WHEEL FROM REAR-ENTRY DROPOUTS

Some time trial and triathlon bikes have very tight clearance at the seat tube; there may even be a cutout in the seat tube for the rear wheel to "hide" from the wind (Fig. i.2). These bikes may employ rear-entry dropouts to allow the rear wheel to fit very tightly behind the seat tube. The dropouts work well but can be daunting if you've never dealt with them. Prepare to get your hands dirty.

2.7 Moving the rear derailleur and chain to remove or install the rear wheel

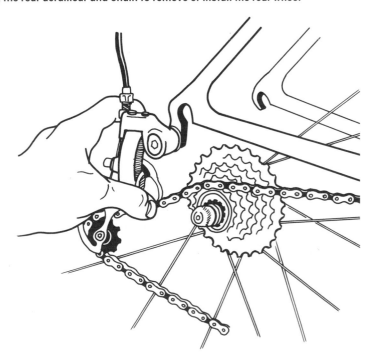

2.8A Removal and installation of rear wheel from rear-entry dropouts

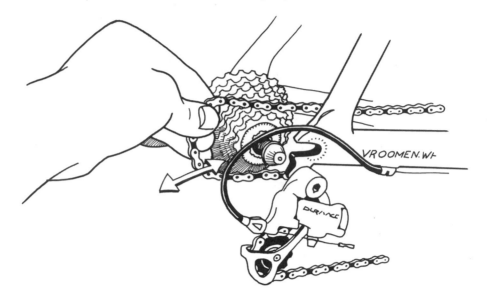

1. Open the brake (or deflate the tire), as outlined in §ii-3.

2. Shift the chain onto the smallest cog: Lift the rear wheel off the ground, turn the cranks, and shift. It's a good idea to shift onto the small chainring as well, to create more chain slack.

3. Open the rear quick-release skewer.

4. **You must move the chain out of the way before you can release the wheel from the rear-facing dropouts.** Grab the chain with your fingers and pull it back (off the rear cog) and to the right (Fig. 2.8a).

5. Open the rear quick-release skewer.

6. With the chain now out of the way, grab the rear wheel and pull it straight back and out of the bike (Fig. 2.8a).

ii-13

INSTALLING THE REAR WHEEL INTO STANDARD DROPOUTS

1. Check to make sure that the rear derailleur is shifted to its outermost position (over the smallest cog).

2. Slip the wheel between the seatstays and between the brake pads. Maneuver the upper section of chain onto the smallest cog (Fig. 2.7).

3. Set the bike down on the rear wheel.

4. **As you let the bike drop down, pull the rear derailleur back with your right hand and pull the axle ends back into the dropouts with your index fingers.** Use your thumbs to push forward on the rear dropouts, which should now slide over the axle ends. (If the axle does not slip into the dropouts, you may need to spread the dropouts apart or squeeze them toward each other as you pull the wheel in.)

5. **Check that the axle is fully seated in the dropouts;** this should result in the rim being centered between the brake pads. If it is not, hold the rim in a centered position as you secure the axle. This procedure should not be necessary if the wheel and frame are both aligned and the brakes are centered. Some dropouts have adjuster screws to adjust the depth to which the wheel slides back into the dropouts (see Fig. 2.8b); adjust

2.8B Horizontal dropouts with adjuster screws to center the rear wheel

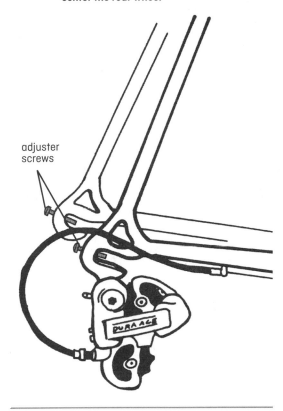

adjuster screws

these as needed to center the wheel between the chainstays.

6. **Tighten the quick-release skewer, bolt-on skewer, or axle nuts as explained for the front wheel.**

7. **Reconnect the rear brake the same way as you did on the front wheel.** Check the brake action. If all's well, you're done. Go ride your bike.

ii-14

INSTALLING THE REAR WHEEL INTO REAR-ENTRY DROPOUTS

Installing the wheel is the reverse of the removal procedure.

1. **While holding the chain off to the side as you did in §ii-12, put the wheel straight into the rear-entry dropouts (Fig. 2.8a).** Slide it forward until it hits the front of the dropout.

2. **Tighten the quick-release to lock the wheel in place.**

3. **Check to see if the wheel is centered in the chainstays and rear brake.** If the wheel is dished correctly and the frame is straight, the wheel should be centered in the frame. If it's not, loosen the quick-release and center the wheel.

   Many bikes with rear-entry dropouts have adjusters to set the depth for the axle. Use these to center the wheel before tightening the skewer.

4. **Grab the chain, pull it backward slightly, and put it back onto the small cog. Retighten the skewer.**

5. **Close the rear brake quick-release (as in §ii-10).**

6. **Operate the rear brake several times to be sure the wheel is centered between the pads.** Also pedal the bike in the stand and shift the rear derailleur to ensure that the shifting is normal.

ii-15

CLEANING YOUR BICYCLE

Most cleaning can be done with soap, water, sponges, and brushes. Soap and water are easier on you and the earth than stronger solvents, which are generally needed only for the drivetrain, if at all.

While using high-pressure car washes to clean your bike is sometimes unavoidable when your bike gets covered with mud while traveling, be careful when using them. The high pressure forces water into bearings and frame tubes, causing extensive damage over time. If you do use a pressure washer, never point it toward hubs and bottom brackets from the side, as it can blow the bearing seals inward; instead, always point it in the plane of the bike. Be careful about pointing the high-pressure water at electronic derailleur connections as well.

The best way to set up your bike for cleaning is to put it in a bike stand. In the absence of a stand, you can hang the bike from a garage ceiling with rope. No good? Turn it upside down so it rests on the saddle and handlebar. Alternatively, you can remove the front wheel and stand the bike on the fork and handlebar, but you'll need to lean it against something too, or it will inevitably pivot around its headset and fall down while you're washing it.

If the bike is really dirty, you can start by washing it with a hose while the wheels are on, letting them spin as you wash. A car-washing brush that screws onto the end of the hose can come in very handy at this point.

1. **Remove the wheels.** The wheels can be cleaned easily while they are on the bike, but even more easily when off. Remove the wheels to clean the frame, fork, and components.

2. **Support the chain.** If the bike has a chain hanger, hook the chain over it (the chain hanger is a little nub attached to the inner side of the right seatstay, a few centimeters above the dropout). If not, pull the chain back over a dowel rod (Fig. 2.9), an old rear hub secured in the dropouts, or a chain keeper (Fig. 1.4 or 1.7).

3. **Fill a bucket with hot water and dish soap.** With a stiff nylon-bristle brush and a big sponge, scrub the entire bike and wheels. Leave the chain, cogs, chainrings, and derailleurs for last; scrub those with a different brush. You can also try bicycle-specific cleaners like Pedro's Green Fizz, Finish Line Super Bike Wash, ProGold Bike Wash, et cetera.

4. **Rinse the bike with water by hosing it off (low pressure!) or wiping it with a wet rag.** Avoid getting water in the bearings of the bottom bracket, headset, pedals, or hubs. Note that most metal frames and forks

2.9 Looping the chain over a dowel rod for cleaning

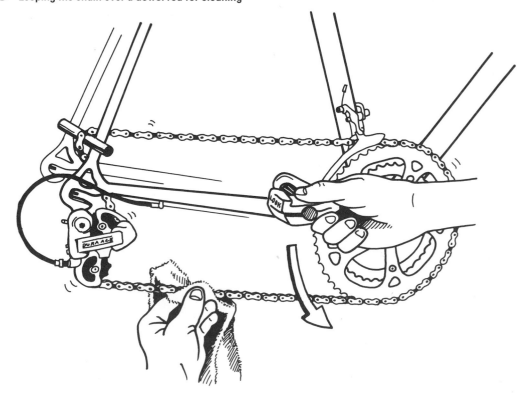

have tiny vent holes in the tubes; these were drilled at the factory to allow hot air to escape during welding. The holes on the seatstays, fork legs, chainstays, and seatstay and chainstay bridges can let water in. Avoid it by taping over the vent holes. Leaving them permanently taped to keep water out when riding is a good idea.

ii-16

CLEANING THE DRIVETRAIN

The drivetrain consists of an oil-covered chain running over gears and through derailleurs. Sounds messy, doesn't it? Because the whole affair is generally exposed to the elements, it picks up lots of dirt.

However, the drivetrain transfers your energy into the bike's forward motion, and so it should be kept fastidiously clean so that it can move freely. Frequent cleaning and lubrication will keep it rolling well and extend the life of your bike.

Fortunately, the drivetrain rarely needs to be completely disassembled for intensive cleaning. If you keep after it, regular maintenance can be confined to wiping down the chain, derailleur pulleys, and chainrings with a dry rag and then lubricating. I recommend wearing rubber gloves to keep your hands clean during this job.

1. **To wipe the chain, turn the cranks while holding a rag in your hand and grabbing the chain (Fig. 2.9).**

2. **Clean the rear derailleur's jockey wheels.** Holding a rag, squeeze the teeth of the rear derailleur's jockey wheels between your index finger and thumb as you turn the cranks (Fig. 2.10). This procedure will remove grease and dirt that have built up on the jockey wheels.

3. **Slip a rag between each pair of rear cogs and work it back and forth until each cog**

is clean (Fig. 2.11). An even better method is to use Finish Line Gear Floss.

4. **Wipe down the derailleurs and the front chainrings with the rag.**

The chain will last much longer if you perform this sort of quick cleaning regularly, followed by dripping chain lube on the chain and another light wipe-down. You will also be able to avoid the kind of heavy-duty solvent cleanings that become necessary when the chain and cogs get really grungy from lack of regular cleaning.

You can remove packed-up road grit from derailleurs and cogs with the soapy water and scrub brush. Note, however, that the soap will not dissolve the dirty lubricant that is all over the drivetrain; rather, the brush will smear it all over the bike if you're not careful. Use a different brush from the one you use for cleaning the

2.10 Cleaning the jockey wheels

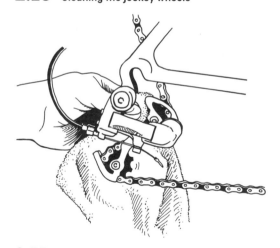

2.11 Cogset flossing with a rag

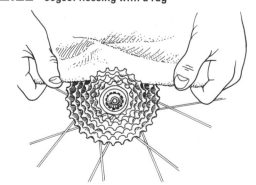

frame. Follow the drivetrain cleanup with a cloth wipe-down of the frame. Follow the lubrication steps 6–8 in the next section.

CLEANING THE CHAIN WITH SOLVENT

When a chain gets really dirty, the only way to rescue it is with an immersion in solvent—a nasty task worth avoiding by performing the regular maintenance just described. In fact, if you are sparing with the chain lube—that is, if you only drip it on the chain rollers where it is needed, rather than spraying it all over the chain—you can minimize, if not avoid, the need for solvent cleaning with its associated disposal and toxicity problems.

If you cannot avoid using a solvent, work in a well-ventilated area, use as little solvent as necessary, and pick an environmentally friendly mixture. There are many citrus-based solvents on the market that will reduce the danger to your lungs and skin and create less of a disposal problem. If you are using a lot of solvents, organic ones such as diesel fuel can be recycled, which may be preferable to citrus solvents, as long as you protect yourself from the fumes with a respirator. All solvents suck the natural oils from your skin, so be sure to wear rubber gloves, even with "green" solvents.

A self-contained chain cleaner with internal brushes and a solvent bath is a quick and convenient way to clean a chain (Fig. 2.12). See instructions given in §iv-3.

A nylon brush or an old toothbrush dipped in solvent is good for cleaning cogs, pulleys, and chainrings, and it can be used for a quick cleanup of the chain as well. Unless the chain has a master link, do not remove it to clean it in a solvent bath. Modern 11-speed, 10-speed, 9-speed, and even 8-speed chains should not be taken apart for cleaning; each chain rivet is so short that it can pop out of a hole enlarged by removal and reinstallation of the rivet. However, chains with

2.12 Solvent cleaning of the chain

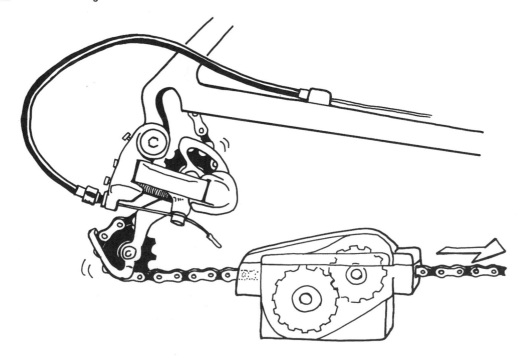

master links, which are available all the way up to supernarrow 11-speed models, can be removed for cleaning without being damaged.

1. **Follow the directions in Chapter 4 (§iv-7) for removing the chain.**

2. **Put the chain in an old water bottle about one-quarter full of solvent.**

3. **Shake the bottle vigorously to clean the chain.** Hold the bottle close to the ground, in case it leaks. Don't leave the chain to soak in the solvent.

4. **Hang the chain to dry completely, especially inside the rollers.**

5. **Install the chain on the bike, following the directions in Chapter 4.**

6. **Drip chain lubricant into each of the chain's links and rollers (Fig. 2.13) as you turn the cranks to move the chain past the drip bottle.** Though it gets more lube on the chain to attract dirt, it's most time-efficient to drip lube on the moving chain by gently squeezing the bottle with the tip on each top edge of the chain for a couple of turns of the crank on each side.

7. **Lightly wipe down the chain with a clean rag.** You want to remove excess lubricant on the outside, where it is not needed.

8. **Wipe down the rest of the drivetrain.** Wipe the jockey wheels (Fig. 2.10), chainrings, front derailleur, and chain with a rag (turn

the crank to pull it through a rag you clasp around it as in Fig. 2.9; there's no need to remove the wheel) and lubricate it (Fig. 2.13) after every ride to avoid another visit to solvent city. Keep rubber gloves and a rag near your bike so you can do this quickly on your return from a ride without having to scrub dirty oil off your hands later.

You can reuse much of the solvent by allowing it to stand in a clear container over a period of days or weeks. Decant and save the clear stuff and dispose of the settled sludge.

---

ii-18

CYCLOCROSS BIKE CLEANING IN THE "RACE PIT"

If you are supporting a cyclocross racer, you will be working in the service pit, the section set aside by the race organizer where racers exchange bikes and get other service. You will be cleaning and lubricating the bike similarly to the method described in §ii-15 through §ii-17, except very quickly, as you will only have a few minutes to do it before your rider is back, trading a dirty bike for the one you've just cleaned and lubed.

You will need the equipment and clothing listed in §i-7 and the tools shown in Figure 1.7. You will have either a hose or a pressure washer supplied by the race (shared with other mechanics) or only water that you brought, perhaps supplemented by buckets of water from a nearby pond. If you are really a pro, you may have brought a portable pressure washer, along with a barrel of water with a hose fitting at the bottom to feed it.

Give yourself enough space to work by keeping your stuff organized in the small area designated for you. Give other mechanics room to work so they will be more apt to reciprocate in the heat of the battle. This is especially important

2.13 Drip oil only where it is needed

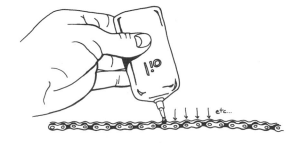

when the riders come through early in the race, as they will be bunched up, and conditions will be quite chaotic. You will be busy handing the clean bike to your rider, so you will need somebody else to grab the dirty bike. Later on, when the riders are spread out, this will no longer be imperative. The rider is not allowed to run without a bike, so he or she must drop the dirty bike close to you.

As soon as you have the dirty bike, get out of the way of incoming riders and other mechanics.

a. If you have a hose or pressure sprayer

1. **Hang the bike on a bike stand or whatever structure the race provided.** Orient yourself so you won't be dousing riders, spectators, or other mechanics as you blast water at the bike. When cleaning near the hubs and crank, always spray in the plane of the bike, not at it from the side, which can force water and grime into the bearings.

2. **First spray right at the tire treads and pedals.** Blast the mud out of them (and all over you and the bike as they spin faster and faster). You did wear waterproof boots, jacket, and pants, right?

3. **Clean from top to bottom.** Once the wheels and pedals are clean, spray down from above, first cleaning the handlebar, saddle, and top tube, working down to the brakes, drivetrain, and bottom bracket area (which you will spray up at from the bottom to complete, as well as the undersides of the saddle and handlebar). Spraying into the bearings is a no-no, hence working in the plane of the bike and from the top and bottom. Turn off the sprayer to avoid wasting your hard-hauled water, unless you are sharing the sprayer and there's somebody else in line waiting to use it. This may be all you have time for, and all that is really necessary, other than a check-over for mechani-cal function and a quick squirt of lube on the chain (continue with step 10).

4. **If you have time, degrease the drivetrain.** Though not usually necessary, if there is time available, you can spray some environmentally friendly degreaser (don't dump anything in this field that you wouldn't want on your own lawn) on the chain, cogs, and derailleurs. Let it sit while you sponge off the rest of the bike. If you have enough time, you can remove the wheels and insert a chain keeper into the rear dropouts or place a dowel rod or a stick across them (Fig. 2.9), and run the chain over it.

5. **Clean the handlebars.** If you have time, carefully sponge off the handlebars and brake levers using your bucket of soapy water and your big sponge, remembering that the only thing the rider will see is the front of the bike. To give your rider confidence, you want him or her to have the impression that the bike is completely clean, even if you did not have the time to clean all of it.

6. **Sponge off the frame, fork, saddle, and other nonsharp, nongreasy areas.**

7. **Scrub the bike where muddy.** With the big scrub brush and soapy water, scrub the brakes (especially the front if you are rushed; see step 5), pedals, cranks, derailleurs, and any areas where mud and foliage may have accumulated. Keep your brushes and sponges separated into those you use on greasy areas and those you don't. Brush off the chain with a stiff brush.

8. **Rinse.** Wipe the chain and the jockey wheels with a rag while turning the crank, as in Figures 2.9 and 2.10.

9. **Pick out gunk from the rear cassette.** Using a stiff cylindrical brush; a flat, narrow stiff brush; a curved plastic cog pick; or a thin screwdriver, flick out mud and grass

jammed between the cogs and chainrings while turning the crank. Dig out anything stuck in the pedals too.

10. **Lubricate.** Run lube into the chain by squeezing the bottle with the tip against it as you turn the cranks (Fig. 2.13). Besides seeing the front of the bike, the rider can feel the smoothness of the drivetrain, the brakes, and the entry into the pedals, so focus on those if time is short.

11. **Dry.** Move to the front of the pit and, while waiting for your rider, quickly dry off the top of the bike, especially the saddle and handlebars, with a rag.

12. **Check the wheels, brakes, and shifting.** If you have extra time, spin the wheels, checking for wobbles and rubbing brakes. Run through the gears and check that the stem is still lined up straight with the front wheel. Correct as need dictates and time allows.

13. **Hand off the bike when your rider comes through for another bike change.** Roll it along the ground and give the saddle a push as the rider mounts if it's a riding section next, or hand it onto the rider's shoulder if a running section is up next.

14. **Get out of the way and go back to step 1.** Repeat.

b. If you have no hose or pressure sprayer or bike stand but do have water nearby for your buckets

1. **Start with the wheels.** For the sake of speed, scrape the mud off the tire sidewalls first, using only your (gloved) thumb and forefinger as you pull the tire through with your other hand. Don't worry about mud left in the tread unless you have time later to work at it with a brush.

2. **Clean the front of the bike.** Grasping the front wheel between your knees, sponge off the stem, handlebar, levers, saddle, fork, and front frame tubes. See §ii-18a, step 5, above, for the psychological explanation.

3. **Clean the rear of the bike.** Grasping the rear wheel between your knees, sponge off the saddle, seat tube, seatpost, and rear stays.

4. **Scrub the pedals with a brush.**

5. **Pick dirt out of the cassette and chainring(s).** To get the big hunks of crud out of the rear cogs and front chainrings, stick a narrow screwdriver or curved plastic cog pick between them as you spin the crank backward.

6. **Unclog the jockey wheels.** Grab them with your fingers or a rag (Fig. 2.10) as you turn the crank, and wipe off the chain as well (Fig. 2.9).

7. **Continue with steps 10–13 in §ii-18a above.**

c. If you have no water or time is very short

1. **Focus only on important items like freespinning wheels, functioning brakes and derailleurs, and pedals that will clip in quickly.** Scrape the mud off the tire sidewalls with the side of a big screwdriver or hex key, and poke dirt, grass, and leaves out from around the brakes.

2. **Pick dirt out of the cassette and chainring(s).** With a thin screwdriver or curved plastic cog pick, poke and drag dirt out from the pedals, chainrings, and cogs.

3. **Continue with steps 6–7 in §ii-18b above.**

---

ii-19

A GENERAL GUIDE TO PERFORMING MECHANICAL WORK

a. Threaded parts

All threads must be prepped before tightening. Depending on the bolt in question (see descriptions in the following list), prep with lubricant,

2.14 Types of wrenches

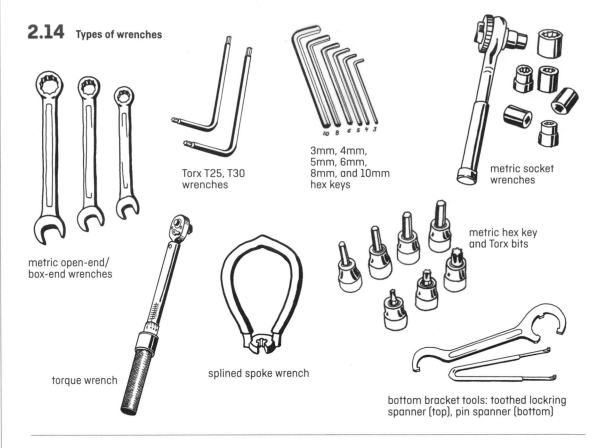

metric open-end/
box-end wrenches

Torx T25, T30
wrenches

3mm, 4mm,
5mm, 6mm,
8mm, and 10mm
hex keys

metric socket
wrenches

metric hex key
and Torx bits

torque wrench

splined spoke wrench

bottom bracket tools: toothed lockring
spanner (top), pin spanner (bottom)

threadlock compound, or antiseize compound. Clean off excess prep compound to minimize dirt attraction.

1. Lubricated threads. Most threads should be lubricated with grease or oil. If a bolt is already installed, you can back it out, smear grease on it, and tighten it back down. Bolts that appreciate lubrication include crank bolts, pedal axles, cleat bolts on shoes, derailleur- and brake-cable anchor bolts, and control-lever mounting bolts.

2. Locked threads. Some threads need to be locked in order to prevent them from vibrating loose. These are bolts that need to stay in place but are not tightened down fully, usually to avoid seizing a moving part, throwing a part out of adjustment, or stripping threads in a soft material. Examples include derailleur limit screws, jockey-wheel center bolts, brake-mounting bolts, spoke nipples, and sometimes crank bolts. Use Loctite,

Finish Line Threadlock, or the equivalent on bolts; use Wheelsmith SpokePrep or the equivalent on spokes.

3. Antiseize threads. Some threads have a tendency to bind up and gall, making full tightening as well as extraction problematic. Use antiseize compound on them to prevent galling. Any bolt threaded into a titanium part (including any parts mounted to titanium frames, like bottom bracket cups), as well as any titanium bolt, must be coated with antiseize compound. Use Finish Line Ti-Prep or the equivalent.

CAUTIONARY NOTE: *Unless specified by the manufacturer, never thread a titanium bolt into a titanium part. These can gall and rip apart when you try to remove them, even with antiseize compound. If you must break this rule, use a liberal coating of antiseize compound on the threads. Every six months, unscrew the bolt, clean it, and reapply the compound.*

Anti-seize paste, or lube, is fine in its place, but there's no need to spread it and its zillions of copper flakes all over your bike. Normal bicycle grease is fine for aluminum and steel threads. You can use it on parts that move and creak, or parts that can get frozen in place: front derailleur band clamps, seat binder clamps, seatposts, stem clamps, and of course on all rolling and sliding parts like bearings and bushings.

However, anti-seize paste must be used on all titanium threads. You can also use it on steel and aluminum threads, but grease is sufficient for them.

Use threadlock compound on bolts that won't be fully tightened to high torque but which need to stay put: Cantilever brake mounting bolts (where overtightening would swell the cantilever post and cause the arm to bind); mounting bolts for caliper brakes, disc-brake calipers and rotors; and rear-derailleur jockey-wheel bolts. For spoke threads, use a spoke-specific compound. You can also use spoke nipples that already have threadlock compound inside.

Carbon assembly paste is the stuff for parts that have slipped or may slip in the future. Definitely use it on a carbon seatpost that has slipped in the past. It can't hurt to put it inside the stem clamp around the handlebar, and it is a must if the bar slips even after the clamp bolts have been tightened to the specified torque.

Wrenches (see Fig. 2.14 for various types) must be fully engaged before tightening or loosening.

1. Hex keys and Torx wrenches must be fully inserted into the bolt head, or the wrench and/or bolt hole will round off. Shallow bolt heads, such as those used on shoe cleat bolts, are especially susceptible, so be careful; tapping the hex key in may be necessary. Be sure to clean dirt and debris from bolt heads before inserting the hex key, and make sure the hex key is inserted all the way before turning the bolt. Do final tightening with the straight end of a hex key, not the ball end, and ideally with a torque wrench set to the recommended torque for the part.

2. Open-end, box-end, and socket wrenches must be properly seated around a hex bolt, or it will round off.

3. Splined wrenches must be fully engaged; if they are not, the splines will be damaged or the tool will snap. Be especially careful when removing a cog lockring; if you strip the splines, you've got a real problem on your hands.

4. Toothed lockring spanners (on a bottom bracket adjustable cup, for example; see Fig. 8.36) need to stay lined up on the lockring. If the teeth slide off, they not only will tear up the lockring but also will damage the frame paint.

5. Pin spanners need to be fully seated in the holes to prevent slipping out and damaging the holes in the part. You'll find holes for a pin spanner in some bottom bracket adjustable cups (Fig. 8.36), hub-adjustment collars, and crank bolt collars.

Tightening torque

Appendix E has a full list of specific tightening torques. To best understand torque values, it helps to know a little about metric bolt sizes, particularly as they are used on bikes. If your torque wrench has a head that clicks over, DO NOT continue to tighten after the head clicks.

The designation M in front of the bolt size number means millimeters and refers to the bolt shaft, not to the hex key that turns it; an M5 bolt is 5mm in diameter, an M6 is 6mm, and so on, but the M designation may not have any relationship to the wrench size. For instance, an M5 bolt usually takes a 4mm hex key (or, in the case of a hex-head style, an 8mm box-end wrench). However, M5 bolts on bicycles often accept wrench sizes that are different from the ones normally used on M5 bolts. Bolts that attach bottle cages to the frame are M5, and although some accept the normal 4mm hex key, many have a rounded cap head and take a 3mm hex key. The bolts that clamp a front derailleur around the seat tube or that anchor the cable on a front or rear derailleur are also M5, but they take a hex key size that is bigger than standard, namely a 5mm. And when you get to the big single-pinch bolts found on old stems, you find lots of different bolt sizes (M6, M7, and even M8), but usually only one wrench size (6mm hex key).

Generally, tightness can be classified in four levels:

1. Snug (10–30 in-lbs, or 1–3 N-m [Newton meters in SI units]): Small setscrews (such as computer-magnet mounting screws), bearing preload bolts (such as on the top cap for a threadless headset), and screws going into plastic parts need to be snug.

2. Firmly tightened (30–80 in-lbs, or 3–9 N-m): Small bolts, often M5 size, such as shoe cleat bolts, cable anchor bolts on brakes and derailleurs, small (M5) stem bolts, and brake-lever-clamp bolts need to be firmly tightened.

3. Tight (80–240 in-lbs, or 9–27 N-m): Wheel axles, old-style single-bolt stem bolts (M6, M7, or M8), and stem-quill wedge bolts, brake-caliper mounting bolts, seatpost binder bolts, and seatpost saddle-rail clamp bolts need to be tight.

4. Really tight (300–600 in-lbs, or 31–68 N-m): Crankarm bolts, cassette lockring bolts, and bottom bracket cups need to be really tight.

b. Cleanliness

1. Do not think you can get parts to work by just squirting or slathering lubricant on them (meanwhile patting yourself on the back for maintaining your bike). The lube will pick up lots of dirt and get very gunky.

2. Unless otherwise instructed, don't lubricate ball bearings with oil; they generally require grease.

3. Do not expect parts to work if you wash them but do not lubricate them. They will get dry and squeaky.

c. Test riding

Always ride the bike—slowly at first, and then harder—after adjusting in the bike stand. Parts behave differently under load.

ii-20

PERIODIC MAINTENANCE SCHEDULE

If you follow this guide, your bike will last longer, and you will have less need for the emergency repairs in Chapter 3.

The interval periods are not written in stone; they depend on the bike, the conditions, and how you ride. In case it is not obvious, a bike used in wet conditions will require more frequent maintenance than one used only in dry, clean conditions. And a bike that's in bad shape will need more frequent attention to provide hassle-free riding than one that is in good shape. Don't add to the stress that your bike riding is intended to relieve by worrying that you're already 30 miles past your 250-mile maintenance interval, and early tomorrow morning you're heading out on a 100-mile ride with some buddies. If you've kept up with it in the past, it probably can wait another 100 miles.

Each maintenance task on this schedule is followed by the section in this book where you can find the instructions for doing it.

You may have other tasks that you want to add to this list; that's why I've added extra lines.

BEFORE EVERY RIDE

1. Pull the brake levers and make sure each brake is working, hits the rim properly, and the quick-release is not open.
2. Check that quick-release hub skewers are tight.
3. Look over the tires for cuts, bulges, and worn-through tread.
4. Check tire pressure, ideally with a tire gauge, but at least squeeze the tire to ensure that it has adequate pressure.
5. Look over the entire bike for anything out of the ordinary, like paint cracks or bulges, frayed cables, rust.
6. _____
7. _____

AFTER EVERY RIDE (OR THREE)

1. Wipe the chain, chainrings, derailleurs, and cogs with a rag, and lubricate the chain (§ii-16).
2. Wipe off the bike and look for damage to the frame or fork.
3. Adjust derailleurs (Chapter 5) and/or brakes (Chapter 7) if they were not working ideally during the ride.
4. Look for the source of any rattles, rubbing noises, or creaks you may have noticed during the ride.
5. If you've ridden in wet conditions, remove the seatpost and turn the bike upside down to drain water. Grease and reinstall the seatpost the following day.

6. _____
7. _____

EVERY 250 MILES (320 km)

1. Check chain wear with a chain-elongation gauge (§iv-6). Replace chain if wear exceeds acceptable elongation.
2. Inspect brake pads for wear and replace if needed (Chapter 7).
3. Clean drivetrain and entire bike if dirty (§ii-15 through §ii-17).
4. Replace tire if tread wear is excessive or you see other tire damage (§vi-1 through §vi-14). Inspect rim strip whenever the tire has been removed.
5. Push rims back and forth to check for play in hub bearings, and correct if loose (§vi-17 through §vi-21).
6. Check crank bolt(s) with torque wrench and tighten as needed (Chapter 8).
7. Push crankarms laterally to check for bearing play, and adjust or replace bottom bracket as needed (Chapter 8).
8. _____
9. _____

EVERY 1,000 MILES (1,600 km)

1. Check that frame pump works or that CO_2 cartridges and inflator are in good condition.
2. Check condition of spare inner tube and presence of appropriate tools in seat bag (§i-6).
3. Drip chain lube on front and rear derailleur pivots.
4. Overhaul derailleur jockey wheel bushings and seals (§v-32). If the derailleur has cartridge-bearing jockey wheels, check for smooth action and regrease if needed after removing bearing covers (§v-33 through §v-34).
5. Check wheel trueness and correct as needed (§vi-15 and §vi-16).

6. Check rim brake-track wear; replace rim if wear indicator dictates it (Chapter 12).

7. Check rims for cracks, particularly at the spoke holes, and replace rim if cracks exist (Chapter 12).

8. Check shoe cleats for wear and replace if needed (§ix-2).

9. Lubricate shift and brake cables (§v-16, §vii-3).

10. _____

11. _____

EVERY 4,000 MILES (6,400 km)

1. Remove and regrease seatpost.

2. Overhaul bearings in hubs (Chapter 6), pedals (Chapter 9), bottom bracket (Chapter 8), and headset (Chapter 11) if loose-ball bearings. If cartridge bearings, replace or grease if they are worn, tight, or grinding or they exhibit play.

3. Replace shift and brake cables and housings if needed (§v-7 through §v-15, §vii-4).

4. _____

5. _____

EVERY 20,000–25,000 MILES (32,000–40,000 km)

1. Replace handlebar.

2. Replace stem.

3. Replace fork.

4. Replace seatpost.

5. Replace saddle.

EMERGENCY REPAIRS

Eat a live toad the first thing in the morning and nothing worse will happen to you the rest of the day.
—Anonymous

TOOLS

Take-along tool kit shown in Figure 1.5 (and Figure 1.6 for epic or multiday rides)

If you ride your bike a fair distance from home, sooner or later you are likely to encounter a situation that has the potential to turn into an emergency. The best way to avoid an unpleasant surprise is to plan ahead and be prepared before it happens, which is what this chapter is all about. Proper planning involves steps as simple as bringing along a few tools, spare tubes, food, water, and extra clothes. And, of course, a little knowledge.

This chapter will acquaint you with ways to deal with most emergencies, whether or not you have all the tools you need. Generally, any prob-

LEVEL 1

lem you're likely to encounter will involve only one component on the bike—a flat tire, a broken derailleur cable, or something similar—and in most cases it is pretty easy to find a workaround that will get you home. True, you always have the option of walking, but this chapter is designed to help you avoid that miserable fate.

Always carry a cell phone on long solo rides, just in case something does break in a big way.

On the other hand, you may find yourself with a perfectly functioning bicycle and a fully charged phone (with service) and still be in dire straits because you're either lost, cold, dehydrated, bonking (i.e., your body has run out of fuel), or injured. Carefully read the final part of this chapter for pointers on how to avoid these possibilities and what to do if the worst does happen.

iii-1

RECOMMENDED TOOLS

The take-along tool kit for your seat bag is described in §i-6. If you're going to be a long way from civilization, take along the extra tools recommended for longer trips.

iii-2

FLAT TIRE PREVENTION

The best way to avoid flats is to keep good tires on your bike. Check them regularly for wear, cracking, and tread cuts. Coat tires you don't ride often with 303 Protectant or ArmorAll to prevent ozone cracking. Steer clear of potholes, broken glass, and nails, and you'll rarely have a problem.

Flat tires can be minimized with the use of tire sealant. Tire sealants usually come either as a viscous liquid containing chopped fibers (Slime is the most common brand), or as a thin solution containing liquid latex or the like that hardens into a rubbery glob to plug holes in the tube as air blows past (Stan's is a common brand). Sealant can be poured into a tubeless tire on installation or injected into an inner tube that has a Schrader valve; liquid latex sealants can be injected into Presta valves if they have removable cores (sealant use is covered in §vi-14). All Schrader valves have removable cores, and a core-remover tool often comes with the bottle of sealant. Most Presta valves, on the other hand, do not have removable cores, and so you cannot inject sealant through the valve except for thin, slow-solidifying sealants like Hutchinson Protect'air or Effetto Mariposa Caffélatex. Even on Presta valves with removable cores (you take the core out with an adjustable wrench or a specific core-removal tool), you can only inject a thin, liquid-latex-type sealant, because the valve stem is so thin that the sealant clogs it up. You can get aerosols with liquid latex designed for Presta valves (Fig. 1.6), or you can use a syringe to inject liquid sealant. You can also purchase tubes (both Schrader and Presta) with sealant already inside.

In a pinch, you can use evaporated milk in any Presta valve tube or tubular tire as a sealant. Just pour some canned evaporated milk into a pump you no longer care about, and pump it right into the tube or tubular tire. It actually works quite well to seal small leaks (it can be a lifesaver with a tubular tire with a slow leak), but if you ever get a blowout, boy, does it stink!

If you do have tire sealant in the tube and the tire gets low owing to a puncture, put in more air and turn the wheel so the hole is at the bottom, or ride the bike for a couple of miles to get the sealant to flow to the hole. Sealant will not fill a puncture if the hole in the tube is on the rim side, because the liquid will be thrown to the outside when the wheel turns.

Sealants cannot fill large punctures and blowouts, although big holes can be plugged sufficiently to get you home if you locate where the sealant is squirting out through the tire. Rotate the wheel so the spot is at the bottom and wait. The sealant may pool up and plug the hole. Add more air and continue. If you have Caffélatex in your tire and it is shooting out through a big hole, you can squirt Effetto Mariposa's ZOT! instant polymerization catalyst into the hole to harden the Caffélatex instantly and fill the hole so you can get home.

Plastic tire liners that fit between the tire and tube are often promoted to ward off flats, but I don't recommend them. Most are so stiff that they roll roughly, decrease traction and cornering ability, and can slip around inside the tire.

iii-3

FIXING FLAT TIRES

a. If you have a spare or a patch kit

Simple flat tires are easy to deal with. The first flat you get on a ride is easily fixed by installing a spare tube (§vi-1 through §vi-5). If you have tubeless tires, simply remove the valve stem from the rim and install a new inner tube, as in §vi-5.

With any tire, make sure you remove whatever caused the flat (you'll probably see it sticking up from the tread), and feel around the inside of the tire for any other sharp objects.

Sometimes inner tubes just fail, particularly near the valve on the rim side. In this case, the solution is to replace the tube.

Pinch flats are not exterior punctures; they are caused by hitting the square edge of a train track, curb, or pothole with insufficient air pressure in the tire. The inner tube gets pinched between the tire and the rim. You know you have a pinch flat if you see two adjacent holes on the top and bottom of the tube (sometimes called a "snake-bite" flat).

If you can't find a thorn, nail, piece of glass, or the like in the tire or tube, check the rim to see whether the flat was caused by the end of a spoke protruding up into the tube, a metal shard from the rim, or the edge of a spoke hole protruding through a worn rim strip. The rim strip is the piece of plastic or rubber that covers the spoke holes in the well of the rim, and you depend on it to prevent punctures to the underside of the tube, so check it carefully. Many rim strips are totally inadequate, being either too narrow or prone to cracking or tearing.

Also, metal hunks left from the drilling of rims during manufacture can work their way into the tube. These flats are so common that I recommend removing the tires and tubes before the first ride on a new bike and checking the rims. Shake out any metal fragments that may be present. If the rim strips consist of limp, narrow strips of soft rubber or cloth, replace them with high-quality plastic or adhesive cotton rim strips, or apply a couple layers of reinforced packing tape (the kind that has lengthwise fibers inside) to cover the spoke holes in place of the rim strips.

After you run out of spare tubes, use your patch kit to fix additional punctures (find the details in §vi-2 through §vi-4).

b. No more spare tubes or patches

If you're out of spare tubes and patches, you can actually tie a knot in the inner tube, pump the tube back up, and ride it home. You'd be amazed how well this works. Simply fold the tube at

the puncture and tie an overhand knot with the folded end (Fig. 3.1). To maximize the length of inflatable inner tube, minimize the length of the folded end sticking out of the knot.

Knotting the tube works fine—and you can ride the bike as if nothing had happened—as long as there is only a single puncture in the tube, a snake bite (pinch flat), or multiple punctures all within a few inches of each other that you can seal off with a single knot. Obviously, if you have widely spaced punctures, multiple knots will seal off sections of the tube from air, leaving them flat.

If tying off the tube won't work because the hole is at the valve, or because the tube has more than one hole in it, continue to the next section.

c. No way to inflate the tube or a section of a knotted tube

If you have neither a pump nor air cartridges, if you have multiple knots in the tube or a hole at the valve and no patches, or if the valve is broken, you will have to ride home without air in the tube or in a section of it. However, riding a flat for a long way will destroy the tire and probably damage the rim too. You can minimize that damage by filling the space in the tire with grass, leaves, or similar materials. Pack the stuff in tightly, and then remount the tire on the rim. This "fix" should make the ride a little less dangerous by minimizing the flat tire's tendency to roll out from under the bike during a turn.

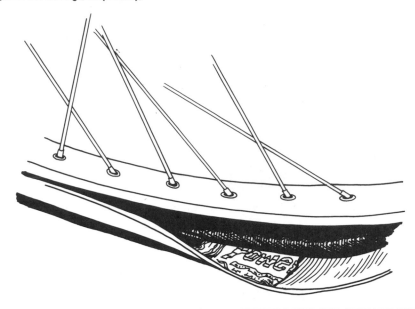

d. Torn sidewall

Rocks and glass can cut tire sidewalls. The likelihood of sidewall problems is reduced if you avoid old tires with rotten and weak cords. If the tire's sidewall is torn or cut, the tube will stick out. Just patching or replacing the tube isn't going to solve the problem. Without reinforcement, the tube will blow out again very soon.

First, you have to look for something to reinforce the tire sidewall (Fig. 3.2). Dollar bills work well as tire boots. The paper is pretty tough and should hold for the rest of the ride if you are careful. (I told you that cash will get you out of bad situations. Credit cards are not acceptable for this purpose.) Business cards are a bit small but work better than nothing. You might even try an energy bar wrapper or a piece of a plastic soda bottle. A small piece of lawn-chair webbing or a piece of old tire sidewall cut in an oval might be a good addition to your patch kit for this purpose. You get the idea.

1. **Lay the cash inside the tire over the gash, or wrap it around the tube at that spot.** Place several layers between the tire and tube to support the tube and prevent it from bulging out through the hole in the sidewall.

2. **Put a little air in the tube to hold the makeshift reinforcement in place.**

3. **Mount the tire bead on the rim.** You may need to let a little air out of the tube to do so.

4. **After making sure that the tire is seated and the boot is still in place, inflate the tube to no more than 75 psi, if you are good at estimating without a gauge.** Pressures lower than this will allow the boot to move around and may lead to a pinch flat, and higher pressures could blow through your boot.

Check the boot periodically on the ride home to make certain that the tube is not bulging out again.

iii-4

JAMMED CHAIN AND TWISTED LINK

When the chain gets jammed between the chainrings and the chainstay, it can be difficult to extract. You may tug and tug on the chain, and it won't come out. Well, chainrings are flexible, and if you apply some mechanical advantage, the chain will come free quite easily.

3.3 Freeing a jammed chain

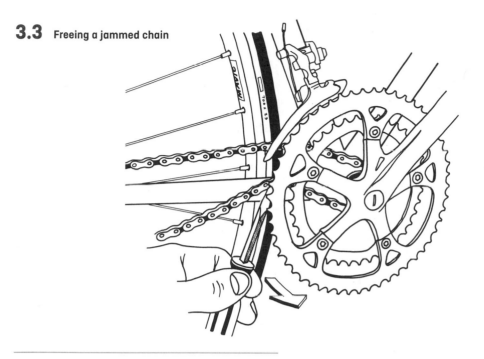

Insert a screwdriver or similar thin lever between the chainring and the chainstay, and pry the space open while pulling the chain out (Fig. 3.3). You will probably be amazed at how easy it is to free the chain this way, especially since lots of tugging would not free it.

If you still cannot free the chain, disassemble it with a chain tool (§iv-7), pull it out, and put it back together (§iv-9 through §iv-12). You can push out a pin on a 9-, 10-, or 11-speed chain, push it back in (Fig. 3.4), and get home. But I would not recommend riding it longer than that, because that link will be very weak; the plate will be prone to pop off the end of the rivet upon shifting.

If you have nine or more cogs on the rear wheel, you need to install a master link (§iv-13) in order to disassemble and reassemble the thin chain on your bike and expect to use it without worry for a prolonged period. If you already have a master link in the chain, fine; otherwise, bring one along that is the proper width for the chain. SRAM (Fig. 3.5), KMC, and Wippermann (Fig. 4.26) make them for all chain widths.

Once you get rolling again, you may experience a common side effect of jamming the

3.4 Fixing a broken chain

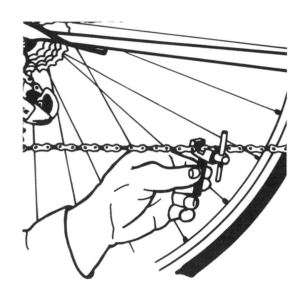

3.5 SRAM or KMC master link

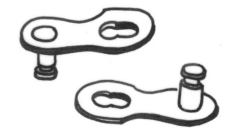

EMERGENCY REPAIRS

3.6 Twisted chain link

3.7 Untwisting a twisted chain link without tools

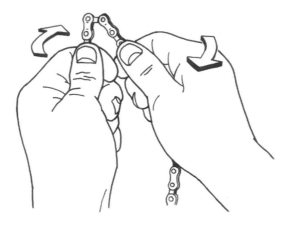

chain and continuing to pedal a split second too long. You may have created a twisted chain link (Fig. 3.6) that will keep popping off the cogs and chainrings and won't stay in gear. Once you find the twisted link, it will be obvious why it was popping out of gear—the chain will be running along nicely with the sides of the links vertical, and all of a sudden you will see some links leaning off to the side.

Untwisting a twisted chain link is easy if you have two pairs of pliers, two adjustable wrenches, or one of each. With the tools, just grab the links on either side of the twisted one at the rivet pins, and twist them to straighten the link.

Without pliers or wrenches, you can still untwist the link. Shift to the smallest rear cog and flip the chain off the inner chainring so it drops around the bottom bracket shell and has no tension on it. Fold the chain at the twisted link so that link alone is at the top, horizontal. Grasp the vertical sections of chain running up to it on either side, and pull one hand toward you and

push the other hand away from you to untwist the link (Fig. 3.7). Repeat until the twist is gone.

iii-5

BROKEN CHAIN

Chains seldom used to break on road bikes, although the problem is becoming more common with supernarrow chains. Chain weakness is compounded by worn cogs, which cause the chain to skip. The chain breaks when a chain plate pops off the end of a rivet. As the chain rips apart, it can cause collateral damage as well. The open chain plate can snag the front-derailleur cage, bending it or tearing it off, or it can jam into the rear dropout.

When a chain breaks, the end link is certainly shot, and some adjacent ones may be as well. Unless you install a master link, a broken chain is unsuitable for further use, although it can often be repaired well enough to ride home carefully, pedaling gingerly.

1. **Remove the damaged links with the chain tool.** (You or your riding partner did remember to bring a chain tool, right?) Again, the procedures for removing the damaged links and reinstalling the chain are covered in Chapter 4, §iv-7 through §iv-12. If the outer chain plates of a single link are damaged, remove them by pushing out the remaining rivet attaching them to the chain, and install a master link (§iv-13), noting proper orientation with a Wippermann master link (Fig. 4.26).

2. **If you have brought along extra chain links, replace the same number you remove.** If not, you'll need to use the chain in its shortened state; it will still work, but you probably won't be able to use the largest cogs when the chain is on the big chainring.

3. **Join the ends and connect the chain (Fig. 3.4);** the procedure is described in Chapter

4, §iv-9 through §iv-12 (§iv-13 with a master link). Some lightweight chain tools and multitools are more difficult to use than a shop chain tool. Some flex so badly that it is hard to keep the pushrod lined up with the rivet. Others pinch the plates so tightly that the chain link binds up. It's a good idea to try yours before you need the tool on the road.

iii-6

BENT WHEEL

If the rim is banging against the brake pads—or, worse yet, the frame or fork—pedaling becomes very difficult. If you haven't hit a pothole or something similar that has bent the rim, the cause is probably a loose or broken spoke. Another culprit could be a broken rim—fairly obvious with aluminum rims but more difficult to detect with carbon-fiber rims.

If the wheel wobble is so bad that you can't loosen the brake (§iii-9) and ride home with it that way, you'll have to perform a temporary fix; see the following sections.

iii-7

LOOSE SPOKES

If a wheel has a loose spoke or two, the rim will wobble all over the place, often too much to ride home with.

1. **Find the loose spoke (or spokes) by feeling all of them.** The really loose ones, which would cause a wobble of large magnitude, will be obvious. If you find a broken spoke, skip to the next section (§iii-8). If there are no loose or broken spokes, skip ahead to §iii-10.

2. **Get out the spoke wrench that you carry for such an eventuality.** If you don't have one, skip to §iii-9.

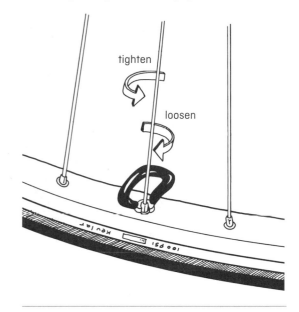

3. **Mark the loose spokes, if necessary.** You can tie blades of grass, sandwich bag twist ties, tape, or the like around them so that you can remember which ones were the culprits as the wheel becomes more true.

4. **Tighten the loose spokes (Fig. 3.8) and true the wheel.** Follow the procedures in §vi-16.

iii-8

BROKEN SPOKES

If you break a spoke, the wheel will wobble so wildly that the tire will hit the chainstay, making it hard to ride as well as wearing away the chainstay.

1. **Locate the broken spoke.**

2. **Remove the remainders of the spoke, both the piece going through the hub and the piece threaded into the nipple.** If the broken spoke is on the freewheel side of the rear wheel, you may not be able to remove it from the hub because it will be behind the cogs. If so, skip to step 6 after wrapping it around a neighboring spoke to prevent it from slapping around (Fig. 3.9).

3.9 Wrapping a broken spoke

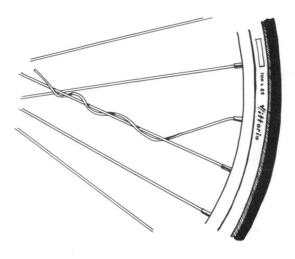

3. **Get out your spoke wrench.** If you have no spoke wrench, skip to §iii-9.

4. **If you brought along a spare spoke of the right length or the Kevlar replacement spoke mentioned in §i-6b, you're in business. If not, skip to step 6.** Put the new spoke through the hub hole, weave it through the other spokes the same way the old one was, and thread it into the spoke nipple that is still sticking out of the rim. Mark it with a pen or a blade of grass tied around it. With the Kevlar emergency spoke, thread the Kevlar string through the hub hole, attach the ends to its included spoke stub, adjust the ends to length, tie them off, and tighten the spoke nipple.

5. **Tighten the nipple on the new spoke with a spoke wrench (Fig. 3.8).** Check the rim clearance with the brake pad as you go. Stop when the rim is reasonably straight, and finish your ride.

6. **If you can't replace the spoke and you have a spoke wrench, bring the wheel into true by loosening the spoke on either side of the broken one.** These two spokes come from the opposite side of the hub and will let the rim move toward the side with the broken

spoke as they are loosened. A spoke nipple loosens counterclockwise when viewed from its top (i.e., from the tire side; Fig. 3.8). Ride home conservatively, as this wheel will rapidly get worse.

7. **Once at home, replace the spoke.** Follow the procedure in §vi-17, or take the wheel to a bike shop for repair. If you break a spoke more than once on a wheel, relace the wheel with new spokes (Chapter 12). The rim may need replacement as well.

iii-9

OPEN YOUR BRAKE TO GET HOME

If the rim is banging the brake pads but the tire is not hitting the chainstays or fork blades, simply open the brake so that you can get home, as detailed here. If the tire is hitting the frame or fork, you may need more extreme measures to temporarily straighten it; see the next section.

1. **Open the brake-caliper quick-release lever as far as necessary for the pads to clear the rim.** If the pads still rub, loosen the tension on the brake cable by screwing in the barrel adjuster on the caliper (Fig. 3.10); it may screw in clockwise or counterclockwise, depending on brand. Remember that braking effectiveness on that wheel will be greatly reduced or nonexistent, so ride slowly and carefully.

2. **If the rim is still banging the brakes and you have a wrench to loosen the brake cable, do so, and then clamp it back down.** The bolt will probably require a 5mm hex key. You now have no brake on this wheel; ride carefully.

3. **If this still does not cut it, you can remove the brake.** Disconnect the cable and remove the brake caliper from the fork or brake bridge, put it in your pocket, and pedal

home slowly. You will usually need a 5mm hex key for this task.

iii-10

BENT RIM

If the wheel is too bent to turn even with spoke truing and/or with removing the brake, you can beat it straight as long as the rim is not broken.

1. **Find the area that is bent outward the most and mark it.**
2. **Leaving the tire on and inflated, hold the wheel by its sides with the bent-outward part at the top facing away from you.**
3. **Smack the bent-outward section of the rim against flat ground (Fig. 3.11).**
4. **Put the wheel back in the frame or fork, and see if anything has changed.**
5. **Repeat the process until the wheel can be ridden.** You may be surprised how straight you can get a wheel this way.

iii-11

DAMAGED FRONT DERAILLEUR

If the front derailleur is mildly bent, straighten it with your hands or leave it until you get home.

If the front derailleur has simply rotated around the seat tube or twisted in the tab that holds it to the frame (the chain, your foot, or a pants leg can catch it and turn it), reposition it so that the cage is just above (Fig. 3.12) and parallel to the chainrings (Figs. 5.13, 5.14). Tighten the derailleur in place (usually with a 5mm hex key).

If the derailleur is broken or so bent that you can't ride, or if the tab that holds the derailleur is bent, you will need to remove the derailleur or route the chain around it as described next. (If the tab is bent, trying to straighten it will either break it, pull it off, dent or crack the seat tube, or cause a crack to form in the near future. You will need to have a frame builder remove the tab and put a new one on.)

EMERGENCY REPAIRS

3.12 Opening the front-derailleur cage

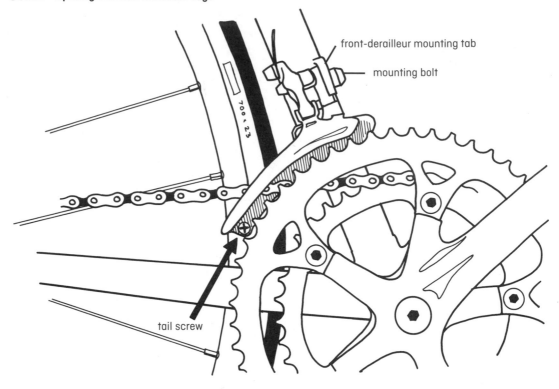

front-derailleur mounting tab

mounting bolt

700 x 23

tail screw

a. If you have only a screwdriver

1. **Get the chain out of the derailleur cage.** To do this, open the derailleur cage by removing the screw at its tail (Fig. 3.12). If the derailleur cage is riveted closed, you'll have to open the chain with a chain tool or by hand at a master link (§iv-7 or §iv-13).

2. **Bypass the derailleur by putting the chain on a chainring that does not interfere with it.** Either shift the derailleur to the inside and put the chain on the big chainring, or vice versa.

b. If you have hex keys and a screwdriver (or a chain tool or master link)

1. **Remove the derailleur from the seat tube, usually with a 5mm hex key.**

2. **Remove the screw at the tail of the derailleur cage with a screwdriver, if it has one.**

3. **Pry open the cage and separate it from the chain.** You can also disassemble the chain,

pull it out of the derailleur, and reconnect it (Chapter 4).

4. **Manually put the chain on whichever chainring is most appropriate for the ride home.** If in doubt, put it on the inner one (or middle one, if you have a triple).

5. **Tie up the derailleur cable so that it won't catch in your wheel.**

6. **Stuff the derailleur in your pocket and ride home.**

iii-12

DAMAGED REAR DERAILLEUR

If the upper jockey wheel gets lost, put the lower one on top and thread a wire or zip tie through three threaded Presta valve collar nuts (off your inner tube valves) as a lower wheel. If one of the jockey-wheel bolts gets lost, and you found the jockey wheel, try replacing the bolt with one of the water bottle cage bolts or a zip tie. If the return spring on the rear-derailleur cage breaks, the chain will hang loosely. If you have a bungee cord, hook it to the lower cage, around the skewer (put the lever on the drive side), and up to the seat-tube bottle cage.

If the rear derailleur gets bent just a bit, you can probably straighten it enough to get home. If it gets really bent or broken or one of the jockey wheels falls off, you will need to bypass the derailleur, effectively turning your bike into a single-speed for the remainder of your ride (Fig. 3.13).

1. **Open the chain with a chain tool or by hand at a master link (§iv-7 or §iv-13) and pull it out of the derailleur.**

2. **Pick a gear combination in which you think you can make it home most effectively, and set the front derailleur over the chainring you have picked.** Be aware that the chain will tend to fall off the chainrings or move down to smaller cogs, unless it is really tight and is lined up as straight as possible with the direction of the bike (i.e., is not crossed at an angle from big to big or small to small chainring and cog).

3. **Wrap the chain over the chainring and the rear cog you have chosen.** Bypass the rear derailleur entirely.

4. **Remove any overlapping chain with the chain tool (§iv-7).** Make the chain as short as you can while still being able to connect the ends.

5. **Connect the chain with the chain tool or by hand at a master link as described in §iv-9 or §iv-13.**

6. **Ride home carefully.**

iii-13

BROKEN FRONT-DERAILLEUR CABLE

The chain will be on the inner chainring, and you will still be able to use all of your rear cogs. Leave it on the inner ring and ride home.

3.13 Bypassing a damaged rear derailleur

3.14 Tightening a high-end limit screw

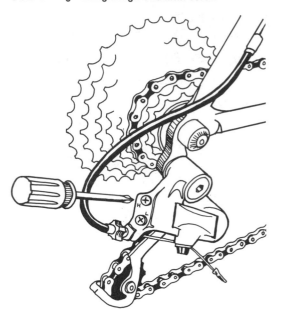

3.15 Wedging the rear derailleur into an easier gear

iii-14

BROKEN REAR-DERAILLEUR CABLE

The chain will be on the smallest rear cog, and you will still be able to use both (or all three) front chainrings. You have three options:

1. **Leave the chain on the small cog and ride home.**

2. **Lock the derailleur in one gear.** Move the chain to a larger cog, push inward on the derailleur with your hand, and tighten the high-gear limit screw on the rear derailleur (usually the upper one of the two screws) until it lines up with a larger cog (Fig. 3.14). Move the chain to that cog and ride home. You may have to fine-tune the adjustment of the derailleur stop screw to get it to run quietly without skipping.

3. **Jam the derailleur in one gear.** If you do not have a screwdriver, you can push inward on the rear derailleur while turning the crank with the rear wheel off the ground to shift

to a larger cog. Jam a stick between the derailleur cage plates to prevent the chain from moving back down to the small cog (Fig. 3.15).

iii-15

NONFUNCTIONING ELECTRONIC DERAILLEUR

If the battery is dead or the wiring harness is faulty, your bike's electronic derailleurs will not work. Check all of the visible wire connections to ensure none have come unplugged, check that the battery is clipped in correctly, and do the standard diagnostic procedures (§v-18 through §v-21) with the programming buttons on the processor and the shifters in an attempt to get it working again. If shifting still is not happening, you can manually move the rear derailleur into a chosen gear, and it will stay there. Push the derailleur into a gear you can get home with, lifting the rear wheel and turning the crank to get the chain to engage. Note that you can damage the derailleur this way; if you manually shift the rear derailleur repeatedly, it may wear out the saver clutch designed to protect it in the case of a crash, and it will then no longer hold a gear.

iii-16

BROKEN BRAKE CABLE

Ride home slowly and carefully. Very slowly. Very carefully.

iii-17

BROKEN SEAT RAILS OR SEATPOST CLAMP

If you can't tape or tie the saddle back on, try wrapping your gloves or some clothing over the top of the seatpost to pad it. Otherwise, remove the seatpost and ride home standing up.

iii-18

BROKEN SEATPOST SHAFT

Ride home standing up.

iii-19

BROKEN HANDLEBAR

It's probably best to walk home (or call for a ride). You could splint it by jamming a stick inside and ride home very carefully, but the stick could easily break, leaving you with no way to control the bike. A sudden impact of your face with the road would follow.

If you decide to splint the handlebar, hold the pieces together with duct tape. If the break is adjacent to the stem, slide the bar left or right into the stem so that both pieces are clamped.

iii-20

FROZEN PARTS

Riding in snow or freezing rain can freeze shift cables where they pass under the bottom bracket or can freeze the derailleurs and fill the cogs you are not using with ice. You will just have to stay in the gear you are frozen in. But if the freehub mechanism freezes, you won't be able to coast for even a second. You may be able to free it by applying any hot liquid available (even urine!) and hitting the freehub with a stick until it rotates counterclockwise again.

iii-21

PREPARE FOR EVERY RIDE

1. **Always take plenty of water and food.**
2. **Tell someone where you are going and when you expect to return.** If you know of someone who is missing, call the police or sheriff, or see to it that someone goes out looking for that person.
3. **Take extra food for any ride over an hour.**
4. **Take a road map or a GPS unit if you don't know the area.** Be willing to ask for directions.
5. **Take a cell phone.**
6. **For long rides in uninhabited areas, take extra supplies.** Carry matches, extra clothing, and perhaps a flashlight and an aluminized emergency blanket, in case you have to spend time huddled under a tree.
7. **Ride carefully and attentively.** Pay special attention to wet roads, gravel-covered turns, turns covered with moss or fallen leaves and other plant debris, and areas with lots of traffic, especially traffic turning into and out of side roads.
8. **Wear a helmet.** It's hard to ride home with a cracked skull.

9. **Don't ride beyond your limits if you are a long way from home.** Take a break. Get out of the hot sun. Avoid dehydration and bonking by drinking and eating enough.

10. **Have your bike in good working order before you leave.**

In short, make appropriate decisions when taking long rides. Prepare well. Just because you have a $4,000 bike and are riding on paved roads, you are not immune to mechanical problems or becoming exhausted, cold, bonked, injured, lost, or caught out in the dark.

THE CHAIN 4

*Take care of the luxuries and the
necessities will take care of themselves.*
—Dorothy Parker

TOOLS

Chain lubricant

12-inch ruler

Chain tool

Lots of rags

Rubber gloves

Optional

Chain-elongation
  indicator

Master-link pliers

Solvent (citrus-based)

Self-contained chain
  cleaner

Old water bottle

Caliper

Pliers

Solvent tank

Rohloff cog-wear
  indicator

The bicycle chain is one of those wondrous technological breakthroughs that we take for granted. Without it a bike would be a clumsy and inefficient contraption. The chain is nothing more than a simple series of links connected by rivets (also called pins). Rollers surround each rivet between the link plates and engage the teeth of the cogs and chainrings. Nothing to it, and yet it is an efficient method of transmitting mechanical energy from the pedals to the rear wheel. In terms of weight, cost, and efficiency, the bicycle chain has no equal, although people have tried endlessly to improve on it.

Perhaps because it is so simple and familiar, the chain is often ignored. To keep your bike running smoothly, though, you have to pay some attention to it. It needs to be kept clean and well lubricated in order to utilize your energy most efficiently, shift smoothly, and operate noiselessly. And because its length increases as it wears, thus contacting gear teeth differently than intended, it needs to be replaced regularly to prolong

the working life of more expensive drivetrain components.

---

iv-1

LUBRICATION

LEVEL 1 For best results, use a lubricant intended for bicycle chains. Most lubes sold for this purpose work reasonably well at the basic task of keeping the chain protected and happy. However, I recommend against wax-based lubricants as they don't lubricate well. Chain life with them is short (1,000–1,500 miles).

If you want to get fancy about it, you can assess the type of conditions in which you ride and choose a lubricant intended for those conditions. Some lubricants are "dry," formulated to pick up less dirt in dry conditions. Other lubes are "sticky" and therefore less prone to wash off in wet conditions. Still others claim to be "metal conditioners" that actually penetrate and alter surface of the metal. Lube makers say you should choose one type and stick with it, though mixing lubes doesn't cause any harm.

Chain lubes are generally sold in spray cans and squeeze bottles. Avoid sprays for regular maintenance chores because they tend to spew oil over everything, and droplets from the spray can end up in your lungs. The chain only needs a reservoir of oil inside each link; on the outside, a thin film is sufficient to keep corrosion at bay. Extra oil on the outside will only attract dirt and gunk; it does nothing to improve the function of the chain.

1. **Ideally, drip a small amount of lubricant across each roller from the inside out (Fig. 4.1), periodically moving the chain to give easy access to the links you are working on.** Regular application is the most important thing you can do with the chain. To speed the process, you can turn the crank slowly while dripping lubricant onto the chain as it goes by. This method will cause you to apply excess lubricant, which will pick up more dirt. But overlubricating is preferable to not lubricating, and if you wipe and lube the chain after each ride or two, it won't build up excessive grime.

2. **Wipe the chain off lightly with a clean rag to remove excess oil.**

3. **If you want to do a champion job, perform this task before you put the bike to bed,**

4.1 Dripping oil only where it is needed

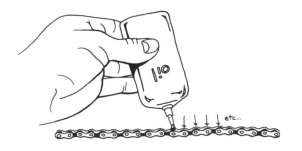

and then wipe the chain clean again the next morning or before the next ride. That way, you'll remove additional oil that has seeped onto the outside of the links, where it isn't needed.

If you're riding in wet conditions, you'll need to apply lubricant frequently (after every ride, or even during a long, rainy ride).

CLEANING BY FREQUENT WIPING AND LUBRICATION

The simplest way to maintain a chain is to wipe it down frequently and then lubricate it. If you follow this scheme prior to every ride, you will never need to clean your chain with a solvent. The lubricant softens the old sludge buildup, which is driven out of the chain when you ride.

The problem is that the fresh lubricant also picks up new dirt and grime, but if this gunk is wiped off before it is driven deep into the chain, and the chain is relubricated frequently, it will stay relatively clean as well as supple. Chain cleaning can be performed with the bike standing on the ground or in a bike stand.

1. **With a rag in your hand, grasp the lower length of the chain (between the bottom of the chainring and the lower jockey wheel of the rear derailleur).**

2. **Turn the crank backward a number of revolutions, pulling the chain through the rag (Fig. 4.2).** Periodically rotate the rag to present a clean section to the chain.

3. **Lubricate each chain roller carefully as in Figure 4.1.** Or take the faster method of running the chain past the dripping bottle tip.

To simplify this procedure, I recommend leaving a pair of rubber gloves, a rag, and some chain lube next to your bike. Whenever you return from a ride, put on the gloves, wipe and lube the

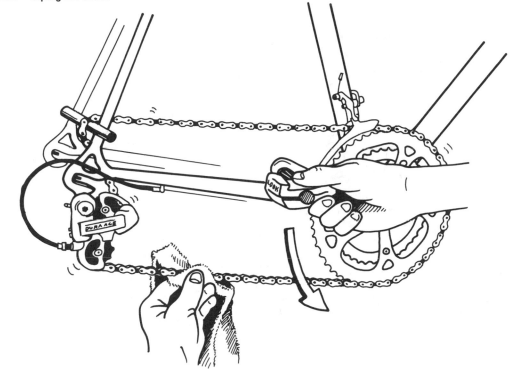

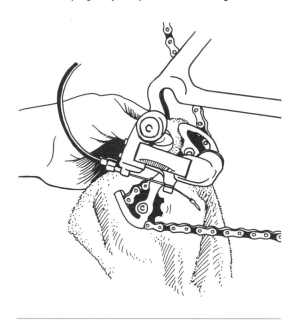

chain, and put your bike away. It takes maybe a minute, your hands stay clean, and your bike is ready for the next ride. Wipe the chainrings, cogs, front derailleur, and jockey wheels (Fig. 4.3) while you're at it, and the entire drivetrain will always work ideally.

iv-3

USING CHAIN-CLEANING UNITS

Several companies make chain-cleaning gizmos that scrub the chain with solvent while the chain is on the bike. These types of chain cleaners are generally made of clear plastic and have two or three rotating brushes that scrub the chain as it moves through the solvent bath (Fig. 4.4). Regularly removing the chain is a pain, as well as inadvisable with 9-, 10-, or 11-speed chains unless you use a master link, hence the need for cleaning the chain on the bike. Not heeding this can result in breaking the chain under high load, driving your foot, and perhaps your entire body, into the asphalt.

Most chain cleaners are supplied with a non-toxic, citrus-based solvent. For your safety and other environmental reasons, I strongly recommend that you continue to use nontoxic citrus solvents with your chain. If you recycle used diesel fuel, then go ahead and use it. In either case,

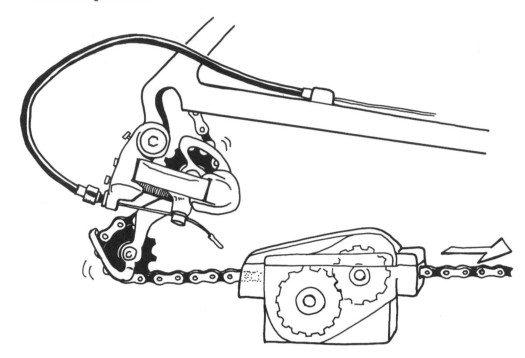

wear gloves and glasses when using any sort of solvent, citrus- or petroleum-based.

Citrus-based chain solvents often contain some lubricants as well, so that they won't dry out the chain. The lubricant carried with the solvent is one reason diesel fuel used to have such a following as a chain cleaner. A really strong solvent without lubricant (acetone, for example) will displace the oil from inside the rollers. The solvent will then evaporate, leaving a dry, squeaking chain that is hard to rehabilitate. The same thing can happen with a citrus-based solvent without an included lubricant, especially if the chain is not allowed to dry sufficiently before it is relubricated.

Here's the procedure for cleaning the chain with a chain-cleaning unit:

1. **Remove the top of the chain-cleaner case and pour in solvent up to the fill line.**
2. **Place the unit against the bottom of the chain, and reinstall the top of the unit so that the chain runs through it (Fig. 4.4).**
3. **Turn the bike's crank backward.**

4. **Remove the unit, wipe off the chain with a clean cloth, and let it dry.**
5. **Lubricate the chain as described in §iv-1.**

iv-4

REMOVAL AND CLEANING

LEVEL 1

You can also clean the chain by removing it from the bicycle and cleaning it in a solvent. I recommend against this approach unless the chain has a master link, because repeated disassembly by pushing rivets in and out weakens the chain by expanding the size of the rivet hole in the outer chain plate, allowing the rivet to pop out more easily.

A hand-opened master link can avoid the chain weakening caused by pushing pins out. Master links are standard on SRAM, Wippermann, Taya, and KMC chains. An aftermarket master link can also be installed into any chain, as long as the master link is of the right width.

If you do disassemble the chain (see §iv-7 or §iv-13 for instructions), you can clean it well, even without a solvent tank. Just drop the chain into an old jar or water bottle half filled with solvent, and agitate. Using an old water bottle or jar allows you to clean the chain without touching or breathing the solvent—even citrus solvents.

Here's the procedure for cleaning the chain if you don't have or don't want to use a chain-cleaning unit:

1. **Remove the chain from the bike (§iv-7 or §iv-13).**
2. **Drop it in a water bottle or jar.**
3. **Pour in enough solvent to cover the chain.**
4. **Shake the bottle vigorously (low to the ground, in case the top pops off).**
5. **Hang the chain to air-dry.**
6. **Reassemble it on the bike (see §iv-8 through §iv-12).**
7. **Lubricate it as described in §iv-1.**

Don't soak the chain for extended periods in citrus-based solvents, since these have a water base and will cause the chain to oxidize (rust), making it move with more friction and making it more prone to breakage. (Some people have two chains they rotate on and off the bike, leaving one soaking in solvent while the other one is on the bike. While this would work with diesel fuel as the solvent, you're asking for a broken chain with water-based solvent.) You gain nothing by soaking it anyway, so just don't do it.

After removing the chain, allow the solvent in the bottle to stand for a few days, decant the clear stuff, and use it again. I'll say it again: Use a citrus-based solvent. It is safer for the environment, gentler on your skin, and less harmful to breathe. Wear rubber gloves when working with any solvent, and use a respirator meant for volatile organic compounds if you are not using a citrus-based solvent. There is no sense in fixing your bike so that it goes faster if you end up becoming a slow, sickly bike rider from breathing solvent fumes.

iv-5

CHAIN REPLACEMENT

LEVEL 1

As the rollers, pins, and plates wear out, the chain will lengthen. That, in turn, will hasten wear and tear on the other parts of the drivetrain. An elongated chain will concentrate the load on each individual gear tooth, rather than distributing it over all of the teeth that the chain is wrapped around. The concentrated load will cause the gear teeth to become hook-shaped and the tooth valleys to lengthen.

If such wear has already occurred, a new chain will not solve the problem, because it will not mesh with the deformed teeth and will skip off them whenever you pedal hard. The only cure is to replace the chain, the chainrings, and the rear cogset, at considerable expense. So before all that extra wear and tear hits your pocketbook, get in the habit of checking the chain on a regular basis (§iv-6) and replacing it as needed.

(Some believe that it's superfluous to replace any part of the drivetrain, choosing instead to let it all wear out together. Since the chain gets longer and the teeth on the cogs and chainrings and jockey wheels all become hook-shaped, everything will tend to still work together, after a fashion at least. This method, which I don't ascribe to, only works if you never interchange cogs, so racers, or anyone with multiple wheelsets or cogsets, would be foolhardy to adopt it. Switch wheels or cogsets for a particular ride destination, or get a wheel change during a race, and your chain will be jumping and skipping like crazy while simultaneously ruining any cogs it lands on.)

Chain life varies depending on chain type, maintenance, riding conditions, and strength and weight of the rider. As a ballpark number, figure on replacing the chain every 1,000–1,500 miles if the bike is ridden in dirty conditions or with infrequent lubrication (or with wax-based lubricants) by a heavy rider. Lighter cyclists riding mostly on clean, dry roads can extend the replacement time to 2,000–3,000 miles with poor maintenance and up to 5,000 miles with a daily high-quality lubrication.

---

iv-6

CHECKING FOR CHAIN ELONGATION

a. Chain-elongation gauges

The most reliable way to see whether the chain is worn out is to employ a chain-elongation gauge. Make sure you check a number of spots on the chain; you'll find variation. The Rohloff gauge (Fig. 4.5) is superquick and easy to use. It's a go/no-go gauge; brace the hook end against a chain roller, and if the opposing curved tooth falls completely into the chain so the length of the tool's body contacts it, the chain is shot. That's it. There's nothing to squint at to determine whether or not to replace the chain. You are supposed to use the tooth marked S for steel cogs and the tooth marked A for aluminum and titanium cogs, but I just use the A side. I find that if the A edge comes down to the chain and I replace it right then, I get

4.5 Checking chain wear with a Rohloff gauge

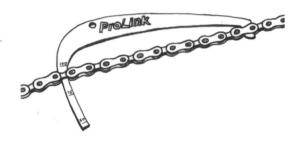

4.6 Using a ProGold chain gauge

almost infinite life out of my chainrings and cogs, even titanium ones. That's worth it to me.

The ProGold chain gauge (Fig. 4.6) offers a quick, easy-to-use alternative to the Rohloff tool. Brace the hooked end against a chain roller and let the long tooth drop into the chain. If it drops in close to the 90 percent mark, that is equivalent to the A side of the Rohloff dropping down flush with the chain.

Feedback Sports makes a digital chain gauge and also offers it under the KMC brand. With it you can monitor chain wear precisely over time.

PRO TIP | Cyclocross Demands Frequent Chain Replacement

If you are racing cyclocross, particularly in the Midwest, Southeast, Northwest, or East Coast (or in northern Europe), the chain is going to wear very quickly due to mud. Replacing the chain frequently under these conditions is critically important, or it will skip or ruin cogs. Cyclocross tends to mandate frequent wheel changes, and a worn chain will screw up the cogs on all the wheels you use on that bike. Chains are pricey, yes, but not nearly as pricey as cogsets, particularly several of them!

If you're riding in the mud a lot, check the chain for elongation weekly. Replace the chain as soon as (or before) the ProGold indicator goes beyond 75 percent (Fig. 4.6) or the Rohloff A side drops fully into the chain (Fig. 4.5).

I've also used some Park and Wippermann chain-elongation gauges, but either I find them less easy to use or they let the chain get longer than I think is a good idea before they indicate replacement.

b. Ruler method

An accurate ruler offers another way to measure for elongation. Bicycle chains are on an inch standard, and they measure a half-inch between adjacent rivets (and nominally have $\frac{3}{32}$-inch-wide rollers on derailleur chains and $\frac{1}{8}$-inch-wide rollers on single-cog bicycles). There should be exactly 12 links in one foot, where each complete link consists of an inner and outer pair of plates (Fig. 4.7).

1. **Set one end of the ruler on a rivet edge and measure to the rivet edge at the other end of the ruler.**

2. **The distance between these rivets should be 12 inches exactly.** If it is 12 $\frac{1}{8}$ inches or greater, replace the chain; if it is 12 $\frac{1}{16}$ inches or more, it is a good idea to replace it (and a necessity if you have any titanium or aluminum cogs or an 11-tooth small cog). The 12 $\frac{1}{16}$-inch measurement is equivalent to the Rohloff A edge indicating a no-go, and to the ProGold gauge indicating 90 percent.

If the chain is off the bike, you can hang it next to a new chain; if it is a third of a link longer or more for the same number of links, replace it.

If you always replace the chain as soon as it becomes elongated beyond the spec I've indicated on these chain-elongation gauges, you will replace at least three chains before needing to change the cogs.

---

iv-7

CHAIN OPENING

The following procedure applies to all derailleur chains when new and when you are shortening them to length. It also applies to removing a chain from a bike, except for those chains with a master link hand-openable without a chain tool (Figs. 4.24–4.27). Wippermann, Taya, SRAM, and KMC chains snap open by hand at the master link (see §iv-13), although they can also be opened at any other link with a chain tool, as described next. First-generation Campagnolo 10-speed chains have a master link that cannot be opened.

1. **Place any link over the back teeth on a chain tool (Fig. 4.8).**

2. **For most road bikes, tighten the chain tool handle clockwise to push the pin most of the way out.** Be careful to leave a millimeter or so of pin protruding inward from the chain plate to hook the chain back together when reassembling. **However, if you have a chain with a master link or a Shimano or Campagnolo chain and its new connecting pin, go ahead and drive the pin all**

4.8 Pushing out the pin (link rivet)

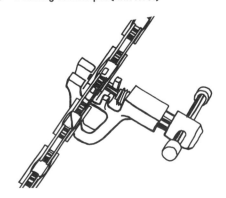

4.7 One complete chain link

the way out. (Campagnolo requires inserting its special chain-assembly pin through "virgin" holes in new outer chain plates, so other than with its 11-speed chains with special pin and tool to mushroom out the rivet head, Campagnolo requires that you buy a section of new chain with virgin outer plates at either end and two assembly pins. Then you remove that many links from the chain and insert this new section of chain.)

3. **Separate the chain by flexing it away from the pushed-out pin if you left the stub in. If you pushed the pin all the way out, the two ends will just pull apart.**

iv-8

DETERMINING CHAIN LENGTH AND ROUTING

a. Methods for determining correct chain length

If you are putting on a new chain for double cranks (including compact doubles), determine how many links you will need in one of the following four ways. Methods 2 and 4 are approximately equivalent, and both work for standard double-chainring setups as well as for compact-drive (smaller) double chainrings. If you have a triple crankset (three chainrings up front) and a long-cage rear derailleur on your bike, however, you should use method 3.

Method 1
Under the assumption that your old chain was the correct length, compare the new with the old chain and use the same number of links.

Method 2
With a standard double-chainring setup, route the chain through the derailleurs and over the large chainring and smallest cog. The jockey

wheels in the rear derailleur should then align vertically (Fig. 4.9). This method will not work if you are using a large cog that is larger than 27 teeth or beyond your rear derailleur's rated capacity; the chain will end up too short and won't reach over the big chainring and big cog simultaneously. Use method 3 instead.

Method 3
Wrap the chain around the big chainring and the biggest cog without going through either derailleur. Bring the two ends together until the ends overlap; one full link (Fig. 4.7) should be the amount of overlap (Fig. 4.10). This method works for triples and for standard doubles and is a must if you are using a double with a big cogset (like an 11–32 or 11–34) and a long-cage (or medium-cage) rear derailleur.

Method 4
Campagnolo suggests a different method with a double crank, routing the chain over the inner chainring and the smallest cog, as shown in Figure 4.11. Check for about 10–15mm of clearance between the chain wrapped around the upper jockey wheel and the lower run of chain (Fig. 4.11). This is not easy to measure; push the bottom of the ruler up against the chain wrapped around the upper jockey wheel.

Remove the excess links (§iv-7, Fig. 4.8) and save them in your spare-tire bag so that you have spares in case of chain breakage on the road.

b. Route the chain properly
Shift the derailleurs so that the chain will rest on the smallest cog in the rear and on the smallest chainring up front. Starting with the rear-derailleur pulley that is farthest from the derailleur body (this will be the bottom pulley once the chain is taut), guide the chain up through the rear derailleur, going around the two jockey

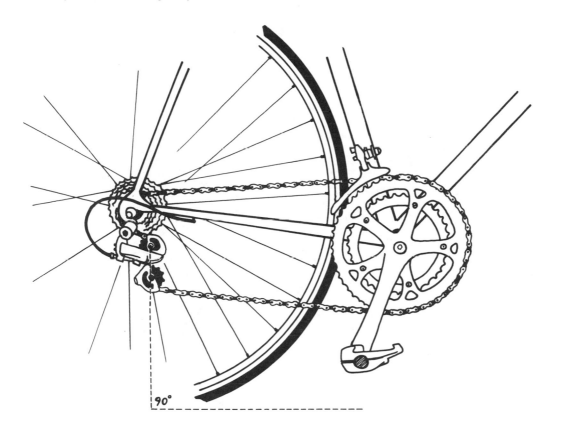

4.10 Determining chain length using the big chainring and the biggest cog

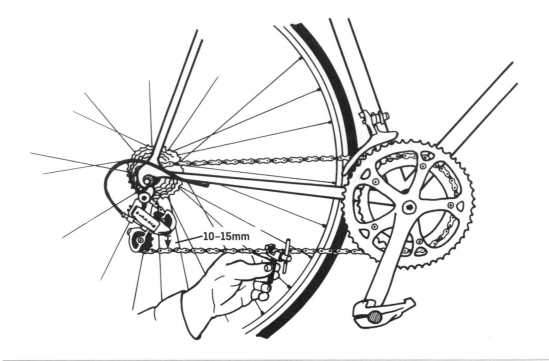

pulleys. Make sure the chain passes inside of the prongs on the rear-derailleur cage. Guide the chain over the smallest rear cog and through the front-derailleur cage. Wrap the chain around the smallest front chainring and bring the chain ends together so that they meet (Fig. 4.11).

iv-9

CONNECTING A 5-, 6-, 7-, OR 8-SPEED CHAIN (WITHOUT A MASTER LINK OR A SPECIAL CONNECTING PIN)

NOTE: *If you have a Shimano chain, a 9-, 10-, or 11-speed chain, or a chain with a master link, go to the appropriate section; don't connect it as described in this section by using the original rivet. Not heeding this warning could result in injury if the chain breaks.*

FURTHER NOTE: *This section applies only to wider chains, such as 5-, 6-, 7-, or perhaps even 8-speed chains. Never use the same pin (except in an emergency on a ride) on a 9-, 10-, or 11-speed chain or on any Shimano or Campagnolo chain.*

Connecting a chain that has no special connecting pin or link is much easier if the link rivet (pin) that was partially removed when the chain was taken apart is facing outward (toward you). Positioning the link rivet this way allows you to use the chain tool (Fig. 4.11) in a much more comfortable manner (driving the rivet toward the bike, instead of back at you). Be sure that the chain length allows about 10–15mm of clearance between the upper jockey wheel and the lower length of chain.

1. **Push the ends together, snapping the end link over the little stub of pin you left sticking out to the inside between the opposite end plates.** You will need to flex the outer chain plates open as you push the link in to get the pin to snap into the hole.

2. **Push the pin through with the chain tool (Fig. 4.12) until the same amount protrudes on either end.** If you have a 9-, 10-, or 11-speed system, or any Shimano chain, you shouldn't be using the original rivet in

4.12 Pushing in the pin (link rivet)

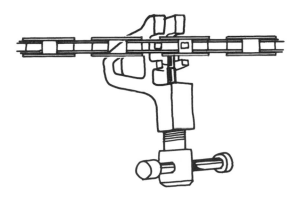

4.13 A stiff link

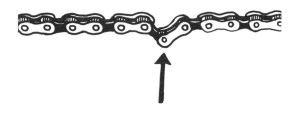

4.14 Freeing a stiff link with your fingers

4.15 Freeing a stiff link using a chain tool

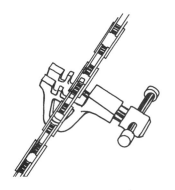

the first place. But if you are, and the chain tool prongs seem to be getting bent as you push the rivet, see the note in §iv-10, step 7.

3. **If there is a stiff link (Fig. 4.13), free it either by flexing it laterally with your fingers (Fig. 4.14) or, better, by using the chain tool's back teeth, as illustrated in Figure 4.15.** Push the pin a fraction of a turn to spread the plates apart.

iv-10

CONNECTING A 7-, 8-, OR 9-SPEED SHIMANO CHAIN

1. **Make sure you have the appropriate Shimano subpin connecting pin.** It looks like a segmented rivet with one segment ending in a pointed tip. It has a breakage groove at the middle of its length. Two subpins come with a new Shimano chain. If you are reinstalling an old Shimano chain, use a new subpin, and make sure it is the right length for the chain (10- and 11-speed subpins are shorter than 9-speed subpins, which are shorter than 7- or 8-speed subpins; see §iv-11). If you don't have a subpin and are going to connect a 7- or 8-speed chain anyway, follow the procedure in §iv-9, but be aware that the chain is now more likely to break than if it had been assembled with the proper subpin. With a 9-speed chain, this is an extremely dangerous approach—don't do it. With a 10- or 11-speed chain, it is a complete no-no to connect the chain without a new connector pin; the chain will likely break immediately. A broken chain is no fun; it can wreck other parts, and you can get injured. For assembling a 10- or 11-speed chain, read §iv-11.

2. **Remove any extra links, pushing the appropriate rivet completely out (§iv-7, Fig. 4.8).**

THE CHAIN

3. **Line up the chain ends.**

4. **Drip some oil on the subpin and push it in with your fingers, pointed end first.** It will go in about halfway.

5. **With the chain tool (Fig. 4.16), push the subpin through until there is only as much left protruding at the tail end as the other rivets in the chain.** It will feel hard, then easy, and then very hard to tighten the tool as you move the pin past its various ridges and valleys. Stop when it gets very hard, and check for binding. Go by feel more than by sight to determine when the pin is seated correctly.

6. **Break off the leading half of the subpin with the hole in the end of a Shimano chain tool or with a pair of pliers (Fig. 4.17).**

7. **The individual links should move freely when the pin is correctly seated.** If not, depending on which end protrudes more, either push the link rivet in a little deeper (Fig. 4.12) or push it back a hair from the other side with the chain on the tool teeth closest to the screw (Fig. 4.15). As a (poor) last resort not recommended with 9-speed or narrower chains, flex the chain back and forth with your thumbs at the stiff rivet (Fig. 4.14).

NOTE: *If you have a 9-speed chain and an older chain tool, you may find that the prongs in the tool to hold the chain are too far from the backing plate of the tool and will get bent. Shimano tools TL-CN23 (Fig. 4.18) and TL-CN32 (Fig. 4.19) work on all Shimano chains. Many other brands made for these chains also work.*

---

iv-11

CONNECTING 10- AND 11-SPEED CHAINS

Breakage can be an issue with 10- and 11-speed chains due to their narrowness. They are narrow because of the tight spacing between the ten cogs required to fit them onto a hub that is the same width as an 8-speed hub. In going from 5-speed to 6-, 7-, 8-, 9-, 10-, and 11-speed systems, the chain width (outside-to-outside) has come down substantially, from 7.3mm to 7.1mm, 6.6mm, 6.1mm, 6.0mm, 5.9mm, and now 5.4mm. But because the cog and chainring teeth did not get significantly narrower, neither did the inner spacing (the roller width) of the chains.

Since the spacing between the inner plates has not decreased, the width decrease has come from shortening the rivets and thinning the steel plates. Minimal protrusion of the chain rivets

---

4.16 Pushing a connector pin into a Campagnolo (or Shimano) chain with a chain tool

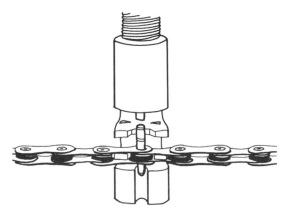

4.17 Breaking off a Shimano or Campagnolo 11-speed subpin

SNAP!

out of the plates means the chain is less secure against breakage under high side loads. To install the short connecting pin on a 10- or 11-speed chain properly, you need a really good chain tool that is intended for use on 10- or 11-speed chains (see Figs. 4.18–4.22, and read the Pro Tip on chain tools). The only exceptions are chains with hand-openable master links (Figs. 4.24–4.27) that allow opening the chain without using a chain tool. If your chain has a master link, skip to §iv-13.

When a chain breaks, it is usually under high pedaling load during shifting. Shifting creates lateral stress, and when the rear derailleur shifts with a modern cogset, the chain is simultaneously engaged on two cogs. And when the front derailleur pushes the chain from one chainring to another, it obviously flexes the links sideways. Easing off on the pedals when you shift will greatly decrease the possibility of a broken chain. However, a chain can break under any high load if a cage plate is just barely hanging on to the end of a rivet. Breaking a chain is dangerous because when the tension on the chain is suddenly removed, your weight drops straight down, as there is no longer anything supporting the pushing foot. You can easily fall hard. Very hard.

So, pay attention to the extra steps required with a 10- or 11-speed chain to ensure its security. To reuse a Campagnolo 10-speed chain, you must have a new section of chain with a "virgin" outer link at either end and two new connector pins. Shimano's 10-speed connector pin can be installed in a used Shimano 10-speed chain. This connector pin is not compatible with CN-7800 (first-generation Dura-Ace 10-speed) chains.

a. Connecting a Campagnolo 10-speed chain

Original Campagnolo 10-speed chains, when introduced in 1999, came with a separate closing link with two pins, called a PermaLink, and it required an expensive installation tool unique to that link. Fortunately, Campagnolo soon abandoned that closing method and replaced it with a pin system similar to Shimano's.

Campagnolo supplies a 10-speed connecting pin, except that it is a two-piece unit that pulls apart, rather than a one-piece pin with a break-off end like Shimano's. Remember, you get only one connecting pin with each Campagnolo chain (as opposed to the two you get with a Shimano chain), so don't lose it! Replacing one ain't cheap!

Campagnolo, like Shimano, has a special chain tool and highly recommends that you use it. Its main feature is a wire retainer that you slide into the tool to hold the chain down (like the 11-speed tool in Fig. 4.23, except without the flip-down peening gate). The Campy tool also has a locator stop for the drive pin specific for its chains. However, although Campagnolo will not guarantee the results with anybody else's tool, I find that, if you are careful to hold the chain down well on a Shimano 10-speed chain tool (Figs. 4.18, 4.19) and push the pin in so that exactly the same amount protrudes at either end, it works fine.

1. **If you need to shorten the chain, cut excess length (§iv-7) only from the end that terminates in an inner link.** That way, the holes in the plates of the outer link you will be connecting will never have had a rivet through them and consequently will not have been enlarged and distorted by the insertion and removal of a rivet, ensuring the strongest possible connection. Campagnolo calls these the "virgin holes," and it ships its chains with a zip tie through this pair of holes at the end of the final outer link so that you will make sure to close the chain at these links.

2. **Remove the zip tie and install the connecting pin as in §iv-10.** Be careful to insert the

4.18 Shimano TL-CN23 tool

4.19 Shimano TL-CN32 tool

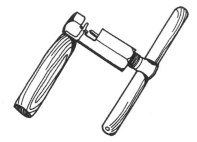

4.20 Pedro's Pro Chain tool

4.21 Rohloff Revolver chain tool

4.22 Park's CT-3 chain tool

connecting pin from the wheel side of the chain outward (the opposite direction from that shown in Fig. 4.11!). If you don't have the Campy chain tool, hold the chain down in the chain tool so that the tool's drive pin lines up exactly with the connecting pin. Note that the Campy connecting pin is in two pieces, and you can just insert the leading "guide pin" segment by hand, with or without the other half of the pin on it. The trailing segment that you will press into the chain has two hole sizes in it, so that only one end will fit on the guide pin, thus ensuring proper orientation. Make sure the same amount of the connecting pin is sticking out of both ends (it will only be about 0.1mm) and that you have no stiff link (Fig. 4.13). If you're sure you've pushed it in far enough and it's still binding, free it by carefully using the back teeth on a chain tool. Set the stiff link over the back teeth closest to the screw handle (Fig. 4.15), and push the pin a fraction of a turn to spread the link.

b. Connecting a Shimano 10-speed chain

IMPORTANT NOTE: *In 2009 with the Dura-Ace 7900 chain, Shimano introduced an asymmetrical 10-speed chain. Since the demands of upshifts are different from those of downshifts, the chain is different on each side. To obtain the correct orientation, make sure that the outer link plates with the Shimano brand and model stamped on them face away from the wheel.*

1. **If you need to shorten the chain, cut excess length (§iv-8) only from the end that terminates in an inner link.** That way, the holes in the plates of the outer link you will be connecting will have never had a rivet through them and consequently will not have been enlarged and distorted by the insertion and

If you ride a lot, you will change the chain frequently. At that point, it becomes worthwhile to have a good chain tool. If you currently just have a cheap little chain tool, you will be glad you made the investment to upgrade.

Shimano says that you should only use its 11-speed chain tool on its 11-speed chains; however, that tool will also work with all Shimano 7-, 8-, 9-, and 10-speed chains as well. Similarly, the Shimano TL-CN23 and pricier TL-CN32 tool were made for its 10-speed chains, and both work on all 7-, 8-, and 9-speed Shimano chains as well. The Shimano TL-CN23 is a small tool (Fig. 4.18), and the TL-CN32 (as well as its predecessors, the TL-CN31 and TL-CN30) is a professional tool with wooden handles (Fig. 4.19) that even has spare driver pins hidden in the base. The TL-CN32 (and the TL-CN31 and TL-CN30) has four locating teeth in a row to hold the chain, rather than just two, as most chain tools have. These extra two teeth, one extending out on either side of the tool, hold the chain well and do much of what Campagnolo's tool accomplishes with its wire loop to hold the chain down. Pedro's Pro Chain tool (Fig. 4.20) also has these extra two locating teeth extending on either side. Pedro's Tutto (everything) tool works on all 8-speed to 11-speed chains; a fourth position on its Speed Dial is the anvil to flare the connecting pin on Campagnolo 11-speed chains.

Holding the chain in place is nothing new. Before special connecting pins came into use, chains still needed to be lined up properly and held in place tightly, because there was no leading tip on a connecting pin to slip in by hand and hold the chain together (§iv-9). The Rohloff Revolver tool (Fig. 4.21), which has been around for well over a decade, has a thumbscrew that tightens against the chain and really holds it in place. It also has a revolving plate with different patterns on it to re-peen the end of the rivet in whatever style you choose. Park's CT-3 (Fig. 4.22)

is a standard shop chain tool, with both a front set of teeth and a back set of teeth, for prying a link apart a bit to free a stiff link, as in Figure 4.15.

If you're strictly a Campagnolo 10-speed or 11-speed rider and don't ride mountain bikes, you might as well get the (very pricey) Campy C10 HD-L 10-speed tool or the C11 11-speed tool (Fig. 4.23). The C10 tool looks similar to the C11 tool in Fig. 4.23, except that it has no swinging gate.

I have used a Shimano TL-CN31 (9-speed tool) for years on every kind of 7-, 8-, 9-, and 10-speed chain from Shimano, Campagnolo, Wippermann, and SRAM. As the chains became narrower, the supporting center section on newer Shimano chain tools was moved closer to the chain-locating teeth, to fully support the rear outer link plate while driving the pin in. If you use an older-generation chain tool (for wider chains) with a one-generation newer (narrower) chain, eventually you will damage the tool as it puts too much lateral load on the chain-locating teeth. A two-generation older chain tool will not seat the chain connector pins, so don't use it. Ideally, the latest tool will do the best job with the latest chains, and it will also be compatible with all the older (wider) chains.

If you are careful and if you are not using a Campagnolo 11-speed chain, you only need one good tool that is at most one generation old (i.e., it is meant for at least 9-speed chains), and you can use it on any chain up through 10-speeds. By careful, I mean that you must make sure that the connecting pin and the holes are all lined up perfectly (which the Campy, Rohloff, Shimano, and Pedro's pro tools definitely help guarantee). Furthermore, you must stop at the right point: Do not go too far or not far enough. For this, you must have a feel for the loose-tight-loose-tight pressure changes as you push a Shimano or Campagnolo connecting pin into place, as well as an eye for when the pin is protruding (or recessed) the same amount on both faces of the chain.

removal of a peened rivet, ensuring the strongest possible connection.

2. **You want the connecting pin you insert to be the pin leading the outer link over the top of the chainring or cog.** Accomplish this link orientation by making sure that, if you are connecting the chain at the bottom as in Figure 4.11, the inner link on one end is to the left (toward the rear derailleur) of the outer link on the other end you are connecting it to.

3. **Lubricate the pin prior to installation.** Make sure that you are using a Shimano 10-speed connecting pin. Two connecting pins come with the chain.

4. **Follow the instructions in §iv-10, except that, rather than having both ends of the connecting pins protruding a bit from their plates (as they are for 7-, 8-, and 9-speed chains), you want the 10-speed connector pin to be slightly recessed, below flush.** Go by feel rather than by how much pin you see exposed. Keep tightening beyond where you would normally stop with a 9-speed chain because it feels hard. It will feel easy and then very hard while you continue to push. At this point, stop to check for binding. The chain is connected perfectly when there is no binding at the connector pin link, without the need for you to flex it sideways to free it. Back off on the chain tool screw, check the link for freedom of movement, and retighten the tool if you feel any binding. According to Shimano, if the link is still binding, there is a 99 percent chance that the pin isn't pushed in far enough to be fully seated. As usual, finish by breaking off the tip of the connecting pin, as shown in Figure 4.17, or by slipping the hole at the end of the Shimano chain tool over the end of the pin and using that to snap it off.

CONNECTING 11-SPEED CHAINS

LEVEL 3

The cog spacing is tighter on 11-speed cogsets than on 10-speed, because they still fit in the same amount of space (namely, the 130mm rear hub width that was introduced with 8-speed cogsets). Thus, the chain is thinner than 10-speed, at 5.4mm outer width. However, the chain rollers (and teeth on the chainrings and cogs) are the same width as they have been all along, so the chain plates are very thin, and the pins are flush with their outer faces, making for even less surface area of pin engagement. You can imagine how thin the chain plates must be, because the spacers on either side of each cog are only 2.2mm thick, and the chain has to be able to run at the most extreme big-to-big or small-to-small cross angles without touching the adjacent cog. Consequently, following recommended assembly procedures is absolutely critical.

a. Connecting a Campagnolo 11-speed chain

Campagnolo's hollow 11-speed connecting pin is a break-off type, very different from the pull-apart version it uses for 10-speed chains. It requires Campagnolo's special (and expensive) 11-speed chain tool (Fig. 4.23) to install it through the virgin holes in the outer link on the end of the chain, which now has a laser etching for identification. If that etching is not on the link with the connecting pin in it, Campagnolo's warranty is void, so make sure you follow this procedure: Push the pin outward from the wheel side (the opposite direction from that shown in Fig. 4.11!), since the end with the break-off pilot protrudes more than the others. Installing the pin from the wheel side out makes the extra length protrude toward smaller cogs, where it won't hang up on the face of the next cog as it could if it were to protrude toward a larger cog.

1. **If you need to shorten the chain, remove excess length (§iv-8) only from the end that terminates in an inner link.** That way, the virgin holes in the plates of the outer link you will be connecting will never have had a rivet through them and consequently will not have been enlarged and distorted by the insertion and removal of a rivet. Campagnolo ships its chains with a zip tie through the virgin holes at the end of the final (laser-etched) outer link so that you will make sure to close the chain at these holes. When removing excess links with the Campagnolo 11-speed chain tool, make sure the tool's swinging gate is open so the old chain rivet can push completely through (Fig. 4.23).

2. **Remove the zip tie and, by hand, slip the connecting pin, pointed end first, from the wheel side of the chain outward through these holes and the opposite end's inner link to hold the chain loop together.**

3. **Flip open the gate and pull out the wire loop on Campagnolo's 11-speed chain tool (Fig. 4.23), back out the tool's driving pin**

4.23 Campagnolo C11 11-speed tool

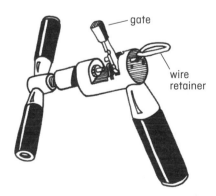

(spin the T-handle counterclockwise), and set the end links into it. Since you will be driving the pin outward, away from the wheel, the tool's T-handle will have to be toward the wheel, making it inconvenient to turn.

4. **Insert the wire loop into the two holes in the end of the tool opposite the T-handle to hold the chain down (Fig. 4.23).**

5. **Push the pin in, going by feel.** You will feel resistance at first, then almost no resistance, and finally a second resistance followed by solid resistance, at which point you should stop pushing.

6. **Open the tool and release the chain.** Check that the link moves easily and that the tail end of the pin is flush with the chain plate.

7. **Turn the tool around, slip its break-off hole (at 3 o'clock on the tool's face) over the pilot pin, and snap it off.**

8. **With the tool facing in toward the wheel as in Figure 4.11, put it back on the same link, lined up with the assembly pin.** Flip the gate of the tool down behind the chain so that the gate's anvil pin backs up the tail end of the connecting pin. Insert the wire loop into the tool to hold the chain in position.

9. **Tighten the chain tool until it mashes out (peens) the head of the assembly pin to lock it in place.**

Unlike Campy 10-speed chains, Campagnolo 11-speed chains can be opened (at any spot other than the connecting pin) and reconnected with a new connecting pin.

b. Connecting a Shimano 11-speed chain

Shimano's 11-speed chains are not asymmetrical like its 10-speed road and mountain counterparts. The connector-pin shape is slightly different, and connecting the 11-speed chain requires a new chain tool. The new chain tool is backward-compatible with Shimano 7- to 11-speed chains. Otherwise, the connecting procedure is the same as with a Shimano 10-speed chain; follow the instructions in §iv-11b, except that either side of the chain can face out. When finished, the link pin should be flush with the chain on the side you pushed it in, and protruding slightly on the other side where you broke off the lead pin.

---

iv-13

CONNECTING AND DISCONNECTING A MASTER LINK

a. SRAM (Sachs) PowerLink, Lickton's SuperLink, and KMC MissingLink

These links are the same; SRAM (which purchased Sachs) licensed the Lickton's SuperLink design (Fig. 4.24), and the MissingLink works the same way. The master link is made up of two symmetrical link halves, each of which has a single pin sticking out of it. There is a round hole in the center of each plate that tapers into a slot on the end opposite the pin.

NOTE: *The SRAM 10-Speed PowerLock Link and the discontinued KMC MissingLink II are not supposed to be openable.*

ANOTHER NOTE: *SRAM 10-Speed PowerLock Links stamped with an "M" or an "N" were recalled in late 2009.*

Connecting

1. **Put the pin of each half of the link through the hole in each end of the chain.** One pin will go down, and one up (Fig. 4.24).
2. **Pull the links close together so that each pin goes through the keyhole in the opposite plate.**
3. **Pull the chain ends apart so that the groove at the top of each pin slides to the end of the slot in each plate.**

4.24 SRAM PowerLink, Lickton's SuperLink, and KMC MissingLink

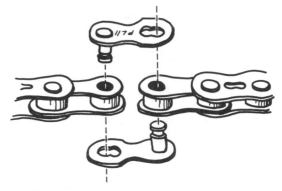

4.25 Using Park master-link pliers

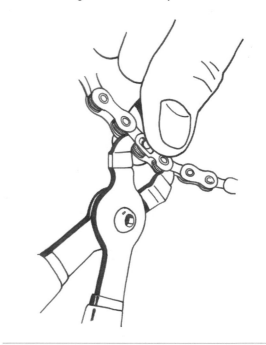

Disconnecting

1. **While squeezing the master-link plates together to free the plate from the groove in the pins, push the chain ends toward each other so that the pins come to the center hole in each plate.** If you have a pair of master-link pliers, use them to grab the two rollers through which the pins of the master link are inserted (Fig. 4.25). Squeeze the pliers while you squeeze the link plates toward each other with your fingers. The link will come right apart. Master-link pliers are

one of the slickest tools in existence; with them you can easily open SRAM 10-speed PowerLock master links, which are not supposed to be openable.

NOTE: *An old, dirty master link may be hard to open without master-link pliers. To disengage the link plates from the pin grooves while you push the ends toward each other, try squeezing the link plates toward each other with a clothespin or a pair of vise grip pliers set on very low pressure. In desperation, you may have to open the chain somewhere else, reassembling it using a second master link.*

2. **Pull the two halves of the master link apart.**

b. Wippermann ConneX link

The Wippermann link works much the same way as the SRAM, KMC, and Lickton's master links just discussed, but the edges of the link plates are not symmetrical. This asymmetry means that there is a definite orientation for the link, and you don't want to install it upside down.

Orient the ConneX link so that its convex edge is away from the chainring or cog (Fig. 4.26). The link plate is bowl-shaped, and if you have the convex bottom of the bowl toward the cog or chainring, then when it is on an 11-, 12-, or maybe

even a 13-tooth cog, the convex edge will ride up on the spacer between cogs, lifting the rollers out of the tooth valleys and causing the chain to skip under load. You will notice that the pair of attached holes where you pop the link together forms a heart shape. When the master link is on the top of the cog or chainring, make sure that the heart is right side up.

Remove and install the ConneX link the same way as the SRAM PowerLink in §iv-13a, but make sure the convex link edge is facing outward from the chain loop (Fig. 4.26), so that the concave edge can run over the cog spacers on the smallest cogs without lifting the chain.

c. Taya Master Link

Taya's "Sigma Connector" is a no-tools master link. Links are made for 1-speed through 10-speed chains.

Connecting

1. **Connect the two ends of the chain together with the master link that has two rivets sticking out of it (Fig. 4.27).**
2. **Snap the outer master-link plate over the rivets and into their grooves.** To facilitate hooking each keyhole-shaped hole over its corresponding rivet, flex the plate with the

---

4.26 Wippermann ConneX link—note its orientation with the link's high bump away from the chainring

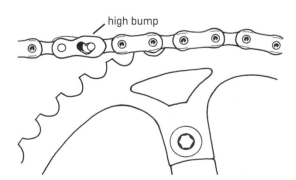

4.27 Taya Sigma Master Link

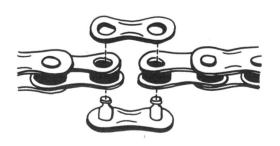

protruding rivets so that the ends of the rivets are closer together.

Disconnecting

1. **Flex the master link so that the pins come closer together.**
2. **Pull the plate with the oval holes off the rivets.**

TROUBLESHOOTING CHAIN PROBLEMS

iv-14

CHAIN SUCK

"Chain suck" occurs when the chain does not release from the bottom of the chainring. Instead, it sticks to the ring and gets "sucked" up until it hits the chainstay. Sometimes the chain becomes wedged between the chainstay and the chainring.

Chain suck is rare on a double-chainring setup on a road bike. It is more likely with a triple crank, but fortunately is still rare.

A number of things can cause chain suck. To eliminate it, try the simplest methods first.

1. **Clean and lube the chain and see if it improves.** A dry, rusty chain will hold the curved shape of the chainring too long.
2. **Check for stiff links (Fig. 4.13).** Watch the chain move through the derailleur jockey wheels as you slowly turn the crank backward. Loosen stiff links by flexing them laterally with your thumbs (Fig. 4.14) or by using a chain tool with back teeth (Fig. 4.22). Set the stiff link over the back teeth closest to the screw handle (Fig. 4.15), and push the pin a fraction of a turn to spread the link.
3. **If chain suck persists, check for bent or torn teeth on the chainring.** Try straightening any broken or torn teeth you find with

pliers, and use a file to remove any burrs you find on the teeth.

4. **If the chain still sucks, replace the inner (and perhaps middle) chainring.** The new, unworn rings will release the chain more easily, and some chainrings have teeth that are thinner than others or have a harder, slicker surface on the teeth that releases the chain better.

iv-15

SQUEAKING CHAIN

Squeaking is caused by dry or rusted surfaces inside the chain rubbing on each other.

1. **Wipe down the chain (Fig. 4.2) and lubricate it (Fig. 4.1) with ProGold ProLink.** This lubricant can penetrate and clean up the surfaces enough to rehabilitate a squeaky chain.
2. **Ride it for a half hour or more, and then wipe and lubricate it with ProLink again and ride it another half hour or more.** Remember not to use a wax-based lubricant, which may have brought on the chain chirp in the first place.
3. **If the squeak does not go away after two rides with fresh ProLink lubricant, replace the chain.**

If the initial remedy does not work, the chain is probably too dry and rusted deep inside. Chains often don't heal from this condition. Life is too short and bike riding is too joyful to put up with the sound of a squeaking chain. Replace it.

iv-16

SKIPPING CHAIN

There can be a number of causes for a chain to skip and jump as you pedal.

a. Stiff links

1. **Turn the crank backward slowly to see whether a stiff chain link (Fig. 4.13) exists.** A stiff link will be unable to bend properly as it goes through the rear-derailleur jockey wheels. It will jump and move the jockey wheels as it passes through.

2. **Loosen stiff links by flexing them laterally between the index finger and thumb of both hands (Fig. 4.14), or by using a chain tool with back teeth (Fig. 4.22).** Set the stiff link over the back teeth closest to the screw handle (Fig. 4.15), and push the pin a fraction of a turn to spread the link.

3. **Wipe down and lubricate the chain (Figs. 4.1–4.2).**

b. Rusted chain

A rusted chain will often squeak as well as skip. If you watch it move through the rear derailleur, it will look like many links are tight; the links will not bend easily and will cause the jockey wheels to jump back and forth.

1. **Lubricate the chain with ProLink (Fig. 4.1).**

2. **If this does not fix the problem after a few miles of riding, replace the chain.**

c. Worn-out chain

If the chain is worn out, it will be elongated and will skip because it does not mesh well with the cogs. A new chain will fix the problem if the condition has not persisted long enough to ruin some cogs.

1. **Check for chain elongation as described in §iv-6.**

2. **If the chain is elongated beyond the specifications in §iv-6, replace it.**

3. **If replacing the chain does not help or actually makes matters worse, see the next section.**

d. Worn cogs

If you just replaced the chain and it is now skipping (despite the derailleurs being in adjustment; see §v-3), probably at least one of the cogs is worn out. If this is the case, the chain will probably skip on the cogs you use most frequently and not on others. However, if it skips only on the smallest cog or two and you have a Wippermann ConneX master link, check to see whether you installed the link upside down (see §iv-13b).

1. **Check each cog visually for wear.** If the teeth are hook-shaped, the cog is shot and should be replaced. For cogs up to 21 teeth, Rohloff makes a simple "HG-Check" tool (pictured in Fig. 1.4) that checks for cog wear by putting tension on a length of chain wrapped around the cog. If, while the cogset is on the freehub, the last chain roller on the tool snags on the tooth and resists being flipped easily in and out of the tooth pocket while the tool handle is under pressure, or, worse, if the entire measurement chain except the first roller slides easily away from the cog teeth while the handle is under pressure, the cog is worn out.

2. **Replace the offending cogs or the entire cassette or freewheel.** See cog installation in §vi-24.

3. **Replace the chain as well, if you have not just done so.** An old chain will wear out new cogs rapidly.

e. Maladjusted rear derailleur

If the rear derailleur is poorly adjusted or bent, it can cause the chain to skip by lining up the chain between gears.

1. **Check that the rear derailleur shifts equally well in both directions and that the chain can be pedaled backward without catching.**

2. **Adjust the rear derailleur by following the procedure described in §v-3.**

f. Sticky shift cable

If the shift cable does not move freely enough to let the derailleur spring over to line up under the cog, the chain will jump off under load. Frayed, rough, dirty, rusted, or worn cables or housings will cause the problem, as will kinked or sharply bent housings. Replacing the shift cables and housings (Chapter 5, §v-7 to §v-15) should eliminate the problem.

g. Loose rear-derailleur jockey wheel(s)

A loose jockey wheel on the rear derailleur can cause the chain to skip by letting it move too far laterally.

1. **Check that the bolts holding the jockey wheel to the cage are tight by using an appropriately sized wrench (usually a 3mm hex key).**
2. **Tighten the jockey-wheel bolts if necessary; hold the hex key close to the bend so that you don't have enough leverage to overtighten them.** If the jockey-wheel bolts loosen regularly, remove and clean them, and then put Loctite or another threadlock compound on the threads and reinstall them.

h. Bent rear derailleur or rear-derailleur hanger

If the derailleur or derailleur hanger is bent, adjustments won't work. You will probably know when it got bent, too. It was either when you shifted your derailleur into your spokes, when you crashed onto the derailleur, or when you kept pedaling as a plastic bag or a tumbleweed blew into your chain.

1. **Unless you happen to have a derailleur-hanger-alignment tool and know how to** use it (Fig. 14.5), take the bike to a shop and have it checked for correct dropout hanger alignment. The majority of modern derailleur bikes have a replaceable (bolt-on) right rear dropout and derailleur hanger, which you can purchase and install yourself.
2. **If a straight derailleur hanger does not correct the misalignment, the rear derailleur is bent.** This is generally cause for replacement (see §v-2). With some derailleurs, you can replace the jockey-wheel cage, if that's all that is bent. If you are careful, you can sometimes bend a bent derailleur cage back with your hands. It seldom works well, but it's worth a try if your only other alternative is to replace the entire rear derailleur. Just make sure you don't bend the derailleur hanger in the process.

i. Worn derailleur pivots

If the derailleur pivots are worn, the derailleur will be loose and will move around under the cogs, causing the chain to skip. Replacing the derailleur is the solution.

j. Bent rear-derailleur mounting bolt

If the mounting bolt is bent, the derailleur will not line up straight. To fix it, get a new derailleur or a new bolt and install it following the "upper-pivot overhaul" in §v-37. Observe how the spring-loaded assembly comes apart during disassembly to ease reassembly.

k. Missing or worn chain rollers

You can have a chain that passes the elongation tests mentioned in §iv-6 yet skips because one of the cylindrical rollers has broken and fallen off its rivet or is so worn that it is spool-shaped. If you don't happen to check that particular link with the chain-elongation gauge, you'll likely miss broken rollers. The width of the gauge is the same as between the inner plates, so that it won't catch worn-out, spool-shaped rollers either, because it will ride up on the edges of the rollers and not fall down into the center of the narrower waist of the worn roller. You might never know the chain is shot without inspecting every roller.

l. Inverted ConneX master link

If you have a Wippermann ConneX master link upside down (described in §iv-13b), the taller link edge will lift the rollers off the cog and will cause the chain to skip. Remove, invert, and reinstall the master link as described in §iv-13b.

THE SHIFTING SYSTEM

Never mistake motion for action.
—Ernest Hemingway

Riding a bike is much more enjoyable when the derailleurs are working well. Feeling the chain respond quickly and positively to shifting commands is sweet. On the other hand, having the chain shift unexpectedly or skip when you pedal hard can ruin your ride.

Derailleurs are simple beasts. When they act up, a few turns of some screws or a cable-tension adjustment will usually get them working again. However, on most current road bikes, the brake levers have the shift levers integrated into them, and so these parts do have considerable complexity. And now some of them are fully electronic! Master this chapter, and you will be able to fix most shifting problems on your bike in seconds, even when you are on the road.

v-1

OPERATING INTEGRATED SHIFT/ BRAKE LEVERS

The derailleur adjustments described in this chapter require that you already know how to operate the levers that go with them. However, there may be nuances you're unaware of, so read this section first. Throughout the book, I will also use the term "dual control" to describe road brake levers with an integrated shift mechanism.

SRAM levers are the least obvious to use, so I'll start with them. Electronic shift levers are described last.

a. Rear SRAM DoubleTap (right-hand lever)

To shift to a larger cog (lower gear), push the shift paddle (the lever behind the brake lever in Fig. 5.1A) to the left (inward) with your fingers far enough that you feel the second click (if you only go to the first click and release, it will upshift instead of downshift). The most you can move the chain is three cogs with a single push.

To shift to a smaller cog (higher gear), push the shift paddle to the left (inward) with your fingers lightly enough to only hit the first click. Release. It will upshift only one cog at a time.

b. Front SRAM DoubleTap (left-hand lever)

To shift to a larger chainring (higher gear), push the shift paddle (the lever behind the brake lever in Fig. 5.1A) to the right (inward) with your fingers. It takes a firm push to get to the second

5.1A Operating a SRAM DoubleTap front shifter

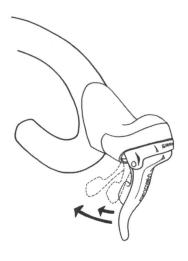

5.1B Operating a Campagnolo Ergopower rear lever

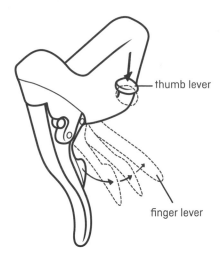

thumb lever

finger lever

click (it will drop back to the inner chainring if you only go to the first click and release).

To shift to a smaller chainring (lower gear), push the shift paddle to the right (inward) to the first click and release.

You can trim the front derailleur so that it does not rub on the chain in some cross-gear combinations (see §v-6 for more on this). When the chain is on the inner chainring on a 2007 unit and rubs the front derailleur in a cross-gear, give the shift paddle a gentle inward push until you hear a soft click. Year 2007 levers have no trim setting on the big chainring. On 2008 and later Red and Rival levers and 2010 and later Force levers, the trim setting is on the big chainring. When the chain is on the outer chainring, give the shift paddle a gentle push until you feel the soft click. This may take some practice, as you can easily overdo it and actually perform the shift.

c. Rear Campagnolo Ergopower (right-hand lever)

To shift to a larger cog (lower gear), push the finger lever (the shift paddle behind the brake lever; see Fig. 5.1B) to the left (inward) with your fingers. Depending on model and year, you can

downshift three to five cogs with a single push.

To shift to a smaller cog (higher gear), push the thumb lever down (yes, with your thumb). A single click upshifts one cog, but depending on model and year, you can move the chain across one to 11 cogs with a single push. High-end Campagnolo Ergopower right levers (Super Record, Record, and Chorus) can shift at least three cogs with a single push on original models; Ultra-shift models with curvier brake levers and a taller knob on the lever body can upshift all 11 cogs with a single go. Campagnolo lower-end Ergopower right levers (Centaur, Athena, Veloce, Mirage, and Xenon) can only upshift a single cog at a time; you can see the difference because the thumb lever does not run in a long slot with a corresponding long slot in the rubber hood, as is seen on Super Record, Record, and Chorus levers. Instead, there is only a hole in the hood for the thumb lever, indicating that the lever can click only one cog smaller at a time.

d. Front Campagnolo Ergopower (left-hand lever)

To shift to a larger chainring (higher gear), push the finger lever (the shift paddle behind the brake lever) to the right (inward) with your fingers. If

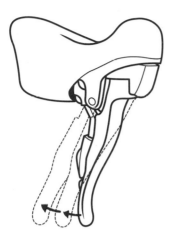

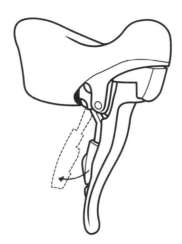

the chain does not climb up the outer ring, give another push. If you have a triple chainwheel, you can shift only one chainring at a time.

To shift to a smaller chainring (lower gear), push the thumb lever down.

You can feather (trim) the front derailleur so that it does not rub on the chain in a cross-gear (see §v-6 for more on this). When the chain is on the inner chainring, give the shift paddle a gentle inward push with your finger to move one click at a time. When the chain is on the outer chainring, give the thumb lever a single-click push at a time; this thumb-lever trim feature is not present on lower-end Ergopower levers.

e. Rear Shimano STI (right-hand lever)

To shift to a larger cog (lower gear), push the brake/shift lever (the larger lever) to the left (inward) with your fingers. The most you can move the chain is three cogs with a single push and two cogs with newer STI levers with under-the-handlebar-tape shift cables.

To shift to a smaller cog (higher gear), push the smaller lever behind the brake lever to the left (inward) with your second finger. It will click only one gear at a time.

f. Front Shimano STI (left-hand lever)

To shift to a larger chainring (higher gear), push the brake/shift lever (the larger lever in Fig. 5.1C) to the right (inward) with your fingers. It takes a firm push. If it moves a small click but the chain does not climb up the outer ring, let it return to center then give it another push. If you have a triple, you can shift only one chainring at a time.

To shift to a smaller chainring (lower gear), push the smaller lever (Fig. 5.1D) to the right (inward) with your second finger. If you have a triple crankset, you can shift only one chainring at a time.

You can trim the front derailleur so that it does not rub on the chain in a cross-gear (see §v-6 for more on this). When the chain is on the inner chainring, give the brake/shift lever a gentle inward push until you hear a soft click. When the chain is on the outer chainring, give the inner lever a gentle push until you feel the soft click; this latter feature is not present on newer STI levers with under-the-handlebar-tape shift cables. Trimming may take some practice, as you can easily overdo it and actually perform the shift.

g. Rear Shimano Dura-Ace Di2 or Ultegra Di2 Electronic Shifter (both drop-bar and aerobar types)

Drop-bar shifter

The shift buttons on the electronic lever for drop handlebars (Fig. 5.29) are oriented along the brake lever blade in approximately the same positions as those shift levers would be on a standard Shimano STI lever. To go to a smaller cog, push the rear button on the right lever. To go to a larger cog, push the longer, forward button on the right lever.

Aerobar shifter

To remember which shift button does what on the electronic aerobar shifters on the brake levers, as well as on the SW-R671 shifters on the aero extensions (both positions have two buttons each; see Fig. 5.2), try this mnemonic device: The upper buttons are for going uphill, and the lower buttons are for going downhill. In other words, the upper buttons on both sides give you easier gears, and the lower buttons on both sides give you harder gears (I don't want to say lower gears with the upper button and higher gears with the lower button, because that's a crappy mnemonic

5.2 Shimano Dura-Ace 7970 Di2 electronic aerobar shifters; SW-R671 shifters shown at ends of aero extensions.

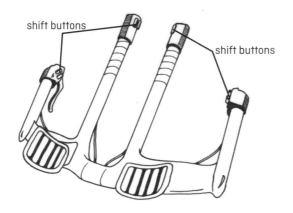

shift buttons

shift buttons

device!). So, whether at the end of the aerobar or on the brake lever on the base bar, push a right lower button to go to a smaller cog and a right upper button to go to a larger cog.

If you don't like which button does what, the shift buttons can be reassigned with the diagnostic computer interface available to shops for troubleshooting the Shimano electronic components.

Shimano also offers a single-button Dura-Ace Di2 electronic aerobar shifter called the SW-9071. There is only a single button on the top of each SW-9071 shifter on each end of the aero extensions, and the left and right shifters both only operate the rear derailleur; the front derailleur can only be operated from the left brake-lever shifter. Generally, the button atop the right SW-9071 shifter upshifts the rear derailleur (goes to a smaller cog), and the left shifter button downshifts the rear derailleur, but, as with all Di2 controls, which shifter does what can be changed in the software. This is a dealer operation, as a special diagnostic interface console is required.

h. Front Shimano Dura-Ace Di2 or Ultegra Di2 Electronic Shifter (both drop-bar and aerobar types)

Drop-bar shifter

To go to the small chainring, push the rear button on the left lever. To go to the big chainring, push the longer, forward button on the left lever.

As you shift through the rear cogs, the Di2 front derailleur automatically trims its position to avoid chain rub.

Aerobar shifter

Whether it is at the end of the aerobar or on the brake lever on the base bar, push a left lower button (Fig. 5.2) to go to the big chainring. Push a left upper button to go to the small chainring.

As with the rear shifter, if you don't like which button does what, the shift buttons can be reassigned with the diagnostic computer available to shops for troubleshooting the Shimano electronic components.

Battery

You must monitor the battery to make sure the Di2 system continues to operate. To view the battery-level indicator, hold down any shift button until the LED indicator hanging on the brake cable lights up. The LED will illuminate green, flashing green, red, or flashing red to indicate a full, half-full, quarter-full, or empty battery. Recharge the battery whenever the upper LED with the battery symbol (Fig. 5.30) next to it turns red.

i. Rear Campagnolo EPS Electronic Shifter (both drop-bar and aerobar types)

Drop-bar shifter

The buttons are the same as on cable-actuated Campagnolo Ergopower. To shift to a larger cog (lower gear), push the finger lever (the shift paddle behind the brake lever; see Fig. 5.1B) to the left (inward) with your finger. Keep pushing it inward for multiple shifts; depending on how long you push the lever, it will shift only a few cogs or through the entire cog range.

To shift to a smaller cog (higher gear), push the thumb lever down (yes, with your thumb). Hold it down for multiple shifts.

Aerobar shifter

Push the right lever down to shift to smaller cog. Pull the right lever up to shift to a larger cog. The lever will return to center after you release it. Hold the lever down or up to shift through multiple cogs up to all 11 cogs.

Base-bar time trial/triathlon shifter

Push the side button on the right brake lever to shift to a smaller cog. Push the button on top of the right brake lever to shift to a larger cog. Holding a button down will shift through multiple cogs up to all 11 cogs.

j. Front Campagnolo EPS Electronic Shifter (both drop-bar and aerobar types)

Drop-bar shifter

The buttons are the same as on cable-actuated Campagnolo Ergopower. To shift to a larger chainring (higher gear), push the finger lever (the shift paddle behind the brake lever) to the right (inward) with your finger (Fig. 5.1B).

To shift to a smaller chainring (lower gear), push the thumb lever down.

As you shift through the rear cogs, the EPS front derailleur automatically trims its position to avoid chain rub.

Aerobar shifter

Push the left lever down to shift to the inner chainring. Pull the left lever up to shift to the big chainring. The lever will return to center after you release it.

Base-bar time trial/triathlon shifter

Push the side button on the left brake lever to shift to the inner chainring. Push the button on top of the left brake lever to shift to the big chainring.

Battery

You must monitor the battery to make sure the EPS system continues to operate by pushing and releasing one of the buttons on either lever adjacent to the thumb switch; the LED on the small interface unit that mounts on the stem, head tube, or brake cable will light up for a few seconds. If the LED glows green, the battery is full; flashing green indicates a nearly full charge; yellow indicates a half charge; flashing red indicates a low charge; and red indicates the need for a charge.

THE REAR DERAILLEUR

The rear derailleur (Figs. 5.3, 5.4) moves the chain from one rear cog to another, and it also takes up chain slack (such as when the front derailleur is shifted or the bike bounces over a bump). The rear derailleur bolts to a hanger on the frame's rear dropout about which the derailleur can pivot (Fig. 5.5).

Two jockey wheels (the upper, or "guide," pulley [1] and the lower, or "idler," pulley [2]), which live in a guide assembly called a chain cage [3], hold the chain tight and help guide the chain to perform shifts. Depending on brand and model, a rear derailleur has a spring [4] in the (lower) p-knuckle [5] and often one in the (upper) b-knuckle [6] as well that pulls the jockey wheels tight against the chain, creating a desirable amount of chain tension.

The shift cable is affixed to the cable-fixing bolt [7]. Increasing the tension on the rear shift cable (as when you shift to a lower gear) moves the derailleur inward toward the larger cogs. When cable tension is released (i.e., when you

5.3 Exploded rear derailleur

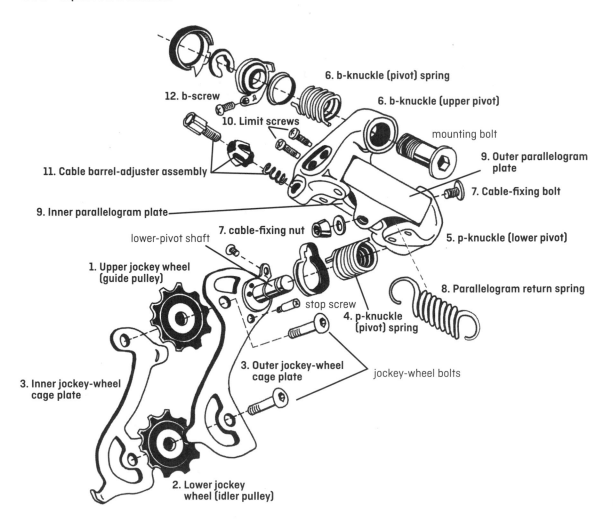

6. b-knuckle (pivot) spring

12. b-screw

6. b-knuckle (upper pivot)

10. Limit screws

mounting bolt

11. Cable barrel-adjuster assembly

9. Outer parallelogram plate

9. Inner parallelogram plate

7. Cable-fixing bolt

lower-pivot shaft

7. cable-fixing nut

5. p-knuckle (lower pivot)

1. Upper jockey wheel (guide pulley)

stop screw

8. Parallelogram return spring

4. p-knuckle (pivot) spring

3. Inner jockey-wheel cage plate

3. Outer jockey-wheel cage plate

jockey-wheel bolts

2. Lower jockey wheel (idler pulley)

5.4 Rear-derailleur limit screws and barrel adjuster

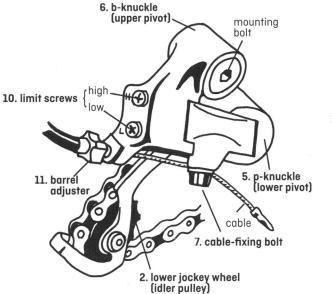

6. b-knuckle (upper pivot)

mounting bolt

10. limit screws { high low

11. barrel adjuster

5. p-knuckle (lower pivot)

cable

7. cable-fixing bolt

2. lower jockey wheel (idler pulley)

5.5 Rear-derailleur right rear dropout-derailleur hanger

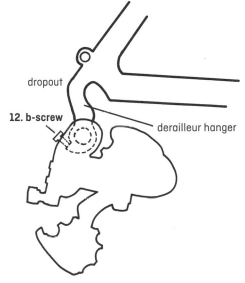

dropout

12. b-screw

derailleur hanger

---

shift to a higher gear), a spring [8] between the derailleur's two parallelogram plates [9] pulls the chain back toward the smallest cogs. The two limit screws [10] on the rear derailleur (Fig. 5.4) prevent the derailleur from moving the chain too far to the inside (into the spokes) or to the outside (into the dropout). The limit screws can be on the back of the b-knuckle or on the side of the outer parallelogram plate.

In addition to limit screws, many rear derailleurs have a barrel adjuster [11] located at the rear of the derailleur, where the cable enters it (Fig. 5.4). The barrel adjuster increases cable tension when it is unscrewed and reduces cable tension when it is screwed in. The barrel adjuster is thus used to fine-tune the shifting mechanism to land the chain precisely on each cog with each corresponding click of the shifter.

Rear derailleurs often have a screw underneath and to the rear (visible in Fig. 5.5). This screw, conventionally called the "b-tension screw" (or "b-screw" [12]), presses against the dropout or a tab attached to the dropout and is largely responsible for controlling the space between the bottom

of the cogs and the upper jockey wheel (Figs. 5.6, 5.7). On a 10- or 11-speed Campagnolo rear derailleur, this adjustment is instead made by a screw on the p-knuckle (Fig. 5.9). The other factor that affects the size of this space is chain length.

The chain length, the balance between the springs in the upper and lower pivots, and the b-screw (Fig. 5.5) adjustment determine how closely the derailleur tracks the cogs during its lateral movement and keep the chain from bouncing off the front chainrings when the bike hits bumps.

v-2

REAR-DERAILLEUR INSTALLATION

LEVEL 1

NOTE: *For Campagnolo and Shimano electronic systems, see §v-18 through §v-20.*

1. **Apply a small amount of grease to the derailleur's mount-ing bolt.** Select the appropriate tool for the mounting bolt. This will most likely be a 5mm or 6mm hex key or a Torx T25 (star) tool.

THE SHIFTING SYSTEM

2. **Rotate the derailleur clockwise so that the b-screw or tab on the derailleur ends up behind the tab on the dropout derailleur hanger (Fig. 5.5).**

3. **Thread the bolt a few turns into the hole on the dropout derailleur hanger.** Check to make sure that the tab and/or b-screw is behind the dropout hanger tab and is not getting smashed into the side of the dropout hanger as you tighten the bolt.

4. **Tighten the mounting bolt until the derailleur fits snugly against the hanger.** Consult the Appendix E torque table for appropriate torque.

5. **Route the chain through the jockey wheels and connect it (§iv-9 through §iv-12).**

6. **Install the cables and housings (§v-7 through §v-15).**

7. **Pull the cable tight with a pair of pliers and tighten the cable-fixing bolt (Fig. 5.24).**

8. **If the chain is not installed, install it as in Chapter 4.** If the chain is already on the bike, remove the old derailleur from it by unscrewing the jockey-wheel bolts and opening the jockey-wheel cage, and install the new derailleur onto it, also by unscrewing the jockey-wheel bolts and opening the jockey-wheel cage. Drape the chain through the cage, put the jockey wheels and inner cage plate back on, and tighten the screws.

9. **Follow the adjustment procedure described in the next section.**

---

v-3

ADJUSTMENT OF REAR DERAILLEUR AND RIGHT-HAND SHIFTER

NOTE: *For Campagnolo and Shimano electronic systems, see §v-18 through §v-20.*

Perform all of the following derailleur adjustments with the bike in a bike stand or hanging from the ceiling. That way, you can turn the crank and shift gears while you put the derailleur through its paces. After adjusting it off the ground, test the shifting while riding. Derailleurs often perform differently under load than in a bike stand.

Before starting, lubricate or replace the chain (Chapter 4) so that the drivetrain runs smoothly.

a. Limit-screw adjustments

Properly set, these screws (Fig. 5.4) make certain that you will not ruin your frame, wheel, or derailleur by shifting into the spokes or by jamming the chain between the dropout and the smallest cog. It is never pleasant to see your expensive equipment turned into shredded metal. Adjustment requires nothing but a small screwdriver; remember, it's lefty loosey, righty tighty for the limit screws.

b. High-gear limit-screw adjustment

This screw limits the outward movement of the rear derailleur. You tighten or loosen this screw until the derailleur shifts the chain to the smallest cog quickly but does not overshift.

How do you determine which limit screw works on the high gear? Often it is labeled H, and it is usually the upper of the two screws (Fig. 5.6). If you're not certain, try both screws. The one that moves the derailleur when the cable tension is released and the chain is on the smallest cog is the one you're looking for. On most derailleurs, you can also see which screw to adjust by looking between the derailleur's parallelogram side plates. You will see one tab on the back end of each plate. Each is designed to hit a limit screw at one end of the movement. Shift to the smallest cog and notice which screw is touching one of the tabs; that is the high-gear limit screw.

All of these adjustments require you to know how to work your shift levers. For a refresher on

5.6 **High gear**

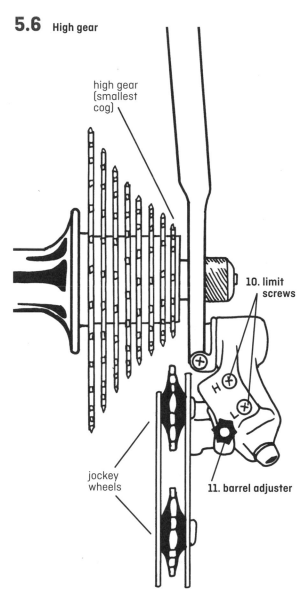

high gear
(smallest
cog)

**10. limit
screws**

jockey
wheels

11. barrel adjuster

shifting Shimano STI, Campagnolo Ergopower, or SRAM DoubleTap, refer back to §v-1.

1. **Shift the chain to the large front chainring.**

2. **While slowly turning the crank, shift the rear derailleur to the smallest rear cog (highest gear) (Fig. 5.6).**

3. **If the chain still won't drop without hesitation to the smallest cog, loosen the high-gear limit screw one-quarter turn at a time, continuously repeating the shift.** Loosen the screw until either the chain repeatedly drops quickly and easily or it is clear that the limit screw is not making any further difference and the chain still won't drop.

4. **If the chain still won't drop onto the small cog with the limit screw backed out, or if there is hesitation in the chain's shifting movement, loosen the cable a little to see if it is stopping the derailleur from moving out far enough.** You loosen the cable by either (a) turning one of the two barrel adjusters in the system clockwise—either the barrel adjuster on the back of the rear derailleur or the barrel adjuster on the threaded boss on the head tube or down tube—or (b) loosening the cable-fixing bolt, letting a little cable out, and retightening the bolt.

PRO TIP | **Rear-Derailleur Limit Screws**

When the cable tension is set correctly so that the derailleur shifts properly on each cog, the high-gear limit screw can be as loose as you like or completely missing, and you won't ever shift the chain into the dropout. This means that you can back out the screw beyond where it needs to be to make sure that it never interferes with the chain dropping onto the smallest cog.

However, note that this also means that whenever you switch wheels, you will need to immediately make sure that the cable tension is accurate so that the derailleur shifts precisely onto each cog. Otherwise, if the cable tension is too loose, which can happen over time or due to switching wheels with a cogset that is set farther inboard, the cable could allow the chain to shift beyond the smallest cog and into the dropout.

THE SHIFTING SYSTEM

5. **If the derailleur throws the chain into the dropout or tries to go past the smallest cog, tighten the cable by turning the barrel adjuster counterclockwise (or tighten the high-gear limit screw one-quarter turn) and redo the shift.** Repeat until the derailleur shifts the chain quickly and easily into the highest gear without throwing the chain into the dropout.

NOTE: *Make sure that the washer under the cable-fixing bolt on the rear derailleur is rotated into the right position, or it may hit the derailleur cage and stop the rear derailleur from getting to the smallest cog. Some derailleurs have a tooth or two on the washer to dovetail into corresponding notches in the derailleur, and a number of positions may seem to fit. Look at the cable groove scored in the washer for a locating hint.*

c. Low-gear limit-screw adjustment

This screw stops the inward movement of the rear derailleur, preventing it from going into the spokes. This screw is often labeled L, and it is usually the bottom screw (Fig. 5.7). You can check which one it is by shifting to the largest cog and, while maintaining pressure on the shifter or by pushing or pulling on the rear-derailleur cable, turning the screw to see if it changes the position of the derailleur.

1. **Shift the chain to the inner chainring on the front.** Shift the rear derailleur to the lowest gear (largest cog; Fig. 5.7). Do it gently, in case the limit screw does not stop the derailleur from moving into the spokes.

2. **If the derailleur touches the spokes or pushes the chain over the largest cog, tighten the low-gear limit screw until the derailleur does neither.**

3. **If the derailleur cannot bring the chain onto the largest cog, loosen the screw one-quarter turn.** Repeat this step until the

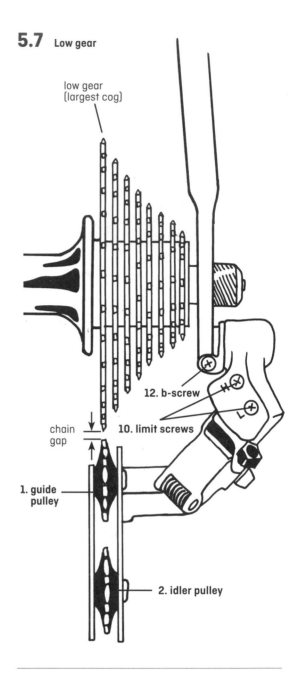

5.7 Low gear

low gear (largest cog)

12. b-screw

10. limit screws

chain gap

1. guide pulley

2. idler pulley

chain shifts easily up to the largest cog but does not touch the spokes or push the chain over the top of the cog.

d. Cable-tension adjustment on indexed rear shifters

With an indexed shifting system (one that "clicks" into each gear), cable tension determines whether the derailleur moves to the proper gear with each click.

1. **With the chain on the large chainring in the front, shift the rear derailleur to the smallest cog.** Keep clicking the shifter until you are sure it will not let out any more cable.

2. **Downshift one click.** This should pull the cable and move the chain smoothly to the second cog.

3. **If the chain does not climb to the second cog, or if it does so slowly, increase the tension in the cable by unscrewing (counterclockwise when viewed from its end where the cable housing enters) either the cable-tension barrel adjuster on the derailleur (Fig. 5.4) or the barrel adjuster on the frame (Fig. 5.8).** (If you have down-tube shifters, the only barrel adjuster is at the rear derailleur.) If you run out of barrel-adjustment range, retighten (clockwise) both adjusters to within a turn or two from their fully in position, loosen the cable-fixing bolt on the derailleur, and pull some of the slack out of the cable. Tighten the cable-fixing bolt and repeat the adjustment.

4. **If the chain overshifts the second cog or comes close to overshifting, decrease the cable tension by turning one of the barrel adjusters clockwise (i.e., screw it in).** If both barrel adjusters are already fully screwed in, you will need to loosen the cable at the cable-fixing bolt.

5. **Keep adjusting the cable tension in small increments while shifting back and forth between the two smallest cogs until the chain moves easily in both directions.**

6. **Fine-tune the adjustment.** Shift the rear derailleur back and forth among the smallest five cogs, again checking for precise and quick movement of the chain from cog to cog. Fine-tune the shifting by making small corrections with the cable-tension barrel adjuster.

5.8 Barrel adjuster on down-tube shifter boss

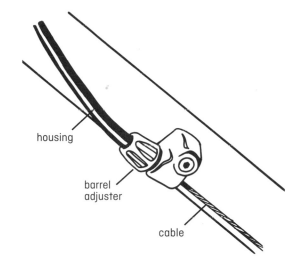

housing

barrel adjuster

cable

7. **Shift to the inner ring in the front and to the largest cog in the rear.** Shift up and down one click in the rear, again checking for symmetry and precise chain movement in either direction between the two largest cogs. Fine-tune the barrel adjusters until you get the shifting just right.

8. **Go back through the gears.** With the chain on the big chainring, the rear derailleur should shift easily on all but perhaps the largest one or two cogs in the rear. With the chain on the inner chainring, the rear derailleur should shift easily on all but perhaps the two smallest cogs. Fine-tune while riding by turning the barrel adjusters at the head tube or down tube.

NOTE: *If you can't get the tension to work properly on all cogs, there is likely an incompatibility between the cogs and the shifter, or something is wrong with the cogset. Check §v-47d and §v-47e regarding compatibility between shifters and cogsets to make sure you don't have mismatched cogs, shifter, or derailleur. If the cogs, shifter, and derailleur are supposed to work with each other, then there may be some spacing off within the cogset. If, for instance, it shifts fine in midsize*

THE SHIFTING SYSTEM

cogs but acts like the cable tension is too high in the large cogs and too low in the small cogs (and your shift cables and housings are new or in good working order; see the Pro Tip on better shifting), you need more spacing somewhere within the cogset. Try cutting a circular shim from a beer can that just fits over the freehub body, and slip the shim between a spacer and a cog somewhere in the middle of the cogset. If it improves things, you can play with the number and position of the shims to get it perfect.

ANOTHER NOTE: *If the derailleur is thwarting your adjustment abilities, or it touches the spokes while it is running smoothly on the largest cog, the derailleur hanger on the dropout may be bent. You can straighten it or replace it (§xiv-4).*

e. Cable-tension adjustment on frictional rear shifters

If you do not have indexed shifting, adjustment is complete after you remove the slack in the cable. With proper cable tension, when the chain is on the smallest cog, the derailleur should move as soon as the shift lever does. If there is free play in the lever, tighten the cable by turning the barrel adjuster on the derailleur counterclockwise. If your rear derailleur has no barrel adjuster, loosen the cable-fixing bolt, pull tension on the cable with pliers, and retighten the bolt.

f. Final details of rear-derailleur adjustment: b-screw adjustment

You can get a bit more precision by adjusting the small screw (b-screw) that changes the derailleur's position against the derailleur hanger tab on the right rear dropout (Fig. 5.5).

View the bike from behind with the chain on the inner chainring and largest cog (Fig. 5.7), and adjust the b-screw so that the upper jockey wheel (the guide pulley) is close to the cog, but not pinching the chain against the cog. Repeat on the smallest cog (Fig. 5.6). You'll know that you've moved the guide pulley in too closely when it starts making noise and even bumping up and down when you turn the crank with the chain on the large cog (i.e., the chain gap shown in Figure 5.7 is narrower than the chain is tall, so that the chain is pinched between the cog and the pulley).

Campagnolo 10- and 11-speed rear derailleurs do not have a b-screw, whereas earlier 8- and 9-speed versions did have one. Instead, you adjust the pulley-to-cog spacing by changing the spring tension in the lower pivot. Set the chain on the large cog. Tighten or loosen the spring-tension adjustment screw under the lower pivot; the screw is up against the jockey-wheel cage plate at the base of the lower derailleur knuckle (Fig. 5.9).

Make the chain gap in Figure 5.7 about 5–7mm, whether it's Campagnolo, Shimano, or SRAM.

Current Campagnolo 11-speed short-cage rear derailleurs are compatible with 12–29 cogsets, but they originally were not because this lower pivot adjustment could not pull the jockey-wheel cage back far enough. You can upgrade an original 11-speed rear derailleur to work with a 12–29 by replacing the toothed ring the lower pivot adjustment screw drives with one with more teeth. You must remove the jockey wheels and unscrew the bolt holding the jockey-wheel cage onto the lower pivot to do it. Replace the ring, start the bolt, wind the spring by rotating the cage past its stop, tighten the bolt, and replace the jockey wheels.

NOTE: *If, despite your best efforts, you cannot get the rear derailleur to shift well and noiselessly, refer to the chainline discussion under "Troubleshooting Derailleur and Shifter Problems" at the end of this chapter.*

5.9 Campagnolo's rear-derailleur lower pivot tension adjustment screw sets the chain gap between the guide pulley and the cogs.

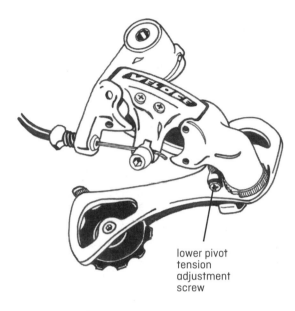

lower pivot tension adjustment screw

THE FRONT DERAILLEUR

The front derailleur (Figs. 5.10, 5.11) moves the chain between the chainrings. The working parts consist of a cage [3, 4], a linkage mechanism, and an arm attached to the shift cable. The front derailleur is attached to the frame, often by a bolt passing through a front-derailleur boss (or tab) attached to the frame's seat tube (Fig. 5.10). A derailleur may also be a "band type" that has an integral band clamp surrounding the seat tube (Fig. 5.11). In an alternative arrangement, a braze-on-type front derailleur may bolt into a separate wraparound clamp that has an integral front-derailleur boss shaped like an ear.

When the front shift cable pulls at the cable-fixing bolt [1] (Fig. 5.11), the derailleur swings out until it is stopped by the outer limit screw [2]; the limit screw prevents the outer cage plate [3] from moving so far outward that the chain shifts past the outer chainring. The inner limit screw stops the inner cage plate [4] from moving inward so far that it allows the chain to fall on the inboard side of the inner chainring.

v-4

FRONT-DERAILLEUR INSTALLATION

LEVEL 1

NOTE: *For Campagnolo and Shimano electronic systems, see §v-18 through §v-20.*

1. **Clamp the front derailleur to the frame boss or around the seat tube.**
2. **Adjust the height and rotation as described in §v-5a.**
3. **Tighten the mounting bolt (Fig. 5.10 or 5.11).**
4. **If the chain is not installed, install it as in Chapter 4.** If it is already on the bike, you can leave it on and remove the old derailleur and install the new one and pass it through it without opening the chain. Remove the old derailleur from the chain by unscrewing the tail screw (Fig. 5.11) and flexing open the front-derailleur cage. Install the new derailleur onto it, also by unscrewing its tail screw, flexing open the front-derailleur cage around the chain, and replacing the tail screw.

v-5

ADJUSTMENT OF FRONT DERAILLEUR AND LEFT-HAND SHIFTER

NOTE: *For Campagnolo and Shimano electronic systems, see §v-18 through §v-20.*

a. Position adjustments

A 5mm hex key is all you need to adjust the position of a front derailleur attached to a frame-mounted front-derailleur tab (Fig. 5.10).

With a band-type front derailleur (Fig. 5.11), the position is adjusted with a 5mm hex key or 8mm box wrench on the band-clamp bolt.

1. **Position the height of the front derailleur so that the outer cage passes about 1–2mm (¹⁄₁₆ to ⅛ inch) above the highest point of the outer chainring (Fig. 5.12).**

NOTE: *The lower edge of the derailleur outer cage plate should roughly follow the curve of the chainring, though the tail of the plate will generally be a bit farther above the chainring than will the leading edge, as shown in Figure 5.12. However, if the tail of the cage is way above the chainring when its leading edge is the correct 1–2mm above it, the derailleur is not properly matched to the bike and chainring and will not shift well. This can happen due to trying to mate a front derailleur (especially an older one) designed for large chainrings (39–53-tooth chainring pairs or the like) with a "compact" crankset (one that accepts smaller chainrings; 34–50T is the most common, but the outer chainring can be much smaller yet). Obviously, getting a front derailleur better mated to the chainring size is ideal, but if it is a braze-on-type front derailleur (Fig. 5.10), you may be able to tip it to approximate the curve of the chainring well enough to work acceptably by placing a wedge-shaped shim between the front-derailleur boss affixed to the frame and the curved mounting face of the front derailleur. You may be able to purchase this shim wedge in a bike shop; otherwise, you can fashion one yourself with a file, a drill, and a little block of aluminum.*

2. **Position the outer plate of the derailleur cage parallel to the chainrings or to the chain in the lowest and highest gears when viewed from above.** When on the inner (smallest) chainring and largest cog, the inner cage plate should be parallel with the chainring or the chain (Fig. 5.13). Similarly,

5.10 Front-derailleur boss (or tab) on seat tube

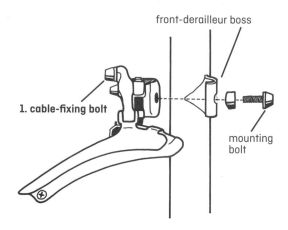

front-derailleur boss

1. cable-fixing bolt

mounting bolt

5.11 Band-clamp front derailleur

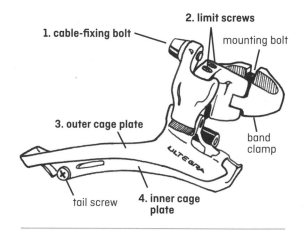

2. limit screws

mounting bolt

1. cable-fixing bolt

3. outer cage plate

band clamp

ULTEGRA

tail screw

4. inner cage plate

check this by shifting to the big chainring and smallest cog and sighting from the top (Fig. 5.14).

b. Limit-screw adjustments

The front derailleur has two limit screws (Fig. 5.11) that stop the derailleur from throwing the chain to the inside or outside of the chainrings. These are sometimes labeled L for low gear (small chainring) and H for high gear (large chainring) (Fig. 5.15). On most derailleurs, the low-gear screw is closer to the frame.

If in doubt, you can determine which limit screw controls which function by trial and error. Shift the chain to the inner ring, and then tighten

5.12 Proper front-derailleur vertical clearance

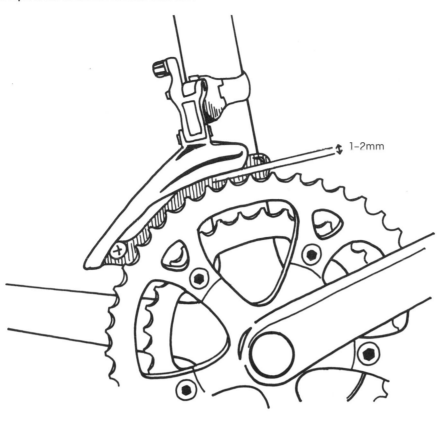

1–2mm

5.13 Proper rotational alignment of front derailleur on smallest chainring

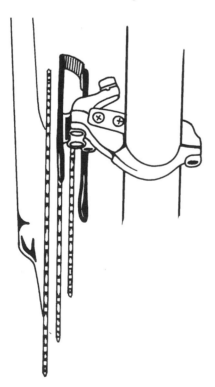

5.14 Proper rotational alignment of front derailleur on largest chainring

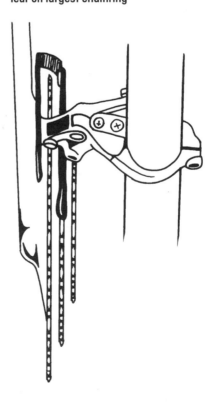

THE SHIFTING SYSTEM

one of the limit screws. If turning that screw moves the front derailleur outward, then it is the low-gear limit screw. If turning that screw does not move the front derailleur, then the other screw is the low-gear limit screw.

c. Low-gear limit-screw adjustment

1. Shift back and forth between chainrings.
2. If the chain drops off the inner ring to the inside, tighten the low-gear limit screw (clockwise) one-quarter turn and try shifting again.
3. If the chain does not shift easily onto the inner chainring, loosen the low-gear limit screw one-quarter turn and repeat the shift.

d. High-gear limit-screw adjustment

1. Shift the chain back and forth between chainrings.
2. If the chain jumps over the big chainring, tighten the high-gear limit screw one-quarter turn and repeat the shift.
3. If the chain is sluggish going up to the big chainring or does not go up at all, loosen the high-gear limit screw one-quarter turn and try the shift again.

e. Cable-tension adjustment

1. With the chain on the inner chainring, remove any excess cable slack. Turn the barrel adjuster on the cable stop (Fig. 5.8) counterclockwise (or loosen the cable-fixing bolt, pull the cable tight with pliers, and tighten the bolt).
2. Check that the cable is loose enough to allow the chain to shift smoothly and repeatedly to the inner chainring.
3. Check that the cable is tight enough that the derailleur starts to move as soon as you move the shifter. Fine-tune while riding.

5.15 Front-derailleur limit screws

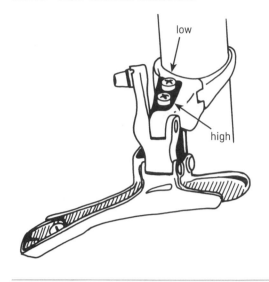

NOTE: *This method of tension adjustment applies to indexed as well as friction shifters. With indexed front shifting, you may want to fine-tune the cable tension to avoid noise from the chain dragging on the derailleur in some cross-gears or to get more precise shifting.*

ANOTHER NOTE: *Some front derailleurs have a cam screw at the end of the return spring to adjust the spring tension. For quicker shifting to the smaller rings, increase the spring tension by turning the screw clockwise one-quarter or one-half turn.*

NOTE ON SHIFTING TROUBLE: *If you cannot get the front derailleur to shift well, or if it rubs in cross-gears and throws the chain off, refer to the chain-line discussion under "Troubleshooting Derailleur and Shifter Problems" at the end of this chapter.*

NOTE ON CHAIN CATCHERS: *If, despite all adjustments, you just can't stop the chain from falling off to the inside, install a "chain catcher" or inner chain stop to nudge the chain back up onto the inner ring whenever it tries to drop off to the inside. Some consist of a long, bent arm and mount under the mounting bolt of a braze-on front derailleur; K-Edge and SRAM are examples. Others are built onto a band clamp, like the*

f you ensure that the cable tension is set correctly (§v-5e) so that the front derailleur stops before dropping the chain off to the inside, then the low-gear limit screw can be as loose as you want (or not even be there at all), and you still won't shift the chain off the inside and into the frame. This means that you can back out

the screw beyond where it needs to be to make sure that it never interferes with the chain dropping onto the smallest chainring.

If you choose to do this, however, you must always keep the cable tension accurate or the front derailleur can drop the chain off to the inside as the cable stretches.

Third Eye Chain Watcher (Fig. 5.55), Deda Dog Fang, K-Edge Clamp-On, or N-Gear Jump Stop.

v-6

FRONT-DERAILLEUR FEATHERING (TRIM) ADJUSTMENT

"Feathering" (also called "trimming") is adjusting the front derailleur slightly so that it will not rub the chain in cross-gears.

a. Shimano front STI shifter

To stop the chain from rubbing the front-derailleur cage while on a small rear cog and the inner chainring of a double crank, push the brake lever blade inward about half as far as you would to shift to the big chainring and let go. You will feel a soft click, and the front derailleur will stay a few millimeters out from its farthest-in position.

If the chain is rubbing in a cross-gear while on the big chainring, move the derailleur inward a couple of millimeters by pushing the chain-dump lever (the smaller lever behind the brake lever) inward lightly a few degrees. When you feel a soft click, let go.

With most road bikes, if the derailleurs are adjusted properly, if the frame is in alignment, and if the chain and chainline are to Shimano specification, these feathering positions will eliminate chain rub in all of the cross-gears except

perhaps a small-small or big-big combination.

NOTE: *You lose the feathering adjustment of an STI lever if you are using it with a triple crank.*

NOTE ON SHIMANO STI LEVERS 2009 AND LATER: *On newer Shimano levers where the shift and brake cables both pass under the handlebar tape, the front derailleur when adjusted properly will not rub the chain in any cross-gear from the big chainring, so the high-gear trim adjustment has been removed from the lever. You can only trim on the small chainring.*

b. Campagnolo front Ergopower shifter

With all original Campagnolo Ergopower other than QS/Escape (QS, or Quick Shift, refers to the left lever, and Escape refers to the right lever), which includes Chorus, Record, and above in all generations, the front shift mechanism has a number of closely spaced click stops in both directions; it does not have two definitive "indexed" positions. This setup means that you can move the derailleur in small increments by a single click in either direction. Trimming is simple and obvious, made with small movements inboard with the thumb lever or small movements outboard with the shift paddle. The front shifter's incremental movements are small enough to find a rub-free position as long as the outer chainring is not bent and the frame is aligned properly. As you ride, you may want to play with the left barrel adjuster a bit to get the chain tension just right for noise-free operation in cross-gears.

Starting in 2007, Campagnolo QS Ergopower left-side shifters appeared on Centaur and lower-end groups. These simpler, lighter lever mechanisms have the small incremental stops only shifting up from the small ring to big ring, so you can trim the derailleur only in combinations from the small chainring. There is not a trim adjustment from the big chainring.

c. SRAM DoubleTap front shifter

Original (2007) Force and Rival shifters only have a trim click for the small chainring. You give the shifter paddle a gentle nudge, and it moves outboard a bit.

Starting in 2008, all of the new or second-generation groups including Red, Force, Rival, and Apex have a feather adjustment for the big chainring. You tap the shift paddle lightly, and it moves inboard a bit. You cannot trim the front derailleur from the inner chainring.

d. Shimano and Campagnolo electronic shifters

Shimano Di2 and Campagnolo EPS electronic front derailleurs trim themselves automatically to ensure rub-free operation in all gears as you move through the rear cogs, no matter which chainring you are on.

REPLACING AND LUBRICATING SHIFT CABLES AND HOUSINGS

LEVEL 2

To function properly, derailleurs need to have clean, smooth-running cables (also called "inner wires"). As with replacing a chain, replacing cables is a maintenance operation, not a repair operation. Do not wait until cables break

to replace them. Replace any cables that have broken strands, kinks, or fraying between the shifter and the derailleur. You should also replace housings (also called "outer wires") if they are bent, mashed, or just plain gritty, or if the color clashes with your bike (this is really important!).

NOTE: *For installing and connecting the cables on Campagnolo and Shimano electronic systems, see §v-18 through §v-20.*

---

v-7

BUYING CABLES

1. **Buy new cables and housing that are at least as long as the ones you are replacing.**

2. **Make sure that the cables and housing are for indexed systems.** These cables will stretch minimally, and the housings will not compress in length. Under its external plastic sheath, indexed housing is not made of steel coil like brake housings; it is made of parallel (coaxial) steel strands of thin wire. If you look at the end (Fig. 5.16), you will see numerous wire ends surrounding a central Teflon tube.

NOTE: *I recommend using 5mm shift housing, rather than 4mm, as I find that the cable friction is reduced with it.*

3. **Buy two cable-end crimp caps (Fig. 5.16) and a tubular cable-housing end (ferrule) for each end of every housing section.** The end caps will prevent fraying, and the ferrules will prevent kinking at the cable entry points, cable stops, shifters, and derailleurs.

4. **It is a good idea to buy extra cables, cable caps, and ferrules (Fig. 5.16) to keep on hand in your work area.** They're inexpensive, and if you have a small supply, you will be able to change cables when you need to without making a special trip to the bike shop to get a little cable-end cap.

NOTE: *If your frame has internal cables, buy thin plastic housing sheaths along with the new cables and housings. Before you pull out the old cables, slide the sheaths onto the cables and through the frame as a way to guide the new cables in. After the new cables are in, you can pull the sheaths back out. Make sure that if the new internal shift cables cross each other inside of the down tube (i.e., if the housings cross in front of the head tube) that they cross a maximum of once. Multiple crosses (i.e., the cables are wound around each other) not only will result in undue friction, but shifting one lever will have an effect on both derailleurs.*

PRO TIP	**Better Shifting**

P erhaps the best thing you can do for your bike—especially a bike with a lot of miles on it—is to replace the cables and housings. Drag on shift cables caused by contamination will prevent accurate and consistent shifts.

---

v-8

CUTTING HOUSING TO LENGTH

1. **Use a special cutter made for the purpose.** Park, Pedro's, Shimano, SRAM, and Jagwire make good ones (Fig. 1.2). Standard wire cutters (i.e., "side cutters") will not cleanly cut index-shift housing.

2. **Cut the housing to the same lengths as the pieces you are replacing.** If you have no old housings for comparison, cut the new pieces so that they curve smoothly. When you turn the handlebar, the housing should not pull or kink. Allow enough length for the rear derailleur to swing backward (Fig. 5.17) and forward (Fig. 5.18) freely.

NOTE: *It is critical that you ensure that the housing loop at the rear derailleur is long enough to allow the cable to slide smoothly inside; a tight bend will prevent the derailleur from shifting well to small cogs, because the derailleur's return spring will not be strong enough to overcome the cable friction.*

3. **With a nail or toothpick, open each end of the Teflon liner that has been smashed shut by the cutter.**

4. **Place a ferrule over each housing end (Fig. 5.16).**

5. **After threading the cable into the housing (see next sections for details), clip the cable 1–2cm past the bolt and crimp a cap onto it to prevent fraying (Fig. 5.19).**

5.16 Cable-housing types and end caps

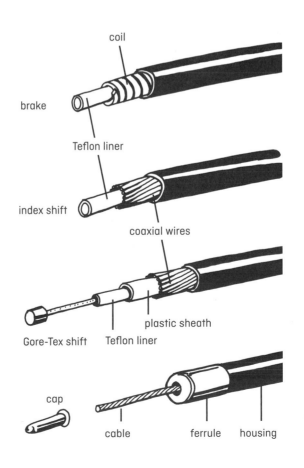

THE SHIFTING SYSTEM

5.17 Rear derailleur swinging backward to check housing length

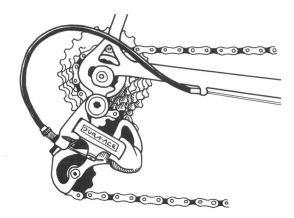

5.18 Rear derailleur swinging forward to check housing length

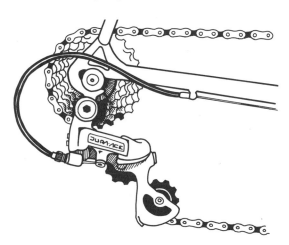

5.19 Crimping the cable-end cap

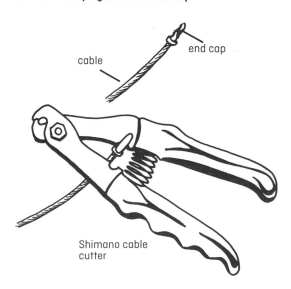

cable

end cap

Shimano cable cutter

REPLACING SHIFT CABLE IN SHIMANO STI SHIFT/BRAKE LEVER

1. **Disconnect the cable at the derailleur and snip off the cable-end cap (if installed).**

2. **Shift the inner lever to the gear setting that lets the most cable out.** This setting will be the highest-gear position for the rear shift lever (small cog) and the lowest for the front (small chainring).

3. **Push the cable until the cable head emerges from the hole far enough to grab it.** Pull out the old cable and recycle it.

   a. On original STI levers (on which the shift cable sticks out of the side of the lever in front of the head tube, not under the handlebar tape), pull the brake lever to reveal the access hole for the shift cable (Fig. 5.20); the hole is on the outboard side of the lever. On Dura-Ace levers with the cable coming out of the side, you must first remove a thin, black plastic cover with a small Phillips screwdriver to get at the access hole.

   b. On newer STI levers where the cable goes under the handlebar tape, the access hole is under a plug in the lever hood, high up on the lever body under the lever, slightly to the outboard side.

4. **The recessed hole into which the cable head seats should be visible through the access hole. Thread the new cable through the hole and out through the inboard side of the lever (Fig. 5.20).** On 2009 and later STI levers where the shift cable goes under the handlebar tape, the cable will pop up out of its passageway and continue in one of two grooves in a white, low-friction material before entering the cable housing end cap at the exit of the lever body. One groove routes

5.20 Threading in a new shift cable into an old-style Shimano STI lever

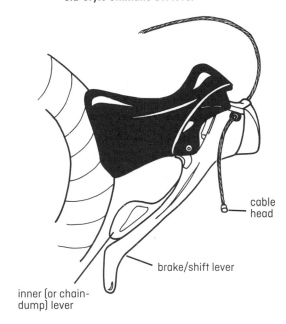

cable head

brake/shift lever

inner (or chain-dump) lever

5.21 Threading in a new Campy Ergopower shift cable

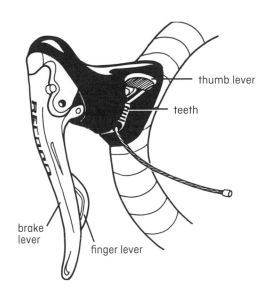

thumb lever

teeth

brake lever

finger lever

the cable in front of the handlebar, and the other routes it behind the bar, so choose the one you wish (I recommend routing the cable in front of the handlebar). The cable may pop that piece of white low-friction material out of the lever; if so, slide it onto the cable and reinsert it in place.

5. **Guide the cable through each housing segment (making sure each housing segment has a ferrule on the end; see Fig. 5.16) and cable guide and cable stop to the derailleur.**

NOTE: *For internal cables, see the Note in §v-7.*

v-10

REPLACING SHIFT CABLE IN CAMPAGNOLO ERGOPOWER LEVER

1. **Disconnect the cable at the derailleur and snip off the cable-end cap (if installed).**

2. **Click the thumb lever until it will click no more.**

3. **Push the cable until the cable head emerges from the cable hole in the slot near the**

bottom of the lever body. It's toward the inboard side—just outboard of the little gear teeth; Fig. 5.21. On QS/Escape levers and 2009 and later Ultra-Shift Ergopower 11- and 10-speed levers with the inward-curved top of the lever body, the access to the cable end is a hole near the base of the lever on the outboard side. Push the cable head out far enough to grab it. Pull out the old cable and recycle it.

4. **Push the new cable in through the hole and up through the lever body until the cable emerges from the housing entry hole at the upper base of the lever body on the outboard side.** On post-2008 Ultra-Shift and Power Shift Ergopower levers, the cable will pop up out of its passageway and continue in one of two grooves in a light-colored, low-friction material before passing through another hole back into the black lever body before exiting it. One groove routes the cable in front of the handlebar, and the other routes it behind the bar, so choose the one you wish

(I recommend routing the cable in front of the handlebar). The cable will not want to follow either groove and pass through that hole without some coaxing. First, push the cable out so it extends above the two grooves, and put a little bend in the end of the cable. Pull it back in a bit until that bend is just visible. Now push the cable forward again, and push down on the end of the cable with a 2mm hex key or other thin implement to get the cable to pass through the little hole at the end of whichever groove you chose and exit the lever. The cable will emerge into a tunnel for the housing, and at its base there is a brass washer to stop the housing; avoid dislodging this brass washer when you push the cable through. If you dislodge the washer and lose it, pop the washer out of the cable tunnel you're not using (i.e., for cable routing around the back of the handlebar), and use it in the tunnel you are using. Note also that these cable tunnels will fit only 4mm housing; they will not fit the 5mm housing of, say, the superlight Gore cable set.

5. **Guide the cable through each housing segment, cable guide, and cable stop to the derailleur.** Except for the end of the housing piece that will insert into a post-2008 (Ultra-Shift or Power Shift) Campagnolo lever (since it doesn't need a ferrule, and one won't fit), place a ferrule on the end of each cable housing segment (Fig. 5.16). Make sure the housing segment at the lever inserts fully into its hole in the lever body. If the housing won't slip in due to shape of the lever body and/or handlebar where the two meet, use a nail to flare the soft lever-body material outward to allow the cable housing to enter. If you insist on installing 5mm housing into an Ultra-Shift or Power Shift lever, you'll have to drill out or cut away the housing tunnel

in the lever body; then you'll need a ferrule to support the end of the housing, because the lever tunnel no longer will.

NOTE: *The Ergopower cable hook (i.e., the enlarged, countersunk hole into which the cable head seats) is too small to fit a Shimano or other cable head—just another of those maddening parts incompatibilities. You can file a cable head to fit in the Campy lever, but unless you are careful to ensure that the cable head is small enough, expect to push hard with pliers to get the cable back out next time. It's simplest to just buy a new Campagnolo-compatible shift cable. Some cables, like Gore Ride On coated road cables, have a smaller Campy-type head on one end and a larger Shimano/SRAM-type head on the other; clip off the one you don't need.*

ANOTHER NOTE: *For internal cables, see the Note in §v-7.*

v-11

REPLACING SHIFT CABLE IN SRAM DOUBLETAP LEVER

1. **Disconnect the cable at the derailleur and snip off the cable-end cap (if installed).**
2. **Click the shift paddle with small pushes (Fig. 5.1) until it won't let out any more cable.**
3. **Push the cable until the cable head emerges from the cable hole at the base of the lever on the inboard side.** Push the cable head out far enough to grab it. Pull out the old cable and recycle it.
4. **Push the new cable in through the hole and up through the lever body until the cable emerges from the housing entry hole at the upper base of the lever body on the outboard side.**
5. **Guide the cable through each housing segment (making sure each housing segment**

has a ferrule on the end; see Fig. 5.16) and cable guide and cable stop to the derailleur.

NOTE: *For internal cables, see the Note in §v-7.*

v-12

REPLACING CABLE IN A DOWN-TUBE SHIFT LEVER OR BAR-END SHIFT LEVER (INCLUDING ON AN AERO HANDLEBAR)

1. **Disconnect the cable at the derailleur and snip off the cable-end cap.**

2. **Flip the lever forward to the gear setting that lets out the most cable.** This setting will be the highest gear position for the rear shift lever (small cog) and the lowest for the front (small chainring).

3. **Push the cable until the cable head pops out of the hole in the shift lever.** Pull out the old cable and recycle it.

4. **Thread the new cable through the hole and out through the other side of the lever (Fig. 5.22).**

5. **Guide the cable through each housing segment (making sure each housing segment has a ferrule on the end; see Fig. 5.16) and cable guide and cable stop to the derailleur.** If the cables run through the frame or handlebars, make sure that there is either cable housing or a plastic liner inside for them to run in (see the Note in §v-7). If there is internal cable housing, is it due for replacement? (Is the cable running smoothly in it without resistance? Is the shifting crisp?) If so, slide a new piece of housing or liner tubing onto the old cable before pulling the old cable from inside the frame or bars, depending on which the frame or bar accepts, and pull it through. Then you can easily slip the new cable in through the frame or bar through the new plastic tube without any fishing around.

5.22 Threading a new cable into a down-tube shifter

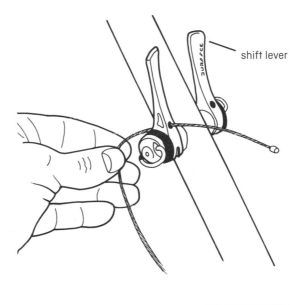

shift lever

v-13

ATTACH CABLE TO REAR DERAILLEUR

1. **Make sure that the rear shifter is on the highest gear setting so that the maximum amount of cable is available to the derailleur.**

2. **Put the chain on the smallest cog so that the rear derailleur moves to the outside.**

3. **Route the cable through each of the frame cable stops and housing segments and the barrel adjuster on the back of the derailleur until you reach the derailleur's cable-fixing bolt.**

NOTE: *For internal cables, see the Note in §v-7.*

On a SRAM rear derailleur, make sure that the cable wraps in the groove around the curved arm behind the fixing bolt and then routes above the bolt (Fig. 5.23), to the side away from the jockey wheels.

4. **Pull the cable taut and into its groove under the cable-fixing bolt (Fig. 5.24).** On all but SRAM rear derailleurs, the cable usually goes on the side of the bolt toward the

5.23 Cable routing to SRAM rear derailleur. (Note that the cable wraps around the curved guide behind the cable fixing bolt and that the cable attaches on the side of the bolt opposite the jockey wheels.)

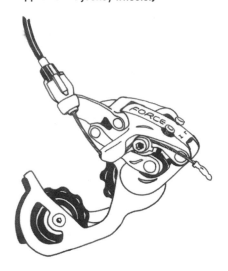

5.24 Attaching rear-derailleur cable

make sure this loop is not too short or kinked

jockey wheels. If you're unsure about which side of the bolt the cable goes on, remove the bolt and look for a groove on the derailleur adjacent to the threaded hole and/or on the underside of the bolt's washer.

5. **Tighten the bolt.** On most derailleurs this step takes a 5mm hex key.

6. Clip the cable 1–2cm past the bolt and crimp on a cap to prevent fraying (Fig. 5.19).

v-14

ATTACH CABLE TO FRONT DERAILLEUR

1. **Shift the chain to the inner chainring so that the derailleur moves farthest to the inside.** This ensures that the maximum amount of cable is available to the derailleur.

2. **With a 5mm hex key, tighten the cable to the cable anchor on the derailleur while pulling the cable taut with pliers.** Be sure that the cable lies in the groove beneath the cable-fixing bolt (Fig. 5.25).

NOTE: *For internal cables, see the Note in §v-7.*

3. **Clip the cable 1–2cm past the bolt and crimp on a cap to prevent fraying (Fig. 5.19).**

5.25 Attaching front-derailleur cable

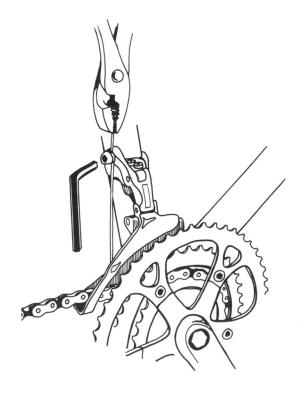

v-15

FINAL CABLE TOUCHES

A high-quality cable assembly includes the cable-housing end ferrules (Fig. 5.16) throughout and crimped cable caps (Fig. 5.19); cables are clipped about 1–2cm past the cable-fixing bolts.

v-16

CABLE LUBRICATION

New cables and housings with Teflon liners do not need to be lubricated. Old cables can be lubricated with chain oil. White lithium grease and other bike greases can slow their movement, so use oil or very light, translucent grease.

1. **Disconnect the cable at the derailleur, and clip off the cable-crimp end.** Be aware that if the cable frays at all when clipped, you may not be able to slide it back in through the housings and may have to replace the cable and perhaps its housings as well.
2. **Coat the areas of the cable that will be inside the cable-housing segments with chain oil.**
3. **Squirt oil into each housing section.**

NOTE: *If you have any trouble reinstalling the cable because of fraying, or the housings are dirty and rusty, you should replace both the cable and the housings.*

ANOTHER NOTE: *On bikes with a slotted chainstay cable stop, pull the housing out of the stop, slide it up the cable, and lubricate that section of cable without disconnecting it from the derailleur.*

v-17

REDUCE CABLE FRICTION

In addition to replacing old cables and housings with good-quality cables and lined housings, the following specific steps can improve shifting efficiency:

1. **The most important friction-reducing steps are to route the cable so that it makes smooth bends (see the Note in §v-8, step 2 on the loop at the rear derailleur).** Make sure that the front cable-housing sections are long enough that turning the handlebar does not increase the tension on the shift cables.
2. **Choose cables that offer especially low friction.** "Die-drawn" cables, which have been mechanically pulled through a die (a small hole in a piece of hard steel), move with lower friction than standard cables. Die-drawing flattens the outer strands, smoothing the cable surface. Thin cables and Teflon-lined housings with a large inside diameter also reduce friction.
3. **If your bike has internal cables, make sure that they aren't crossing each other multiple times inside the down tube.**

v-18

INSTALLING SHIMANO DI2 AND CAMPAGNOLO EPS ELECTRONIC DERAILLEURS AND SHIFTERS

LEVEL 2

It is likely that you might have trepidation the first time you install one of these, as electronic systems are so different from cable-operated shifting systems. However, after performing a few installations of electronic shifting systems, you will likely find that it is quicker, if not easier, than installing a cable-shift system. And though you may be worried about durability relative to standard cable systems, you'll find that the warranties from both Campagnolo and Shimano are many years long on these parts and wiring harnesses.

THE SHIFTING SYSTEM

Make sure that you have the appropriate parts for your frame. Make sure that you have the correct front-derailleur adapter—if one is required—to fit the seat tube. If your frame will have external wires, get the external-wire kit. If your frame takes internal wiring, make sure you have purchased the correct battery mount to fit the mounts on the frame and that the hole in the frame for it is in the correct spot to route the battery wire through it.

The motors that drive the derailleurs are extremely powerful, and if the front-derailleur upshift button is pushed when a finger is between the derailleur and the large chainring, the finger can be pinched, cut, or wedged. For your own safety, rotate the cranks whenever shifting, and disconnect the battery whenever installing electronic components.

To disconnect the Shimano Di2 battery, unplug the battery (or unplug its wire if you're using a seatpost-mounted battery). Removing a Di2 battery from the mount requires flipping open the lever on the back of the mount and pressing the button on the side of the mount while pulling on the battery (Fig. 5.26). To install the battery, slide it in along its grooves and flip the lever to secure it.

To disconnect the Campagnolo (EPS) battery, plug in the "EPS shutoff magnet," a cylindrical magnet with a plastic key-ring loop that plugs into the Power Unit battery housing on the curved end below the large connector plug (Fig. 5.27).

1. **Install the rear derailleur (Fig. 5.28) just as in §v-2.**

2. **Install the levers (Fig. 5.29) as in §v-21, and install the brake cables as in §vii-4.** Di2 levers have a lever-reach adjustment on the rear upper part of the lever body, under the rubber hood; turn it clockwise with a screwdriver to decrease lever reach, and vice versa. Campagnolo levers are short reach as shipped; install the "big hands" insert (Fig. 5.38) under the front edge of the lever body for more brake-lever reach.

If you're using supplementary Shimano satellite shifters for Dura-Ace Di2, install them now; they connect to the second plug in the lever body.

5.26 Removing Shimano Di2 battery; open the lever, pull the battery, and push the button

5.27 Disconnect the Campagnolo EPS battery by removing the EPS shutoff magnet

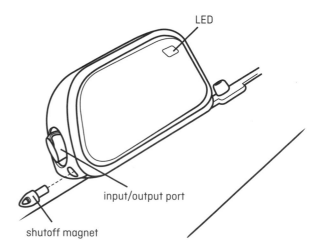

The "sprint shifters" mount to the inboard side of each curved drop of the handlebar so that the rider can shift with each thumb while sprinting in the drops of the bars. Generally, the left sprint shifter shifts to a larger cog, and the one for the right hand shifts to a smaller cog, but this can be reversed if you so choose using a shop tool to select button function (see §v-19 "Diagnostics").

The SW-7970 satellite shifter is a pod with a pair of buttons that is usually mounted on the top of the bar, just to the right of the stem clamp. This allows the rider to shift the rear derailleur while grasping the tops of the bar.

3. **Install the battery mount to the frame.** For internal wiring, temporarily mounting it using only a single, partially screwed-in bolt at the top of the mount allows access to the hole in the frame for wires connected to the battery. Use the supplied spacers between the mount and the frame (with Campy, you first bolt the EPS mount itself to the battery/ Power Unit). Different electronic-compatible frames have different battery-mounting locations. For bikes without a specific battery mount, use the bottle-boss battery mount and bolt it underneath the bottle cage on the down tube.

   Skip to step 6 for Campagnolo EPS.

   On Di2, ensure that there is at least 108mm from the base of the mount to the bottom of the bottle cage; this allows enough room to slide the battery up toward the bottle sufficiently to remove it.

   Aftermarket seatposts with integrated Di2 batteries or saddle bags with a Di2 battery inside require no additional battery mount but do require a long battery wire routed up the seat tube.

5.28 Shimano Dura-Ace 7970 Di2 electronic rear derailleur

limit screws

5.29 Shimano Dura-Ace 7970 Di2 electronic STI right lever

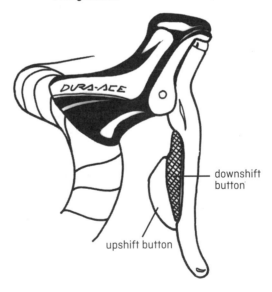

downshift button

upshift button

4. **On Di2, plug the wires from Junction A (Fig. 5.30) into the levers, ensuring the proper orientation of the indexing protrusions and grooves on the connectors.** Slip the end of the wire into the slender plastic TL-EW02 tool for Ultegra 6770 Di2 and TL-EW01 for

Dura-Ace 7970 Di2 so that the projection on the connector is aligned with the groove on the narrow end (Ultegra 6770 and Dura-Ace 7970 Di2 wires and connectors are incompatible with each other). Peel back the rubber hood, lift the terminal cover hatch, and plug the electrical wire end into the lever terminal with the TL-EW02 or TL-EW01 tool until it snaps in with a click. Use either the top or bottom terminal; the remaining terminal is for a satellite shifter (see step 2) or for plugging in the system checker.

If you're using sprint or satellite shifters, plug them in now—plug one sprint shifter into each lever; plug a SW-7970 satellite shifter into the right lever.

Cover unused terminals with dummy plugs, again using the TL-EW02 or TL-EW01. Close the hatch and flip the rubber lever hood back down.

When disconnecting wires, pry connectors off with the other end of the TL-EW02 or TL-EW01, flat side against the component you're disconnecting from.

5. **Zip-tie the Shimano Junction A unit (Fig. 5.30) to a brake cable so you can see the LED while riding.**

6. **Route the wires through the frame (or along the frame for external mount).**

EPS internal routing

Campagnolo supplies a super-useful thin cable with a magnet on the end for internal wire routing in nonsteel frames and aero handlebars. In addition to EPS wires, you can also use it to guide steel cable housing through frames and handlebars. The Campy magnet kit comes with the cable with a magnet on the end (the "metallic cable"), a dummy wire with an EPS connector on one end and a magnet on the other end (the "lead wire"), and a separate large, cylindrical magnet (Fig. 5.31).

EPS wires are color coded: green = rear derailleur; yellow = front derailleur; red = EPS interface; purple = right Ergopower lever; and blue = left Ergopower lever. Arrows on the male and female ends of the connectors must line up; it's useful to mark the arrows with a silver or white paint pen so you can see them easily.

a. Magnet end first, push the metallic cable in through the hole in the right chainstay or seatstay near the dropout for the rear derailleur wire; push it through until the magnet appears in the bottom bracket shell. Plug the

5.30 Shimano Di2 electronic Junction A (upper junction box) zip-tied to the front brake cable

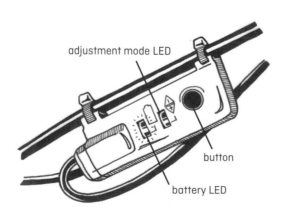

5.31 Campagnolo EPS magnet kit for guiding wires through the frame

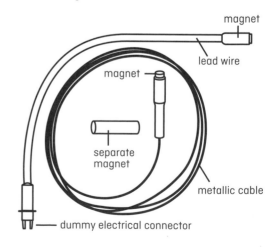

end of the green-banded wire from the Power Unit into the end of the lead wire and drop the lead wire, magnet end first, down into the hole at the Power Unit, pushing it until it appears in the bottom bracket shell. Bring the magnets of the lead wire and metallic cable together so they stick, and pull the other end of the metallic cable until it pulls the lead wire and the first few inches of the green-banded wire out through the hole near the dropout. Plug the green-banded connector into the (green-banded) wire emanating from the rear derailleur.

b. Magnet end first, push the metallic cable in through the hole in the frame. Using the separate magnet on the outside of the frame, guide the magnet end of the metallic cable into the down tube (Fig. 5.32). Keep pushing the cable until the magnet end appears inside the bottom bracket shell. Plug the end of the red-banded wire from the Power Unit into the end of the lead wire, and drop the lead wire, magnet end first, into the hole at the Power Unit, pushing it until it appears in the shell.

Bring the magnets of the lead wire and metallic cable together so they stick to each other. Pull the other end of the metallic cable until it pulls the lead wire and the first few inches of the red-banded wire out through the hole at the head tube. Connect the red-banded wire from the Power Unit to the red-banded wire from the EPS interface.

c. Use the rubber band and plastic hook or zip ties to attach the EPS interface under the stem, to a cable, or to the head tube. (On time trial and triathlon bikes, zip-tie the EPS interface to one of the aerobar extensions.)

d. Magnet end first, push the metallic cable in through the hole in the seat tube near the front derailleur braze-on or clamp area; push it in until the magnet appears in the bottom bracket shell. Plug the end of the yellow-banded wire from the Power Unit into the end of the lead wire, drop the magnet end of the lead wire down into the hole near the Power Unit, pushing it until it appears in the shell. Bring the magnets of the lead wire and metallic cable together so they stick to

5.32 Guiding Campagnolo EPS metallic cable from the head tube into the down tube with external magnet

5.33 Opening cover on Campagnolo EPS Ergopower right lever to access wires.

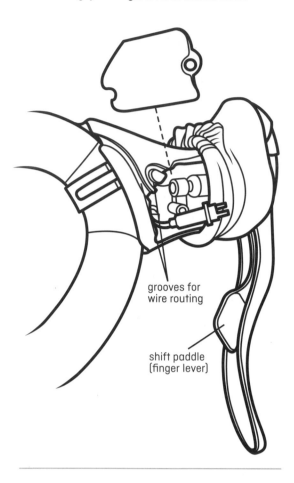

grooves for
wire routing

shift paddle
(finger lever)

Di2 internal routing

a. Route all of the wires into the bottom bracket shell (Fig. 5.34A): the wires from Junction A (Fig. 5.30) at the front, from the front derailleur (Fig. 5.35), from the rear derailleur (Fig. 5.28), and from the battery (Fig. 5.26). When pushing the wires in through the holes in the frame, push the end in so that the zip ties around the wire fold back rather than prevent the wire from going through the hole. The preattached zip ties prevent the wires from rattling inside the frame, but they also make sliding the flexible wires through the frame more difficult. Do not be afraid to shorten a zip tie or two to make the task more doable. If you're having trouble getting the wires through the frame, you can try pushing in a stiff wire from the other end with a hook bent into the end, and fish your Di2 wire through.

b. Pull the ends of the wires out of the bottom bracket shell and plug all of them into Junction B (Fig. 5.34A)—the lower junction box—until they click, using the TL-EW02 or TL-EW01 tool to fully insert them. On Dura-Ace 7970, slide the supplied shrink tubing over the connection and heat it with a blow dryer to seal water out; Ultegra and 11-speed Dura-Ace Di2 connections are watertight without the need for the shrink tubing.

c. Plug in the wires from the lower junction box to the front derailleur, rear derailleur (labeled FD and RD on Dura-Ace 7970 Di2 wires, whereas all wires are universal on Ultegra 6770 Di2 and available in myriad lengths), and battery. Push the lower junction box up into the down tube (Fig. 5.34B) so that the only wires visible inside the bottom bracket shell are the wires going to the front and rear derailleur (Fig. 5.34C); in the case of a seatpost battery, there will also be a battery wire visible running up into the seat tube.

each other. Pull the other end of the metallic cable until it pulls the lead wire and the first few inches of the yellow-banded wire out through the hole in the seat tube. Fold the first inch or so of the wire over and tape it down so it doesn't slip back into the hole before you are ready to connect it to the front derailleur.

e. Peel back the outer bottom edge of the rubber hoods on the Ergopower levers and, with a small Phillips screwdriver, remove the covers on the outboard side of each lever body (Fig. 5.33). Plug the purple-banded wire from the interface into the purple-banded wire from the right Ergopower, and plug the blue-banded wire from the interface into the blue-banded wire from the left Ergopower.

5.34A Connecting Di2 wires at the lower junction box (Junction B) at the bottom bracket

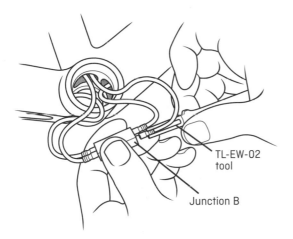

TL-EW-02 tool

Junction B

5.34B Shove the lower junction box (Junction B) into the down tube

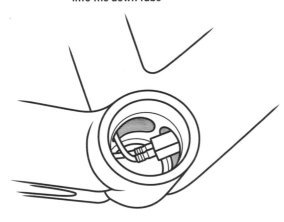

5.34C Ensure that the front- and rear-derailleur wires don't interfere with the bottom bracket

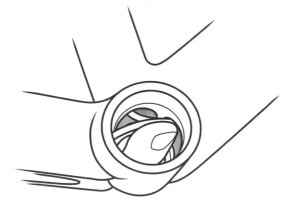

Di2 external routing

NOTE: *As of this writing, Campagnolo does not offer an EPS wiring harness for external frame routing.*

a. Route all of the wires along the outside of the frame to the bottom bracket: the wires from Junction A at the front, the front derailleur, the rear derailleur, and the battery.

b. Provisionally tape the wires to the frame, and later cover the wires with the supplied adhesive cover strips (after cleaning the area with alcohol). Route the rear-derailleur wire under the chainstay so the chain can't drop on it.

c. Take up any wire slack in the Di2 Junction B looping pegs (under the cover); you can wind 120mm of slack into it.

d. Bolt Junction B to the threaded cable-guide hole under the bottom bracket shell with 13–18 in-lbs (1.5–2.0 N-m) of torque.

NOTE: *If the bike frame has internal routing holes for shift cables rather than electrical wires, you will still have to route the electrical wires externally unless (1) the cable holes in the frame are large enough to pass the wire plug ends (Dura-Ace 7970 wire ends are much bigger than Ultegra 6770 or 11-speed Dura-Ace Di2 connectors); (2) there are no internal shift cable liners; (3) the hole into the bottom bracket shell from the down tube is large enough to plug in the junction box and push it up into the down tube (Fig. 5.34B); and (4) the holes into the bottom bracket shell from the seat tube and right chainstay are properly located to allow proper wire routing without interference with bottom bracket cups (Fig. 5.34C). Even if you can route the wires internally, the external frame holes may not be the correct size or shape to accept the rubber grommets to seal out moisture, so you'll have to improvise a method to cover the holes.*

7. **Install the bottom plastic sleeve and bracket bearings (Chapter 8).** Ensure that

both derailleur wires (and battery wire for a seatpost battery) pass above the sleeve (Fig. 5.34C), and the bearing or bearing cup threads do not impinge on the rear derailleur wire.

8. **Install the crankset (Chapter 8).**

9. **Install the front derailleur (Fig. 5.35) as in §v-4.**

On an EPS front derailleur, do this just as you would on a cable-operated one. Its nut takes a 7mm open-end wrench (Fig. 5.36). Plug its yellow-banded wire to the yellow-banded wire sticking up out of the hole in the seat tube.

On Di2 front derailleurs with a band clamp adapter, rotate the derailleur so that the tail of the outer cage plate is slightly inboard of the tip. While not necessary when using the band-clamp adapter, with Shimano Di2 front derailleurs mounted to a frame braze-on, adhere the supplied metallic seat tube protector to the seat tube so that the portion of it without foam adhesive sits behind the front derailleur support bolt (this is necessary to prevent the pointed tip of the support bolt from driving straight into the seat tube). Choose the flat or curved protector depending on seat tube shape at the support bolt contact point.

With a 2mm hex key, turn the Di2 support bolt (Fig. 5.35) to align the front derailleur outer cage plate parallel with the large chainring.

10. **Test the system.**

On Di2, plug in the battery (Fig. 5.26). Press the lever buttons to ensure that the derailleurs move properly without the chain. If they are working properly, remove the Di2 battery.

On EPS, remove the EPS shutoff magnet from the Power Unit (Fig. 5.27). Hold down

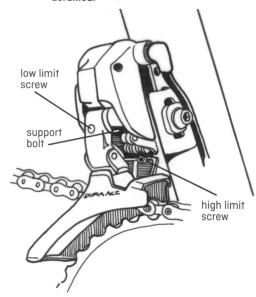

5.35 Shimano Dura-Ace 7970 Di2 electronic front derailleur

low limit screw

support bolt

high limit screw

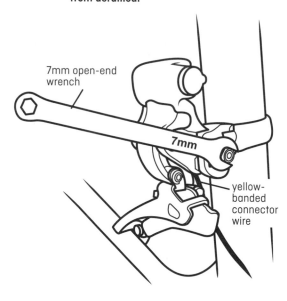

5.36 Installing Campagnolo Super Record EPS front derailleur

7mm open-end wrench

7mm

yellow-banded connector wire

both mode buttons, one on each lever, for a couple of seconds. Press the lever buttons to ensure that the derailleurs move properly without the chain. Plug the EPS shutoff magnet back in.

11. **Install the chain as in Chapter 4.** Ensure the proper orientation with Shimano 10-speed asymmetric chains (the outer chain plates

with the logos stamped into them face away from the bike; the slotted outer cage plates face toward the bike; see §iv-11b).

12. **If you haven't already done so, install the additional screw(s) in the battery mount and tighten it down.** The EPS Power Unit (Fig. 5.27) requires a rubber vibration washer under its tail, whereas the bottle-mount type Di2 battery mount (Fig. 5.26) requires a zip tie at its tail (or a third bolt hole in the frame) to keep the battery from bouncing around.

13. **Install the Di2 battery (Fig. 5.26), or plug in the battery wire to a seatpost battery, or remove the EPS shutoff magnet from the Power Unit (Fig. 5.27).** If the bottom of the seat-tube water bottle hits the battery, Shimano offers an accessory spacer (SM-BA01) that the bottle cage bolts to. The accessory spacer offsets the cage upward; its position is adjustable from 32mm to 50mm higher than with the cage bolted straight into the seat tube.

14. **Clean up the wiring.**

    On EPS, push the connectors into the side compartment on the Ergopower lever bodies, route the wire through the grooves (Fig. 5.33), and replace the compartment covers. Wrap the curly wire cover on the exposed wires at the Power Unit.

    Tape the shifter wires to the handlebar.

    Tape wire covers over external wiring.

15. **On internally routed wires, slip a rubber sealing grommet around each wire where it protrudes from the frame.** Push the grommet into the hole (Fig. 5.37) until it engages properly and creates a seal. The grommets come in different shapes and sizes depending on frame hole shape and wire size. The standard frame hole size (and hence standard grommets from both Shimano and Campagnolo) is 8 × 7mm, with the hole for

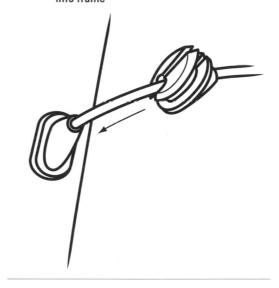

5.37 Installing sealing grommet on wire entry into frame

the battery wires being 14 × 7.7mm, but Shimano also offers round 7mm grommets. Additionally, frame manufacturers using nonstandard hole sizes will generally supply grommets with the frame. Hardware stores carry lots of rubber grommets if you need an odd size.

After reading the important details below, continue to initial system adjustment: §v-19 for Di2 or §v-20 for EPS.

Other electrical details

Battery care

Whenever replacing or reinstalling electronic components, disconnect the battery and wait at least 10 seconds before reconnecting it. The system must individually recognize each component of the electronic shifting system to operate correctly.

As with any battery, do not wet the battery or charger terminals; do not subject the battery to temperatures in excess of 140°F (60°C) or cover the battery or charger when charging; do not allow metal objects or wet objects to connect across the battery or charger terminals; do not use if the battery shows signs of leakage; and do not get battery acid in your eyes or on your skin.

THE SHIFTING SYSTEM

Use the charger only with AC voltages within the range printed on the unit. Do not use the charger with electrical transformers designed for overseas use.

Sealing out the elements

Although EPS and Di2 components are designed to be fully waterproof and able to withstand wet weather riding conditions, avoid submerging in water or solvents and do not subject to high-pressure spray, as in a car wash. Avoid lubricating the rear-derailleur links, as some lubricants can damage the O-rings that seal the electronic components inside. When washing the bike, ensure that all electrical connections are fully snapped in place to properly seal out water. Campagnolo and Shimano rubber sealing grommets (Fig. 5.37) are compatible with electric-ready frames.

Each of the electrical connections on EPS and on Ultegra and 11-speed Dura-Ace Di2 have O-ring seals that require no heat-shrink tubing over the connection. Only one EPS wire length is available for each color-coded wire attached to the interface and Power Unit; bigger bikes require extension wires with the same connectors. Conversely, Shimano Di2 wires plug in on both ends and can be obtained in different lengths; all Ultegra Di2 wires are completely interchangeable.

Secure external electrical wires with tape or zip ties to prevent snagging them on the chainrings, cogs, and tires.

Charging

You can charge the battery with any amount of charge remaining. Leaving the battery uncharged for extended periods can damage it, and storing it with at least a half charge is preferable. If storing for an extended time, recharge it periodically. Except in the case of an aftermarket battery

built into the seatpost and charged with a cord, Di2 batteries are made to be removed from the bike and charged in a charging pod. Conversely, the EPS Power Unit is more than just a battery; it houses the brain of the EPS system and is not to be removed from the bike. To charge, pull off the cover over the input/output plug on the more curved end of the Power Unit (Fig. 5.27), and plug in the charger cord.

Dura-Ace 7970 Di2 battery life is about 1,000 km (600 mi) on a single charge; Ultegra 6770 Di2 battery life is about 700 km (400 mi). The Di2 battery is uncharged at the time of purchase; charge it fully before riding. Campagnolo EPS battery life is around 1,500–2,000 km (900–1,200 mi), and it comes fully charged. Charge time for EPS and Di2 batteries is approximately 1.5 hours.

On Di2, always connect and disconnect electric wires with the TL-EW01 (Dura-Ace 7970) or TL-EW02 (Ultegra 6770) special tool; make sure the connection snaps together with an audible click to ensure a proper water seal. EPS connectors snap together by hand, but they require the UT-CG020EPS tool to disconnect them. Inserting the UT-CG020EPS's attached fork between the tool and the connector and rotating it clockwise pries the male end out; the pin pushes the female end out of the tool.

Crash protection

If an EPS or Di2 rear derailleur is hit in a crash, it protects itself by uncoupling the electronic motor from the mechanical shaft. You'll know this has happened when it won't shift properly. To recouple an EPS derailleur, you can repeatedly press the upshift button without pedaling until it hooks up and will again allow shifting to the smallest cog. To recouple a Di2 motor with its derailleur link, hold down the button on Junction A for five seconds or more.

Alternatively, you can stop and engage the two parts of either type of rear derailleur by pushing inward on the derailleur body with your hand until you hear it click back into place. Unless the derailleur hanger was also bent in the crash, it should now shift properly again.

NOTE: *The uncoupling feature can be used to set the rear derailleur on any cog to ride back home when, for instance, the wire has been cut in a crash, or the battery has been completely discharged.*

---

v-19

ADJUSTING SHIMANO DURA-ACE 7970 AND ULTEGRA 6770 DI2 ELECTRONIC DERAILLEURS AND SHIFTERS

a. Rear derailleur

LEVEL 1

1. **Shift to the fifth-largest rear cog.** See §v-1g and §v-1h for shifting instructions with Di2 electronic shifters.

2. **Hold the button down on Junction A (Fig. 5.30) until the LED with the "+−" lights up red, indicating that the system is in the adjustment mode.**

3. **Listening for noise while turning the chain and observing the vertical alignment of the upper jockey wheel under the cog, tap the right-hand upshift or downshift button until the jockey wheel lines up straight under the cog and the chain moves silently.** Shimano's suggested method (not possible while riding) is to bump the downshift button until the chain makes noise against the next largest cog. Then bump the upshift button four times to center the guide pulley under the cog.

NOTE: *In the adjustment mode, each push of a shift button moves a derailleur less than a single click of a barrel adjuster on a cable-shift system would.*

4. **Push the button on Junction A again until the LED turns off.** Check for silent operation when shifting through all cogs. If not shifting perfectly, repeat steps 1–4.

5. **Shift to the largest cog. Tighten the low-gear limit screw (the inboard one; Fig. 5.28) until it touches the link and ensures that the derailleur cannot shift into the spokes.** If you tighten it too tightly, either it won't shift to the largest cog or it will continue to run the motor, wearing down the battery rapidly; back the low-gear limit screw off appropriately if that happens.

6. **Shift to the smallest cog (it will overshift and then come back to center under the cog). Tighten the high-gear limit screw (the outboard one; Fig. 5.28) until it touches the link, and then back it off (counterclockwise) one full turn.** This allows for the over-shift-and-return shift method the derailleur utilizes, yet it still ensures that the derailleur cannot shift into the dropout.

7. **Set the b-screw as in §v-3f.** By turning the crank backward in both the small front–big rear and small-small combinations, check that the guide pulley is as close to the cog as possible without bumping up and down as the chain moves. Check that on the smallest cog the guide pulley doesn't interfere with the chain's movement.

b. Front derailleur

1. **Shift to the inner chainring and largest rear cog.** See §v-1h for shifting instructions.

2. **With a 2mm hex key, turn the front derailleur low-gear limit screw on the face of the upper link (Fig. 5.35) to bring the inner cage plate within 1.0–0.5mm from the chain.**

3. **Shift to the outer chainring and smallest rear cog.**

4. **With a 2mm hex key, turn the front derailleur high-gear limit screw to bring the outer cage plate 0.5–1mm from the chain.** The screw is set back just above the front-derailleur cage; it's below the support bolt you turned in §v-18, step 1 (Fig. 5.35).

NOTE: *You want both front-derailleur limits and the rear low-gear limit to be "hard" stops to prevent the rear derailleur from moving too far in either direction, and you want the rear-derailleur high-gear limit to be a "soft" stop to allow overshift, ensuring fast shifting to the smallest cog.*

The Di2 front derailleur shifts quickly, but in two steps; it pushes hard and fast to derail the chain without pushing so far that it overshifts the chainring, and then it carefully lines up the cage over the chain depending on what cog it is on in the rear.

On either chainring, the front derailleur automatically trims itself twice in either direction when the chain is shifted from one extreme of the cogset to the other. If you set the front-derailleur position properly, this auto-trim feature will ensure chain-rub-free riding in any gear combination.

c. Battery

To view the battery-level indicator, hold down any shift button on either lever (Fig. 5.29) until the LED battery indicator on Junction A (Fig. 5.30) lights up. The LED will illuminate green, flashing green, red, or flashing red to indicate a full, half-full, quarter-full, or empty battery. Recharge the battery whenever (or before) the upper LED with the battery symbol next to it turns red. The optional wireless Flight Deck computer, which features heart rate, altitude, incline, and PC downloading, also has a battery indicator for the shifting system on its screen.

TROUBLESHOOTING DI2

When the battery runs out of charge, the front derailleur stops working first, then the rear derailleur. They stop at the last gear positions they were in.

If you drop the chain off to the inside, hold the front upshift lever down and keep pedaling to drive the chain back up to the big chainring.

a. Diagnostics

1. On the bike.shimano.com website, in the drop-down menu under "Tech Support," go to "Tech Docs," hover the mouse over "Road Bike" (or go to techdocs.shimano.com and hover over "Road Bike"), and click on "Ultegra" or on "Dura-Ace."

2. For first-generation Di2 (Dura-Ace 7970), scroll down and click on "System Checker." To perform the diagnostics, you need the SM-EC79 system checker unit. If you have the unit, you can plug it into each component in the system and push the button on its face. If a green light appears, that component is fine. The LED indicators on the SM-EC79 system checker illuminate or flash green, red, or orange, and the online instructions guide you through diagnosing problems in the system. You can also use the SM-EC79 system checker to switch the shift commands to change which direction the derailleur moves in response to pressure on a given switch.

3. For Ultegra 6770 Di2, click on "E-tube Project." If you have a Windows computer, you can download the software and plug into your bike's Di2 system with Shimano's

SM-PCE1 PC interface device for Ultegra Di2. You can then diagnose and correct problems in the system on your computer screen.

v-20

ADJUSTING CAMPAGNOLO EPS ELECTRONIC DERAILLEURS AND SHIFTERS

LEVEL 1

Front and rear EPS derailleurs can be adjusted with the bike on a stand or while riding. Mode buttons are on the inboard side of each Ergopower lever adjacent the thumb switch, while they are under each lever at the end of the aero extensions on EPS aerobar shifters.

NOTE: *You may find it simpler to adjust the system by performing the quick adjustment mode used for on-ride adjustments: Hold down a single mode button until the LED on the EPS interface glows pink, rather than holding both down until the LED glows blue. Then adjust the derailleur as below. If you do this, be sure to adjust the rear derailleur first (see the Note below).*

ANOTHER NOTE: *The brains of the EPS system are supposedly in the Power Unit. But the front derailleur seems to have its share of intelligence and has more to say about how things will behave than does the rear derailleur. The adjustment can get screwed up if you adjust the front derailleur before the rear derailleur, which confuses it. At that point, the rear derailleur may shift only half of the cogs. If it gets confused, install the shutoff magnet (Fig. 5.27) to shut down the system and allow it to reboot itself; then remove the magnet and hold both mode buttons down six seconds or more to move into the master adjustment mode (LED glows blue). You may need to repeat this a number of times.*

a. Adjustment mode, initial setup

1. **Shift to the big front ring/biggest rear cog gear combination or big front ring/second-biggest rear cog if it won't go to the biggest cog.** See §v-1i and §v-1j for shifting instructions with EPS electronic shifters.

2. **Get into adjustment mode by pressing both mode buttons—one on each lever behind the thumb lever on the inboard side—for at least six seconds; the LED on the EPS interface (zip-tied to a front cable or rubber-banded around the head tube) will glow blue.**

3. **When you've finished each adjustment below, hit one of the mode buttons once to memorize the setting; the LED will flash blue.** Then hit any mode button one more time to get out of standby mode.

b. Rear derailleur initial adjustment

1. **Shift into the second-smallest cog, leaving the chain on the large chainring.**

2. **In the adjustment mode (LED glowing blue; see a.2 above), bump whichever rear shift lever is necessary for the chain to be quiet and lined up on the second-smallest cog.** Each touch of the lever will move the derailleur about the same amount that a single click of a barrel adjuster will on a cable-actuated system.

3. **Press the right mode button to save the adjustment (the LED will glow white).**

4. **Shift into the second-largest cog (chain still on the big chainring).**

5. **Bump whichever rear shift lever is necessary for the chain to be quiet and lined up on the second-largest cog.**

6. **Press the right mode button to save the adjustment (the LED will flash blue and then go back to solid blue).** Press the mode

button again to exit adjustment mode.

7. **Shift to the largest cog and the inner chainring.**

8. **As in §v-3a and §v-3c, adjust the rear derailleur inner limit screw (to keep the chain out of the spokes), except back the screw out a half turn after bringing it into contact with the derailleur tab when the upper jockey wheel is lined up directly under the largest cog (to allow for the overshift used by the electronic system).**

9. **As in §v-3f, adjust the b-screw on the rear derailleur, if present, to adjust the distance from the cog to the upper jockey wheel to 5–7mm.** The rear derailleur is adjusted.

c. Front derailleur initial adjustment

1. **Shift to the inner chainring and the largest cog.**

2. **In the adjustment mode (LED glowing blue; see a.2 above), bump whichever front lever is necessary to move the front derailleur the direction you want.** Hold that lever until the front derailleur's inner cage plate is 0.5mm from the chain. Holding the left thumb lever down drives the inner front-derailleur cage plate away from the chain; holding the left finger lever inward drives the inner front-derailleur cage plate toward the chain. There are no limit screws or other front-derailleur adjustments; easy schmeezy.

3. **Touch the left mode button to memorize the setting; the LED will flash blue and then turn off after a few seconds.** If it doesn't turn off, hit any mode button again to make sure it is out of standby mode (LED off).

4. **Take your bike for a road test.** On either chainring, the front derailleur automatically trims itself twice in either direction when the chain is shifted from one extreme of the cogset to the other. If you have set the front-

derailleur position properly, this auto-trim feature will ensure chain-rub-free riding in any gear combination.

d. Adjustment mode, fine-tuning, or ride setting

This is the mode you use if you've gotten a wheel change and the rear shifting is off, or if, after initial setting, shifting is sluggish at some point in the cogset. You can also use this if you have chain rub on the front derailleur.

1. **Get into fine-tune mode by holding only one mode button down (the one for the derailleur that you want to adjust) for six seconds; the LED on the EPS interface will glow pink.**

2. **Bump whichever shift button is necessary to move the chain in the direction you want to eliminate the noise or rub, or to move it toward the cog which is sluggish in shifting.**

3. **Hit the same mode button again to memorize the setting.** The LED will flash pink and then go out after a few seconds.

e. Diagnostics

It is easy to check battery level—simply push and release one of the mode buttons on either lever; a light on the EPS interface unit that mounts on the stem, head tube, or the brake cable will light up for a few seconds. The color code is similar to a traffic light; if it's green, the battery is full, yellow indicates half charge, and red indicates the need for a charge. Additionally, flashing green indicates a small drop from full, and flashing red indicates that the red light is coming soon. Campagnolo claims a battery life of more than three months for riders putting in 500 km/month (300 mi), and one month or more for those riding 2,000 km/month (1,200 mi). The 12V lithium ion battery can be recharged more than 500 times without losing significant performance.

Full diagnostics are built into the Power Unit. While sophisticated circuit boards and indicator LEDs in the Digital Tech Intelligence (DTI) Power Unit preclude aftermarket EPS batteries integrated into seatposts (as Calfee and others do for Shimano Di2 batteries), it does make it possible for the user to perform all diagnostics and electronic adjustments on the road. Firmware and the device configuration memory can be updated, and system diagnosis can be accomplished through the input/output plug on the Power Unit.

THE SHIFTERS

v-21

REPLACING AND INSTALLING INTEGRATED BRAKE/SHIFT LEVERS

LEVEL 2

Shifters can be replaced as an entire unit and sometimes as separate parts. Brake/shift levers are generally labeled right and left, but if you're in doubt, you can tell which is which because the levers should flip to the inside. Here are the steps for you to replace the entire brake/shift lever unit:

1. **Remove the handlebar tape and bar plugs.**
2. **Remove the old brake/shift lever by loosening its mounting bolt with a 5mm hex key or a Torx T25 key and sliding the lever assembly off.** The position of the bolt varies, but it is always on the outside of the lever body, under the lever hood on the outboard side. Slip the hex key (or Torx T25 key; if the 5mm hex key doesn't fit, your lever probably takes one of these) down from the top between the lever body and the hood, or roll back the hood far enough to get at it from outside of the hood (Fig. 7.11).
3. **Slide the new lever on the bar to where you like it.** A good rule of thumb is to put

a straightedge against the bottom of the bar and slide the lever down until its end touches the straightedge. The lever can sit a little higher than this, but generally not any lower. Put a long straightedge across the top of both levers before they are fully tightened to make sure that they are level with each other.

4. **Post-2008 Campagnolo Ultra-Shift and Power-Shift Ergopower levers have a "big hands" insert.** If you want the lever body cocked back so that the reach to the levers is increased, push the insert onto the bottom of the lever base under the hood (Fig. 5.38). They are asymmetrical but not labeled L and R, so line up the hole on the insert with the cable-access hole on the lever body to ensure you have it on the correct lever.
5. **Tighten the mounting bolt.** Again, this will likely take either a 5mm hex key (it's best to have a long one without a ball end that can strip the bolt head) or a Torx T25 key.
6. **Install the cables (§v-7 through §v-15; §vii-4) and barrel adjusters, if not already in place.**
7. **Wrap the handlebar with tape (§xi-12).**

5.38 Installing "big hands" insert onto Ultra-Shift Ergopower

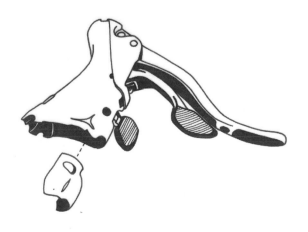

REHABILITATING OR REPLACING SHIFTER UNIT ON SHIMANO STI INTEGRAL BRAKE/SHIFT LEVER

LEVEL 1

If you have a jammed Shimano STI shifter, you cannot really go into the mechanism like a watchmaker and replace parts. Shimano doesn't sell the internal parts separately, and opening the mechanism voids the warranty. But, with a little lube, you can often rehabilitate a sticky mechanism or an STI lever that does not always engage when you try to shift. Use the thin tube attachment on an aerosol chain lube to flush the guts of the lever from the side by sticking the aerosol tube into the little hole visible when you pull the brake; the hole is above the rounded upper section of the main lever on the noncable side. Many riders have used this technique to get years of extra life out of levers that otherwise looked

destined for replacement. Don't do this over your carpet.

If that does not work, you can replace the entire shifter unit of two blades and internal ratchet (Fig. 5.39). Note that this approach may be false economy; you save the lever base, rubber hood, and band clamp, but you generally pay more than half the cost of a pair of levers for a single blade assembly. But if you find a bargain somewhere, here's the procedure:

1. **Remove the shift and brake cables and the brake-cable hook from its notches.**
2. **With a 2mm hex key, remove the setscrew holding the pivot axle (Fig. 5.39) in place under the lever.** Expect it to make noise while being unscrewed and for it to be hard to remove. There is a lot of threadlock compound on it to keep it from vibrating loose.
3. **Push out the axle with a blunt nail struck by a hammer, and catch the spring.**
4. **Pull off the old blade assembly and insert the new blade assembly.**

5.39 Exploded Dura-Ace 9-speed STI lever

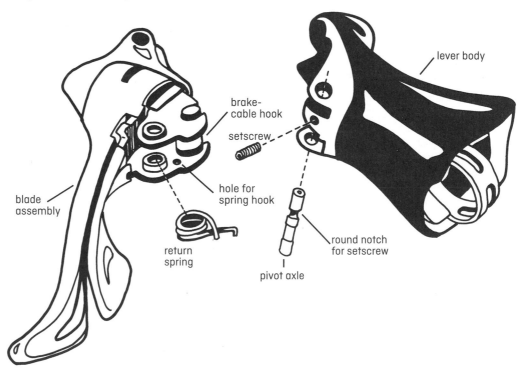

NOTE: *If you have a lever that is Flight Deck–computer compatible, you will need to unscrew the cover on the inboard side of the lever under the gum hood and push the end of the wiring harness up through the lever as you pull off the blade. Fish the wires of the new blade back in the same way, and replace the cover to hold the little rubber part and the four terminals in place.*

5. **Replace the return spring and axle.** The return-spring hook goes in the hole adjacent to the cable-hook notches, and its other end must sit on the shelf adjacent to the setscrew, not down in the wide notch in the lever body. Line up the rounded groove in the axle with the setscrew.

6. **Replace the setscrew, putting some thread-lock compound on it first.**

7. **Replace the cable hook into its notches.**

<hr/>

v-23

OVERHAULING ORIGINAL CAMPAGNOLO ERGOPOWER LEVERS

This is an extremely satisfying maintenance task. As with any mechanism that has lots of precision internal parts, it can be great fun, if you are in the right state of mind, to take an Ergopower (EP) lever entirely apart, clean it up, put it back together, and hear it click more loudly while engaging more firmly and working more smoothly afterward. You can also change the number of speeds in the lever.

Every Record and Chorus Ergopower lever through 2008 and every Centaur, Veloce, Mirage, and below lever through 2006 has two little G-shaped springs (Figs. 5.40, 5.41) that click into teeth in a ratchet, providing the indexing steps as the shift lever behind the brake lever advances the ratchet to pull cable, or as the thumb lever drives the ratchet in the opposite direction to release cable. Since these springs are constantly riding over the gear teeth on every shift in either direction, the G-springs can get worn, flattened, or broken, and shifting performance will drop off or cease to exist, since they will no longer be able to stop the index gear from turning. These G-springs are the same for every model and year, so get a couple, if you think you need them, and follow along. Your EP levers will be good as new again!

As is typical with Campagnolo components, every little Ergopower part is replaceable. However, only the entire shifter mechanism as a single unit is available for QS/Escape levers, which appeared on Centaur and groups below it starting in 2007. QS/Escape levers have different guts than the 8-, 9-, and original 10-speed levers described here. Replacement of the shift mechanism in QS/Escape levers is described in §v-24. Starting in 2009, 10- and 11-speed Ultra-Shift levers appeared, which sport a distinctly different lever and body shape; their mechanism is completely different and eliminates the fast-wearing G-springs; find Ultra-Shift overhaul in §v-25. In 2010 came Power-Shift levers sharing the lever and body shape with Ultra-Shift, a mechanism similar to QS/Escape, and the only spare parts available being the lever blade and the entire shift assembly, so refer to only the first few steps of §v-25 for that.

Refer to the exploded diagrams, Figure 5.40 (8-speed right-hand lever) and Figure 5.41 (9- or 10-speed right-hand lever). You can also magnify all those parts and find their part numbers for your particular year and model of lever on campagnolo.com.

The following instructions cover overhaul and lubrication, as well as replacing broken or damaged index springs and other parts. They also cover replacing ratchets to change the number of speeds. When I mention 8-speed levers, I am referring to 1992–1997 Ergopower levers (Fig. 5.40), both right and left. The lever body

5.40 Exploded Campagnolo Ergopower lever (8-speed)

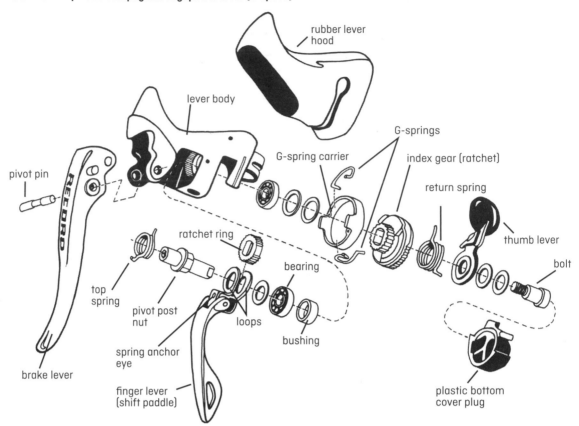

- rubber lever hood
- lever body
- pivot pin
- G-springs
- G-spring carrier
- index gear (ratchet)
- return spring
- thumb lever
- bolt
- ratchet ring
- bearing
- top spring
- pivot post nut
- loops
- spring anchor eye
- bushing
- brake lever
- finger lever (shift paddle)
- plastic bottom cover plug

5.41 Exploded Campagnolo Ergopower lever (9-speed) (Note: 10-speed has a different bottom bushing and washer, but is otherwise the same)

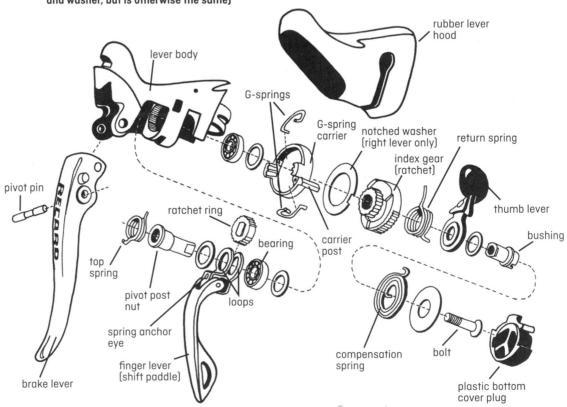

- rubber lever hood
- lever body
- G-springs
- G-spring carrier
- notched washer (right lever only)
- return spring
- index gear (ratchet)
- thumb lever
- pivot pin
- ratchet ring
- bearing
- carrier post
- bushing
- top spring
- pivot post nut
- loops
- spring anchor eye
- compensation spring
- bolt
- brake lever
- finger lever (shift paddle)
- plastic bottom cover plug

and the rubber hood come to a point on top of these (and the lever body allows a brake cable to be installed old-style straight into the top of the lever, as well as aero-style under the handlebar tape). The reference to 9- and 10-speed levers applies to left and right 1999–2008 Record and Chorus EP levers and 1999–2006 Centaur and below EP levers whose lever body and rubber hood are rounded on top (Fig. 5.41) and only allow the brake cable to be routed under the tape to the base of the lever.

NOTE: *The internals of 1998 9-speed levers are similar to those of an 8-speed lever. On the outside, 1998 levers look like the lever in Figure 5.41, but a 1998 lever will not have a bump on the inboard side of the rubber cover for the button to control an ErgoBrain computer. Also, a Record 1998 lever will be aluminum, whereas from 1999 on, the lever will be carbon fiber.*

1. **Remove the rubber hood.** It's easier to pull it off the base of the lever, but it will come off over the top as well. On composite lever bodies, pull off the plastic piece that covers the bottom of the shift mechanism; use pliers if necessary.

2. **Push out the lever-pivot pin by tapping it out with a blunt nail and a hammer.** Support the lever body near the pin so that the edge of the lever does not flex outward as you tap. Holding the lever body flat on a block of wood with a drilled hole that is lined up under the pin does the trick nicely. Pull off the brake lever.

3. **Clamp the lever body onto the end of a handlebar held in a vise so that the bar-clamp strap is right at the edge of the bar and the lower part of the lever body is hanging off the end of the bar.** You want to be able to get at the lever's mechanism from the bottom. Hold the bar in the vise so that the lever is upside down.

   a. With a 9- or 10-speed lever, shift to the lowest-gear position with the finger lever (shift paddle) to release tension on the flat coil "compensation" spring at the bottom of the lever; you can see it stick out around the large, flat washer when you get to the low-gear position.

   b. With an 8-speed lever, you do the opposite; shift the thumb lever to the highest-gear position.

4. **Hold the top (pivot post) nut with one hex key while you unscrew and remove the bottom bolt with another hex key.** On a 9- or 10-speed lever, the top nut takes a 5mm hex key, and the lower bolt takes a 3mm hex key (avoid using a 3mm ball-end hex key to start turning this bolt, as you can snap it off—leaving the ball in the bolt head) or a Torx T20 (left lever). On an 8-speed lever, the nut and bolt both accept 4mm hex keys, and the bolt may have a brass washer or two on it, so watch for them.

IMPORTANT NOTE: *The bolt on a right-hand 8-speed lever is left-hand threaded, so it unscrews in a clockwise direction! Also note that 1998 9-speed levers are configured this way.*

5. **With an 8-speed lever, skip to step 7. With a 9- or 10-speed lever, remove the bottom washer, pop the flat compensation spring out with a thin screwdriver, and take out the thin, play-removing washer, if installed.**

6. **Hold the (9- or 10-speed) assembly together with your thumb while shifting to the high-gear position with the thumb lever. Hold the thumb lever in place and, with needle-nose pliers, pull out the next part: the bushing in the center of the thumb lever return spring.**

7. **Pop out the thumb lever, the spring, the ratchet (also known as the index gear; see Figs. 5.40, 5.41), and, on a 9- or 10-speed**

right-hand lever, the notched washer. The two G-shaped index springs, which are the most common replacement item in Ergopower levers, are now visible. One or two washers that sit against the cartridge bearing underneath may come out with the ratchet. If they are dirty, you can push out the bearings after step 8 and clean, grease, and replace them at that time.

8. **Pop the G-spring carrier and G-springs out. Clean and grease all parts.**

9. **With an 8-speed lever, unless the top ratchet ring is worn out, skip to step 11.** To upgrade from a 9- to a 10-speed, you need to install a new ratchet ring in the finger-lever assembly, which will come out as an assembly. Flip the lever over so that it is clamped upright on the bar. It is hard to get the top spring out; grab it with thin needle-nose pliers and twist it upward with the other end still hooked into the anchor eye in the loop atop the finger lever. Pull the finger-lever assembly out. Push the center pivot post nut out. Now you can slip the ratchet ring out and replace it with a 10-speed ring.

10. **Orient the ratchet ring with the number 9 or 10 or letter L up (it will be pointed forward when the lever is installed on the bike).** Push the pivot nut and washer through the ratchet ring (line up the flats). Hook the top spring's short hook onto the anchor eye atop the upper finger lever loop. Push the assembly back in place, hooking the long spring end into the notch in the lever body with needle-nose pliers. Flip the lever back over to get at the bottom side again.

11. **Put the new (or clean and regreased) G-springs on the underside of the G-spring carrier, and coat them with grease to hold them in place.** Push the G-spring carrier back into place in the lever body.

12. **On a right-hand 9- or 10-speed lever, replace the thin washer on top of the G-spring carrier with the washer's tab facing down.** The notch (if the washer has it) fits around the vertical post on the G-spring carrier. This washer (and the vertical carrier post) do not exist in left-hand levers or in 8-speed ones, so ignore this step for them.

13. **Drop the (greased) indexing ratchet (index gear) down onto the pivot post nut so that the flats in both parts interlock.** Now is the time to put in a new ratchet if you are changing speeds (for instance, from 8 to 9 or from 9 to 10) or if the ratchet is worn (check the teeth near the cable hole). Make sure that the cable-hook tab on the ratchet butts against the outboard side of the lever body. Slip the long end of the return spring down into the ratchet, out the ratchet's slot, and into the hole in the lever body (the hole goes clear through, out the back, starting at the base of the notch in the body for the thumb lever), dropping the (greased) spring into the ratchet with the short end of the spring sticking up.

14. **Push the small hole in the thumb-lever ring onto the upward-pointing or hooked end of the thumb lever return spring inside the ratchet; the convex side of the ring should face the spring.** Push back on the thumb-lever ring to align it over the ratchet. Make sure the thumb lever is up at the top of its slot in the lever body, so that when you push it back into place it winds the spring tighter, rather than unwinding it.

15. **On 9- or 10-speed levers, while holding the thumb-lever ring down, push the central bushing (with its washer) down through the ring.** Push down and turn the bushing (on a 1998 9-speed lever, use a 5mm hex key; on later 9-speed and all 10-speed levers,

use a large screwdriver in the larger set of slots) until the flats on the end of the bushing engage the flats on the end of the pivot post nut protruding into the ratchet. If there were washers on the bushing, make sure you have reinstalled them.

a. On 1999 and later 9-speed and on all 10-speed levers, the bushing is larger in diameter and has flats that engage over the flats on the pivot post nut, rather than inserting into them. An unfortunate consequence of this larger diameter of the bushing is that it is harder to push the bushing into place without disengaging the return spring from the thumb lever. Keep at it until you get it.

b. On 8-speed levers, insert the bolt, with any washers it had on it, down through the thumb-lever ring until it engages the nut. While holding the nut with a 4mm hex key inserted into the top of the lever, tighten the bolt with another 4mm hex key. Remember that the bolt is reverse-threaded on a right-hand 8-speed lever! Skip to step 19 now.

16. **Steps 16–18 apply only to 9- and 10-speed levers.** While holding the bushing in place (it will turn), shift the finger lever all the way to the lowest-gear position.

17. **Lay the flat compensation spring on top of the thumb-lever ring.** The inner end of the spring hooks into a notch in the end of the bushing, and the outer spring end hooks around either the post on the spring carrier (right-hand lever) or the outboard edge of the lever body (left-hand lever).

18. **Holding the flat spring down, tip the bushing back and forth until you feel the flats in the end of the bushing disengage from the flats on the top bolt (use the 5mm hex key on a 1998 9-speed lever and the large screwdriver on 1999 and later 9- and 10-speed levers).** Still holding the spring down, turn the bushing about a half turn to wind the spring (counterclockwise on the right lever; clockwise on the left lever), and jiggle the bushing back and forth with the 5mm hex key or large screwdriver until its flats reengage the top bolt.

NOTE: *For a harder shift feel, leave the compensation spring out. Alternative method for steps 17 and 18: Hook the compensation spring's inner end into a more advanced bushing slot; the outer end of the spring will be squished up against the back wall of the lever body. While holding the bushing with the hex key or screwdriver (or install the bolt to hold the bushing in place), pull the outer spring end with a hooked awl, a small crochet hook, or a paper clip with a small hook bent into the end and pull it to the post (right-hand lever) or to the notch in the lever body's outboard wall (left-hand lever).*

19. **Holding the flat spring down with your finger, slide the large washer under your finger and on top of the flat spring so that it snaps over the end of the bushing.** The 1999 and later 9- or 10-speed washer has two notches to fit the larger slots in the bushing. Start the bolt while holding the other end of the pivot shaft with a 5mm hex key. Snug the bolt down with a 3mm hex key.

20. **Check the mechanism, taking note of step 21 in §v-24.** If it works smoothly, unclamp the lever from the bar, reinstall the brake lever, bottom cap, and rubber hood (engaging the hood's nubs into holes, slots, and protrusions in the lever body). It's usually easier to pull the hood on over the levers from the front rather than from the base of the lever body, and lubricating it with rubbing alcohol or water makes it easier yet. Congratulations! You are done!

THE SHIFTING SYSTEM

OVERHAULING CAMPAGNOLO QS/ ESCAPE ERGOPOWER LEVERS

LEVEL 3

This mechanism (Fig. 5.42), which appeared on Centaur, Veloce, and other EP levers below Chorus, eliminates the full swing of the thumb lever and has only a simple hole in the lever body (and in the rubber hood), rather than a long slot, for it to swing through. A hinged pawl clicks into each successive index-gear tooth as a push on the shift lever behind the brake lever rotates the gear to pull cable. The index gear is spring-loaded (and the spring in the derailleur is pulling on the cable), and each time the thumb-lever linkage pops the pawl out of a gear tooth, the springs rotate the index gear in the opposite direction to release cable. The pawl then drops into the next tooth to stop the index gear from rotating any farther than a single shift, and the rear derailleur shifts to the next smaller cog (in the case of the right lever), or the front derailleur shifts to the next smaller chainring (in the case of the left lever).

This mechanism is not as durable as earlier EP levers or later EP Ultra-Shift levers. When worn, it tends to upshift multiple cogs with a single light push of the thumb lever. If this happens, you not only may find a worn small part or two but also may have a hard time finding individual parts; instead, you may have to replace the entire lever body with the shifter assembly already integrated into it.

1. **Remove the rubber hood.** It is easier to pull it off the base of the lever, but it will come off over the top as well, and lubricating inside with rubbing alcohol will make it slide off easily.

2. **Unscrew the handlebar band clamp.** Alternatively, you can leave it on and use it to clamp the lever body to the end of a handlebar fixed in a vise so that the lower part of the lever body overhangs the end of the bar, allowing you to get at the underside of the mechanism.

3. **Push out the brake-lever pivot pin by tapping it out with a blunt nail and a hammer.** Support the lever body near the pin so that the edge of the lever does not flex outward as you tap. Holding the lever body flat on a block of wood with a drilled hole that is lined up under the pin does the trick nicely. Pull off the brake lever, keeping its plastic bushings with it.

4. **Pull off the plastic bottom cover plug.**

5. **With a 2.5mm hex key, remove the bottom bolt.**

6. **Pull off the large, thin washer and flat compensation spring and the plastic cable hook gear, which has a recessed cable entry hole.**

7. **Pull off the steel index gear and the tiny, thin washer it conceals.** Turn the lever body upright.

8. **With needle-nose pliers, unhook and pull off the finger-lever return spring (top spring) out through the front of the lever body.**

9. **With a hex key, push the central pivot post nut straight up and out through the top of the finger-lever assembly.**

10. **Pull out the finger-lever assembly and the flat washer under it.** Pull out the ratchet ring from between the loops extending from the top of the finger lever.

11. **Disassembly of the lever is now complete (Fig. 5.42). Clean all of the parts and put a thin layer of clean grease on them.**

12. **Replace the greased ratchet ring between the finger lever's extending loops with its engraved 0 up against the top loop (so that**

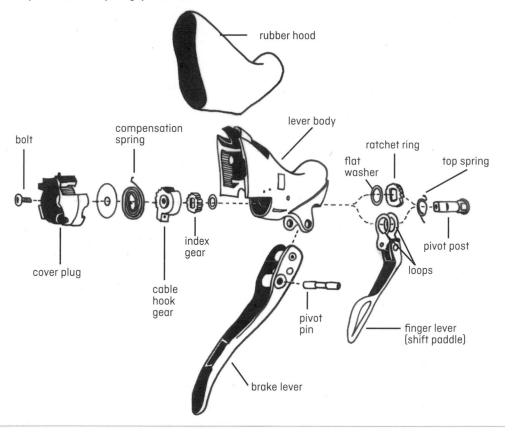

5.42 Exploded QS/Escape Ergopower levers

- rubber hood
- lever body
- bolt
- compensation spring
- ratchet ring
- flat washer
- top spring
- cover plug
- index gear
- pivot post
- cable hook gear
- loops
- pivot pin
- finger lever (shift paddle)
- brake lever

it will be pointing forward when on the bike). Push the greased pivot post nut down through the assembly so that its larger flats engage the flats in the ratchet ring.

13. **With grease, stick the flat washer to the bottom extending loop, around the pivot post nut.**

14. **Push the pivot post nut up so that it does not protrude through the bottom of the finger-lever assembly, and slide the finger lever into its place in the lever body.** Push the pivot post nut down through the assembly and through the brass bushing in the lever body. If the pivot post nut does not come all the way down so that its flange once again contacts the top extending loop, grab its smaller flats extending out of the bottom of the brass bushing with needle-nose pliers. Rotate the post while pulling down until its larger flats line up with the

ratchet ring flats and it pulls down until its top flange contacts the top extending loop.

15. **Hold the finger-lever return spring so that its short, hook end is on the bottom and its long, straight end is on the top. Maneuver it in from the top of the lever body so that the long, spring end sits in the little groove at the top of the wide notch in the lever body for the finger lever.** Stick a 4mm or smaller hex key down through the spring coil into the hole in the top of the pivot post nut. With a small hook (a small crochet hook works; I've also used a thin nail by grinding it thinner at the tip and bending it into a hook with needle-nose pliers), pull the hook end of the spring so that it catches on the anchor eye on the top extending loop (the anchor eye is not visible in Fig. 5.42; you can see it in Fig. 5.41). You can also try holding the spring with needle-nose pliers and hooking the short, hook

end onto the anchor eye first. Then grab the long end of the spring with the pliers and pull it into its notch in the lever body. Turn the lever over to view it from the bottom.

16. **Replace the tiny, thin washer followed by the index gear onto the end of the pivot post nut with the gear's recessed base away from you and its engraved 0 toward you.** Push it in place while pushing the thumb lever to move the pawl riveted into the lever body away and give the index gear clearance to drop into place.

17. **Grease the teeth on the thick plastic cable hook gear.** Push its rectangular recess onto the end of the pivot post nut (the engraved 0 will be toward you). Turn it and the finger lever as required to engage the recess onto the end of the pivot post nut.

18. **Push the outboard tip of the flat compensation spring into the small hole in the lever body on the side opposite from the thumb lever.** With needle-nose pliers, wind it an extra turn before pushing its inner end into the slot in the plastic gear.

19. **Grease the spring and stick the big flat washer against it.**

20. **Push the bottom screw through the hole in the big flat washer and tighten it into the end of the pivot post nut with a 2.5mm hex key.**

21. **Test the shift mechanism function.** Check that when the finger lever returns, its outboard edge lines up with the outboard edge of the brake lever. This is necessary for the finger lever's engagement teeth to fully disengage from the ratchet ring so that operating the thumb lever properly releases the cable and allows it to advance. If the finger lever does not line up properly, the inboard end of the tiny return spring surrounding the rivet of the finger lever has become dis-

engaged. It needs to hook in diagonally over the outboard notch in the chromed steel flat loop inside the notch at the top of the finger lever. Push the spring tip back into place with a small screwdriver.

22. **Push the plastic bottom cover plug back into the base of the lever body.**

23. **Replace the brake lever, including its plastic bushings, into the lever body, line up the holes in the lever and body, and hold the parts together by pushing the pivot pin back in partway by hand.** The pin is symmetrical; you can push it in from either side.

24. **Tap the pin in with a hammer or set the end of the pin on a wooden surface, and tap the side of the lever body down onto it with the mallet until the pin is fully inserted with the same amount protruding on either side.**

25. **Install the handlebar band clamp.**

26. **Lube the inside of the rubber hood with rubbing alcohol and slide it back onto the lever body.**

You're done! Cable it up to a derailleur and see how it works.

v-25

OVERHAULING CAMPAGNOLO ULTRA-SHIFT ERGOPOWER LEVERS

LEVEL 3

The mechanism in Campagnolo's Ultra-Shift EP levers introduced in 2009 in Super Record, Record, Chorus, and Centaur (Figs. 5.38, 5.43), whether 10-speed (Centaur) or 11-speed, is very robust. It requires less maintenance and is less prone to failure than the mechanism in prior Ergopower designs, mainly because it has no G-springs to wear out. It is also easier to overhaul, requiring less dexterity when winding the springs.

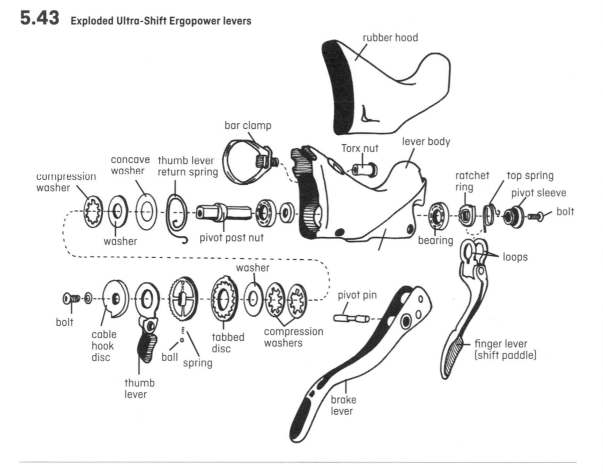

In 2010, Campagnolo ceased producing 10-speed Ultra-Shift levers and instead introduced EP Power-Shift levers in Athena (11-speed) and 10-speed Centaur, Veloce, and lower levels. Power-Shift levers are shaped like Ultra-Shift levers, sharing the more curvaceous lever and taller knob atop the lever body than earlier Ergopower and QS/Escape levers. Like Escape levers (§v-24), Power-Shift levers can only upshift one cog at a time on the rear, and on the front can only make a complete shift from one chainring to the next, rather than in smaller increments. Just as on QS/Escape EP levers, eliminating the full swing of the thumb lever results in a simple hole in the lever body (and in the rubber hood) for it, rather than a long slot for the lever's swing. Power-Shift levers also have a directional pivot pin holding the brake lever on, so follow step 2 for removing it. No parts are available

for Power-Shift EP, other than entire lever body/shifter assemblies, brake levers, and handlebar band clamps, so if yours won't shift, you're probably looking at replacing the lever body/shifter assembly, in which case you will only need steps 1–3 and 31–34 below.

When originally introduced, Campagnolo offered all of the Ultra-Shift spare parts; now it only offers an entire lever body/shifter assembly (as well as brake lever and band clamp as individual parts).

These instructions apply to the right lever (rear-derailleur control); the left lever is similar, but there are significant differences, including that the thumb-lever return spring is integrated into the cable-hook disc. Note that running changes to the washers inside Ergopower levers may occur.

1. **Remove the rubber hood.** It is easier to pull it off the base of the lever, but it will come off

THE SHIFTING SYSTEM

over the top as well. Lubricating inside with rubbing alcohol will help it slide off easily.

2. **Push out the brake-lever pivot pin by tapping it out with a blunt nail and a hammer from the inboard side out.** Unlike on other Ergopower levers, on Ultra-Shift levers the pivot pin has an enlarged head, which goes on the outboard side. Support the lever body near the pin so that the edge of the lever does not flex outward as you tap. Holding the lever body flat on a block of wood with a hole lined up under the pin does the trick nicely. Pull off the brake lever.

3. **With a Torx T25 key, unscrew the band-clamp bolt and remove the handlebar band clamp.** You may instead wish to clamp the lever body to the end of a rigidly fixed handlebar so that the lever is securely held as you work on it. Have the band clamp right at the end of the bar with the lower part of the lever body overhanging so that you can get at the underside of the mechanism.

4. **With a 2.5mm hex key in the bolts at the top and bottom of the lever body, unscrew the bottom bolt and remove it along with its tiny brass washer.**

5. **With needle-nose pliers, pull out the thick plastic disc with the recessed cable entry hole (called "cable hook disc" in Fig. 5.43).**

6. **With a thin crochet hook or similar tool, unhook the end of the thumb-lever return spring from the spool-shaped pin on the thumb lever.**

7. **Pull the thumb lever straight out to remove it along with the flat ring it's joined to.**

8. **With needle-nose pliers grabbing its raised lips at its center (or by pushing it up from below with a thin screwdriver through the lever-body slot), pull out the big, flat, toothed disc, taking care not to lose the two tiny springs and two tiny ball bearings** that sit in slots on its hidden face (see one ball and spring exploded away in Fig. 5.43; don't let this happen to you!).

9. **With needle-nose pliers or by pushing it up from below with a thin screwdriver through the lever body slot, remove the tabbed disc with raised teeth on its face; two thin, flat washers; a slotted concave compression washer; a mating slotted convex compression washer; a third slotted compression washer concave side up; a thin, flat washer; and a large, thin, concave plastic washer (some levers differ in how many and the orientation of these washers; note how yours were arranged when removing them).**

10. **Pull out the flat thumb-lever return spring.** Although not imperative, it's easier to now work on the top of the lever body with it fixed in place; you can clamp it onto the end of a handlebar clamped in a vise.

11. **Unscrew and remove the top bolt with a 2.5mm hex key and, with needle-nose pliers, pull the central pivot post nut down and out of the bottom of the lever body.** The cartridge bearing and spacer above it may come out with the pivot post nut; if not, remove them separately after step 12 below. You can use the pivot post nut to wiggle the bottom bearing out and then use it to push the upper bearing out.

12. **Unless it fell out when you pulled out the pivot post nut, pull straight out on the finger lever (shift paddle) to remove it, while holding the parts (shown in Fig. 5.43) held between its extending loops with your finger to keep them from falling out.**

13. **Pull out the pivot sleeve, finger-lever return spring, and ratchet ring from between the extending loops.** Disassembly of the lever now is complete.

14. **Clean and grease all parts.** If any are worn out or broken, stop now and go buy a new entire lever body/shifter assembly; the parts are not otherwise individually available.

15. **If you removed them, push the cartridge bearings and the spacer between them back in with your finger or thumb.**

16. **Orient the ratchet ring with its flat side up (stamped with the number 10 or 11 on a right lever) so that it points forward when the lever is installed on the bike.** Slip the ratchet ring between the loops extending from the finger lever so its raised central lip drops into the hole in the lower loop. Rotate the ratchet ring so its tab rests against the flat base between the extending loops.

17. **Install the finger-lever return spring above the ratchet ring, hooking its short end in the anchor eye adjacent to the upper extending loop.**

18. **Push the pivot sleeve through the upper loop and the return spring.**

19. **Push the assembly back in place, bracing the long end of the return spring against the notch in the lever body.**

20. **Insert the pivot post nut up through the bearing and finger-lever assembly while pushing back on the finger lever to line up the ratchet ring.** Compress the spring. This is not an easy step. Check that the flats on the pivot post nut line up with those inside the ratchet ring before pushing the pivot post nut up.

21. **Tighten the top bolt into the pivot post nut.** Ensure that the finger-lever return spring hook end is properly hooked in the eye alongside the top loop riveted to the lever. Turn the lever body over to get at the bottom side again.

22. **Install the flat thumb-lever return spring with its central, downturned end inserted** into the tiny hole in back adjacent to the bearing, and its outboard end hooked around the edge of the thumb lever's slot in the lever body. To do this, you'll probably find it easiest to slip it in through the slot from the side and then angle it so that its hooked end sits up high in back when the downturned end is lined up above the hole. Pull back and push down on the hooked end with needle-nose pliers, pushing the spring down so the downturned end goes into the hole. Holding the spring down to keep the end in the hole, pull the hooked end out to the edge of the lever-body slot with the pliers or with a hook.

23. **Drop the following parts in over the pivot post nut in this order from the bottom: large, thin, plastic washer with concave side facing you; thin, large-diameter flat washer; one smaller-diameter flat washer; slotted compression washer with concave side facing you; mating slotted compression washer with convex side facing you; third slotted compression washer with concave side facing you; and other smaller-diameter flat washer.** Not all levers have the same stack of washers; yours may not have the third slotted compression washer. Also, the smaller-diameter flat washers can both go on last.

24. **Install the tabbed disc; the tab must point away from you, and the side with raised teeth around the outer edge must face toward you.** As you push the disc down onto the pivot post nut, its tab needs to slide down the square groove running longitudinally in the lever body past the cable access hole.

25. **Ensuring that the tiny springs pushing outward on tiny steel balls are in place in their slots on its face, drop the toothed disc down onto the pivot post nut.** The balls

and springs will be on the side facing down toward the tabbed disc below. The teeth around the outer edge of one side of the disc should face out through the thumb-lever slot in the lever body.

26. **Install the thumb lever from the side, through the slot in the lever body.**

27. **Install the thick plastic disc over the end of the pivot post nut so that its tab with recessed hole for the cable head is at the cable access hole in the lever body.**

28. **Slip the tiny brass washer onto the bottom bolt and tighten the bolt into the pivot post nut with a 2.5mm hex key.**

29. **Loosen the bolt just enough to tip the thumb lever up and allow the hooked end of its return spring to pass by the spool-shaped pin on the thumb lever. With your thin hook, pull the hooked end of the spring onto the spool-shaped pin on the thumb lever.** You may find it easiest to pull it past the pin, tighten the bolt so it pushes the lever down, and bring the hook back to the pin.

30. **With 2.5mm hex keys in the top and bottom bolts, tighten both bolts.**

31. **Replace the brake lever, including its plastic bushings, into the lever body, line up the holes in the lever and body, and hold the parts together by pushing the pivot pin back in from the outboard side as far as you can by hand.**

32. **Tap in the pin with a mallet, with the inboard side of the lever body on a block of wood.** You can also set the end of the pin on a wooden surface and tap the side of the lever body down onto it with the mallet until the pin is fully inserted.

33. **With a Torx T25 wrench in the cap nut, install the handlebar band clamp.**

34. **Lube the inside of the hood with rubbing alcohol and slide it back onto the lever body.**

You did it! Congratulations! Try it and see how it works.

v-26

OVERHAUL BAR-END SHIFTERS

LEVEL 2

Bar-end shifters that stick out in front of the bike will eventually get dirty and perform less well after being ridden in the rain, especially behind other riders whose rear tires kick up dirty water. You cannot overhaul Shimano or SRAM bar-end shifter mechanisms, but you can lubricate them.

1. **Release the cable at the derailleur so the lever will be free to pull away from its mount housing.**

2. **Remove the screw holding the shifter to its mount, and pull the shifter off.** At this point, it is possible to remove the lever mount housing (by loo sening the expander bolt in its throat with a hex key and releasing the expander plugs and pulling the whole thing out), but there is no need to do so.

3. **Left lever:**

    The Shimano (Fig. 5.44A) and SRAM lever mechanisms cannot be disassembled, but you can rinse or blow grit out of them.

    To get the Campagnolo frictional shifter (Fig. 5.45A) working smoothly, simply clean the parts and put them back together. You generally do not want to grease the mechanism, since that will only demand higher bolt-tightening torque to get the lever to hold its position.

4. **Right lever:**

    If you have a Shimano indexed shifter (Fig. 5.44B), the mechanism cannot be ser-

5.44A Exploded left lever, Shimano bar-end shifters

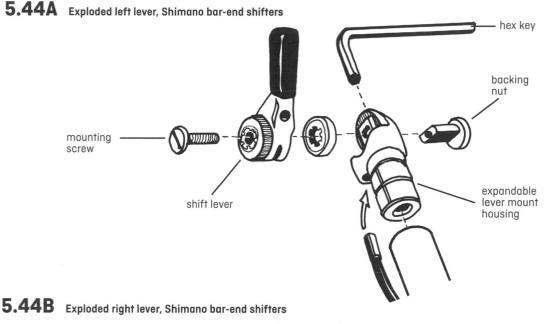

hex key

backing nut

mounting screw

shift lever

expandable lever mount housing

5.44B Exploded right lever, Shimano bar-end shifters

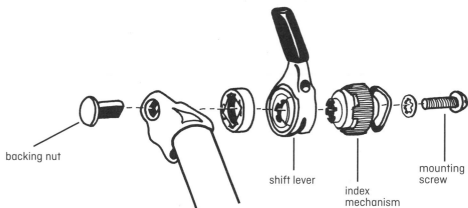

backing nut

shift lever

index mechanism

mounting screw

viced; buy a new lever if the mechanism has failed.

With SRAM, you can blow out the area around the index gear with compressed air and grease the teeth and the three G-springs, which might rehabilitate it fully.

With Campagnolo (Fig. 5.45B), pull the T-shaped (or pedestal-shaped) bushing out of the center of the outboard side of the lever. Now you can see the index gear and the three G-springs that click into the teeth. To get the plastic G-spring carrier out of the hollow in the base of the lever, push on

the index gear and, with a screwdriver, pry on the edge of the plastic carrier protruding from the lever as well. You can blow out the area and grease the G-springs and gear teeth, but you can also push the index gear out if you want to clean or replace the springs or change the index gear to change the number of speeds. Pull or pry the index gear up out from the springs. Clean and grease the G-springs and index gear. Line up the arrow on the index gear with the G-spring prong on the side of the G-spring carrier that has a nub on it to engage a notch

THE SHIFTING SYSTEM

5.45A Exploded Campagnolo frictional left-side bar-end shifter

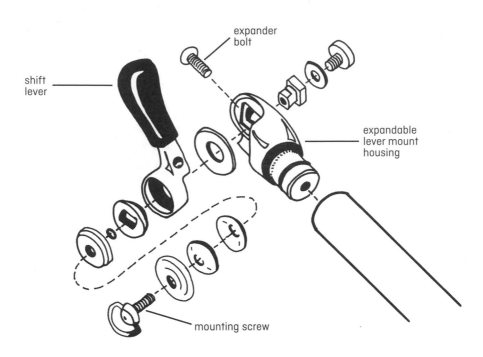

shift lever

expander bolt

expandable lever mount housing

mounting screw

5.45B Exploded Campagnolo right-side 8-, 9-, or 10-speed indexed bar-end shifter

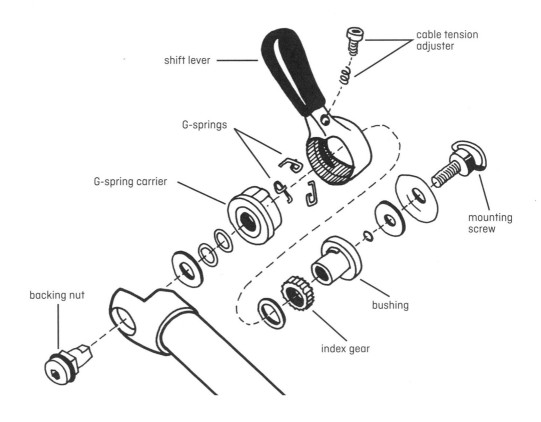

shift lever

cable tension adjuster

G-springs

G-spring carrier

mounting screw

backing nut

bushing

index gear

under the cable hole on the lever; the index gear's arrow marking will point toward the rubber cover on the shift lever. Tip the index gear down to engage two springs, fit a screwdriver in between the third spring and the other side of the gear, and pry with it, while pushing the gear down into place. Push the plastic spring housing back into the lever, lining up the nub with the notch in the hollow of the lever. Make sure you replace any washers that may have fallen out. Push the T-shaped (or pedestal-shaped) bushing back into place, lining up its two teeth on the underside of its flange with the two notches in the index gear.

5. **Line up the lever in its cable-release position (i.e., flipped down) and fit the notches inside the bushing's bore over the ledges on the backing nut, once you have pushed it back through the shifter mount housing.**

6. **Tighten the mounting screw into the backing nut snugly.** It must be tight enough that the lever does not wobble, but not so tight that it binds.

7. **Install the cable and tighten it at the derailleur.**

OVERHAUL OR REPLACE DOWN-TUBE SHIFTERS

LEVEL 1

1. **Remove the screw holding the shifter to the frame's shifter boss, and pull the shifter off.**

2. **If you have a frictional shifter (Fig. 5.46), all of its pieces come apart.** To get the shifter working smoothly, simply clean the parts, grease them, and put them back together. If you have an indexed Shimano shifter, the mechanism cannot be serviced. Buy a new lever if the mechanism has failed.

3. **Replace the stop piece that fits over the square base of the shifter boss.** With old frictional shifters, the shifter stop boss is simply a washer with a square hole and a bent tab (Fig. 5.46). With more recent shifters (Fig. 5.22), the stop is a cast piece that has a square stop on it that is to be lined up along the down tube projecting forward.

4. **Put on the brass or plastic washer, slip the shifter on, and install the top washer(s) and the screw.** Some Shimano left-hand

5.46 Exploded Campagnolo Nuovo Record frictional lever

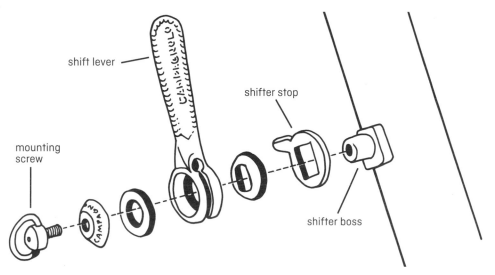

shift lever

mounting screw

shifter stop

shifter boss

shifters have a return spring in them and must be installed with the lever flipped down in order to fit properly over the stop on the base. It is not until the screw is tightened down that one of these spring-loaded levers will stay in place when rotated counterclockwise to its starting position, pointed forward, parallel with the down tube.

5. **Install the cable at the derailleur.**

CYCLOCROSS SHIFTING CONSIDERATIONS

Cyclocross, in all its dirty glory, is a winter sport often contested in deep mud, snow, ice, and freezing temperatures. Mechanical breakdowns are rampant due to the nature of the sport. You can minimize shifting problems with good maintenance, as well as with good frame and component choice and good planning.

You can reduce shifting problems in general by routing the derailleur cables internally or over the top tube, following the instructions in §v-28 below for the front derailleur (either way, the frame must be set up for this cable routing either with the correct holes or cable stops) instead of under the bottom bracket where they can get glommed up in the muck or frozen in accumulated snow. The over-top rear shift cable needs to run from the top tube down the right seatstay to the rear derailleur.

Use a short-cage rear derailleur for snappier shifting and a reduced chance of snagging the rear derailleur on course detritus, unless you either insist on using larger cogs than the short derailleur is rated for (see tips in §v-42 to still use a short-cage derailleur) or are running a triple-chainring setup in front (not advisable for 'cross racing; see the Note in §vi-30). Tighten the lower knuckle spring tension as in §v-39 so the rear derailleur will keep the chain tight. Do this with short-cage as well as long-cage derailleurs.

You can completely eliminate front shifting problems by running only a single front chainring (somewhere in the 39- to 42-tooth range is standard). Set it up to keep the chain on either with toothless chain-guard rings on both sides of the chainring or with a single chain-guard ring to the outside and three Third Eye Chain Watchers (Fig. 5.55), Deda Dog Fangs, or N-Gear Jump Stops, clamped around the seat tube, one atop the other (if you use only a single one, it won't retain the chain as well, and if the chain somehow gets under it, you will not be able to get it out without some tools; your race will be over). If you choose to run a single front chainring, note also that if the chain pops off, you won't be able to pedal it back on, as you often can with a front derailleur, so make sure the chain is not too long but is long enough (it will reach the big chainring without tearing up the rear derailleur—set it up as in §iv-8, method 3).

With a front derailleur, run the front cable over the top tube, following the instructions below.

v-28

ROUTING THE FRONT SHIFT CABLE OVER THE TOP TUBE

Unlike front derailleurs for mountain bikes with over-the-top cable routing, road front derailleurs are bottom-pull, not top-pull (i.e., the cable needs to pull from the bottom, not the top). So, if the shift cables go over the top, you need to route the front shift cable down the back of the seat tube and around a little pulley on the back of the seat tube and up to the front derailleur (Fig. 5.47). If your frame does not have a roller or a threaded hole to accept one, you can buy a roller

5.47 Over-the-top cyclocross cable routing with front-derailleur cable roller on the back of the seat tube

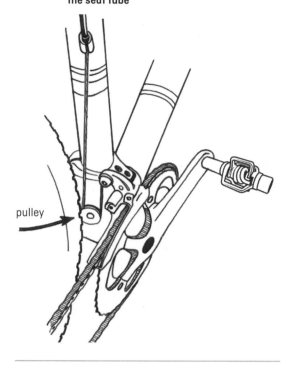

pulley

that is attached to a band clamp. In a pinch, you can wrap the cable around the chainstay bridge and back up to the front derailleur.

Note that a mountain bike top-pull front derailleur could be an option to avoid a cable roller, but it will only work well with a triple crank, and the cage curvature is designed for smaller mountain bike–size chainrings, so it won't track close enough to bigger road rings to shift particularly well. It also may not match the cable pull of your shifter.

De-gutsing the left shift lever for a single chainring

On a cyclocross bike with a single chainring, why carry the weight of the shift mechanism in your left brake lever if it's never going to be used? If you were to replace your left brake/shift lever with a simple brake lever, its shape would not match that of the right lever. However, if you

pull the shifter mechanism out of your existing left lever, it becomes a superlight brake lever that is shaped just like the other lever.

v-29

REMOVE SHIFTER MECHANISM FROM LEFT CAMPAGNOLO ERGOPOWER LEVER

Depending on which type of Ergopower (EP) lever you have, follow the overhaul instructions in §v-23, §v-24, or §v-25 until you have the lever completely disassembled. Remove the two bearings and spacer between them from the center of the plastic lever body. Then, instead of reinstalling all of the shifter parts, just replace the brake lever. Now you have a really light lever that matches your right lever in shape and feel.

v-30

REMOVE SHIFTER MECHANISM FROM LEFT SRAM DOUBLETAP LEVER

This is not a recommended or authorized procedure by SRAM, but you will see these gutted left levers on the start lines at cyclocross races. And if you store the 35–45 grams' worth of parts you removed in a safe place, you can reinstall them if you change your mind in the future and want a front derailleur after all.

1. **Disconnect the brake and shift cables at the brake caliper and front derailleur.**
2. **Pull the brake lever.** Push the brake cable out of it and remove it.
3. **Remove the shift cable.** Click the shift lever with the short-throw, single-click downshift motion to the fully released (small chainring) cable position. Peel up the skirt of the lever hood and push the shift cable out of its access hole on the inboard side of the lever and remove it.

5.48 SRAM DoubleTap lever shift mechanism removal

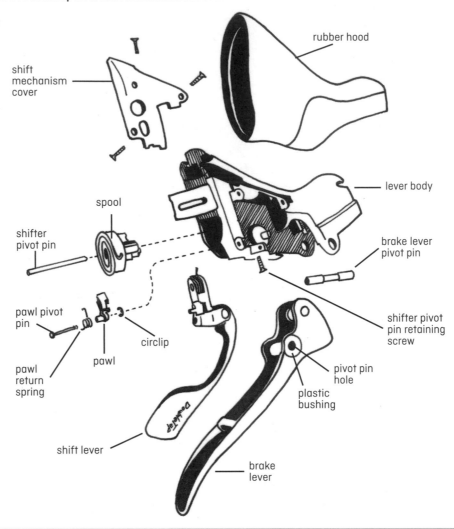

rubber hood

shift
mechanism
cover

lever body

spool

shifter
pivot pin

brake lever
pivot pin

pawl pivot
pin

circlip

shifter pivot
pin retaining
screw

pawl

pawl
return
spring

pivot pin
hole

plastic
bushing

shift lever

brake
lever

4. **Remove the hood.** Wipe rubbing alcohol on the lever body and the exposed underside of the hood skirt, and get it inside the upper part of the hood as well. Flip the hood skirt back down, twist the hood around on the slippery alcohol layer, and slide the hood off over the top or bottom.

5. **Remove the access cover.** With a small Phillips screwdriver fully inserted into the head of each screw to avoid stripping it, remove the three screws holding the inboard shifter mechanism access cover on, and remove the cover itself (Fig. 5.48).

6. **Push out the brake lever's pivot pin by tapping it out with a blunt nail and a mallet.**

To prevent the edge of the lever from flexing outward, support the lever body near the pin as you tap by holding the lever body flat on a block of wood that has a drilled hole under the pin. Because of the bowed shape of the lever body, it's probably easier to place the outboard side over the hole in the wood block and tap the pin out from the inboard side. Pull off the brake lever, with its plastic pivot bushings still in place (Fig. 5.48).

7. **With the small Phillips screwdriver, remove the shifter pivot pin retaining screw from the outboard side of the lever body or simply unscrew it until you can see that its tip is no longer impeding the shifter pivot**

pin. You can see the bottom of the pin and retaining screw across its end from the bottom side of the lever body; look just forward of the handlebar band clamp.

8. **Remove the pivot pin.** Find the top of the shifter pivot pin (it goes straight up through the shifter mechanism and protrudes inside the lever body behind the top of the shift lever; see Fig. 5.48). With the short end of an L-bend 2mm hex key, push the pivot pin down so it protrudes enough from the bottom of the lever body that you can pull it completely out with your fingers (or, if necessary, a pair of pliers).

9. **Remove the shift lever (along with its assembly of pivot body, pawl, and three springs).** Rotate it inward to release it from the spool, then lifting it out of the lever body. Put the assembly in the container where you're keeping all the parts.

10. **Push the circlip (C-shaped retaining ring) off the top of the pawl pivot pin located at the very front of the lever body.** Use a knifepoint or a sharp pick.

11. **Push the pawl pin out the bottom of the lever body while keeping parts from flying out of the mechanism with your thumb.** Use the short end of the L-bend 2mm hex key.

12. **Pull the pawl, pawl return spring, spool (large metal piece with the plastic base), and spool return spring out of the lever body.**

13. **Replace the brake lever, including its plastic bushings, into the lever body.** Line up the holes in the lever and body, and hold the parts together by pushing the brake lever pivot pin back in partway by hand. The pin is symmetrical; you can push it in from either side.

14. **Replace the brake lever pivot pin.** Set the end of the pin on a wooden surface, and tap the side of the lever body down onto it with the mallet until the pin is fully inserted with the same amount protruding on either side.

15. **To reinforce the lever body vertically against impacts, you can reinstall the shifter pivot pin from the bottom and tighten its retaining screw from the outboard side of the lever body to hold it in place.** This is probably worth doing; it adds only 5 grams.

16. **Replace the hood.** Lube the inside of the rubber hood with rubbing alcohol and slide it back onto the lever body.

DERAILLEUR MAINTENANCE

v-31

JOCKEY-WHEEL MAINTENANCE

LEVEL 2

With proper attention, the jockey wheels on the rear derailleur will last a long time. They should be wiped off every time you wipe down and lubricate the chain (daily is a good idea). The only other maintenance involved is a light overhaul every 1,000–2,000 miles in dirty conditions; otherwise an overhaul every time you replace the chain should be frequent enough.

The mounting bolts on jockey wheels also should be checked regularly. If a loose jockey-wheel bolt falls off while you are riding, you'll need to follow the procedure for a damaged rear derailleur in §iii-12.

Standard jockey wheels turn on a bushing made of steel or ceramic. Some high-end models have cartridge bearings. A washer with an inward lip is usually installed on both sides of a standard jockey wheel. Some jockey wheels also have rubber seals around the edges of these washers to keep dirt and grit at bay.

5.49A Exploded derailleur

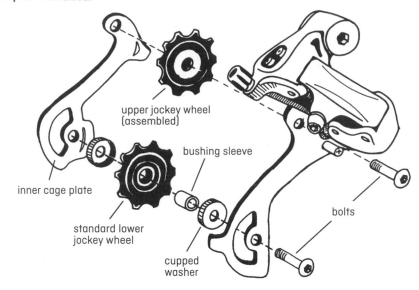

upper jockey wheel
(assembled)

bushing sleeve

inner cage plate

standard lower
jockey wheel

bolts

cupped
washer

---

v-32

OVERHAULING STANDARD JOCKEY WHEELS

1. **Remove the jockey wheels by undoing the bolts that hold them to the derailleur (Fig. 5.49A).** The bolts usually take a 3mm hex key.

2. **Wipe all parts clean with a rag.** Solvent is usually not necessary but can be used.

3. **If the teeth on the jockey wheels are broken or badly worn, replace the wheels.**

4. **Smear grease over each bolt and bushing and inside each jockey wheel.**

5. **Reassemble the jockey wheels onto the derailleur.** Be sure to orient the inner cage plate properly so that its larger part is at the bottom jockey wheel.

v-33

OVERHAULING CARTRIDGE-BEARING JOCKEY WHEELS

If the cartridge bearings in high-end jockey wheels (Fig. 5.49B) do not turn freely, they can usually be overhauled.

1. **Remove the jockey wheels by undoing the bolts that hold them to the derailleur (Fig. 5.49A).** The bolts usually take a 3mm hex key.

2. **Remove the bearing seals.** With a single-edge razor blade, pry the plastic cover (bearing seal) off one side or—preferably—both sides of the bearing (Fig. 6.33). (Steel covers on bearings cannot be removed. If such a bearing is not turning freely, the entire bearing needs to be replaced.)

3. **With a toothbrush and solvent, clean the bearings.** Use citrus-based solvent, and wear gloves and glasses to protect skin and eyes.

4. **Blow the solvent out with compressed air or your tire pump, and allow the parts to dry.**

5. **Squeeze new grease into the bearings and replace the covers.**

6. **Reassemble the jockey wheels onto the derailleur.** Be sure to orient the inner cage plate properly (the larger part of the inner cage plate should be at the bottom jockey wheel).

v-34

UPGRADING JOCKEY WHEELS

You can reduce your bike's drivetrain friction by upgrading the jockey wheels to ones that spin more easily. Simply upgrading from pulleys with bushings (Fig. 5.49A) to cartridge-bearing jockey wheels (Fig. 5.49B) can make a substantial difference. There are many brands available, and they constitute a relatively inexpensive, simple, and quick upgrade.

If you already have cartridge-bearing jockey wheels that are in good shape, you can still upgrade from cartridge bearings containing steel balls to cartridge bearings containing much pricier, harder, smoother, and rounder ceramic balls. The simplest and most advisable way to do a ceramic jockey-wheel-bearing upgrade is to replace the pulleys with complete jockey wheels with ceramic bearings; since the plastic wheel will wear out soon enough anyway, you might as well replace the entire thing. Top-end Campagnolo Super Record 11-speed rear derailleurs already come with ceramic-bearing jockey wheels, and Tiso, SRAM, FSA, KCNC, Enduro, and Wheels Mfg. sell such jockey wheels.

1. **Remove the jockey wheels by undoing the bolts that hold them to the derailleur (Fig. 5.49A).** The bolts usually take a 3mm hex key.

2. **Reassemble the new jockey wheels onto the derailleur.** Be sure to orient the inner cage plate properly (the larger part of the inner cage plate should be at the bottom jockey wheel).

NOTE: *If you want to just buy a ceramic bearing and upgrade an existing jockey wheel, it can be done, but not with all jockey wheels. You cannot replace a bushing (a metal or ceramic sleeve within the jockey-wheel bore; Fig. 5.49A) with a bearing; you must buy an entire ceramic-bearing jockey wheel.*

5.49B Exploded jockey wheel with cartridge bearing

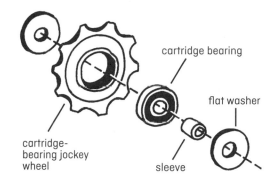

cartridge bearing

flat washer

cartridge-bearing jockey wheel

sleeve

If you do have a cartridge-bearing jockey wheel, you must look at it to determine how to get the bearing out. Some have no obvious stop against the bearing outside diameter (OD). In that case, find a socket that just fits around the outside of the new bearing (which is the exact same size as the old bearing, right?). Place the new ceramic bearing (of the same size, of course) on a flat surface; set the jockey wheel lined up perfectly on top of it; heat the jockey wheel with a heat gun; set the socket, open end down, on the jockey wheel so it surrounds the bearing; and smack it with a hammer. The old bearing will pop out, and, voilà, the new bearing will have replaced it. You can also do this in a vise or arbor press.

Some jockey wheels are injection-molded around the bearing. To get those out, you are going to have to push through 1mm or so of plastic that's lapped over the OD of the bearing. Locate two sockets, one whose internal diameter (ID) is just bigger than the bearing's OD, and another whose OD is just smaller than the bearing's OD. With a hand arbor press, a drill press, or a vise, place one socket on one side of the jockey wheel and one on the other, both open toward each other. Apply pressure with the press or vise until the bearing pops out. Clean up the torn plastic edges with a sharp knife and push a new bearing in with the same press or vise, using the old bearing or the smaller socket to do so.

REAR-DERAILLEUR OVERHAUL

LEVEL 1

Except for the jockey wheels and pivots, most rear derailleurs are not designed to be disassembled. If the pivot springs seem to be operating effectively, all you need to do is overhaul the jockey wheels (see previous section) and clean and lubricate the parallelogram and spring, as described next.

REAR-DERAILLEUR WIPE AND LUBE

1. Clean the derailleur as well as you can with a rag, including between the parallelogram plates.
2. Drip chain lube on both ends of every pivot pin.
3. If the derailleur has a clothespin-type spring between the plates of the parallelogram (as opposed to a full coil spring running diagonally from one corner of the parallelogram to the other), put a dab of grease where the spring end slides along the underside of the outer parallelogram plate.

REAR-DERAILLEUR UPPER PIVOT OVERHAUL

These steps apply to Shimano derailleurs.

CAUTION: *Don't undertake this job unless you absolutely must to rehabilitate a poorly functioning rear derailleur. The strong spring resists*

your best intentions at reassembly, and you may not be able to get the derailleur back together properly, even with a second set of hands.

1. **Remove the rear derailleur.** It usually takes a 5mm hex key to unscrew it from the frame and to disconnect the cable.
2. **With a screwdriver, pry the circlip (Fig. 5.50) off the threaded end of the mounting bolt.** Don't lose it; it will tend to fly when it comes off.
3. **Pull the mounting bolt and the upper pivot spring out of the derailleur (Fig. 5.3).**
4. **Clean and dry the parts with or without the use of a solvent.**
5. **Grease liberally, and replace the parts.**
6. **Attach the spring.** Each end of the spring has a hole that it needs to go into. If there are several holes and you don't know which one it was in before, try the middle one. (If the derailleur does not keep tension on the chain well enough, you can later try another hole that increases the spring tension.)
7. **Push it all together and replace the circlip with pliers.**

5.50 Rear-derailleur pivots

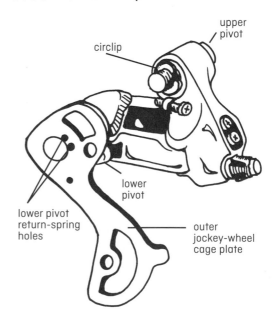

REAR-DERAILLEUR LOWER PIVOT OVERHAUL AND SPRING-TENSION ADJUSTMENT

On its 10- and 11-speed rear derailleurs, Campagnolo has eliminated the b-screw (Fig. 5.7), the traditional means of adjusting the spacing between the upper jockey wheel and the cogs (§v-3f). Instead, an external screw engaging a number of external teeth around the base of the rear derailleur's lower pivot performs the adjustment (Fig. 5.9).

If shifting is sluggish but the cable tension is correct (§v-3d), try adjusting the lower pivot spring by turning the b-screw or the Campy lower-pivot adjustment screw until the upper jockey wheel is close to the cog but not pinching the chain against it. Perform this adjustment when the chain is on the inner chainring and on the largest cog, as described in §v-3f.

Similarly, if the drivetrain is making noise or running roughly in low gears (because the chain is bumping along or being pinched between the cog and the upper jockey wheel), turn the b-screw or the Campy lower-pivot adjustment screw counterclockwise to loosen the lower pivot spring. This drops the upper jockey wheel down away from the cogs.

On a Shimano rear derailleur, fine-tuning the lower pivot spring tension is a secondary adjustment to turning the b-screw, and the derailleur must first be disassembled to perform the lower pivot spring-tension adjustment.

1. **Remove the derailleur from the bike.**
2. **Shimano derailleurs can be divided into two types: those that have a setscrew on the side of the lower pivot, and older ones that do not.**
   a. If yours has a setscrew (Fig. 5.51), remove it using a 2mm hex key and

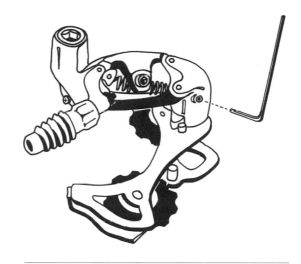

pull the jockey cage away from the derailleur.

b. If your derailleur has no setscrew, find and unscrew the tall cage-stop screw on the derailleur cage (Fig. 5.52); it is located near the upper jockey wheel. It is designed to maintain tension on the lower pivot spring and prevent the cage from springing all the way around. Once the stop screw is removed, slowly guide the cage around until the spring tension is relieved. Remove the upper jockey wheel and unscrew the pivot bolt from the back with a 5mm (sometimes 6mm) hex key (Fig. 5.53). Be sure to hold the jockey-wheel cage to keep it from twisting.

3. **Remove the spring.** Determine and mark, if necessary, which hole the spring end has been placed in, and then remove it.
4. **Clean and dry the bolt and the spring with a rag.** A solvent may be used if necessary.
5. **Grease all parts liberally.**
6. **Replace the spring ends in their holes in the derailleur body and jockey-wheel cage**

THE SHIFTING SYSTEM

(Fig. 5.54). Put the spring in the adjacent hole in the jockey-wheel cage plate if you want to increase its tension. Increasing the lower pivot spring tension pulls the chain tighter; if you have problems with the chain drooping or falling off, or you will be racing cyclocross, increasing the spring tension may solve the problem.

7. **Reassemble the derailleur.**

   a. If the derailleur has a setscrew, push the assembly together, wind the spring, and replace the setscrew (Fig. 5.51).

   b. If the derailleur does not take a set-screw, wind the jockey-wheel cage back around, screw it together with the pivot bolt (Fig. 5.53), and replace the stop screw (Fig. 5.52).

---

v-39

REAR-DERAILLEUR PARALLELOGRAM OVERHAUL

Few derailleurs can be completely disassembled. Those that can (Mavic cable-actuated derailleurs) have removable pins holding them together. The pins have circlips on the ends that can be popped off with a screwdriver. If you have such a derailleur, disassemble it in a box so that the circlips do not fly away, and note where each part belongs so that you can get it back together again. Clean all parts, grease them, and reassemble.

---

v-40

REPLACING STOCK REAR-DERAILLEUR BOLTS WITH LIGHTWEIGHT VERSIONS

Lightweight aluminum and titanium derailleur bolts are available as replacement items for some rear derailleurs. Removing and replacing

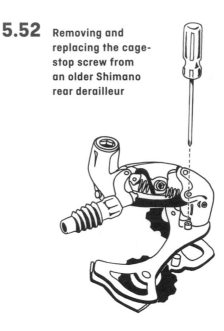

5.52 Removing and replacing the cage-stop screw from an older Shimano rear derailleur

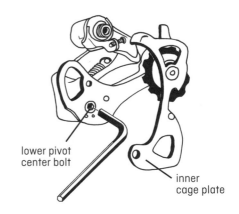

5.53 Removing and replacing the lower pivot center bolt from an older Shimano rear derailleur

lower pivot center bolt

inner cage plate

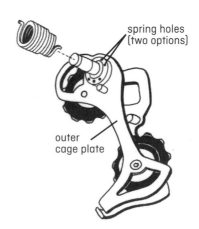

5.54 Removing and replacing the lower pivot return spring in one of the two holes in the jockey-wheel inner cage plate

spring holes (two options)

outer cage plate

jockey-wheel bolts is simple, as long as you keep all of the jockey-wheel parts together (Fig. 5.49) and put the inner cage plate back on the way it was. Upper and lower pivot bolts (Fig. 5.50) are replaced following the instructions outlined earlier in this chapter for overhauling the pivots (§v-37 and §v-38).

TROUBLESHOOTING DERAILLEUR AND SHIFTER PROBLEMS

Once you have made the adjustments outlined previously in this chapter, the drivetrain should operate quietly and shift smoothly. The drivetrain should stay in gear, even if you turn the crank backward. If you cannot fine-tune the adjustment so that each click with the right shifter results in a clean, quick shift of the rear derailleur, you need to check some of the following possibilities. For chain problems of skipping and jumping, see also the "Troubleshooting Chain Problems" section at the end of Chapter 4.

v-41

SHIFTER COMPATIBILITY

Make certain that the shifter and derailleur are made by the same company, are compatible models, and are made for the cogset you have (brand, model, and number of cogs). If the brands are different, make sure that they are designed to work together. For instance, Modolo makes an integral brake/shift lever that can be set up to work with either Campagnolo or Shimano derailleurs, and it has different settings for different numbers of speeds as well. If the shifter and derailleur are incompatible, you will need to change one of them (probably whichever item is less costly). For more on compatibility, see §v-47.

v-42

HOW DO I GET MORE GEAR RANGE?

At some point, everybody gets on a climb they wish they had a lower gear for. If this is a recurring theme for you, maybe it makes sense for you to expand your gear range. In Chapter 8, I discuss compact triple cranks and double cranks (i.e., a "compact" accepts an inner chainring as small as 34 teeth, rather than the 38- or 39-tooth minimum of standard double cranks).

If you've already made one of those changes and still don't have a low enough gear, or you have a compact crank but don't want to go to the extra expense, hassle, weight, or slower shifting of a triple (which requires changing the left shifter, both derailleurs, and the crank), then you can address the rear cogs. All rear derailleurs have a maximum tooth-count capacity for the largest cog, as well as a maximum range of teeth over which they can take up chain slack. On modern rear derailleurs for doubles, we're getting a lot more range than we used to, so much more is possible, and I'll show you how to expand that range a bit as well. Current Shimano short-cage (i.e., double) rear derailleurs have a maximum rear cog size of 28 teeth, a maximum tooth difference on the front chainrings of 16 teeth, and a total capacity of 33 teeth (the sum of the difference in front chainrings, for instance, 50 – 34 = 16, and the total tooth difference over the rear cogs, for instance, 28 – 12 = 16, yielding a total of 32T). This range is similar for SRAM and Campagnolo double rear derailleurs, and all three companies also offer rear derailleurs with a longer jockey-wheel cage and hence a larger maximum rear cog size and a wider total capacity.

You may want to keep your existing rear derailleur, however, and simply get a larger rear cogset, so what do you do if your cogset is beyond the published range of the rear derailleur? There are two things you can do—one simple and one more complex. The first is to simply tighten the b-screw (§v-3f) as far as it will go. This will rotate the rear derailleur back and move the guide pulley farther from the largest cog. Just by doing this, you may find that your Shimano Ultegra 6700 10-speed rear derailleur, rated to a maximum rear cog size of 28 teeth and a total capacity of 33 teeth, will now work with 34–50 compact front chainrings and a 12–30 Shimano Tiagra road or 11–32 Shimano XT mountain 10-speed cogset (total range of 34T and 36T, respectively). You will probably need to have a chain with one or two more links in it; you need to (carefully, in a bike stand!) check that the chain is long enough that shifting to the big-big gear combination won't rip apart the rear derailleur.

If it almost works with the b-screw tightened all of the way in but is still noisy on the largest cog, with the guide pulley noticeably bumping up and down over each tooth, you can remove the b-screw and turn it around to get it to rotate the derailleur farther back. You'll need to remove the derailleur to do this as well as to adjust it. When reinstalling the derailleur, make sure that you twist it back far enough when screwing the mounting bolt into the derailleur hanger that the b-screw is behind the tab on the hanger (§v-2, steps 2–4).

Finally, if you want even more range, like an 11–34 or 11–36 10-speed mountain bike cogset, you'll generally need a longer jockey-wheel cage on the rear derailleur. This is as simple as buying a compatible rear derailleur with a longer cage—for example, you can replace a Shimano Ultegra 6700-SS rear derailleur with an Ultegra 6700-GS medium-cage rear derailleur, and then perform the same b-screw manipulation detailed in the preceding two paragraphs to increase its capacity. Figure on adding at least two links to the chain length.

If you have an electronic rear derailleur and want a much wider gear range than it is rated for, there is something you can do beyond tightening in or turning around the b-screw; you can put a longer pulley cage on it! For instance, if you have a Dura-Ace Di2 7970 rear derailleur, you can interchange its pulley cage with an Ultegra 6700-GS rear derailleur (its pulley cage fits the mechanical Dura-Ace RD-7900 as well), following the instructions in §v-38. You'll have to buy the Ultegra 6700-GS rear derailleur, as you won't be able to find the parts singly, but you can put the carbon pulley cage from the Dura-Ace derailleur on it and upgrade it to a lighter short-cage derailleur as well. Add at least two links to the chain length, and experiment very carefully in a bike stand with the big-big combination to make sure you have enough chain length to not ruin your superpricey derailleur that you've added your sweat equity to before you head out on the road.

Additionally, if you want to turn to Chapter 8 and address chainring sizes, too, the advent of 2x10 mountain bike drivetrains means that you can replace a road double crank with a mountain bike double crank (say, with 30–42 chainrings). If you go down this path, the one complication will be that the MTB crank will be made for a mountain bike bottom bracket shell, which is 5mm wider than a road bottom bracket shell, and the chainline (§v-50 and §v-51) will be too wide. With a threaded bottom bracket, you can space the non-drive bearing out to get the right chainline, and some threadless bottom bracket types allow some respacing as well.

v-43

STICKY CABLES

Check to see whether the derailleur cables run smoothly through the housing. Sticky cable movement will cause sluggish shifting. Lubricate the cable by smearing it with chain oil or a specific lubricant that came with the shifters (§v-16). If lubricating the cable does not help, replace the cable and housing (§v-7 through §v-15).

v-44

BENT REAR-DERAILLEUR HANGER

A bent hanger will hold the derailleur crooked and bedevil shifting. Instructions for straightening the hanger are in §xiv-4.

v-45

BENT REAR-DERAILLEUR CAGE

A bent derailleur cage will align the jockey wheels at an angle. Mild bending can be straightened by hand; eyeball the crankset for a vertical reference.

v-46

LOOSE OR WORN-OUT REAR DERAILLEUR

Grab the derailleur and twist it with your fingers to feel for excessive play. Loose pivots, a symptom of a worn-out rear derailleur, will cause the rear derailleur to be loose and floppy. Replace it if it has this problem.

A loose mounting bolt will also mess up shifting by allowing the derailleur to flop around. Tighten the bolt.

v-47

DRIVETRAIN COMPATIBILITY ISSUES BETWEEN BRANDS, MODELS, AND SPEEDS

The number of rear cogs on a road bike keeps going up every few years. But does any of the old stuff work with any of the new stuff? And can you mix Shimano, SRAM, Campagnolo, and FSA drivetrain parts?

If you have resolutely stuck with your old frictional down-tube shifters, you can let Campagnolo and Shimano throw however many cogs they want at you, and you will still be able to shift. That old Campagnolo Nuovo Record shifter and derailleur shifted the chain across 5 cogs, and it will probably work on 11 cogs! Modern indexed systems shift more precisely, but they don't offer that kind of flexibility.

Compatibility problems occur because the chain required gets narrower as the number of cogs goes up. The spacing also narrows between chainrings, between rear-derailleur jockey-wheel plates, between front-derailleur cage plates, and between the right rear hub flange and the largest cog. Also, the rear hub axles have gotten longer. The spacing between rear dropouts (and hence the rear axle "overlock" length dimension) was at 120mm during 5-speed days, was 126mm during the 6- and 7-speed era, is now 130mm for 8-, 9-, 10-, and 11-speed hubs, and is 135mm for disc-brake hubs.

a. Threaded freewheels

The 5-, 6-, and 7-speed era marked the beginning of the transition from freewheels that threaded onto the rear hub to cassette freehubs built into the hub onto which separate cogs could be installed. With some minor exceptions, freewheels were completely compatible with every hub, since nearly all shared the same threading. Spacers sometimes had to be moved around from one end of the axle to the other to prevent the chain from dragging on the frame in the smallest cog. And, of course, you had to get a longer axle and re-dish the rear wheel when frames went from 120mm to 126mm rear spacing. But that was about it.

Freewheels did appear with eight speeds, so you could still space your old hub one more time with a new axle to 130mm. But freewheel makers threw in the towel when we hit nine speeds.

Five-speed freewheel cogs were spaced farther apart than current cogs, and there was no consistency of cog spacing between brands. There did not have to be, since the rider was manually lining up the derailleur with each cog. You were also lucky to have a 13-tooth first cog, rather than the 14-tooth that the previous generation saw as a high gear.

The first SunTour 6-speed freewheels were called "Ultra-6" and had narrower spacing between cogs (and a narrower chain) so they would fit on a 120mm rear hub. Not everyone embraced narrowness, but many riders wanted the 12-tooth cogs that SunTour offered. Splitting the difference, many frames of the era (especially Italian ones) were built with 126mm rear spacing and equipped with 6-speed freewheels with cogs set at the old wide spacing. SunTour answered with "Ultra-7" narrow-spaced freewheels and chains. Sedis started making narrow chains as well, and narrow spacing became the standard, carrying on into 8-speed.

b. Cassette freehubs

Shimano's spacing between cogs has narrowed from 3.70mm for 5- and 6-speeds to 3.10mm for 7-speed, 3.00mm for 8-speed, 2.56mm for 9-speed, 2.35mm for 10-speed, and 2.18mm for 11-speed. Shimano freehubs appeared around 1980 and accepted six speeds widely spaced (at 3.70mm apart) on a 126mm hub. The first five cogs were splined to fit on the splined freehub body, and the last cog threaded on. Shimano Uniglide chains were wide and had a bent-plate configuration. Shimano began making its first indexed shifting systems in the mid-1980s as well.

When SunTour introduced narrow Ultra-7 freewheels in the early 1980s, Shimano countered with wider freehub bodies that fit seven widely spaced cogs (at 3.70mm apart) and the wide Shimano chain.

In the second half of the 1980s, Shimano succumbed to the rising popularity of narrow chains and made narrow bent-plate (Uniglide) chains. Its new freehub body was the old 6-speed length, and it fit seven narrowly spaced cogs (at 3.10mm apart). But the new cogs would not fit on the old freehub bodies because a lockring now secured the cogs instead of a threaded small cog, and one spline groove was wider than the others.

The 1990s began with Shimano's introduction of 8-speed cogsets with 3.0mm cog spacing. Shimano had dictated that frames now had to have 130mm rear ends to accommodate new hubs with wider freehub bodies. Its one-wide-spline arrangement and threaded lockrings continued, but eight cogs would not fit a 7-speed body.

This set the stage for 9-speed Shimano cogsets, which had narrower (2.56mm) spacing and a narrower chain, and fit on 8-speed freehubs at first. But the desire for an 11-tooth cog forced the reduction of the freehub diameter by removing the outboard 2–3mm of spline ridges, which required new hubs (unless you were handy enough with a grinder to knock off the last couple of millimeters of the spline ridges flush with the freehub outer diameter).

With the advent of 10-speed cogs, Shimano's freehub body changed again, utilizing deeper spline valleys so that soft aluminum freehub bodies would not get torn up by the cogs. The outer diameter of the bottom of the spline valleys in the freehub body remained unchanged, so 10-speed cogs will fit on 9-speed freehub bodies. But 9-speed Shimano cogs will not fit Shimano 10-speed freehub bodies. Fortunately, by 2008 Shimano had abandoned the deep-spline freehub bodies and was back to using the same freehub dimensions that it has used since the introduction of nine speeds.

As for SunTour, Mavic, and Campagnolo, all began making freehub bodies and cogs with their own spline configurations, and only Campagnolo's systems survived the shakeout. SunTour disappeared completely from the road market, while Mavic went with the flow, making Shimano- and Campagnolo-compatible hubs, wheels, and cogs. Other hub and wheel makers followed suit.

Campagnolo, the great, reliable, and unchanging bastion of compatibility and small parts availability in the 1970s and early 1980s, changed its 8-speed freehub body when it came out with nine speeds. Campagnolo 9-speed freehub bodies have deeper splines that do not fit Campy 8-speed cogs, but its 10- and 11-speed cogsets, fortunately, fit on the same Campy 9-speed freehub bodies. The ultranarrow, 5.9mm- to 6.1mm-wide 10-speed chain allows 10 cogs to fit in the same space that used to accept only 9 with the wider 9-speed chain and cogset, and now the even narrower 5.4mm-wide 11-speed chain allows 11 cogs to fit in that same space. The thickness of the spacers on either side of each cog has come down to 2.2mm with 11-speed, whereas the width of each chain roller and thickness of each cog have stayed the same. The tooth-to-tooth distance is 4.55mm on Campagnolo 9-speed, 4.15mm on Campagnolo 10-speed, and 3.9mm on Campagnolo 11-speed.

SRAM, Shimano, and FSA 10-speed cogs fit on all Shimano-compatible 9- and 10-speed freehub bodies other than Shimano 10-speed aluminum ones (only Shimano 10-speed cogs fit on those).

c. Chainrings

The spacing between chainrings keeps getting narrower as the number of cogs at the rear increases, as do the width and index spacing of the front derailleur. If you have upgraded piecemeal, you may find your 9-, 10-, or 11-speed chain falling between the two chainrings held over from an earlier 7- or 8-speed system. The narrow chain will generally slip uselessly as you pedal, but it can jam between the rings as well, causing all sorts of expensive havoc.

Chainring teeth are made to fit closer together either by reducing the thickness of the chainring mounting flats on the crank spider arms or by offsetting the teeth to one side of the chainring. Shimano 7-, 8-, 9-, and 10-speed spider arm mounting tabs are all the same thickness, but the teeth on Shimano 9- and 10-speed chainrings are offset toward each other. The tab thickness on 11-speed Shimano cranks is irrelevant, because with a four-arm spider, only Shimano's 11-speed chainrings fit them.

Campagnolo's spider arms got thinner when going from 7- and 8-speed to 9-speed, but the chainring teeth got offset going to 10- and 11-speed, and the spider arms stayed the same as 9-speed. You can upgrade a Campagnolo 9-speed crank to 10- or 11-speed by changing the rings.

In general, I have encountered no problems using 9-speed cranks and chainrings of any brand with 10-speed drivetrains from Campagnolo, Shimano, or SRAM. Nor have I had any trouble using 10-speed cranks with Campagnolo 11-speed drivetrains.

Compact-drive double cranks have smaller chainrings, with tooth counts like 34–48, 34–50, 36–50, or 36–52. These cranks have a 110mm bolt circle diameter (BCD), rather than the 130mm BCD of Shimano/FSA/SRAM or the 135mm BCD of Campagnolo. With the smaller curvature to the chainrings, standard front derailleurs do not always work well on compact cranks, although recent derailleurs from Shimano, Campagnolo, and SRAM are designed to work on both. Campagnolo's CT system had a dedicated compact crank with a dedicated compact front derailleur. An IRD or FSA compact front derailleur can improve shifting with compact cranks relative to some front derailleurs not designed for them.

THE SHIFTING SYSTEM

d. Shifting compatibility within brands

All Campagnolo shifting system components can be interchanged within models with the same number of speeds. In other words, you can use Athena 9-speed Ergopower shifters with a Veloce 9-speed rear derailleur, Mirage front derailleur, Record 9-speed cogs, Chorus crank, and Centaur hub. The same holds true if all components are 8-, 10-, or 11-speed.

Shimano components have more inter-changeability exceptions. Until 9-speed came out, the stroke length for Dura-Ace rear derailleurs was different from all other Shimano rear derailleurs, mountain or road. Put another way, you could use any Shimano shifter you wanted with any Shimano derailleur except that Dura-Ace was compatible only with Dura-Ace for the rear derailleur.

With the advent of 9-speeds and then 10-speeds, all Shimano road rear derailleurs and shifters worked together. However, 10 speeds on mountain bikes brought incompatibility; Shimano 10-speed MTB Dynasis rear derailleurs are incompatible with 9-speed shifters or any other Shimano shifter that came before. Dura-Ace 9000 11-speed rear shifters have a unique stroke length between 10-speed road and 10-speed Dyna-Sys MTB stroke lengths; presumably 11-speed Ultegra will follow with a matching stroke length.

Compatibility is more of an issue with Shimano front derailleurs. When the Dura-Ace 7900 front shifter with zero trim premiered in 2009, it featured a new stroke length and wouldn't work well with the prior Dura-Ace 7800 10-speed front derailleurs, or those of any other model. Ultegra 6700 and 105 5700 front shifters didn't adopt the 7900 stroke length nor that of pre-2009 shifters, but the differences are small enough that you can generally mix and match 10-speed front derailleurs and shifters from Shimano com-

ponent lines and adjust them to work acceptably. If you try to use a road STI shift/brake lever with a Shimano mountain bike front derailleur (you might do this for a triple on a hybrid bike, for instance), it won't work very well.

All current Shimano cassettes fit on any Shimano freehub model designed for the same number of speeds.

All SRAM Red, Force, Rival, and Apex components are interchangeable. However, SRAM mountain bike derailleurs do not work with SRAM road shifters and vice versa.

e. Shifting compatibility between brands

Until the advent of 9-speeds, a Campagnolo cogset did not shift acceptably on a Shimano indexed drivetrain, and vice versa. But the limited amount of space available for nine speeds brought Shimano's and Campagnolo's cog spacing close enough that rear wheels could be switched back and forth between the two with decent shifting performance—not as good as you would get if you paid big bucks, but acceptable for normal riding and for wheel changes during races. Neutral-support vehicles only had to stock one variety of 9-speed wheels to cover every rider in the peloton.

Of course, 10-speed systems changed all of that again. For instance, in a Shimano 10-speed drivetrain, a Campy 10-speed cogset shifts acceptably in maybe 8 of the 10 gears, the 9th cog just barely, and the 10th cog not at all. Shimano 10-speed cogsets work flawlessly in SRAM road drivetrains and vice versa.

The Mavic Zap system was designed for Shimano 8-speed systems, and Mavic Mektronic was built for Shimano 9-speed systems, but it works decently on Campagnolo 9-speed cassettes as well.

As for front derailleurs and cranksets, mixing parts seems to cause few problems as long as you use parts designed for the same number of speeds. Campagnolo and Shimano road front derailleurs and cranksets work fine with each other's road shifters.

Any 8-speed chain works on any 7- or 8-speed system. All 9-speed chains work with all 9-speed systems. For 10-speeds, you'd better stick with a 10-speed chain meant for that system, and you'd certainly better keep 11-speed chains with 11-speed cogsets. It is worth experimenting among chain brands, though, to see if you can improve performance. The 7- and 8-speed chains are 7.0–7.2mm wide; 9-speed chains are 6.5–6.7mm wide; 10-speed chains from Shimano, Campagnolo, and SRAM, as well as KMC and Wippermann, are 5.88–6.1mm wide. Campagnolo's 11-speed chains are 5.44mm wide, while Shimano's 11-speed chains are 5.62mm wide.

v-48

CHAIN SUCK

Though relatively rare on road bikes, chain suck (where the chain sticks to the chainring and is dragged around until it jams between the chainring and the chainstay) can occur. See §iv-14.

v-49

CHAIN FALLS ONTO THE GRANNY RING ON A TRIPLE

An inadvertent shift to the smallest chainring on a triple can happen spontaneously when you are riding on the middle chainring and the largest rear cog, and is common on bikes with a 30–39–53 chainring combination. The extra four-tooth difference of the 39–53 outer pair (previously found on Shimano Dura-Ace 7803, slightly morphed to the 30–39–52 of Ultegra 6603 and 6703 triples) over a 42–52 pair (found on 105

and 9-speed Ultegra, which almost always works great) is more than the system can handle. The derailleur on a 30–39–53 triple is placed so much higher relative to the middle chainring than on a 30–42–52 (or on 10-speed 105's 30–39–50) that it would have difficulty derailing the chain down to the smallest chainring if the teeth weren't lowered to let it drop more easily or the derailleur weren't set to overshift to the inside, increasing the danger of throwing the chain off to the inside.

Shimano first addressed this problem by changing the tooth profile to derail more easily, but it often derailed too easily. Shimano then redesigned the middle chainring, but the problem often persists because of the inherent geometry problems of the higher front derailleur. Replacing the outer rings with 42–52 chainrings usually fixes the problem. If you don't want to do that, adjust the front derailleur so that its inner cage plate is very close to the chain when it is on the middle ring.

Campagnolo Comp Triple cranksets come with 30–40–50 or 30–42–53 combinations, which keep the derailleur a bit closer to the middle chainring. Auto-dropping to the granny ring is consequently rarely a problem with them. That's good because, unlike with Shimano's 130/74mm bolt circle diameter, inexpensive aftermarket chainrings that fit Campagnolo's 135/74mm BCD are nonexistent.

Also, when shifting from a bigger ring to a smaller one, the derailleur may overshift and throw the chain to the granny ring or completely off to the inside. This is more of a problem with stiff shift levers, since they derail the chain so suddenly that it can jump. My recommendation is to always install an inner stop like a Third Eye Chain Watcher (Fig. 5.55), Deda Dog Fang, or N-Gear Jump Stop with any triple crankset, and it's not a bad idea with a double, too. SRAM,

5.55 Third Eye Chain Watcher

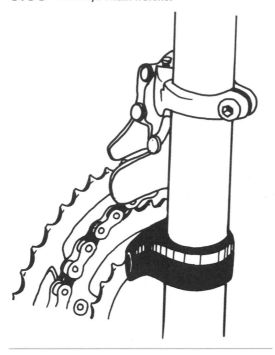

K-Edge, and others make chain stops that mount onto a braze-on front derailleur boss.

If you don't want to shell out 10 bucks for an inner stop, you can minimize the possibility of a dropped chain with a simple adjustment of the front derailleur. Turn the derailleur cage's tail slightly more inboard than its leading tip. This decreases the downshift force it applies. More important, it allows you to tighten the inner limit screw farther in without rubbing in the small-small gear. Then the inside plate of the front-derailleur cage acts similarly to an anti-chain-drop device.

v-50

CHAINLINE

Chainline is the relative alignment of the front chainrings with the rear cogs; it is the imaginary line connecting the center of the middle chainring with the middle of the cogset (Fig. 5.56). In theory, this line should be straight and parallel with the vertical plane of the bicycle.

Even owners of new bikes may discover poor chainlines on their bikes, due to mismatched cranks and bottom brackets.

Assuming that the frame is aligned properly, adjust chainline by moving or replacing the bottom bracket to move the cranks left or right. You can roughly check the chainline by placing a long straightedge between the two chainrings and back to the rear cogs; it should come out in the center of the rear cogs. (If that's not good enough for your purposes, a more precise method is outlined below.)

If the chain falls off to the inside no matter how much you adjust the derailleur's low-gear limit screw, cable tension, and derailleur position, or you have chain rub, noise, or auto-shift problems in mild cross-gears that are not corrected with derailleur adjustments, a likely culprit is poor chainline (or poor frame alignment).

v-51

PRECISE CHAINLINE MEASUREMENT

You will need a caliper with a vernier dial or digital scale.

The position of the plane centered between the two chainrings, as measured from the center of the seat tube to the center between the chainrings, is often called the chainline, although this is only the front point of the line.

1. **Find the position of the plane centered between the chainrings, or front point of the chainline (CL_F in Fig. 5.56).**

   a. Measure from the left side of the down tube to the outside of the large chainring (d1 in Fig. 5.56). (Do not measure from the seat tube; this tube is often ovalized at the bottom.)

   b. Measure the distance from the right side of the down tube to the inside of the inner chainring (d2 in Fig. 5.56).

5.56 Measuring chainline

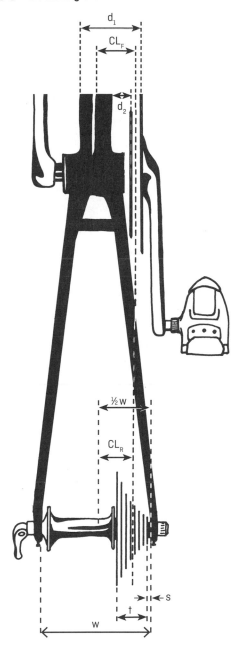

from the center of the plane of the bicycle to the center of the cogset.

a. Measure the thickness of the cog stack, end to end (t in Fig. 5.56).

b. Measure the space between the face of the smallest cog and the inside face of the dropout (s in Fig. 5.56).

c. Measure the length of the axle from dropout to dropout (w in Fig. 5.56); this length is also called the "axle overlock dimension," referring to the distance from locknut face to locknut face on either end. Generally, on any road bike built since the late 1980s, this will be 130mm.

d. To find CL_R, subtract one-half of the thickness of the cog stack and the distance from the inside face of the right rear dropout from one-half of the rear axle length.

$$CL_R = w \div 2 - t \div 2 - s$$

3. **If $CL_F = CL_R$ (the rear chainline), the chainline is perfect.** This may not be possible to attain, however, due to considerations of chainstay clearance and prevention of chain rub on large chainrings in cross-gears. Shimano specifies a "chainline" (meaning CL_F, the front point of the chainline) of 43.5mm for a double and 45.0mm for a triple on road bikes. On the other hand, CL_F, the rear end point of the chainline, usually comes out around 42.6mm for Shimano 9-speed, 41.8mm for Campagnolo 9-speed, and 41.7mm for Campagnolo 8-speed.

a. Your bike will shift best and run quietest if you get the chainline (CL_F) at around 42mm. However, this ideal may cause problems on your particular bike because (a) the inner chainring might rub the chainstay; (b) the front derailleur

c. To find CL_F (the front chainline), add these two measurements, and divide the sum by two.

$$CL_F = (d_1 + d_2) \div 2$$

2. **Find the rear end point of the chainline (CL_R in Fig. 5.56), which is the distance**

THE SHIFTING SYSTEM

150

may bottom out on the seat tube before moving inward enough to shift to the inner chainring (this is particularly a problem on bikes with triples and large-diameter seat tubes); or (c) when crossing to the smallest cog from the inner chainring, the chain may rub on the next larger ring (simply avoid those cross-gears).

b. My general recommendation is to have the chainrings in toward the frame as far as possible without rubbing the frame or bottoming out the front derailleur before it shifts cleanly to the inner chainring.

4. **To improve the chainline, move the chainrings (bikes with conventional bottom brackets only; this is not possible with an integrated-spindle crank).** The chainrings can be moved by using a different bottom bracket, by exchanging the bottom bracket spindle with a longer one, or by moving the bottom bracket right or left (bottom bracket installation is covered in Chapter 8).

NOTE: *The chainline can also be off if the frame is out of alignment. If that's the case, it is probably something you cannot fix yourself.*

5. **If improving the chainline does not fix the problem, or if you don't want to mess with the chainline, buy and install an anti-chain-drop device like a Third Eye Chain Watcher (Fig. 5.55), Deda Dog Fang, or N-Gear Jump Stop.** These are inexpensive gizmos that clamp around the seat tube next to the inner chainring. Similarly, SRAM and K-Edge inner stops mount onto a braze-on front derailleur boss. Adjust the inner stop's position so that it nudges the chain back on when the chain tries to fall off to the inside.

WHEELS AND TIRES

All you need in this life is ignorance and confidence, and then success is sure.
—Mark Twain

TOOLS

Tire levers

Pump

Patch kit

Spoke wrench

Grease

5mm hex keys

13mm, 14mm, 15mm
  cone wrenches

Metric open-end or
  adjustable wrenches

Freehub cassette
  lockring remover

Pedro's Vise Whip or
  chain whip

BBQ grill-cleaning pad
  or brush

Table knife

Optional

Citrus solvent

Truing stand

Tire sealant

Tubular gluing tape

Tubular rim cement

VM&P Naphtha/acetone/
  white gas as glue
  solvent

Teflon tape

Pliers

Miter clamp

Leather sewing needle

Braided high-test
  fishing line

Thimble

continues p. 152 >

Most road bike wheels are strung together with spokes connecting the hub to the rim. The rim, which usually is made of aluminum but can also be made of carbon-fiber composite, steel, or magnesium, supports the tire and forms the surface on which the brakes are applied. It in turn is supported and aligned by the tension of the spokes. Bearings in the hub, when clean and properly adjusted, allow the wheel to turn freely around the axle.

Composite (i.e., carbon fiber) wheels can use rigid members instead of wire spokes to connect the hub and rim, as is the case with disc wheels or three-, four-, or five-spoke wheels. The spokes in this case are in compression, like the wooden spoked wheels on a Conestoga wagon, not in tension as with a wire-spoke wheel. A composite wheel cannot be trued, although some can be returned to the manufacturer for rim replacement. Some composite wheels use composite spokes in tension, much like a wire-spoke wheel, but the spokes are usually bonded to the rim and hub and hence can't be adjusted to true the wheel. One attempt to bridge the gap between the tension

wheel and the wagon wheel is the Mavic R-Sys TraComp (i.e., TRAction/COMPression) wheel. It has thick, rigid carbon spokes backed up against a shell inside the hub to support the rim somewhat in compression, yet the spokes are also in tension and have threaded nipples to allow truing.

Wheels intended for aerodynamic efficiency have either solid sides made from sheets of fiber (disc wheels) or aerodynamically shaped rims and few spokes, which often are aerodynamic in shape. The spokes can be steel, aluminum, titanium, or composite (which generally means carbon fiber).

A cassette freehub or freewheel with cogs attached (Fig. 6.1) allows the rear wheel to spin independently of the chain and pedals while you are coasting, and it engages when force is applied to the pedals. The tires provide suspension as well as grip and traction for propulsion and steering. The air pressure in the tire is the primary suspension system on a road bike.

Three types of road bike tires are available. "Clinchers" (Fig. 6.2), which are C-shaped in cross-section, are held into a C-shaped rim by a steel or

6.1 The whole thing

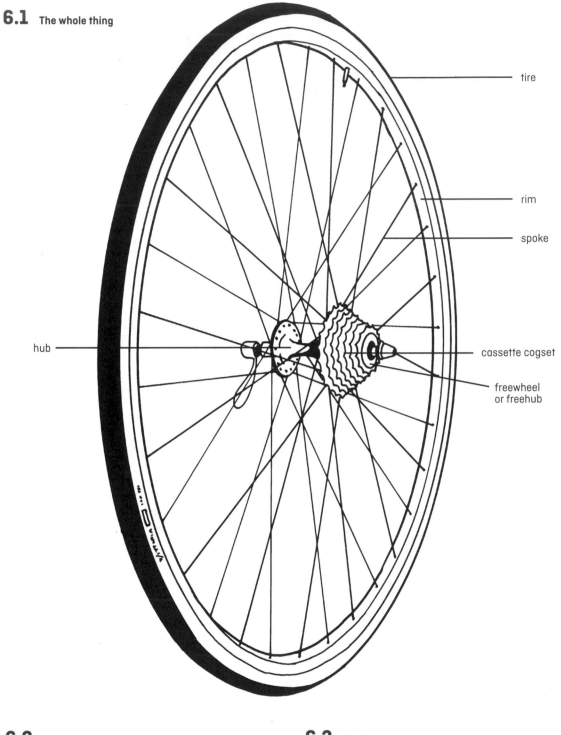

tire

rim

spoke

hub

cassette cogset

freewheel or freehub

6.2 Clincher tire

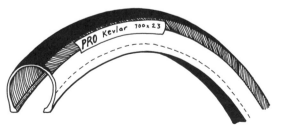

6.3 Tubular tire

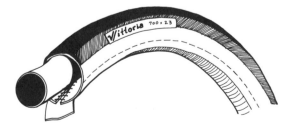

Kevlar bead on each edge of the tire. A separate inner tube inside of the clincher holds the air. "Tubulars" (Fig. 6.3), which are circular in cross-section, have a casing that is wrapped around an inner tube and stitched or glued together. The tire is glued onto a box-section rim that has no vertical rim walls like a clincher rim. The third and most recent type is a tubeless road tire that resembles a clincher tire, but the rim is sealed, and there is no inner tube—merely a valve sealed into the rim (Fig. 6.17). Tubeless tires are generally used with a sealant inside.

This chapter addresses how to fix a flat or replace a tire or tube, true a wheel, fix a broken spoke or bent rim, overhaul hubs, change rear cogs, and lubricate cassettes and freewheels. Have at it.

6.4 Presta valve

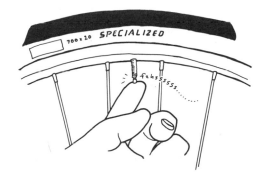

6.5 Schrader valve

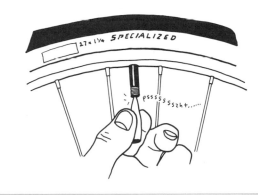

CLINCHER TIRES

vi-1

REMOVING THE TIRE

LEVEL 1

1. **Remove the wheel (§ii-2 and §ii-11).**

2. **If the tire is not already flat, deflate it.** First remove the valve cap (if installed) to get to the valve.

Most road bike tires have Presta valves (also known as Sclaverand or French valves). These valves are thinner (6mm vs. 8mm) than Schrader valves (the kind found on cars) and have a small threaded rod with a tiny nut on the end. To let air out, unscrew the little nut a few turns, and push down on the thin rod (Fig. 6.4). To seal, tighten the little nut down again (with your fingers only!); leave it tightened for riding.

To deflate a Schrader valve, push down on the valve pin with something thin enough to fit in that won't break off, like a pen cap or a paper clip (Fig. 6.5).

NOTE: *If the rims on your bike have a deep section (i.e., with a rim depth greater than 30mm; these are generally carbon rims), the air valves for the tires either will be extremely long or will be fitted with valve extenders—thin threaded tubes that screw onto the Presta valve stems.*

One type of valve extender is simply a thin tube like a drinking straw with threads inside one end to screw onto the cap threads of the valve (Fig. 6.6A). Due to the wrench flats on a removable Presta valve core's cap threads, these don't work well with Presta valves with removable cores, which are found on most high-quality tubular tires. They also require the valve to be always open, by unscrewing the little nut atop it hard enough that it stays open and does not screw closed on its own. If the valve has a problem such as an imperfect seal or a bent rod, it can leak when the nut is not tightened down.

To deflate tires that have simple drinking-straw-type valve extenders installed, you need to insert a thin rod (a spoke is perfect) into the valve extender to release the air.

To install drinking-straw-type valve extenders so that they seal properly and allow easy inflation, you need to unscrew the little nut on the Presta valve until it is against the mashed threads at the top of the valve shaft (they are mashed to keep the nut from unscrewing completely). Back the nut firmly into these mashed threads with a pair of pliers so that it stays unscrewed and does not tighten back down against the valve stem while riding, which would prevent air from going in when you pump it. Wrap a turn or two of Teflon pipe thread tape (plumbing tape) around the top threads on the valve stem before screwing on the valve extender; if you do not, air will leak out when you are pumping, and the pressure gauge on your pump will not give an accurate reading of the pressure in the tire. Tighten the valve extender onto the valve with a pair of pliers.

Alternatively, valve extenders for removable-core valves will be threaded at the base with the same thread as on the base of a valve core (Fig. 6.6B), and they will have threads inside the other end to accept a valve core. Deflating and inflating the tire with one of these valve extenders are no different than deflating and inflating any tire with a standard Presta valve. To install one of these valve extenders, unscrew the valve core (counter-clockwise) with an adjustable wrench or specific Presta valve-core wrench and remove it. Screw the valve extender into the valve body where the core was; tighten it firmly with pliers or a wrench on its wrench flats. Screw the valve core into the valve extender and tighten it with an adjustable wrench or specific Presta valve-core wrench.

Some valve extenders are straws with a thin knurled knob on top with a shaft running all the way down to a cup that grabs the nut atop the valve (Fig. 6.6C). They actually allow you to tighten or loosen the valve nut with the extender

6.6A Straw-type valve extender

6.6B Removable-core valve extender (showing separate valve core)

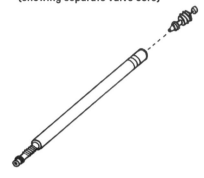

6.6C Topeak/Spinergy valve extender

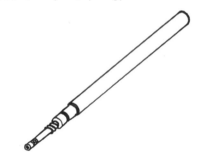

6.6D Vittoria tube stub with different valve lengths

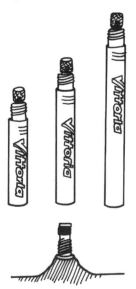

in place, thus behaving like a standard Presta valve. With this type, unless it has a rubber seal at its base, you should also wrap a turn or two of Teflon pipe thread tape around the top threads on the valve stem before screwing on the valve extender; if you do not, air will leak out when you are pumping, and the pressure gauge on the pump will not give an accurate reading of the pressure in the tire. Tighten the valve extender onto the valve stem with a pair of pliers.

Note too that some Vittoria tubulars have a threaded stub where the valve would go, and you thread in a complete valve of the length you need for your specific rim (Fig. 6.6D). It operates like any other Presta valve.

3. **If you can push the tire bead off the rim with your thumbs without using tire levers, by all means do so.** There is a lesser chance of damaging the tube or the tire if you avoid the use of levers or other tools. It's easiest if you start just to one side or the other of the valve, after squeezing the tire beads into the center of the rim all of the way around (see the Pro Tip on tire removal and installation).

4. **If you can't get the tire off with your hands alone, use tire levers.** Insert a lever (with its scoop toward you) between the rim sidewall and the tire (again, close to the valve stem; see the Pro Tip on tire removal and installation) until you catch the edge of the tire bead. Make sure you do not pinch the tube between the lever and the tire.

5. **Pry down on the lever until the tire bead is pulled out over the rim (Fig. 6.7).** If the lever has a hook on the other end, hook it onto the nearest spoke. Otherwise, keep holding it down.

6. **Place the next lever a few inches away, and do the same thing with it (Fig. 6.7).**

7. **If needed, place a third lever a few inches farther on, pry it out, and continue sliding**

this lever around the tire, pulling the bead out as you go (Fig. 6.8). Some people slide their fingers around under the tire bead, but beware of cutting your fingers on a sharp bead.

NOTE: *There are quick-change tire levers on the market that work differently and more quickly than the separate standard tire levers. If the tire bead is very tight on the rim, however, using separate tire levers may be the only method that works effectively.*

8. **Once the bead is off the rim on one side, pull the tube out (Fig. 6.9).**

6.7 Removing clincher tire with levers

6.8 Pulling out the bead with the third lever

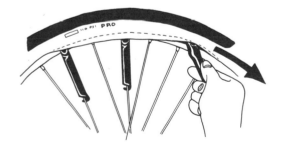

6.9 Removing the inner tube

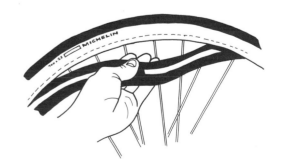

Removal of a clincher or tubeless tire is most easily accomplished by starting near the valve stem, and tire installation is similarly best accomplished by finishing at the valve stem. That way, the beads of the deflated tire can fall into the dropped center (valley) of the rim on the opposite side of the wheel, making it effectively a smaller-circumference rim. If you instead try to push the tire bead off (or on) the rim on the side opposite the valve stem, the circumference on which the bead is resting is larger, because the valve stem is forcing the beads to stay up on their seating ledges opposite where you are working. Adhering to this method is particularly critical with a tubeless road tire, because the bead is very tight, it does not stretch at all, and you install the tire without tire levers to avoid damaging the tire's edges that seal the air inside.

With a standard (i.e., nontubeless) clincher tire, another reason to finish at the valve stem is to avoid ending up with a bit of inner tube trapped under the tire bead where you finished pushing the tire onto the rim. If that happens, it may immediately blow the tire off the rim when you pump it up to pressure (temporarily deafening you; the explosion is very loud) or it may explode later on a ride. In either case, you will have an unpatchable tube with a long rip down its length, possibly endangering your life if the tire blows at high speed on a turn.

You can minimize explosions and flats by finishing the tire installation at the valve stem (Fig. 6.15). First, take the appropriate precaution of having some air in the tube to keep it from twisting and getting under the bead as you push the tire on. Deflate that last bit of air only when it prevents you from getting the final few inches of the tire bead on. Note that the edge of the flat tube can still slip under the bead edge as it pops into the rim at that point. But pushing up on the valve stem after the tire is on (Fig. 6.16) can lift the adjacent sections of inner tube completely into the tire chamber and ensure that none is caught under the edge, waiting to blow the tire off the rim. Always inspect around the tire bead before inflating as in §vi-5, step 11.

9. **If you are patching or replacing the tube, you do not need to remove the other side of the tire from the rim.** If you are replacing the tire, the other bead should come off easily with your fingers. If it does not, use the tire levers as just outlined.

vi-2

PATCHING AN INNER TUBE

1. **If the leak location is not obvious, inflate the tube until it is two to three times larger than its deflated size.** Be careful. You can explode it if you put in too much air, especially with lightweight latex or urethane tubes.

2. **Listen for air, and mark the leak(s).**

3. **If you cannot find the leak by listening, submerge the tube in water or sponge soap suds on it.** Look for air bubbling out (Fig. 6.10) and mark the spot(s). Make sure you check the valve for air leaking out.

NOTE: *You can only patch small holes. If the hole is bigger than a pencil eraser, a round patch is not likely to work. A slit as long as an inch or so can be repaired with an oval patch.*

6.10 Checking for a puncture

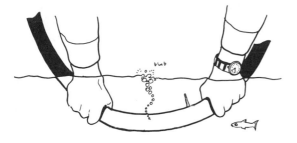

---

vi-3

STANDARD PATCHES

Use a patch designed for bicycle tires; it will generally have a thin gummy edge, usually orange, surrounding a slightly thicker patch of black rubber.

1. Dry the tube thoroughly near the puncture and mark the location of the hole with a pen.

2. **To provide a suitable surface for the patch, clean and then rough up the tube surface within about a 1-inch radius around the hole with a small piece of sandpaper (usually supplied with the patch kit).** Do not touch the sanded area. If the patch kit you are using has a little metal "cheese grater" for the purpose, discard it and replace it with sandpaper. The grater-style rougheners tend to do to a tube what they do to cheese.

3. **Apply glue (patch cement) in a thin, smooth layer all over an area centered on the hole (Fig. 6.11).** Use the end of the glue container or a brush, rather than your finger, to spread the glue around. Cover an area that is bigger than the size of the patch. By the way, the glue is similar to rubber cement, so if the tube in your patch kit has dried out, you can use any rubber cement sold in office supply and hardware stores. If you do this, and use the brush attached to the top of the bottle cap, wipe the brush almost dry before spreading the cement on the tube. You only need a thin layer for the patch.

4. **Let the glue dry 10 minutes or so until there are no more shiny, wet spots.**

5. **Peel the patch from its foil backing (but do not remove the cellophane top cover yet).**

6. **Stick the patch over the hole and push it down in place, making sure that all of the gummy edges are stuck down.** With the tube sitting on a hard surface, burnish the patch with the plastic handle of a screwdriver to stick the edges down securely.

7. **Optional: Remove the cellophane top covering, being careful not to peel up the edges of the patch (Fig. 6.12).** Often the cellophane top patch is scored. If you fold the patch, the cellophane will split at the scored cuts, allowing you to peel outward and avoid

---

6.11 Applying glue

6.12 Removing cellophane

pulling the newly adhered patch up off the tube. If you can't get the cellophane off without peeling up the patch or you don't mind it being there, just leave it alone. It won't harm the tire.

vi-4

GLUELESS PATCHES

There are a number of adhesive-backed patches on the market that do not require cement. Simply clean the area around the hole with an alcohol pad supplied with the patch. Let the alcohol dry, peel the backing, and stick on the patch.

Glueless patches are quick to use and take little room in a seat bag; also, you never open your patch kit to discover that your glue tube is dried up. On the downside, I have not found a glueless patch that sticks nearly as well as the standard type. With a standard patch installed, you can inflate the tube to look for more leaks without having it in the tire. If you do that with a glueless patch, the patch usually lifts enough to start leaking. With glueless patching, you must install the tube in the tire and on the rim before putting air in it. And glueless patches are probably not a permanent fix.

vi-5

INSTALLING PATCHED OR NEW TUBE

If you fix a flat, feel around the inside of the tire to see whether there is anything sticking through that can puncture the tube again. Sliding a rag all the way around the inside of the tire works well. The rag will catch on anything sharp and will save your fingers from being cut by whatever is stuck in the tire.

1. **Replace any tire that has damaged areas (inside or out) where the casing fibers appear to be cut or frayed.**

6.13 Installing a rim strip

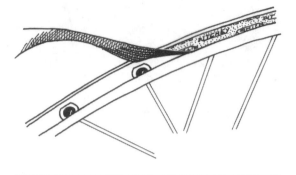

2. **Examine the rim to be certain that the rim strip is in place and that there are no spokes or anything else sticking up that can puncture the tube.** Replace the rim strip if necessary (Fig. 6.13). Use a stretch-on rim strip or, lacking that, two layers of fiberglass strapping tape. Don't use tape that doesn't have reinforcing fibers in it, since it can stretch or tear into the spoke holes and allow the spoke ends to puncture the tube.

3. **By hand, push one bead of the tire onto the rim.**

4. **Optional: Smear talcum powder around the inside of the tire and on the outside of the tube so the two do not adhere to each other.** Don't inhale this stuff, by the way.

5. **Put just enough air in the tube to give it shape.** Close the valve, if it's a Presta.

NOTE: *If the rims have a deep section (more than 30mm) and the tube has a standard-length Presta valve, you will need to install a valve extender (Figs. 6.6A–D) so that you can get air into the tire once it is on the rim. See the Note in §vi-1, step 2, for instructions on installing the various types of valve extenders.*

6. **Push the valve through the valve hole in the rim.**

7. **Push the tube up inside the tire all the way around.**

8. **Starting at the side opposite the valve stem (see the Pro Tip in §vi-2 on tire removal and**

6.14 Installing a tire by hand

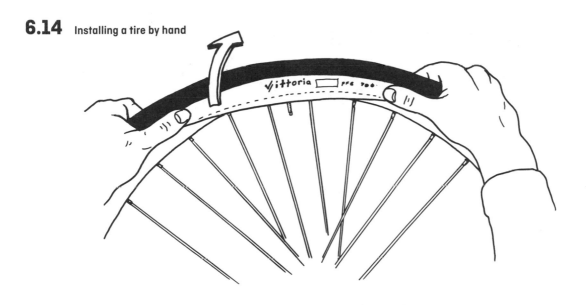

6.15 Finishing at the valve

6.16 Seating the tube

installation for why to start there), push the tire bead onto the rim with your thumbs. Be sure that the tube doesn't get pinched between the tire bead and the rim.

9. **Work around the rim in both directions toward the valve with your thumbs, pushing the tire onto the rim (Fig. 6.14).** Finish from both sides at the valve (Fig. 6.15), deflating the tube when it gets hard to push more of the tire onto the rim. (See the Pro Tip in §vi-2 on tire removal and installation for why you should finish at the valve.) Using this method, you can often install a tire without tools. If you cannot, use tire levers, but make sure you don't catch any of the tube under the edge of the bead. Finish the same way, at the valve.

10. **Reseat the valve stem by pushing up on the valve after you have pushed the last bit of bead onto the rim (Fig. 6.16).** You may have to manipulate the tire so that all the tube is tucked under the tire bead.

11. **Go around the rim and inspect for any part of the tube protruding from under the edge of the tire bead.** If you have a fold of the tube under the edge of the bead, it can blow the tire off the rim when you inflate it or while you are riding. It will sound like a gun went off next to you and will leave you with an unpatchable tube.

12. **Pump up the tire.** Generally, 85–110 psi is correct for a good-quality 23–25mm-wide road bike tire (see the Pro Tip on tire pressure), unless you weigh more than 200

Many road riders make the mistake of using very high air pressure to reduce rolling resistance. The likelihood of hurting yourself in a blowout is high, and, contrary to popular belief, using extremely high pressure does not make the tire roll faster, and it reduces traction. If the tire cannot absorb small bumps into its surface because it is pumped up too high, the bike will roll slower, even though it may feel fast because it is so stiff and bouncy. Every little bump lifts the bike and rider, providing a backward force on impact as well. This costs energy compared with absorbing the bump into the tire while the bike and rider continue to roll along smoothly without up-down motion.

Pressures of 140 psi and higher are fast only on the very smooth surfaces found on a velodrome (banked racetrack). On a road surface, anything higher than 120 psi costs you speed.

Regarding rolling resistance, a handmade tire with a casing made of thin, tightly packed threads will generally roll faster than a casing made of fewer thicker, stiffer threads. So, if you want to roll fast, choose a tire with a high thread count that feels supple when you fold it in your hand, and forget the bomber tire pressures that also endanger your life!

pounds (in which case you need more air). If you increase the pressure further, you will be pushing the limits of some tires and increasing ride harshness. If you put in less air than recommended, you run the risk of a pinch flat (or "snake-bite" flat).

vi-6

PATCHING TIRE CASING (SIDEWALL)

Unless it is an emergency, don't patch a clincher tire! If the tire casing is cut, get a new tire. Patching the tire casing is dangerous. No matter what you use as a patch, the tube will find a way to bulge out of the patched hole, and when it does, the tire will go flat immediately. Imagine coming down a steep hill and suddenly the front tire goes completely flat . . . you get the picture.

In an emergency, you can put layers of non-stretchable material between the tube and tire (§iii-3d, Fig. 3.2). Candidates for this duty include a dollar bill, an empty energy bar wrapper (or two), or a small piece cut from an old tire sidewall.

TUBELESS ROAD TIRES

LEVEL 1

Tubeless tires cannot pinch flat (i.e., the pinching of the inner tube between the tire and the rim when hitting a sharp object, which punctures the tube with two "snake-bite" holes), since there is no tube to pinch. With liquid sealant inside, tubeless tires also will not lose a significant amount of air to a small puncture. When used in conjunction with tubeless-specific road rims, road tubeless tires also will tend to stay on the rim better than a clincher in the event of sudden pressure loss. You can also run a road tubeless tire at 10–20 psi lower pressure than a clincher and get better traction without sacrificing rolling resistance or worrying about pinch flats.

vi-7

REMOVING A TUBELESS ROAD TIRE

Tubeless road tires fit very tightly because they must. Since there is no inner tube pressing the tire sidewalls against the rim walls, the tire bead is more critical for retaining the tire. It must not stretch in order to prevent the air pressure from pulling the tire beads right up off the rim. Consequently, road tubeless tires are harder to remove than most clinchers. You will likely need tire levers. To avoid breaking the carbon bead or damaging the rubber edge along it, compromising its sealing ability, make sure you use only plastic levers with no sharp edges. Hutchinson Stick'Air tire levers are specifically made for tubeless road tire installation and removal.

If you intend to patch the tire, find the hole before removing the tire from the rim (§vi-8).

1. **Remove the wheel (§ii-2 and §ii-11).**
2. **If the tire is not already flat, deflate it.** First remove the valve cap (if installed) to get to the valve. To let air out of the valve (it's a standard Presta valve), unscrew the little nut a few turns, and push down on the thin rod (Fig. 6.4). To seal, tighten the little nut down again (with your fingers only!); leave it tightened for riding.
3. **If you can push the tire bead off the rim with your thumbs without using tire levers, by all means do so.** There is less chance of damaging the tire's sealing edges if you unseat the bead by hand. It's easiest if you start just to one side or the other of the valve, after squeezing the tire beads into the center of the rim all the way around (see the Pro Tip in §vi-2 on tire removal).
4. **If you can't get the tire off with your hands alone, use tire levers.** Insert a tire lever (with its scoop toward you; the pointed end of the tire lever should be on the rim side) between the rim sidewall and the tire until you catch the edge of the tire bead. Again, start near the valve after squeezing the tire beads into the rim valley all the way around to put as much slack into the tire as possible.
5. **Pry down on the lever until the tire bead is pulled over the rim (Fig. 6.7).** If the lever has a hook on the other end, hook it onto the nearest spoke. Otherwise, keep holding it down.
6. **Place the next lever a few inches away, and do the same thing with it (Fig. 6.7).**
7. **If needed, place a third lever a few inches farther on.** Pry it out, and continue sliding this lever around the tire, pulling the bead out as you go (Fig. 6.8) until you can get it the rest of the way off with your hands.
8. **Remove the other bead, by hand if you can.**

vi-8

PATCHING A TUBELESS ROAD TIRE

You must find the hole before removing the tire from the rim. If the tire has a cut that is more than a few millimeters long, it's best to replace the tire to avoid endangering yourself from a blowout. If a number of casing threads are cut, the tire will also have a bulge and will not ride smoothly.

You can usually eliminate the need to patch the tire by simply deflating the tire and inflating it with a latex-based tire sealant (see §vi-9, step 7 below).

1. **Inflate the tire to no more than 100 psi.**
2. **Listen for where air is coming out, or coat the tire with soap suds or submerge it in water to find bubbles locating the hole.** Make sure you check all the way around, in case there are numerous holes.
3. **Mark the hole(s).**
4. **Remove the tire (§vi-7).**

5. **Dry the inside of the tire, and rough up and patch the hole(s) from the inside, using the patches in the same way as instructed in §vi-3.** Install the tire as in §vi-9 below.

vi-9

INSTALLING A TUBELESS ROAD TIRE

Tubeless road tires have carbon-fiber beads to ensure that the beads do not stretch and yet are thin enough to allow both beads to drop into the rim valley together to reduce the mounting circumference of the wheel and make the tire easier to install.

Tubeless-specific road rims have a little hump on the edge of the tire-mounting ledge to seal against the tire (Fig. 6.17). They also have no holes in the upper rim wall for accessing the spoke nipples.

You can mount a road tubeless tire on a rim not specifically denoted as a tubeless rim by using a latex sealant, but doing so runs counter to the tire manufacturer's warnings. Either you would need a rim that has no spoke holes in the upper rim wall, or, in a rim with spoke holes, you would need to use an airtight rim strip like the

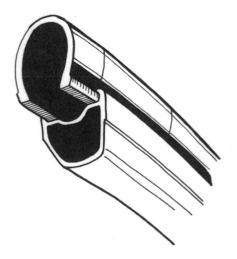

6.17 Tubeless road tire with rim cutaway view

Stan's NoTubes or Caffélatex rim strip to seal the spoke-nipple access holes. You would also need a valve specifically designed for using a road tubeless tire on a standard road wheel, which will seal the valve hole. One danger of using a road tubeless tire on a rim not specifically designed for it is that the bead may not stay locked on in the case of sudden air loss, allowing the tire to come off the rim easily.

IMPORTANT SAFETY WARNING: *NEVER, EVER mount a road clincher tire without an inner tube unless it is specifically branded as a tubeless tire (yes, I know running standard tires tubeless is often done with mountain bike tires and even with cyclocross clinchers, but the pressures are lower). The beads of a standard clincher tire are not sufficiently resistant to stretching and are not precise enough in size to prevent the tire from blowing off the rim. This, compounded with the fact that the tire will have latex sealant inside to get it to hold air in the first place, is extremely dangerous. If the tire does blow off, the rim will be slipping around on the liquid latex in the tire, allowing the rim to slide off of the tire, a situation almost impossible for the rider to control without crashing. Don't do it.*

1. **Install the valve into the rim.** Make sure that the rubber washer on the outside and rubber seal on the inside are properly seated. Put some sealant (like Caffélatex or Stan's NoTubes) around the valve hole before installing the valve; otherwise, wet the rubber base of the valve with soapy water before installing it.

2. **Wet the tire edges either with water alone or with soapy water on a sponge.**

3. **By hand, push one bead of the tire onto the rim.** Start opposite the valve stem and finish at the valve stem to minimize the rim's mounting circumference (see the Pro Tip in §vi-2 on tire removal and installation).

4. **Starting opposite the valve stem (again, see the Pro Tip in §vi-2 on tire removal and installation), push the second tire bead onto the rim with your thumbs.**

5. **Work around the rim in both directions toward the valve with your thumbs, pushing the tire onto the rim (Fig. 6.14).** Finish from both sides at the valve (Fig. 6.15). The Pro Tip on tire removal and installation explains why you should finish at the valve. Using this method, you should be able to mount the tire without tools. If not, use tire levers, but make sure you use plastic levers with no sharp edges (like Hutchinson Stick'Air), finishing at the valve.

6. **Make sure that the beads are well down into the channel of the rim.**

7. **If you're not going to use a sealant, you can now inflate the tire with a high-volume floor pump, air compressor, or gas cartridge to 120 psi maximum.** A small hand pump may not push enough air volume fast enough to get the beads to seat; air will leak out around the edges while you pump until you're blue in the face. You may find that you need the air compressor or cartridge to seat the tire.

Personally, I don't see the point of not using a tire sealant. A tubeless tire has the possibility of eliminating not only pinch flats but also punctures. The sealant ensures that if you get a puncture, it seals up immediately, and it also can prevent slow leaks around the bead. I therefore recommend one of two methods to inflate the tire the first time: Use either an aerosol sealant or a liquid sealant. Method 1 is to inject sealant through the valve with a syringe or with an aerosol canister like Hutchinson Fast'Air or Vittoria Pit Stop (Fig. 6.19A); follow the directions in §vi-14a. Method 2 is to pour in a couple of tablespoons of liquid sealant while mounting the tire at the point where there are only a few more inches of the second bead to push on the rim. The other way to get liquid sealant into the tire is to use a Stan's or Caffélatex valve, both of which have removable valve cores, and put the sealant in as in §vi-14b. Then inflate the tire with a high-volume floor pump, air compressor, or gas cartridge to 120 psi maximum.

8. **Spin the wheel and ensure that the tire is aligned properly and has no bulges or places where the bead is not fully seated.**

TUBULAR TIRES

LEVEL 3

Tubular tires, or sew-ups, are expensive, slow to install (they must be glued to the rim), hard to repair, and can even be hard to find. So why bother with them?

For one thing, tubular wheelsets (front/rear wheel pairs) are generally lighter than clincher wheelsets, because tubular rims do not require flanges for the tire bead; superlight carbon-fiber tubular rims in particular have made tubulars popular again. Tubular tires by themselves are often lighter than clinchers, too.

Another reason is that most riders find that tubulars ride and corner better than clinchers, particularly for cyclocross. Since the tubular casing is sewn together around the inner tube, tubulars can hold extremely high air pressures, which is why they're almost always used for track racing.

Tubulars can also operate at low air pressures with less risk of a pinch flat, since the rim has no flanges. That's why you'll find most high-end cyclocross bikes equipped with tubulars; reduced air pressure minimizes rolling resistance on rough surfaces and enlarges the tire contact area with the ground for increased traction.

But perhaps the main reason to consider tubulars is their inherent safety. In the event of a blowout, they stay on the rim. Clincher tires, when flat, fall into the rim well, and you may find yourself trying to ride on the slippery metal rim, rather than on rubber.

Tubulars usually deflate more slowly when punctured than clinchers because the air can escape only through the puncture hole. Clinchers let air escape all the way around the rim, and the next thing you know you're skittering around on metal. (Tubeless tires also solve this problem, and they don't require any glue; see §vi-7 through §vi-9 for more information.)

If the advantages appeal to you—and the disadvantages don't put you off—tubulars are a worthwhile alternative to the standard clincher setup.

vi-10

REMOVING A TUBULAR

1. **Remove the wheel (§ii-2 and §ii-11).**
2. **If the tire is not already flat, deflate it.** Tubular tires have Presta (or French) valves. To let air out, unscrew the little nut atop the valve stem a few turns, and push down on the thin rod (Fig. 6.4). See the Note in §vi-1 for instructions on dealing with valve extenders of various types.
3. **Push the tire off the rim in one section with your thumbs pushing up against one side.** If you can't get it up any farther than the center of the rim, then work at it the same way from the other side (in the same area) until the entire underside is unstuck there. Avoid using tools, because if you use a tool to pry the tire away from the glue, you will likely tear the base tape at the least and quite likely tear casing cords as well. The tire will always be lumpy in that area after such damage.

If you absolutely cannot get it off by hand in any area of the tire, carefully slide a thin screwdriver blade under it in an area where you have peeled it up as much as possible, working it under without damaging the base tape (alternating from each side if necessary) until the tip extends out from the other side. Then gently roll the screwdriver shaft along the rim, separating the tire as you go.

Stop when you've gone far enough that you can get your hand under the tire.

4. **Peel the tire off the rest of the way around the rim by hand.**

vi-11

GLUING (OR TAPING) TUBULAR TIRES

Gluing tubular tires to the rims properly is critical to continuing the attachment you have with your epidermis. Follow these steps, and your tire will really be secure! Pay particular attention to the second step, because all the rim cement in the world will not keep a tire on if the cement is not adhered to the tire.

1. **Before gluing a new tubular, first stretch it over the rim (Fig. 6.18A), inflate it, and leave it for at least a few hours, or overnight if possible.** To stretch it on, install the tire without any glue by using the method described in step 9.

NOTE: *If the wheel has a deep-section rim (deeper than 30mm) and the tubular has a standard-length Presta valve, you will need to install a valve extender (Figs. 6.6A–C) so that you can get air into the tire once it is on the rim. See the Note in §vi-1, step 2, for instructions on installation of the various types of valve extenders.*

Note too that some Vittoria tubular tires have a threaded stub where the valve would go, and you thread in a complete valve of the

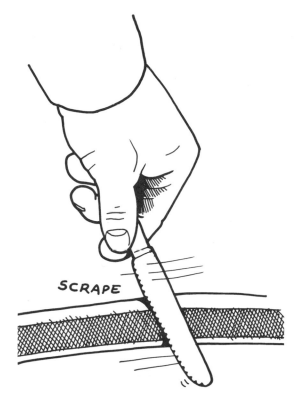

length you need for your specific rim (Fig. 6.6D). It operates like any other Presta valve. If you don't have a sufficiently long valve stem, you can use a removable-core valve extender (Fig. 6.6B) between the valve and the stub on the tube; the valve extender would be inverted from the way it works on standard removable-core valves.

2. **Remove the tubular after stretching.** The base tape on most tubulars is cotton and in many cases has a neoprene coating over it to which the rim cement will not bond well. If yours has this slick neoprene coating, scrape the base tape of the tubular with a serrated knife edge or metal file edge to produce a good gluing surface; the tire can roll off with an otherwise good glue job if the base tape has not been properly prepared. This step does not apply to most Challenge, Continental, and Tufo tubulars, which usually have no latex over the base tape.

3. **Start by pumping the tire (not on the rim) until it turns inside out and the base tape faces outward.** By using the serrations of a table knife or the rough side of a metal file, scrape the base tape back and forth (Fig. 6.18B) until its neoprene coating balls up into little sticky hunks. I have also heard of people brushing rubbing alcohol on the base tape to make the surface tacky. I generally discourage the use of solvents on the base tape for fear of solvent penetrating the tape and dissolving the glue holding the tape onto the tire, but rubbing alcohol is probably too mild to be an issue. I have seen many a tire roll right off the base tape because it was not glued well to the tire, even though the tape was well adhered to the rim, so stay away from stronger solvents.

4. **Prepare the rim for glue.** With a new rim, clean off any oil that may be present with

WHEELS AND TIRES

alcohol, VM&P Naphtha, or acetone (while wearing rubber gloves and a respirator) and a rag, followed by sandpaper. Roughing up the gluing surface with sandpaper may not help the tire stick to the rim better, but solvent will not remove everything (Teflon, for instance), and sandpaper can remove invisible contaminants that would prevent the glue from sticking to the rim.

NOTE ON TUBULAR GLUING TAPE: *Tire gluing is such a hassle that some riders prefer to use tubular rim tape, but it will not hold as well as a superior gluing job. For triathlons and time trials on moderate terrain without sharp corners, gluing tape may be sufficient, once you get through step 4, above, to properly prepare the tire and rim. I personally would not race a criterium, ride fast on a mountainous switchback descent, or do a cyclocross race with taped-on tires, especially on a hot day. It's not just the bond strength; there are instances of the tubular tape splitting down the middle, leaving a layer on the rim and a layer on the rolled-off tire. You will find opinions both raving about and warning against tubular tape and will have to make your own decision. Don't ride any tire that you can push off easily by hand.*

Tufo gluing tape (Fig. 6.18C) and "Belgian Tape" from cyclocrossworld.com are easy-to-use, double-sided tapes to attach a tubular to a rim without using rim cement. Tufo offers "standard" tubular gluing tape, which has backing on one side only, and "Extreme," which has backing on both sides.

To use Tufo standard single-sided tape, peel the backing off, stick it on the rim, cut through the tape to open the valve hole, and then install, center, and inflate the tire.

To use Tufo Extreme double-sided tape, first remove the backing from the bottom side, labeled as meant to adhere to the rim, and stick

6.18C Tufo tubular gluing tape

the tape onto the rim. Peel back the corners of the top-side (tire-side) backing at each end so that the corners stick out from the sides of the rim. Cut through the tape to open the valve hole and then install, inflate, and center the tire. Centering is easy with the slick backing allowing the tire to move. Pull the backing out from under the entire tire before inflating it to 130 psi. Ride on the tire for five minutes. Tufo tapes are ready to ride immediately after inflating and five minutes of riding on the tire.

Cyclocross mechanics often use cyclocrossworld.com's Belgian gluing tape along with rim cement to get a stronger bond (see step 7).

5. **With a rim that has been glued before, you can just apply a uniform layer of glue, unless there is a thick, lumpy layer of old glue on the rim.** In this case, knock the edge globs off with a knife; scrape or brush off the big lumps with a knife, screwdriver, or barbecue grill pad or brush to get the surface as uniform as you can; or strip the entire rim with acetone, VM&P Naphtha, or white gas. Be sure to wear rubber or nitrile gloves when working with these solvents, and remember that the fumes are dense and extremely flammable. Be sure to have plenty of ventilation, and don't work in an enclosed room where an exposed flame may be present, such as in a water heater or furnace.

6. **Put a thin layer of glue on the rim, edge to edge, and a thin layer edge to edge on**

the base tape of the inflated tire. The best way is to brush glue from a can with an acid brush (hardware stores sell them for welding and brazing); you can even squeeze tubes of glue into a can if you didn't buy it by the can. Otherwise, I recommend squeezing a bead out of the tube onto the rim or tire and then putting a plastic bag over your finger and spreading the glue thinly and uniformly. If you let the layer on the tire get too thick, the base tape of the tubular may become so rigid that it will tear; keep the tire layers especially thin. Let it dry (overnight is best) with the tire deflated so it won't shrink while drying. Repeat two more times.

7. **Alternatively, for cyclocross, apply double-sided Belgian Tape (from cyclocrossworld .com) on the rim after the second glue layer while it's tacky.** Press it into the rim bed. Peel off the backing, apply a third layer of glue to the rim (on top of the Belgian Tape) and tire, wait 15–30 minutes, and skip to step 9. For more on gluing cyclocross tires, see the Pro Tip on the subject in the 'cross section at the end of this chapter.

NOTE ON GLUE TYPE: *Except for carbon rims (see the Pro Tip on gluing a tubular to a carbon rim), I recommend using clear tubular rim cement, ideally Vittoria Mastik'One or else Continental rim cement, rather than red glues. Red glues can harden up, making the tire base tape rigid and the glue bond weak after a year.*

8. **After the three layers of glue on the rim and tire have dried (overnight), smear or brush another thin layer of glue on the rim.**

9. **If you have a spare tubular wheel with a rim free of glue, first stretch the tire onto this rim as below in step 10. Inflate it and then deflate it.** Then pull it off and repeat step 10 on the freshly glued rim. This will make stretching the tire over the glued rim much easier, and you will end up with less glue smeared all over you and the rim.

10. **Mount the (deflated) tire as follows:**

    a. Stand the wheel with the valve hole facing up.

    b. Put the valve stem through the hole, and, leaning over the wheel, grab the tire and stretch outward as you push the base tape into the top of the rim. Keep stretching down on the tire with both hands, using your body weight, as you push the tire down around the rim (Fig. 6.18A). I like to lean hard enough on the tire that my feet lift repeatedly off the ground. The farther you can stretch the tire at this point, the easier it will be to get the last bit of tire onto the rim.

    c. Lifting the rim up to horizontal with the valve side against your belly, roll the last bit of the tire onto the opposite side of the rim. If you can't get the tire to pop over the rim, peel the tire back and start over, pushing down again from the valve stem. Avoid prying a stubborn tire onto the rim with screwdrivers or other tools, as you will likely tear cords in the base tape and tire casing, leading to a bulge in the tire in this area.

11. By pulling the tire this way and that, get the edge of the base tape aligned with the rim. You want to see the same amount sticking out from the rim all the way around on both sides around the wheel.

12. Pump the tire to 100 psi (50 psi for a cyclocross tubular) and spin the wheel, looking for wobbles in the tire. If you find that the tread snakes back and forth as you spin the wheel, deflate the tire and push it over where required. Reinflate and check again, repeating the process until the tire is as straight as

Carbon rims are notoriously hard to glue to. The thick, gloppy Clément red glue of yesteryear seems to adhere best, but it is no longer available unless you know somebody with a stash. Otherwise, Vittoria Mastik'One seems to be the best choice, according to research done at the University of Kansas.

Tires tend to snap off carbon rims rather than peel off; they require about the same amount of force to get them started off the rim, but then they can continue to roll right off, rather than needing additional force to remove, as with a well-glued tubular on an aluminum rim. Follow the above multiple-layer gluing procedure with clean rims and scraped base tape. It is worth pulling your tire off after you have it glued on and cured to see how well you did. Then reglue it the same way again, especially if all of the glue pulled off the rim in the process. For cyclocross, see the Pro Tip on gluing 'cross tires at the end of this chapter.

you are able to get it. The final process will depend somewhat on how accurately the tubular was made; some brands and models glue on straighter than others.

13. Pump the tire up to 120–130 psi (60 psi for a cyclocross tubular) and leave it overnight to bond firmly. You can get an even better bond by using a woodworker's band (miter) clamp around the entire inflated tire. The miter clamp (see Fig. 1.2) is a piece of nylon webbing with a ratchet-lock buckle on it. Depress the tab on the buckle to let out enough strap to surround the inflated tire and wheel. Pull the end of the strap to tighten the loop around the tire. Use a wrench to tighten the clamp and put extra pressure down on the tire to conform its bottom surface to the rim and bond it tightly. Tomorrow you can release the miter clamp (by using the release [thumb] tab) and go ride or race on this wheel.

vi-12

CHANGING A TUBULAR TIRE ON THE ROAD

If you get a puncture out on the road with a tubular tire, it may be easier to deal with than a flat clincher, provided you can peel the old tire off without too much struggle and too many blood blisters on your thumbs. Be sure to carry a spare tubular that already has glue on the base tape. For your spare, carry an old tubular that has been glued to a rim in the past, or, with a new tire as a spare, either apply glue to the base tape as instructed in §vi-11 before packing the tire as a spare, or bring along gluing tape.

Remove the wheel and pull the flat tire off the rim. If you did a good gluing job, this may take some doing. (On the other hand, if the tubular is easy to peel off, you need to improve your gluing technique.) Stretch the spare tire onto the rim as in Fig. 6.18A. Pump it up hard (over 100 psi) to get it to stay on the rim for the rest of the ride. Corner carefully going home, as the glue bond is marginal. When you get home, glue a tire securely on the rim before riding that wheel again.

vi-13

PATCHING TUBULAR TIRES

In the early 1980s, my racing buddies and I spent countless hours patching tubular tires, often while sitting in the car on the way to distant races. Now that everyone trains on clinchers, nobody seems to patch tubulars anymore. Tubulars arguably are the best tires for racing, being lighter, working on lighter rims, staying on the rim when punctured, and having excellent cornering and descending characteristics. However, even though tubulars are expensive, it makes no sense to patch a racing tire because you invest too much time, energy, and money competing in races to run the risk of getting a puncture due to a weakened tire. Also, tubulars with slow leaks can be easily and permanently fixed by injecting liquid sealant into them (§vi-14).

If for some reason you still wish to patch a tubular, here are the steps involved:

1. **Remove the tire from the rim.**
2. **Pump up the tire to 70 psi (50 psi for a cyclocross tubular), or as high as you can, and find the leak by submerging the inflated tire in a bucket of water.** If you're lucky, air will come out through a hole in the tread. In the case of a pinched tube, though, the air may seep out through the casing randomly at the stitches, and be hard to pinpoint. See the next step for help.
3. **For 2 inches on either side of the puncture, peel away the base tape covering the stitching.** If you were unable to precisely locate the hole, try submerging the inflated tire now to watch the bubbles coming out through the stitching. Peel more base tape back if necessary until you are sure that you have exposed the stitching nearest the hole.
4. **Deflate the tire and carefully cut the outer layer of stitching threads for an inch or so on either side of the hole.** Pull the casing open in that spot, and pull enough of the tube out through the hole to find (§vi-2) and access the hole(s) in it.
5. **Patch the tube in the same manner as outlined in §vi-3.** Use the same type of recommended patches.

6. **Push the tube back in place, and sew the opening in the stitching closed by hand.** I recommend using a needle made for leather with a triangular cross-section tip and braided high-test fishing line. Stitch one way across the opening, turn the tire around, and double back over the stitches again. For obvious reasons, be careful not to poke the tube. You may need a thimble to push the needle in and a pair of pliers to pull it out on each stitch.
7. **Inflate the tire to 70 psi or so (50 psi for a cyclocross tubular) to make sure all of the leaks have been patched.**
8. **Deflate the tire and coat the peeled-back section of base tape and the exposed stitching area with contact cement.** Barge cement (a brand originally made for shoes and available in hardware stores) works great. Wait 15 minutes or so for the glue to set, and carefully stick the base tape back down over the stitching. (If the tape stretched when you pulled it loose, it's permissible to cut it and overlap the ends.)
9. **Coat the rim and the tire base tape with a thin layer of rim cement.** Let it sit 15 minutes to an hour. Because this is an old tire, there should already be a good layer of rim cement on the tire and the rim.
10. **Glue the tire onto the rim (§vi-11).**

vi-14

TIRE SEALANTS

Tire sealants can virtually eliminate flat tires caused by tread punctures; they generally do not fix sidewall cuts or holes, pinch flats, or rim-side punctures. A typical tire sealant, Slime, is a green goo full of chopped fibers; when poured into an inner tube, it flows to punctures and seals them. There are other brands and colors of fibrous tire sealants as well; these instructions generally apply to them all, and I will use the word "Slime" to refer to the entire class of them.

Another type of sealant is thinner and has a liquid latex or similar base. It can come as a liquid in a bottle, like Stan's NoTubes, Caffélatex, or Schwalbe Doc Blue sealant, or it can come as an aerosol, like Vittoria Pit Stop or Hutchinson Fast'Air.

NOTE: *You can also purchase tubes with sealant already inside.*

a. Latex sealant foam installation into a Presta valve, inner tube, tubular tire, or tubeless tire

This is a great way to get extra life out of a tubular with a slow leak. This method is also useful prophylactically or as an on-the-road fix for a slow leak in an inner tube. It's also highly recommended for any tubeless road tire and can be a necessity to get a tubeless tire to seal against the rim.

The tire (and tube, if applicable) should be installed on the rim before adding sealant.

1. **Deflate the tire, if it is not already deflated.**
2. **Screw or push the end of the nozzle onto the open Presta valve (Figs. 1.1B, 6.4).**
3. **Depress the button on the aerosol sealant can (Fig. 6.19A) and hold it down until the full contents are deployed into the tire.** This will inflate the tire as well as fill it with sealant.
4. **If the tire has a leak, rotate the wheel until the hole is at the bottom, and hold it that way until the sealant has filled the hole and no more air is escaping.** Go for a ride, or spin the wheel for a while to further spread the sealant around in the tube.

Alternatively, the old-school way to seal a slow leak in a tubular or an inner tube, or

6.19A Aerosol latex-based tire sealants

to add some puncture resistance to either, is to pour a can of evaporated milk into a pump you don't care about and pump it in through the Presta valve. It works quite well for tiny leaks, but if you get a blowout, boy, does it ever stink!

b. Sealing a tubular, Presta-valve inner tube (especially with a removable valve core) or tubeless tire with liquid latex-type tire sealant

The Presta valve must have a removable core, which separate inner tubes rarely have, but which good tubulars and some tubeless valves do have. If the valve core is removable, there will be two wrench flats present on opposite sides of the small valve-cap threads.

1. **Unscrew the valve core (counterclockwise) with an adjustable wrench or specific Presta valve-core wrench and remove it.** (You can use the Caffélatex with its injector even without a removable valve core, since it won't seal the valve, but Stan's sealant will.)
2. **With the valve at the bottom, jam the tip of a squeeze bottle of liquid latex sealant into the valve stem (or the Caffélatex syringe hose without its brass fitting onto the valve stem) and squeeze.** Inject a couple of fluid ounces inside.

6.19B Injectable tire sealants

3. Screw the valve core back in (clockwise).

4. Pump the tire to full pressure.

5. If the tube has a leak, rotate the wheel until the hole is at the bottom, and hold it that way until the sealant has filled the hole and no more air is escaping. Go ride, or spin the wheel for a while to further spread the sealant in the tube.

c. Slime installation into a Schrader-valve inner tube

Only use Slime (Fig. 6.19B) in an inner tube with a Schrader valve (Figs. 1.1B, 6.5); you cannot insert Slime into a Presta valve because it will block the valve. You can fix small punctures this way and/ or protect the tube against future punctures.

The tire and tube should be installed on a rim before adding sealant.

1. Shake the Slime bottle.

2. Remove the Schrader valve core by using a valve-core remover. One is usually packaged with the Slime.

3. Rotate the wheel so that the valve stem is at the four o'clock position.

4. Cut off the bottle spout, and connect the bottle spout and valve stem with the supplied tubing.

5. Squeeze the bottle slowly to inject the Slime.

6. Stop squeezing after injecting 4 fluid ounces. Wait several minutes to clear the stem.

7. Remove the tubing from the valve.

8. Screw the valve core firmly back into the valve stem in a clockwise direction.

9. Inflate the tire.

10. If the tube has a leak, rotate the wheel until the hole is at the bottom, and hold it that way until the Slime has filled the hole and no more air is escaping. Go ride, or spin the wheel for a while to further spread the Slime around in the tube.

d. Maintaining sealant-filled tires

Inflating or deflating

Always have the stem at four o'clock and wait a minute for the sealant to drain away; if you don't, sealant will leak out, eventually clogging the valve.

Sealing punctures

1. If you find the tire has gone flat, pump it up and ride it a bit to see if it seals.

2. If you get numerous punctures, you may need to pump repeatedly and ride before the tube seals up.

3. Embedded nails and other foreign objects can be removed. Rotate the wheel to place the hole at the bottom to seal the hole.

4. Pinch flats, caused by pinching the tube between the tire and rim, are nearly impossible to seal because one of the two "snake-bite" holes is on the rim side. You will need to replace the tube.

5. Punctures on the rim side of the tube will not seal because the sealant is thrown to the outside by centrifugal force.

6. Sidewall gashes need to be patched, and the tire needs to be replaced.

vi-15

CHECKING RIM CONDITION

LEVEL 2

After the tires, your bike's rims are your next line of contact with the road. You never want a wheel to fail on you while you are riding, as the consequences can be severe. To ensure that this won't happen to you, replace any rim that has a significant defect. Chapter 12 describes how to rebuild a wheel with a new rim, should you decide to do it yourself.

Check over the rims for cracks, particularly at the spoke holes, the valve hole, and the seam (opposite the valve hole). If you find a crack, the rim should be replaced immediately.

Inspect the rims for a wear indicator. Modern rims have indicators to let you know when brakes have worn the rim sidewalls too thin. On a clincher rim, if the sidewalls become too thin, the tire can push the sidewalls out and fold them open like a limp taco shell, causing braking and tire-retention issues. On a tubular rim, a rim worn thin from braking simply becomes weak enough to collapse.

Safety indicators take different forms. In some cases, they consist of small holes drilled partway into the brake track that, once gone, indicate that too much sidewall material has been worn off. Others have a dark spot underneath the surface that appears once the wear limit has been reached. Mavic rims have a dark hole that appears when the rim is deeply worn; the hole is directly opposite the valve stem hole and is identified by a sticker.

vi-16

TRUING A WHEEL

For more information on truing wheels, see Chapter 12 on wheel building (§xii-4).

You can fix a mild wobble by adjusting the tension on the spokes. An extreme bend in the rim cannot be fixed by spoke truing alone, because the spoke tension on the two sides of the wheel will be so uneven that the wheel will rapidly fall apart. If you have a bent rim that cannot be corrected with spoke truing, you can try banging it into shape to use temporarily to get yourself home (see §iii-10 and Fig. 3.11).

1. **Check that there are no broken spokes in the wheel, or any spokes that are so loose that they flop around.** If there is a broken spoke, follow the replacement procedure in §vi-17. If there is a single loose spoke, check to see that the rim is not dented or cracked in that area. If the rim is damaged, replace it. If the rim looks okay, mark the loose spoke with a piece of tape and tighten its nipple with a spoke wrench (see step 5 regarding tightening direction) until it feels like it has tension similar to other spokes coming from the same side of the hub (pluck the spoke and feel for tension as well as listen to the tone). Then continue with the truing procedure.

2. **Grab the rim while the wheel is on the bike, and flex it side to side to check the hub-bearing adjustment.** If the bearings are loose, the wheel will clunk side to side. The play in the bearings will have to be eliminated before you true the wheel or the rim will wobble erratically because of the loose hub. Follow the hub-adjustment procedure in §vi-20d, steps 29–32.

3. **Put the wheel in a truing stand, if you have one.** Otherwise, leave it on the bike and suspend the bike in a bike stand or from the ceiling, or turn it upside down on the handlebar and saddle.

4. **Adjust the truing stand feeler, or hold one of the brake pads so that it scrapes the rim at the biggest wobble.**

5. **Where the rim scrapes, tighten the spoke (or spokes) that come(s) to the rim from the opposite side of the hub, and loosen the spoke(s) that come(s) from the same side of the hub (Figs. 6.20, 6.21).** This process will pull the rim away from the feeler or brake pad. Spokes and nipples have standard right-hand threads: righty tighty, lefty loosey. See the Note below to help keep things straight.

NOTE: *When correcting a wheel that is laterally out of true (wobbles side to side), always adjust spokes coming from both sides of the wheel.*

NOTE ON DIRECTION TO TURN THE NIPPLES: *Adjusting spokes is like opening or closing an upside-down jar. With the jar right side up, turning the lid to the left (counterclockwise) opens the jar, but you'd turn the lid the opposite (clockwise) direction when you turn the jar upside down (try it and see). Spoke nipples are just like the lid on that upside-down jar. When the nipples are at the bottom of the rim (Fig. 6.22), counterclockwise tightens (shortens the spoke, like closing the lid shortens the jar plus lid), and clockwise loosens (lengthens the spoke, as unscrewing the lid lengthens the jar plus lid until the jar opens). The opposite is true when the nipples to be turned are at the top. It may take you a few attempts before you catch on, but you will eventually get it. If you temporarily make the wheel worse, simply undo what you have done and start over.*

Note that rotation direction for the nipples on some Shimano wheels is the opposite of this because the nipples screw into the rim. There is also a little sleeve that screws onto the (right-hand) threads on the hub end of the spoke, after the spoke has been slid through its hub hole.

Tighten and loosen about a quarter turn at a time, decreasing the amount you turn the spoke nipples as you move away from the spot where the rim scrapes the hardest. If the wobble gets worse,

6.20 Lateral truing if rim scrapes on the left

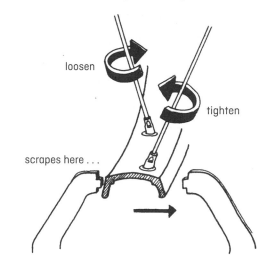

6.21 Lateral truing if rim scrapes on the right

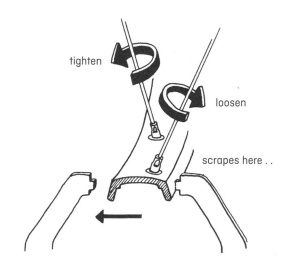

6.22 Tightening and loosening spokes

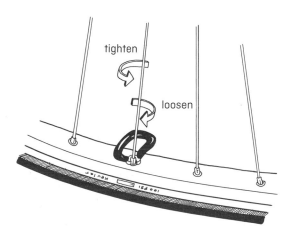

WHEELS AND TIRES

you are turning the spokes in the wrong direction.
NOTE ON TWISTED SPOKES: *As you turn the nipple on a tight spoke, particularly a thin one or a flat, aero one, it will tend to twist. To avoid this, when you tighten or loosen a spoke, twist it in the direction that corrects the problem, and then twist back half as far. This will be enough to unwind most spokes, but aero ones or superlight ones will still have a twist in them. With superthin round ones, you won't really be able to tell until you go for a ride; the wheel may then "ping" at first as the spokes unwind and settle in. You may need to re-true the wheel once they have settled in. With aero spokes, it is best to hold the spoke from twisting as you turn the nipple. The best tool for steel aero spokes, from DT Swiss, is a red plastic spoke key with a long, conical groove down the spoke side to fit an L-shaped steel tool to keep the spoke from twisting (§i-4, Fig. 1.4). The long part of the L-shaped tool is slotted for the aero spoke to keep it from twisting as you turn the nipple, and its conical exterior fits in the groove in the spoke key. For Mavic aluminum flat spokes, use Mavic's plastic ring with slots.*

NOTE ON INTERNAL NIPPLES: *Some deep-section wheels have the nipples inside the rim to reduce aerodynamic drag. To adjust the nipples, you must remove the tire and, in the case of a clincher, the rim strip as well. Then you reach down into the spoke holes with the correct-size socket. The simplest tool for this is either a Y-wrench with 5mm and 5.5mm hex sockets and a square-drive socket (for upside-down standard nipples inside the rim) on the ends of its three long arms (§i-4, Fig. 1.4) or a specialty wrench for the internal spoke nipples.*

NOTE ON NIPPLES AT THE HUB: *Some wheels have the spoke nipples at the hub, not at the rim. Before you turn them, think carefully about which way tightens and which way loosens. Remember that if you want the spoke tighter (shorter), it*

is like tightening a jar lid. So if you are looking down the spoke toward the hub, it's like looking at an upside-down jar, whose lid you would thus tighten by turning it counterclockwise.

6. **As the rim moves into proper alignment, readjust the truing-stand feeler or the brake pad so that it again finds the most out-of-true spot on the wheel.**

7. **Check the wobble first on one side of the wheel and then the other, adjusting spokes accordingly.** You want to make sure that you don't end up pulling the whole wheel off center by chasing wobbles only on one side. As the wheel gets closer to true, you will need to decrease the amount you turn each spoke; otherwise, you will overcorrect.

8. **Accept a certain amount of wobble if you are truing the wheel in a bike.** The method is not very accurate and is not at all suited for making a wheel absolutely true. If you have access to a wheel-dishing tool, check to make sure that the wheel is centered (§xii-5, Figs. 12.22, 12.23).

NOTE ON ROUNDNESS: *I have discussed only lateral truing here, but a wheel can also get out of round from banging something hard; it's much less likely to lose radial trueness from spokes loosening than it is to lose lateral trueness. If the wheel is not dented, you may be able to improve its roundness without having so large a tension difference in the spokes from section to section of the wheel that it is unstable and falls apart rapidly. Consult §xii-4b, Figures 12.20, 12.21, to see how to radially true the wheel.*

vi-17

REPLACING A BROKEN SPOKE

Go to the bike store and get a new spoke of the same length. Remember, the spokes on the front wheel are usually not the same length as the spokes on the rear wheel. Also, the spokes on the drive (right) side of the rear wheel are almost always shorter than those on the non-drive (left) side.

1. **Make sure you are using a replacement spoke of the proper thickness and length.**

2. **Thread the spoke through the spoke hole in the hub flange in the same direction (from the inside out or from the outside in) that the broken one went through.** If the broken spoke is on the drive side of the rear wheel, you will need to remove the cassette cogs or the freewheel to get at the hub flange (§vi-24 and §vi-25).

3. **Weave the new spoke in with the other spokes just as it was before (Fig. 6.23).** It may take some bending to get it in place.

4. **Thread it into the same nipple, if the nipple is in good shape.** Otherwise, use a new nipple; you'll need to remove the tire, tube, and rim strip (or the tubular tire) to install the nipple.

5. **Mark the new spoke with a piece of tape and tighten it about as snugly as the neighboring spokes coming from the same side of the hub (usually multiples of two away on either side).**

6. **Follow the steps for truing a wheel as outlined in §vi-16.**

HUBS

vi-18

OVERHAULING HUBS

LEVEL 2

Hubs should turn smoothly and noiselessly. If you maintain them regularly, expect them to run smoothly when you are ready to give up on the rest of your bike.

All hubs have a hub shell that contains the axle and bearings and is connected to the rim

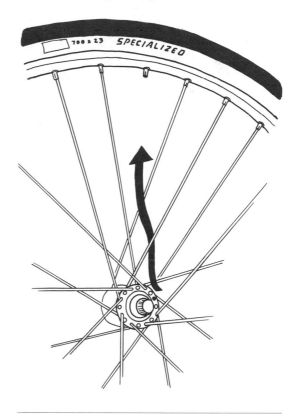

with spokes or, in the case of disc wheels, with sheets of composite material. Beyond that, they diverge into two types: the loose-bearing cup-and-cone type (Fig. 6.24) and the sealed-bearing (or cartridge-bearing) type (Fig. 6.25).

Cup-and-cone hubs have loose ball bearings that roll along very smooth bearing surfaces called "races" or "cups." An axle runs through the center of the hub. Conical nuts, called "cones" (Fig. 6.24), thread onto the axle. The cones create an inner race for the bearings. In high-quality hubs, the cup-and-cone surfaces that contact the bearings are precisely machined to minimize friction. The operation of the hub depends on the smoothness and lubrication of the cones, ball bearings, and bearing cups. The cones are held in place on the axle by one or more spacers (washers) followed by threaded locknuts that tighten down against the cones and spacers to keep the hub in proper adjustment. In the absence of a locknut,

6.24 Cup-and-cone front hub with standard ball bearings

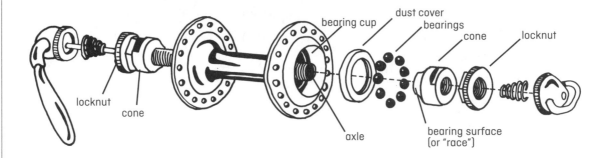

6.25 Front hub with cartridge bearing

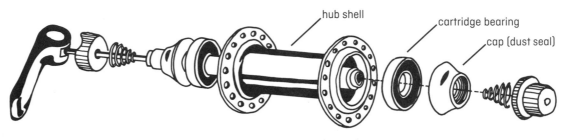

the cone will be slotted at the end and will have a pinch bolt, which, when tightened, prevents the cone from unscrewing. The rear hub will generally have more spacers than the front, especially on the drive side (Fig. 6.37).

The term "sealed-bearing" hub is a bit of a misnomer, because some cup-and-cone hubs offer better protection against dirt and water than some sealed-bearing hubs. The phrase "cartridge-bearing hub" is more accurate, because the distinguishing feature of these hubs is that the ball bearings, races, and cones are assembled as a complete unit—the cartridge—that is then plugged into a hub shell. Cartridge-bearing front hubs have two bearings, one on each end of the hub shell (Fig. 6.25). Rear hubs may have a cartridge bearing on either end of the hub (Fig. 6.36) with loose balls inside of the freehub; they may have multiple cartridge bearings and/or bushings inside the freehub as well as the two on the ends of the hubs (Fig. 6.45); or they may have a cartridge bearing in the left (non-drive) side only

and may employ a stock Shimano freehub with loose hub bearings as well as loose freehub bearings on the drive side.

Cartridge-bearing hubs can have any number of axle-assembly types. Some have a threaded axle with locknuts (Fig. 6.36), similar to a cup-and-cone hub. More common in high-end hubs are aluminum axles (sometimes carbon-fiber or very thin-wall steel axles), often very large in diameter with correspondingly large bearings. Their end caps usually snap on (Fig. 6.45) or are held on with setscrews or circlips. The end caps may also thread into the axle and accept a 5mm hex key in the end of each cap.

vi-19

ALL HUBS, PRELIMINARY

1. Remove the wheel from the bike (§ii-2 and §ii-11).

2. Remove the quick-release skewer or the nuts and washers holding the wheel onto

the bike. (This step is unnecessary for hubs that have solid axles held on with nuts or wing nuts, rather than having skewers that pass through hollow axles.)

vi-20

OVERHAUL STANDARD CUP-AND-CONE HUB (FRONT OR REAR)

To isolate problems, take some time to evaluate the hub's condition before disassembling it. Spin the hub while holding the axle, and turn the axle while holding the hub. Does it turn roughly? Is the axle bent or broken? Wobble the axle side to side. Is the bearing adjustment loose?

a. Disassembly

1. **Set the wheel flat on a table or workbench.** On a rear wheel, work on the left (non-drive) side. Slip a cone wrench of the appropriate size (usually 13mm, 14mm, or 15mm) onto the wrench flats on one of the cones. If the cone has a slot and a pinch bolt on it (and takes a much bigger cone wrench than those listed here), read the Note below.

NOTE ON CAMPAGNOLO AND FULCRUM: *On current Campagnolo and Fulcrum high-end hubs, you must unscrew the axle into two pieces with 5mm hex keys inserted into either end of the axle. Loosen the setscrew on the large, aluminum, split locknut with a 2.5mm hex key (loosen the setscrew three turns). Unscrew and remove the locknut with your fingers or with a 22mm (or adjustable) wrench. Push the axle end toward the hub to free the slide-on cone. Follow steps 7–27, and then assemble in the reverse order. For a rear hub, see §vi-26e for hints on reinstalling the freehub pawls into the hub shell. Adjust the hub by turning the locknut by hand or with a 22mm (or adjustable) wrench until the bearing end play is removed, and tighten the setscrew*

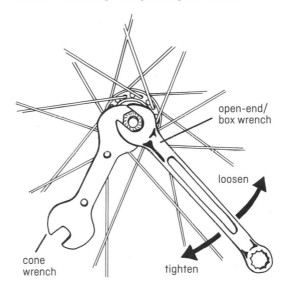

with a 2.5mm hex key. This adjustment can even be performed while the wheel is installed in the frame or fork to get it extremely precise—free-running with no end play.

2. **Put an appropriately sized wrench or adjustable wrench on the locknut on the same side.**

3. **While holding the cone with the cone wrench, loosen the locknut (Fig. 6.26).** This may take considerable force, because the parts are usually tightened against each other securely to maintain the hub's adjustment. Make sure that you are unscrewing the locknut counterclockwise (lefty loosey, righty tighty).

4. **As soon as the locknut loosens, move the cone wrench from the cone on top to the cone on the opposite end of the axle, in order to hold the axle in place as you unscrew the locknut.** On a rear hub, put another open-end wrench on the opposite locknut. Unscrew the loose locknut with your fingers; use a wrench if necessary.

5. **Slide off any spacers, keeping track of where they came from.** If they will not slide

off, the cone will push them off when you unscrew it. Note that some spacers have a small tooth or "key" that corresponds to a lengthwise groove in the axle. Keep these lined up to facilitate removal.

6. **Unscrew the cone from the axle.** Again, you may need to hold the opposite cone with a wrench.

7. **Keep track of the various nuts, spacers, and cones by placing them on your workbench in the order they were removed.** If that seems too casual, you can slide a twist tie, zip tie, or string through the axle and all of the parts in the correct order and orientation. Either method serves as an easy guide when reassembling the hub.

8. **To catch any bearings that may fall out, put your hand over the end of the hub from which you removed the nuts and spacers and flip the wheel over.** Have a rag underneath the wheel to catch stray bearings.

9. **Pull the axle up and out, being careful not to lose any bearings that fall out of the hub or stick briefly to the axle.** Leave the cone, spacers, and locknut all tightened together on the opposite end of the axle from the one you disassembled. If you are replacing a bent or broken axle, measure the amount of axle sticking out beyond the locknut. Put the cone, spacers, and locknut on the new axle identically.

10. **Remove all of the ball bearings from both sides of the hub.** They may stick to a screwdriver with a coating of grease on the tip, or you can push them down through the center of the hub and out the other side with the screwdriver. Tweezers or a magnetic screwdriver may also be useful for removing bearings. Put the bearings in a cup, a jar lid, or the like. Count the bearings, and make sure you have the same number from each side.

6.27 Removing the dust caps

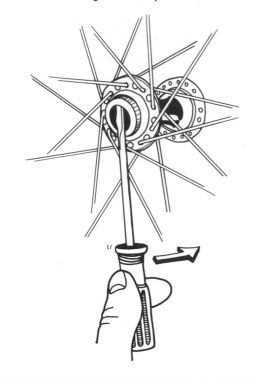

11. **With a screwdriver, gently pop off the seals (i.e., the dust caps) that are pressed into either end of the hub shell (Fig. 6.27).** Be careful not to deform them; leave them in if you can't pop them out without damage. If they are not removed, it is tedious, but not impossible, to clean the dirty grease out of their concave interior with a rag and a thin screwdriver and perhaps some solvent.

b. Cleaning

12. **Clean the hub shell parts.** Wipe out the hub shell with a rag. Remove all dirt and grease from the bearing surfaces. With a screwdriver, push a rag through the hub shell and spin it to clean out the hub-shell axle hole. Wipe off the outer faces of the shell. Finish with a very clean rag on the bearing surfaces, which should be shiny and completely free of dirt or grease. If the hub has been neglected, the grease may have solidi-

fied and glazed over so completely that you will need a solvent to remove it. Wear gloves while working with the solvent. If you are working on a rear cassette hub, take this opportunity to lubricate the freehub. (See §vi-26 on lubricating freehubs.)

13. **Clean the running parts.** Wipe down the axle, nuts, and cones with a rag. Clean the cones well with a clean rag; strive for spotless. Again, solvent may be required if the grease has solidified. Get any dirt out of the threads on the disassembled axle end to prevent the cone from pushing the dirt into the hub upon reassembly.

14. **Wipe the grease and dirt off the seals.** A rag over the end of a screwdriver is sometimes useful to get inside. Again, glaze-hard grease may have to be removed with a solvent. Keep solvent out of the freehub body.

15. **Clean the bearing balls.** Wipe off the bearings by rubbing all of them together between two rags. This may be sufficient to clean them completely, but small specks of dirt can still adhere to them, so I advise the next step as well.

16. **Polish the bearings.** (If you are overhauling low-quality hubs, you can skip to the next step.) I prefer to wash bearing balls in a plugged sink with an abrasive soap like Lava, rubbing them between my hands as if I were washing my palms. This really gets them shining, unless they are caked with glaze-hard grease. Make sure you have plugged the sink drain! This method has the added advantage of getting my hands clean for the assembly step. It is silly to contaminate your superclean parts with dirty hands. If there is hardened glaze on the bearings, soak them in solvent. If that does not remove it, buy new bearings at the bike shop. Take a few of the old bearings along so that you get the right size.

17. **Dry all bearings and any other wet parts.** Inspect the bearings and bearing surfaces carefully. If any of the bearings have pits or gouges in them, replace all of them. Same goes for the cones. A patina or lack of sheen on balls and cones indicates wear and is cause for replacement. Most bike shops stock replacement cones. If the bearing races (or cups) in the hub shell are pitted, the only thing you can do is buy new hubs. Regular maintenance and proper adjustment can prevent pitted bearing races.

NOTE ON BEARING INSPECTION: *Using new ball bearings when overhauling standard cup-and-cone hubs ensures round, smooth bearings; however, do not avoid performing an overhaul just because you don't have any new ball bearings. Inspect the bearings carefully. If there is even the slightest hint of uneven wear or pitting on the balls, cups, or cones, throw the bearings out and complete the overhaul with new bearings. Err on the side of caution.*

c. Assembly and lubrication

18. **Press the seals or dust covers in on both ends of the hub shell.**

19. **Smear grease with your clean finger into the bearing race on one end of the hub shell.** I like using light-colored or clear grease so that I can see if it gets dirty, but any bike grease will do. Grease not only lubricates the bearings, but also forms a barrier to dirt and water, so use enough grease to cover the balls halfway. Too much grease will slow the hub by packing around the axle.

20. **Stick half of the ball bearings into the grease, making sure you put in the same number of bearings that came out.** Distribute them uniformly around in the bearing race.

21. **Smear some grease on the cone that is still attached to the axle, and slide the**

6.28 Pushing inward on the axle   **6.29** Seating the bottom cone in the bearings

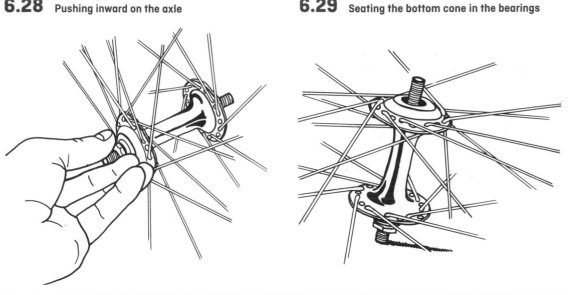

axle into the hub shell. Lift the wheel up a bit (30-degree angle), so that you can push the axle in until the cone slides into position, keeping all the bearings in place. On rear hubs, it is important to replace the axle and cone assembly into the same side of the hub from which it was removed to preserve drive-side cog spacing.

22. **Holding the axle pushed inward with one hand to secure the bearings, turn the wheel over (Fig. 6.28).**

23. **Smear grease into the bearing race that is now facing up.** Lift the wheel and allow the axle to slide down just enough so that it is not sticking up past the bearing race. Make sure no bearings fall out of the bottom. If the race and bearings are properly greased and the axle remains in the hub shell, they are not likely to fall out.

24. **While the top end of the axle is still below the bearing race, place the remaining bearings uniformly around in the grease.** Make sure you have inserted the correct number of bearings.

25. **Slide the axle back up into place.** Set the wheel down on the table, so that the wheel

rests on the lower axle end, seating the cone into the bearings (Fig. 6.29).

26. **Cover the top cone with a film of grease and then, with your fingers, screw it into place, seating it snugly onto the bearings.**

27. **In correct order, slide on the washer and any spacers.** Properly align any washers that have a little tooth or "key" that fits into a lengthwise groove in the axle.

28. **Use your finger to screw on the locknut.** Note that the two sides of the locknut are not the same. If you are unsure about which way the locknut goes back on, check the orientation of the locknut that is on the opposite end of the axle (this locknut was not removed during this overhaul and is assumed to be in the correct orientation). As a general rule, the rough surface of the locknut faces out so that it can get a good purchase on the dropout.

d. Hub adjustment

29. **Thread the cone onto the axle until it lightly contacts the bearings.** The axle should turn smoothly without any roughness or grinding, and there should be a small amount of

6.30 Tightening the locknut with another wrench

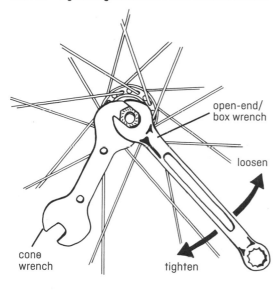

cone wrench

open-end/box wrench

loosen

tighten

lateral play. Thread the locknut down until it is snug against the cone.

30. **Tighten the locknut.** Place the cone wrench into the flats of the hub cone. While holding the cone steady, tighten the locknut with another wrench (Fig. 6.30). Tighten it about as snugly as you can against the cone and spacers, in order to hold the adjustment. Be sure that you are tightening the locknut and not the cone; you can ruin the hub if you tighten the cone hard against the bearings. On a Campagnolo or Fulcrum hub with a split cone, tighten the cone's pinch bolt now.

31. **Check and adjust play.** If there is too much play in the axle when you are done, or if the bearings are tight, loosen the locknut while holding the cone with the cone wrench. If the hub is too tight, unscrew the cone a bit. If the hub is too loose, screw the cone in a bit. You may need to put a wrench on the opposite-side cone to effectively tighten or loosen the cone you are adjusting.

32. **Repeat steps 29–31 until the hub adjustment feels right.** There should be a slight amount of axle-end play so that the pres-

sure of the quick-release skewer will compress it to perfect adjustment. (A hub held on with a nut—no quick release—should be adjusted with no bearing play.) Tighten the locknut firmly against the cone to hold the adjustment.

NOTE ON HUB ADJUSTMENT: *You may find that tightening the locknut against the cone suddenly turns your "Mona Lisa" perfect hub adjustment into something slightly less beautiful. If it is too tight, back off both cones (with a cone wrench on either side of the hub, each on one cone) a fraction of a turn. If too loose, tighten both locknuts a bit. If it's still off, you may have to loosen one side and go back to step 30. It's rare that I get a hub adjustment perfectly dialed in on the first try, so don't be dismayed if you have to tinker with the adjustment a bit before it's right. You have to have the wheel tightened into the bike to assess the hub adjustment; grab the rim and push it back and forth to check for bearing play.*

33. **Put the skewer back into the hub.** Make sure that the conical springs have their narrow ends toward the inside (Fig. 6.24).

34. **Install the wheel in the bike and tighten the skewer.** Check that the wheel spins well without any side play at the rim. If it needs readjustment, go back to step 32.

35. **Congratulate yourself on a job well done!** Hub overhaul is a delicate job, and it makes a difference in the longevity and performance of your bike.

vi-21

OVERHAUL OR REPLACE HUB CARTRIDGE BEARINGS

Compared with inexpensive hubs with cup-and-cone bearings, cartridge-bearing hubs generally do not need much maintenance, though some

WHEELS AND TIRES

are certainly much better sealed than others. If you ride in rain a lot or clean your bike with a high-pressure sprayer, however, you can expect water and dirt to get through any kind of seal. If the ball bearings inside the cartridges get wet or dirty, the cartridge bearings will soon seize up and should be overhauled or replaced.

a. Removing the bearings

If you can easily get at the rubber bearing seal, you may not need to remove the bearings to grease them. See step 1 below.

There are many types of cartridge-bearing hubs (Figs. 6.25, 6.31, 6.46, 6.47), and it is outside the scope of this book to explain how to disassemble every one of them, but the instructions below certainly cover the vast majority of them (and see specific details of rear Mavic hub overhaul in §vi-26d). It is usually not too hard to figure out how to take apart any hub.

Most cartridge-bearing hubs generally have axle end caps that butt up against the bearings and must be removed to remove the axle. The axle removal can be initiated by one of the following approaches:

- Pulling or prying off the end caps. You may need an axle-clamp tool (§i-4, Fig. 1.4) clamped in a vise to grab the tip of the end cap securely enough to pull it off by pulling up on the wheel.
- Unscrewing the end caps with a 5mm hex key inserted into the central 5mm hex holes in either axle end cap; generally only one cap will come off this way. You may find a receptacle for an 8mm or 10mm hex key in the bore of the axle after one end cap is off; insert that hex key and, with a 5mm hex key still in the opposite-end cap or with your fingers on a smooth, conical end cap, unscrew that cap (Fig. 6.45).
- Unscrewing the caps on either axle end with cone wrenches engaged on wrench flats on each cap (Fig. 6.25); generally only one cap will

come off this way. You will then tap the axle out from the end whose cap came off; it will drive the bearing on the opposite side out with it. There will sometimes be an enlarged flange with wrench flats behind that bearing; if yours has one, put an open-end wrench on it and a cone wrench on the end cap, and unscrew the end cap to free the bearing.

- On Mavic, unscrewing the axle with a 5mm hex key while holding the other end with either a pin tool in the adjuster ring (front) or a 5mm hex key (front) or 10mm hex key (rear; Fig. 6.45) in the bore of the axle, often after pulling off the end cap on the adjuster end.
- Loosening a tiny setscrew pinching each collar-type end cap around the axle. On a Zipp front hub, one collar is threaded and will unscrew once the setscrew is loosened, and the other (unthreaded) will slide off. Push out the axle bearing and the aluminum bearing cover by pushing on the threaded end of the axle. The rear Zipp hub has a collar with a tiny setscrew; remove the screw and push the axle out of the drive side, and then pull off the freehub body. You can remove the bearings on each end of the freehub body and both ends of the front and rear hub shells with light finger pressure.
- Yanking the rear cassette cogset straight off of the hub by hand (DT Swiss); the freehub body will come off with the cogset and will take off the end cap with it (Fig. 6.47).
- Sliding the end caps off after loosening a setscrew on the side of each cap.
- Loosening three radial setscrews (with a tiny—2mm—hex key) on the axle collar (on the non-drive side on a rear hub), which sometimes must be accessed through a tiny hole in the end of the hub shell (rotate the axle to line each setscrew up under the hole in succession). Once the collar is loose, pull out the end

cap, and then pull the entire axle assembly (including the freehub on a rear hub) out from the opposite side.

If you see hex flats inside the axle bore, try sticking a hex key in there (except Zipp; see above). If both axle ends have them, put a 5mm hex key in each end and unscrew the end caps. If only one end fits a hex key, the other end must first pull off to reveal a hex hole into which you can insert a second hex key to work against the first to unscrew the axle (Fig. 6.45).

If you see no hex hole in the end, then usually the end cap will pull off; it is usually held on by a rubber O-ring engaging grooves at the end of the axle and inside the end cap, so a good yank will get it off. In practice, this often requires more than just your fingers, however. If you have an axle-clamp tool (§i-4, Fig. 1.4), put it in a vise and grab the end of the axle with it to pull the cap off. Without that, you can just grab the outside of the cap with a vise and yank up on the wheel.

Some (generally very old) cartridge-bearing hubs have threaded axles with locknuts that tighten against each other to hold the bearing adjustment, much like a loose-bearing hub (Figs. 6.24, 6.37). You remove the axle just as you would for a loose-bearing hub (§vi-20).

On many rear cartridge-bearing hubs, once the axle or drive-side axle end cap is out, you can (carefully) pull the freehub body off the hub while turning it counterclockwise. Sometimes the freehub body comes off when you push the axle out. In either case, be ready to catch pawls, springs, or ratchet rings (Figs. 6.45–6.47).

If you were able to pull the axle out (and the freehub as well on a rear hub), you can now drive the bearings out of the hub shell.

Some axles have a shoulder against the inner face of the bearing that allows you to push it out. In this case, smack the end of the axle with a soft hammer (Fig. 6.31) to drive the bearing out (or if the axle end is recessed, with a rod, hex key, or drift punch just smaller in diameter than the end of the axle). Or you can set the end of the axle down on the workbench and push down on the hub or the spokes emanating from it. If it's too stubborn to just tap it out while you're holding the wheel, first stand the hub up, bearing to be removed down, on two wood blocks or padded vise jaws separated by enough space to allow the

6.31 **Tapping out a cartridge bearing using the axle's shoulder**

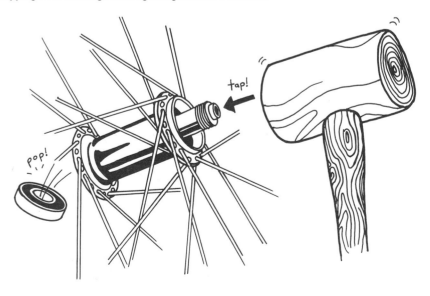

6.32 Tapping out a cartridge bearing with a hex key

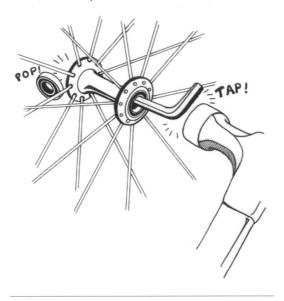

bearing to pass between them as it comes out. Unless the fit is very tight, driving the bearing out with the axle usually does not damage a bearing. On a DT Swiss rear hub (Fig. 6.47), you can get the non-drive bearing out this way, but you cannot remove the drive-side bearing without first unscrewing and removing the large threaded ring with inwardly radiating teeth that engage the freehub star ratchets. This requires a special DT Swiss tool held in a very solid vise.

The best way to remove a bearing from a hub whose axle does not have a shoulder designed to push the bearing out is with a specialty tool called a blind-hole bearing puller that slides into the bore of the bearing and then expands to grip it and has a rod with a sliding weight on it that you slide backward against a stop to pull the bearing farther out with each impact. I'm guessing you don't have one, but if you do have one of the right size, by all means use it! Otherwise, with the hub shell standing vertically on two wood blocks or padded vise jaws separated by enough space to allow the bearing to pass between them, slide in a large screwdriver or hex key, and cock it at an angle to hit the backside of the opposite bearing.

Smack it with a hammer, alternately moving its tip around the bearing (like around a clock face) to slowly work it out until the bearing pops out (Fig. 6.32). This is likely to damage the bearing enough to require replacement. Besides the fact that most cartridge bearings are vulnerable to lateral stress, the tip of a screwdriver can damage the seals and retainers.

If the bearing is reusable, you can remove the seals (and even the bearing retainer and the balls themselves if it has a plastic bearing retainer inside); see §viii-13 for bearing disassembly instructions.

Driving the bearing(s) out of the freehub body, once it's been removed from the hub, is often simple with a hex key of appropriate diameter, but some freehub bearing systems can only be serviced by the factory that made them.

b. Cleaning and greasing the hub cartridge bearings

Once the cartridge bearings are out (and sometimes without removing them at all), you may be able to overhaul them if removing them did not damage them; otherwise you'll need to buy new ones. To overhaul:

1. **Remove the seal.** The most common type of hub bearing is also the simplest to access; it has a rubber-coated metal seal on each side. Gently pop off the rubber-coated bearing seal by sliding a single-edge razor blade (Fig. 6.33) or box-cutter knife blade under the edge and prying it up. Avoid tearing or cutting the rubber edges of the seal, but if you bend the seal, you can easily flatten it out again; it is soft aluminum. If the bearing seals are steel instead, you may find a thin, flat circlip (C-shaped retaining ring) around the outer edge that you can remove; slip a thin blade under one tip of the circlip and work around to pop it out. The bearing

6.33 Removing the bearing seal

cover should come right out with some help from a razor blade. If the bearing has steel seals and no circlip, you probably cannot remove them without damaging them (you would remove them by pounding a sharp awl into the edge of the seal and prying up); it's best to buy new bearings.

2. **Clean the bearing.** Squirt citrus-based solvent into the bearing (wear rubber gloves and protective glasses) to wash out the grease, water, and dirt. Scrub with a clean toothbrush.

3. **Dry the bearing with compressed air.** Do not spin it at high speed, however, which can overheat the surfaces and damage them.

4. **Pack the bearing with grease and snap the bearing covers back on.** If the bearing does not now spin smoothly, replace it. If you really want to rescue this bearing (for instance, if it's an expensive ceramic bearing whose steel bearing races have rusted), you can disassemble it completely, polish the bearing races and bearings, and bring it close to new. This is possible only if it has a plastic bearing retainer inside; forget it if the bearing retainers are metal (i.e., when the seals are off, you are looking at a bumpy silver metal ring on either side as in Fig. 6.33, rather than a smooth plastic one). See §viii-13 for how to disassemble a cartridge bearing.

c. Installing the bearings and adjusting the hub

The closest thing the average home mechanic will have to a proper tool for pressing in a cartridge bearing is a quick-release skewer and a socket wrench or the old bearing. The ideal tool is a hub bearing press (Fig. 1.4), which has a central threaded shaft and discs of different sizes to fit various bearing sizes; tightening the wing nut on the end with the proper pair of discs against the bearings drives them in evenly.

NOTE: *Installing a bearing with a hammer can deform or chip the bearing and prevent it from spinning smoothly. Use a bearing press or a skewer with an appropriately sized socket or old bearing against the bearing to ensure that you are pressing only against the outer race of the bearing.*

1. **Grease the bearing and press it into place.** Put a layer of grease around the outside of the new bearing, and place it in proper alignment where it's going to go in. Place a socket whose outside diameter (OD) is just slightly smaller than the bearing's OD against the new bearing, or place the old bearing atop the new bearing (but note that if the bearing seat is deeper than the bearing, the old

6.34 Pressing the bearing in with the skewer and socket

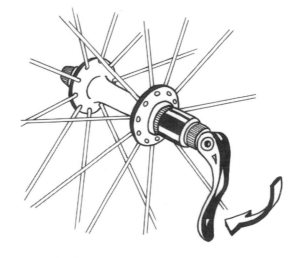

WHEELS AND TIRES

bearing can get stuck). It's generally better to install one bearing at a time to ensure that it's going in straight, especially because you may have only one socket of the right size anyway. Using washers or something of the sort to protect the bearing seat on the opposite end, install the skewer (without the springs on it) and tighten it until the bearing is fully pressed in place (Fig. 6.34).

When you install ceramic cartridge bearings or other high-quality bearings, it is worth thinking ahead of time about maintenance when you are determining the orientation of the bearings. You may as well keep it rolling smoothly, since you don't want to be making this investment frequently. Ceramic bearings for hubs will most likely be "hybrid ceramic" bearings, so even though their ceramic balls cannot rust and are more than twice as hard as steel balls, their races are still steel, may not be stainless, and can rust. Full ceramic bearings (if you thought hybrid ceramics were pricey . . .) are generally not used in hubs, as their brittle outer races can crack when pressed into a tight hole.

Cartridge bearings have bearing retainers (Fig. 6.33) that separate the balls from each other. This design reduces friction by preventing neighboring balls, whose adjacent sides are turning in opposite directions, from rubbing against each other. The bearing retainer may be plastic and asymmetrical, so when you remove the bearing seals (with a razor blade slipped under the edge), you'll see the balls on one side and you'll see only the plastic retainer from the other side. Proper maintenance requires cleaning out the bearing and slathering new grease into it, so before you press the bearings in, determine on which side the balls are visible and make sure that side faces outboard. That way, you can pry off the bearing covers and clean and grease them easily. If you were to completely disassemble and overhaul this bearing instead (§viii-13), you would need to remove it from the hub to get at the other side of the bearing retainer.

If the bearing has a symmetrical retainer (usually steel; Fig. 6.33) concealing the balls on both sides, the best you can do to clean them out is to squirt solvent in followed by compressed air. Overhauling the bearing effectively requires disassembling it and cleaning and polishing its parts as described in §viii-13, but this is only possible with a plastic, asymmetrical bearing retainer. Removing a steel bearing retainer (Fig. 6.33) ruins it, and you won't be able to reassemble the bearing.

2. **Reassemble the hub axle, second bearing, and end caps the reverse of the way they came apart.** Install the axle (put a bit of grease on it first) and press in the other bearing, generally using the same method you did with the first bearing. When you press in the second bearing with the socket, you'll need another, bigger socket that is large enough to slip around the outside of the bearing. Place the bigger socket with its open end toward the hub on the other side; otherwise, you'll just be tightening against the axle end and not pressing the bearing into its seat in the hub shell. If one bearing was originally tightened between a shoulder on the axle and a thread-on end cap, tighten the new bearing onto the axle that way first, and then tap the axle assembly in.

On many hubs, you can also press in the outer bearing in the freehub body with a socket and the skewer once the freehub body is in place on the hub (Fig. 6.35).

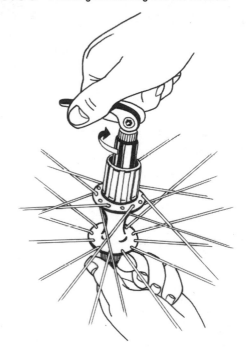

6.35 Pressing the bearing into the freehub

would dramatically shorten their lifespan as well as increase their rolling friction.

On Mavic hubs, you adjust the bearing with a pin tool on the adjuster ring once the hub is tightened into the frame or fork with the quick-release skewer. A little threadlock on the adjuster's threads is a good idea when putting the hub back together.

On White Industries and original Mad Fiber hubs, there are three setscrews pointing radially inward through a sliding collar on one end of the hub. Each setscrew is at 120 degrees from the next, and on some hubs must be accessed through a hole in the hub shell that must be rotated over each setscrew. Loosen the three setscrews with a 2mm hex key and slide the collar inward against the bearing to remove the end play. If the adjustment is still loose, try rotating the collar on the axle end cap first; it may be that the setscrews keep going back into the indentations they made in the collar before and thus prevent changing the adjustment unless you rotate them to a new area of the collar.

3. **Check the bearing adjustment.** Sometimes the bearings will be out of alignment slightly after installation, making the hub noticeably hard to turn. A light tap on either end of the axle with a soft hammer will sometimes free them. If you have threaded end caps and you find that tightening them binds up the hub, then you'll want to put Loctite on the threads and tighten them only enough to make the hub adjustment perfect once the wheel is tightened with the skewer into the frame or fork; the threadlock compound will prevent the end caps from loosening.

Many hubs have no adjustment; a tubular spacer between the inner races of the two bearings keeps them at the proper separation, and the end caps push against the other side of the inner bearing races. Other systems have no spacer between the bearings; the bearings just sit in a pocket in each end of the hub, and pressure from the outside has to be adjusted to remove axle end play without side-loading the bearings, which

vi-22

UPGRADING BEARINGS

Following the instructions in §vi-20 or §vi-21 above, depending on whether it's a loose-bearing hub or a cartridge-bearing hub, you can replace old bearings with supersmooth ceramic bearings, higher-grade steel bearings, or simply new bearings of the same type. Ball bearings are higher-grade if the balls are smoother, harder, rounder, and more uniform in size. Cartridge bearings are higher-grade if both the balls and races are smoother, harder, and more uniform. Ceramic bearings are generally higher-grade than even the best steel ones, because the balls are harder, polished smoother, and rounder and more uniform in size. Expect to pay a lot for ceramic bearings and even for high-grade steel bearings. Ceramic bearings should run more smoothly and last longer, since, besides being rounder, smoother, more uniform in size, and harder, the balls cannot rust or be scratched by grit and are less sensitive to lubrication.

Hybrid ceramic bearings are cartridge bearings with ceramic balls and steel races; full-ceramic bearings have ceramic races as well as ceramic balls and are the most expensive. Full-ceramic bearings should be installed at the factory; the ceramic race cannot be pressed in, as it has no flexibility and may crack. Instead, the seat into which it fits must be larger than the bearing OD so that the bearing fits in without pressure, and then it must be glued into place. These sometimes have no bearing seals, as the balls and races are harder than any grit that could get into them.

FREEHUBS, FREEWHEELS, AND COGS

LEVEL 2

Freehubs and freewheels allow the rear wheel to turn freely, in the reverse direction of the chain driving direction. Most rely on a series of spring-loaded pawls (Fig. 6.45) that engage internal teeth when pressure is applied to the pedals and disengage from the teeth when the rider is coasting; the springs cause the pawls to bounce off the teeth as they pass by—that's the clicking sound you hear when coasting.

A freehub is an integral part of the rear hub. The cogs slide onto the longitudinal splines of the freehub body (Fig. 6.36). Changing gear combinations is accomplished by removing the cogs from the freehub body and putting on different ones. A freehub can usually be lubricated without removing it from the hub.

A freewheel is a separate unit with the cogs attached to it. The entire freewheel threads onto the drive side of the rear hub (Fig. 6.37). Thread-on freewheels have fallen out of fashion relative to freehubs; changing cogs on freewheels is difficult, and freewheels do not support the hub axle, leaving a long section of axle on the drive end sticking out of the hub unsupported. Freewheels can only be removed with a freewheel tool that matches the shape at the end of the particular freewheel. Entire freewheels with different gear combinations can be interchanged in this way.

6.36 Rear freehub with cartridge bearings and cassette cogs

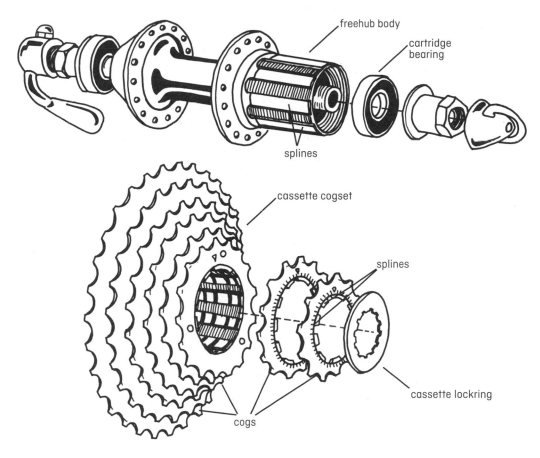

freehub body

cartridge bearing

splines

cassette cogset

splines

cassette lockring

cogs

6.37 Threaded rear hub with standard ball bearings and freewheel

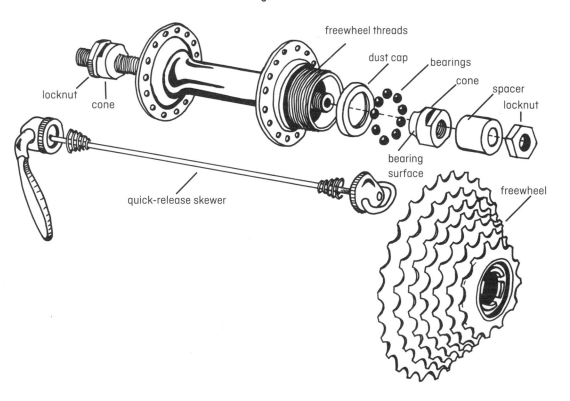

freewheel threads

dust cap

bearings

cone

spacer

locknut

locknut

cone

bearing surface

quick-release skewer

freewheel

WHEELS AND TIRES

Fixed-gear cogs, as used on track bikes, urban fixies, or some road bike winter-training setups, do not freewheel; the cog drives the chain forward whenever the wheel is rotating. Single-speed freewheels, on the other hand, allow coasting and are found on BMX bikes and other single-speed bikes without coaster brakes. Both fixed gears and single-speed freewheels screw onto a threaded hub.

There are two widths of fixed gears and single-speed freewheels: those that take a standard $\frac{3}{32}$-inch-width derailleur chain, and those that take the $\frac{1}{8}$-inch-width chain of track, internal-gear, and standard single-speed bicycles. With either type, the frame needs to have horizontal dropouts with long slots to allow the wheel to be moved rearward sufficiently to tension the chain, or they need a spring-loaded chain tensioner that pulls the lower section of chain taut; these can thread onto the derailleur hanger for the dropout or be bolted to the chainstay.

When put on a standard threaded wheel for a road bike, a fixed-gear cog can unscrew when pedaled backward, but it's best to use a track hub. On a track hub, there is a second set of threads outboard of the standard hub threads. These threads are smaller in diameter and are left-hand threaded. A left-hand-threaded lockring holds the cog on and is tightened whenever the rider pushes backward on the pedals. The cog is removed by unscrewing the lockring in a clockwise direction with a lockring spanner, and then unscrewing the cog in a counterclockwise direction with a Vise Whip (Fig. 1.2) or a chain whip.

vi-23

CLEANING REAR COGS

The quickest, albeit perfunctory, way to clean the rear cogs is to slide a rag back and forth between each pair of cogs while they are on the hub (Fig. 6.38). An improvement on this is Finish

6.38 Cleaning cogs

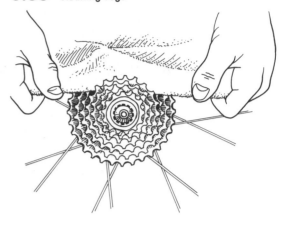

Line's Gear Floss—thick string with which to do the same thing. The other way—usually unnecessary unless the bike has been neglected—is to remove them (§vi-24) and wipe them off with a rag or immerse them in solvent.

vi-24

CHANGING CASSETTE COGS

1. **Make sure you have the tools you need.** Get out a Pedro's Vise Whip or a chain whip, a cassette-lockring remover, a wrench (adjustable or open) to fit the remover, and the cog(s) you want to install. (Some very old freehubs have a threaded smallest cog instead of a lockring. These require two Vise Whips or chain whips and no lockring remover.)

2. **Remove the quick-release skewer.**

3. **Secure the cassette so it cannot spin when you remove the lockring.** Adjust the Vise Whip's jaw-adjustment screw on the end of the handle to fit on any cog you choose, and clamp onto it (Fig. 6.40), or wrap the chain whip around a cog (Fig. 6.39) at least two up from the smallest cog. Wrap in the drive direction (clockwise) so that the cassette is held in place, and keep tension on it so it doesn't fall off.

4. **Remove the lockring.** Insert the splined lockring remover into the lockring. The lockring is the internally splined ring that holds the smallest cog in place. With a wrench on the lockring remover, unscrew the lockring in a counterclockwise direction while using the Vise Whip or chain whip to keep the cassette from turning (Figs. 6.39, 6.40). If the lockring is so tight that the tool pops out without loosening it, install and tighten the skewer, sans springs, through the hub and lockring tool. Once you have broken the lockring free and unscrewed it a fraction of a turn, remove the skewer so you don't snap it; now unscrew the lockring the rest of the way.

5. **Pull the cogs straight off.** Some cassette cogsets are composed of single cogs separated by loose spacers; some cogsets are bolted together with one or two loose cogs and perhaps a spacer or two (Fig. 6.36); some cogsets have groups of two or three cogs attached to splined aluminum carriers along with some loose cogs and spacers; and some SRAM cogsets are machined in a single piece.

6. **Clean the cogs with a rag or a toothbrush.** Use solvent if necessary, observing the usual precautions.

7. **Inspect the cogs for wear.** If the teeth are hook-shaped, they may be worn out and ripe for replacement. Rohloff makes a cog-wear indicator tool; if you have access to one, use it according to its supplied instructions.

8. **Replace the cogs.** If there was a spacer behind the cogset, make sure you replace it; otherwise, you may find your rear derailleur going into the spokes on shifting to your largest cog.

   a. If you are replacing the entire cogset, just slide the new set on. Usually, you'll find that one spline is wider than

6.39 Removing a cassette lockring with a chain whip and a locknut remover

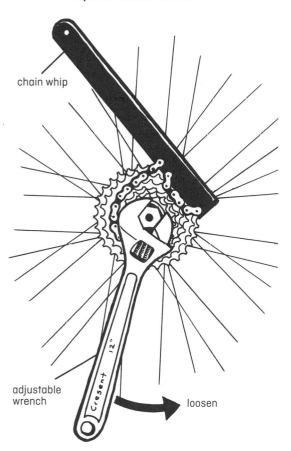

6.40 Using a Vise Whip to remove a cassette lockring

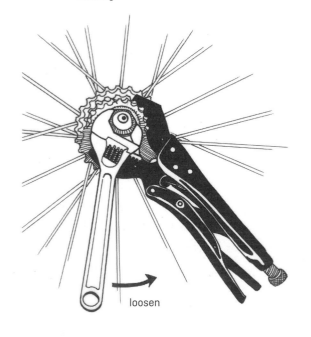

6.41 Large spline

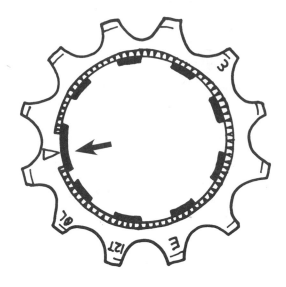

the others (Fig. 6.41), so line them up accordingly.

b. If you are installing a 9-, 10-, or 11-speed cassette, see the first note under step 9.

c. If you are replacing individual cogs within the cogset, be certain that they are of the same type and model. For example, not all 16-tooth Shimano cogs are alike. Most cogs have shifting ramps, differentially shaped teeth, and other asymmetries. They differ by model as well as by sizes of the adjacent cogs, so you need to buy one for the exact location and model. Install cogs in decreasing numerical sequence with the numbers facing out.

NOTE: *Some bolt-together cogsets can be disassembled for cleaning and cog interchanging and then reinstalled onto the freehub as separate cogs to facilitate future cog changes and cleaning. Note that there are two kinds of bolt-together cogsets: (1) those with three long, thin bolts holding the stack of cogs and spacers together (Fig. 6.36) and (2) those with pairs or groups of cogs bolted or riveted to aluminum*

spider-shaped carriers that have internal splines to fit on the cassette body. For the type with the three bolts, just unscrew the bolts, take it apart, and put in the replacement cogs. The other type is not to be disassembled from the aluminum spider, and the individual cogs are not to be replaced; you replace each carrier with its attached cogs as a complete assembly.

9. **Install the lockring.** First, ensure that the lockring you are using is the right one for both the freehub and the particular cogset. The diameter of the lockring depends on the size of the first cog, and its thread pitch and diameter depend on the brand of the freehub. With everything back in place, tighten the lockring with the lockring remover and wrench. (If you have the old-type 6- or 7-speed Shimano freehub with the thread-on first cog, tighten that with a Vise Whip or chain whip instead.) Make sure that all of the cogs are seated and can't wobble from side to side, which would indicate that the first or second cog is sitting against the ends of the splines, or that you didn't install all of the spacers. If the cogs are loose after tightening the lockring, loosen the lockring, line up the first and second cogs to make sure they are in place, and tighten the lockring again.

NOTE ON COMPATIBILITY: *These instructions for removing and replacing cogs apply for 6-, 7-, 8-, 9-, 10-, and 11-speed cogsets. But freehub-body dimensions vary with number of speeds, so make sure you only use a 7-speed cogset on a 7-speed freehub body, and so on.*

NOTE ON 11-TOOTH COGS: *Although all Shimano 8-speed freehubs are wide enough for a 9- or 10-speed cogset, some 8- and 9-speed freehub bodies will not accept 11-tooth cogs (for instance, 1992–1994 Shimano 8-speed freehub bodies will not accept 11-tooth cogs). To accept the small, 11-tooth cog, the freehub splines stop* *about 2mm before the outer end of the freehub body. You can grind the last 2mm of splines off an old-style 8-speed freehub so that it will accept an 11-tooth cog. The steel is very hard on high-end freehubs, so a grinder, rather than a file, will be needed for this job.*

vi-25

CHANGING FREEWHEELS

If you have a freewheel (Fig. 6.37) and want to switch it with another one, follow this procedure. Replacing individual cogs on an existing freewheel is beyond the scope of this book, since it is rarely done these days owing to the preponderance of freehubs and to the lack of availability of spare freewheel parts.

1. **Obtain the appropriate freewheel remover for your freewheel.** Take the wheel to the bike shop to make sure you get the right tool. Round up a big adjustable wrench to fit it.

2. **Remove the quick-release skewer and take off the springs.**

3. **Install the freewheel remover.** Slide the skewer back in from the left side, place the freewheel remover into the end of the freewheel so that the notches or splines engage, and thread the skewer nut back on, tightening it against the freewheel remover to keep it from popping out of its notches.

4. **Unscrew the freewheel.** Put the big adjustable wrench onto the flats of the freewheel remover and loosen it (counterclockwise). It may take considerable force to free it, and you may even need to put a large pipe on the end of the wrench for more leverage. Set the tire on the ground for traction as you do it. As soon as the freewheel pops loose, loosen the skewer nut before continuing; otherwise, you may snap the skewer in two.

5. **Loosen the skewer nut a bit.** Unscrew the freewheel a bit more, and so on, until it spins off freely and there is no longer any danger of having the freewheel remover pop out of the notches.

6. **Remove the skewer and spin off the freewheel.**

7. **Grease the threads on the hub and the inside of the new freewheel.**

8. **Thread on the new freewheel by hand.** You can snug it down with the freewheel remover and a wrench or with a Vise Whip or chain whip, if you like, but it will tighten itself into place with the first few pedal strokes anyway.

9. **Replace the skewer with the narrow ends of its conical springs facing inward (Fig. 6.37).**

vi-26

LUBRICATING FREEHUBS

a. Simple, minor freehub lubrication

Often neglected, freehubs need lubrication and can usually be lubricated for the short term simply by dripping chain lube into them. It's not a long-term fix, as the thin lubricant will not protect it for long, and the chain lube can get into the wheel bearings and dilute the grease protecting them. Do not dunk a freehub in a solvent bath; it will pull in dirt along with the solvent.

Some freehubs have grease-injection holes on the freehub body, visible after removing the cogs. Remove the cogs to get at the hole, and meticulously clean any dirt out of the hole before injecting the oil or grease. Add oil or very lightweight grease (frequently) to avoid thickening of the grease inside. To be thorough, before injecting the grease, inject diesel fuel or biodegradable chain cleaner into the hole from a squeeze bottle with its thin tip pressed into the hole. Keep adding solvent until the freehub spins without any crunching noises. Rather than using bearing grease in the grease gun, inject a thinner lube into them, such as outboard-motor gear oil or Morningstar Freehub Soup by means of an oil squeeze bottle or a fine-tip grease gun (Fig. 1.3). Using heavy oil like this will avoid the problem of grease thickening up inside and sticking the pawls in cold temperatures, preventing engagement of the freehub. In most freehubs (but not DT Swiss and other star-ratchet freehubs), the springs are very light, and it does not take much in the way of sticky or cold-thickened lube to stop them from pushing the pawls radially outward. It's a dark day if you apply power to the pedal and the freehub slips.

If the freehub has teeth on the faces of the hub shell and freehub (DT Swiss, Hügi, or old Mavic freehubs have these radial teeth), drip oil into the crease between the freehub and the hub shell as you turn the freehub counterclockwise for a short-term fix. These freehubs come off easily, so you might as well lubricate them well; see §vi-26f below.

For most loose-bearing freehubs, here is the general procedure. The details for lubricating the major types of freehubs follow in separate sections.

1. **Disassemble the hub-axle assembly (§vi-20a, b).**
2. **Clean the parts.** Wipe clean the inside of the drive-side bearing surface and inspect it. Look for discoloration or wear.
3. **Lubricate the freehub.** With the wheel lying flat and the freehub pointed up toward you, flow chain lube between the bearing surface and the freehub body as you spin the freehub counterclockwise. You will hear the clicking noise of the freehub pawls smooth out as lubricant reaches them. Keep it flowing until old black oil finishes flowing out of the other end of the freehub.

4. **Wipe off the excess lube and continue with the hub overhaul (§vi-20c, d).**

b. Thorough Shimano freehub lubrication without disassembling the freehub body

An effective way to lubricate a Shimano freehub is to inject lubricant under pressure with a Morningstar Freehub Buddy tool (Fig. 6.42). Once the hub is apart, most of the work is done. This tool is easy to use, but first you may want to order a reusable dust cap from Morningstar (see the Note after step 4).

1. **To use this tool, you must first disassemble the hub-axle assembly as described in §vi-20a, b.**
2. **Pry out the freehub dust cover with a screwdriver.** Work your way around. On an old Shimano freehub, the Morningstar J-tool (Fig. 6.43) is ideal for this.
3. **Once the dust cover is off, push the Freehub Buddy into the bearing race (Fig. 6.44).**
4. **Clean the mechanism with solvent first, if necessary.** If the freehub has a crunchy feel to it, first inject diesel fuel or a citrus solvent followed by a lubricant into the threaded hole (or the smaller tapered section below the threads) in the center of the Freehub Buddy; it will exit through the lube galley hole in the side of the tool between the two rubber O-rings (Fig. 6.42). The smaller O-ring at the closed end of the Freehub Buddy seals

6.42 Morningstar Freehub Buddy tool

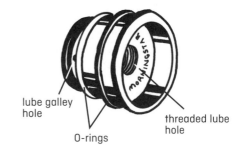

lube galley hole

threaded lube hole

O-rings

6.43 Prying out the freehub dust cover with a J-tool

POP!

6.44 Freehub buddy installed in the end of a Shimano freehub

BUDDY

off the center of the hub to prevent lubricant from going in there, and the larger O-ring prevents lube from squirting back out the front of the freehub.

a. I recommend force-threading the tip of a turkey baster filled with a strong citrus solvent or diesel fuel into the threaded hole in the center of the Freehub Buddy and squirting it in as you slowly turn the freehub. Tilt the wheel with a bucket below to catch the dirty solvent. Then force-thread the tip of a tube of outboard motor gear oil or Morningstar's Freehub Soup syringe (Fig. 1.3) into the Freehub Buddy's threaded hole (Fig. 6.42) and inject the lube. Either one is the perfect weight for a freehub; the Soup has specific ingredients for longer freehub life. The gear oil comes in a huge tube whose end fits nicely into the center hole of the tool, while the Soup is already packaged in a syringe designed to fit the tool. You can also force-thread a tube of grease or, better, the tip of a glue syringe or turkey baster filled with oil or your own custom mixture of compatible (i.e., synthetic with synthetic or petroleum with petroleum) oil and grease into the Freehub Buddy. Chain lube can also be squirted into the Freehub Buddy.

b. Whatever lubricant you use, squeeze it into the Freehub Buddy until all the old dirty lubricant squeezes through the freehub and out the back end of it. Keep going until clean lube oozes out.

c. Other than by disassembling the entire freehub, the Freehub Buddy is the only way you can get a lubricant thicker than thin chain lube into the freehub, and a thicker lubricant protects better. Be certain that it's not too thick, however. Filling a freehub with thick grease may cause the pawls to stick in cold weather and not spring back into the freehub teeth to lock it up when you want to pedal forward. You could end up free-wheeling in both directions! Always spin it by hand and check it first; if it does not engage well, purge it again with lighter oil that is compatible with the grease you put inside, or start over with the citrus solvent or diesel fuel.

NOTE: *Many freehub dust caps will be ruined upon removal; they are usually made of stamped sheet metal. Shimano does not sell them separately, complicating freehub service considerably. Morningstar Tools (morningstartools.com) sells machined removable dust caps with an O-ring seal as well as freehub tools and lubricants.*

5. **Once the freehub is lubricated, overhaul the hub and replace the axle assembly.**

c. Alternative method of thorough Shimano freehub lubrication without complete disassembly

1. **Disassemble the hub-axle assembly as described in §vi-20a, b.**

2. **If the freehub feels crunchy when you spin it, remove the freehub body with a 10mm hex wrench inserted into the internal freehub-fixing bolt.**

3. **Completely flush out the freehub.** With a rubber stopper from a hardware store, close off the bottom of the freehub body. Pour solvent into the outer opening, spinning the mechanism and letting contaminants run out. If there is a rubber seal, remove it. Repeat until clean.

4. **Lubricate the parts.** Squirt in a quantity of outboard gear lube, then park the body on paper towels and let the excess drain off. With this method, you do not need to remove the freehub body dust seal.

NOTE: *You can also disassemble a Shimano freehub by unscrewing (clockwise—it's a left-hand thread) the hub's end bearing race on the outboard end of the freehub. Morningstar sells a tool that fits into its two notches. I won't go into the details here, but I do illustrate it in my out-of-print* Mountain Bike Performance Handbook *published by MBI.*

d. Mavic freehub lubrication (or swap)

1. **Remove the axle.** Depending on model, removing the axle usually involves first pulling the non-drive-side dust cap straight off (Fig. 6.45), or unscrewing external locknuts from external threads on a steel axle.

2. **Unscrew the parts.** Depending on the model, using two hex keys (two 5mm hex keys, or one 10mm and one 5mm), one in either end, loosen counterclockwise, unscrew, and remove (Fig. 6.45).

3. **Turn the wheel on its side, freehub up, on a clean surface where you can catch—or at least see—any pawls or pawl springs that fly away.**

4. **Rotate the freehub body slowly counterclockwise as you pull up on it, and remove it (Fig. 6.45).**

6.45 Removing a Mavic Ksyrium axle and freehub in order to lubricate the freehub and pawls

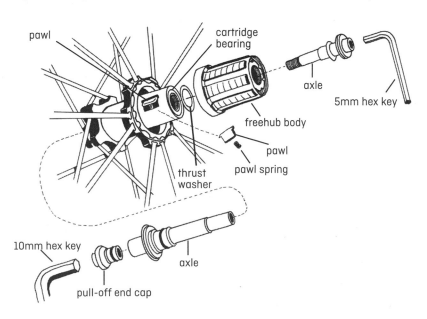

5. Clean the pawls, springs, and hub shell.

6. **Replace the springs and pawls, and put 10–20 drops of Mavic mineral oil M40122 into the freehub (on the plastic bushing and the ratchet teeth).** There is no need to lubricate the rubber seal.

7. **Reinstall the freehub body.** Turn it counterclockwise while holding the pawls down with your fingers.

8. **Replace the axle.** Simple.

NOTE: *This same procedure can be used to change Mavic freehub bodies from, say, a Shimano-compatible type to a Campagnolo-compatible type.*

e. Campagnolo/Fulcrum freehub lubrication

1. **Begin by removing the skewer.**

2. **Unlock the freehub from the hub.** On high-end Campagnolo or Fulcrum rear hubs, insert a 5mm hex key into the drive-side axle, and put a 17mm open-end or box wrench on the drive-side locknut. While holding the 5mm hex key, unscrew the locknut clockwise (it has left-hand threads, and you need to unscrew it in the opposite direction from what you would expect). Older Campagnolo models instead have a little setscrew on the 17mm locknut that must be loosened with a 2mm hex key in order to unscrew the locknut.

3. **Now pull the freehub straight off.** Older Campagnolo models have individual coil springs under each of the three pawls. These can go flying, and they are hard to clean and to insert back into the hub shell. Newer Campagnolo and Fulcrum models have a single, circular wire spring wrapped around all three pawls (it fits in a groove in the freehub body as well as one cut across the flanks of each pawl; Fig. 6.46). With the

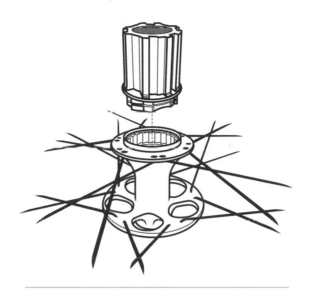

new style, you can pull the freehub off with abandon, and nothing will go flying. When removing the freehub body, older models require wrapping a twist tie around the three pawls as they expose themselves from the hub shell as you pull; if you don't do this, the three pawls and the three springs will fly away.

4. **Clean and grease the three pawls and the radial teeth inside the hub shell.**

5. **Slide the freehub back in while slowly turning it backward.** If necessary, push inward on each pawl with a pencil tip as you do this, until all three are engaged and the freehub body drops into place. Again, older Campagnolo models require using a twist tie to hold the pawls in place as you push the body in. Pull the twist tie off after the pawls are started inside the hub shell and before the freehub is pushed all the way in.

6. **While holding the drive-side end of the axle with a 5mm hex key inside its bore, tighten the locknut counterclockwise— it's left-hand threaded!—with a 17mm hex key.** Complete the bearing adjustment as in §vi-20d.

NOTE: *This same procedure can be used to change Campagnolo or Fulcrum freehub bodies from, say, a Campagnolo-compatible type to a freehub body that accepts Shimano (or SRAM) cogs.*

f. Lubricating freehubs with three radial pawls mounted on cartridge-bearing hubs

The freehub body is essentially the same as the Campagnolo and Fulcrum bodies mentioned above, but they exist on myriad cartridge-bearing hubs. The hub shell has radial teeth pointing inwardly on its drive end, and the base of the freehub body slips down inside and has three pawls that flip outward to engage the teeth (Fig. 6.46). Usually, there is a circular spring around all three pawls that flips them outward; it also generally keeps them from flying away when you pull the freehub body off. But it is always possible that the freehub body is the older style with a single tiny coil spring behind each pawl, and these parts definitely can go flying when you pull the freehub body off unless you put a twist tie around them as mentioned above (§vi-26e).

1. **Access the freehub body by first removing the axle as in §vi-21.**
2. **Pull the freehub straight off.** Again, a single, circular wire spring will generally be wrapped around all three pawls (it fits in a groove in the freehub body as well as one cut across the flanks of each pawl; Fig. 6.46). Nonetheless, exercise care that nothing goes flying.
3. **Clean and lightly grease the three pawls and the radial teeth inside the hub shell.**
4. **Slide the freehub back in while slowly turning it backward.** Push inward on each pawl with a pencil tip as you do this, until all three are engaged and the freehub body drops into place.
5. **Reassemble the hub as in §vi-21.**

6.47 DT Swiss freehub removal and lubrication

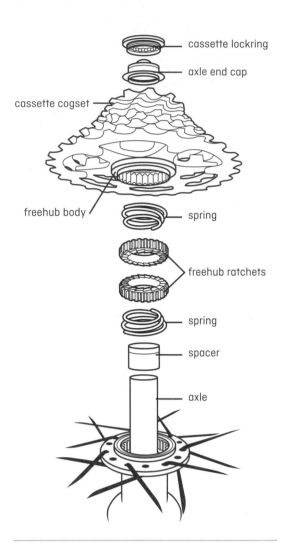

cassette lockring
axle end cap
cassette cogset
freehub body
spring
freehub ratchets
spring
spacer
axle

g. DT Swiss/HüGI freehub lubrication

DT Swiss and older DT and HüGI high-end star-ratchet freehubs pull apart easily for cleaning and lubrication.

1. **Remove the skewer.**
2. **Lay the wheel on its side, cogs up; grasp the cogset; and pull up.** The freehub body will come off, bringing the axle end cap with it.
3. **Clean and grease the spring, both star-shaped ratchets (Fig. 6.47), and the teeth that engage on the freehub body and hub shell.**
4. **Push the freehub and end cap back on, and replace the skewer.** That's it!

LUBRICATING FREEWHEELS

1. **Clean the parts.** Wipe dirt off the face of the fixed part of the freewheel surrounding the axle (Fig. 6.37).

2. **With the wheel lying flat and the cogs facing upward, drip lubricant into the crease between the fixed and moving parts of the freewheel as you spin the cogs in a counterclockwise direction.** You will hear the clicking noise inside become smoother as you get lubricant in there. Be sure to keep the flow of lubricant going until the old, dirty oil flows out the backside around the hub flange. Do not dunk a freewheel in a solvent bath; it will pull in dirt along with the solvent.

3. **Wipe off the excess oil.**

CYCLOCROSS WHEELS AND TIRES

vi-28

TIRE SELECTION

LEVEL 1

a. Tire type

You need to select the tire type before you can decide on a wheel type (see §vi-29). There is quite a selection these days of both clincher and tubular cyclocross tires. And tubeless cyclocross clinchers (or "tubeless-ready," meaning that they require sealant) offer some unique advantages.

Clinchers are the cheapest choice, but they probably also roll slowest. They are easy to mount, rivaled in that category only by tubeless clinchers. For training, an unsponsored rider should use clinchers, because all it takes is an errant piece of sharp metal or a few thorns to reduce an expensive tubular tire to a piece of junk and condemn yourself to yet more hours of tire gluing (§vi-11).

Modern liquid tire sealants can breathe new life into a tubular with small punctures (§vi-14), but with a clincher, you can change the inner tube and keep riding it for many more miles.

Downsides of clinchers include weight, rolling resistance, likelihood of pinch flats, and limited capability of riding when flat. Not only are a clincher tire and its tube heavier than a good tubular, but a clincher wheel is also heavier than a tubular wheel of similar strength and stiffness. Rolling resistance is generally understood to be higher for a clincher, which has stiffer sidewall cords and a thicker tube than a more supple tubular. The tall, sharp edge of a clincher rim (Fig. 6.48A), when hitting a sharp edge at speed, can pinch a tube inside the tire casing to give you a two-hole "snake-bite" puncture, and the rim edges are easily dented.

6.48A Blunt-nose shallow-section clincher rim cross-section

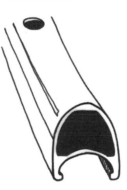

6.48B Deep-section tubular rim cross-section

Tubular tires sit on flatter rim surfaces (Fig. 6.48B) and are less prone to pinch flats, while tubeless tires have no tubes to pinch. Finally, if you get a flat on a clincher and try to ride it back to the pit, it's unlikely to stay on the rim long enough for you to do that.

Tubulars, besides being lighter and having lighter rims, lower rolling resistance, and less proclivity to pinch flats, are glued to the rim and will stay in place if you have to ride back to the pit on a flat. Their supple casings keep more tread on the ground than a clincher, unless you were to run the clincher at such low pressure that pinch flats would be a certainty. Tubulars are generally going to be faster than clinchers. But you will pay a high price for tubulars both at the cash register and in time spent gluing (§vi-11 and the Pro Tip below).

Tufo tubulars are tubeless and are sold with a sealant, so they combine a tubular's supple casing, low tire weight, low rim weight, and ride-ability when flat, with the invulnerability to pinch flats and punctures of a tubeless clincher.

To protect your investment in cyclocross tubulars, use Caffélatex sealant (§vi-14b) or a sealant that came with the tire after small punctures and perhaps as a prophylactic measure beforehand if you ride where there are lots of thorns. The downside of sealant in tubulars is that if you don't remove it after the season is over, it will solidify inside the tube over the off-season,

---

PRO TIP — **Gluing Tubular Cyclocross Tires**

LEVEL 3

Gluing a cyclocross tire is the same as gluing a road tubular (§vi-11), except there are three important distinctions that make gluing a cyclocross tubular more problematic:

- A cyclocross tire is fatter than a road tire, but most rims used for cyclocross are road rims. Since a tubular tire will always be round in cross-section when inflated (Fig. 6.3), this means that the curvature of, say, a 700 × 33mm 'cross tire will be lower than the curvature of the concave top surface of the rim, which is designed to fit a 700 × 23mm road tubular.

- A cyclocross tire, if inflated as intended, will be ridden at much lower pressure than a road tubular, in order to get better traction, cushion the ride, and reduce rolling resistance on bumpy sections of the course. Tire-gluing studies show that tire adhesion to the rim decreases with decreasing tire pressure (you can see this yourself by putting an unglued tire on a rim and trying to push it off at varying air pressures).

- The continual washing that cyclocross bikes get (§ii-18), combined with the constant splashing through mud, sand, and water, will tend to dry out the glue joint and infiltrate it with dirt.

All three may be reasons to use both glue and cyclocrossworld.com's "Belgian" tubular gluing tape (§vi-11, step 7). The center of the rim does not usually touch the entire base tape of the tire with a cyclocross tire bigger than 28mm. The glue-plus-Belgian-Tape method of §vi-11, step 7, should hold on any 'cross tire if done correctly, but if not, you can use the following method to shim up the center of the rim to better fit the tire's shape:

1. Peel the base tape off an old tubular and split it down the center with scissors.

2. After applying the second glue layer as in §vi-11, step 6, smear glue down one side of the half-width strip of old base tape, and stick it down the center of the rim channel. Apply the third glue layer over it.

3. Continue with §vi-11, step 8.

4. With a carbon rim, also read the Pro Tip in §vi-11 on gluing a tubular to a carbon rim.

---

and rinsing the inner tube and drying it out is not easy. Sealant removal is much easier with a Tufo tubular tire, since it has no inner tube; you can flush it with water via a big syringe, and you can suck air out with a vacuum cleaner necked down to the valve with tape.

Tubeless tires offer benefits and drawbacks versus clinchers and tubulars. Tubeless tires cannot pinch flat, so you can run them at very low pressures to get better traction, a smoother ride, and lower rolling resistance on bumpy sections. If you install them with sealant (§vi-14), they are essentially impervious to small punctures (you can use sealant in a tubular or clincher, too, by injecting it through the valve, ideally with the valve core removed).

"Tubeless-ready" clinchers have a stiff casing like a clincher, but they don't have a tube stiffen-ing and chafing them and can be run at low pressures without fear of pinch flats, so they arguably have rolling resistance comparable to an expensive, supple tubular. Tubeless-ready clinchers are as fast to install and remove as a clincher and cost only marginally more, and wise riders have successfully ridden and raced on many standard cyclocross tubeless clinchers. Mounted on a tubeless-specific clincher rim, tubeless-ready clinchers are designed to stay on if ridden when flat, because the "humps" on the rim shelves should "lock" the tire bead on (Fig. 6.17).

The big caveat with tubeless cyclocross tires is that the low tire pressure and intermediate tire diameters used in cyclocross have a tendency to defeat tubeless features that work on road and mountain bike tubeless tires, and "burping" (allowing air to escape suddenly under the bead

PRO TIP | Setting Up Tubeless Cyclocross Tires

You have to be committed to some experimentation (ideally before the season) to get tubeless tires to work reliably in cyclocross, especially for a big rider racing with them. The bead needs to fit tightly to not burp air, and there is evidence to suggest that stiffer tire casings are also more likely to burp air than more flexible ones. A common method of addressing burping issues is to add additional layers of rim strip to make the rim bead seat effectively larger in diameter.

You can start with a tubeless-specific road rim, or you can convert a standard rim to tubeless by sealing off the rim's nipple holes. NoTube's yellow tape is the ticket here. You will generally be less likely to burp air if you add an extra layer or two of tape. NoTube's full tubeless conversion kit includes a thick rubber rim strip, and this is perhaps an even better method; like additional tape layers, it also increases the bead seat diameter and effectively reduces the sidewall height

(allowing the tire to flex more), but it also seals better around the tire bead.

You can use tubeless-ready or standard clincher tires, and there are many standard clinchers that seem to work as well for running without a tube as tubeless-ready clinchers. With any of them, you have to use quite a bit of sealant (up to ¼ cup). Also, some tires have little vertical sipes along the bead on the outside of the tire, which obviously hinders making a seal to the rim. In this case, you at a minimum have to use the most aggressive sealant, which is probably the Stan's NoTubes sealant.

When running any rim and tire tubeless with sealant, you should remove the tire periodically and check for corrosion of the rim; especially remove the valve stem and check there. Rim corrosion can be a problem with some rims and some sealants, and you don't want to let it go until the rim fails.

edge) is often a problem on sharp turns. Also, like any clincher rim, the rim edges are susceptible to denting on rocks, stairs, and curbs, and tubeless-specific wheel and tire choices are limited. See the Pro Tip on setting up tubeless cyclocross clincher tires.

b. Tire size

Don't get a tire smaller than 28mm (i.e., 700 × 28). On the other hand, tires wider than 33mm are banned in races sanctioned by the UCI (Union Cycliste Internationale, the governing body of the sport). Make sure your bike has sufficient mud clearance around the tire; check with the tire mounted on a wheel under the fork crown, between the chainstays, behind the chainstay bridge, behind the front derailleur and the cable roller on the back of the seat tube, under the brake bridge, and between the seatstays.

A bigger tire gives more cushioning and can be run at a lower pressure, both of which are advantages, but its drawback is extra weight. A tire smaller than 30mm will rattle your teeth out and invite pinch flats. On frozen, rutted, bumpy, or sandy courses, use a 34mm width unless the race checks tire diameter, in which case use 33mm. For general use, 32mm or 33mm are the universal sizes.

With clinchers, don't use a road-size inner tube; it will be stretched too thin for durability inside a big cyclocross tire. And running sealant inside a too-small inner tube will be less effective; if it punctures, the hole will widen due to the stretched tube. Get a 700 × 28–35 inner tube. While you're at it, make sure the rim strip (Fig. 6.13) is in good shape and can't become dislodged due to water, mud, and being bumped around.

c. Tire tread pattern

With tubulars, you have the choice of a mud tread (Fig. 6.49A), an open knobby tread (6.49B),

6.49A Cyclocross mud tread pattern (Challenge Limus)

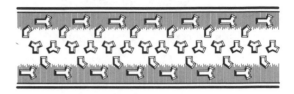

6.49B Cyclocross knobby tread pattern (Schwalbe Racing Ralph)

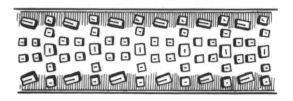

6.49C Cyclocross chevron tread pattern (Vittoria Cross XG Pro)

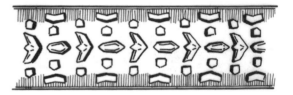

6.49D Cyclocross file tread pattern (Challenge Grifo XS)

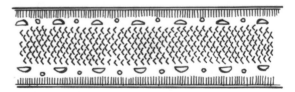

a chevron tread (Fig. 6.49C), or a file tread (Fig. 6.49D). File-tread tires are great in grass and tacky dirt but have insufficient traction for muddy or loose course conditions, so don't bother purchasing a pair of these unless you have many specific-condition wheels. Obviously, pick the mud tread for muddy courses and the knobby or chevron tread for everything else.

Clinchers offer the above tread choices and more, and they're cheaper and easier to change, so experiment; try trading wheels with friends.

'Cross pros often coat their tire sidewalls with either Aquaseal urethane adhesive or Tent Sure tent-floor sealant (both McNett products) to seal the casings from mud and allow the mud to wash off more easily.

Also, regular use of 303 Protectant on the tread and the sidewall will extend the tire's life.

Tubeless-ready clinchers are also available from Hutchinson, Kenda, NoTubes, and others.

d. Tire pressure

'Cross riders coming from a road-riding background tend to use too much tire pressure. Suffice it to say that the best riders in the world are often running 20–28 psi in tubular tires (and you thought 50 psi was superlow!). Traction and rolling resistance improve with lower pressures, up to a point, so 45 psi should be the maximum for racing, save for on a completely hardpacked, smooth course or if you're a big rider running clincher tires not big enough to evade pinch flats.

If you have tight-fitting, supple clinchers that you're running tubeless and don't have burping problems with them (see the Pro Tip on this above), you can run very low pressures with them, too, but the sharp rim edges are more vulnerable to denting than tubeless rims.

vi-29

WHEEL SELECTION

In cyclocross, you're carrying your bike a lot, and you're adding weight to it whenever you go through the mud, so you want it as light as possible while still being reliable. This is especially true with the wheels and tires, because you are constantly accelerating them and decelerating them.

Another consideration is steering. It will come as no surprise that a stiff wheel steers and tracks better than a laterally flexible one. But you may not have considered that in deep mud and sand, a tall (deep-section) rim (Fig. 6.48B) will cut through and track better than a shallow one (Fig. 6.48A).

Mud-shedding ability is also something to consider, and a deep-section, aero-shaped rim will not collect mud the way a shallow, flat rim will.

Trumping all of this will be tire choice. If you're using tubular tires, you can find lighter rims than you can for clinchers or tubeless clinchers, because you don't have the extra rim wall for the clincher to "clinch" into (Fig. 6.48A). And tubeless (or "tubeless-ready") tires are designed as a system with tubeless-specific wheels, of which there are few choices. You can mount tubeless tires on standard clincher wheels (§vi-9 and the Pro Tip "Setting Up Tubeless Cyclocross Tires"). Even if you're using tubeless-specific tires and wheels, don't count on a tubeless 'cross tire to stay on the rim if you try to ride it flat back to the pit; you certainly can't count on that with standard clincher tires or rims set up tubeless.

All other things being equal, a shallow-rim wheel will be lighter and more vertically compliant, both good features for 'cross. So in dry conditions, there's your solution. However, 'cross is often muddy, and a deep-section wheel will be your friend there. But while a wheel with a shallow aluminum rim can be quite light, that is not the case for a deep aluminum rim—you're better off dragging the mud around and losing steering precision on shallow rims. So the best of both worlds for mud will be a wheelset with deep-section carbon rims that are light, stiff, and strong. You will need carbon-specific brake pads to get decent, nongrabby braking on them; more on this in Chapter 7.

WHEELS AND TIRES

If you're pursuing cyclocross with the intent of being competitive, you need multiple sets of wheels for training and racing (not to mention two bikes), so it makes sense to have wheelsets for different race conditions, as well as inexpensive clincher wheels for training. If you have approximately the same rim width on all of your wheelsets, or if you are using disc brakes with the rotors on all your wheels spaced the same distance from the axle end, you won't have to readjust your brakes whenever you switch wheels. And if their cogsets are all spaced the same distance inward from the dropout's inner face, you won't have to adjust your rear derailleur every time you switch wheels, either.

vi-30

COG SELECTION

You might think that you'd want lower gears on a cyclocross bike than on a road bike, but that's not true. The hills are short in 'cross races, and there's usually insufficient traction in mud or even on dry dirt or grass to pedal up the steepest hills; you'll be running up them with your bike. The high gears on a 'cross bike, however, are usually lower than on a road bike. That's because the speeds are lower on flat sections of dirt, grass, mud, or sand than on pavement, and the steep downhills in 'cross are usually short and technical, emphasizing staying upright rather than powering the pedals.

Your smallest rear cog will depend on the size(s) of your front chainring(s). A fairly standard 'cross double-chainring combination is a 39–46-tooth, although compact (see §viii-7 for the difference between "compact" and "standard" double cranks) 36–46 and 34–50 combinations are becoming common. The standard single-chainring choice is somewhere between a 39-tooth and a 44-tooth. A 46 × 12 high gear is usually plenty for all but the fastest riders, as is a 39 × 11 (see the gear chart in Appendix B); indeed, even a 39 × 12 high gear is fine for most riders (it's just not great if you do a lot of road riding on a 'cross bike). So, with a double, you'd be using somewhere between a 12–25 and a 12–28 cogset (pros generally use an 11–27 or smaller), and with a single chainring, you'd be using those same cogsets, possibly starting with an 11-tooth. Many short-cage road rear derailleurs cannot handle a cog larger than 28 teeth, and even that may be a stretch; a conservative approach is to max out at 27 teeth.

NOTE ON TRIPLES: *A triple is not a realistic option on a 'cross racing bike. The only reason to use a triple on a 'cross bike is if you use it for winter training or endurance racing on mountain dirt roads or use it as a mountain bike. Otherwise, the extra weight, lower shifting precision, additional chainrings and derailleur cage in the front to collect mud and grass, and longer derailleurs more vulnerable to being torn off make a triple a net liability. You'd never be pedaling in a 'cross race at a slow enough speed to use a granny gear (innermost triple chainring); you'd be much faster running.*

It should go without saying that you should use the same number of cogs and compatibility type as your shifter; in other words, don't pair a 9-speed cogset with a 10-speed shifter, or vice versa. And almost as important, don't try mixing Shimano-compatible and Campagnolo cogsets or shifters. Shimano and SRAM cogsets are interchangeable; they fit the same freehub bodies, and they shift well with either Shimano or SRAM derailleurs. Campagnolo cogsets, however, whether 9-, 10-, or 11-speed, should only be used with Campagnolo shifters and rear derailleurs dedicated to the same number of speeds. It's probably obvious, but given the great challenges the shifting system already faces in cyclocross, there is no sense in using combinations of questionable compatibility.

BRAKES

What do I say to complaints that my brakes are no good? I'll tell you this: Anyone can stop. But it takes a genius to go fast.
—Enzo Ferrari

TOOLS

2mm, 3mm, 4mm, 5mm, 6mm hex keys

Torx T25 wrench

Cable cutter

Wet chain lube

Grease

Pliers

Optional

8mm socket wrench

8mm, 10mm open-end wrenches

13mm, 14mm cone wrenches

Adjustable wrench

The most popular brake for road bikes is the dual-pivot sidepull (Fig. 7.1). Its predecessor was the center-pivot sidepull brake (Fig. 7.2), which is also a powerful, lightweight brake. And going way back to the 1970s, dual-pivot center-pull brakes (Fig. 7.3) were the standard. A couple of other dual-pivot center-pull brakes that did not require a cable hanger (cable stop) or a straddle cable (notably Shimano AX, and Campagnolo C-Record, and Croce d'Aune Delta brakes) experienced brief popularity in the 1980s.

Center-pull cantilever brakes (simply called cantilever brakes; Fig. 7.4) or sidepull (or "direct-pull") cantilever brakes (generally called V-brakes; Fig. 7.5) are found on cyclocross bikes, hybrid bikes, and many touring bikes and tandems. Both brake types are light and simple and offer good clearance for mud, fenders, and big tires, and both pivot on bosses attached to the frame and fork. V-brakes offer the advantage of not requiring a cable hanger fixed to the frame or fork (as a canti-

lever brake does), because the cable routes directly to the brake arm. But most road bike brake levers do not pull enough cable to operate a V-brake without some sort of adapter installed to increase cable pull—hence the near-universal use of cantilevers on cyclocross bikes until disc brakes came along. Mini V-brakes work reasonably well with current Shimano road levers, but clearance to the rim is still closer than a cantilever and thus presents more resistance in muddy cyclocross conditions.

Due to rule changes in 2010 allowing them in races, disc brakes, both cable-actuated (Fig. 7.48) and hydraulic (Fig. 7.49), are the rage now for cyclocross bikes, so this book is now chock full of information on maintaining and adjusting them. They provide the best braking in the rain of any bicycle brake, and they don't limit clearance for fenders or big tires, or for mud and detritus to pass through.

A tiny contingent has always preferred hydraulic rim brakes. Road bike models mount in

205

7.1 Shimano dual-pivot sidepull brake caliper

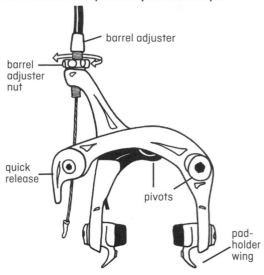

barrel adjuster

barrel adjuster nut

quick release

pivots

pad-holder wing

7.2 Center-pivot sidepull brake caliper

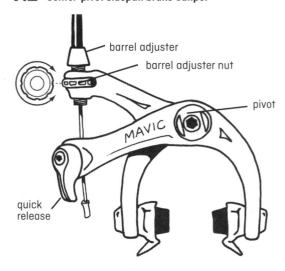

barrel adjuster

barrel adjuster nut

pivot

MAVIC

quick release

7.3 Dual-pivot center-pull brake caliper

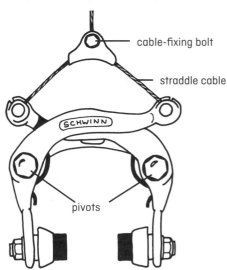

cable-fixing bolt

straddle cable

SCHWINN

pivots

the same bolt hole as standard road bike brakes, but mountain bike versions that mount on the cantilever bosses can be used on cyclocross bikes and touring bikes with cantilever studs.

RELEASING BRAKES TO REMOVE A WHEEL

Road bike tires are often narrow enough to slip past the brake pads without opening the brakes. With a wide tire or with a brake adjusted for very little clearance between the rim and the pads, the brake will need to be opened a bit. The following instructions describe how to open the vast majority of road bike brakes out there, both old and new. When you put the wheel back in, remember to follow these instructions in reverse so that your brakes will work when you need them.

1. **Opening dual-pivot sidepull brakes:** For most dual-pivot sidepull brakes (Fig. 7.1), flip open the quick-release lever on the brake arm. Campagnolo and Mavic dual-pivot sidepull brakes for Campagnolo levers do not have a quick-release mechanism on the brake caliper. Instead, there is a cable-release button on the brake/shift lever. On a Campagnolo Ergopower lever (Fig. 7.6), push the button inward so that it clears the edge of the lever housing and allows the lever to open wider.

2. **Opening center-pivot sidepull brakes:** Flip open the lever on the brake arm (Fig. 7.2), the same as on a Shimano dual-pivot side-pull brake. Although older Campagnolo brakes open this way (after the mid-1980s), modern Campagnolo center-pivot sidepull brakes have the quick-release on the brake/shift lever (as in Fig. 7.6) and not on the caliper.

7.4 **Center-pull cantilever brake caliper**

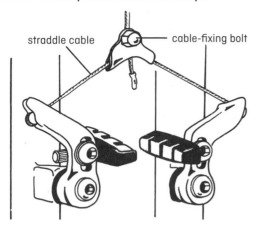

straddle cable — cable-fixing bolt

7.5 **Sidepull cantilever brake (V-brake) caliper**

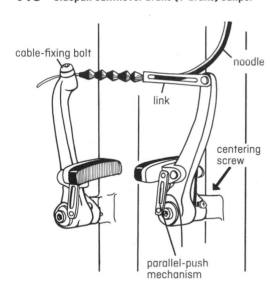

cable-fixing bolt

noodle

link

centering screw

parallel-push mechanism

7.6 **Cable-release button on a Campagnolo Ergopower lever**

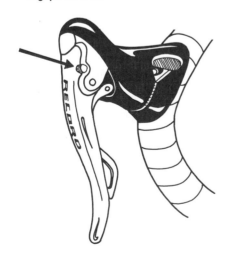

3. **Opening cantilevers and ancient dual-pivot center-pull brakes:** For cantilevers (Fig. 7.4) and 1970s and older dual-pivot center-pull brakes (Fig. 7.3), hold the pads against the rim and pull the head of the straddle cable out of the hook at the end of one brake arm.

4. **Opening V-brakes:** For V-brakes (Fig. 7.5), hold the pads against the rim and pull the cable noodle back and up to release it from the brake-arm link.

5. **Opening Shimano AX and Campagnolo Delta (both from the 1980s) dual-pivot center-pull brakes:** On Campagnolo Delta brakes, push the cable-release button on the brake lever (Fig. 7.6), as described in step 1. On Shimano AX brakes, pull the cable-tensioning barrel adjuster up and out.

CABLES AND HOUSINGS

LEVEL 1

Given that cables transfer braking force from the levers to the brakes, proper installation and maintenance are critical to brake performance. Excess friction in the cable system will prevent the brakes from working properly, no matter how well the brakes, calipers, and levers are adjusted. Cables with broken strands should be replaced immediately.

vii-2

CABLE TENSIONING

As brake pads wear and cables stretch, the cable needs to be tightened to remove slack in the system. The barrel adjuster on the brake arm of any road bike sidepull brake (Fig. 7.7) and on top of Shimano AX and Campagnolo Delta center-pull brakes serves exactly this purpose.

Center-pull brakes, cantilever brakes, and V-brakes (Figs. 7.3–7.5) have no barrel adjuster

7.7 Turning the barrel adjuster on the brake arm of sidepull brakes

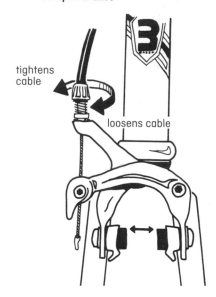

tightens cable

loosens cable

on the brake lever (or brake/shift lever). Cable tensioning for cantilever brakes and for ancient center-pull brakes requires either turning a barrel adjuster on a cable hanger on the frame or fork (Fig. 7.8) or sometimes on the brake arm (Fig. 7.18), or loosening the cable-fixing bolt on the straddle cable carrier (Figs. 7.3, 7.4, 7.35), pulling the cable taut, and tightening the bolt again. V-brakes generally are set up with a flat handlebar and flat-bar levers, which usually have a barrel adjuster on the lever to adjust cable tension; otherwise, cable tension is increased by loosening the cable-fixing bolt at the brake caliper (Fig. 7.5), pulling the cable taut, and tightening the bolt again.

The cable should be tight enough that the lever cannot be pulled to the bar, yet loose enough that the brakes—assuming they are centered and the wheels are true—are not dragging on the rims.

a. Increasing cable tension

1. **For brakes with the barrel adjuster on the caliper, back out the barrel adjuster to tighten the cable.** Not all of them turn the same way to tighten the cable, so pay atten-

tion to which direction tightens the cable and which direction loosens it on yours. On brakes with a nut on the barrel adjuster (Figs. 7.1, 7.2), turn the nut clockwise when viewed from above; the barrel adjuster will be pulled straight upward out of the D-shaped hole in the brake arm. The underside of the adjuster nut usually has bumps that drop in and out of notches in the top of the brake arm to hold its adjustment, so holding the pads against the rim with your thumb and fingers will make turning the nut easier; stop when it clicks into a notch, not between notches. On brakes whose barrel adjuster threads into the brake arm (Figs. 7.7, 7.9), turn the barrel adjuster counter-clockwise to tighten the cable. For cantilever brakes, recall that the barrel adjuster may be on a cable hanger (Fig. 7.8) and/or on a brake arm (Fig. 7.18); unscrew the barrel adjuster (counterclockwise) to tighten the cable, and secure it in position by tightening the knurled nut against the cable hanger or straddle cable end.

2. **Increase the cable tension sufficiently that the brake lever (or the shift lever behind it) does not hit the handlebar when the brake is applied fully.** Be careful not to make the tension so tight that the brake rubs or comes on with very little movement of the lever.

3. **If the barrel adjuster cannot take up enough cable slack to get the brakes as tight as you want, you need to tighten the cable at the brake.** First, screw the barrel adjuster back in most of the way; this step leaves some adjustment in the system for brake setup and cable stretch over time. Loosen the cable-fixing bolt clamping the cable at the brake (Figs. 7.5, 7.9, 7.35). Check the cable for wear. If it's badly frayed, replace it (see §vii-4.) Otherwise, pull the cable tight

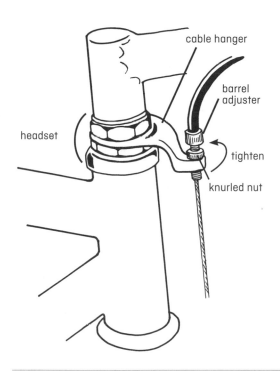

cable hanger

barrel adjuster

headset

tighten

knurled nut

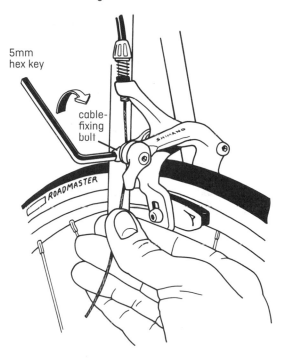

5mm hex key

cable-fixing bolt

SHIMANO

ROADMASTER

and retighten the clamping bolt. Tension the cable as needed with the barrel adjuster.

b. Reducing cable tension

1. **On brakes with a nut on the barrel adjuster (Figs. 7.1, 7.2), turn the nut counterclockwise (when viewed from the top) until your brake pads are properly spaced from the rim.** On brakes whose barrel adjuster threads into the brake arm, turn the barrel adjuster clockwise (Figs. 7.7, 7.9). You want some movement of the lever before the pads contact the rim, but not so much that the lever comes back to the handlebar under hard braking. Within that range, it is up to your personal preference. On a cantilever, turn the barrel adjuster on the cable hanger or brake arm clockwise after loosening the knurled nut (Figs. 7.8, 7.18).

2. **Let the notches in the barrel adjuster and brake arm engage to lock in the adjust-** ment (or tighten the knurled nut).

3. **Double-check that the cable is tight enough that the lever cannot be squeezed all the way to the handlebar.**

vii-3

CABLE MAINTENANCE

1. **If the cable is frayed or kinked or has any broken strands, replace it (§vii-4).**

2. **If the cable is not sliding well, lubricate it.** Use an oil-based chain lubricant (not a chain wax or other dry lube) or molybdenum disulfide grease, if possible. Lithium-based greases and chain waxes can eventually gum up cables and restrict movement.

   To lubricate, open the brake (via the cable quick-release as when you remove a wheel; see §vii-1).

   If the bike has slotted cable stops for the rear brake, pull the ends of the rear brake-cable-housing segments out of each stop. On the front brake—and on the rear brake if your bike does not have slotted cable stops—you will have to disconnect the cable at the brake, clip off the cable end, and pull out the entire cable.

Slide the housing up the cable, wipe the cable clean with a rag, rub chain lubricant on the cable section that was inside the housing, and slide the housing back into place. If you have pulled the housing completely off the cable, squirt chain lube through the housing as well.

3. **If the cable still sticks, replace the cable and housing.**

---

vii-4

CABLE REPLACEMENT AND INSTALLATION

1. **Disconnect the cable at the brake caliper, clip off the cable-end cap, and pull out the old cable from the lever.** You will need to pull the lever and then let it back a bit to free the head of the cable from the cable hook in the lever.

NOTE: *When installing a new cable, it is a good idea to replace the housings as well, even if they seem okay. Daily riding in dirty conditions may require cables and housings to be replaced every few months. As with chains and derailleur cables, brake-cable replacement is a maintenance operation, not a repair operation; don't wait until a cable breaks or seizes up to replace it.*

2. **Purchase good-quality cables and lined housings.** For cables, try using "die-drawn" cables; the exterior strands have been flattened by being pulled through a constricting die. They will move with less friction. Brake-cable housing is spiral-wrapped to prevent

splitting under braking pressure (Fig. 5.16). Plastic-lined housing (i.e., Teflon) reduces friction and is a must.

3. **Cut the housing sections long enough to reach the brakes, and route them so that they do not make any sharp bends.** If you are replacing existing housing, look at the bends before removing the old housings (after unwrapping the handlebar tape to get at them). If the housing bends are smooth and do not bind when the front wheel is swung through its arc, cut the new housings to the same lengths. Otherwise, cut each new segment longer than you think necessary and keep trimming it back until it gives the smoothest path possible for the cable, without the cable tension being affected by steering. Use a cutter specifically designed for cutting housings, or a sharp side-cutter to cut between two coils, rather than trying to cut across a couple of coils, which will mash them flat.

4. **After cutting, make sure the housing's end faces are flat.** If not, square them off with a file or a clipper.

5. **If the end of the Teflon liner is mashed shut after cutting, open it up with a sharp object like a nail or a toothpick.**

6. **Slip a ferrule (a cylindrical cap; see Fig. 5.16) over each housing end for support at each frame cable stop and at the caliper and lever, if required.** Some brake-arm barrel adjusters and ports in brake-lever bodies function as a ferrule and are too narrow for a ferrule to fit in; they are designed to accept only bare cable housing.

7. **Decide which hand you want to control which brake.** (The U.S. bike standard is that the right hand controls the rear brake, but if you're the only one riding the bike, you can

switch it around to match the setup on your motorcycle, for example.) Install the housings into each housing stop, brake lever (or brake/shift lever), and brake caliper.

8. **Turn the adjusting barrel on the brake caliper or cable hanger to within one turn of being screwed all the way in (Fig. 7.7 or Fig. 7.8).**

9. **Insert the cable into the lever, through the lever's cable hook (Fig. 7.10), and out the cable exit hole in the lever body.** Make sure that the cable head is countersunk into its seat in the cable hook. Some brakes have a cylinder through which the cable passes perpendicularly. The hole on one side may be countersunk but not on the other, so rotate the cylinder so that the countersunk hole is forward. On recent brakes, the cable exits the inboard side of the lever under the edge of the lever hood so that it can be wrapped under the handlebar tape. Many brake levers prior to 1988 or so, and almost all of them prior to 1980, had the cable coming out the top of the lever.

10. **Slide the cable through the housings and to the brake caliper.** Make sure there is a

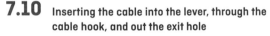

7.10 Inserting the cable into the lever, through the cable hook, and out the exit hole

ferrule on the end of the housing, if one will fit into the barrel adjuster.

NOTE: *Lubrication is not necessary. New cables slide well in new, lined housing, and to avoid attracting dirt it is usually best not to use a lubricant on the cable. Also, some greases can gum up inside the housing. (Down the road when the cable starts to stick, however, you may need to lubricate it; see §vii-3.)*

11. **Attach the cable to the brake.** (See the section entitled "Brake Calipers" for details on your type of brake caliper.) Pull it taut and tighten the cable-fixing bolt (Figs. 7.3, 7.4, 7.5, 7.9, 7.35). Pull the lever as hard as you can and hold it for sixty seconds to stretch the new cable.

12. **Adjust cable tension with the barrel adjuster (as in §vii-2).**

13. **Cut off the cable about an inch past the cable-fixing bolt.** Crimp an end cap on the exposed cable end to prevent fraying (Fig. 5.19). Wrap the handlebar tape (§xi-12).

14. **Check for free movement.** Once the cable has been properly installed, the lever should snap back quickly when released. If it does not, recheck the cable for kinks and fraying, and check the housing for sharp bends. Release the cable quick-release and hold the pads to the rim with your hand while checking the lever for free movement. With the cable still loose, check that the brake pads do not drag on the tire as they return to the neutral position. Make sure the brake arms rotate freely on their pivots, and check that the brake-arm return springs snap the pads away from the rims. If the lever and caliper move freely and spring back strongly, and if there are no obvious binds in the system, check for frayed strands within the housing sections and then try lubricating the cable as in §vii-3.

BRAKE LEVERS

The levers must operate smoothly and be set up so that you can reach them easily while riding.

vii-5

LUBRICATION AND SERVICE

LEVEL 1

1. **Oil all pivot points in the lever.**
2. **Check return-spring function on the lever.** Note that not all levers have springs in them.
3. **Make sure that the lever or lever body is not bent in a way that hinders movement.**
4. **Check for stress cracks. If you find any, replace the lever.**
5. **Replace torn or cracked lever hoods.**

vii-6

REMOVAL, INSTALLATION, AND POSITIONING

LEVEL 1

Most current brake levers integrate the brake lever and the shifter in a single unit (Figs. 7.6, 7.11–7.13). Brake/shift levers are generally labeled right and left, but if you're in doubt, you can tell which is which because the levers flip to the inside. Here are the steps to replace the entire brake/shift lever unit, or a simple brake lever on bikes that have bar-end or down-tube shifters:

1. **Remove the handlebar tape and bar plugs.**
2. **Remove the old brake/shift lever by loosening its mounting bolt with a 5mm hex key and sliding the lever assembly off (post-2008 Campagnolo Ultra-Shift Ergopower levers require a Torx T25 wrench).** The position of the bolt varies, but it is always on the outside of the lever body under the

7.11 Tightening a Shimano STI brake/shift lever to the bar with a 5mm hex key

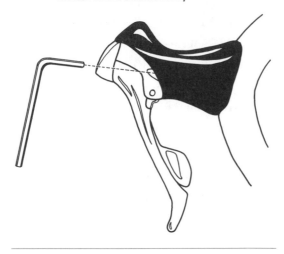

lever hood on the outboard side. Slip the hex or Torx key down from the top between the lever body and the hood (Fig. 7.11) or roll back the hood far enough to get at it from outside of the hood.

Old-style brake levers without shifters in them have the mounting bolt in the center of the lever body; reach it by pulling the lever and sticking the hex key straight in. Campagnolo and other European levers from the early 1980s and before used a hex nut (accessed with an 8mm socket wrench) rather than an Allen bolt.

3. **Slide the new lever on the bar.** Campagnolo lever bands have an arrow indicating direction of sliding onto the bar, in case they become separated from the lever; use this as a guide for proper orientation. Slide the lever up the bar to where you like it. A good rule of thumb is to put a straightedge against the bottom of the bar and slide the lever down until its end touches the straightedge. The lever can sit a little higher than this if you like (and the current style is often to have the levers quite high on the handlebar), but generally not any lower. Put a long straightedge across the top of both levers after they

are tightened to make sure that they are level with each other.

4. **Tighten the mounting bolt.**

5. **Post-2008 Campagnolo Ultra-Shift Ergopower levers have a "big hands" insert.** If you want to increase the reach to the levers, shove the insert onto the bottom of the lever base under the hood (Fig. 5.38). The inserts are asymmetrical but not labeled per side, so line up the hole on the insert with the cable-access hole on the lever body to ensure you have it on the correct lever.

6. **Install the cables (see §vii-4 and §v-7 through §v-17).**

7. **Wrap the handlebar with tape (see §xi-12).**

---

vii-7

REACH

Reach adjustment is a recent feature for dual-control brake/shift levers.

a. SRAM

SRAM's first-year (2007) Force and Rival levers did not have a reach adjustment, but since the introduction of the RED group in 2008, all RED, Force, and Rival levers have a reach adjustment. On the SRAM system, you reduce the reach of the shift lever first, then move the brake lever inward to avoid having them overlap and interfere with each other.

1. **Pull the shift lever back, independently from the brake lever.** On the outboard side, up near the pivot, you will see either a small screw with a 2.5mm hex hole, or a tiny cam about the diameter of brake-cable housing; either will be easier to access once the lever is pulled back.

2. **Insert a 2.5mm hex key in the screw, or push the cam inward with your finger or the tip of a pen (Fig. 7.12). The can is spring-**

loaded and will snap back unless you keep pushing inward on it.

3. **Turn the screw or cam counterclockwise until you find its next adjustment position (there are six altogether).** Be aware that on some levers it is possible to knock off the circlip retaining this cam, and the cam will go flying and be very hard to find. It takes very little force to turn this cam, as long as it is pushed in. If you're having trouble turning it, push it in more; if you try to turn it when it's not pushed in, you can apply too much force and knock parts off, so just move the parts as they are intended to move. Once you've turned it a notch (or more), let the cam pop back out against its stop. When you let go of the shift lever, it will have pulled in a bit, leaving a space between it and the back of the brake lever.

4. **Peel back the lever hood.**

5. **Tighten (clockwise) the brake lever reach adjustment screw on the back of the lever body with a 2.5 or 3mm hex key until the brake lever comes back and once again just touches the shift lever.**

6. **Readjust the brake-cable tension (§vii-2) as needed.** (Decreasing lever reach will have

---

7.12 SRAM reach adjustment

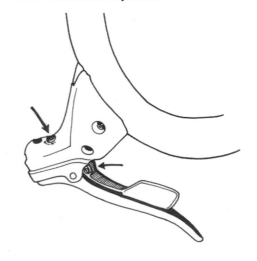

pulled the brake pads closer to the rims.)

7. **Repeat steps 1–6 until you get the reach you desire.** Or do the steps in reverse to increase lever reach.

b. Shimano

Shimano introduced reach adjustment beginning in 2009 with the Dura-Ace 7900 group. It's a simple turn of a single screw, but you have to remove a cover to get at it.

1. **Pull the brake lever.**

2. **Loosen the little Phillips-head screw that is revealed when you pull the lever back.** You do not need to remove this screw all the way; it's a good idea not to, because it is very easy to lose.

3. **Using your fingernail, flip the top of the little chrome cover plate (about the size of a thumbnail) forward and remove it (Fig. 7.13).**

4. **You will now see the head of the brake cable, and you will see a small slotted screw in the hole just outboard of it. This is the reach adjustment screw.** To get at it, you may need to loosen the little Phillips screw more than you loosened it to remove the cover plate, because it comes down across the hole right in front of that screw.

7.13 Shimano Dura-Ace 7900 reach adjustment (beneath cover)

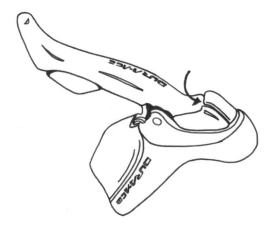

5. **With a small screwdriver, tighten (clockwise) that screw (Fig. 7.13).** The lever will tip forward, bringing the lever tip closer to the bar. There are many turns of adjustment to this screw; keep turning it until you find the position you like.

c. Campagnolo

With the introduction of Ultra-Shift Ergopower levers (which first became available in late 2008) throughout the Campagnolo range, small hands had fewer reach problems, since the new lever shape brought the tip closer to the handlebar. But for some riders with large hands, the reach reduction resulted in a constrained feeling, so Campagnolo began packaging a small, plastic "big hands" insert with its Ultra-Shift levers. It fits between the lever and the handlebar under the bottom edge of the lever body and tips the lever back to increase the distance from the handlebar to the lever blade (Fig. 5.38).

d. Other levers

Even if you don't have adjustable-reach levers, there are a few things you can try if you have difficulty reaching the levers.

First, you can try moving the lever to a different position on the bar. This may bring the lever closer to the bar.

Another option is to buy a bar with a different bend that puts the palm of the hand closer to the lever. There are some bars specifically made to accomplish this feat.

Finally, you can try to buy a smaller lever. This used to be relatively simple when brake levers were just brake levers. But now, with dual-control levers that incorporate the shifters, you cannot swap a shorter lever from another manufacturer, and the levers made by derailleur manufacturers do not come in different reaches, with one midrange exception from Shimano. You can buy a whole new brake and derailleur system to get one with a reach you prefer or that you can adjust, but I recommend investigating a different handlebar first.

BRAKE CALIPERS

LEVEL 1

The caliper of a brake is the mechanism that pinches the pads inward against the wheel rim. In most cases, a road bike caliper is a side-pull device that bolts on through a hole in the brake bridge or fork crown (Figs. 7.1, 7.2, 7.14, 7.15). But "caliper" can also refer to the pair of arms of a cantilever or V-brake that attach to pivot posts welded onto the frame and fork (Figs. 7.4, 7.5). And then there are those old center-pull Weinmann and Universal calipers (Fig. 7.3) from 1970s Raleighs and Peugeots.

vii-8

DUAL-PIVOT SIDEPULL BRAKES

Dual-pivot sidepull brakes (Figs. 7.1, 7.15) have become the industry standard. They are powerful and easy to keep in adjustment.

Campagnolo and Mavic dual-pivot brakes have some features distinct from Shimano dual-pivot brakes. Asian copies of Shimano brakes generally share the same features.

a. Installation

Stick the center bolt through the hole in the brake bridge or fork crown and tighten it in place with a 5mm hex key inserted into the recessed nut (Fig. 7.14). Hold it roughly centered over the wheel as you tighten the nut. Ensure that you have at least six turns of engagement (this is only an issue on the fork). Get a longer recessed brake nut if needed to ensure sufficient thread engagement.

b. Cable hookup

Open the quick-release on the caliper (or on the lever on Campagnolo or Mavic) before you do the cable hookup. Route the cable housing into the barrel adjuster on the upper brake arm. On the end of the housing, install a ferrule if one will fit into the barrel adjuster (§vii-4). Push the cable through the housing and the barrel adjuster and under the cable-fixing-bolt washer on the lower brake arm. Pull the cable taut and tighten the bolt with a 5mm hex key (Fig. 7.9). Close the quick-release after the cable is connected.

c. Centering

You are trying to achieve an equal amount of space between the pad and the rim on each side. The simplest and quickest way to center these brakes requires no tools. Just grab the brake and twist the entire thing into position (don't mess with the mounting bolt; leave it tight). Or just pull outward on the pad that is closer to the rim. But do make sure before riding that the recessed nut on the back of the brake bridge or fork is tight (Fig. 7.14).

7.14 Tightening a caliper to the brake bridge with a 5mm hex key

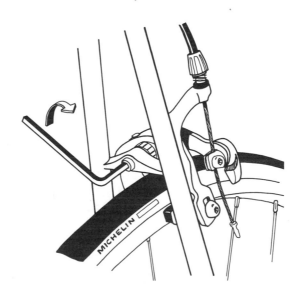

The centering method built in by Campagnolo and Shimano consists of a setscrew; you can center SRAM and Mavic calipers with a 12mm or 14mm cone wrench, respectively.

Campagnolo has a 2mm hex setscrew on the side opposite the cable, just above the pad on the arm. As you tighten the screw, the pad on that side moves away from the rim. Loosen the screw, and the other pad (the one on the cable side) moves away from the rim.

Shimano's setscrew is on the upper end of the opposite brake arm. It takes a 3mm hex key (Fig. 7.15), and tightening it moves the pad on that side away from the rim. Loosen it, and the other pad (the one on the cable side) moves away from the rim.

SRAM and Mavic dual-pivot sidepull brakes require working a 5mm hex key in the recessed mounting nut while rotating the nut behind the brake caliper with a 12mm or 14mm cone wrench, respectively (similar to center-pivot centering; see Fig. 7.17).

d. Pad adjustment

Loosen the pad-mounting bolt with a hex key (generally 4mm or 5mm). Slide the pad up or down along the slot in the arm to get the pad even with the height of the rim's braking surface. Twist the pad in the vertical plane to have the top edge of the pad follow the curve of the top edge of the rim (Fig. 7.16). While squeezing the brake lever to hold the pad against the rim, tighten the pad-mounting bolt. Make sure the pad does not twist as you tighten (if it does, you will have to hold it with your fingers as you cinch the bolt). Also make sure that the pad does not contact the tire. If it does, it will quickly wear a hole in the tire sidewall, causing a blowout.

Higher-end brakes also have an orbital adjustment of the pads to align the face of the pad flat against the rim and to allow a toe-in

7.15 Turning a setscrew with a 3mm hex key to center a Shimano dual-pivot brake caliper

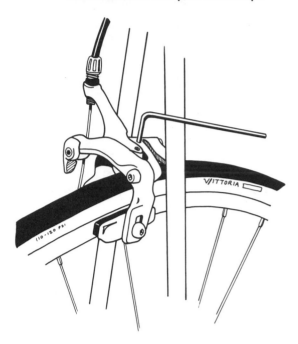

7.16 Line the pad up with the rim

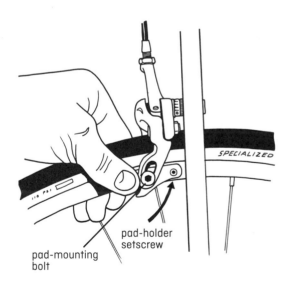

pad-holder setscrew

pad-mounting bolt

adjustment of the pad by means of a concave washer that nests against the convex face of the pad holder. If the brake squeals or is grabby, toe the pads in a bit so that the forward end of the pad is a little closer to the rim than the rearward end. A 1mm toe-in is sufficient to eliminate squeal and grabbiness.

NOTE: *Users of first-generation Shimano pre-built wheels with the spoke elbows at the rim and with turn-of-the-millennium Dura-Ace or Ultegra brakes will want to remove the little plastic screw in the pad-holder wing, if present (below the pad; Fig. 7.1). Otherwise, as soon as the pad wears a bit, that screw will thump-thump-thump against the bend in the spoke where it exits the side of the rim.*

e. Spring-tension adjustment

Campagnolo dual-pivot brakes have a setscrew that pushes on the end of the return spring. It is located on the side of the arm above the cable-side pad. If you tighten this screw (with a 2mm hex key), you will also tighten the spring, thus making the brake both harder to pull and quicker to snap back. There is no tension adjustment on Shimano brake springs or on the leaf spring in Mavic brakes. Some springs can be bent with pliers to increase tension.

f. Cable-tension adjustment

Follow the instructions in §vii-2.

g. Pad replacement

When the pads wear to the point that the grooves molded into the pads are almost gone, replace them. Low-end pads often are molded in one piece with the mounting nut insert or stud,

---

PRO TIP | Brake Pad Selection for Carbon Rims

It is absolutely critical to get the right pad if you are using all-carbon rims. The pad compound for carbon rims is quite different from the compounds made for aluminum rims because normal high-rubber brake pads cannot take the heat of braking on carbon rims and can actually melt. Carbon is an insulator and retains heat well, while aluminum is a conductor and disperses heat well. Carbon rims are also generally lighter than aluminum rims, with less thermal mass to absorb heat. And you are talking some hot pads.

Carbon rims often come with pads made for them, and approaches vary in their manufacture. Cork pads are also often used for carbon rims due to cork's high coefficient of friction and its resistance to heat.

Even with specific carbon-rim pads, wear rates are very high on most carbon braking surfaces. After descending a few kilometers of switchbacks, you will notice melted pad material building up on the front of the pads. Make sure that you check the pads frequently and replace them before they get too worn. You would not be the first to have brake failure on a carbon rim.

The pad buildup on the braking surface of carbon rims is a good thing; when you clean the rims, braking performance may drop, so don't clean the braking surfaces too often. On the other hand, buildup in the pads is not beneficial. Clean the pads and also dig out any chunks of foreign matter from them before you chew up the expensive carbon braking surface.

If you switch back and forth between aluminum rims and carbon rims, you may need matching sets of pads to switch along with the rims. If you do not, braking distance may increase substantially, which is not a good thing for safety or for maximizing speed when racing.

By the way, if you are interested in trying wooden rims (an old technology that is making a small comeback), you will find that good carbon-specific pads work far better on them than do standard pads; be prepared for the smell of burning wood under hard braking, though!

so you just unscrew the old pad and holder assembly and bolt the new one in place.

High-end dual-pivot brakes surround the pad with an aluminum holder that is bolted to the brake arm. The pad can be replaced separately by sliding it from the holder. Some pad holders have a setscrew (Fig. 7.16) that must first be backed out to free the pad. Buy the correct pad according to the year and model of brake.

Sliding the pad in or out of the holder can be difficult. You may have to yank out the old pad with pliers and slide in the new pad with the aid of a vise, or hold the post in a vise while you push on the pad grooves with a screwdriver.

Be sure to put the proper pad in the proper holder; look at the old one for guidance. Pads often say R or L on the backside and indicate the forward direction; Campagnolo pads may say DX (right) or SX (left) on the backside. Be prepared for some work pushing the new pads into the holders, at least with Campagnolo; use a vise or slip-joint pliers and keep cutting off the burrs of pad material that may get peeled back by the edges of the pad holder.

When you reinstall the pad on the brake arm, make sure that the closed end of the pad holder faces forward. Otherwise, the first time you brake hard, you may see two pieces of rubber fly ahead of you and feel two more hit the backs of your legs. You may not remember anything after that.

vii-9

CENTER-PIVOT SIDEPULL BRAKES

Center-pivot sidepull brakes (Fig. 7.2) are still found on lots of bikes because they were the standard from the late 1970s to the early 1990s, and current high-end Campagnolo brake sets use them on the rear to save weight and reduce braking power (most braking is done with the front brake; an overly powerful rear brake can easily lock up the rear wheel). Center-pivot side-pulls work very well and are easy to set up and adjust. Many adjustments are the same as those on dual-pivot brakes.

a. Installation

Stick the center bolt through the hole in the brake bridge or fork crown and tighten it in place with a 5mm hex key inserted into the recessed nut (Fig. 7.14). Hold the brake roughly centered over the wheel as you tighten the nut. Ensure that you have at least six turns of engagement (this is only an issue on the fork). Get a longer recessed brake nut if needed to ensure sufficient thread engagement.

Some older bikes do not have a countersunk hole in the back of the brake bridge and fork crown. With these, you need a brake with a longer center bolt and a standard nut, which you tighten with a 10mm box wrench.

b. Cable hookup

Open the quick-release on the caliper (or on the lever on some current Campagnolo levers) before you make this hookup. Route the cable housing into the barrel adjuster on the upper brake arm. If a ferrule will fit into the barrel adjuster, install one on the end of the housing (§vii-4). Push the cable through the housing and the barrel adjuster and under the cable-fixing bolt washer on the lower brake arm. Pull the cable tight and tighten the bolt with a 5mm hex key (same as with a dual-pivot brake; Fig. 7.9) or an 8mm box wrench.

c. Centering

You want an equal amount of space between the pad and the rim on each side. Turn the brake in the direction you need with a cone wrench (usually 13mm or 14mm) slipped onto the flats of the center bolt between the brake and the frame

7.17 Centering a center-pivot sidepull brake with a cone wrench

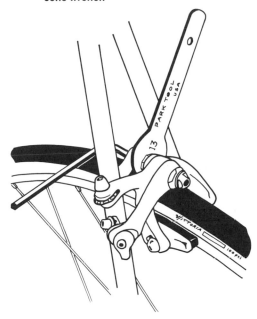

(Fig. 7.17). Hold the brake-mounting nut at the same time, making sure that it is tight when you are finished.

d. Pad adjustment

Loosen the pad-mounting bolt with a hex key or box wrench. Slide the pad up or down along the slot in the arm to get the pad even with the height of the rim's braking surface. Twist the pad in the vertical plane to make the top edge of the pad follow the curve of the top edge of the rim (the same as with a dual-pivot brake; Fig. 7.16). While squeezing the brake lever to hold the pad against the rim, tighten the bolt. Make sure the pad does not twist as you tighten (if it does, you will have to hold it with your fingers as you cinch down on the bolt). Also make sure that the pad does not contact the tire; if it does, it will quickly wear a hole in the tire sidewall, causing a blowout.

e. Spring-tension adjustment

Some center-pivot sidepull brakes have a spring-tension adjusting screw. And on some Shimano center-pivot brakes, the piece of plastic at each end of the spring can be reversed to tighten or loosen the spring. The hole through which the end of the spring slides is offset in the wafer-shaped plastic piece. Push inward on the end of the spring to free the plastic wafer from the brake-arm tab, flip the wafer over, and push it back in place under the tab. If the hole is to the outside, the spring is looser; if the wafer is flipped so that the hole is toward the inside, the spring is as tight as it is going to get.

f. Cable-tension adjustment

Follow the instructions in §vii-2.

g. Pad replacement

When the pads are worn to the point that the grooves molded into the pads are almost gone, replace them.

Most pads are molded in one piece with the mounting nut insert or mounting stud, so you just unscrew the pad and bolt the new one in place.

High-end brake pads are fitted into a holder that is bolted to the brake arm. You slide the rubber pad to remove it from the holder, but often it is not easy. You may have to yank out the old pad with pliers and slide in the new pad with the aid of a vise; see §vii-8g for more on this.

When you reinstall the pad to the brake arm, make sure that the closed end of the pad holder faces forward. Otherwise, the pads will be pulled out of the holders the first time you use the brakes. This will be very bad news for the second time you need the brakes.

CANTILEVER BRAKES

Whether traditional "cantis" with a straddle cable (Fig. 7.4, §vii-10) or sidepull cantilevers (a.k.a. "V-brakes" or "direct-pull cantilevers;" Figs. 7.5, 7.42), cantilever brake calipers consist of two separate brake arms that pivot on posts pro-truding from the fork legs and rear seatstays. Standard cantilever brakes have relatively short arms and work well with drop-bar brake levers, but long-arm cantilevers, including standard mountain bike V-brakes, require more cable pull than standard road bike levers are able to muster and have enormous (too much!) braking power with them (see §vii-12 for solutions).

Traditional cantilevers are some of the only bicycle brakes that allow the user to substantially adjust their mechanical advantage or lever-age—the ratio between how much force the hand applies at the lever and the amount of force the brake pads apply at the rim. This is because the user can adjust the angle of the straddle cable as well as the offset of the brake pad from the brake arm, and, on some models, the angle of the arms from vertical as well.

---

vii-10

CANTILEVER BRAKE CALIPERS, CYCLOCROSS

Found on cyclocross bikes as well as some touring bikes and tandems, standard cantilever brakes offer greater clearance over the tire for mud to pass through than other rim brakes, and they provide clearance for fenders and large tires as well. Their two separate arms mount onto brake posts integral to the frame and fork and are pulled toward each other when the brake cable pulls up on a transverse cable (a.k.a. "straddle cable") connecting the arms (Figs. 7.18–7.19).

In order to mount cantilevers, a cable stop is required at the rear on the frame's seatstays or hanging off the seat binder bolt, and another one for the front brake is needed on the fork steering tube above the headset (Fig. 7.8), on the fork crown (Fig. 7.18), or hanging from the stem

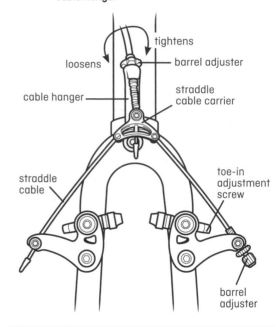

7.18 TRP EuroX cantilever brake assembly connected via a fork-crown-mounted cable hanger

(decades ago, some stems had integrated cable hangers or even through-holes for the cable, and some cable hangers slip in between the stem and the stem front cap of modern stems and hang from one or two handlebar clamp bolts).

Whether it is on the front or rear, the cable stop often includes a barrel adjuster to pull up cable slack, as on the cable hangers in Figures 7.8 and 7.18. The barrel adjuster makes brake setup easier, because there is no cable-tension adjuster on a drop-bar brake lever, and only recently (and only at the high end) have cantilever brakes included a barrel adjuster at the caliper (Fig. 7.18).

a. Brake arm installation

1. **Grease the outside of the brake posts (Fig. 7.19).** Avoid getting grease inside the brake post threads; brake-mounting bolts are treated with threadlock goop to prevent them from vibrating loose. If your brake has an adjustment for brake arm angle (Fig. 7.20), skip to step 11.

7.19 Cantilever brake assembly with spring-tension adjusting nut in front

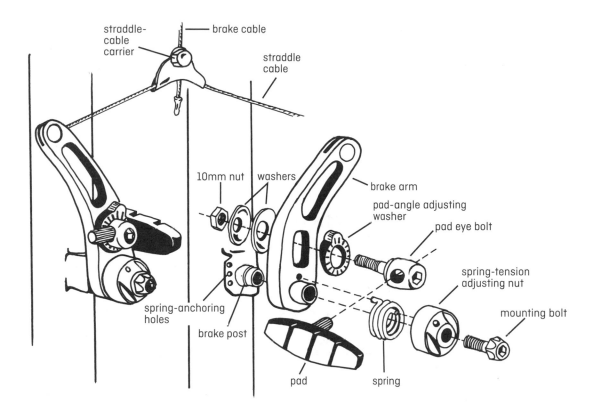

7.20A Wide- and narrow-stance options on an Avid Shorty Ultimate cantilever brake

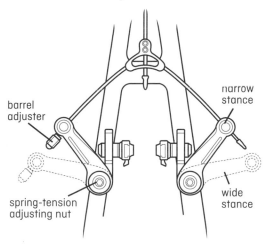

7.20B Removal and replacement of Torx T10 bolts to change stance on Avid Shorty Ultimate brake

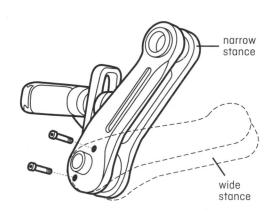

2. **Make sure you install the brakes with all of the parts in the order in which they were originally in the package (or on a previous bike).** The springs often are of different colors and are not interchangeable from left to right.

3. **If the brake has a separate inner sleeve bushing to fit over the cantilever boss, install that first.** Slip the brake arm and return spring over it.

4. **Determine what sort of return system your brakes use.**

a.   If the brake arms have no spring-tension adjustment (Fig. 7.18), or a setscrew on the side of one of the arms for adjusting spring tension (Fig. 7.37), proceed to step 5; the spring in such brakes anchors in a hole in the cantilever boss.

b.   If there is a large nut at each arm for adjusting spring tension, skip to step 7, since these brakes do not use a hole in the cantilever boss as a spring anchor. This spring-tension-adjusting nut is usually in front of the brake arm, surrounding the mounting bolt (Fig. 7.19, 7.20A), but it can also be behind it (Fig. 7.28).

5.   **Slip the brake arm onto the boss, inserting the lower end of the spring into the hole in the cantilever boss.** If the boss has three holes as in Figure 7.19, try the center hole first; use a higher hole to make the brake response snappier, a necessity with lower-quality or old brakes. You want to make sure that the top end of the spring is inserted into the corresponding hole (or notch or slot as in Fig. 7.18) in the brake arm as well.

6.   **Install and tighten the mounting bolt into the cantilever boss. Skip steps 7–9.**

7.   **If step 4b brings you here, install the spring so that one end inserts into the hole in the brake arm and the other inserts into the hole in the adjusting nut (Fig. 7.19).**

8.   **Slide the brake-arm assembly (with any included bushings) onto the cantilever boss.**

9.   **Install and tighten the mounting bolt.** Do this while holding the adjusting nut with an open-end wrench that fits it so that the pad is touching the rim to facilitate pad adjustment later.

10. **Some brakes are sensitive to the length of the cantilever post on the frame or fork.** There are two standard post lengths: 21mm or 22mm, measured from the shoulder to the

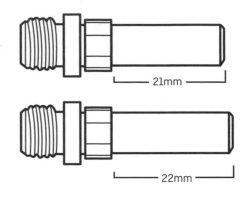

7.21 **Standard cantilever brake pivot post lengths**

21mm

22mm

end (Fig. 7.21). If your brake binds up when you tightened the bolt, the post may be too short. You may need to switch to a 22mm post or use a 1mm washer ring under the bolt head (possibly supplied with the brake). Similarly, if the brake has play and rattles up and down on the pivot, you can get a shorter post or slip a 1mm spacer over the post (possibly supplied with the brake) in front of or behind the brake arm.

11. **If your brake is adjustable for brake-arm angle or stance (Fig. 7.20) and you want to change the arm stance, you must do that before installing it on the brake posts.** This consists of disassembling the brake arm from the pad-mounting tab, changing their angle relative to each other, and reassembling.

Why would you want to change the cantilever arm angle? Well, in the wide stance, with the arms sticking out almost horizontally, mud clearance is maximized, as the leverage is reduced. This results in the pads moving farther from the rims. The narrow stance offers higher power due to increased leverage, and it offers more heel clearance on the rear brake. A full explanation of this is below in step d on straddle-cable adjustment. In cyclocross, I like to have more power and heel clearance in the rear (narrow stance) to be able to always get as much rear brake as I want without excessive hand force as well as to prevent me from kicking a brake arm into the rear spokes on a botched remount. I like lower power in the front (wide stance) to prevent me from grabbing too much front brake and washing out the front tire, and I always appreciate more mud clearance.

To change the cantilever angle with Avid Shorty Ultimates (Fig. 7.20), unscrew the twin Torx T10 bolts at each pivot (Fig. 7.20B) to free the separate plates that form each arm, rotate the arms relative to the pad-mounting tabs, and reengage them at the new angle by inserting the locating pin on each pad-mounting tab into the next hole in the arm plate to change the angle. Then tighten up the arm assembly again with the Torx T10 bolts.

To change the cantilever angle with FSA K-Force cantilevers, unscrew the collar nut at each pivot to free the separate plates that form each arm, rotate the arms relative to the pad-mounting tabs, and reengage the central shaft at the new angle by engaging the splines of the plastic bushings inserted into each arm plate to fix their relative angles. Then tighten up the arm assembly again with the collar nut.

After you have changed the stance adjustment, return to step 2 and continue with installation.

b. Pad installation and replacement

Older cantilevers had the brake pad integrated with the brake shoe. So if the pad was worn out, you replaced the entire shoe. The shoe could have an unthreaded (Fig. 7.19) or threaded post (Fig. 7.23), depending on brake style.

Modern cantilever brakes have shoes that hold replaceable road pads (Fig. 7.20A). The shoe (a.k.a. "pad holder") usually has a threaded post, but it sometimes has an unthreaded one—sometimes even with a thin, internal bolt that allows pivoting the pad on the end of the post to adjust toe-in (Fig. 7.18).

1. **Remove the old pad, if applicable.** With newer, road-style pads, you'll remove the pad-holder screw (Fig. 7.16) and slide the pad out by hand or by pushing it with a screwdriver. Otherwise, you'll remove the entire shoe, which can have a threaded or unthreaded post.

2. **Install the new pad or shoe with integrated pad.** With a road-style pad, slide the new pad in and replace the pad-holder screw (Fig. 7.16).

   When installing a brake shoe with a threaded post (Figs. 7.5, 7.20, 7.23), note the thickness and orientation of the nesting concave and convex washers that come with it. Nest a pair of concave/convex washers on each side of the pad-mounting tab, and select the appropriate washers to get the best spacing from the mounting tab. If in doubt, put the thinner washers between the pad and the mounting tab and the thicker pair between the tab and the nut; doing it the other way around increases the brake leverage and decreases pad clearance with the rim.

   Many cantilevers rely on an eyebolt with an enlarged head and a hole through it to accept the pad post (Figs. 7.19, 7.22, 7.28). Some cantilevers have the hole in the eyebolt between two plates forming the brake arm (Fig. 7.18). Lubricate the threads on the eyebolt, slip the post through, and tighten the nut.

3. **If the brake has a spring-tension nut (Figs. 7.19, 7.20A, 7.28), temporarily adjust the spring so that it holds the pad against the**

7.22 Cantilever brake with pad clamps on cylindrical brake arms

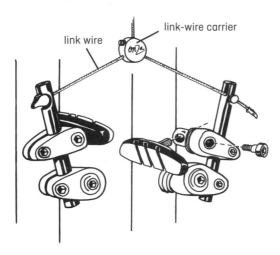

link wire — link-wire carrier

7.23 Threaded brake-pad-post on a one-piece shoe and pad

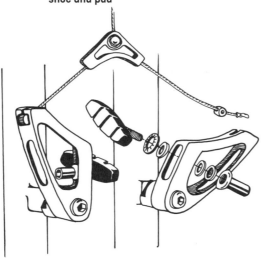

rim. It will make the pad adjustments easier with unthreaded pad posts. If not, you will have to push each arm toward the rim or pull the brake lever as you adjust the pad.

c. Pad adjustment

Pad adjustments are quite easy with some brakes and a real pain with others. Five separate adjustments (a through e in Figs. 7.24–7.26) must be made for each pad:

- Offset distance of the pad from the brake arm (extension of the pad post; distance a in Fig. 7.24)
- Vertical pad height (distance b in Fig. 7.25)
- Pad swing in the vertical plane for mating with the rim's sidewall angle (angle c in Fig. 7.24)
- Pad twist to align the face of the pad with the rim's curvature (angle d in Fig. 7.25)
- Pad swing in the horizontal plane to set toe-in (angle e in Fig. 7.26)

Threaded brake pad posts with nesting concave/convex washers (Figs. 7.20A, 7.23) make pad adjustment straightforward. Of brakes with unthreaded posts, cantilevers with a thin central bolt to adjust toe-in (Fig. 7.18) are easy to adjust. So are those that feature a cylindrical brake arm (Fig. 7.22), because the pad is held to the cylinder with a clamp that offers almost full range of motion. Other cantilevers employ a single eyebolt to hold all five pad adjustments (the eyebolt and washers are exploded in Fig. 7.19 and are seen from above in Fig. 7.26). Manual dexterity is required to hold all five adjustments simultaneously while tightening the bolt. Here is the pad-adjustment procedure for all types of cantilevers:

1. **On brakes with unthreaded posts, loosen the pad-clamping bolt and set the pad offset (distance a in Fig. 7.24) by sliding the post in or out of the clamping hole. On brakes with threaded posts, organize the nesting concave/convex washers (Figs. 7.20A, 7.23) to have more washer stack either on the pad side or on the other side.** The farther the pad is extended away from the brake arm, the greater the angle of the brake arm will be from the plane of the wheel. A benefit of this geometry is that leverage is increased (see the Pro Tip on the mechanical advantage of cantilever brakes). However, there are two drawbacks: (a) clearance between the rim and pad is reduced (higher leverage requires more cable pull and hence a closer adjustment to the rim to ensure that the lever does not hit the han-

ZINN & THE ART OF ROAD BIKE MAINTENANCE

7.24 Distance of pad to fixing bolt (a, pad offset) and angle against rim (c, pad swing in vertical plane)

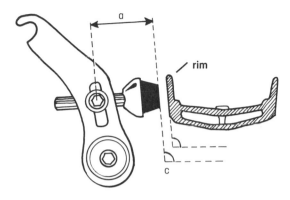

7.25 Up and down (b, vertical pad height) and rotate (d, pad twist)

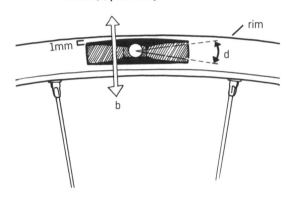

7.26 Brake-pad toe-in (e, horizontal pad swing)

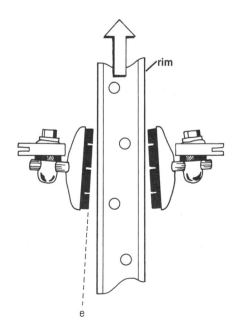

dlebar before fully applying the brake), and (b) clearance between the rider's heel and the rear brake arms is reduced. Also, the brake feels less firm, because less force is required to pull the lever (a powerful brake feels spongy, because it is so powerful that it is compressing the pads). A good initial position is with the post clamped in the center of its length or the thinner nesting concave/convex washers on the pad side.

2. **Roughly adjust the vertical pad height (distance b in Fig. 7.25) by sliding the pad-clamping mechanism up or down in the brake-arm slot.** For cantilever brakes with pad clamps surrounding cylindrical brake arms (Fig. 7.22), loosen the bolt clamping the pad holder to the brake arm, and snug the bolt back up once the rough adjustment is reached. With all other types, leave the pad bolt just loose enough to move the pad easily.

3. **Adjust pad swing in the vertical plane (angle c in Fig. 7.24).** You want the face of the pad to meet the rim flat with its top edge 1–2mm below the top of the rim. Fine-tune this adjustment by simultaneously sliding the pad up or down while rotating it to meet the rim flat.

4. **Adjust the pad twist (angle d in Fig. 7.25).** You want the top edge of the pad parallel to the top of the rim and at least 1mm below it. Make sure that the pads do not contact the tire. With a threaded pad post, you can pull the brake lever to hold the pad against the rim, move it around to the desired position, and tighten the pad-fixing nut (or bolt). For cantilever brakes with pad clamps on cylindrical brake arms (Fig. 7.22), the pad-securing bolt may now be tightened.

5. **Finally, adjust the pad toe-in (angle e in Fig. 7.26).** The pad should be adjusted either flat to the rim or toed in so that when the

forward end (note the arrow in Fig. 7.26) of the pad touches the rim, the rear end of it is 1–2mm away from the rim.

On brakes with a thin central bolt within an unthreaded pad post (Fig. 7.18), adjust toe-in after the large pad-fixing nut has been tightened down by loosening the thin central bolt and rotating the pad holder on the end of the post to the desired angle; then tighten the bolt.

On cylindrical-arm brakes with two fixing bolts (Fig. 7.22), the toe-in is adjusted by again loosening the bolt that holds the vertical-height adjustment of the pad. Because you have already tightened the other bolt that holds the pad in place, you simply loosen this second bolt and swing the pad horizontally until you arrive at your preferred toe-in setting. Tighten the bolt again, and you are done with pad adjustment.

Toed in, flat, or toed out—what's the difference? If the pad is toed out, the heel of it will catch the rim and will tend to chatter, making an obnoxious squealing noise, so avoid that. If the brake arms are not stiff, they fit loosely on the cantilever boss, or the fork steering tube is overly flexible (see §vii-11), the same thing will happen when the pad is flat. Toe-in is a must with flimsy brake arms and will have to be adjusted frequently as the pads wear in order to keep them quiet; it may be insufficient with a flexible fork steerer (§vii-11 offers solutions). If the brakes work smoothly and powerfully with the pads flat, leave them that way; you'll get the most even pad wear and longest pad life with them set that way. But if the brakes begin to squeal or judder, set the pads with a little toe-in.

6. **Tighten the pad-fixing nut (or bolt).** That's simple enough with a threaded post or unthreaded posts on brakes as in Figures 7.18 and 7.22. However, with any brake using a single bolt to hold the pad as well as control its rotation, you now have the tricky task of holding all of the adjustments you have made and simultaneously tightening the nut. Most eyebolt systems are tightened with a 10mm wrench on the nut on the back of the brake while the front is held with a 5mm hex key (Fig. 7.19). Help from someone else to either hold or tighten is useful here. Probably the trickiest brake to adjust has a big toothed or notched washer between the head of the eyebolt and a flat brake arm (Fig. 7.19). The adjusting washer is thinner on one edge than the other, so rotating it (by means of the tooth or notch) toes the pad in or out. With this type, you must hold all of the pad adjustments as you turn this washer, and then keep it and the pad in place as you tighten the nut. It's not an easy job, and the adjustment changes as you tighten the bolt. At some point, you will want to slug the guy who came up with this system. Be patient.

Another common type of brake has a convex or concave shape to the slotted brake arm (Fig. 7.27). Cupped washers separate the eyebolt head and nut from the brake arm. The concave or convex surfaces allow the pad to swivel, and tightening the bolt secures everything. Again, you may not get it on the first try. Threaded posts also employ such washers.

NOTE: *Some of these curved-face brakes do not hold their toe-in adjustment well; you may need to sand the brake-arm faces and washers to create more friction between them.*

Brakes with a cylindrical arm and a clamp secured only by the pad eyebolt are adjusted functionally the same as the curved-face ones with cupped washers.

A rare but simple-to-adjust type of brake has a ball joint at each pad's eyebolt (Fig. 7.28).

7.27 Curved-face cantilever brake (Ritchey)

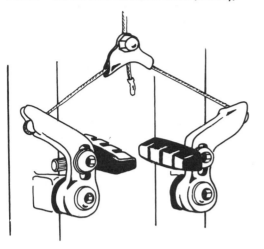

7.28 Ball-joint cantilever brake (Campagnolo)

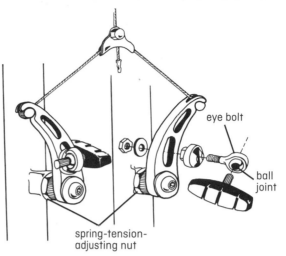

eye bolt

ball joint

spring-tension-adjusting nut

PRO TIP | **Cantilever Brake Mechanical Advantage**

With any lever arm, the mechanical advantage is highest when the force is applied at right angles to the lever arm. This applies to the straddle cable as well as to the brake arm. Three things determine the leverage of a cantilever brake: (1) the brake lever's mechanical advantage, (2) the ratio of the distance from the pivot (or fulcrum) to the pad face (length FP in Fig. 7.29) to the perpendicular distance from the straddle cable to the pivot (or fulcrum) (length FC), and (3) the angle of the straddle cable relative to horizontal (angle S in Fig. 7.29). Looking at Figure 7.29, you can see that each arm of a cantilever brake is just like a bent teeter-totter of length FC + FP.

1. The mechanical advantage of the brake lever is the ratio of the length of the lever (from its pivot to where your finger pulls it) to the distance from the lever pivot to the cable head. Most drop-bar levers are about the same length, and you can't do much about your lever's mechanical advantage, other than pulling closer to the tip. That said, Shimano road levers with shift cables concealed under the handlebar tape beginning with the Dura-Ace 7900 (Fig. 7.13) in 2008 have lower mechanical advantage (due to a longer pivot-to-cable-head distance), and hence higher cable pull, than do most dual control road levers.

2. The "cantilever angle" (angle BFP in Fig. 7.29), which is adjustable on Avid Shorty Ultimate

---

7.29 Defining angles and lengths on a cantilever brake

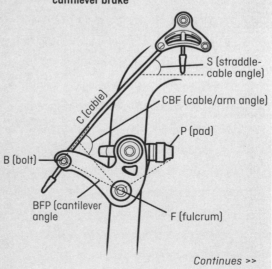

S (straddle-cable angle)

CBF (cable/arm angle)

C (cable)

P (pad)

B (bolt)

BFP (cantilever angle)

F (fulcrum)

Continues >>

BRAKES

(Fig. 7.20) and FSA K-Force cantis, is a big determinant of the mechanical advantage of a cantilever brake, arguably more so than the actual length of the brake arm. You can see that as the cantilever angle becomes larger, length FC decreases, thus reducing the ratio FC/FP and hence the brake's mechanical advantage. It is akin to trying to lift a kid sitting on a teeter-totter when you move closer to the fulcrum—it becomes progressively harder.

3. The closer the straddle cable is to being horizontal (S = 0), the higher the mechanical advantage, although achieving a horizontal straddle cable obviously requires a low cantilever angle ("narrow stance" or "low-profile" cantilever brakes; the one in Fig. 7.22 is an example) as well as tall brake arms. And while the leverage is enormous initially, angle S increases rapidly as the brake is applied, thus rapidly reducing its mechanical advantage. Obviously, a smaller angle S means that the straddle cable is closer to the tire, thus reducing mud clearance and options for larger tires.

The perpendicular distance from the pivot (fulcrum) to the straddle cable is at its greatest when it is equal to the brake arm length (FC = FB); in other words, the straddle cable pulls at 90 degrees to the brake arm (Fig. 7.30). Some argue that, once the pad hits the rim, the actual lever arm is the line from the face of the pad to the cable attachment point on top of the arm because the pad face, not the brake post, now becomes the fulcrum (Fig. 7.31), and you are prying the brake post outward rather than pushing the pad any further inward.

Since the leverage of your brake levers is not adjustable, you are balancing the straddle-

7.30   Straddle-cable angle when open

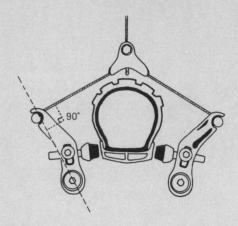

7.31   Straddle-cable angle when closed

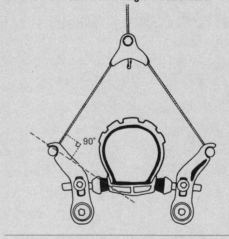

cable angle S and its angle with the brake arm (angle CBF) to determine leverage. From Figure 7.29, you can see that you reduce leverage the longer you make the straddle cable, and vice versa. And the longer you make the straddle cable, the greater the mud clearance over the tire and the greater the clearance between the pads and the rim when the lever is released. Understanding that, now you can experiment with what you prefer in your brake setup. Make sure that you allow at least an inch of cable clearance over the tire to prevent mud or a bulge in the tire from engaging the brake.

d. Straddle-cable adjustment, and how to maximize cantilever performance

The straddle (or transverse) cable has a lot to do with the brake's mechanical advantage and should be set so that it pulls on the brake arms in such a way as to provide optimal overall performance. This is not always the adjustment that produces the highest leverage, for sometimes brake feel and modulation (i.e., stiffness opposing you when pulling the lever) are improved when leverage is reduced, because you are doing more of the work. In general, I recommend initially setting the straddle cable for relatively high leverage and reducing it from there to improve lever feel, pad clearance with the rim, and mud clearance over the tire.

The straddle cable (Figs. 7.32–7.34) usually has a metal blob on one end. On an old-school straddle cable (Fig. 7.32), the other end is clamped to one brake arm by the cable-fixing bolt, as in Figure 7.37. The blob fits into the slotted brake arm and acts as a quick-release for the brake.

With some cantilevers built since 1988, the cable from the brake lever passes through a round link-wire carrier (Fig. 7.22) and connects directly to one brake arm, and a link wire attached to the carrier hooks to the other arm. The brakes generally came with a plastic gauge to set the distance from the link-wire carrier to the brake arm. If you have this type and no gauge, simply set the cable length from the link-wire carrier to the brake arm the same on both sides. Some post-1993 cantilevers use the same system except that the brake cable passes through the link-wire carrier and through a fixed length of cable housing attached to it (Fig. 7.33) to reach the brake arm. The mechanic has no choice of straddle-cable settings; it is predetermined by the lengths of the link wire and housing segment integrated into the link-wire carrier.

Instead of a cable-fixing bolt on one arm, some brakes have slotted hooks on both arms

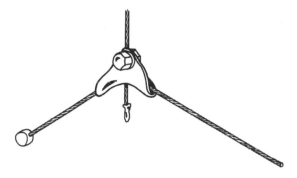

7.32 Straddle-cable carrier, old-school

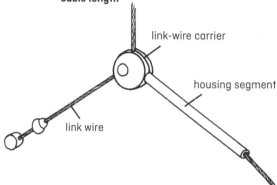

7.33 Straddle cable: link-wire carrier with pass-through housing segment to set straddle cable length

link-wire carrier

housing segment

link wire

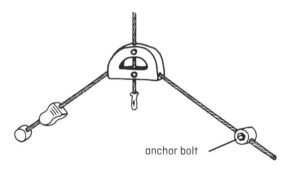

7.34 Straddle cable, double-ended

anchor bolt

to accept the blob on the end of a straddle cable or link wire; see Figures 7.18, 7.19, 7.22, 7.23, 7.28, 7.30, and 7.31. In this case, you tighten a small cylindrical clamp on the end of the straddle cable to form a cable end blob (Fig. 7.34); one end may also incorporate a cable barrel adjuster into which the blob on the end of the link wire nests (Figs. 7.18, 7.20A). A link-wire carrier that holds two separate link wires may also be used.

With any straddle cable, after you set its length, the straddle-cable carrier's vertical position is set by loosening the bolt or setscrews that secure it and sliding it on the brake cable. Tighten it in place (Fig. 7.35). The cable length is set properly when the brake engages quickly, and the lever cannot be pulled closer than a finger's width from the bar.

Setting cable length is considerably easier with brakes like those in Figures 7.18 and 7.20A, as they incorporate a cable barrel adjuster on the straddle cable that allows you to adjust cable length simply by loosening the locknut (if included; the brake in Fig. 7.18 has a locknut, and the brake in Fig. 7.20A does not), rotating the barrel adjuster, and retightening the locknut. A barrel adjuster on one of the cable stops in the system (Figs. 7.8, 7.18) accomplishes the same thing.

To adjust the right-left balance of the brake pads, you can adjust the lateral position of the straddle-cable carrier. Modern straddle-cable carriers (Figs. 7.18, 7.20A), unlike old-school ones (Figs. 7.32, 7.35), provide friction to fix the carrier's lateral position; the one in Figure 7.20A has a friction bump pressing on the straddle cable, while the ones in Figures 7.18, 7.34, and 7.36 have setscrews pinching the straddle cable. The carrier should generally be centered on the straddle cable, but some brake cables pull asymmetrically as they come around the seat tube or from the headset cable hanger. In these cases, the straddle-cable carrier may need to be offset for the brake pads to be centered (Fig. 7.36).

e. Spring-tension adjustment

The spring-tension adjustment, where present, centers the brake pads about the rim and also determines the return spring force. There is only one adjustment to make on brakes with a single setscrew on the side of one brake arm. Turn the screw (Fig. 7.37) until the brake arms are

7.35 Securing cantilever brake cable to straddle-cable carrier

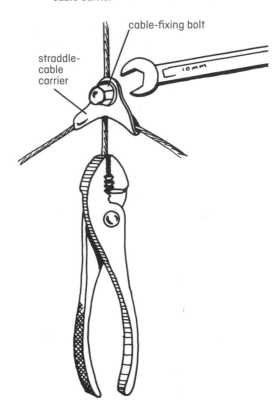

7.36 An offset straddle-cable stop requires an offset straddle cable carrier

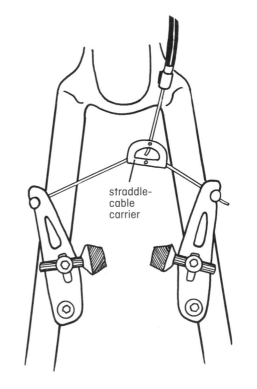

centered and the pads hit the rim simultaneously when applied. Higher spring tensions can be achieved by moving the spring to a higher hole in the brake post.

Some brakes rely on a large spring-tension adjusting nut (Figs. 7.19, 7.20A, 7.28) surrounding the mounting bolt and do not use the holes in the brake posts as anchors. On these, the tensioning nuts may be turned on both arms to get the combination of return force and centering you prefer. You must loosen the mounting bolt while holding the tensioning nut with a wrench. Turn the nut to the desired tension and, while holding it in place with the wrench, tighten the mounting bolt again (Fig. 7.38).

On brakes without a tension adjustment screw, tension adjustment is accomplished by removing the brake arm and moving the spring to another hole (if present) on the post. It is a rough adjustment at best, and newer posts have only one hole. When this adjustment fails, you can twist the arm on the post to tighten or loosen the spring a bit. That, of course, is an even rougher adjustment. **NOTE:** *If the brake arms do not rotate easily on the brake post, there is too much friction. Remove the brake and check that the post is not bent or split, in which case a new one needs to be screwed in or welded on. If not bent, the post is probably too fat to slide freely inside the brake arm, because of paint on it or bulging or mushrooming of the post due to overtightening of the brake-mounting bolt. In this case, if it's the replaceable type (Fig. 7.21), screw a new post into the frame or fork. Otherwise, file or sand the circumference of the post to reduce its diameter. Remove material uniformly, and only a little at a time; avoid making it too thin.*

f. Lubrication and service

The only lubrication necessary on cantilever brakes is on the cables, levers, and brake

7.37 Adjusting return-spring tension with a set-screw

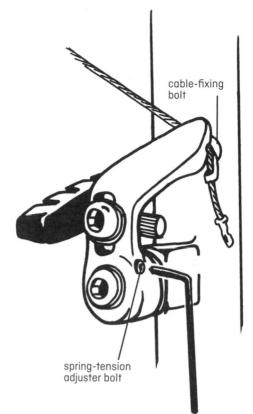

cable-fixing bolt

spring-tension adjuster bolt

7.38 Adjusting return-spring tension with tensioning nut

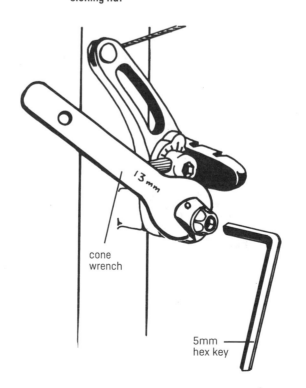

13 mm

cone wrench

5mm hex key

arms. Lubrication should be performed whenever braking feels sticky. Cable lubrication and replacement and lever lubrication are covered in §vii-3 through §vii-5. Cantilevers can be lubricated by removing them, cleaning and greasing the pivots, and replacing them (§vii-10a).

g. Top-mount brake levers

Top-mount or "cross-top" levers (Fig. 7.39) allow the brakes to be accessed from little levers mounted on the top, straight section of the handlebar as well as from the normal levers on the drops of the handlebar. The brake cable from the normal lever passes through the top-mount lever and can hence be pulled from either lever.

Top-mount levers are simple to set up as long as you are using modern brake levers with the brake cable running under the tape along the front of the handlebar. For installation, follow these steps:

1. **Clamp the top-mount lever onto the handlebar.** The lever tip must face outward, toward the brake lever it will be connected to, and lever logos should face up (in other words, the mounting bolt is usually underneath).

   a. If you have a standard-diameter handlebar (i.e., with a 26mm-diameter clamping section at the stem), you will be mounting the levers just beyond the bulged stem-clamping section, on the 24mm-diameter part of the handlebar (Fig. 7.39).

   b. If you have a larger-diameter handlebar (i.e., with a 31.8mm stem clamp), you will need top-mount levers with large clamps, because there probably will not be enough room for a standard top-mount lever between the point where the bar tapers down to 24mm and the bend. You can get top-mount levers with a 31.8mm clamp diameter, and you

7.39 Top-mount brake lever connected to standard brake lever on a standard 26mm-clamp-size handlebar

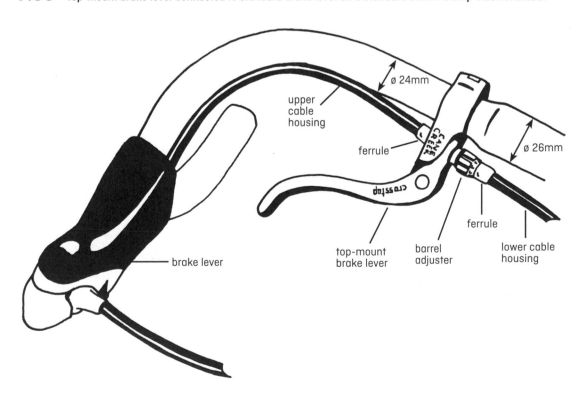

should mount these up on the bulged clamping section of the bar.

2. **Orient the levers in a comfortable position for your hands.**

3. **Cut a section of brake-cable housing so that it runs from its insertion point on the brake lever, along the front of the bar, to the bottom of its insertion hole in the top-mount lever clamp.** If your bike is already set up, you can just pull the brake cable out (or at least until the end is between the top-mount lever and the brake lever). Then you can cut the housing at about the centerline of the top-mount lever.

4. **Install the housing from the brake lever to the insertion hole in the top-mount lever clamp (Fig. 7.39).** Reinforce each end of the housing with a ferrule (Fig. 5.16), if possible.

5. **Cut a piece of housing to run to the brake caliper (front) or frame cable stop (rear) from the other cable-insertion point on the top-mount lever.** This cable-insertion point will be on the moving part of the lever and usually will have a barrel adjuster on it. If you are just cutting the old brake housing of your preexisting setup, then you already cut this piece of housing (because it was left over) when you made your cut in step 3.

6. **Run the housing section you just cut from the top-mount lever's barrel adjuster to the brake or frame cable stop (Fig. 7.39).** Use ferrules (Fig. 5.16) to reinforce the ends.

7. **Install the brake cable, running it right through the top-mount lever to pass from one housing section into the next.** If you are using the old cable and it is frayed, it may not pass through the holes, so you may need to buy a new cable.

8. **Hook up the brakes as usual.** Turn the barrel adjuster to get the right cable tension so that the brakes apply properly. You're ready to ride and now have another position from which to brake!

vii-11

CANTILEVER BRAKE/FORK SHUDDER, BRAKE CHATTER, AND SQUEAL

Squeal and chatter can occur on the front brake with cantilever brakes. This can get to the point where the fork shudders, even when the front brake is only applied lightly. This is due to an overly flexible steering tube on the fork combined with a cable hanger above the headset.

Here's the mechanism at work: When the brake pads apply pressure on the rim, the wheel slows and pushes the fork tips back (Fig. 7.40). The fork steering tube and perhaps also the upper part of the fork between the lower headset bearing and the cantilever pivot bosses can flex. If the front brake's cable hanger is above the headset, this will tend to tighten that cable, pulling the brake on harder. This will push the fork back yet farther, thus tightening the cable even more and applying the brake yet harder (Fig. 7.40). Eventually, something has to give. Either the bike must come to a stop, conceivably flipping the rider over the front if his or her weight is not back far enough, or the momentum of the bike and rider will force the rim to push through the brake pads. If the latter happens, the fork will relax back toward its original shape, and the cable will loosen. But the pressure of continued braking will again push the fork back, and tighten the cable, which tightens the brake more, which flexes the fork back yet farther, which tightens the brake yet more until something gives again, and the cycle repeats, resulting in a scary fork shudder. Since the bike is essentially applying the brake, it can happen with relatively light finger pull on the brake lever.

7.40 Fork shudder in cantilever brake

What to do?

The least expensive and first thing to try is to adjust the front brake pads with more toe-in (§vii-10c). This may be enough to fix the problem if the shudder is minor. Some people also have had success with cutting the brake shoes shorter so that there is less pad area to grab. This of course takes away some braking power as well.

A solution that sometimes works with minor shudder and costs nothing except a new straddle cable is to run the front straddle cable very long (combined with more toe-in). As you learned in §vii-10d, this reduces your mechanical advantage and also increases the cable pull. This means that the brake power won't increase as much as the cable tightens due to steering-tube flex.

Another, more expensive, solution is to get a fork with a much stiffer steering tube. This is the method many cyclocross bike manufacturers have chosen: using forks with steering tubes tapering from 1.5-inch diameter at the fork crown to 1.125-inch at the top (instead of 1.125-inch or 1-inch throughout, as used to be the standards).

Due to the huge steering tube joining it, the fork crown area and upper fork legs naturally become deeper, thus stiffening those parts in a fore-aft direction as well. Unless your frame already accepts a 1.5-inch lower bearing, you can't install a tapered fork, so you are left seeking a stiffer fork with a standard cylindrical steering tube. For a tall bike, you may not be able to find one stiff enough, as the steerer will be so long.

A much less expensive and more effective fix is to use a fork-crown-mounted cable hanger (Figs. 7.18, 7.41), rather than one surrounding the steering tube above the headset (Figs. 7.8, 7.40). This completely eliminates the steering tube from the equation, and the distance is so short from the fork crown to the pivot bosses that flex there cannot significantly increase brake-cable tension when the brake is applied. Also, two fork legs and a fork crown are stiffer than a single steering tube. The hitch with this solution is that, unless your fork already has a hole through the fork crown, you can't bolt on a hanger as in Fig. 7.41. If you have a steel or aluminum fork crown, you may be able to safely drill a hole through the crown for the hanger bolt, but I certainly cannot recommend this for a carbon fork. Ruckus Components, a carbon-repair shop in Portland, Oregon, will mount a cable hanger to a carbon fork using carbon wrapping. This is the most elegant solution, albeit a pricey one.

Yet another solution is to put a V-brake (Fig. 7.42) on the front. This completely eliminates any flex in the fork from the equation—neither the steerer nor the crown and upper legs affect braking. But, as I discuss in §vii-12, even with the shortest V-brake, you will have considerably more brake power and considerably less pad-to-rim clearance and mud clearance over the tire. This setup may be acceptable with a Shimano 7900 or 6700 or 5700 brake lever, as these have less leverage and more cable pull than most other

7.41 Fork-crown-mounted cable hanger

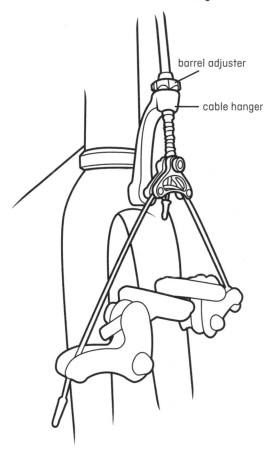

barrel adjuster

cable hanger

road levers, but it still won't offer the clearance of a cantilever and in my opinion must have the cable tension backed off so far that the brake just comes on as the lever comes to the bar; otherwise, you can apply it too hard in a panic situation and flip over the front. A good solution is a V-brake-specific drop-bar brake lever, but you can only use this with a single chainring setup unless you're willing to use a bar-end or downtube shift lever for your front derailleur.

Finally, you can use a disc brake (§vii-13) to eliminate fork shudder. You will need to add a disc-specific fork and disc brake (and new front hub or wheel) to your bike. However, carbon forks for disc brakes that don't have a tapered steering tube are rare, so this solution won't fit your frame if yours accepts a 1-⅛-inch or 1-inch steering tube.

If the rear brake is chattering, more pad toe-in or different pads better suited to the rims are generally the answer. Less flexy brake arms also may be required.

---

vii-12

SIDEPULL CANTILEVER (A.K.A. V-BRAKE) CALIPERS

Some hybrid, touring, and tandem bikes have V-brakes, which, like cantilevers, mount on pivot studs attached to the frame and fork.

V-brakes (Figs. 7.5, 7.42) have tall, cantilever-like arms, a horizontal cable-hook link on top of one arm, and a cable clamp on the top of the other. A curved aluminum guide pipe, or "noodle," hooks into the horizontal link and takes the cable from the end of the housing and out through the link and then directs the cable toward the cable-fixing bolt on the opposite arm. V-brakes usually have long, thin brake pads with threaded posts. Some V-brakes have "parallel-push" linkages (Fig. 7.5) that move the brake pads horizontally rather than in an arc around the brake post like a cantilever. Simple V-brake designs (Fig. 7.42) mount

---

7.42 Simple V-brake (a.k.a. sidepull cantilever brake)

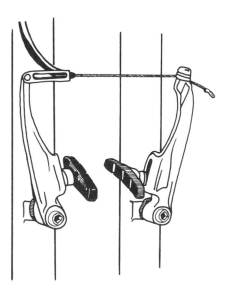

the pad directly to the arm so that the pads move in a cantilever-like arc.

V-brakes are extremely powerful but require more cable pull than road bike brakes and don't generally work with road bike levers unless (1) you have mini V-brakes with shorter arms coupled to Shimano 7900 (Fig. 7.13), 6700, 5700, or similar low-leverage levers; (2) you have V-brake-specific drop-bar levers (these have longer cable pull and lower leverage); or (3) you install a cam unit that increases the cable pull. This cam unit usually replaces the noodle and bolts onto the cable-fixing bolt. A cable stop is bolted onto the end of the cable and hooks into the brake link.

Because of this leverage problem and consequent need for a cable-pull multiplier (as well as poor mud clearance), V-brakes are rare on drop-bar bikes. Unless you're using a cam multiplier or a V-brake lever, I recommend reducing the cable tension to the point that the lever almost reaches the bar when the brake pads hit the rim to avoid pulling them on too hard in a panic stop.

V-brakes set up easily, with a spring pin that goes into the brake pivot hole; just bolt each arm on. Run the cable through the noodle and to the cable-fixing bolt on the opposite arm. Loosen the pad nuts, squeeze the lever, set the pad adjustment, and tighten the pad nuts. If you have V-brakes and want more setup information, please consult Chapter 7 of *Zinn & the Art of Mountain Bike Maintenance* for details on adjusting them.

DISC BRAKES

LEVEL 1

Disc brakes can offer great stopping and modulation, but installing them correctly is a must. Once properly installed, discs require less maintenance than do rim brakes, because the tire does not drag dirt and mud into them. There is no need to be intimi-

dated by them; although disc brakes are small and enclosed and therefore somewhat mysterious, they are really quite simple.

Disc brakes have calipers that operate either mechanically or hydraulically. A mechanical disc brake uses a standard brake cable to connect the brake lever to the caliper. A hydraulic disc brake has a master cylinder at the lever filled with hydraulic fluid; the fluid is pumped by lever action through a hose connected to the caliper. Since air is compressible (but fluid is not), a bleed screw is provided in the system to remove air bubbles that can form when the fluid is replaced. Inside the caliper, two pistons actuated by the cable or the hydraulic fluid push brake pads against the brake disc (or "rotor"), which is mounted to the wheel hub.

NOTE: *Never squeeze the lever on a hydraulic disc brake without a disc or another spacer between the pads, as you can push a piston in the caliper all of the way out. For bike travel with the wheel out, insert a spacer between the pads—either one that came with the brake or a chunk of corrugated cardboard you cut for the purpose.*

vii-13

DISC-BRAKE PAD CHECK AND REPLACEMENT

Disc-brake pads are less easy to see than rim-brake pads, so you should be diligent about checking them for wear. The friction material needs to be at least the thickness of a dime (about 1.2mm); with most pads this means that the pad and backing plate together should be thicker than 2.5mm. Some brakes specify as much as 3–4mm minimum.

The wheel must be removed to remove disc-brake pads.

On cotterless types of pads, grab a tab on the pad with your fingers or needle-nose pliers and pull it toward the center of the caliper slot and out

(Fig. 7.43). You have to do this from underneath the caliper, so it's often not easy to get to. The pads need space to pull toward the other pad and out, one at a time (although some, like the Avid BB7, will come out together with the spring). With a hydraulic brake, you may need to first slip a plastic pad spacer, tire lever, or flat-bladed screwdriver between the pads and carefully rock the spacer or lever back and forth to push the pistons back into their bores and separate the pads without damaging them; with a cable-actuated brake, back out both pad-adjustment knobs first.

Cottered pads require that you remove a cotter pin or bolt and then pull the pads out (Fig. 7.44), but they're usually easy to get out because they come out of the top of the brake. The cotter pin may be a threaded bolt, a pin with a retaining clip holding it in, or both. Catch the pad spreader spring, too, if there is one.

Clean the pads with isopropyl alcohol or a dry, oil-free rag, or by rubbing them against each other. Check for pad wear, scoring, or glazing—anything that could damage the rotor or reduce braking effectiveness. Brakes fade when the pads and rotors get too hot, after which blue discoloration of the rotor and glazing of the pads occur, indicating that resins holding the pad material have broken down and recrystallized on the surface. Glazed pads must be discarded. Always replace pads in pairs.

While not mandatory, you'll reduce the potential for introducing dirt into a hydraulic caliper if, before replacing the pads, you clean around the pistons with a Q-tip soaked in the brake fluid used in that brake.

Replace the new pads the way the old ones came out, noting that the left and right pads may differ; it should be obvious if you try to put a pad in the wrong side.

Cotterless pads usually snap back in with a retaining clip (Fig. 7.43), a wire catch, or

7.43 Removing cotterless brake pads (Avid BB7 shown)

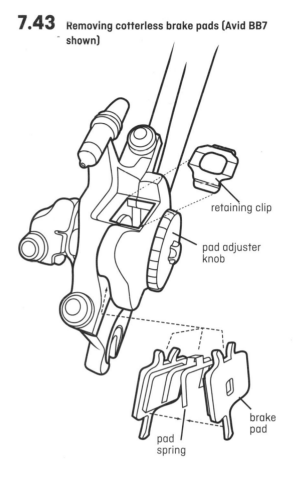

retaining clip

pad adjuster knob

brake pad

pad spring

7.44 Removing cottered brake pads

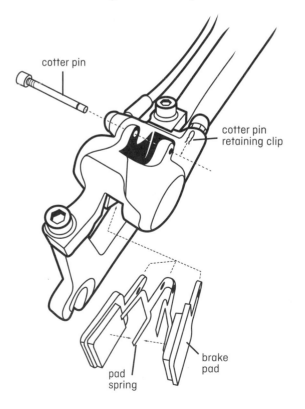

cotter pin

cotter pin retaining clip

brake pad

pad spring

magnetically. If the pads are not symmetrical and you reverse them, they may not snap back into place because the piston is often offset from the center of the cutaway for the pad. If there is a spring steel pad spreader clip between cotterless pads, it may go in after the pads are inserted, or it may go in like a sandwich with the pads. Push the pads deep into the caliper until they click into place.

With cottered pads, the ears on the pads may not line up with the cotter hole if reversed. On cottered pads that have a little butterfly-shaped spring-steel piece that pushes the pads apart (Fig. 7.44), make a sandwich of the new pads and the butterfly spring and push them back in together. Then push in or screw in the cotter pin and replace its circlip, if it has one.

vii-14

DISC-BRAKE PAD SELECTION AND BURN-IN

Make sure you buy pads meant for your exact make and model of brake; there are myriad shapes to disc-brake pads, and they're not interchangeable.

When buying pads, you may have a choice of pad compounds, and your choice should be based on the type of riding you do. Metallic pads deal with heat and grit better, whereas resin pads give better initial brake power. Resin pads also wear out faster than metallic pads, especially in wet conditions.

New pads need to be burnished (or "burned in" or "bedded in") with repeated braking before they reach full braking power. If you slam on the brakes when the pads are new, you can damage them so that they won't reach full power, and they may squeal mercilessly to remind you on every ride.

Burn in the pads by braking firmly and evenly without letting the brake get too hot. It's best to do this with one brake at a time, rather than by applying both brakes at the same time. Every manufacturer has a different procedure, but all say that it takes somewhere in the range of 20 to 40 stops to bed in the pad. I recommend starting out by applying the brake 20 times to bring the speed down from about 10mph to walking speed. Then increase the speed to 15–18mph and brake to walking speed 10 more times. This works the heat cycle evenly over the rotor and reduces the potential for squeal problems. Do not bring the bike to a full stop or lock up the wheel when bedding in the pads.

vii-15

PUSHING HYDRAULIC DISC-BRAKE PISTONS BACK IN WHEN PADS RUB

Sometimes hydraulic pistons get pushed so far out that they drag on the rotor or even won't let the rotor back in when the wheel is replaced. This can easily happen if the lever is applied without a rotor or spacer between the pads. You will have to push the pistons back in, and on some brakes this is best done with the pads out, while on others it is best done with the pads in.

If the wheel is out and the rotor will not go in, you will first have to push the pads and pistons back by jamming in the plastic pad spacer that is supplied with the brakes (which you should have had in when you pulled the lever when the wheel was out; it would have prevented this from happening). Once you have some space between the pads, you might as well try pushing the pistons back with the pads in. Using a plastic tire lever or a flat-bladed screwdriver, carefully (so you don't gouge the pads) twist the tire lever or screwdriver back and forth until there is enough space between the pads to accept the rotor without rubbing.

On some brakes, you can more successfully get the pistons fully back in place by removing the pads (§vii-13) and carefully pushing the pistons back in with the box end of a wrench. Then reinstall the pads.

Sometimes, a hydraulic brake in normal usage doesn't retract the pads fully and they rub. This indicates contamination, and you'll have to clean around the piston to get this to stop.

On most hydraulic disc brakes, each piston is pulled back in by an O-ring seal with a square cross-section surrounding the waist of the piston (Fig. 7.45A). This "square seal" sits in a groove running around the bore of the piston cylinder; you can see it in cross-section in Figure 7.45B. When fluid is forced in behind the piston by squeezing the lever, the piston moves outward, and the square seal will start to twist out into the tapered section of the groove shown in Figure 7.45B. When the hydraulic pressure is relieved by releasing the lever, the square seal will untwist back to its original configuration, bringing the piston back with it, as long as the seal is not damaged and the seal is not broken by contamination.

If dirt is present, it can inhibit piston retraction, either by breaking the seal or by creating more friction around the sides of the piston than the square seal can overcome. In this case, simply forcing the pistons back into their bores exacerbates the problem by pushing even more dirt under or against the square seal. So, you want to clean around the piston and lubricate it.

If you have this problem of pad spacing from the rotor being reduced to almost nothing while riding, remove the pads (§vii-13). While holding one piston in place with a plastic tire lever or a box-end wrench, carefully squeeze the lever to push the other piston out a bit more to expose more of it for lubrication. Using a cotton swab soaked in hydraulic fluid of the type that's in your brake, wipe off any grime from around the piston and lubricate it the same way with clean hydraulic fluid.

7.45A Piston and square seal

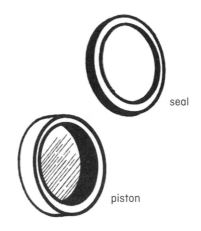

seal

piston

7.45B Caliper cylinder cutaway view

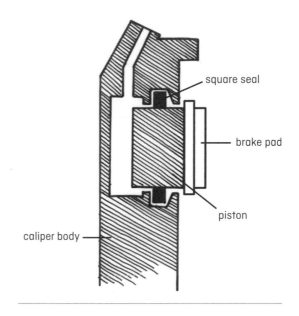

square seal

brake pad

piston

caliper body

Carefully prying against the opposite side of the caliper, push the piston back into its bore with the plastic tire lever or box-end wrench. Repeat the procedure to clean and lube the other piston, push it back in as well, and replace the pads.

If you use the wrong implement to push directly on the piston, you can crack it.

Also, if the piston gets out too far and you cannot push it back in far enough against fluid pressure, open the bleed screw slightly while pushing it back, and close it back up immediately to prevent the entry of air.

DISC-BRAKE INSTALLATION AND ADJUSTMENT

LEVEL 2

Simply stated, you just bolt the rotor to the hub, tighten the lever onto the handlebar (see §vii-6 for instructions on this), bolt the caliper to the mounts on the frame or fork, and tie down the hose or cable. But the space between the pads and rotor is small, and the speed of accurate mounting depends on you, the brake, and the type of mount the brake accepts.

The two types of mounts built into frames and forks are "post mounts" (Fig. 7.48) and "International Standard" (IS) mounts (Fig. 7.49). IS mounts are drilled transversely (across the frame and toward the wheel) and are not threaded, whereas post mounts are threaded directly into the frame or fork. IS mounts, front or rear, are 51mm apart; the post-mount standard for frames and forks is 74mm. Fortunately, the forks, frames, brakes, and rotors (two mounting standards) of the major manufacturers are completely cross-compatible.

After installation, follow the pad bed-in procedure in §vii-14 to get full brake performance.

Avoid touching the rotor's braking surface and getting grease or oil on it. If brake performance drops off, clean the rotor and pads with alcohol. And for obvious reasons, never touch a rotor that's hot after heavy braking.

a. Rotor mounting and removal

Installation

The two rotor-mounting systems are the six-bolt standard (Fig. 7.46) pioneered by Hayes, and Shimano's Center Lock (Fig. 7.47), in which a splined aluminum adapter riveted to the steel rotor slips onto the splines of the hub; a single lockring holds it in place. Theoretically, the rotor

should be positioned in the same place relative to the axle end with either system, so a wheel with a Center Lock rotor should work fine in a brake set up for a bolt-on rotor of the same diameter. However, if you have a number of wheels you interchange—cyclocross racers will have this concern—the rotors may not all line up in exactly the same place. This is a bummer, since you don't want to have to readjust the caliper every time you switch wheels. If you have this problem, you can get thin shim washers to space a six-bolt rotor away from the hub shell and hence slightly closer to the axle end to get it to more precisely match your other wheel(s).

Six-Bolt Rotor

1. **Loosely bolt the rotor to the hub flange (Fig. 7.46).** The logo on the rotor should face outward so that the rotor turns in the proper direction.

2. **Gradually snug the bolts, alternately tightening opposing bolts, rather than adjacent**

7.46 Bolting rotor onto hub

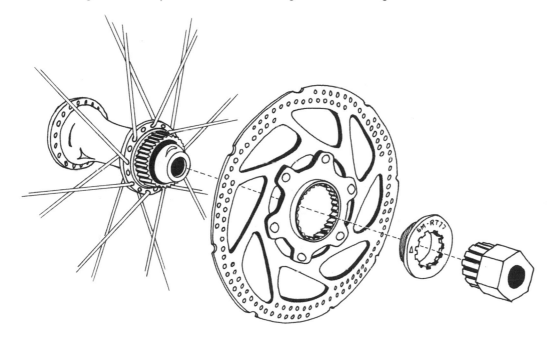

bolts. A size T25 Torx wrench (like a hex wrench, but with a star-shaped end) is usually required for this. Torque for rotor bolts ranges from 18 in-lbs (2 N-m) for some manufacturers to 55 in-lbs (6 N-m) for others.

Center Lock Rotor

1. **Slip the rotor splines over the hub splines (Fig. 7.47) with the logo on the rotor facing you.**

2. **Thread on the rotor-securing lockring, and tighten it with the same splined lockring-remover tool used for rear gear cassettes.** If you have a torque wrench that fits the lockring tool, tighten it to 350 in-lbs (40 N-m).

Removal

Six-Bolt Rotor

When removing a bolt-on rotor, you must loosen all of the screws a fraction of a turn before unscrewing any of them fully. On braking, the rotor may rotate relative to the hub a bit and

lean against one side of each screw. If you remove one screw while the others are still tight, the rotor hole's wall will still be pressed against the side of the screw, and the threads on the screw will be damaged. You will then wreck the threads in your hub when you put the damaged screw back in.

Center Lock Rotor

Unscrew the lockring with the splined lockring-removal tool (Fig. 7.47), and pull the rotor off.

NOTE: *Adapters are available to convert Center Lock hubs to accept six-bolt rotors.*

b. Installing a disc-brake caliper

The beauty of post mounts, whether on the fork (Fig. 7.48), frame, or IS adapter bracket, is that the brake can be moved laterally to center it over the rotor.

1. **If you are using a post-mount caliper on an IS frame or fork, tighten the correct adapter bracket to the IS mounts first.** Torque is usually 55–70 in-lbs (6–8 N-m).

7.48 Mounting a cable-actuated post-mount brake caliper on fork post mounts (Avid BB7 shown)

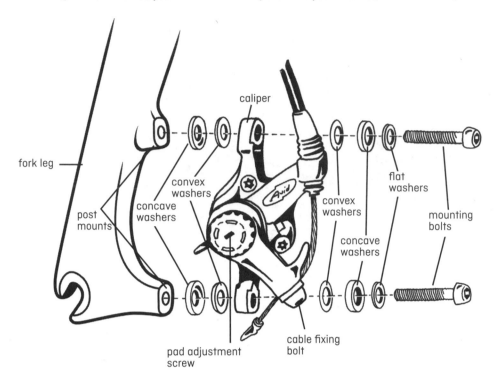

caliper

fork leg

convex
washers

concave
washers

post
mounts

convex
washers

concave
washers

flat
washers

mounting
bolts

pad adjustment
screw

cable fixing
bolt

7.49 Mounting a hydraulic post-mount brake caliper on rear IS mounts

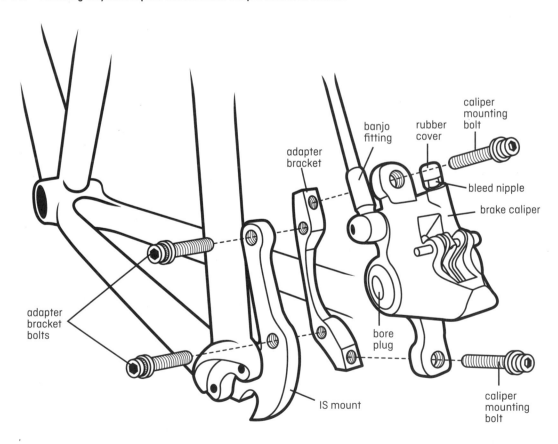

caliper
mounting
bolt

banjo
fitting

rubber
cover

adapter
bracket

bleed nipple

brake caliper

adapter
bracket
bolts

bore
plug

IS mount

caliper
mounting
bolt

2. **Loosely bolt the post-mount caliper to the post mounts on the fork (Fig. 7.48), frame, or adapter bracket (Fig. 7.49).** If the brake has concave and convex washers, keep them in the same order as in Figure 7.48.

NOTE: *If you are installing a hydraulic caliper that is not connected to its lever, skip to section d to cut the hose to length; then skip to §vii-17a to fill it with fluid and bleed it; and then come back here and begin with step 3.*

3. **Install the wheel.** The caliper slot will be over the rotor, and the caliper will have some lateral freedom of movement.

4. **While squeezing the brake lever, shake the caliper to get it to find its natural position over the rotor, and tighten the mounting bolts.** With a cable-actuated brake (Fig. 7.48), you need not hook up the cable yet to do this. Instead of squeezing the lever, first turn the adjuster knob on the wheel side clockwise a few clicks to bring the inboard pad closer to the rotor so that the pads look equally extended toward the rotor. With an Avid BB5 or BB7, it is easier on the knuckles to use a Torx T25 key through the spokes to turn the knob; some other types take a hex key. Then turn the outboard knob clockwise until it stops, which will cause the pads to squeeze the rotor from both sides. Now tighten the mounting bolts to the correct torque setting. Ultimately, you want a third of the gap between pads and rotor to be on the inboard side and two-thirds of it to be on the outboard side, so after hooking up the cable (§vii-4 and §vii-16c) and tightening the cable anchor bolt to torque, back the two knobs out appropriately to achieve this. Be aware that, while hydraulic disc-brake pads self-adjust to maintain the same spacing to the rotor as they wear, cable-actuated ones do not. As the pads wear, adjust them farther toward the rotor by turning in (clockwise) the knobs at the caliper; don't tighten the cable at the fixing bolt or barrel adjuster.

5. **Spin the wheel to check for brake rub.** If you hear rub, peer through the gap between the rotor and the pads, and, with a white background for contrast, note which pad (or worse, which side of the caliper slot) is rubbing. Loosen the bolts again, and slip a business card or two between the rubbing pad and the rotor.

6. **Repeat steps 4 and 5 until the rotor spins without rub.** If desperate, just loosen the bolts, eyeball the gap, push the caliper as you see fit, and tighten while holding the caliper; expect some frustration.

7. **If the rotor is bent, straighten it.** See §vii-18 on rotor truing.

NOTE ON CENTERING BRAKES THAT HAVE ONLY ONE MOVING PAD: *Some disc brakes work by flexing the rotor toward a fixed pad. This applies to some hydraulic disc brakes and to all cable-actuated disc brakes. The above procedure will work for installing hydraulic ones, provided you first tighten the fixed-pad adjuster screw about a half turn. Once the caliper is bolted in place, back out the fixed-pad adjuster screw so the pad just barely clears the rotor.*

For cable-actuated disc calipers (Fig. 7.48), follow step 4 above.

NOTE ON BENT ROTORS: *A bent rotor will rub or at least reduce pad adjustment range. See §vii-18 on rotor truing.*

c. Hookup of cable-actuated disc brakes

Route the cable housing to the brake following the procedures in §vii-4 on cable installation. Tie it down with zip-ties where there are no cable stops. Push the cable through the housing stop on the caliper, and tighten it under the cable anchor bolt.

d. Cutting hydraulic disc-brake hoses to length

When you route the hose to the brake, make it curve smoothly without kinks, and without large loops that can catch on things, and not so short that it is tight across spans where it is vulnerable. If the frame has disc-brake hose guides, use those. Otherwise, tie the hose down to the frame or fork with zip-ties, tape, guides that clip or screw into cable guides, or adhesive-backed hose guides.

Don't expect aftermarket brake hoses to be the right length for your bike; you may need to cut them. If one end of the hose has a permanent crimped end on it, don't cut that end. Generally, on the end you can cut, there will be a brass, olive-shaped ring around the end of the hose crushed by a sleeve nut to seal against leaks. This brass "olive" will need to be replaced after you cut the hose.

When you cut a hose, point the end up immediately to try to maintain a dome of fluid at the end, rather than letting any drip out. This may prevent air from being trapped after you reconnect the hose and may save you the trouble of having to bleed the system afterward.

1. **Remove the wheel and the brake pads (§vii-13).** You don't want to get brake fluid on the rotor or the pads.

2. **Disconnect the hose from the fittings.** This can be done at either the lever or the caliper, but it can't be done at an end that has a permanent crimped fitting. Unscrew the sleeve nut holding the hose. The sleeve nut may be concealed under a plastic or rubber cover; slide it up the hose for access. If the hose attaches at a banjo fitting, it is usu-

ally not necessary to remove the banjo bolt, and hence the banjo itself, from the lever or caliper.

3. **If possible, gently pull the hose straight off and skip to step 6.** Be very careful, because on some brakes you can break a thin barbed nipple that runs up into the tube. As part of the sealing system, many brakes have a thin barbed nipple extending up inside the hose under the brass olive ring; the olive, compressed by the sleeve nut, tightens around the nipple's barbs. While this barbed nipple is generally a separate piece that presses into the end of the hose, it may also be part of the lever, and if you bend the hose sideways while you pull on it, you can break it off.

4. **If the hose did not pull off easily (i.e., the barbed nipple must be integral to the lever), carefully cut the brass olive open with a hacksaw and peel it away from the hose.**

5. **Pull the hose off and slide the sleeve nut and rubber cover up the hose beyond where you plan to cut.**

6. **Cut the hose to length with a sharp, perpendicular cut.** Measure twice, cut once. Make sure that you will have enough hose length for full rotation of the handlebars. Ideally, use a hydraulic hose cutter (Fig. 1.4). You can also do a good job with a sharp knife while the hose is clamped in a vise, held by a pair of plastic grooved blocks, which many brakes come with and which bike shops get so many of that they throw them away. Again, tip the hose end up to prevent loss of fluid and consequent addition of air into the system.

7. **Slide the connection parts onto the hose.** Slip on the rubber hose-nut cover, the hose nut, and the new brass olive.

8. **If the brake has a separate barbed fitting,** tap it into the hose while held in a vise between the grooved blocks.

9. **Push the hose in place and tighten the sleeve nut (maximum torque: 40 in-lbs/4.5 N-m).** Slide the plastic or rubber nut cover back into place over the nut.

10. **Confirm that the hose routing works.** Make sure that the hose does not get yanked when you turn the handlebars. Some brakes allow adjustment of the angle of the banjo at the caliper (or at a satellite master cylinder) by loosening and retightening the banjo bolt to smooth the hose routing.

11. **Skip to §vii-17 on bleeding hydraulic disc brakes.** However, if the brake was previously connected, and you think you might have prevented the entry of air into the system, then install the pads and wheel again and squeeze the lever. If the lever feels firm, you're done. If it doesn't, there is air in the line, and you must bleed the air from the system (see §vii-17).

e. Lever reach, lever pull, and pad spacing

The reach adjustment, if present, may be like those in §vii-7.

Lever pull and pad spacing are closely related, as the closer the pads are to the rotor, the less pull it takes to stop. But the pads will rub if too close. The lever on a hydraulic brake may or may not have a lever pull adjustment.

Lever pull with cable-actuated brakes can be adjusted by the cable barrel adjuster at the caliper. Pad spacing on cable-actuated disc brakes, which affects lever pull, can be adjusted with the knobs or screws on either side of the caliper. Same goes for hydraulic brakes that have only one moving piston, but only the pad on the wheel side is adjustable.

HYDRAULIC DISC-BRAKE BLEEDING (OR FILLING)

LEVEL 2

Brakes must be bled whenever they have air in the system. The symptom is a lever that is not firm when pulled and/or becomes more firm with repeated pumping of the lever. Separately, given enough usage in dirty conditions, dirt can get past the seals and contaminate the fluid, so flushing the old fluid out with new fluid will improve performance.

The procedure for filling an empty brake system is the same as for bleeding one. In general, you either move fluid down through the system by filling the reservoir at the top and forcing fluid through by pulling the lever or by sucking from a syringe at the caliper, or you force fluid up from a syringe or squeeze bottle through the caliper to the lever reservoir. Air bubbles float up to the top of the fluid, toward the lever.

It is unrealistic to include complete bleeding instructions here for every brake, especially as road hydraulic disc brakes are in their infancy as of this printing. With one of the three following methods, you should be able to bleed almost any brake, but it is of course preferable to follow specific instructions that come with a brake's bleed kit.

With all brakes:

1. **Remove the wheel.**

2. **Remove the brake pads (§vii-13).**

3. **Install a spacer block (Fig. 7.50) between the pistons.** The spacer allows you to apply hydraulic pressure while keeping the pistons pushed back in their bores. Many brakes come with a bleed spacer.

IMPORTANT—PAD PROTECTION: *Avoid getting fluid on the pads, which will ruin them. Replace* pads contaminated by brake fluid, and clean rotors contaminated by brake fluid with rubbing alcohol.

IMPORTANT—FLUID TYPE: *Use the recommended brake fluid for your brake. Some systems use mineral oil, and some use DOT (automotive) brake fluid. DO NOT interchange mineral oil and DOT fluid in a brake; doing so will ruin the seals inside.*

Not all mineral oil is the same (viscosity, purity, boiling point, etc. varies), nor is all DOT fluid. DOT (which stands for Department of Transportation) has a standardized numbering system. The higher the DOT number, the higher the boiling point, and your brake was designed to operate in a certain temperature range with a DOT fluid for that range. If you were to use DOT 3 or DOT 4 fluid, for instance, in a brake designed for DOT 5.1, you might be without brakes when you need them the most—when they get really hot under heavy braking (see warning below). Again, use the fluid your brake was designed for.

WARNING—BOILING FLUID: *With brakes using DOT fluid, only add fluid from a container that has never been opened before. DOT fluid absorbs water, and the more water it has absorbed, the lower its boiling point. Opening the container for a short time can be enough to bring the boiling point down significantly (if you leave a glass of DOT fluid out overnight in a humid area, it will overflow the glass by morning!).*

Why is the boiling point of the fluid important? A hydraulic brake works because liquids are essentially noncompressible, so pushing on a piston at one end of a column of liquid (at the lever, a.k.a., the master cylinder) can push a piston just as forcefully at the other end of the column of liquid (at the caliper). Gases, on the other hand, are compressible; that's why you have compressed air in your tires. But if hydraulic fluid boils, gas bubbles form in the hydraulic lines, and pulling the lever will only compress the gas; it won't forcefully push the caliper pistons.

"Vapor lock" occurs when the caliper gets so hot that the fluid inside boils. Your only braking hope is to pump the lever rapidly to compress the bubbles enough to partially function. Once vapor lock occurs, you need to replace the fluid in a DOT-fluid brake with new DOT fluid. With mineral oil, you need only let the brake cool down, since oil doesn't absorb water.

IMPORTANT: *DOT fluid can dissolve paint, so wipe it off wherever it dripped on the bike, and rinse with isopropyl alcohol quickly. Obviously, don't get it on your skin or in your eyes, either. It is soluble in water as well as in isopropyl alcohol.*

a. Bleeding up from the caliper

1. **Orient the lever so the bleed screw is at the top.** Mount the bike in a stand, turn the handlebar, and rotate the lever on the handlebar such that the lever is the highest point in the system. Turn the lever and/or handlebar until the bleed screw is at the top.

2. **Push the pistons fully back into their cylinders.** Carefully push the pistons back in with the box end of a wrench.

3. **Remove the rubber cover from the caliper bleed fitting (Fig. 7.49).**

4. **Push a short section of clear tube onto the tip of a syringe or squeeze bottle.** Push it on so it stays on.

5. **Fill the syringe or squeeze bottle.** Use the recommended fluid for your brake. If it is DOT fluid, take it from a previously unopened container (see note on boiled fluid above).

6. **Push the other end of the tube over the caliper bleed nipple.** Put the box end of a wrench on the bleed nipple (Fig. 7.50).

7. **Connect a tube to the master cylinder bleed hole.** The bleed kit should have come with a fluid exit tube and a fitting to hold

7.50 Bleeding TRP Parabox hydraulic disc-brake caliper: note spacer in place of brake pads.

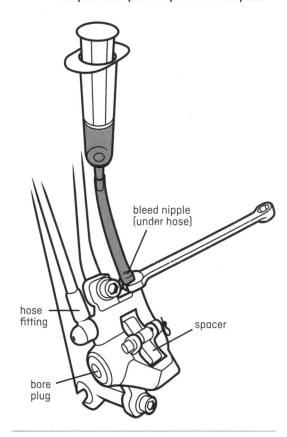

bleed nipple (under hose)

hose fitting

spacer

bore plug

tube before you stick it on the nipple. Push the olive down over the hose and nipple so it won't pull off.

11. **Pull back slightly on the syringe plunger (or let off for about three counts so the squeeze bottle returns to its natural shape).** This draws air out of the caliper and up into the syringe or bottle.

12. **Push for five, let off for three.** Repeat until no more bubbles come out of the caliper.

13. **Push firmly on the syringe or bottle until clean fluid without bubbles comes out of the tube at the lever.** Tap the syringe or bottle, its tube, and the brake hose, caliper, and master cylinder to break free any stuck bubbles.

14. **While still pushing the syringe or bottle, quickly pull the lever to the handlebar and release.** Look for air coming out of the bleed tube at the lever. Repeat until no more air emerges.

15. **While still pushing the syringe or bottle, close the caliper bleed fitting.** Don't over-tighten the fitting—it is small, and you only need to tighten it enough to create a seal!

16. **Remove the tubes from the caliper and lever.**

17. **Replace the lever bleed screw or plug.**

18. **Replace the rubber cover on the caliper bleed fitting.**

19. **Install the pads (§vii-13) and wheel, and pump the lever.** The lever should feel firm, and it should not come back to the grip. Repeat bleed if it feels spongy.

20. **Clean DOT fluid off the lever and bike.** Wipe it first, then spray it with isopropyl alcohol and wipe again.

21. **Check for fluid leaks by putting a zip-tie overnight around the lever.** If the zip-tie is still tight around the lever and the handlebar grip the next day, the system is completely sealed.

it into the bleed hole. Plug the proper fitting into the tube. Remove the screw or plug from the master cylinder bleed hole, and push or thread the fitting into it.

8. **Hang a container from the handlebar with wire or a zip-tie.** Direct the other end of the tube into it.

9. **With the caliper bleed fitting closed, squeeze the syringe or fluid bottle repeatedly until any air bubbles in the tube come back into the syringe or bottle.** The syringe or bottle should be pointed straight down; keep it that way throughout the following steps.

10. **Loosen the bleed fitting on the caliper one-fourth turn, and squeeze in new fluid from the bottle or syringe for a count of five.** If the tube is popping off the caliper bleed nipple, put an "olive"—the barrel-shaped brass hose fitting ring seal—on the bottle's bleed

b. Bleeding brakes down from a reservoir with a screw-on cover

One way to bleed brakes is to add extra fluid to the reservoir at the master cylinder (the lever) and squeeze old fluid and air out at the caliper as well as allow bubbles to come up to and out of the fluid in the reservoir.

1. **Turn the handlebar and the lever so the reservoir is level and the hose trends downward the entire way to the caliper.** You can unbolt the caliper so that it hangs by the hose.

2. **Remove the reservoir cover and diaphragm.** Tiny screws secure it; make sure your screwdriver or wrench is completely engaged in each one.

NOTE: *Make sure you remove the rubber diaphragm under the cover! You would not be the first one to think you were looking at the inside of the reservoir and not the top of the diaphragm, wondering why the fluid you keep adding does not disappear and why the brakes don't tighten up!*

3. **Add fluid at the lever reservoir.** Use fluid specified by the brake manufacturer.

4. **Remove the rubber cover from the bleed nipple (Fig. 7.49).**

5. **Put a box-end wrench on the bleed fitting.** Size will vary with application. If you don't have a box-end wrench, a standard open-end wrench will do, but be mindful not to round off the nipple hex as you work.

6. **Put a clear tube on the caliper bleed fitting nipple leading into a catch container.** It is preferable to put a box-end wrench on the bleed fitting before pushing the hose onto the nipple—the wrench then stays in place as you open and close the fitting.

7. **Unscrew the bleed fitting one-eighth turn.**

8. **Squeeze the lever repeatedly.** Make sure you have a spacer (you can make one out of a chunk of wood) between the pistons (Fig. 7.50) before squeezing the lever! Tighten the bleed fitting before releasing the lever each time. This pushes fluid in and air out. Push until fluid flows out into the bleed tube you attached at the caliper.

9. **Use the following three techniques to ensure removal of all the air:**

   a. Push air bubbles out of the caliper: Squeeze the lever with the bleed nipple open, tighten the nipple, release the lever, open the bleed nipple, squeeze the lever, tighten the nipple, release the lever, and repeat, keeping the reservoir topped up, until no more bubbles appear in the bleed tube.

   b. Repeatedly squeeze the brake lever with the bleed nipple closed, making sure that you keep the fluid level in the reservoir topped up. While you are squeezing, air bubbles should rise through the port into the reservoir.

   c. Tap the hose, caliper, and reservoir to break free any stuck air bubbles.

10. **While squeezing the brake lever, open and close the bleed nipple in rapid succession for about half a second each time.** This optional procedure can release trapped air bubbles from the caliper. Repeat two or three times (refilling as needed at the reservoir), and finish by tightening the bleed nipple.

11. **Squeeze the lever fully.**

    a. If it feels solid, as it should—meaning that it comes inward perhaps a third of the way toward the handlebar grip at most—then skip to step 12.

    b. If it still does not feel solid, squeeze the lever and hold it while you shake the hose and the caliper, and tap on the hose and the caliper with the plastic head of a screwdriver to free any stuck air bubbles. When they have all been removed, the lever should feel firm, and the lever should sink back to the grip. Continue with step 12.

12. **Refill the reservoir to the top.**

13. **Replace the diaphragm, cover, and cover screws.**

14. **Install the pads and wheel and check the brake function.**

15. **Retighten the brake lever.** Tighten to the handlebar in riding position.

16. **Clean DOT fluid off the lever and bike.** Wipe it first, then spray it with isopropyl alcohol and wipe again.

17. **Zip-tie the lever around the handlebar overnight to check for fluid leaks.** If the zip-tie is still tight around the lever and the handlebar grip the next morning, there are no leaks.

c. Vacuum-bleeding SRAM brakes

There is some air trapped in any DOT fluid, and exerting a vacuum over the fluid can draw some of that air out. The method here uses a bleed kit from SRAM. The bleed kit has a pair of syringes with screw-on fittings.

1. **Remove the gas from the fluid in one syringe.** Fill one syringe halfway with DOT fluid from a previously unopened container (see note on boiled fluid above). Holding a rag over the end of the syringe hose, point the syringe up, push the plunger, and expel any air bubbles. Close the clamp on the hose firmly, though not hard enough to break the seal, and pull the plunger so tiny bubbles appear in the fluid. Open the clamp and expel collected air.

2. **Screw the syringes onto the bleed ports.** The syringe you degassed goes on the caliper; the empty syringe goes on the lever (peel back the rubber lever hood to reveal the bleed screw; it's atop the tall knob on the lever body). The clamps on both syringe hoses should be open.

3. **Push the air out of the system.** Push the caliper syringe plunger to force half of its fluid up through the system to the lever syringe, along with any air bubbles. Close the clamp on the lever syringe.

4. **Pull the brake lever to the handlebar and secure it with a strap or rubber band.** This closes the reservoir fluid passage.

5. **Suck the air out of the caliper.** Without pulling so hard that you break the seal, pull a vacuum on the syringe plunger with the syringe pointed down, drawing air bubbles up through the fluid in the syringe. Push and pull the syringe plunger a few times. Close the clamp on the syringe hose.

6. **Hold the brake lever to the bar and remove the strap or rubber band from it.**

7. **Push the caliper syringe plunger in while slowly allowing the brake lever to open.** Close the caliper syringe clamp.

8. **Remove the caliper syringe and replace the caliper bleed screw.**

9. **Firmly pull on the lever syringe plunger.** This sucks air out of the lever. Make sure the syringe is pointed down. Gently push the plunger without blowing out the bladder in the lever. Pull and release the brake lever repeatedly to free bubbles. Lightly push the syringe plunger to pressurize the system and prevent entry of air.

10. **Close the syringe clamp.** Remove the syringe and replace the bleed screw.

11. **Clean DOT fluid off the lever, caliper, and bike.** Wipe it first, then spray it with isopropyl alcohol and wipe again.

12. **Install the brake pads and wheel.** Squeeze the lever and check brake function.

TRUING DISC-BRAKE ROTORS

LEVEL 2

Even when you get a caliper perfectly centered over a rotor (disc), the brake will squeal and howl if the rotor gets bent. The spacing between brake pads and rotor is so tight on a bicycle disc brake—around 0.015 inch (0.4mm)—that there is almost no room for any rotor wobble whatsoever. And unlike car brake discs, bicycle rotors are thin and unprotected; they can be bent by rocks thrown up while riding, in a crash, or when packing your wheel in a car or a bike bag. They can also warp due to heat buildup on a long, steep descent. One way or another, the rotors will likely get bent eventually, so you need to be able to straighten them.

If a rotor is really potato-chipped, you will first need to remove it from the hub and pound it as flat as you can with a hammer on an anvil. Then you can proceed with any of the following methods.

a. Eyeballing rotor in caliper

By eyeballing, you can often do an adequate job to at least minimize brake-pad rub, but be forewarned that this approach requires patience, because it can be hard to tell on which pad the rotor is rubbing as the gap is so small. Place a piece of white paper on the floor or the wall, below or level with the caliper, so that you can see the space between the rotor and the pads. Slowly turn the wheel, marking where the disc rubs on each pad with a felt-tipped pen. Carefully bend the disc into alignment with your fingers, rechecking it constantly by spinning it again through the brake. A rotor bends easily by hand.

b. Using a gauge that grazes the rotor

A more accurate way is to attach a pointer to a truing stand or to the frame or fork in such a way that you can adjust it to graze the rotor similar to a feeler on a truing stand. The best solution is the Park DT-3 Rotor Truing Gauge, which bolts to a Park TS-2 or TS-2.2 truing stand. It has a microadjustable threaded rod that you can move to just graze the rotor and indicate where its alignment is off.

You can also make a pointer to graze the rotor while the wheel is on the bike. This pointer may be made of wire bent around the caliper. You can also remove the caliper and screw a piece of metal with a hole in it onto one of the caliper-mounting tabs. Bend the rotor away from the pointer where it touches as you rotate the wheel. The pointer must be mounted securely for this method to work; otherwise, you can make mistakes, thinking the rotor is bent one way when it is actually bent the other.

c. Rotor truing with a Park DT-3i or Morningstar ROC dial indicator

If you straighten rotors often, the Park DT-3i or Morningstar Rotors on Center (ROC) dial indicator (Fig. 7.51) will show the lateral position of the rotor within 0.001 inch (0.025mm), so you can get the rotor as straight as it was when it was brand new. Either dial indicator will clamp to a Park truing stand (the DT-3i attaches to the DT-3 mentioned above in step b, which bolts to the truing stand), and Morningstar also offers a base with a long mounting screw that clamps through the center of the hub axle in place of the skewer.

Set the dial indicator foot against the rotor. Rotate the indicator face cover so that the needle is on zero; wherever the needle indicates the greatest deflection in either direction, bend the rotor back, continually rechecking it with the dial indicator.

You can bend the rotor back with your thumbs, and I have aligned badly bent rotors to

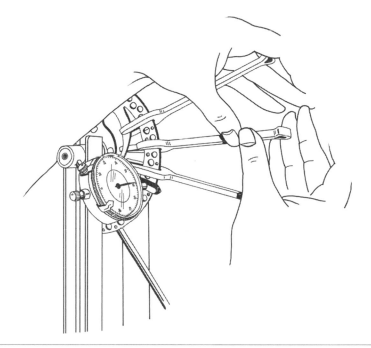

near perfection this way. Better yet, Park's DT-2 Rotor Truing Forks or Morningstar's "Drumstix" rotor-tuning forks slip onto the rotor and provide leverage to precisely bend the rotor. It's best to have three of them: Stabilize the rotor in position with two DT-2s or with the two symmetrical Drumstix, one on either side of the bent spot, and with the third DT-2 or Drumstix (which has an angled slot for the rotor), bend the rotor to eliminate the warped spot (Fig. 7.51).

vii-19

OVERHAULING DISC BRAKES

LEVEL 3

Regular bleeding and fluid replenishment cleans dirt out of the system and lengthens the time between overhauls of hydraulic brakes. On many disc brakes, overhaul is relatively simple, but you will need an air compressor to get the pistons out of the caliper. There are two kinds of hydraulic calipers: clamshell models whose two pieces bolt together, and single-piece calipers. Buy new seals for the part of the brake you are overhauling before you start. A speck of dirt or hair in a hydraulic disc brake can cause a leak, so work in a clean area with clean methods.

a. Overhauling clamshell hydraulic caliper

1. **Remove the caliper from the bike (Figs. 7.48 and 7.49).**
2. **Remove the brake pads (§vii-13).**
3. **Disconnect the hose.** If it has a banjo fitting (Fig. 7.52), unscrew the hollow banjo bolt holding it on, but don't disconnect the hose from the banjo. Save the two O-rings if you did not get new ones.
4. **Remove the bridge bolts (Fig. 7.52) holding the caliper clamshell halves together.** One of these may be a banjo bolt, which you already removed.
5. **Remove the piston(s).** This is best done by blowing compressed air into the fluid-entry hole. If a banjo bolt holds the caliper together, you are blowing into the banjo

7.52 Clamshell hydraulic disc-brake caliper, exploded view

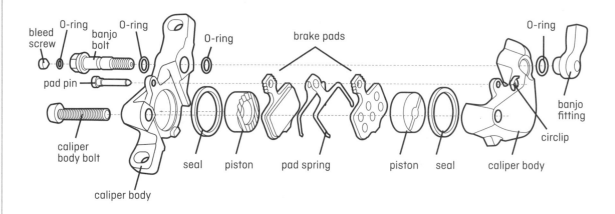

bleed screw · O-ring · banjo bolt · O-ring · O-ring · brake pads · O-ring · banjo fitting · circlip · pad pin · caliper body bolt · seal · piston · pad spring · piston · seal · caliper body · caliper body

hole and there is nothing else to plug; do the same on both sides. However, if there are two caliper-body bolts, then blow compressed air into the fluid-transfer hole while plugging either the bleed hole or the fluid-entry hole with your finger, depending on which piston you are removing. Be careful to not get hit with fluid or parts. Wear safety glasses and cover the piston with your hand or hold the piston side of the caliper half face down so that no parts fly away.

6. **Dig the piston seals out of their grooves in the cylinder bores.** Use a fingernail or a toothpick to avoid scratching the bores, or stick an awl straight into the seal without touching the caliper body. You'll find there are relatively few parts inside the caliper (an object that you might assume is much more complicated); generally there are just two pistons and two seals (Fig. 7.52).

7. **Clean all parts carefully with isopropyl alcohol.** Inspect. Replace any cracked or scratched parts.

8. **With compressed air, clean the caliper-seal grooves and the bleeder hole.** Wear safety glasses. Check that the seal grooves are completely clean.

9. **Let the parts dry.** Compressed air is humid, which contaminates DOT fluid.

10. **Lubricate the pistons and new seals with brake fluid.**

11. **Put all of the parts back together in the way that you found them.**

12. **Bolt the caliper together to the recommended torque.**

13. **Reinstall the hose.**

14. **Install and center the caliper (§vii-16b).**

15. **Bleed the system (§vii-17).**

b. Overhauling one-piece hydraulic caliper

1. **Remove the caliper from the bike.**

2. **Remove the brake pads (§vii-13).**

3. **Disconnect the hose.** If it has a banjo fitting (Fig. 7.50), unscrew the hollow banjo bolt holding it on, but don't disconnect the hose from the banjo. Save the two O-rings if you did not get new ones.

4. **Remove the bore plug (Fig. 7.50).** You will need a tool specific to the brake caliper.

5. **Push outer piston out.** Reach in with your finger through the open bore to push the piston into the rotor gap so it will fall out.

6. **Blow inner piston out.** Blow with compressed air through the fluid-entry (banjo)

hole to push the piston into the rotor gap so it will fall out.

7. **Clean all parts carefully with isopropyl alcohol.** Inspect. Replace any cracked or scratched parts.

8. **With compressed air, blow out the caliper-seal grooves and the bleeder hole.** Wear safety glasses. Check that the seal grooves are completely clean.

9. **Let the parts dry.** Compressed air is humid, which contaminates DOT fluid.

10. **Lubricate the pistons and new seals with brake fluid.**

11. **Install the square seals in the cylinder grooves.**

12. **Install the inner piston.** Slide the piston up into the rotor gap and push it in place with your finger through the open bore.

13. **Install the outer piston.**

14. **Install a new bore plug seal.**

15. **Tighten in the bore plug.**

16. **Reinstall the hose.**

17. **Install and center the caliper (§vii-16b).**

18. **Bleed the system (§vii-17).**

c. Overhauling cable-actuated disc-brake calipers

Cable-actuated disc brakes (Fig. 7.48) usually push the pistons by means of a number of ball bearings rolling in curved, ramped tracks. If they become dirty inside, they won't work as well. Methods to disassemble them vary; you won't find the how-to in their accompanying instruction manual; and it would require too many pages in this book for each one to realistically devote to a task that few readers are likely to undertake. Consult the manufacturer's website for a service manual. It is not particularly complicated to take cable-actuated disc brakes apart and put them back together; it just takes a lot of steps specific to each one.

SHIMANO AX AND CAMPAGNOLO C-RECORD DELTA AND CROCE D'AUNE DELTA CENTER-PULL CALIPERS

Not many of these brakes were produced, but they were coveted as high-end brakes, so there are still some around. They attach in the same manner as sidepull calipers, and the pad adjustment and cable-tension adjustment procedure is pretty much the same as well. The major differences have to do with cable connection and centering.

The cable housing stops at a barrel adjuster above the center of the brake. The cable goes straight down through a crosswise hole in the cable-fixing bolt. The Shimano fixing anchor is in a separate triangular yoke that tends to turn as you tighten the bolt.

Centering either of these brakes could not be simpler. Just grab the part sticking straight up (with the cable entry on top) and twist it as needed. Make sure the mounting nut is tight behind the fork or brake bridge.

TROUBLESHOOTING

a. Squealing

Possible causes for squealing brakes include the following:

- Grease or oil or fine dust on the rim or disc rotor and/or pad.
- Toe-out of the pads under hard braking so that the heel of the pad does the work.
- Brake arms that are too flimsy for the rider (and which therefore chatter or toe-out when the brakes are applied).
- Carbon-fiber or ceramic-coated rims paired with pads not intended for those braking surfaces.

- Fork shudder on cantilever brakes, which includes squealing and brake chatter, is caused by flex in the fork steering tube. Get a stiffer fork or eliminate the fork steerer's flex from the equation by using a fork-crown-mounted cable hanger, a mini V-brake, or a disc brake (which also requires a different fork). See §vii-11 for a full discussion.
- Squealing or howling disc brake due to vibration.
- Squealing disc brake due to road de-icer splashed on rotor in winter.

  Solutions include the following:

  a. If the rims or disc rotors are dirty or oily, clean them with solvent (rubbing alcohol only on disc rotors) and wipe them clean. If the pads are dirty, reveal a clean layer of the pad with sandpaper; never use solvent other than rubbing alcohol on them, particularly disc-brake pads.

  b. If the pads toe out while braking, you should toe them in (Fig. 7.26). Some pads (recent high-end Shimano and Campagnolo) have an orbital adjustment on the pads that allows toe-in. Otherwise, the only way to toe road brake pads is to remove the pad, put an adjustable wrench on the end of the brake arm, and twist it. This will help eliminate squeal on a brake with flimsy arms too. If the arms flex too much for you, get new brakes.

  c. Carbon rims or rims with ceramic braking surfaces can squeal if the pads are not specifically made for carbon or ceramic rims. Easy enough—get new pads.

  d. Tighten caliper bolts, adapter bolts, and rotor bolts on disc brakes to the proper torque specification.

  e. Replace or true a bent disc rotor.

  f. Perform fork-shudder fixes (§vii-11).

b. Low power

Insufficient braking power is available. Possible causes include the following:

- Flexing of brake arms or lever.
- Stretching of cable.
- Compression of brake housing.
- Squishing of pads.
- Insufficient coefficient of friction between the pads and rim.
- Oil and grime on the rims or discs and pads (or water, but that will dry off soon).
- The pads may not work with your particular rim.
- Overly long straddle cable on cantilever brake (see §vii-10d).
- Disc-brake rotors and/or pads are dirty or oily.
- Hydraulic brake system has a leak or has air in it.

  Try the following solutions:

  a. If the brake arms or levers are too flexible, the only sure solution is to install new brakes, but you can try eliminating the other factors first and see if braking power comes up enough for you.

  b. If the cables and housings are old, frayed, thin, or cheap, chances are the cable is stretching more than a new one would, and the cable housing is compressing more than new housing would. Replace both. Use compressionless housing with cable-actuated disc brakes.

  c. If the pads are too soft, they will squish rather than apply full pressure against the rim. Replace them with higher-quality ones.

  d. Insufficient friction is common with chromed steel rims (found only on cheap bikes). The only cure is to fit especially aggressive pads (or replace the rims—not a bad idea, because chromed steel rims do not provide much braking power when wet).

e. Another cause of weak braking power can be oil and grime on the rims or rotors and pads (or water, but that will dry off soon). The pads may also be overly worn and need replacement. Clean the rims, rotors, and pads with rubbing alcohol.

f. And finally, try different pads. With carbon rims in particular, you will find a vast difference in performance between different pads. Always start with the pads recommended by the rim manufacturer. With disc brakes, organic pads offer higher power, while metallic pads offer greater durability.

g. Check hydraulic brake system for leaks, replace parts as needed, and bleed the system.

c. Too much lever travel

The levers come back all the way to the bar before the bike slows down enough.

a. Check that the brake quick-release is closed. If so, the cable needs to be tightened. See §vii-2.

b. The causes and solutions in item 2 (insufficient braking power) may also apply.

c. Tighten brake cable.

d. Replace worn brake pads.

e. With cantilevers, see §vii-10d.

f. Check hydraulic brake system for leaks, replace parts as needed, and bleed the system.

g. Tighten pad-adjustment knobs on cable-actuated disc brakes as the pads wear.

d. Pad drag

Brake rubs on wheel because of off-center caliper, the brakes are too tight, or a wheel is untrue:

a. If one pad rubs all the way around the rim, see the sections regarding centering the caliper for your type of brakes.

b. If both pads rub all the way around, loosen the cable as in §vii-2.

c. If the wheel wobbles back and forth against the pad(s), true the wheel; see §vi-15 or §xii-4.

d. High-power, low cable-pull brake like a V-brake with a road lever (§vii-12) offers insufficient clearance.

e. Disc-brake caliper is not centered over rotor. Center the caliper (§vii-16b), and push the pistons back on a hydraulic brake (§vii-15).

f. Disc-brake rotor is bent. Replace or true the rotor (§vii-18).

e. Angled pads

Pads do not meet flat to the rim.

a. Other than on late-model, high-end road brakes, if the pad will not mount so that it meets the rim flat or slightly toed in, the only way to adjust it is to remove the pad and twist the end of the arm with an adjustable wrench. (Late-model, high-end road brakes generally have an orbital pad mount that allows freedom of adjustment in all planes, once the pad bolt is loosened.)

b. If one pad toes in and one toes out, either the brake center bolt is bent or the brake hole in the frame or fork is drilled crookedly.

f. Slow return

Brake caliper returns slowly or not at all. Possible causes include the following:

• The caliper's center bolt or secondary pivot bolt is bent, or the nuts on it are too tight where it passes through the brake arm.

- The end of the spring is not riding in its plastic friction piece, or it needs lubrication.
- The cable is sticking.

  Solutions include the following:

  a. You can adjust the tightness of the pivot-bolt nuts and replace bent bolts.

  b. Replacing the end of the spring in its plastic friction-reducing piece is easy, or you can put a dab of grease between the spring and the spring tab on the arm for those springs without the friction-reducing piece.

  c. If the cable is sticking, replace or lubricate it (§vii-3 and §vii-4), or thaw and dry it if frozen.

g. Loose caliper

Brake arms are loose, or the front nut or bolt is loose or missing from a center-pivot sidepull brake or a cantilever or V-brake, or the caliper mounting bolts are loose or missing on a disc brake:

  a. The nut(s) holding the caliper together are missing. Replace any missing nuts.

  b. Tighten the nuts until there is no play in the caliper, yet it still moves freely. If the brake has two nuts, make sure they are both there (the end of the bolt should be covered by the front cap-nut). Hold the back one with one wrench while you tighten the front one against it with another wrench.

h. Pads won't reach the rim

You just got new brakes for your old (pre-1980) racing bike or for a touring bike and (a) the pads will not slide down far enough to hit the rim, and/or (b) the hole on the back of the fork crown and/or brake bridge is too small for the recessed brake nut.

  a. You need to get a long-reach brake for the pads to hit the rim, and to fit the small, unrecessed brake hole, you need to get a brake with a long center bolt and a standard nut and washer. This means you need to either buy a new brake with these features, which will be a low-end brake, or find a good old brake. In the 1980s, Campagnolo and others made top-quality brakes with your choice of brake reach and center-bolt style.

  b. You can get drop-style center bolts for old Campagnolo single-pivot sidepull brakes to lower a short-reach brake so that the pads can reach the rim on a long-reach frame.

i. Grinding noise

The brakes sound like there is sand on the pads. There probably was at one point, and it tore into the rim. Dig the aluminum bits out of the pads. On disc brakes, clean the rotor and pads.

j. Soft lever or lever pulls to bar with no resistance

- Broken brake cable or loose cable-fixing bolt.
- Hydraulic brake system has a leak or has air in it.

  Solutions include the following:

  a. Replace brake cable and tighten cable-fixing bolt.

  b. Check hydraulic brake system for leaks, replace parts as needed, and bleed the system.

k. Soft lever that pumps up and gets firmer

- Hydraulic brake system has air in it.

  Check hydraulic brake system for leaks, replace parts as needed, and bleed the system.

CRANKS AND BOTTOM BRACKETS

8

*When someone tells you something
defies description, you can be pretty sure
he's going to have a go at it anyway.*

—Clyde B. Aster

The crankset consists of the crankarms, bottom bracket, chainrings, chainring bolts, and crank bolt, sometimes incorporating two chainrings (Fig. 8.1A) and sometimes three chainrings (Fig. 8.1B). In modern integrated-spindle cranksets the bottom bracket spindle is permanently pressed into one of the crankarms. The bottom bracket is thought of as the spindle and its bearings, but on integrated-spindle cranksets, what is called the bottom bracket has become just the bearings, or the bearing cups and bearings.

The forces applied through the crankset are large, so all parts need to be tight to prevent creaking noises as well as to avoid ruining expensive components by using them when loose. In addition, bottom bracket bearings need to run smoothly under high loads so that they don't sap your energy.

NOTE: *Cartridge bearings for bottom brackets are specified by their dimensions, according to their inside diameter (ID) or outside diameter (OD), as* *well as their width. When you need to replace bearings, be sure to get exact replacements.*

CRANKARMS AND CHAINRINGS

viii-1

CRANKARM REMOVAL

LEVEL 2

Most modern cranks are simple to remove with a single hex key (5mm, 8mm, or 10mm). The two-piece (Fig. 8.2) design means that only the left arm needs to come off; the spindle pulls out of the bearings along with the right crankarm.

NOTE: *"Right," in this chapter and generally throughout this book, refers to the drive side of the bike, and "left" refers to the non-drive side.*

To remove a traditional three-piece crankset (Fig. 8.1), you will need either a thin-wall 14mm (sometimes 15mm or 16mm) socket wrench or a

TOOLS

5mm, 6mm, 7mm,
    8mm, 10mm hex
    keys or socket drivers

Torx T30 wrench or
    socket driver

14mm socket wrench

$^3/_8$-inch drive ratchet
    or torque wrench

$^3/_8$-inch drive
    extension

Chainring nut tool

External-bearing
    splined bottom
    bracket wrench or
    socket

Shimano TL-FC16
    splined left arm cap
    installation tool or
    equivalent

Internal bottom
    bracket splined
    socket with large
    opening for ISIS/
    Octalink

Snapring pliers

Crank puller with ends
    for square-taper and
    splined spindles

Pin spanner (or
    adjustable pin tool)

Toothed lockring
    spanner

Adjustable wrench

Pliers

Flat hand file

Single-edge razor
    blade or box cutter

Grease

continues p. 258 >

8.1A Square-taper "three-piece" double crankset

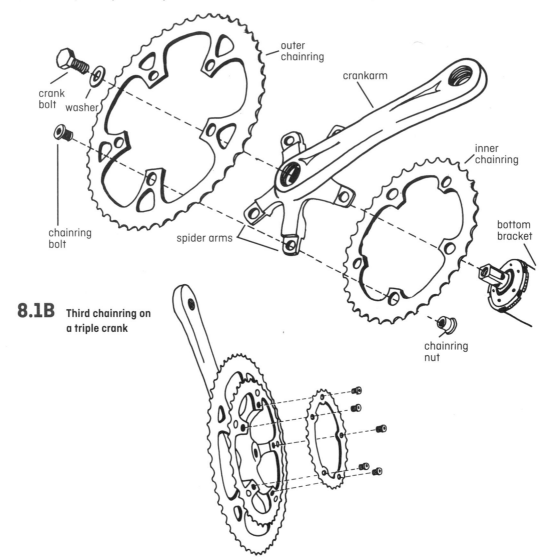

8.1B Third chainring on a triple crank

8.2 Integrated-spindle (a.k.a. "two-piece") crankset (Shimano Hollowtech II shown)

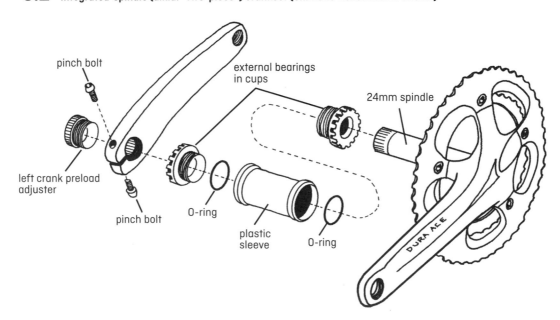

large, 8mm hex key in order to remove the crank bolt. Pre-1980 French (TA, Stronglight) cranks have 15mm crank bolts. Campagnolo cranks from the 1980s take a 7mm hex key or a 15mm socket. Early 1980s Shimano Dura-Ace and 600 Dyna-Drive cranks are self-extracting and come off with just a 6mm hex key. You may or may not need a crank puller (Fig. 8.7) to take off the crankarms.

Really old bikes (pre-1970) may have steel cottered cranks, requiring a wrench and a hammer to remove them.

a. Integrated-spindle cranks with two pinch bolts on the left arm

LEVEL 1

1. **Unscrew the bearing preload cap from the left arm completely (Fig. 8.2).** This takes a special splined tool for Shimano; others require a hex key.
2. **Loosen the two pinch bolts holding the arm onto the spindle (Fig. 8.3).** Use a 5mm hex key.
3. **Pull off the left arm.**
4. **Pull the right arm (and attached spindle) straight out.** You may need to tap the end of the spindle with a rubber mallet to get it started. If there is a bearing seal stuck on the spindle, leave it there; when you install the crank, it will go back against the bearing.

b. Integrated-spindle cranks with a single crank bolt other than Campagnolo, Fulcrum, and Specialized

LEVEL 1

1. **Unscrew the crank bolt as in Figure 8.4, except with a large (8mm or 10mm) hex key.** The arm will come right off. Do not unscrew the cap that surrounds and partially covers the bolt head (it takes a

8.3 **Removing and installing a left Shimano Hollowtech II crankarm**

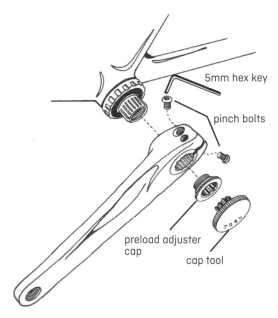

5mm hex key
pinch bolts
preload adjuster cap
cap tool

8.4 **Removing and installing the crank bolt**

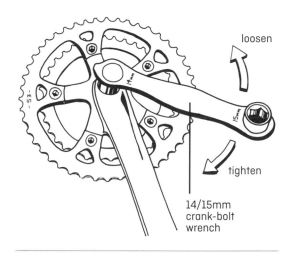

loosen
tighten
14/15mm crank-bolt wrench

pin tool or a 10mm or larger hex key to get it off); that cap traps the bolt head so that the arm comes off simply by unscrewing the bolt.

2. **Pull the right arm (and attached spindle) straight out.** Tap the end of the spindle with a mallet if it's stuck. If a bearing seal comes off with the arm, you can clean it in place or pull it off and put it back on the bearing.

CRANKS AND BOTTOM BRACKETS

8.5 Removing and installing a Campagnolo/Fulcrum bottom bracket bearing retaining clip with pliers

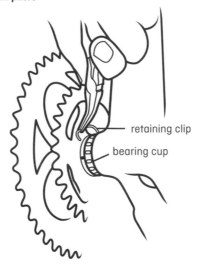

retaining clip

bearing cup

8.6 Positioning a Park CBP-3 puller to pull off a Campagnolo Power Torque left crankarm

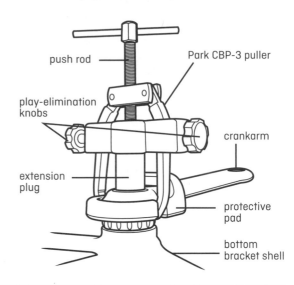

push rod

Park CBP-3 puller

play-elimination knobs

crankarm

extension plug

protective pad

bottom bracket shell

c. Campagnolo Ultra-Torque, Fulcrum Racing-Torq, and Specialized S-Works integrated-spindle cranks

LEVEL 2

1. **Unscrew the crank bolt with a long hex key.** Reach into the spindle from the drive side with a long 10mm hex key (6mm on Specialized) or with a torque or socket wrench with an extension and a 10mm hex driver (6mm on Specialized). Unscrew the bolt and remove it.

NOTE: *On Campagnolo Super Record cranks with a titanium Ultra-Torque spindle, the crank bolt is left-hand threaded.*

2. **On Campagnolo and Fulcrum, remove the retaining clip.** Find the wire retaining clip around the drive-side bearing cup (Fig. 8.5), and pop both of its ends out of the holes in the cup into which they are inserted. You can pull the retaining clip completely off or leave it on the cup with the ends just off to the sides of the holes. (Campagnolo Ultra-Torque and Fulcrum Racing-Torq cranks have half of the spindle attached to each arm and the bearing pressed onto the spindle, against the

arm. The cups are merely receptacles for the bearings, and the side-to-side position of the crank is maintained by the retaining clip's ends penetrating the holes in the drive-side cup and trapping the drive bearing.)

3. **Pull the cranks out.** On Campagnolo and Fulcrum, grab the wavy washer out of the left cup (this washer takes up lateral slack in the system).

d. Campagnolo Power Torque

LEVEL 3

This job requires special tools, namely, the Park CBP-5 and CBP-3, or the equivalent.

1. **Unscrew the crank bolt as in Figure 8.4, except with a 14mm hex key.** The arm will not come off.

2. **Remove the washer.** If the washer did not come off with the crank bolt, get it out of the crankarm hole. If you don't, you won't be able to pull the crank off and may wreck your tool and your crank trying.

3. **Pad the crank.** If it's a carbon Power Torque crank, install one of the cardboard curved pads under the head of the crank. If it's an

aluminum crank, slip the molded plastic cup pad shown in Figure 8.6 under the head of the crank. (The head of the aluminum Power Torque crank has a curved edge terminating in a ridge around the end, and the feet of the CBP-3 bearing puller that you will be employing to pull the crank off cannot grab it well without marking it, hence the plastic molded cup pad to protect the crank finish. The carbon Power Torque crank, by contrast, has a flat back face that mates well with the bearing puller's fingertips, so a cardboard pad is sufficient to protect it.)

4. **Insert the extension plug.** The plug will push on the end of the spindle (as long as you removed the washer that was under the crank bolt) when the bearing puller's push rod pushes on it.

5. **Install the CBP-3 bearing puller.** Hook the puller's fingers under the pad surrounding the head of the crank (there are little recesses for the fingertips under the edges of the molded plastic cup pad), and tighten the two side knobs to remove play from the puller's fingers so they can't slip off (Fig. 8.6).

6. **Pull the crank off.** Tighten the push rod until the crankarm comes off.

7. **Remove the retaining clip.** See §viii-1c and Figure 8.5.

8. **Yank out the drive arm.** Pull the spindle out by pulling on the drive crank. If it's stubborn, tap the end of the spindle with a soft hammer. Catch the wavy washer.

e. Three-piece cranks (square-taper, Shimano Octalink, and ISIS)

LEVEL 2

1. **Remove the dust cap covering the crank bolt if present.** This requires either a 5mm hex key, a two-pin dust cap tool, or a screwdriver.

2. **Remove the crank bolt with the appropriate wrench (Fig. 8.4).** Unless the crankarm comes off when you unscrew the bolt, make sure that you extract the washer (Fig. 8.1) with the bolt. If you leave it in, you will not be able to pull the crank off.

NOTE: *Some cranks that accept a hex key in the crank bolt are self-extracting and don't require a crank puller (Fig. 8.7). The crank bolt is held down by a retaining ring threaded into the crank; as the bolt is unscrewed, its lip pushes on the ring and pushes the crank off.*

ANOTHER NOTE: *"Square taper," "Octalink," and "ISIS" are three different bottom bracket and crankarm interface standards. Square-taper bottom bracket spindles are square on the end (Fig. 8.1) and fit into a square hole in the crankarm. The spindle ends are tapered (at a 2-degree angle) to tighten into the crank as the arm is pushed into the spindle. ISIS (Fig. 8.25) and Shimano Octalink (Fig. 8.24) are both oversized hollow spindles (a.k.a. "pipe spindles") with longitudinal splines on the ends. The spline patterns look similar, but the measurements are different and cannot be interchanged.*

3. **Unscrew the crank puller's center push bolt (Fig. 8.7) so that its tip is flush with the face of the tool.** Make sure the flat end of the push bolt is the right size for the bottom bracket; the push bolt end is much smaller for a square-taper spindle than for an ISIS or Shimano Octalink splined spindle.

4. **Thread the crank puller into the hole in the crankarm.** Be sure that you thread it in (by hand) as far as it can go; otherwise, you will not engage sufficient crank threads when you tighten the push bolt, and you will damage the threads. Future crank removal depends on those threads being in good condition.

5. **Tighten the push bolt clockwise (Fig. 8.7) until the crankarm pulls off of the spindle.**

CRANKS AND BOTTOM BRACKETS

8.7 Using a crank puller; be sure to thread in the crank puller completely.

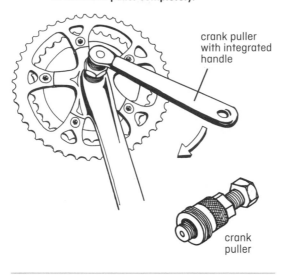

crank puller with integrated handle

crank puller

Use a socket wrench or the included handle.

6. Unscrew the puller from the crankarm.

f. Old steel cottered cranks

A steel cottered crank is secured to the spindle by means of a tapered, wedge-shaped cotter bolt with a nut on the end. The cotter bolt runs transverse to the crankarm and wedges into a notch in the spindle. To remove these cranks, first remove the nut from the bolt, and then smack the cotter pin on the threaded end with a mallet to knock it loose.

---

viii-2

CRANKARM INSTALLATION

a. Integrated-spindle cranks with two pinch bolts on the left arm

LEVEL 1

1. Grease the spindle tip and the bore of each bearing (Fig. 8.2).
2. Push the spindle (which is attached to the right crankarm) in through the bearings from the drive side.

3. Slide the left arm onto the end of the spindle. Check that the crank is at 180 degrees from the right arm.

4. **Gently tighten the left-side preload adjuster cap (Fig. 8.3).** Use the special plastic splined cap tool for Shimano or a hex key for FSA, Easton, and others. Torque is not high—3.5–6.2 in-lbs (0.4–0.7 N-m)—just enough to pull the right and left cranks over against the bottom bracket cups, so do not overtighten.

5. **Tighten the two opposing (greased) pinch bolts (Fig. 8.3).** Using a 5mm hex key, alternately tighten each bolt one-quarter turn at a time. Torque is 88.5–133 in-lbs (10–15 N-m).

6. **Recheck the torque after one ride as the crank may settle in and the bolt will need retightening.**

b. Integrated-spindle cranks with a single crank bolt other than Campagnolo, Fulcrum, and Specialized

LEVEL 1

1. Grease the spindle tip and the bore of each bearing.
2. Push the spindle (which is attached to the right crankarm) in through the bearings from the drive side.

3. Slide the left arm onto the end of the spindle. If there is a wavy washer, put it onto the spindle before the left arm. Check that the crank is at 180 degrees from the right arm.

4. **Tighten the crank bolt with an 8mm or 10mm hex key.** Torque for this bolt is high; see Appendix E.

5. **Recheck the torque after one ride as the crank may settle in and the bolt will need retightening.** Periodically check the torque from then on.

c. Campagnolo Ultra-Torque, Fulcrum Racing-Torq, Campagnolo Power Torque, and Specialized S-Works integrated-spindle cranks

1. **Prepare the clip.** On Campagnolo and Fulcrum, set the wire retaining clip (Fig. 8.5) so that its ends are not in the holes in the drive-side cup but are just adjacent to them.

2. **Install Specialized washers.** Apply a film of grease at the base of each spindle where the Specialized spindle meets the crankarm. Install the bearing spacers on the arms; the cone-shaped side faces the crankarm, and the stepped side faces the bearing. Install the wavy washer on the left arm.

3. **Push the drive-side crank into the right cup.**

4. **Install the wavy washer.** On Campagnolo Power Torque, slide the bearing seal, then the wavy washer, and then the rubber cup-shaped dust cover on the end of the spindle, which should now be sticking out of the left bearing. On Campagnolo Ultra-Torque and Fulcrum Racing-Torq, place the wavy washer into the left cup (Fig. 8.8).

5. **Install the left arm.** Push the left arm onto the spindle on Power Torque, and push the left bearing into the cup on Ultra-Torque and Racing-Torq. Clock the arms so that the teeth at the ends of the spindle stub attached to each crankarm engage with the cranks at 180 degrees from each other.

6. **Install the (greased) crank bolt with washer.** Except on Power Torque, put it in from the drive side.

NOTE: *On Campagnolo Super Record cranks with a titanium Ultra-Torque spindle, the crank bolt is left-hand threaded.*

If you have a long 10mm hex bit for a socket wrench (6mm on Specialized), use a torque wrench on it and tighten it to 372 in-lbs (42 N-m), or 300 in-lbs (34 N-m) on Specialized. If you only have a long hex key, tighten it as hard as you can. Ideally, you should use a hex key with a square end for this; a hex key with a ball end will not engage the bolt well enough for such high torque. On Power Torque, put the washer and bolt into the left arm and tighten to torque with a 14mm hex key.

8.8 Campagnolo Ultra-Torque crankset assembly

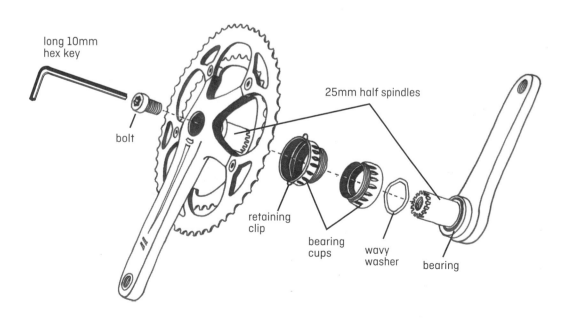

long 10mm hex key

25mm half spindles

bolt

retaining clip

bearing cups

wavy washer

bearing

CRANKS AND BOTTOM BRACKETS

7. **On Campagnolo and Fulcrum cranks, push the retaining clip in (Fig. 8.5).** Pop its ends into the holes in the right cup, thus securing the crankset in the proper lateral position.

d. Three-piece cranks (square-taper, ISIS, and Octalink)

1. **Slide the crankarm onto the bottom bracket spindle.** With square-taper spindles, clean off all grease from both parts. Grease may allow the soft aluminum crank to slide too far onto the spindle and deform the square hole in the crank. With an ISIS or Shimano Octalink splined spindle, however, do grease the parts. With ISIS and Octalink cranks you must be careful to line up the crank splines with those on the spindle before tightening the crank bolt.

2. **Install the crank bolt.** Apply grease to the threads and tighten (Fig. 8.4). Apply titanium-specific antiseize compound for titanium spindles and for titanium crank bolts. If you have aluminum or titanium crank bolts, first tighten the cranks with the greased steel bolt to the specified torque, then replace the steel bolt with the lightweight bolt and tighten it to spec.

NOTE: *Here is where a torque wrench comes in handy; tighten the bolt to about 300–435 in-lbs (32–49 N-m), and as high as 522 in-lbs (59 N-m) for some steel oversized bolts in ISIS spindles (see the torque table, Appendix E). If you're not using a torque wrench, make sure the bolt is really tight, but don't muscle it until your veins pop.*

3. **Replace the dust cap.**

4. **Check the front derailleur adjustment (see §v-5).** Removing and reinstalling the right crankarm could affect chainring position and hence shifting.

5. **Recheck the torque after one ride as the crank may settle in and the bolt will need retightening.** Periodically check the torque from then on.

e. Old steel cottered cranks

To reinstall a steel cottered crank-arm, you need to buy a new pair of cotter bolts at a bike shop because after removal, the old ones will be deformed and will not secure the crankarms properly. Installation consists simply of inserting the new (greased) cotter once the crankarm is slid back into place on the spindle and tightening the nut to pull the cotter tightly into the notch in the spindle.

viii-3

CHAINRINGS

Get into the habit of checking the chainrings regularly. They do wear out and need to be replaced. It's hard to say how often, so include chainrings as part of your regular maintenance checklist. Always check the chainring teeth for wear when you replace the chain. Check the chainring bolts periodically for tightness and the chainrings themselves for trueness by watching them as they spin past the front derailleur.

1. **Wipe the chainring clean and inspect each tooth.** The teeth should be straight and uniform in size and shape. If the teeth are worn into a hook shape (Fig. 8.9), the chainring needs to be replaced. The chain should be replaced as well (§iv-7), because this tooth shape effectively changes the spacing between teeth and accelerates wear on the chain, and it indicates that the chain was already worn in order to cause the hook shape in the first place.

CAUTION: *Don't be deceived by the erratic tooth shapes (some tall, some short) and bulged spots below the teeth on modern chainrings; the shapes are designed to facilitate shifting (Fig. 8.10). Shifting ramps on the inboard side, meant to speed chain movement between the rings, often look like cracks on inexpensive chainrings, where they are pressed into the ring rather than being a separate steel piece riveted on like the one shown in Figure 8.10.*

NOTE: *Another wear evaluation method is to lift the chain from the top of the chainring; the greater the wear of either part, the farther the chain separates. If it lifts more than one tooth, the chain and perhaps the chainring as well need to be replaced.*

2. **Remove minor gouges in the chainrings with a file.**

8.9 Worn teeth

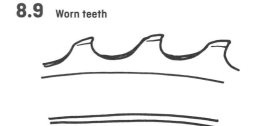

3. **Straighten bent teeth carefully.** If an individual tooth is bent, try bending it back carefully with a pair of pliers or a Crescent wrench (Fig. 8.11) and smooth it with a file. If it breaks off, take the hint and buy a new chainring.

4. **Check chain release.** While turning the crank slowly, watch where the chain exits the bottom of the chainring. See if any of the teeth are reluctant to let go of the chain. If the chain gets pulled up a bit as it leaves the bottom of the chainring, it can get sucked up between the chainring and the chainstay. Locate any offending teeth and see if you can correct the problem. If the teeth are really chewed up or cannot be improved with pliers and/or a file, the chainring should be replaced.

NOTE ON CHAINRING POSITION: *Never rotate the chainring position relative to the spider arms of the crank, because the shifting ramps (Fig. 8.10) will not be in the proper places to function correctly in picking up the chain as you shift. The outer chainring will generally have a protruding pin to locate it behind the crankarm, and each of the other two rings will have a radially inward-*

8.10 Chainring shifting ramps and asymmetrical teeth

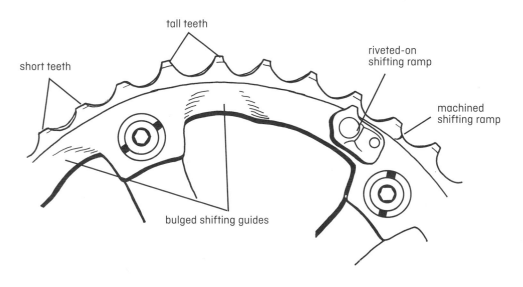

pointed tooth or a small engraved triangle to mark where it is designed to line up behind the crankarm.

viii-4

CHAINRING BOLTS

Check that the bolts are tight, and tighten them (Fig. 8.12) by turning them clockwise. In the past, this job always required a 5mm hex key, but now it often requires a star-shaped Torx T30 key. As you turn the bolt, its nut may also turn. If so, hold the nut with a two-pronged chainring-nut tool (Fig. 8.12), a 6mm hex key, or a screwdriver, depending on what the nut requires.

Some lightweight aluminum chainring bolts cannot take much tightening and will snap off easily. Be careful not to overtorque them (see Appendix E).

If you're having trouble with chainring bolts loosening, put some threadlock compound on the threads. If you're having trouble with the chainring bolts creaking when pedaling (or you're trying to eliminate that as a possible source of creaking while pedaling), try grease on the threads and heads; you can do this right over dry threadlock compound.

viii-5

WARPED CHAINRINGS

Looking down from above, turn the crank slowly to check whether the chainrings wobble back and forth relative to the plane of the front derailleur.

If they do wobble, push the crankarms back and forth to make sure there is no play in the crank or bottom bracket. If there is play, tighten the chainring bolt(s); with a loose-bearing bottom bracket, also adjust the bottom bracket (§viii-11, step 15). A small amount of chainring lateral flex is normal when you pedal hard, but excessive wobbling will compromise shifting. Small, localized bends can be straightened with an adjustable wrench (Fig. 8.11). If a ring is really bent, replace it.

8.11 Straightening warped chainrings

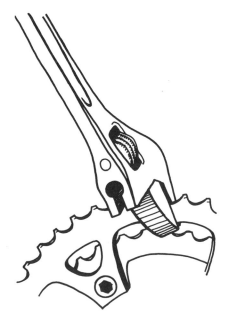

8.12 Removing and installing chainring bolts

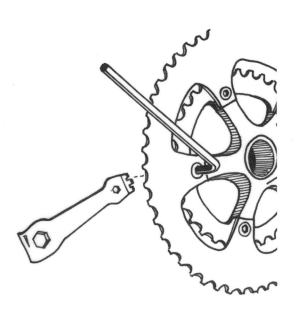

viii-6

BENT CRANKARM SPIDERS

If you installed a new chainring and are still seeing serious back-and-forth wobble, chances are good that the spider arms on the crank are bent. If the crank is new, this is a warranty item, so return it to your bike shop.

If you insist on fixing it, you can find which spider arm is bent by tracking the movement of the chainring relative to the front derailleur outer cage plate. Wrap the spider arm with a rag, grab it with an L-shaped adjustable wrench or pipe wrench, and give it a little tweak in the appropriate direction by pushing on the end of the wrench handle. Obviously you can't do this with a carbon crank, because carbon won't bend. And you can only do it on a crank with a standard double-chainring spider; the arms on a triple or compact double crank neither will allow the wrench to fit nor will bend easily, due to the short spider-arm length on a compact and the threaded standoffs for the granny gear on the spider arms of a triple crank.

viii-7

CHAINRING REPLACEMENT

Road cranks generally have five spider arms, but if you're replacing a chainring, you need to know more details about your crank to ensure that your new chainrings will fit.

A standard double crank has a bolt circle diameter (BCD) of 130mm—the circle formed by the chainring bolts has a 130mm diameter. The smallest chainring you can mount on it has 38 teeth.

A standard Campagnolo double crank has a 135mm BCD, and the smallest chainring you can mount on it has 39 teeth.

A compact double crank has a bolt circle diameter of 110mm (the spider arms are 10mm shorter than on a standard double crank), and you can mount a 34-tooth chainring on it. A Campagnolo compact double crank also has a 110mm BCD, but one bolt hole is offset so it only accepts Campagnolo compact chainrings.

A standard road triple crank has a BCD of 130mm for the outer two chainrings and 74mm for the inner ("granny") chainring, which can be as small as 24 teeth.

You want to get chainrings in pairs (or in threes, in the case of a triple) to ensure that their chain ramps are appropriately positioned for optimal shifting; you want the correct tooth to be there to pick up the chain as it moves from one ring to the next. Chainrings nowadays sometimes have not only their own size (number of teeth) stamped on them, but the number of teeth on the adjacent chainring they're meant to work with as well (Fig. 8.13). Also look for a stamp on the chainring that indicates the number of rear cogs it should be used with (for example, if you have an 11-speed cogset, be sure to get 11-speed-compatible chainrings).

a. Double chainrings

Replacing either of the chainrings on a double (Fig. 8.12) or the two largest chainrings on a triple is easy.

8.13 Chainring tooth-number and speed-number stamps on a 10-speed chainring pair

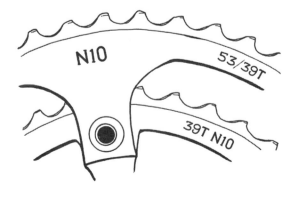

1. **Unscrew the chainring bolts.** They will take either a 5mm hex key or a Torx T30 wrench (Fig. 8.12). You may need to hold the nut on the backside with either a chainring-nut tool, a 6mm hex key, or a thin screwdriver.

2. **Install the new chainrings.** Lubricate the bolts and the little recesses that accept them in the chainring faces, and tighten them (Fig. 8.12). The outer chainring has a protruding pin meant to keep the chain from falling between it and the crankarm. Make sure this pin lines up behind the crankarm and faces away from the bicycle. The middle ring (and the inner ring on a triple) has a little chainring-orientation bump protruding radially inward or an engraved triangle that is also to line up with the crankarm. And both (or all three) chainrings have recesses for the heads of the chainring bolts and nuts, so make sure that these recesses receive those parts and are not facing inward toward the spider. If the chainrings are rotated relative to the crank or inverted, the shift ramps will not work.

NOTE: *If you're positioning a Rotor chainring, the ring is not round, and how you clock the ring changes the effect it has on your pedaling. There will be at least three positioning options and sometimes five: three on one side of the chainring and two on the other that are effectively half steps between the other three positions. These holes will be marked with a number of dots above them. Start by locating the middle of the three marked holes (the one with two dots) aligned with the crankarm. Install the chainring bolts as described here. Down the road you can change the position if you wish to experiment further.*

  a. Be careful not to overtighten lightweight aluminum chainring bolts.

  b. If you're having trouble with chainring bolts loosening up, you can put some threadlock compound on the threads instead of grease, but the latter will do a better job of eliminating creaking noises. You can grease right over the dried threadlock compound that comes on many new chainring bolts.

NOTE: *Whenever you change the size of the outer chainring, you must reposition the front derailleur for proper chainring clearance, as described in §v-5.*

b. Replacing the inner chainring on a triple

1. **Pull off the crankarm (§viii-1).** If you don't remove the crankarm, you will have to remove the two outer chainrings to get at the inner chainring, which is more work.

2. **Remove the bolts holding the chainring on.** Use a 5mm hex key (or, for some, a Torx T30 key). With the exception of a Dura-Ace triple (Fig. 8.1B), they are threaded directly into the crankarm. On a Dura-Ace triple, the inner ring is attached to a special middle chainring with long tabs extending radially inward.

3. **Install the new chainring and then lubricate and tighten the bolts.** The ring will have a little chainring-orientation bump protruding radially inward or an engraved triangle; make sure it lines up under the crankarm. Some inner chainrings have two of these indexing bumps to clock the chainring differently depending on the size of the adjacent chainring. The chainring combination will be stamped near the bump. So if your outer chainring is a 50-tooth and you're installing an inner 36-tooth ring, position the bump labeled "36-50" behind the crankarm, not the one labeled "36-52."

8.14 Removing and installing a chainring spider on a first-generation FSA carbon ISIS road crank or on a Shimano 1996-2002 XTR or 1997-2003 XT crank

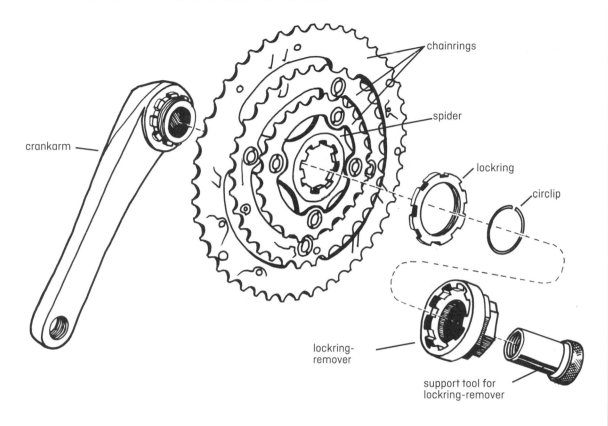

Make sure that the heads of the chainring bolts and nuts are recessed into the countersunk holes (i.e., make sure the countersunk holes are not facing inward toward the spider). Some lightweight aluminum chainring bolts cannot take much tightening and will snap off easily; don't overtorque them.

If you're having trouble with chainring bolts loosening, you can put threadlock compound on the threads instead of grease, but grease will do a better job of eliminating creaking noises. You can grease right over the dried threadlock compound that comes on many new chainring bolts.

NOTE: *Some cranks have a removable spider or chainrings attached together as a set. At the more expensive end, first-generation FSA carbon ISIS road cranks and Sibex titanium cranks use the same splined slip-on spider system as the Shimano 1996–2002 XTR and 1997–2003 XT cranks shown in Figure 8.14. After removing a circlip (by prying it off with a screwdriver), a special lockring-remover tool loosens the chainring-spider-securing lockring; a female-threaded tool that goes on the crank bolt holds the lockring-remover tool in place (Fig. 8.14). Once the spider is off, you can interchange chainrings within the set or simply pop on a whole new set.*

Inexpensive cranks sometimes have chainrings riveted to the crank or riveted to each other and bolted to the crank as a unit. If these chainrings are damaged, you may have to replace the entire crankset.

4. **Replace the crankarm (§viii-2, Figs. 8.3, 8.4).**

CRANKS AND BOTTOM BRACKETS

PRO TIP   **Advantages of a Compact-Drive Double Crank**

If you want lower gears for climbing but do not want a triple crank (which is heavier than a double and spaces the feet farther apart), consider a compact-drive double crank. A compact-drive road crank has a 110mm bolt-circle diameter, considerably less than the standard 130mm or the 135mm of Campagnolo, which limit the minimum inner chainring size to 38 teeth (or 39T). The "compact crank" allows the use of a 34-tooth inner chainring.

You can switch from, for example, a 39–53 chainring setup to a 34–50 setup (lowering the front derailleur accordingly). You generally will need to replace the bottom bracket as well, but the new crank may work with the existing one,

and you may wish to use the rest of your components as is (possibly shortening the chain by one link).

The tighter curvature of the compact chainrings, and the larger 16-tooth jump (50 minus 34) versus the 14-tooth jump (53 minus 39) that you had before means that the double front derailleur you have been using may not shift crisply. Current front derailleurs are compatible with both compact and standard chainring sizes, but if yours is pre-2005 or so, it may only be intended for standard chainrings (i.e., 52T or 53T outer chainring). Its tail may be too high above the chainring for optimal shifting. In this case, you may need to install a new front derailleur as well.

BOTTOM BRACKETS

Traditionally, bottom brackets other than on the most inexpensive of bicycles thread into the frame's bottom bracket shell. Originally, these were cottered cranks (cranks held on by a cotterpin) and then were square-taper bottom brackets (Fig. 8.20). In both cases, the cranks were separate from the bottom bracket spindle (three-piece cranks). External-bearing bottom brackets for two-piece (integrated-spindle) cranks (Fig. 8.2) then took over.

Now, however, the trend is toward frames with unthreaded bottom bracket shells into which the bottom bracket bearings are pressed. These are available in a number of different widths and diameters.

Bottom bracket bearings tend to be fairly well sealed toward the outside but not toward the inside, and water can come in around the seatpost. So, if your frame's bottom bracket shell does not have a drain hole in it and you ride it in the rain, I recommend drilling one to let water out. Drill it as close to straight under the bottom when the complete bike is standing upright, but place it so that it will not be covered by the screw-on derailleur cable guide.

Threadless bottom brackets

Eliminating bottom bracket threads reduces machining and assembly time in bike factories and allows the use of full-carbon bottom bracket shells, sometimes straight out of the frame mold without any machining afterward, so threadless bottom brackets with press-in bearings have become the wave of the future. However, there is so far no standard for width or diameter of the frame's bottom bracket shell. Apart from some early designs with small bearings for three-piece cranks, threadless bottom brackets take integrated-spindle cranks, but that spindle can be either 24mm or 30mm (and even bigger in isolated cases).

8.15 BB386 crank assembly

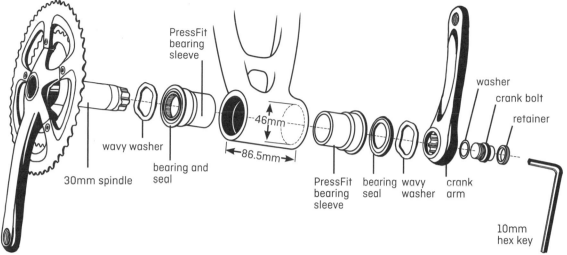

PressFit bearing sleeve

washer
crank bolt
retainer

46mm

86.5mm

wavy washer

30mm spindle

bearing and seal

PressFit bearing sleeve

bearing seal

wavy washer

crank arm

10mm hex key

BB386

Let's begin here, because BB386 cranks (Fig. 8.15) are currently the most versatile; they fit in more bike frame types than any other. BB386 cranks have 30mm-diameter bottom bracket spindles and pass through 30mm inside diameter (ID) cartridge bearings. They will also fit in BB30 and PF30 bottom brackets with 9mm spacers on either side as well as BBRight bottom brackets with a drive-side spacer. They have longer spindles than BB30 and PF30 cranks, however, which allows them to fit threaded bottom bracket shells, since the crankarms are far enough apart to allow external bearings to fit between them and a threaded bottom bracket shell (Fig. 8.16B). Bottom bracket face to bottom bracket face distance is 90mm, the same as threaded external-bearing systems. Adapters are available to allow the use of any 24mm or 25mm integrated-spindle crank into a BB386 shell, too.

A BB386 bottom bracket shell is 86.5mm-wide (Fig. 8.16A); this, combined with the "3" for

8.16A BB386 bottom bracket shell cutaway with PF30 bearings; if this shell were 68mm-wide, this would be a PF30 bottom bracket shell.

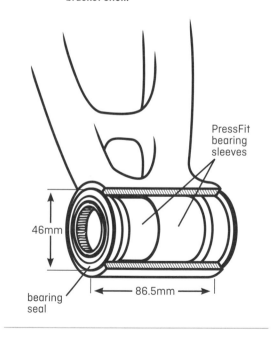

PressFit bearing sleeves

46mm

86.5mm

bearing seal

the 30mm spindle, explains what "386" denotes. The bearings are housed in plastic, press-fit sleeves that press into the 46mm ID shell from either end and overlap inside.

CRANKS AND BOTTOM BRACKETS

8.16B Threaded BSA/ISO bottom bracket shell cutaway with BB386 external bearings; threads are 1.37 in × 24 TPI.

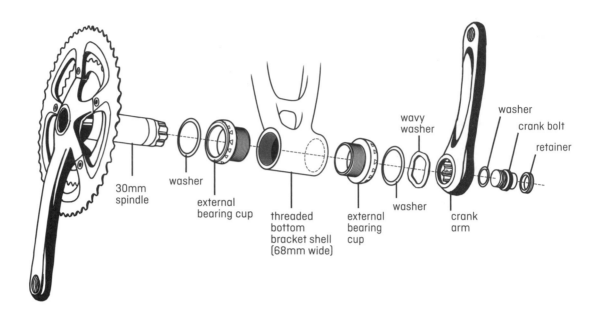

8.16C BB30 bottom bracket shell cutaway with BB386 cranks and spacers; the shell is 68mm-wide with a 42mm inside diameter.

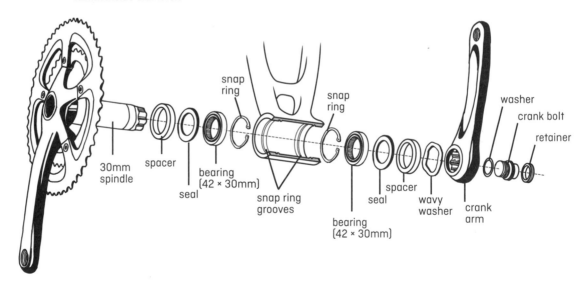

BB30 and PF30

Both BB30 and Press Fit 30 (a.k.a. "PF30") bottom brackets fit BB30 cranks, which have 30mm-diameter bottom bracket spindles that are shorter than BB386 spindles. The difference between BB386 cranks and BB30 cranks is the spindle length and consequent shaping of the crankarms.

On BB30 road bikes, the bearings press into a 68mm-wide bottom bracket shell (Figs. 8.16C, 8.17) with a 42mm inside diameter (ID). The bearings are prevented from going in farther by snaprings seated in grooves in the inner diameter of the shell (Fig. 8.16C). To fit the longer spindle of a BB386 crank into a BB30

8.17 BB30 crank assembly; note the absence of the two thick spacers in Figure 8.16C that are required to adapt a BB386 crank to fit a BB30 bottom bracket shell.

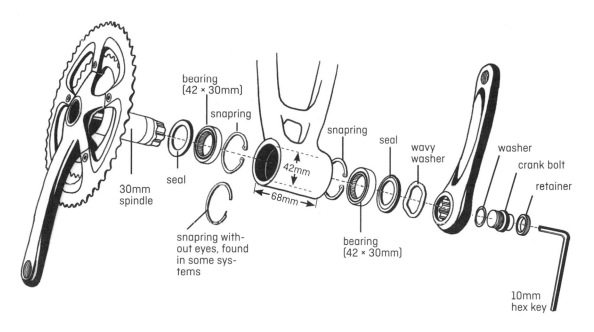

bottom bracket shell, you only need a pair of thick spacers (Fig. 8.16C).

PF30 bearings are the same size as BB30 bearings (42mm OD, 30mm ID), but they are housed inside plastic sleeves that are 46mm in diameter that press straight into the bottom bracket shell without any need for snaprings. The bottom bracket is the same as BB386 (Fig. 8.16A) other than the length of the plastic sleeves being shorter on PF30; it's PF30 when it's in a 68mm-wide PF30 bottom bracket shell, and BB386 when it's in an 86.5mm-wide BB386 shell.

PF24 (BB86)

BB86 and BB92 are often called the "Shimano press-fit system" standards for road and mountain bikes, respectively, even though other crank manufacturers make bottom brackets for this standard as well. In an attempt at more clarity with the morass of bottom bracket standards, I'll call it "Press Fit 24" or PF24, since the spindle

diameter is 24mm and it has the same type of plastic cups (adapters) as PF30. PF24 bottom brackets accept standard integrated-spindle cranks for external-bearing bottom brackets (Fig. 8.2), which have a 24 × 90 road integrated crank spindle (24 × 90 refers to its 24mm diameter and the 90mm distance from the outside face of one bearing to the outside face of the other).

A BB86 road shell is 86.5mm wide and has a 41mm ID. The PF24 (BB86) system is similar to BB386 and PF30 (Fig. 8.16A); the bearings are incorporated into plastic sleeves that press into the bottom bracket shell. On PF24, however, the bearings have a 37mm OD, and the sleeves have a 41mm OD. Each sleeve's shoulder is 1.75mm wide, creating a 90mm overall width for road BB86 (86.5mm + 1.75mm + 1.75mm), exactly the same as the Trek system below or as a threaded external-bearing system.

You cannot install a BB30 or BB386 crank into a PF24 (BB86) shell.

BB90 (Trek system)

BB90 and BB95 are Trek's slip-fit bearing systems for road and mountain bikes, respectively. The road bottom bracket shell is 90mm wide and has a 37mm ID for the bearing seat, which is molded directly into the frame (Fig. 8.18). The 37mm OD × 24mm ID bearing is the same as you would find inside the threaded cup of external-bearing cups for 24mm spindles, and it is compatible with any standard external-bearing/integrated 24mm-spindle crankset (Fig. 8.2).

Trek supplies bearing sets for all 24mm integrated-spindle cranksets, and the bearings slip into place with finger pressure alone. Campagnolo Ultra-Torque and Fulcrum Racing-Torq cranksets fit right in without cups or retaining clips, but you have to insert a flat washer into each side under the bearings, a wavy washer under the left bearing, and covers on both bearings.

You cannot install a BB30 or BB386 crank into a BB90 shell.

BBRight

Cervelo's BBRight system is designed for 30mm-spindle cranks and is neither as wide as BB386 nor as narrow as BB30. The bottom bracket shell is 79mm wide and is not centered on the down tube; the added width is on the non-drive side. Two frame types with two different shell diameters are available: BBRight PF, which has a 46mm ID and fits PF30 or BB386 press-fit bearing sleeves, and BBRight CA (only on California-made Cervelo frames), which has a 42mm ID and fits BB30 press-in bearings. BBRight shells fit BB386 cranks with an additional spacer on the drive side or can be adapted to 25- or 24mm-spindle cranks.

BB94

Wilier Triestina's BB94 system has a 94mm-wide bottom bracket shell into which a Campagnolo Ultra-Torque or Fulcrum Racing-Torq crankset fits directly without cups, wavy washers, or a retaining clip. Using composite spacers from

8.18   SRAM GXP crank in the BB90 shell of a Trek Madone carbon frame

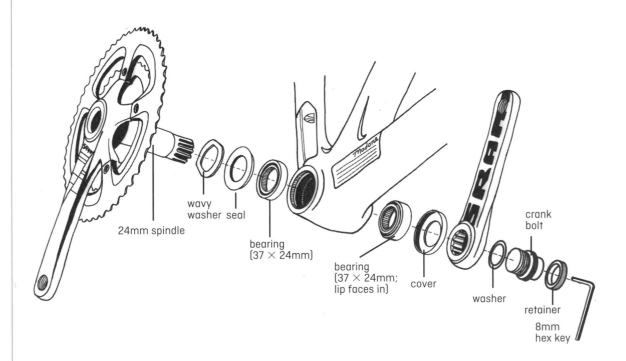

24mm spindle

wavy
washer   seal

bearing
(37 × 24mm)

bearing
(37 × 24mm;
lip faces in)

cover

washer

crank
bolt

retainer

8mm
hex key

Wilier Triestina and 37mm OD × 24mm ID bearings like the Trek system, you can install Shimano, SRAM, FSA, and other 24mm-spindle cranks on it.

Look ZED

Look's ZED system consists of a one-piece carbon crank/bottom bracket spindle. The shell has a 65mm inside diameter and is 68mm wide.

Early press-in

Some old bottom brackets with a square-taper spindle do not thread into the bottom bracket shell. One type, found on old Fisher, Klein, and Fat Chance frames, uses cartridge bearings held into an unthreaded bottom bracket shell by snaprings in machined grooves, much like BB30 but with a much smaller-diameter shell and a spindle with square-taper ends. Early Merlin titanium frames used a similar system except that the bearings are pressed and glued into place with Loctite, without a snapring.

Threaded bottom brackets

Until the recent renaissance of threadless bottom brackets, the bottom bracket type on most bike models simply threads into the frame's bottom bracket shell and accepts the crankarms (Figs. 8.19, 8.20). Simple enough, but not all threaded bottom bracket shells are the same.

Almost all current threaded bottom bracket shells in bicycle frames have ISO (a.k.a. "English" or "BSA") standard threads; these have a 1.37-inch diameter and a thread pitch of 24 threads per inch and, on a road frame, are 68mm wide. The diameter and thread pitch are usually engraved on the bottom bracket cups. If you are replacing a bottom bracket, make sure that the new cups have the same threads. It is important to remember that the drive side (right side) of an

8.19 Installing and removing threaded BSA/ISO external-bearing cups

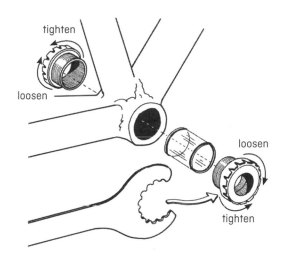

tighten

loosen

loosen

tighten

8.20 Cup-and-cone bottom bracket assembly

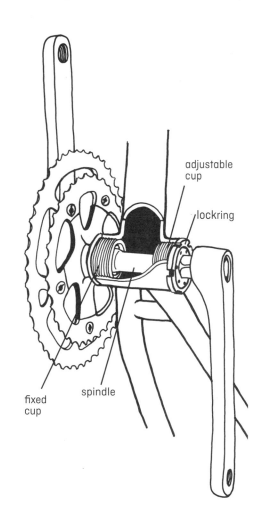

adjustable cup

lockring

fixed cup

spindle

CRANKS AND BOTTOM BRACKETS

English/ISO standard bottom bracket has left-hand threads. Turning counterclockwise tightens the drive-side cup (Fig. 8.19), while turning clockwise tightens the left cup into its standard right-hand threads (Fig. 8.19).

Other bottom bracket threads you may run across are Italian (with a 36mm diameter, and note that both cups have right-hand threads), French, and Swiss (both of these come in 35mm diameter, but use different thread directions). The latter two thread patterns are rare, although French threading was common until the early 1980s.

Currently the most common threaded crank system on high-end bikes is an external-bearing bottom bracket with an integrated-spindle crank (Fig. 8.2). The bearings are external to the bottom bracket shell, have a 37mm OD with a 24mm (usually) ID, and are housed in threaded cups (Fig. 8.19). The spindle and crankarm on at least one side are a single piece; most systems use a 24mm spindle permanently pressed into the drive crankarm (Fig. 8.2), although Race Face X-Type left crankarms are integrated with their spindles. Campagnolo Ultra-Torque and Fulcrum Racing-Torq cranks have a 25mm-diameter spindle; half of it is integrated into the left arm and half into the right arm (Fig. 8.8). The spindle meets in the middle, with the crank bolt pulling the teeth on each end together.

Two-piece threaded cranksets

With the bearing cups of integrated-spindle, external-bearing cranksets (Fig. 8.2) being external to the bottom bracket shell (Fig. 8.19), the bearings and spindle can be far larger (and hence stiffer) than prior designs (whose bearings are contained within the bottom bracket shell). The external bearings can also be right up against the crankarms (Fig. 8.3), adding more stiffness. These are called "two-piece" to mean two crankarms with an integrated bottom bracket spindle; the bearings and cups are not counted in the name.

For integrated-spindle bottom brackets to work properly, the threads on both sides of the frame's bottom bracket shell must be aligned, and the end faces of the shell must be parallel. If you are installing an expensive bottom bracket and have any doubts about the frame, it is a good idea to have the bottom bracket shell tapped (threaded) and faced (ends cut parallel) by a qualified shop possessing the proper tools. These tools are pictured in Figure 1.4. This procedure will improve durability and freedom of movement and will reduce the likelihood of creaking while pedaling.

Three-piece threaded cranksets

For three-piece cranks (i.e., two crankarms and a bottom bracket unit), the most common type of bottom bracket is probably the cartridge type (Fig. 8.21 or 8.25); it has cups that accept the splined removal tool shown in Figure 8.25. These bottom brackets can have a square-taper spindle (Fig. 8.21), an ISIS splined spindle (Fig. 8.25), or a Shimano Octalink splined spindle (Fig. 8.24).

While most Octalink bottom brackets are the cartridge type (Fig. 8.21 or 8.25) with an Octalink spindle, the first generation of Shimano Dura-Ace Octalink bottom brackets had four sets of loose, adjustable, and overhaulable bearings: two sets of tiny ball bearings and two sets of needle bearings (Fig. 8.24). Once Octalink cartridge bottom brackets came out, Octalink split into version 1 and version 2, which vary in the depth of mounting grooves on the spindle.

To counter Shimano's patented Octalink designs, which offer increased stiffness and lower weight than the square-taper designs shown in Figures 8.21–8.23, a number of manufacturers banded together in the late 1990s to create the ISIS standard for bottom brackets. Like Octalink,

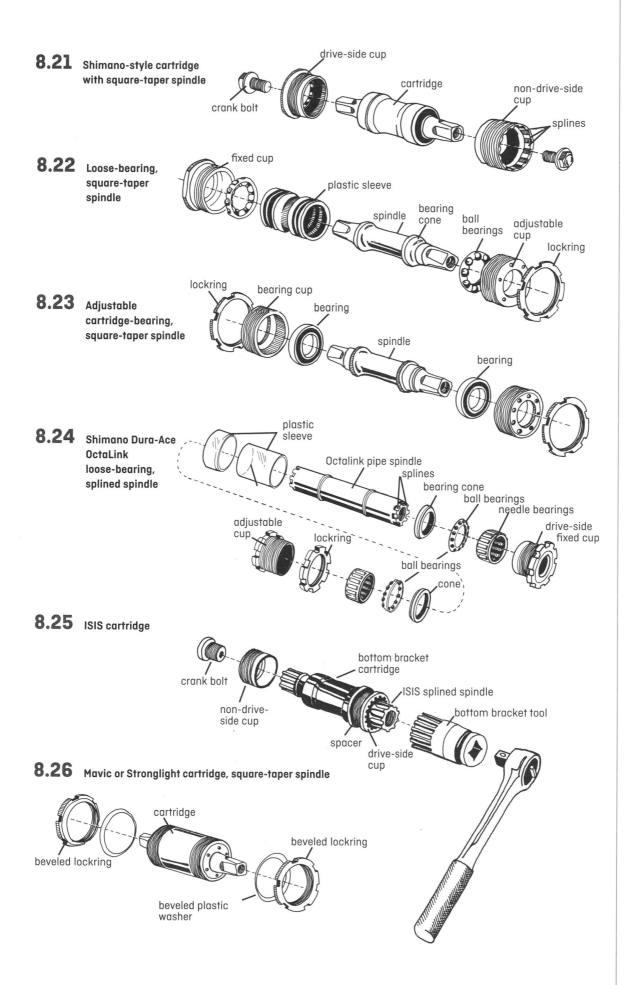

8.21 Shimano-style cartridge with square-taper spindle

drive-side cup

cartridge

non-drive-side cup

crank bolt

splines

8.22 Loose-bearing, square-taper spindle

fixed cup

plastic sleeve

spindle

bearing cone

ball bearings

adjustable cup

lockring

8.23 Adjustable cartridge-bearing, square-taper spindle

lockring

bearing cup

bearing

spindle

bearing

8.24 Shimano Dura-Ace OctaLink loose-bearing, splined spindle

plastic sleeve

Octalink pipe spindle

splines

bearing cone

ball bearings

needle bearings

drive-side fixed cup

adjustable cup

lockring

ball bearings

cone

8.25 ISIS cartridge

bottom bracket cartridge

crank bolt

non-drive-side cup

ISIS splined spindle

bottom bracket tool

spacer

drive-side cup

8.26 Mavic or Stronglight cartridge, square-taper spindle

cartridge

beveled lockring

beveled lockring

beveled plastic washer

ISIS has a larger-diameter splined spindle (Fig. 8.25), but it features longer and deeper splines than Octalink.

The most common bottom bracket prior to the 1990s was the square-taper "cup-and-cone" style with loose ball bearings (Figs. 8.20, 8.22). As discussed earlier regarding two-piece threaded cranksets, the bottom bracket shell for cup-and-cone bottom brackets must be threaded concentrically, and the faces of the shell must be "faced" parallel to each other and perpendicular to the spindle. Otherwise, the bearings will drag and wear excessively.

Another older bottom bracket type has cartridge bearings secured by an adjustable cup and lockring at either end (Fig. 8.23).

Another type made first by Mavic and then by Stronglight includes a cartridge that is externally threaded on each end (Fig. 8.26). It slips into the bottom bracket shell and is held in place by tapered lockrings threaded onto the cartridge. The lockrings have a convex 45-degree taper to bind against the bottom bracket shell, which is machined with a matching 45-degree concave taper on its ends.

The most important item in bottom bracket installation is to put the correct bottom bracket in. If a bike has a bottom bracket spindle of the wrong length for the crankarms, the chainrings will not line up well with the rear cogs. The center ring should be in line with the center of the cogset; this is called the chainline (Fig. 5.48). No amount of fiddling with the derailleurs will get a bike with a chainline that is way off to shift properly. Get a bottom bracket with the proper spindle length, thread, and cartridge width for the frame, crank, and bottom bracket shell width. Before installing a new bottom bracket of a different brand and model than the crank, see Figure 5.56 and read the chainline section (§v-50).

BOTTOM BRACKET INSTALLATION

Threaded bottom brackets

The most important item in the installation of a separate (non-integrated-spindle) threaded bottom bracket is to make sure that the axle length in the bottom bracket is correct. If it's incorrect, the chainrings will not line up with the rear cogs (i.e., the chainline will be off; see §v-50 and §v-51). No amount of fiddling with the derailleurs will get such a bike to shift properly. Get a bottom bracket specifically recommended for the crankset, and double-check that it has the proper threading for the frame. Before installing a new bottom bracket of a brand and model different from the crank, see Figure 5.56 and read the chainline sections (§v-50 and §v-51).

With one-piece cartridge-style bottom brackets (Figs. 8.21, 8.25, 8.26), absolute precision of the threads and faces of the bottom bracket shell is not critical. However, for integrated-spindle cranksets (Figs. 8.2, 8.8) and cup-and-cone bottom brackets (Figs. 8.20, 8.22, 8.23) to spin freely and not wear rapidly, the threads inside both ends of the frame's bottom bracket shell must be lined up with each other, and the end faces of the shell must be parallel. If you have any doubts about the frame and are installing an expensive bottom bracket, it is a good idea to have the bottom bracket shell tapped (threaded) and faced (ends cut parallel) by a qualified shop possessing the proper tools. Doing so will reduce binding and the likelihood of creaking with integrated-spindle cranksets and will improve adjustment and freedom of movement with loose-bearing bottom brackets.

Always grease the threads of the bottom bracket cups and the threads in the frame when installing bottom brackets (or use an antiseize compound on them).

viii-8

THREADED EXTERNAL-BEARING/ INTEGRATED-SPINDLE BOTTOM BRACKET INSTALLATION AND REMOVAL

LEVEL 2

1. **Grease the threads.**
2. **Start the cups by hand.** Turn the right (drive-side) cup counter-clockwise and the left cup clock-wise with ISO (English-threaded) frames. Turn them both clockwise with Italian threads.

NOTE: *A removable plastic sleeve (Fig. 8.19) keeps contamination away from the back side of the bearings. Keep the sleeve on the right cup when installing the cup.*

ANOTHER NOTE: *Even if the bottom bracket cups came with spacers, do not install either of them on a double crank.*

3. **Tighten the cups.** Use the splined tool designed for the purpose (Fig. 8.19). Sockets as well as a crow's-foot splined out-board bottom bracket cup tool from RWC (OBBCT2; Fig. 1.4) are available to allow use of a torque wrench; turn the OBBCT2 at 90 degrees to the torque wrench so that the torque reading is accurate. You need a bigger socket for BB386 threaded external-bearing bottom bracket cups. Torque is high (310–442 in-lbs, or 35–50 N-m). For this task you are not likely to have a splined tool that works with a torque wrench; if that's the case, simply yank on the tool pretty hard.

4. **Install the spindle and crankarms.** Follow the instructions in §viii-2a, b, or c, depending on type.

Bottom bracket removal is obviously done by reversing the rotation directions in step 2. Use a standard wrench, not a torque wrench, to unscrew the bolts (it's not a good idea to use a torque wrench to unscrew bolts, as it can stretch the spring and thus throw off the torque readings).

viii-9

PRESS-IN BOTTOM BRACKET INSTALLATION

LEVEL 2

There is no room for error with a press-in bearing system in a bottom bracket, be it BB386, PF30, BB30, PF24 (BB86), BB90, BB94, or some other system. The bearings must line up straight with each other and must fit tightly enough that they won't rattle or move around, yet loosely enough that they won't become deformed when pressing them in. Proper preparation of the bottom bracket shell must be done at the factory; you cannot expect to correct a malformed shell.

Threadless bottom bracket installation is similar to threadless headset installation (§xi-22).

1. **Clean and grease the inside ends of the bottom bracket shell.**
2. **Grease the outside of the bearings or PressFit bearing sleeves.**
3. **Press in the bearings and install the spindle and crankarms.** Follow one of the procedures below, depending on the bottom bracket shell and crank type.

a. PressFit bearings housed in plastic cups: PF30, BB386, PF24 (BB86)

1. **Press in the plastic bearing cups.** The plastic bearing cups (or "adapters") are specific to the bottom bracket shell and the crankset. Each plastic cup has a bearing inside and slips into or over the other cup (Fig. 8.27). Using a headset press, press in one cup at a time (Fig. 8.28). Ideally, use bushings in the bearings that fit their ID and outer face; the

8.27 PressFit bottom bracket: PF30, BB386, or PF24 (BB86)

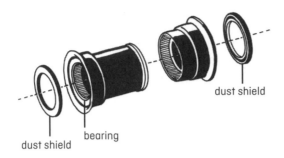

dust shield

dust shield

bearing

8.28 Pressing a bearing into a threadless bottom bracket shell with a headset press

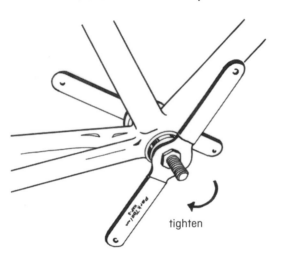

tighten

8.29 Pressing Campagnolo adapter cups into a threadless bottom bracket shell

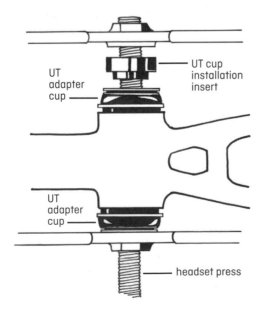

UT adapter cup

UT cup installation insert

UT adapter cup

headset press

flat faces of the headset press will also work. Ensure that both bearing cups are seated fully. Place the manufacturer-supplied seals over them (Fig. 8.27).

a. Campagnolo Ultra-Torque, Fulcrum Racing-Torq, and Campagnolo Power Torque cranksets can't be installed in threadless bottom brackets until the correct Campagnolo adapter cups have been installed into the ends of the shell. Push them in by hand until the O-ring disappears from view and resistance increases. To press them the rest of the way in, you can use the Campagnolo shop tool designed for the job or the correct bushings (like from Park's BB30/BB86 bearing installer; Fig. 1.4) and a headset press. Run the headset press or the Campy press through the cups and bushings and carefully turn the handle until the cups just meet the bottom bracket shell (Fig. 8.29). Without these tools, have a shop install the cups, or use a headset press without inserts, and do it one at a time to increase your odds of getting them in straight. Make sure you don't crush the walls of the cups in the process. Once the cups are pressed in, install the cranks as in §viii-2c.

2. **Slide in the spindle and tighten the crank-arms.** Follow the instructions in §viii-2a, b, or c, depending on type.

b. BB90: Trek frame with a 90mm-wide bottom bracket shell

1. **Push the bearings into the frame by hand (Fig. 8.30).** Trek has a plastic bearing-installation tool for its BB90 frames, but you don't need it.

   a. For Shimano, FSA aluminum MegaExo, Race Face X-Type, Easton (and others), place the Trek-supplied seals over the bearings (except FSA, where the seal is already in the bearing). Install the crankarms as in §viii-2a.

b. For SRAM/Truvativ GXP, make sure to put the bearing with the smaller bore (22mm, rather than 24mm) in the left side with the inner bearing ring's lip facing inward. Place the flat, rubbery bearing seal against the right bearing, and slip the wavy washer onto the crank spindle. Install the crankarms as in §viii-2b.

c. Campagnolo and Fulcrum cranks: You install the bearing as in Figure 8.30 only with Power Torque cranks, and only on the left (non-drive) side. It is a 6805 bearing, $37 \times 25 \times 7$mm. With a Campagnolo Ultra-Torque or Fulcrum Racing-Torq crankset, first Loctite the Trek-supplied seals for the bearing seats into the shell on either side only with Power Torque) and let sit for 24 hours. The next day, place the Trek-supplied thin washer into the seat on either side with Ultra-Torque and Racing-Torq, and on the right side only with Power Torque. Install the crankarms (Fig. 8.31) as in §viii-2c.

c. BB30: All types

1. **Clear the bottom bracket shell of any metal chips or other detritus.**

2. **Grease the contact surfaces.** Apply a thin layer of grease to the snapring grooves and surfaces outboard of them, and to the snaprings themselves.

3. **Insert the snaprings.** If the snapring has a hole (eye) on either end, push the tips of the snapring pliers into the holes, squeeze the handles to reduce the snapring's diameter, and install it into the groove inside one end of the bottom bracket shell (Fig. 8.32). If

8.30 Pressing in bearing by hand in a Trek Madone BB90

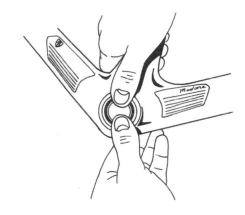

8.31 Installing a Campagnolo Ultra-Torque crankset in a Trek Madone BB90; bearing seal seat and thin washers not shown.

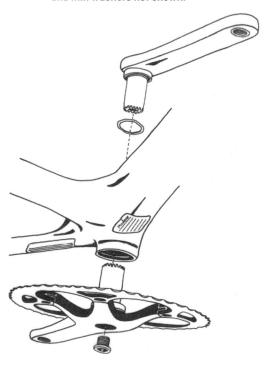

the snapring does not have holes, push the ring into the shell to compress it, push its square-cut end to the groove so that it drops into it, and work around, pushing the rest of it in place. Check that the snapring is fully engaged in the groove all of the way around. Repeat for the other snapring in the other end. (To remove a snapring with holes on the ends, compress it with snapring pliers and pull it out. To remove a snapring without eyes, slip a screwdriver blade under the pointed end of the snapring, push it inward, beyond the groove, and keep pushing on it, working from that end toward the square-cut end until the snapring is free.)

4. **Press in the bearings.** Beg, borrow, or buy tool bushings for BB30 bearings (FSA, Park, and Cannondale sell such bushings). With a headset press and depending on the bushings you have, press in both bearings simultaneously or one bearing at a time (Fig. 8.25). Obviously, you are pressing them in until they stop at the snapring. Without a headset press, if you're careful and have BB30 tool bushings, you should be able to press the bearings in straight using a large bench vise.

5. **Grease the back side of each bearing.** This protects it from water trapped in the shell.

6. **Place the supplied aluminum bearing shields against the bearings.** Their machined grooves face inward, toward the bearings.

7. **Push the spindle in from the drive side.** First, lightly grease the spindle bearing areas, splined end, and threads. You'll probably need a rubber mallet to push in the spindle, since BB30 spindles are designed to be a light interference fit.

8. **If supplied, put a wavy washer on the left end of the spindle.** It goes between the bearing shield and the crankarm and takes out lateral play.

9. **Push on the left crankarm and tighten the crank bolt.** Ideally, use a torque wrench (8mm or 10mm hex driver) to torque spec (torque is often less than with external-bearing cranks; see Appendix E for torque specs).

10. **Check the wavy washer.** It should be compressed somewhat, but not flattened. If it is not slightly compressed, remove the crank,

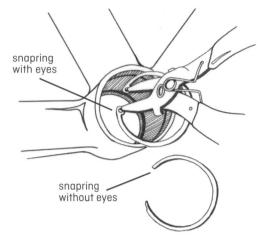

8.32 Installing a snapring in a BB30 shell

snapring with eyes

snapring without eyes

add as many spacers against the bearing shields as are required to fill the space so that the wavy washer will be slightly flattened when the crankarm is on, and reinstall the crankarm.

11. **If the bearings fit loosely or creak, they need Loctite.** Remove them (§viii-14c), smear a thin layer of Loctite 609 retaining compound where they sit inside the bottom bracket shell, and reinstall them.

NOTE ON CAMPAGNOLO BB30: *Campagnolo Ultra-Torque, Fulcrum Racing-Torq, and Campagnolo Power Torque cranksets can't be installed in BB30 or other threadless bottom brackets until the correct Campagnolo adapter cups have been installed into the ends of the shell. Push them in by hand until the O-ring disappears from view and resistance increases. To press them the rest of the way in, you can use the Campagnolo shop tool designed for the job or the correct bushings (such as the ones from Park's BB30/BB86 bearing installer, Fig. 1.4) and a headset press. Run the headset press or the Campy press through the cups and bushings and carefully turn the handle until the cups just meet the BB shell (Fig. 8.29). Without these tools, have a shop install the cups, or use a headset press without inserts, and do it one at a time to increase your odds of getting* *them in straight. Make sure you don't crush the walls of the cups in the process. Once the cups are pressed in, install the cranks as in §viii-2c.*

d. BB94: Wilier Triestina frame with a 94mm-wide bottom bracket shell

1. For Shimano, SRAM/Truvativ GXP, FSA MegaExo, Race Face X-Type, Easton (and others), push the bearings in by hand and place the Wilier-supplied seals over them. Install the cranks as in §viii-2a or §viii-2b.

2. With a Campagnolo Ultra-Torque or Fulcrum Racing-Torq crankset, install the arms at 180 degrees from each other by hand into the bottom bracket shell. Tighten the cranks as in §viii-2c. For Power Torque, push the left (non-drive) side bearing in by hand and install the right (drive) arm as in §viii-2c.

e. Square-taper press-in

Small-diameter, unthreaded bottom bracket shells with snapring grooves were popular in the 1980s. Two snaprings retain the bearings in the shell, and the spindle has a square taper. If the shell is bored to the correct diameter, you can probably seat the cartridge bearings by hand. If not, you can press them in with a vise or a headset press (Fig. 8.28), using a large socket or other flat-ended cylindrical object as a drift pushing against the bearing, as long as it is just slightly smaller in diameter than the OD of the bearing. The inboard bearing stops are usually shoulders or snaprings on either end of the axle, rather than lips inside the shell.

If the bearings will go in by hand, install one snapring with snapring pliers into the groove in one end of the shell. Push the entire assembly of axle and two bearings in from the other side of the bottom bracket shell. Install the other snapring, and you're done.

If you can't press them in by hand, press one bearing in as far as the snapring groove by using

one vise jaw or headset-press face against the shell face, the other against first the bearing, until it reaches the shell, and then against the drift to push the bearing into the bottom bracket shell's bore. Install the snapring. Install the spindle and push the other bearing in the same way until you can install the other snapring.

---

viii-10

THREADED CARTRIDGE BOTTOM BRACKET INSTALLATION

These instructions apply to square-taper or ISIS cartridge bottom brackets like those shown in Figures 8.21 and 8.25, as well as to ones with this type of cartridge body and a Shimano Octalink splined spindle (Fig. 8.24). Most cartridges fit a Shimano splined socket (similar to Fig. 8.25), but Campagnolo cartridges require a different socket.

1. **Thread the left cup (clockwise) in three to four turns by hand.**

2. **Slide the cartridge into the bottom bracket shell, paying particular attention to the "right" and "left" markings on the cartridge.** The cup with the raised lip is the drive-side cup (the cup shown on the left in Fig. 8.21 and the cup on the right in Fig. 8.25). The drive-side cup is left-hand threaded on an English-threaded bottom bracket and right-hand threaded on an Italian-threaded one.

3. **Tighten the drive-side cup.** By using the splined cup socket (again, Campagnolo bottom brackets require a socket with slightly different splines than all of the other brands) with either an open-end wrench or a ⅜-inch drive socket or torque wrench on it, tighten the drive-side cup into the drive side of the bottom bracket shell until the lip seats against the face of the shell (as in Fig. 8.33, except on the drive side instead of the

non-drive side as illustrated). Note that a splined bottom bracket socket meant for ISIS and Octalink cartridge bottom brackets (Fig. 8.25) will also fit square-taper cartridge bottom brackets (except Campagnolo), but the reverse is not true; the bore of the square-taper bottom bracket socket will be too small to swallow the ISIS or Octalink splined spindle end. Recommended torque is high: 442–620 in-lbs (50–70 N-m); see Appendix E).

NOTE: *On most bikes, this drive-side cup will tighten counterclockwise. On Italian-threaded bikes, it will tighten clockwise.*

4. **With the same tool, turn the left (non-drive) cup clockwise until it tightens against the cartridge (Fig. 8.33).** The torque required is the same as for the right cup (see Appendix E). There is no adjustment of the bearings to be done; the bottom bracket is now ready for crank installation (§viii-2d).

8.33 Tightening or loosening the non-drive-side bottom bracket cup

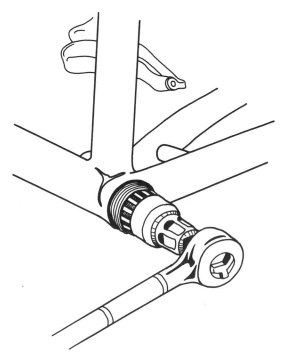

CUP-AND-CONE BOTTOM BRACKET INSTALLATION

Cup-and-cone (or "loose-ball") bottom brackets (Figs. 8.20, 8.22, 8.24) use ball bearings that ride between cone-shaped bearing surfaces on the axle and cup-shaped races in the threaded cups. One cup, called the fixed cup (the cup on the left in Figs. 8.20 and 8.22, and on the right in Fig. 8.24), has a lip on it and fits on the drive side (right side) of the bike. The other, called the adjustable cup (the right cup in Figs. 8.20 and 8.22, and on the left in Fig. 8.24), has a lockring that threads onto the cup and against the face of the bottom bracket shell. The individual ball bearings are usually held together by a retaining cage, which varies in shape depending on bottom bracket. Some folks prefer to do without the retainer; it works fine either way.

In order for cup-and-cone bottom brackets to turn smoothly, the bearing surfaces of the cups must be parallel. Because the cups thread into the bottom bracket shell, the threads on both sides of the shell must align, and the end faces of the shell must be parallel. If you have any doubts about the frame, it is a good idea to have the bottom bracket shell tapped (threaded) and faced (ends cut parallel) by a qualified shop possessing the proper tools.

1. **Unless you have a fixed-cup tool, have a shop install the fixed cup for you.** The shop tool ensures that the cup goes in straight and very tight. The tool pictured in Figure 8.34 can be used in a pinch, but it can let the cup go in crooked and will slip off before you get it really tight. The fixed cup must be tight (see Appendix E for torque) so that it does not vibrate loose. Remember that English-threaded fixed cups are tightened counterclockwise.

8.34 Tightening and loosening the drive-side fixed cup

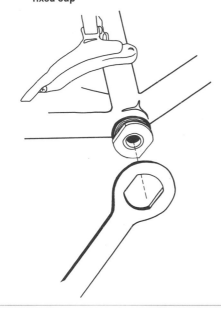

8.35 Placing the axle and drive-side bearings in the bottom bracket shell

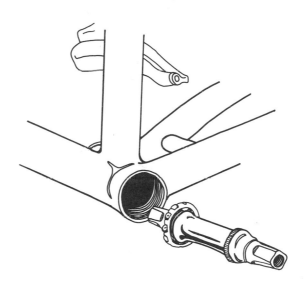

2. **Lubricate the cups.** Wipe the inside surface of both cups with a clean rag, and put a layer of clean grease on the bearing surfaces. Apply enough so that the balls will be half covered; more than that will be wasted and will attract dirt.

3. **Wipe the axle (also called a spindle) with a clean rag.**

4. **Figure out which end of the bottom bracket axle is the drive side.** The drive side may be marked with an R; if not, you can tell by choosing the side with the longer end (when measured from the bearing surface). If there is writing on the axle, it will usually read right side up for a rider sitting on the bike. If there is no marking and no length difference, the axle orientation is irrelevant.

5. **Slide one set of bearings onto the drive-side end of the axle (Fig. 8.35).** If you're using a retainer cage, make sure you put it on right. The balls, rather than the retainer cage, should rest against the bearing surfaces. Because there are two types of retainers with opposite designs, you need to be careful to avoid binding as well as smashing the retainers. If you're still confused, there is one easy test: If it's in right, it will turn smoothly; if it's in wrong, it won't. If you have loose ball bearings with no retainer cage, stick them into the greased cup. Most setups rely on nine balls; you can confirm that you are using the correct number by inserting and removing the axle and checking to make sure that they are evenly distributed in the grease with no extra gap for more balls.

6. **Slide the axle into the bottom bracket so that it pushes the bearings into the fixed cup (Fig. 8.35).** You can stick your pinkie in from the other side to stabilize the end of the axle as you slide it in.

7. **Insert the protective plastic sleeve (shown in Figs. 8.22 and 8.24) into the shell against the inside edge of the fixed cup.** The sleeve keeps dirt and rust from falling from the frame tubes into the bearings; if you don't have one, get one.

8. **Now turn your attention to the other cup.** Place the bearing set into the greased

adjustable cup. If you are using a bearing retainer, make sure it is properly oriented. If you are using loose balls, press them lightly into the grease so that they stay in place.

9. **Without the lockring, slide the adjustable cup over the axle and tighten it clockwise by hand into the shell, being certain that it is going in straight.** Screw the cup in as far as you can by hand—ideally, all the way until the bearings seat between the axle and cup.

10. **Locate the appropriate tool for tightening the adjustable cup.** Most cups have two holes that accept the ends, or pins, of an adjustable cup wrench called a "pin spanner" (Fig. 1.2). The other common type of adjustable cup has two flats for a wrench; on this type, you may use an adjustable wrench.

11. **Carefully tighten the adjustable cup against the bearings, taking great care not to overtighten.** Turn the axle periodically with your fingers to ensure that it moves freely. If it binds up, you have gone too far; back off a bit. The danger of overtightening is that the bearings can force dents into the bearing surfaces of the cups, and the bearings will never turn smoothly again.

12. **Screw the lockring onto the adjustable cup.**

13. **Tighten the lockring against the face of the bottom bracket shell with the lockring spanner while holding the adjustable cup in place with a pin spanner (Fig. 8.36).** Lockrings come in different shapes, and so do lockring spanners; make sure yours mate with each other. If you turn the bicycle upside down, you can pull down harder on the wrenches.

14. **As you snug the lockring against the bottom bracket shell, check the axle periodically.** The lockring can pull the cup out of the shell minutely and loosen the adjustment.

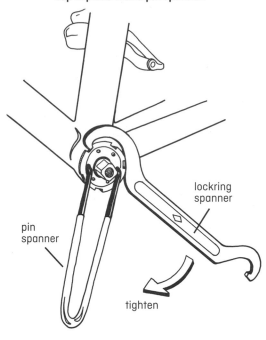

8.36 Tightening the lockring: Hold the adjustable cup in place with a pin spanner.

lockring spanner

pin spanner

tighten

The axle should turn smoothly without free play in the bearings. I recommend installing and tightening the drive-side crankarm onto the drive end of the axle (Fig. 8.4) at this time so that you can check for free play by wiggling the end of the crank; it will give you a better feel for any play in the system.

15. **Adjust the cup so that the axle play is just barely eliminated.** While holding the cup in place, tighten the lockring as much as you can (Fig. 8.36) so that the bottom bracket does not come out of adjustment while riding (recommended torque is in Appendix E; tightening it as much as you can is about right). You may have to repeat this step a time or two until you get the ideal adjustment.

viii-12

INSTALLING OTHER TYPES OF BOTTOM BRACKETS

The four bottom bracket types just described probably represent about 95 percent of the road bikes in circulation. There are, however, a few variations worth mentioning.

a. Cartridge-bearing bottom brackets with adjustable cups

Cartridge-bearing bottom brackets with adjustable cups (Fig. 8.23) are reasonably easy to install. They have an adjustable cup at each end. With this type, you simply install the drive-side cup and lockring, slide the cartridge bearing in (if it is not already pressed into the cup), slip the axle in, and then install the other bearing, cup, and lockring. Tighten each lockring while holding the adjustable cup in place with a pin spanner (Fig. 8.36). Adjust for free play as in §viii-11, steps 11–15.

The advantage of having two adjustable cups is that you can center the cartridge by moving it side to side in the bottom bracket shell. If the chainrings end up too close or too far away from the frame (see chainline discussion in §v-50 and §v-51), you can shift the position of the spindle.

Sometimes cartridge-bearing bottom brackets bind up a bit during adjustment and installation. A light tap on each end of the axle usually seats them.

b. Stronglight (or Mavic) cartridge-bearing bottom brackets

Stronglight (or Mavic) cartridge-bearing bottom brackets (Fig. 8.26) require each end of the bottom bracket shell to be chamfered at an angle to seat the angled lockrings. You need to have the chamfer cut by a shop equipped with the correct cutting tool. Once the shell has been cut, simply slip the cartridge into the shell, slide on one of the angled plastic rings from either end (pictured in Fig. 8.26), and screw on a lockring, angled side inward, from either side. Holding the cartridge with a pin spanner, tighten the lockrings on each side (Fig. 8.36). The beauty of these bottom

brackets is that they work independently of the shell threads, so they can be installed in shells with ruined threads or nonstandard threads. Mavic stopped producing them in 1995, but Stronglight resumed production.

OVERHAULING THE BOTTOM BRACKET

A bottom bracket overhaul consists of cleaning or replacing the bearings, cleaning the axle and bearing surfaces, and regreasing the bearings. Both crankarms must be removed first (§viii-1).

viii-13

OVERHAULING INTEGRATED-SPINDLE BOTTOM BRACKETS

a. Simple bearing scrub and lube from one side.

LEVEL 1

1. **Remove the crankarms as in §viii-1a, b, c, or d.**

2. **With Campagnolo or Fulcrum, skip to step 3. With all others, remove the rubber bearing seal or shield covering the bearing.** In many cases, the drive-side cover seal stays stuck on the crank spindle and pulls off with the right crank (with Race Face X-Type, the left bearing cover seal comes off with the left crank). To get this cover seal off to reveal the bearing, slip a blade under the edge and pry it up (Fig. 8.37), possibly working around the outside with a thin screwdriver for FSA and Shimano cover seals that extend inside the bearing bore.

3. **Remove the seal.** Now that the bearing is visible, you'll see that it has a circular seal between its inner and outer rings that covers the balls inside. With a razor blade or knife blade, get under the edge of it and pry it off (Fig. 8.38).

4. **Clean the bearings.** With a clean, dry cloth, or with solvent and a clean toothbrush, scrub the bearing to clean the dirty grease off the ball bearings which usually will be concealed under a bearing retainer. You can blow the bearing out with compressed air; wear safety glasses. Repeat until clean. You can't get at the other side of the bearing without removing it from the cup (see §viii-14a), but do your best to flush the bearing and dry it out afterward.

5. **Repack the bearing with clean grease and replace the bearing seal and the bottom bracket cover seal.**

6. **Reinstall the crankarms as in §viii-2a, b, or c.** If the bearings still do not turn well after this or are gritty, you'll need to overhaul (see §viii-13b below) or replace the bearings; see §viii-14 below, or simply replace the entire cup and bearing (§viii-8).

8.37 Prying the bearing cover up off of the external bearing with a box cutter blade

8.38 Prying the bearing seal out of the external bearing with a box cutter blade

b. Disassembling and overhauling a cartridge bearing

LEVEL 3

This only works with high-end bearings with plastic bearing retainers separating the balls. You would ruin a steel bearing retainer trying to get the balls out. If you remove the bearing seal as in Figure 8.38 and see a shiny steel flat ring underneath it with a bump over each ball bearing, you cannot reassemble it if you take it apart, so don't even start. And even if you have a plastic bearing retainer, for inexpensive bearings, the amount of time and effort it takes does not make much sense economically. But I do think it makes sense to overhaul expensive hybrid ceramic bearings.

1. **Remove the bearing seal.** Do this while the bearing is still in the frame to determine if it can be disassembled. Pry off the cover seal (Fig. 8.37); get underneath the seal with a box cutter or razor blade and pry it up (Fig. 8.38). Don't cut the rubber edges, but if you bend it a bit, don't be concerned—you can easily straighten it back out; it's soft aluminum.

2. **Wipe the grease away and inspect what's inside.** If you're looking at a shiny steel bearing retainer that has a bulge at each ball, you can't disassemble it without ruining it. You'll need to either replace the bearing or do the simple clean and grease in the section above (viii-13a). Go on to step 3 below if it's a plastic bearing retainer; one side will be smooth, concealing the balls; the other side will have prongs coming up between each ball, so that each ball is clearly visible. With a threaded external bearing cup, read §viii-14a, step 8, first. If the spine of the plastic bearing retainer is facing you, you may be able to overhaul the bearing without removing it from its external cup (which is

an involved process; see §viii-14a). If this is the case, skip to step 5.

3. **Separate the cartridge bearing from the bottom bracket as in §viii-14a, b, c, d, or e.**

4. **Pry off the other bearing seal as in step 1.**

5. **Remove the bearing retainer.** With its spine facing you, pry it up with an awl at each ball.

6. **Push all of the balls together on one side of the bearing.** You can slide them around in their tracks with the awl.

7. **Pull out the inner bearing race.** Loop your finger through the inner race opposite the collected balls and pull it over until it touches the outer race. The balls should now fall out, freeing the race.

8. **Clean the balls and races.** Wipe the races clean with a rag and polish them with a polishing or rubbing compound. Clean the balls and the bearing retainer by wiping them and then by washing them by hand with soap in a (plugged!) sink. Dry everything thoroughly.

9. **Group all of the bearings in the track together inside the outer bearing race.** Each ball should be touching its neighbors. Use grease to hold them in place.

10. **Install the inner bearing race.** Push it in on the opposite side from the balls.

11. **Space the balls evenly around the bearing between the races.** You can slide them around in their tracks with the awl.

12. **Carefully push in the bearing retainer.** You may find that you will have to snip the ears off of the last prong of the bearing retainer to go in, as the balls can no longer move laterally once there is a prong between each pair of balls all of the way around except the last pair.

13. **Pack the bearing with grease from both sides.** For ceramic bearings, it's preferable to use grease designed specifically for them.

14. **Install the bearing covers with your fingers.**

15. **If required, press the cartridge bearings back into the cups or onto the spindle.**

16. **Take pride in a complicated job well done.** The bearing is good as new again!

viii-14

REPLACING THE BEARINGS IN INTEGRATED-SPINDLE BOTTOM BRACKETS

You can replace the bearings with the same type you had before to bring your bottom bracket back to the way it was. Or you can make it spin better than ever by replacing the cartridge bearings with upgraded steel ones or with ceramic bearings. Ceramic bearings are expensive, but they give the performance advantage demanded by top pro cyclists. Ceramic balls are lighter, smoother, 2.5 times rounder, 2.5 times harder, and 50 percent stiffer than steel balls and are less affected by heat.

If you're replacing only the bearings and not the entire cup assembly with bearings in place, first select the bearings you will need from WheelsMfg.com, EnduroForkSeals.com, CeramicSpeed.com, BocaBearings.com, or your bike shop; make sure they are the correct ones for your crankset.

a. Interchanging the bearings inside external-bearing cups

LEVEL 3

In most cases, replacing or upgrading the bearings means replacing the cups with new ones that contain new bearings, unless you have access to the specialty tool required to pull the bearings out of external-bearing cups. SRAM, FSA, and others offer cups with ceramic bearings inside. Instructions for installing the new cups are in §viii-8; removal is just the opposite, after removing the cranks as in §viii-1a. But if you want to get the tool and upgrade the bearings inside external-bearing cups, the instructions are below.

You need a special tool to remove bearings from external-bearing cups without marring the cups and to install new ones ensuring complete bearing insertion and proper alignment. Enduro has a nice one made by Sonny's Bike Tools (Fig. 8.39), and Phil Wood also makes such a tool. The key to the external bottom bracket bearing puller is a two-piece collet with a band around it. The instructions here are for the Enduro tool; the Phil Wood tool is slightly different. Bearing installation into the cups is the same for Shimano Hollowtech II, FSA MegaExo, and Race Face X-Type bottom brackets; an extra step is required for SRAM/Truvativ GXP cups.

1. **Remove the crankarms (§viii-1b).**
2. **Unscrew the cups from the frame with the proper tool (§viii-8, Fig. 8.19).** Remember, the driveside cup will be left-hand threaded unless it is an Italian-threaded frame.
3. **Remove the bearing cover seals.** These are the seals covering the face of the outboard cup, not the seals on the cartridge bearings. You could also leave them on, in which case the bearings will push the cover seals off when you push out the bearings with the remover tool. To remove a cover seal, slip a razor blade under the edge and pry it up (Fig. 8.37), possibly working around the outside with a thin screwdriver blade for FSA and Shimano cover seals that extend inside the bearing bore.
4. **Drop the collet into the bearing from the inboard side.**
5. **Expand the collet.** Push the rounded-nose cylindrical "collet expander" into the collet to spread it inside the bearing bore. The lips of the collet will catch the back of the inner bearing race. Many bearing cups have an

8.39 Pressing the new bearing into the external-bearing cup with an Enduro tool

internal shelf that would prevent you from being able to push the bearing out if you did not have this collet.

6. **Put the bearing cup's outboard end face down into the tool's cup holder.**
7. **Push the bearing out by applying pressure on the collet expander.** In the Enduro tool, you accomplish this by running a big bolt through it and tightening it. This often takes considerable force. And especially in the case of Truvativ/SRAM GXP, the bearing finally comes free with a loud pop.
8. **Determine bearing orientation.** When you install cartridge bearings, it is worth thinking ahead about maintenance. Even though ceramic balls cannot rust and are more than twice as hard as steel balls, the races are made of steel and can rust. Ceramic cartridge bearings, like all cartridge bearings, have bearing retainers that separate the balls, but the ones in ceramic bearings are always plastic and can be removed to

disassemble, clean, polish, and repack the bearing as in §viii-13. The retainers reduce friction by preventing neighboring balls, whose adjacent sides are turning in opposite directions, from rubbing against each other. A plastic bearing retainer will be asymmetrical, so when you remove the bearing seals (with a razor blade slipped under the edge), you'll see the balls with the peaks of the plastic retainer between them on one side and you'll only see the spine of the plastic retainer from the other side. The simplest maintenance, which is sufficient if done frequently enough (SRAM recommends a service interval of 100 hours for the ceramic bearings in its Red crankset), is to simply pry off the bearing cover, wipe the dirty grease as much as possible out of the bearing, repack it with new grease, and replace the bearing cover (§viii-13a). You can do this most effectively from the side of the bearing where you see the balls and not the spine of the bearing retainer, so if this will be your method of maintaining your expensive bearing, before you press the bearings in, ensure that the spine of the bearing retainer faces inboard. On the other hand, if you orient the bearing so that the bearing retainer's spine faces outward, you can completely disassemble the bearing without removing it from the cup; you'll be able to remove the retainer, balls, and inner race in order to do a complete bearing overhaul as in §viii-13b without having to break out this Enduro or Phil Wood tool. This is a good thing, because each time you press a bearing in and out of the cup, you may stretch it slightly or scrape off some aluminum from its bore, so the press fit within the cup may become slightly loose. Plan ahead for the maintenance you intend to perform with the bearing orienta-

tion you choose. If the new bearing has a symmetrical retainer (i.e., a shiny steel one with bumps concealing the balls on both sides), so be it; you'll have to just do your best to clean and grease the bearings or replace them when the time comes.

9. **Place the new bearing on an insert that fits snugly in the bearing's ID.** One end of the insert is 24mm in diameter, and the other is 25mm. Stock bearings for FSA and Shimano have a 25mm ID; a thin plastic shim integral with the outer bearing cover brings the bore down to the 24mm diameter of the spindle. If you are simply replacing the bearings and reusing the stock seals, get 25mm ID bearings. Otherwise, Enduro's Shimano/ FSA replacement kit instead uses a 24mm ID bearing and a thin outer silicone cover seal instead of the stock one.

10. **Place the insert and bearing inside the bore of the tool's cup holder, facing upward.**

11. **Place the bearing cup over it and put a support ring atop it.**

12. **Run the bolt through and tighten it.** Tighten with an 8mm hex wrench until it hits a dead stop (Fig. 8.39).

13. **Check that the bearing is in as far as the old one was.** If not, flip the bearing cup over, with the insert still inside of the bearing bore, and put it back into the tool's cup holder with the cup's threaded section down inside. Reinstall the bolt and tighten it until it stops. This second pressing step is always necessary with Truvativ and SRAM GXP cranks (24mm ID bearings), because the replacement bearing (a standard size, 7mm thick) is 1mm narrower than the (proprietary) bearing employed by Truvativ.

14. **On a non-drive-side Truvativ/SRAM GXP bearing, install its sleeve.** GXP cranks require an 11.5mm-wide, 1mm-thick sleeve

that stops the non-drive shoulder of the GXP spindle and establishes the side-to-side position of the crankset. Use the special GXP insert in the tool to install the sleeve.

15. **Install the cups as in §viii-8 and the crank-arms as in §viii-1.** Spin them and smile.

b. Interchanging bearings on BB30

With a BB30 crank (Fig. 8.17), you'll need a special bearing puller. Enduro has a removal/installation tool that works similarly to the tool described in §viii-13a. As in §viii-13a, you insert the collet and collet expander into the bearing and drive it out by tightening the tool's center bolt.

The following instructions are for Park's BBT-39 T-shaped BB30 bearing puller (actually, it's a pusher-outer).

1. **Angle the BBT-39's T-end in through one bearing and push it straight in against the other bearing (Fig. 8.40).** Make sure it does not hit the snapring's eyes (Figs. 8.17, 8.32).

2. **Center the BBT-39 shaft with the dummy bearing insert in the near side.**

3. **Smack the handle with a hammer.** The bearing on the far side will pop out.

If you don't have the correct tool, you'll probably want to have a shop do this to avoid mauling the inside of the bottom bracket shell, but if you're careful, you can reach in against the back side of the opposite bearing (not against the snapring!) with a rod or big hex wrench that you tap with a hammer. Work a little bit on each side of the bearing, moving the end of the rod or wrench from side to side and around the bearing as you tap it to slowly walk the bearing out.

Install the new bearings as in §viii-9c.

c. Interchanging PressFit bottom bracket bearings

Remove a PF30 and BB386 plastic bearing adapter cup by sliding in a "rocket" headset cup remover tool so it expands behind the bearing. Smack the bearing out just like you would a headset cup (see Figs. 11.37, 11.38; §xi-20, steps 3–5).

Remove PF24 (BB86) cups in like manner, but you'll need a smaller-diameter cup-remover rocket. The diameter of a headset rocket is usually 1 inch (25.4mm), which is of course larger than the ID of a PF24 bearing, as it's intended for a 24mm spindle. The Park BBT-90.3 rocket tool is specifically designed for removing PF24 (BB86) bearing adapters.

You will mangle the plastic adapters if you try to remove the bearings from them. Interchanging bearings means buying and installing a new bottom bracket, whether it's PF24 (BB86), PF30, or BB386. The molded plastic adapters are inexpensive.

Install the new bearings as in §viii-9a.

d. Interchanging bearings on BB90 or BB94

LEVEL 1

With a BB90 (Fig. 8.18) or BB94 system, you can pull the bearings out with your finger. If need be, walk it out a bit at a time by placing a big hex key against it from the opposite side and gently tapping it with a hammer as you move the hex key tip around from side to side on the backside of the bearing.

Put the new bearings in as described in §viii-9b.

e. Interchanging Campagnolo Ultra-Torque or Power Torque or Fulcrum Racing-Torq bearings

LEVEL 3

For Campagnolo Ultra-Torque and Fulcrum Racing-Torq cranks (Fig. 8.8), you need a special puller like the Park CBP-3 to get the bearing off the spindle (Fig. 8.41B); for Campagnolo Power Torque cranks, you'll need the CBP-5 tool set (Fig. 8.41A) as well as the CBP-3. If you don't have such a puller, I recommend you take the cranks to a shop that does. You definitely do not want to pry with a screwdriver against a carbon crank to get a bearing off!

Removal

1. **Remove the crankarms as in §viii-1c or d, depending on type.**
2. **Remove the circlip holding the bearing onto the spindle.** With a screwdriver, push one end of the circlip out of its groove, and

8.41A Park CBP-5 tool set for removing and replacing bearings on Ultra-Torque, Power Torque, and Racing-Torq cranksets

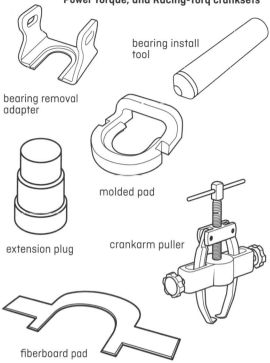

bearing install tool

bearing removal adapter

molded pad

extension plug

crankarm puller

fiberboard pad

8.41B Pulling the bearing off of a Campagnolo Power Torque crank spindle

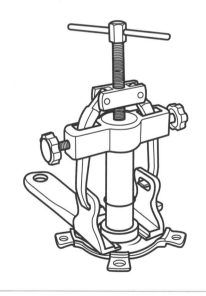

then work around with the screwdriver to pop the entire clip out. This applies to both arms of Campagnolo Ultra-Torque and Fulcrum Racing-Torq cranks and only to the drive arm of Campagnolo Power Torque cranks.

CRANKS AND BOTTOM BRACKETS

3. **Install the bearing puller.** On Ultra-Torque and Racing-Torq, hook the fingers of the CBP-3 puller under the edge of the bearing and tighten the two side knobs to remove play from the puller's fingers as in Figure 8.6 so they can't slip off. On Power Torque, first slip the steel extension basket CBP-5 under the bearing to extend the reach of the CBP-3 puller sufficiently to reach the Power Torque's full-length spindle; then hook the CBP-3's fingers into the slots at the top edges of the basket (Fig. 8.41B) and tighten the two side knobs to remove play from the puller's fingers as in Figure 8.6 so they can't slip off. On a compact Power Torque crank (with a 34- or 36-tooth inner chainring), you must first remove the chainrings in order to get the extension basket under the bearing. You must also break off the plastic tab in the Torx hole of the bolt behind the crankarm in order to insert the Torx key.

4. **Tighten the push bolt of the CBP-3 puller clockwise until the bearing pops off.**

5. **On Campagnolo Power Torque cranks, remove the left bearing.** Get it out of its cup using the same method as in §viii-14a above, or replace the cup and bearing.

Installation

1. **Replace the bearing seal on the spindle.**

2. **Slide the new bearing on the spindle as far as you can by hand.**

3. **Tap the bearing into place.** Use the CBP-3 or CBP-5 bearing setter and a hammer; on Power Torque, you'll need the longer CBP-5 setter. Lacking that tool, set the old bearing on top of it, and tap it down with a tube that just fits over the spindle. Pull off the old bearing.

4. **Slide on the snapring and push it into its groove.**

5. **Reinstall the crankarms.**

OVERHAULING CARTRIDGE BOTTOM BRACKETS

Cartridge bottom brackets with a spindle integrated into them (Figs. 8.21, 8.25) are sealed units and cannot be overhauled. They must be replaced when they stop performing properly. Remove the cranks as in §viii-1c. Remove the bottom bracket by unscrewing the cups with the splined cup tool (Fig. 8.33), and install a new bottom bracket as directed in §viii-10.

OVERHAULING CUP-AND-CONE BOTTOM BRACKETS

Cup-and-cone bottom brackets (Fig. 8.22) can be overhauled entirely from the non-drive side, after you have removed the crankarms as described in §viii-1c.

1. **Remove the lockring with the lockring spanner.** Use the tool as in Figure 8.36, except the lockring spanner and its rotation direction will be reversed.

2. **Remove the adjustable cup with the correct tool.** This is usually a pin spanner (Fig. 1.2), installed into the cup as in Figure 8.36.

3. **Check that the fixed cup is tight.** Put a fixed-cup wrench on it and try to tighten it (counterclockwise for English thread, clockwise for Italian; Fig. 8.34).

4. **Clean the cups and axle with a rag.** There should be no need for a solvent unless the parts are glazed with hardened grease.

5. **Clean the bearings with a citrus-based solvent.** Don't remove them from their retainer cages. A simple way to clean them is to drop the bearings in a plastic bottle, fill it with solvent, cap it, and shake it. A toothbrush may be required afterward, and a solvent

tank is certainly handy if you have access to one. If the bearings are not shiny and in perfect shape, replace them. Balls with dull luster and/or rough spots or rust on them should be replaced.

6. **Wash the bearings in soap and water.** This will remove the solvent and any remaining grit. Towel them off thoroughly and then let them dry completely. An air compressor is handy here.

7. **Follow the installation procedure described in §viii-11.**

8. **Install the crankarms as in §viii-2d, Figure 8.4.**

OVERHAULING OTHER TYPES OF BOTTOM BRACKETS

If any cartridge-bearing bottom bracket becomes difficult to turn, the bearing seals must be removed (Fig. 8.38) and the bearings scrubbed and flushed with solvent, dried, and regreased. If that doesn't fix the problem, the bearings must be replaced. If they are pressed into cups, you may also have to buy new cups, if you can find them.

1. **Reverse the installation procedure outlined in §viii-12a to remove the bottom bracket.**

2. **Replace the bearings.**

3. **Reinstall the bottom bracket (§viii-12a) and crankarms (§viii-2).**

CYCLOCROSS CRANK SETUPS

For cyclocross, you don't need excessively large or small chainrings; sizes right in the middle are perfect. It is faster to run up short, steep, muddy dirt hills than to ride them in a superlow gear, so there is no need for a triple crank or even for a compact double with a 34-tooth inner chainring (some modern cyclocross cranks are compact doubles with 34–50 chainrings, but a 36–46 compact option is preferable for racing). It is advisable to avoid a triple, since the long rear derailleur required would be a liability; it could easily get caught on shrubbery or be torn off in a crash. A compact double can save money; you can buy a complete crankset with a 34–50 chainring combination, rather than buying separate chainrings in addition to the crank. The compact's 50-tooth outer chainring is a better choice than the 53-tooth of a standard double; the downside is that the jump in size between chainrings is so big that double shifts are common (shifting in the rear whenever you shift in the front to compensate for a big change in gear ratio with a front shift).

Cyclocrossers are split, however, between those favoring two chainrings and those favoring a single ring. A single chainring eliminates the possibility of missed front shifts in the adverse conditions that define cyclocross. It also saves some weight and eliminates another place that mud can collect, namely, on the front derailleur. And having 10 or 11 rear cogs ranging from 11 teeth to 25 or 27 teeth means that you still have plenty of gear choices with a single chainring.

Not all bikes have chainstay clearance for double chainring guards for a single chainring, so an inner chain minder (§v-49, Fig. 5.55) with an outer chainring guard may be the only way to run a single ring successfully. The downside of a single chainring is that if the chain does come off—which it almost never does if set up properly—it can jam between the ring and the guard so you have to stop to put it back on, losing a bunch of time and probably getting passed by a number of riders. The poor chainline (§v-50) to the big cogs from the single chainring in the big-ring position, combined with a chainring meant for shifting rather than for single-ring use, can lead to frequent chain derailment.

If you lose the chain with a double, however, you can often pedal it back on, carefully turning the cranks under no load while you use the front derailleur to shift back onto the chainring.

Take your pick of downsides: complexity, weight, a cable to gum up, shifting to mess up, and the mud-catching topography of two chainrings and a front derailleur, or fewer gear choices and a remote possibility of a bigger downside if you lose the chain with a single chainring.

a. Setting up a single-chainring cyclocross crank

With two chainring guards

A standard cyclocross single chainring usually is no smaller than 39 teeth and no larger than 44 teeth; 40 or 42 teeth are common. The chainring generally sits on the outer chainring shelf of the crank and is sandwiched between two toothless chainring guards just 3mm or 4mm larger in diameter than the chainring; they must be larger than the chainring or they won't keep the chain on, which is the whole idea! If you have enough room between the crank and the right chainstay, you may instead be able to put the single chainring on the inner chainring position, one chainring guard inboard of that, and the other guard on the big chainring position outboard of the spider arms (Fig. 8.42). This improves the chainline (§v-50), by having the chainring at the inner-ring position, but few bikes can fit it. Instead, you would normally have the chainring in Figure 8.42 be on the outer chainring spider-arm shelves, and the spacer would go between it and the outer chainring guard. The inner chainring guard would go in the inner-chainring position on the crank.

1. **Gather the chainring, two chainring guards of the right size for the chainring, a set of extralong chainring bolts meant for this, and five 2mm chainring spacers.** Installing these parts is easier with the crank-

8.42 Bolting together a single-chainring cyclocross setup: 2 chainring guards, 5 spacers, chainring, long bolts and nuts

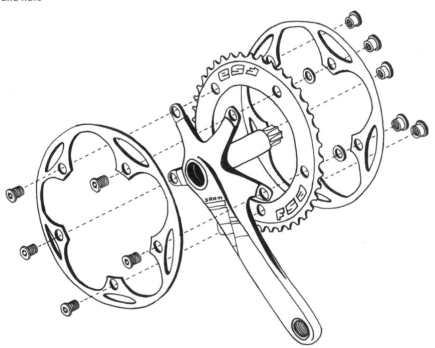

arm off and lying flat, so follow the applicable instructions in §viii-1 to remove the right crankarm.

2. **Flip the crank over so its backside is up.** Install the inner chain guard in the small chainring position on the inboard side of the spider arms.

3. **Insert the chainring nuts in the chainring guard.** Tape them in from the inboard side to hold them in place for assembly. Flip the crankarm over.

4. **Put the chainring on the big chainring position on the outboard side of the spider arms.**

5. **Set a spacer on the chainring surrounding each bolt hole.**

6. **Set the outer chainring guard on top of the spacers.**

7. **Screw the bolts through the outer guard, spacers, spider arm tabs, and inner guard.** Tighten them as in §viii-7.

8. **Install the crankarm and make sure that the inner guard does not drag on the chainstay.** If there is a lot of available space, you can try removing the rings and installing them again with the chainring on the inner ring position, the outer chainring guard on the big ring position, the spacers inboard of the chainring, and the inner chainring guard inboard of that (Fig. 8.42). If it rubs, you have three choices:

   a. You can try a smaller chainring and chainring guards.

   b. You can remove the inner chainring guard and install a seat-tube-mounted inner stop as below.

   c. You can remove the bottom bracket, put a thin spacer between the right cup and the bottom bracket shell, and reinstall it. This will generally not work with integrated-spindle cranks; if it makes

the cup-to-cup spacing too wide on an external-bearing crank, it will side-load and bind the bearings.

With one chainring guard

A second option is to have the single chainring at the inner chainring position inboard of the spider arms, a single chainring guard in the big chainring position, and an inner stop (such as a Third Eye Chain Watcher, an N-Gear Jump Stop, or two or three Deda Dog Fangs, one above the other) attached to the seat tube to keep the chain from jumping off to the inside (Fig. 5.55). This is generally less effective at keeping the chain on than two chainring guards, but the chainline may be better on average through all of the gears (§viii-50, Fig. 5.56) and hence less likely to try to jump off than the single chainring in the big ring position on the outside of the spider arms.

If the chainring is not too large, installation of a single ring and guard follows the procedure for a pair of chainrings as in §viii-7, with the chainring on the inner-ring position, and the chainring guard on the outer-ring position. Otherwise, the chainring will need to go in the big ring position, and you will need spacers to install the guard. Clamp the inner stop or stops around the seat tube so that its top edge is a couple of millimeters higher than the chain. Rotate it on the seat tube until it is so close that it almost touches the chain when the chain is on the largest rear cog.

b. Setting up a two-chainring cyclocross crank

The standard 'cross double chainring combinations have traditionally been 39–46 or 39–44, which offer sufficient high and low gears while making the gear ratios close enough that a front shift need not mandate a rear shift. Now, with compact cranks, a 36–46 is becoming a standard setup. A 46 × 12 and certainly a 46 × 11 high gear is usually tall enough for even the fastest pros. A recommended cogset would be a 12–25 or a 12–28 on anything but the very fastest of courses, where an 11–26 or 11–23 might be useful.

Installing the chainrings is explained in §viii-7. Set up the chain length and front derailleur position as in Chapters 4 and 5, noting the cable-routing tips in §v-28.

TROUBLESHOOTING CRANK AND BOTTOM BRACKET NOISE

viii-19

CREAKING NOISES

Mysterious creaking noises can drive you nuts. Just when you think you have your bike tuned to perfection, a little noise comes along to ruin your ride. What's worse is that these annoying little creaks, pops, and groans can be a bear to locate.

Pedaling-induced noises can originate from almost anything connected to the crankset, including movement of the cleats on your shoes, loose crankarms on the bottom bracket axle, loose chainrings, and poorly adjusted pedal or bottom bracket bearings. Of course, noise could also originate from seemingly unrelated components like the seat, seatpost, frame, wheels, or handlebar. A front derailleur with a band clamp on an unpainted titanium or stainless steel frame can creak with each pedal stroke; grease under the band usually silences it.

Before spending hours overhauling the drivetrain, spend some time trying to isolate the source of the noise. Try different pedals, shoes, and wheels. Grease the faces of the front and rear dropouts and the wheel skewer end faces and clamping mechanism. Pedal out of the saddle, and pedal without flexing the handlebar. If the source of the creak turns out to be the saddle, seatpost, pedals, wheels, or handlebar, turn to the appropriate chapter for directions to correct the problem.

If the creaking is definitely in the crank area, here are some steps to resolve it:

1. **Check to make sure that the chainring bolts are tight, and tighten them if they are not (Fig. 8.12).**

2. **Make certain that the crankarm bolts are tight (Figs. 8.3, 8.4).** If they are not, the resulting movement between the crankarm and the bottom bracket axle is a likely source of noise. If the crank is of a different brand than the bottom bracket, check with the manufacturers or your local shop to make sure that they are recommended for use together. Incompatible cranks and axles will never properly join and are a potential problem area.

3. **Rusting can break the glue bond between a cartridge bottom bracket and one or both of its cups (Figs. 8.21, 8.25), allowing movement between cartridge and cup.** This movement can make creaking noises when pedaling. To quiet the noises, remove the cartridge, grease the inside of the cup(s) as well as the threads, and reinstall the bottom bracket.

4. **The bottom bracket cups can move in the frame threads, causing creaking.** Remove the cups, grease the threads, reinstall them, and tighten them to the correct torque (Appendix E).

5. **The bottom bracket itself can creak owing to improper alignment or adjustment, lack of grease, cracked bearings, worn parts, or loose cups.** All of these things require adjustment or overhaul procedures, outlined in §viii-9 through §viii-12. Many external-bearing designs (Fig. 8.19), as well as cup-and-cone bottom brackets (Fig. 8.20), are very sensitive to being out of parallel, and creaking can occur if the bottom bracket

shell is not perfectly tapped and faced. This is a job for a good bike shop.

6. **Check to make sure the front-derailleur clamp is tight.** The noise from a loose clamp while pedaling, especially under heavy load, can seem to emanate from the crankset.

7. **Now for the bad news.** If creaking persists, the problem could be rooted in the frame. Creaks can originate from cracks in and around the bottom bracket shell. Or the threads in the bottom bracket shell could be so worn that they allow the cups to move slightly. Neither of these is a good sign—unless, of course, you were hoping for an excuse to buy a new frame.

viii-20

CLUNKING NOISES

1. **Crankarm play: Grab the crankarm and push on it side to side.**

    a. If there is play, tighten the crankarm bolt (Figs. 8.3, 8.4; torque spec is in Appendix E).

    b. If there is still crankarm play, and you have a cup-and-cone bottom bracket (Figs. 8.20, 8.22, 8.24) or a cartridge-bearing bottom bracket with a lockring on each side (Fig. 8.23), adjust the bottom bracket axle-end play (§viii-11, steps 11–15).

    c. If bottom bracket adjustment does not eliminate crankarm play, or you have a nonadjustable cartridge bottom bracket (Figs. 8.21, 8.25), the bottom bracket is loose in the frame threads. With a cup-and-cone bottom bracket, you can go back to §viii-8 and start over, making sure that the fixed cup is very tight. Adjustable-cup lockrings also need to

be tight (Fig. 8.36), once the axle-end play is adjusted properly.

    d. The lockrings and fixed-cup flanges must be flush against the bottom bracket shell all the way around (Fig. 8.20); if they are not, the bottom bracket must be removed, and the bottom bracket shell must be tapped (threaded) and faced (cut parallel) by a shop equipped with the tools.

    e. If the crankarm play persists and the crankarm won't stay tight, the square hole is damaged due to riding it while insufficiently tight. A new crankset is in order.

    f. If the bottom bracket fixed cup or lockring will not tighten completely, then either the bottom bracket cups are stripped or undersized or the frame's bottom bracket shell threads are stripped or oversized. Either way, it's an expensive fix, especially the frame replacement option! Get a second opinion if you reach this point. If your bike has a square-taper crank and you can find a Mavic or Stronglight cartridge-bearing bottom bracket (§viii-12b, Fig. 8.26), you can still use a frame with stripped threads.

2. **Pedal-end play: Grab each pedal and wobble it to check for play.** If you find axle-end play, see the section on overhauling pedals in Chapter 9.

viii-21

HARD-TO-TURN CRANKS

If the cranks are hard to turn, you need to overhaul the bottom bracket (see §viii-13 through §viii-17), unless you want to continue intensifying your workout or boost the egos of your cycling companions. The bottom bracket may be shot and need to be replaced.

viii-22

INNER CHAINRING DRAGS ON CHAINSTAY

If the inner chainring drags on the chainstay, the bottom bracket axle may be too short or the square hole in the crankarm may be so deformed that the crank slides on too far. If you have switched to a larger inner chainring and the chainring is too large, get a smaller one. A misaligned frame, with either bent chainstays or a twisted bottom bracket shell, can cause chainring rub as well. A badly misaligned frame needs to be replaced.

With an adjustable cartridge-bearing bottom bracket (Fig. 8.23) with a lockring on each end, it is possible to fix the problem by offsetting the entire bottom bracket to the right (Fig. 8.36). If the bottom bracket axle is too short, replace it with one of the correct length. If the square hole in the crank is badly deformed, replace the crankarm. There's no other cure; it will continue to loosen up and cause problems otherwise.

NOTE: *See §v-50 and Figure 5.56 concerning the chainline to establish proper crank-to-frame spacing.*

PEDALS | 9

To best serve its purpose, a bicycle pedal only needs to be attached to the crankarm and provide a stable platform for the shoe. A simple enough task, but you'd be amazed at the different approaches that have been taken to achieve this goal.

There are two basic types of road pedals: (1) The standard cage-type pedal, with or without a toeclip and strap, is the simplest and cheapest. A "quill" pedal is a standard pedal in which the cage is asymmetrical on the two sides (Fig. 9.1). The cage is thinner on the bottom side and curves up on the outboard end to improve cornering clearance. (2) "Clip-in"–type pedals (Fig. 9.2) retain the foot with spring-loaded clips (like a ski binding) and are almost universal on mid- to high-end road bikes. Clip-in pedals are sometimes called "clipless," because they have no toeclip.

Cage-type pedals are fairly common on lower-end bikes. They are relatively unintimidating for the novice rider, and the frame (or "cage") that surrounds the pedal provides a large, stable platform (Fig. 9.1). A symmetrical, mountain bike–style, cage-type pedal has an identical top and bottom, and it can be used with just about any type of shoe. If you mount toeclips on these without straps, your feet won't slide forward and will release easily in almost any direction.

One-sided road bike quill pedals (Fig. 9.1) are designed to be used exclusively with toeclips, because they cannot be pedaled upside down very well. A toe strap keeps your foot on the pedal and also allows you to pull on the upward part of the pedal stroke, giving you more power, a fluid pedal stroke, and balanced muscle development. Of course, as you add clips and straps, the pedal becomes harder to enter and to exit, and running shoes with aggressive tread become increasingly difficult to use. A tab on the cage plate opposite the toeclip is there so that you can flip the pedal up with your toe in order to slide your foot into the toeclip.

Clip-in models (Figs. 9.2–9.4) offer all of the advantages of a pedal firmly coupled to a stiff shoe by means of a slotted cleat mounted on the

9.1 **Standard cage-type "quill" pedal with toeclip and strap**

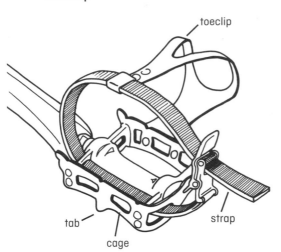

9.2 **Clip-in pedal**

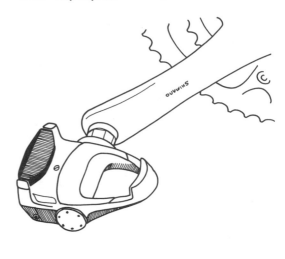

sole, snapped down onto the cage, and held in place with a toeclip and strap, yet they allow easier entry and exit from the pedal. Clip-in pedals are more expensive and require special shoes and accurate mounting of the cleats. Your choice of shoes is limited to stiff-sole models that accept cleats for your particular pedal. Once you have them properly mounted and adjusted, you will find that clip-in pedals waste less energy through flex and slippage and allow you to transfer more power directly to the pedals.

Clip-in models for cyclocross and mountain bikes have an open design to help clear mud. The cleat is small, and it mounts into a recess in the knobby outsole of a treaded shoe that is easier to run and walk in than a road shoe with an attached cleat.

This chapter explains how to remove and replace pedals, how to mount the cleats and adjust the release tension with clip-in pedals, how to troubleshoot pedal problems, and how to overhaul and replace spindles on almost all road pedals. Incidentally, I use the terms "axle" and "spindle" interchangeably, as you are likely to hear either one when visiting bike shops for spare parts.

ix-1

PEDAL REMOVAL AND INSTALLATION

LEVEL 1

Note that the right pedal axle is right-hand threaded, and the left is left-hand (reverse) threaded. Both unscrew in the pedaling direction.

There's an interesting bit of history behind the threading of pedal axles this way. In the early days of cycling, fixed-gear bikes were the norm, and it was decided that if the pedal bearings were to seize up, the pedal should unscrew from the crank rather than tear up the rider's strapped-in feet. If the pedals have bushings rather than bearings, indeed they will unscrew in the pedaling direction if the bushings seize. But in pedals with bearings, the opposite is true, because the side of each ball that is up against the bearing race on the pedal body is going one direction, but its opposite side, which is up against the bearing race on the spindle, is going the opposite direction. So when pedaling, the rotation of pedals with bearings will tend to tighten the pedals in more. And pedals that have both bushings and bearings, of which there are many, will have the unscrewing force counteracted by the screwing-in force!

9.3 Removing or installing a pedal with a 15mm wrench

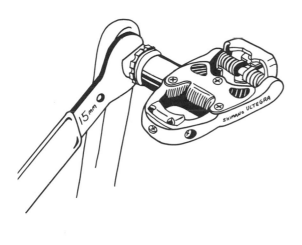

9.4 Removing or installing a pedal with a 6mm hex key

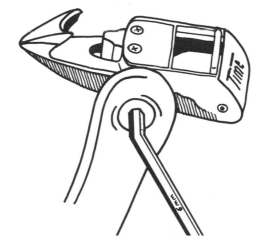

a. Removal

1. **Slide a 15mm pedal wrench onto the wrench flats of the pedal axle (Fig. 9.3).** Or, if the pedal axle is designed to accept it, you can use a 6mm or 8mm hex key from the backside of the crankarm (Fig. 9.4). The latter is particularly handy on the road, because you probably won't be carrying a 15mm wrench. But if you are at home and the pedal is really tight, it will be easier to use the standard pedal wrench, assuming the pedal axle has wrench flats.

2. **Unscrew the pedal in the appropriate direction.** The right, or drive-side, pedal unscrews counterclockwise when viewed from that side. The left-side pedal is reverse threaded, so it unscrews in a clockwise direction when viewed from the left side of the bike. Once loosened, either pedal can be unscrewed quickly by turning the crank forward with a 15mm pedal wrench engaged on the pedal spindle and the rear wheel off the ground. You can remember that they unscrew in the pedaling direction from the story above about the concern with seized pedal bearings in the early days of cycling!

b. Installation

1. **Clean the threads.** Use a rag to wipe the threads clean on the pedal axle and inside the crankarm.

2. **Apply a light coat of fresh grease to pedal threads.**

3. **Start screwing the pedal in with your fingers.** Pedals go in clockwise for the right pedal, counterclockwise for the left.

4. **Tighten the pedal.** Use a 15mm pedal wrench (Fig. 9.3) or a 6mm or 8mm hex key (Fig. 9.4). This can be done quickly by turning the cranks backward with a 15mm pedal wrench engaged on the pedal spindle.

SETTING UP CLIP-IN PEDALS

Setting up clip-in pedals involves installing and adjusting the cleats on the shoes and adjusting the pedal-release tension.

There are a number of different mounting platforms for road pedals, and your shoe sole must be compatible with your pedal cleats. The original clip-in road bike pedal system was the Look, which has three M5-threaded holes arranged in a triangular pattern (Fig. 9.5) to accept a three-hole cleat (Fig. 9.10). The original Time pedal system required a flat surface with four smaller threaded holes (Fig. 9.6), and all Speedplay pedal cleats can be mounted on these as well, without the curved bottom cleat layer. Shimano Pedaling Dynamics, or SPD, began as a system for mountain bikes with tiny cleats (Fig. 9.9) that were easy to walk in and less likely to clog with mud. SPD cleats mount with two side-by-side M5-thread screws, spaced 14mm apart. They screw into a movable threaded cleat-mounting plate behind two longitudinal grooves in the sole (Fig. 9.7). Crank Brothers cleats mount on this system, as do all mountain bike cleats. For their road bike, some riders prefer an SPD-compatible system that uses either a single-sided road bike pedal or a double-sided mountain bike pedal so that they are able to use a mountain bike shoe, which is far easier to walk in than a road bike cycling shoe. And for cyclocross, mountain bike pedals and shoes are a must.

Shimano's SPD-R pedal (since abandoned) required a shoe having a single lengthwise slot in the sole with an M5-threaded hole at either end moving on a threaded backing plate behind the slot (Fig. 9.8). (Diadora pedals have yet another mounting pattern, but they are long gone from the market.)

After a long shakeout, Look's original three-hole mounting system (Fig. 9.5) has emerged victorious on road bikes. The two-adjacent-hole system pioneered by Shimano is the only game in town when it comes to cyclocross and mountain bikes, and, as already noted, many riders and at least one pedal system use it on the road as well. Now Shimano SPD-SL, Time, Speedplay, and all other road pedals save for Crank Brothers Quattro (Fig. 9.24), Ritchey V4 road, and a few others mount on the standard three-hole system.

9.5 Three-hole (Look) cleat drill pattern

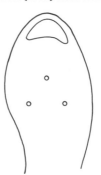

9.6 Original Time cleat drill pattern

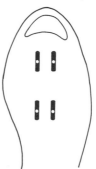

9.7 SPD cleat drill pattern

9.8 SPD-R cleat drill pattern

INSTALLING AND ADJUSTING PEDAL CLEATS ON THE SHOES

LEVEL 1

The cleat position determines the fore-and-aft, lateral (side-to-side), and rotational position of your foot. If the cleats aren't properly oriented, the misalignment could eventually cause hip, knee, or ankle problems.

1. **Put the shoe on and then mark the position of the ball of your foot (the big bump behind your big toe) on the outside of the shoe.** This mark will help you position the cleat so that the ball of your foot will be straight above or in close proximity to the pedal spindle. Take the shoe off, and continue drawing the line straight across the bottom of the shoe.

NOTE: *On SPD-R cleats, the pontoon mounts on the rear bolt, pointing back.*

2. **Grease the cleat screw threads, and screw the cleat that came with the pedals onto the shoe.** This usually requires a 4mm hex key or a Phillips-head or standard screwdriver. If the cleats come with adhesive-backed sandpaper cut to the shape of the cleat, adhere it to the bottom of the cleat so that it faces the sole.

Make sure you orient the cleat in the appropriate direction. Some cleats have an arrow indicating forward (Fig. 9.9); if yours do not, the instructions accompanying the pedals will specify which direction the cleat should point, and in some cases, on which shoe an asymmetrical cleat should be mounted. If mounted on a road shoe, SPD and SPD-R cleats require rubber "pontoons" on a plate mounted under the cleat (Fig. 9.9). The pontoons guide the small cleat into the

9.9 Cleat centered 1cm behind the ball-of-foot line

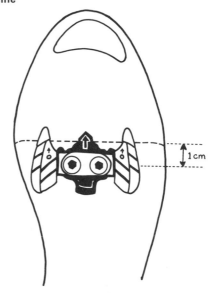

9.10 Look cleat with a mark for the pedal center

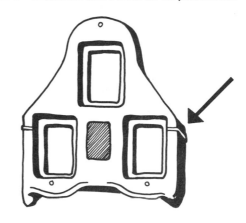

pedal. The pontoons are not necessary on a mountain bike shoe, as the recessed area in its tread will guide the cleat.

3. **Position the cleat.** Temporarily place it in the middle of its lateral- and rotational-adjustment range. Setting the fore-and-aft position requires knowing where the pedal spindle is positioned relative to the cleat. Many cleats have a mark on the side indicating the spindle position (Fig. 9.10). If your cleat has such a mark, line it up 0–1cm behind the line you drew in step 1 across

the shoe sole. With an SPD pedal, line up the mounting screws 0–1cm behind the mark you made in step 1 (Fig. 9.9). With a Speedplay cleat, place the center of the hole in the middle of the cleat 0–1cm behind the mark you made in step 1. If you're not sure, tighten the screws and set the shoe in the pedal. When the shoe is level, the standard is for the ball of the foot to be between 0cm and 1cm forward of the pedal spindle. Putting the ball farther forward is usually helpful to develop power, while high-cadence spinning is usually enhanced with the ball of the foot farther back. If you know which type of rider you are, you can set the shoe as appropriate; a gear-masher will like the cleat farther back than will a spinner. Very small feet sometimes do better with the cleat farther forward on the shoe, placing the ball of the foot behind the spindle. Riders with large feet often prefer the cleat all the way back, so the foot goes as far over the pedal as possible. The long lever that is the rider's foot and which must be controlled from ankle to foot attachment point on the pedal will be reduced. And pedaling force from a large rider, concentrated on the same-size cleat as for a small rider, is better distributed over the shoe if the cleat is located behind the ball of the foot, resulting in less pain under the metatarsals. Speedplay offers a cleat extender base plate kit to offset the cleats either 14mm farther rearward or 2mm farther forward than the standard black, plastic base plates.

NOTE: *If you have an old-style Time pedal (Fig. 9.4), make sure you don't put an old-style Time rear cam on the wrong shoe, or you will not be able to release by twisting outward.*

4. **Snug the screws down.** Tighten them enough to prevent the cleat from moving when clipped in or out of the pedals, but don't tighten them fully. Follow the same steps with the other shoe. Check that the curvature of the cleat matches that of the shoe. If it does not, the cleat may bow when tightened, which will make it hard to clip in or release. Some pedal manufacturers offer cleat shims to fill spaces and keep the cleat flat; see your bicycle dealer for assistance.

5. **To set the lateral cleat position, put the shoes on, sit on the bike, and clip into the pedals.** Ride around a bit. Notice the position of your feet. Generally, the closer your feet are to the plane of the bike, the more efficient your pedaling will be, but you don't want them in so far that your ankles bump the cranks. Take the shoes off and adjust the cleats laterally, if necessary, to move the feet side to side. Get back on the bike and clip in again.

Speedplay Zero cleats offer independently adjustable fore-and-aft, side-to-side, and rotational foot positions; each can be set or changed without affecting the position of the other two adjustments. Note that early Time pedals have no lateral cleat adjustment; recent Time models offer it by means of interchanging the left and right cleats.

6. **To set the rotational cleat position, ride around and notice if your feet feel twisted and uncomfortable.** You may feel pressure on one side of your heel from the shoe. If so, remove your shoes and rotate the cleat slightly in the direction that relieves that pressure.

NOTE: *Most pedals now offer free-float, allowing the foot to rotate freely for a few degrees before releasing. Precise rotational cleat adjustment is less important if the pedal is free-floating.*

I recommend starting with the greatest amount of free-float angle the system allows. You can reduce the float later if you desire.

Some pedals have a dial on the back of the clip to set the amount of free-float rotation, and some cleats (Speedplay Zero) can be adjusted to set the amount of float. Many companies also offer a number of cleat styles having increased or reduced (or eliminated) free-float range.

SPD-R cleats (for the discontinued pedals in Figs. 9.3, 9.13, and 9.17) come in three styles: one with a wide tip for fixed operation, and two narrower-tip models for different amounts of free-float. Vertical cleat play can be eliminated by raising rubber bumpers on the pedal body. Dura-Ace SPD-R pedals have a 3mm nut on the bottom of the pedal to push the bumper up, and Ultegra SPD-R pedals require removing three screws on the face of the pedal to interchange the two pads with thicker ones.

7. **Once your cleat position feels right, trace the cleats with a pen or a scribe.** That way, you can tell if the cleat stays put.

8. **While holding the cleat in place, tighten the bolts down firmly.** Hold the hex key close to the bend so that you do not exert too much leverage and strip the bolts. There is little danger of overtightening with a screwdriver, but do take care that the blade (or Phillips tip) fits well in the screw slot (or Phillips cross). Push down firmly while tightening to avoid stripping the head of the screw.

NOTE: *If you have a small torque wrench, tighten the cleat screws to 35–43 in-lbs (4–5 N-m); see Appendix E).*

9. **Check the screw length.** Remove the insole and feel around inside above the cleat to ensure that the screws are not too long and are pushing up on the cardboard lasting sole. Get shorter screws or shorten these ones if that is happening. You don't want bumps sticking up into the balls of your feet while riding!

10. **When riding with new shoes or pedals, bring cleat-tightening tools along.** You may want to fine-tune the cleat adjustment over the course of a few rides.

11. **Retighten the cleat bolts after every ride for the first few rides.** After that, the cleat will have pushed itself into the shoe sole as far as it can go. This is particularly important with a mountain bike shoe, where the cleat is harder and smaller and the surface of the outsole is generally softer than a road shoe outsole. This is the key to keeping the cleat bolts from falling out as well as preventing the cleats from slipping. Threadlock compound on the bolts also can help. Once the bolts stop turning at the same torque setting, you can stop doing this daily, but do check them from time to time.

---

ix-3

ADJUSTING RELEASE TENSION OF CLIP-IN PEDALS

LEVEL 1

If you find the factory-set release adjustment to be too loose or too restrictive, you can change it on many clip-in pedals; notable exceptions without a spring-tension adjustment are Crank Brothers (Figs. 9.24, 9.29) and some Speedplay (Fig. 9.22), Look Quartz mountain pedals, and some Time models (Figs. 9.4, 9.28). The adjusting screws are usually located on or near the spring-loaded rear clip (Figs. 9.11, 9.12). The adjuster screws are usually operated with a small (usually 3mm) hex key or a small screwdriver.

1. **Locate the tension-adjustment screws.** Older Looks have a screw (either slotted or 2.5mm or 3mm hex head) on top of the platform (Fig. 9.11); Look Anatomics and Campagnolo ProFits (Fig. 9.14) have a

9.11 Release-tension adjustment screw on a Look pedal

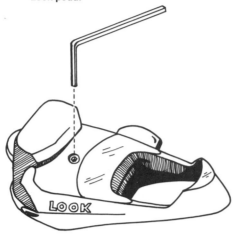

9.12 Release-tension adjustment screw on a Shimano SPD pedal

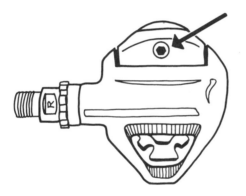

9.13 Tool for removing a Shimano pedal-axle assembly

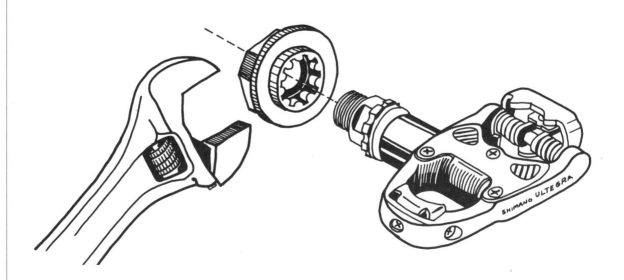

3mm hex screw on the side. Look Keos and Shimano SPD-SLs have a 3mm hex screw on the top of the rear clip. Ritchey, Shimano SPD (Fig. 9.12), and SPD-R (Fig. 9.13) have a 3mm hex screw on the back of the clip.

NOTE: *There are many SPD- and Look-style pedal clones under various brand names on the market. The cleat-mounting and tension-adjustment instructions for SPD or Look pedals generally apply to these pedals as well.*

2. **To loosen the tension adjustment, turn the screw counterclockwise; to tighten it, turn it clockwise (Figs. 9.11, 9.12).** It's the classic lefty loosey, righty tighty approach. There usually are click stops in the rotation of the screw. Tighten or loosen one click at a time (one-quarter to one-half turn), then ride the bike to test the adjustment. Many types include an indicator that moves with the screw to show relative adjustment. Make certain that you do not back the screw out so far that it comes out of the spring plate or so far that it can vibrate loose; feel for at least the first "click" to hold it in place.

9.14 A 22mm wrench fits the axle assembly of a Campagnolo ProFit pedal.

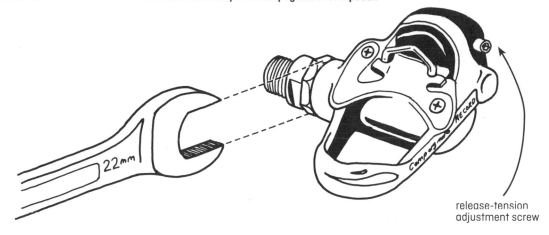

release-tension
adjustment screw

NOTE: *With some pedals, you will decrease the amount of free-float in the pedal as you increase the release tension.*

OVERHAULING PEDALS

LEVEL 2

Like a hub or bottom bracket, pedal bearings and bushings need to be cleaned and regreased periodically.

There is a wide variation in road bike pedal designs. This book is not big enough to go into great detail about the inner workings of every model. Speaking in general terms, pedal guts fall into two broad categories: those that have loose ball bearings (Figs. 9.17, 9.18, 9.25–9.27, 9.31), and those that have cartridge bearings (Figs. 9.15, 9.16, 9.19–9.24, 9.28, 9.30, 9.32). Furthermore, there are two other broad categories that overlap the above two categories, namely, pedals that are closed on the outboard end and have a nut or a snapring surrounding the axle on the inboard end holding the assembly together (Figs. 9.13–9.21, 9.28, 9.31), and pedals that have a dust cap on the outboard end with a nut on that end holding the assembly together (Figs. 9.22–9.24, 9.26–9.27, 9.29–9.30). I've organized the instructions below based on these

divisions rather than on whether the pedals have loose balls or cartridge bearings. There is also a small category of pedals that come apart like a clamshell (Fig. 9.32); I have lumped these in with pedals that have a dust cap on the outboard end.

NOTE: *Whether the pedals have ball bearings or cartridge bearings, you can return a pedal to like-new performance by replacing rusted or otherwise compromised bearings with new ones. You can also replace loose steel balls with ceramic balls or steel cartridge bearings with ceramic cartridge bearings. Ceramic bearings are harder, stiffer, generally rounder, and more uniform in size than steel balls; can't rust; and spin with less resistance. They are, however, more expensive than steel bearings.*

Getting started on pedal overhaul

1. **Remove the pedal from the bike (Figs. 9.3, 9.4).**
2. **Examine the pedal style.** Before you start, figure out how the pedal is put together so that you will know how to take it apart; the following paragraphs and the illustrations on subsequent pages should help. In a few cases, the workings of the pedal guts may not be clear until you have completed step 1 in the overhaul process.

9.15–9.21 Exploded views of clip-in pedals closed on the outboard end

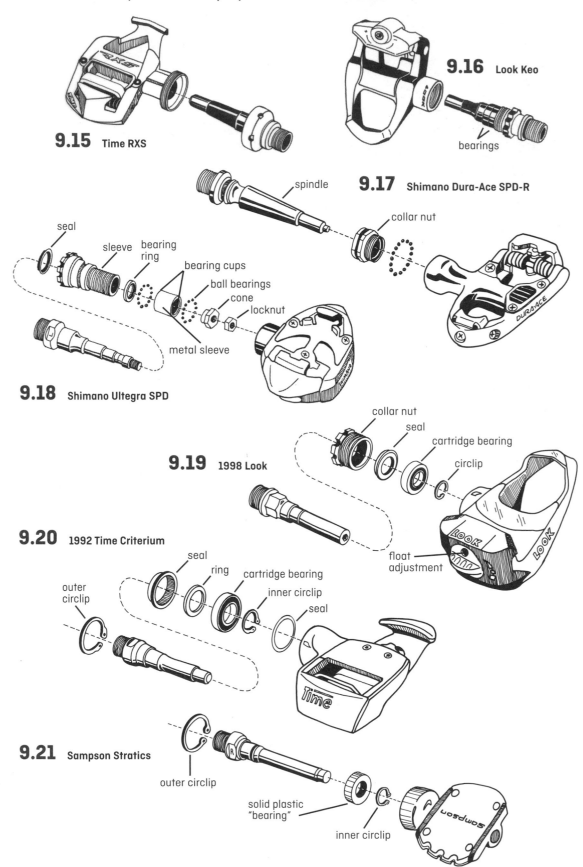

9.15 Time RXS

9.16 Look Keo

bearings

9.17 Shimano Dura-Ace SPD-R

spindle

collar nut

seal

sleeve

bearing ring

bearing cups

ball bearings

cone

locknut

metal sleeve

9.18 Shimano Ultegra SPD

collar nut

seal

cartridge bearing

circlip

9.19 1998 Look

float adjustment

9.20 1992 Time Criterium

seal

ring

cartridge bearing

inner circlip

seal

outer circlip

9.21 Sampson Stratics

outer circlip

solid plastic "bearing"

inner circlip

9.22–9.24 Exploded views of clip-in pedals openable from the outboard end

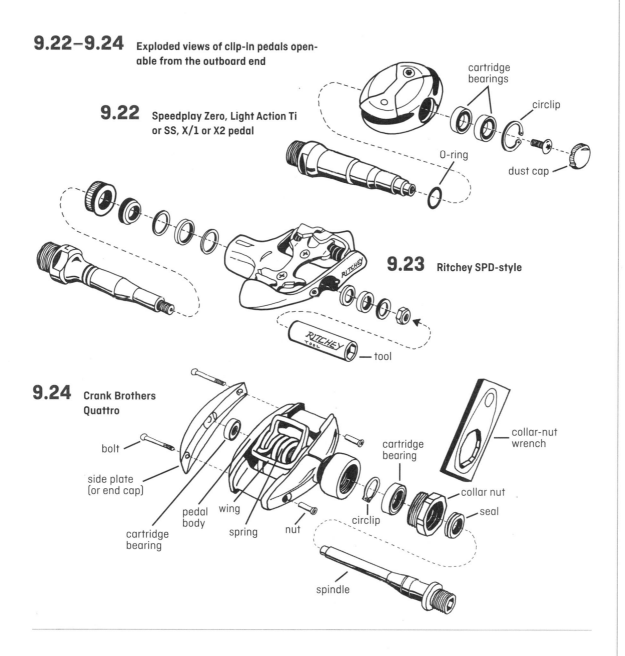

9.22 Speedplay Zero, Light Action Ti or SS, X/1 or X2 pedal

9.23 Ritchey SPD-style

9.24 Crank Brothers Quattro

Most Shimano pedals, road and mountain, have two sets of loose bearings and a bushing (Figs. 9.18, 9.31). The bearings and bushing will come out with the complete axle assembly (Fig. 9.25); you can see the tiny ball bearings at the small end of the axle behind the wrenches in Figure 9.25. Shimano's Dura-Ace model SPD-R (Fig. 9.17) and SPD-SL pedals have a set of ball bearings on each end of the spindle and a set of 6mm-inside-diameter (ID) needle bearings (not shown) in between them.

Speedplay X/3 pedals have an inboard 10mm ID, Teflon bushing, and an outboard 6mm ID cartridge bearing. Speedplay X/5, Light Action Chrome-Moly, and Frog (Fig. 9.32) pedals have a clamshell body with an inboard needle bearing and an outboard cartridge bearing. Speedplay X/1, X/2, Zero, and high-end Light Action pedals have an inboard pressed-in needle bearing (not shown) and an outboard pair of cartridge bearings (Fig. 9.22).

The Campagnolo Record ProFit (Fig. 9.14) pedal has one inboard and two outboard

17mm-outside-diameter (OD) cartridge bearings.

Older Look, Diadora, and older Time pedals have an inboard cartridge bearing (19mm, 24mm, and 24mm OD, respectively) and one or two pressed-in outboard needle-bearing sets (not shown) (Figs. 9.19, 9.20).

Of the newer, carbon-composite-body road pedals, Look Keos (Fig. 9.16) have a pair of 15mm OD inboard cartridge bearings and an 8mm ID outboard needle bearing, whereas Time RXS pedals (Fig. 9.15) have a 21mm OD inboard cartridge bearing and an 8mm ID outboard needle bearing.

Older Time mountain pedals were closed on the outboard end and accessed by means of a snapring (Fig. 9.28) or a threaded collar. They had a needle bearing deep inside and a cartridge bearing at the inboard opening like Time road pedals (Figs. 9.15, 9.20). Later Time mountain pedals have an outboard dust cap and cartridge bearings or a bushing and a cartridge bearing (Fig. 9.30).

Crank Brothers Quattros (Fig. 9.24) constituted a brief foray into road pedals for the company, but they have been discontinued. Quattros have two cartridge bearings: a large one on the inboard side and a smaller one on the outboard side. Depending on model, some Crank Brothers mountain bike pedals, like the Eggbeater (Fig. 9.29), Candy, Mallet, and Acid, either share this spindle arrangement or have one cartridge ball bearing (outboard) and one bushing (inboard).

Sampson Stratics (Fig. 9.21) pedals have a 24mm OD, solid-plastic "bearing" on the inboard side, and a plastic bushing inside the pedal body.

Ritchey SPD-style road pedals (Fig. 9.23) have two sets of pressed-in needle bearings, one with an ID of 10mm and the other with an ID of 7mm.

OVERHAULING PEDALS CLOSED ON THE OUTBOARD END

LEVEL 3

1. **Make sure the pedal does not have a dust cap or screw cover on the outboard end.** If it does, skip to §ix-5. The exception is the Crank Brothers Quattro (Fig. 9.24), which has a removable end cap but still is overhauled by unscrewing the inboard collar nut. Unless you have an old Time, Diadora, or Sampson pedal, remove the axle assembly by unscrewing the nut surrounding the axle (collar nut) where it enters the inboard side of the pedal (Figs. 9.13, 9.14). You can usually hold the pedal in your hand and unscrew the collar nut, but you may want to hold the pedal body in a padded vise while unscrewing the nut. The collar nut is often made of plastic and can crack if you turn it the wrong way, so be careful. Hold the pedal body with your hand or a vise while you unscrew the assembly. The fine threads take many turns to unscrew.

NOTE: *The threads on the pedal body are reversed compared with the crankarm threads on the axle. That means the right-axle assembly unscrews clockwise, and the left-axle assembly unscrews counterclockwise.*

a. Most Shimano pedals disassemble with a special plastic, splined tool (Fig. 9.13); some Looks and Crank Brothers Quattros (Fig. 9.24) also have their own special tools. Use a large adjustable wrench or a vise to hold the tool (Fig. 9.13). Most other pedals take a 19mm, 20mm, or 22mm open-end wrench (Fig. 9.14). The collar nut on a Time RXS requires a special tool, but in its absence, the nut is easy to unscrew with a pair of pliers wrapped in cloth to avoid marring the nut's surface.

b. Campagnolo ProFit (Fig. 9.14) and many Look pedal-axle assemblies unscrew with a 22mm open-end or box wrench. Removal of the Dura-Ace SPD-R (Fig. 9.17) and SPD-SL axle assemblies requires a 20mm wrench, and Look Keos (Fig. 9.16) take a 19mm wrench. Some older Look axles are accessed with a special Look splined tool similar to the one that unscrews most Shimano pedals (Fig. 9.13). Note that original Shimano clip-in road pedals are actually Looks with Shimano axle assemblies, and Campagnolo clip-in pedals prior to 1997 (other than an unfortunate attempt by Campagnolo itself in the late 1980s) are also Looks with Campagnolo axle assemblies.

c. Older Time, Diadora, and Sampson pedal axles are retained by a snap-ring on the crank side (Figs. 9.20, 9.21, 9.28). Popping the snapring out usually requires inward-squeezing snapring pliers (Fig. 8.32), but the snapring on a Time Impact requires only a thin screwdriver to remove, once you move the end of the snapring under the little notch in the inboard pedal-body face so that you can pry it up with the screwdriver. Skip to step 3 after removing the snapring.

2. **Once you have removed the pedal body, take a look at the axle-bearing-bushing assembly.** You will notice either one or two nuts on the thin end of the axle that serve to hold the bearings and/or bushings in place. Remove the nut or nuts as follows:

a. If the axle has a single nut on the end (Fig. 9.23), simply hold the axle's large end with the 15mm pedal wrench and unscrew the little nut with a 9mm or 12mm wrench (or whatever fits it). The nut will be tight, because it has no locknut.

b. If the axle has two nuts on the end (Figs. 9.18, 9.31), they are tightened against each other. To remove them, hold the inner nut with one wrench while you unscrew the outer nut with another (Fig. 9.25). On Shimano pedals, the inner nut does double duty as the bearing cone; be careful not to lose the tiny ball bearings as you unscrew the cone!

3. **Clean all of the parts as follows:**

a. If it is a loose-bearing pedal, use a rag to clean the ball bearings, the cone, the inner ring that the bearings ride on at the end of the plastic sleeve (it looks like a washer), the bearing surfaces on either end of the little steel cylinder, the axle, and the inside of the plastic or metal axle sleeve (Fig. 9.18). To get the bearings really clean, wash them in the sink in soap and water with the sink drain plugged; the motion is the same as washing your hands, and results in both the bearings and your hands being clean for a sterile reassembly. Blot dry.

b. On a pedal with a cartridge bearing (Figs. 9.15, 9.16, 9.19–9.24), if the bearing is dirty or worn out and has steel bearing covers that cannot be pried off without damaging them, then replace it. Pry off plastic cartridge-bearing covers that can be pried off (Fig. 8.37), and clean and grease the bearing.

c. Needle bearings (not visible in the figures because they are pressed inside) on Dura-Ace SPD-R/PD-7700 and SPD-SL/PD-7800, Look, Time, and Diadora (Figs. 9.17, 9.19, 9.20, 9.28) can be cleaned with solvent and a thin toothbrush slipped inside the pedal-body bore. The needle bearings usually just need grease, though, because they are well isolated from dirt.

d. On a Sampson (Fig. 9.21), just wipe down the axle, the plastic bearing, and the pedal-body bore. Do the same for an inexpensive bushing-only pedal.

4. **Lightly grease everything and reassemble the parts.** This is a simple process with bushings, cartridge bearings, and needle bearings, but not so simple with loose bearings!

a. With a loose-bearing pedal, you have some exacting work to place the bearings on their races and screw the cone on while they stay in place. For most Shimano guts (Fig. 9.18), grease the bushing inside the axle sleeve, and slide the axle into the sleeve. Slide the steel bearing ring, on which the inner set of bearings rides, down onto the axle and against the end of the sleeve. Make sure that the concave bearing surface faces away from the sleeve. Coat the ring with grease and stick half of the bearings (usually 12) onto the outer surface of the ring. Slip the steel cylinder onto the axle so that one end rides on the bearings. Make sure that all of the bearings are seated properly and that none are stuck inside of the sleeve.

b. To prevent the bearings from piling up on each other and ending up inside the sleeve instead of on the races, grease the cone and start it on the axle a few threads. Place the remaining half of the bearings on the flanks of the cone. Being careful not to dislodge the bearings, screw the cone in until the bearings come close to the end of the cylinder without touching it. While holding the axle sleeve, push the axle inward until the bearings seat against the end of the cylinder. Make sure that

the first set of bearings is still in place. Screw the cone in without dislodging the inboard bearings by avoiding turning the axle or the cylinder. Tighten the cone with your fingers only, and loosely screw on the locknut.

c. Pre-1997 Look-style Campagnolo pedal guts are similar to Shimano's, except that the bearing race is machined into the axle (rather than being a separate ring), and there are two sleeves, not one. Orient the sleeves so that their bearing races face outward, and then follow the previous steps.

d. With Dura-Ace SPD-R/PD-7700 (Fig. 9.17) or Dura-Ace SPD-SL/PD-7800 pedals, you needed to push back on the bearing cup (on the end of the 20mm nut that holds the axle into the pedal body) to remove the ball bearings in the first place. Grease the cup and push back on it again to allow enough space between the cup and the cylinder to set each of the 17 balls onto the edge of the cup with a small screwdriver.

5. **Adjust the axle assembly.** (For Time, Look, Diadora, and Sampson pedals, skip this step.)

a. Pedals with a small cartridge bearing and a single nut on the end of the axle, such as Campagnolo Record ProFit (Fig. 9.14), require that you tighten the nut against the cartridge bearing while holding the other end of the axle with the 15mm pedal wrench. Tighten it enough to remove play but not enough to bind the axle.

b. On pedals with two nuts on the end of the axle, hold the cone or inner nut with a wrench and tighten the outer locknut down against it (Fig. 9.25). Check the adjustment for freedom of rotation, and

9.25 Most Shimano axles have a cone and a lock-nut, used to adjust bearing play.

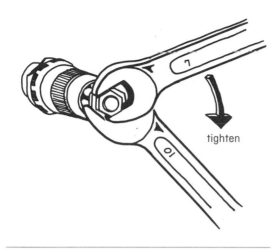

tighten

be sure there is no lateral play. Readjust as necessary by tightening or loosening the cone or inner nut and retightening the locknut.

6. **Replace the axle assembly in the pedal body.** Smear grease on the inside of the pedal hole; this will ease insertion and act as a barrier to dirt and water. Screw the sleeve in with the same wrench you used to remove it (Figs. 9.13, 9.14).

NOTE: *Pay attention to proper thread direction (see the Note in step 1)! Tighten carefully; it is easy to overtighten, which can crack a plastic nut.*

Put the pedals back on your bike, and go ride.

ix-5

OVERHAULING PEDALS WITH A DUST CAP ON THE OUTBOARD END

LEVEL 2

NOTE: *Assess the value of the pedals and your time before continuing. Well-made, older, classic quill-racing pedals like Campagnolo (Figs. 9.1, 9.26) deserve careful attention, but many non-clip-in pedals may not be worth the effort of overhaul.*

1. **Remove the dust cover from the outboard end of the pedal with the appropriate tool.** This could be a pair of pliers, a flat or Phillips screwdriver, a coin, a hex key, or a splined tool made especially for the pedals; it's pretty easy to figure out which one is needed to remove the cap. Dig the dust cap out from SPD-style Ritcheys (Fig. 9.23) and Speedplay X/1, X/2, Zero, and Light Action Ti and SS (Fig. 9.22) with a sharp pick. (Ritchey pedals first require removal of a 2.5mm hex screw holding down the corner of the dust cap.)

NOTE: *Speedplay bearings can be regreased without removing the axle and on newer models without removing the dust cap. On current X/1, X/2, X/5, Light Action, or Zero, and recent X/3, after removing the screw from the outboard end, pump grease in with a fine-tip grease gun while slowly turning the spindle until you see grease at the opposite end. On an older X/1 or X/2, remove the dust cap as just described in step 1, insert Speedplay's Speedy Luber grease-injection fitting, and squirt grease in with a fine-tip bicycle grease gun until it squirts out the other end.*

Older Crank Brothers Eggbeater and Candy pedals (not the Quattro) have a similar feature, and the screw-in grease adapter (which screws in where the dust cap was and accepts the grease gun tip) is included with every pair of pedals. Improved internal seals and sealed cartridge bearings that were phased into Crank Brothers pedals in 2006 made the system too tight to flush grease through with a grease gun. You need to remove the end cap as well as the nut on the end of the spindle, and slide the pedal body off the spindle to regrease it.

2. **Unscrew the locknut.** Hold the wrench flats on the inboard end of the axle with a pedal wrench, and unscrew the locknut with the appropriate-size socket wrench (or box wrench, if there is room for it).

315

9.26 Loose-bearing "quill" pedal

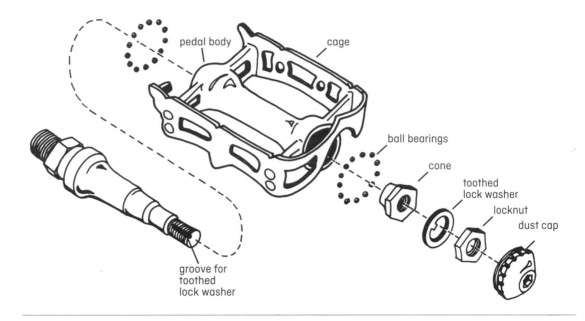

pedal body

cage

ball bearings

cone

toothed lock washer

locknut

dust cap

groove for toothed lock washer

a. Original Ritchey road pedals (Fig. 9.23) require a deep, thin-wall 8mm socket; Ritchey makes a double-ended, thin 8mm socket for the purpose that you can turn with an 8mm hex key in the other end.

b. On a Speedplay X/1 or X/2 pedal, remove the Torx T15 or T20 screw on the outboard end under the dust cap (Fig. 9.22) with the appropriate Torx driver. You may have to heat the bolt with a soldering iron to soften the threadlock compound.

c. On a Speedplay X/3, X/5, Frog (Fig. 9.32), or Light Action Chrome-Moly, carefully pry the halves of the pedal apart with a knife or razor blade after removing the 2.5mm hex pedal-body screws from either side. Lift out the axle assembly and remove the 9mm locknut from the end of the spindle. Pull the bearings and bushing (all located in an alloy sleeve) and O-ring off the spindle. Clean and grease the parts, and replace the cartridge bearing and bushing if necessary.

Reassemble the parts onto the axle, and tighten the locknut snugly against the bearing (35–40 in-lbs/4–5 N-m). When you reassemble the pedal, seal it from water by caulking the inside edges of the pedal-body halves and putting on a new O-ring.

3. **Remove the axle.** If it is a loose-bearing pedal (Fig. 9.26), hold the pedal over a rag to catch the bearings and then unscrew the cone. Keep the bearings from the two ends separate in case they differ in size or in number. Count them so that you can put the right numbers back in when you reassemble the pedal. The guts should look like Figure 9.26. If the pedal does not have loose bearings (Figs. 9.22, 9.23), the procedure is different, as detailed next.

a. With an old Ritchey (Fig. 9.23) pedal, once you have removed the 8mm locknut, you can pull the axle out. The pedal has two pressed-in needle bearings inside. Scrub them with solvent and a rag or thin brush, if they are dirty. Removal of bad needle bearings requires a special tool to pull them out.

b. With a Speedplay X/1, X/2, Zero, or high-end Light Action pedal (Fig. 9.22), pull out the axle and reinstall the Torx screw in the end of the axle. Remove the little snapring from the outboard end of the pedal bore with inward-squeezing snapring pliers (Fig. 8.32). Push the axle back in and carefully push the cartridge bearings out. The cartridge bearings are easily replaceable, but if the needle bearings are in bad shape, you will have to buy a new pedal body from Speedplay with the needle bearings already pressed in. You can clean them as just described for Ritchey pedals.

c. With Ritchey or Speedplay pedals, dry and grease the needle bearings and put the pedals together by reversing the process of disassembly. Do not over-tighten the Ritchey locknut; remove bearing play, but don't bind the axle. Put threadlock compound on the Speedplay Torx end bolt and tighten it snugly (35–40 in-lbs/4–5 N-m). Then skip to step 11.

4. **Clean the bearings, cones, and bearing races.** Use a rag to clean the inside of the pedal body by pushing the rag through with a screwdriver. If there is a dust cover on the inboard end of the pedal body, you can clean it in place, or pop it out with a screwdriver and clean it separately.

    If you want to get the bearings really clean, wash them in a plugged sink with soap and water. The motion is the same as washing your hands, and it results in both the bearings and your hands being clean for a sterile reassembly. Blot dry.

5. **Press the inboard dust cover back into the pedal body (if you removed it earlier).**

9.27 Dropping in bearings

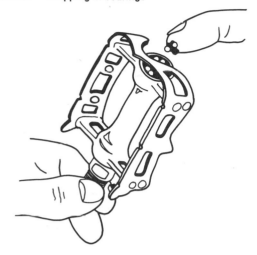

6. **Smear a thin layer of grease in the inboard bearing cup and replace the bearings.** Once all of the bearings are in place, there will be a gap equal to about half the diameter of one bearing.

7. **Drop the axle in and turn the pedal over so that the outboard end is up.** Smear grease in that end and replace the bearings (Fig. 9.27).

8. **Screw the cone in until it almost contacts the bearings, then push the axle straight in to bring the cone and bearings together.** This prevents the bearings from piling up and getting spit out as the cone turns down against them. Without turning the axle (which would knock the inboard bearings about), screw the cone in until it is finger-tight.

9. **Slide on the washer and screw on the locknut.** While holding the cone with a cone wrench, tighten the locknut (similar to Fig. 9.25, but you will be holding the cone with a 13mm or similar cone wrench, not the pictured 10mm standard open-end wrench).

10. **Check that the pedal spins smoothly without play.** Readjust as necessary by tightening or loosening the cone and retightening the locknut.

11. Replace the dust cap.

12. Install the pedals and go for a ride.

ix-6

CYCLOCROSS PEDALS

Mountain bike pedals with high mud-clearing ability are the ticket for cyclocross. The first pedal to offer exceptional mud performance was the Time ATAC (Fig. 9.28). When Crank Brothers came along with the Eggbeater (Fig. 9.29), into which you can clip on any of the four sides, it became the 'cross pedal of choice. More and

more pedals offer great mud clearing, though it's hard to imagine any ever exceeding the Eggbeater. Newer Time ATAC models have a more open design than the original ones, and the low-priced Time Alium (Fig. 9.30) is as good at clearing mud as the original ATAC. Other pedals good for cyclocross using the loop spring design include the Crank Brothers Candy—an Eggbeater with a small platform around it—the newer, more open and angular Time ATAC models, and the Look Quartz. Shimano pedals continue to use steel plate clips (Fig. 9.31), but they and similar pedals like the Ritchey V4 have become more

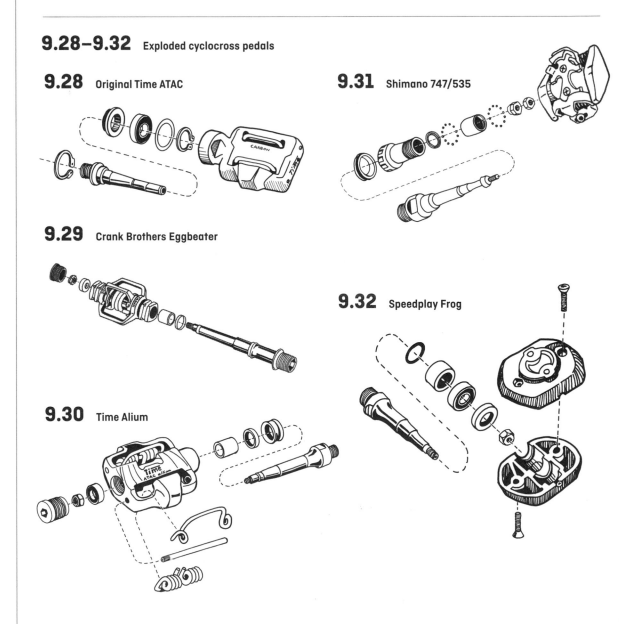

9.28–9.32 Exploded cyclocross pedals

9.28 Original Time ATAC

9.29 Crank Brothers Eggbeater

9.30 Time Alium

9.31 Shimano 747/535

9.32 Speedplay Frog

open to allow mud through more easily, with the latest Shimano XTR and XT having a minimalist design excelling in that capacity. Stepping into a Speedplay Frog pushes accumulated mud away, making this a great 'cross performer as well.

With carbon-sole shoes, install "shoe shields," which are thin steel plates that go between the cleat and the shoe sole. They prevent carbon soles from becoming deeply indented and eventually cracking due to pressure from the wire loops on Crank Brothers, Time, and Look mountain/cyclocross pedals.

If the shoe rocks side to side, it is due to insufficient tread contact with the ends of the pedal body. Another symptom can be the foot popping down farther under high pedaling efforts on pedals with wire-loop cleat engagement systems; since the tread is not supporting the shoe from dropping down farther toward the pedal, the spring can open farther under high pressure from the shoe, allowing the sole to pry the loops apart until the cleat hits the center of the pedal and stops. On the upstroke, the loops spring back, lifting the shoe higher off of the pedal again, and the cycle will recommence on the next hard downstroke. There are two things you can do to fix this. The first is to replace the shoe with one with taller tread, or if you have a shoe with replaceable tread, then replace it. The second is to shim the pedal ends to bring them into contact with the shoe tread when the cleat is engaged. On Eggbeaters, riders often did this in the past by wrapping tape or heat-shrink tubing around the ends. Today, Crank Brothers offers tread contact sleeves for both Eggbeater and Candy models.

Washing off the pedals and cleats after they get muddy is critical to good clip-in/clip-out performance. Apply a dry lubricant like Pedro's Extra Dry or Ice Wax to the cleat tips. Doing so will help them clip in and out, won't pick up dirt, and won't leave oily stains on carpets.

ix-7

CREAKING NOISE WHILE PEDALING

1. **Cleats need attention.** The shoe cleats need grease on the tip, or they are loose and need to be tightened, or they are worn and need to be replaced (§ix-2).
2. **Pedal bearings and pedal-body threads need cleaning and lubrication.** See the "Overhauling Pedals" section in this chapter and especially §ix-4 and §ix-5.
3. **The noise is originating from somewhere other than the pedals.** See "Troubleshooting Crank and Bottom Bracket Noise" in Chapter 8 or Appendix A.

ix-8

RELEASE OR ENTRY WITH CLIP-IN PEDALS IS TOO EASY OR TOO HARD

1. **Release tension needs to be adjusted. See §ix-3.**
2. **The pedal-release mechanism needs to be cleaned and lubricated.** Clean off mud and dirt, and drip chain lubricant on the springs (Fig. 9.33) and a dry lubricant (like Pedro's Extra Dry or Ice Wax) on the cleat-contact surfaces of the clips.
3. **The cleats themselves need to be cleaned and lubricated.** Clean off dirt and mud, oil the springs, and put a dry chain lubricant like Pedro's Extra Dry or Ice Wax on the contact ends of the cleats.
4. **The cleats are worn out.** They cannot be repaired; replace them (§ix-2).
5. **The clips on the pedal are bent or the guide plates on top of the pedal are worn, bent, broken, or missing.** Straighten bent clips or replace them. If you can't repair the clips,

9.33 Lubricating the springs and cleat contact areas

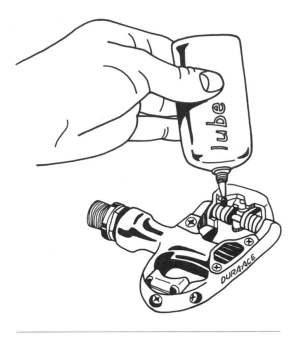

you may have to replace the entire pedal. On Speedplays (Fig. 9.22), the top and bottom metal plates may need to be replaced.

6. **The cleat guide needs attention.** If it is hard to clip in, check the metal cleat guide plate at the center of an SPD-type pedal. It is held with Phillips screws (Figs. 9.18, 9.23, 9.31). They may be loose or missing, or the guide plate may be bent or broken. Tighten loose screws and replace missing or damaged guide plates.

7. **The cleat is not flat.** If you have small feet and have difficulty getting in and out of a pedal that has a large cleat (Look and copies, Campagnolo) or a large adapter plate, the curvature of your shoe sole may be so extreme that the center of the cleat hits the center of the pedal before the ends have clipped in. Try removing the little rubber plug from under the Look cleat (Fig. 9.10).

You may also need to shim the front and rear of the cleat away from the shoe or file down the center of the cleat to make the cleat flat.

---

ix-9

YOU EXPERIENCE KNEE AND JOINT PAIN WHILE PEDALING

1. **The cleats need to be realigned.** Cleat rotational misalignment often causes pain on the sides of the knees. Loosen and realign the cleats the way your feet want to be oriented when pedaling (§ix-2).

2. **You need more rotational float.** Consider a pedal that offers more float (or replace fixed cleats with floating ones, or adjust pedals with a float adjustment; Fig. 9.19).

3. **You need orthotics.** If your foot naturally needs to tip inward for proper pedaling mechanics, yet your shoe and cleat tip your feet farther out (this correction is built into some shoes), then there is likely to be an increase in the tension on the iliotibial (IT) band, which is the tendon connecting the hip and calf. This tension will eventually cause pain on the outside of the knee. You need to see a specialist about custom orthotics for your shoes to correct the problem.

4. **You need to adjust saddle height.** Fatigue and improper seat height can also contribute to joint pain. Pain in the front of the knee right behind the kneecap can indicate that your saddle is too low. Pain in the back of the leg behind the knee suggests that your saddle is too high.

CAUTION: *If any of these problems result in chronic pain, consult a specialist.*

SADDLES AND SEATPOSTS

I do most of my work sitting down.
That's where I shine.
—Robert Benchley

TOOLS

4mm, 5mm, 6mm hex
  keys

Screwdriver

Grease

Optional

Soft hammer

Securely mounted vise

Penetrating oil

Hacksaw

Flex hone

Electric drill

Cutting oil

After a few hours on your bike, you will be most keenly aware of one of its components: the saddle. It is the part of your bike with which you are most . . . uh . . . intimately connected. Nothing can ruin a good ride faster than a poorly positioned or uncomfortable saddle.

And the seatpost is critical, as it connects the saddle to the frame. It must hold the saddle firmly in the proper position without letting it tilt or slide down or back.

x-1

SADDLES

Most bike saddles are made of a flexible plastic shell suspended like a hammock between attachment points with the rails at the tip and tail, along with some padding and a cover (Fig. 10.1). Not much to it, which perhaps explains why there are countless variations on this theme. To make the shell suspended on the rails stiffer or lighter or conformable to the rider over time, it can be made of carbon-filled nylon, carbon fiber, or thick leather. To reduce pressure on sensitive areas, the shell can have depressions, holes, or splits in it. To reduce weight, the rails can be made of solid titanium rod, hollow titanium tubing, hollow steel tubing, or braided carbon fiber. Or, to reduce manufacturing cost, add or remove suspension, or fit a new saddle-clamping standard, the rail and shell can be molded out of the same piece of nylon and may even require a unique seatpost by virtue of being shaped like a single I-beam rather than like two pieces of thick wire. To create more comfort, the padding can be extra thick or have high-tech gel cushions within it. The cover over the padding can be leather, synthetic leather, Kevlar, or any of an infinite array of materials.

You can expect to spend anywhere from $20 to $300 and more for a decent saddle, yet comfort is the best indicator of what makes a saddle really good. My best advice is to ignore weight, fashion, and looks, and choose a saddle that is comfortable.

High-zoot gel padding, scientifically designed shells that support some parts, don't contact others, and flex just right, as well as all sorts of factors that engineers consider when designing a saddle, mean nothing if a saddle turns out to be a giant pain in the rear. People are different and saddles are different. Try as many as you can before buying one.

The marketing war raging over saddles that are designed to prevent male impotency (Fig. 10.2) can ruin a consumer's ability to select appropriately. If you buy a saddle out of fear and it is uncomfortable, you have done yourself a disservice. Don't take it on faith or accept without question from scientific studies that such a saddle must be protecting you, even if you don't particularly like it; if it hurts or you get numb, it isn't working for you. What works for one person won't necessarily work for another.

Determine which saddle shape and design are the most comfortable for your body. Then—and only then—start looking at things like titanium rails, fancy covers, and all of the other things that improve a saddle and add to its cost. Some people can only find comfort on 400-gram saddles with tons of thick padding. Others can ride for hours on a skinny little sub–100-gram saddle. It's a matter of preference. Any decent bike shop worth its weight in titanium should let you try a saddle for a while before locking you into a sale. And keep in mind that the position of the saddle can be as important as the shape.

Brooks and Ideale saddles have no plastic shell, foam padding, or cover. They are constructed from a single piece of thick leather attached to a steel frame with large brass rivets (Fig. 10.3). This was the main type of saddle up until the 1980s. Brooks still makes them this way, updated with titanium rails in some models. This type of saddle requires a long break-in period

10.1 Modern lightweight saddle

10.2 Saddle designed not to contact the perineum

10.3 Brooks leather saddle

and frequent applications of a leather-softening compound that comes with the saddle or from a shoe store. As is the case with a lot of old or retro bike parts, either you love 'em or you hate 'em. If you're not familiar with them by now, you'll probably hate 'em, so go out and buy a nice comfortable modern saddle (Figs. 10.1, 10.2).

A saddle with a plastic shell and foam padding requires little maintenance, except to keep it clean. Check the rails periodically for bends or cracks (clear signs that you need to replace the saddle).

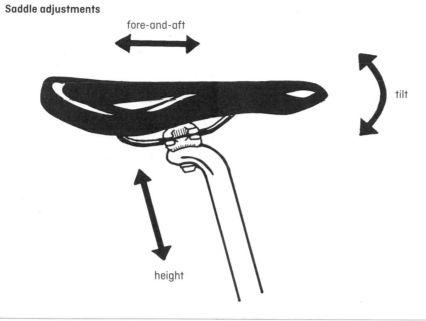

fore-and-aft

tilt

height

---

x-2

SADDLE POSITIONS

Even the perfect saddle will feel like a medieval torture device if it isn't properly positioned. Saddle placement is the most important part of finding a comfortable riding position. Not only does saddle position affect how you feel on the bike, but it affects your control and efficiency as well. With the saddle in the right place, you suddenly become a much better rider. See Appendix C, §C-3, for a detailed explanation of setting saddle and handlebar positions. The following are some brief guidelines.

There are three basic elements to saddle position: tilt, fore-and-aft position, and saddle height (Fig. 10.4). Proper saddle height is key to effectively transferring power to the pedals. The ideal height on a road bike places your leg in a 90 to 95 percent extension (knee bend of 25–30 degrees) when your foot is at bottom dead center in riding position (Fig. 10.5). If your frame is the correct size, you should have no trouble achieving this without pulling the seatpost beyond its

height-limit line. Appendix C has more detail on this sizing factor.

A common cause of numb crotch and butt fatigue (and even sore arms and shoulders) is an improperly tilted saddle. The rule of thumb is that you should set the saddle level when you first install it. If you have a lot of seatpost sticking out of the frame or the saddle is pushed way back on its rails, you may need to tilt it slightly down (maybe 2 degrees or so) at the nose so that it will come to level when you sit on it, flexing the seatpost and saddle rails. After a while, some people find that they prefer a slight upward or downward tilt to their saddles. I strongly recommend against making that tilt much more than ¼ inch. Too much upward tilt places too much of your body weight on the nose of the saddle. Too much downward tilt will cause you to slide down the saddle as you ride. That puts unnecessary pressure on your arms, back, and shoulders as they fight to oppose the forward slide.

Fore-and-aft position (Fig. 10.4) determines where your butt sits on the saddle, the position

10.5 Knee bend at bottom dead center should be 25–30 degrees from straight

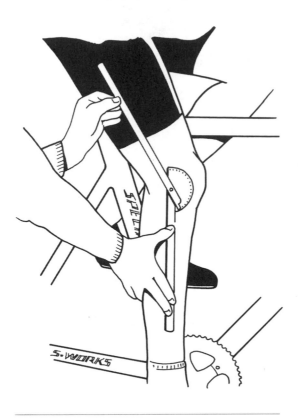

of your knees relative to the pedals, and how much of your weight is transferred to your hands. Regardless of manufacturer, all saddles are designed to have your butt centered over the widest part. If this is not where you sit, reposition the saddle. You want to have a comfortable bend in your arms, without feeling cramped or stretched out. If you find that your neck and shoulders feel tighter than usual and your hands are going numb, redistributing your weight by moving the saddle back and leveling it could make a difference.

Fore-and-aft saddle position also affects how your legs are positioned relative to the pedals. Ideally, your knee should push straight down on the forward pedal when the crankarms are in a perfectly horizontal position. Appendix C explains how to determine this precisely.

Butt pain is intimately connected to handlebar position, as are other aches and pains. The shorter the upper-body reach and higher the handlebar, the more weight will go on the butt. On the other hand, the longer the reach and lower the bar, the more the pelvis rotates forward and the pressure point moves from the sit bones to the soft tissue of the perineum and genital area. As a general rule, a novice rider will want a shorter reach and higher bar, and perhaps a correspondingly wider saddle, than an experienced rider. Once again, consult Appendix C.

x-3

SEATPOST MAINTENANCE

A standard seatpost requires little maintenance other than removing it from the frame every few months. Wipe down the seatpost, regrease it, dry out and grease the inside of the frame's seat tube (turn the bike upside down to pour out any trapped water), and then reinstall the seatpost. This procedure keeps it clean and able to move freely if you want to adjust it. It also should prevent the seatpost from getting stuck in the frame (a very nasty and potentially serious problem), and it will prevent a steel seat tube from rusting out from the inside.

The procedures for installing a new seatpost and for removing a stuck seatpost are outlined later in this chapter.

If you have a carbon seatpost, make sure that you read the Pro Tip on the subject.

Regularly check the seatpost for cracks or bends so that you can replace it before it breaks with you on it.

Because suspension seatposts are rare on road bikes, maintenance of them is not covered here, but it is covered in *Zinn & the Art of Mountain Bike Maintenance*.

Carbon-fiber seatposts can break if the pinch-bolt assembly digs in and cuts some fibers or makes a notch in the post. Point-loading on a thin carbon part is not a good idea. Some carbon seatposts, like Campagnolo, come with a special binder clamp meant to distribute the clamping force. If the post comes with such a clamp, make sure you use it. In the absence of one, at a minimum you should reverse the binder clamp so that its slot is not lined up with the seat-tube slot (Fig. 10.6); that way, it will pull more evenly around the circumference and not push the slot into the seatpost. And if you have a slotted seat-tube shim that some bikes have to fit the seatpost, you want to offset that slot from the other two slots as well. You can imagine how the top corners of the slot could dig into the back of the seatpost (where the load on it is also highest) if you crank down on the bolt with the slots of the binder clamp and seat tube and perhaps a seat-tube shim all stacked up there. This is where carbon seatposts break.

Carbon seatposts often slip, which of course also leads to further tightening of the bolt, increasing the probability of snapping it off. If the post slips, apply some carbon assembly paste or spray (Fig. 10.6) to the post shaft. This stuff has small plastic spheres in the solution that press back

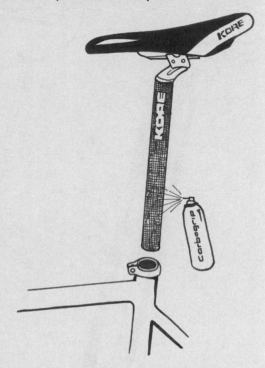

10.6 Spraying CarboGrip carbon assembly compound on a carbon post

against the clamp to increase the pressure uniformly and avoid point-loading. In the absence of carbon assembly paste, you can try not greasing the post. Unlike an aluminum or steel seatpost, a carbon post itself cannot corrode, so grease to prevent seizure is less of an issue. However, corrosion of an aluminum seat tube or seat-tube sleeve surrounding it can nonetheless seize it, so the best solution is carbon assembly compound.

---

x-4

INSTALLING A SADDLE

LEVEL 1

Remember the heavy steel posts with the skinnier section on top that you had on your bike as a kid (or on a cheap adult bike)? Those seatposts had a single horizontal bolt that pulled together a number of knurled washers with ears to hold the saddle rails. They are cheap to make but do not hold up well to adult use. If your bike has that style of post and it fails, you can upgrade the post with a stronger style, but note that you may have to upgrade the saddle as well, if it has flat rails rather than round ones.

Much more secure (and generally lighter) is a post with one or two vertical bolts holding an aluminum clamshell together. Most posts have

10.7 Single-bolt seatpost   **10.8** Single-bolt seatpost with small adjusting bolt   **10.9** Two-bolt seatpost

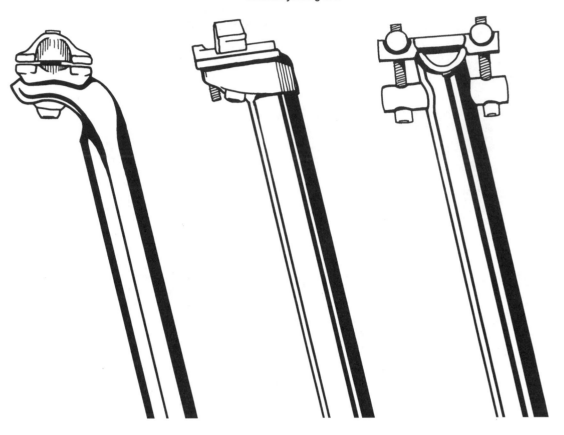

either one or two bolts for clamping the saddle. A single-bolt post can have a vertical bolt pulling the clamshell clamp halves together (Figs. 10.4, 10.7), or it can have a horizontal bolt pulling two ears of the clamp toward each other to clamp the rails; the ears can even slide on angled ramps so that tightening the bolt pulls the rails down onto the saddle cradle as well as clamps them from the sides. Two-bolt posts usually rely on one of three systems. In one, the two bolts work together by pulling the saddle into the clamp (Fig. 10.9). On others, a smaller second bolt holds the tilt angle (Fig. 10.8). Yet another type has two side-by-side bolts holding the saddle clamp together. It is reasonably easy to figure out how to remove, install, and adjust the saddle, no matter what kind of post you have.

x-5

SADDLE INSTALLATION ON SEATPOST WITH A SINGLE VERTICAL BOLT

Posts with a single vertical bolt (Figs. 10.4, 10.7) usually have a two-piece clamp that fastens onto the saddle rails. On most models, saddle tilt is controlled by moving the clamp and saddle along a curved platform. Before you tighten the clamp bolt, make sure there is not a second, smaller bolt (setscrew) that adjusts seat tilt. If one is present, skip to the next section (§x-6).

1. **Loosen the bolt until there are only a couple of threads holding the upper clamp.**
2. **Turn the top half of the clamp 90 degrees.** Put a dab of grease on each clamp contact point to prevent squeaking. Slide the saddle

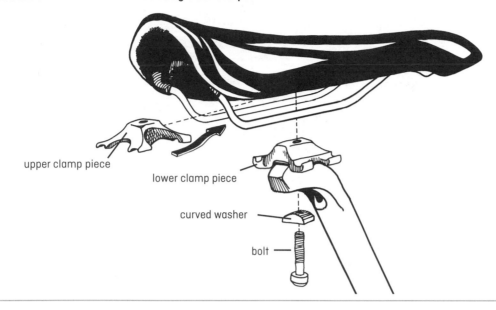

upper clamp piece

lower clamp piece

curved washer

bolt

rails into position. Do it from the back where the space between the rails is wider. You may need to remove the top clamp piece completely from the bolt if it is too large to fit between the rails. If you disassemble the clamp, pay attention to the orientation of the parts so that you can put it back together the same way.

3. **Set the seat rails into the grooves in the lower part of the clamp.** Then set the top clamp piece on top of the rails (Fig. 10.10). Slide the saddle to the desired fore-and-aft position.

4. **Tighten the bolt and check the seat tilt.** Readjust if necessary. Wipe off any excess grease on the rails.

x-6

SADDLE INSTALLATION ON SEATPOST WITH LARGE CLAMP BOLT AND SMALL SETSCREWS

This post type is illustrated in Figure 10.8.

1. **Loosen the large bolt.** Unscrew it until the top part of the clamp can be moved out of

the way or removed so that you can slide the saddle rails into place.

2. **Put a dab of grease on the clamp contact areas to prevent squeaking.** Set the saddle rails between the top and bottom sets of grooves in the seat clamp. Slide the saddle to the desired fore-and-aft position. Tighten the large bolt. Wipe off any excess grease.

3. **Adjust the tilt.** To change saddle tilt, loosen the large clamp bolt, adjust the saddle angle as needed by turning the setscrew, and retighten the clamp bolt. Repeat until the desired adjustment is reached.

CAUTION: *Do not use the setscrew to make the clamp tight! Do not adjust the setscrew unless the clamp bolt is loose!*

NOTE: *On this type of seatpost, the setscrew may be vertical or horizontal. On posts with a vertical setscrew, the screw is usually adjacent to the clamp bolt, as in Figure 10.8.*

You will find a horizontal setscrew at the top front of the seatpost, pushing back on the clamp. When setting saddle tilt, push down on the back of the saddle with the clamp bolt loose to make sure the clamp and horizontal setscrew are in contact.

10.11 Saddle installation on two-bolt seatpost

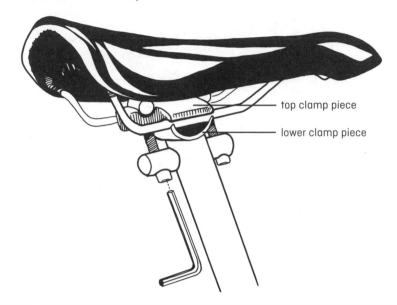

top clamp piece

lower clamp piece

Another type of post has a horizontal tilt-adjusting bolt that passes crosswise through a slot in the seatpost clamp. On this type, the saddle can be fully tightened down, yet the tilt-adjust screw can be loosened, the saddle tilt adjusted, and the screw retightened without adjusting the clamp bolt.

x-7

SADDLE INSTALLATION ON SEATPOST WITH TWO EQUAL-SIZED CLAMP BOLTS

This post type is illustrated in Figure 10.9.

1. **Loosen or remove one or both of the bolts.** Unscrew them sufficiently to open the clamp enough to slide the saddle rails into the grooves of the clamp. Put a dab of grease on the clamp contact areas to prevent squeaking.

2. **Slide the saddle to the desired fore-and-aft position.** Tighten down one or both of the clamp bolts completely.

3. **Adjust tilt.** Loosen one clamp bolt and tighten the other to change the tilt of the saddle (Fig. 10.11). Repeat as necessary.

4. **Finish by tightening both bolts.** Wipe off any excess grease.

Seatposts with two identical side-by-side bolts work in the same basic way as a seatpost with a single vertical bolt (§x-5). The saddle clamp slides over a curved platform to vary the saddle tilt. Follow the directions in §x-5, except you may need to remove one or both of the bolts completely to get the saddle rails into the clamp.

x-8

SEATPOST INSTALLATION INTO THE FRAME

LEVEL 1

1. **Inspect the seat tube.** Check for irregularities, burrs, and other problems inside the seat tube visually and with your finger; if there are some, you may need to sand or otherwise clean up inside the seat tube. A bike shop can ream the seat tube if a post of the correct size will not fit.

2. **Grease the seatpost and the inside of the seat tube.** If you have a carbon-fiber seatpost, use carbon assembly paste on the post,

especially if it slips with grease on it (see the Pro Tip on carbon seatposts earlier in this chapter). Grease the seatpost binder bolt. If you are using a sleeve or shim to adapt an undersized seatpost to fit the frame, grease it inside and out, and insert it.

3. **Insert the seatpost (Fig. 10.12) and tighten the binder bolt.** Some binder bolts are tightened with a single wrench (usually a 5mm hex key), and some require two wrenches (usually two 5mm hex keys or two open-end wrenches). If you have a carbon-fiber seatpost, make sure the binder clamp surrounding the seat tube either is an angled-slot type designed for the seatpost or that you rotate the binder clamp 180 degrees so that its slot and the seat-tube slot are not lined up over each other (see the Pro Tip).

4. **After the saddle is attached, adjust the seat height to your desired position.** If you mark this height on the post with an indelible marker or a piece of tape, you can just

10.12   Seatpost installation into the frame

slide it right back into the proper place if you remove it.

IMPORTANT: *Periodically remove the seatpost, invert the bike to drain water out of the seat tube, and let it dry out. The frequency depends on riding conditions. With a steel frame, spray oil (or Frame Saver, a product made for the purpose that is available in bike shops) into the seat tube to arrest the rusting process. Regrease the post and the inside of the seat tube, and then reinstall it (use carbon assembly spray or paste if it's a carbon post; see the Pro Tip).*

x-9

INTEGRATED SEAT MASTS

Some lightweight carbon frames do not have a seatpost that inserts into the frame at the seat-tube/top-tube junction. Rather, the seat tube continues past the intersection with the top tube and forms a mast onto which the saddle attaches (Fig. 10.13). Reasons for incorporating a seat mast into the frame include reducing weight, improving aerodynamics, increasing strength or stiffness or otherwise changing the physical characteristics of that area of the frame, and producing a unique look to the bike. Downsides include difficulty fitting the bike into a travel case, likelihood of damage if clamped in a standard bicycle work stand, and, for bikes with masts requiring cutting to length, reduced resale value once cut.

When you work on an integrated-seat-mast frame, finding a way to hold it in a conventional workstand can be difficult. You cannot use the stand clamp on the seat mast or on any of the tubes without risking cracking the frame. If the frame has a system like the one employed on some Time or BH frames with a standard seatpost, you can put in a long seatpost and clamp to it. Probably the best solution, however, is the one

SADDLES AND SEATPOSTS

10.13 Integrated seat mast on a Trek madone

already mandated by aero bikes without a round seatpost: Use a Euro-style race team mechanic's bike stand that supports the bottom bracket and has a long arm with a quick-release clamp to hold the fork ends or the rear dropouts (Fig. 1.4). Or you can use a special adaptor clamp from the frame manufacturer intended to allow you to clamp the seat-mast cap in the arm of a standard bike stand (Fig. 1.2).

There are a number of variations on the integrated seat-mast theme, and the method for clamping the saddle to the mast varies. Some have a short, hollow seatpost split at the bottom with a binder bolt or two to clamp it; I'll call this a seat-mast cap. Others have a short seatpost with a standard binder clamp around the seat mast. Yet others have a seat clamp that inserts inside the seat mast and is held in place either with a bolt going in radially through the seat mast or with an expander wedge expanding the bottom of the seat clamp against the interior walls of the seat mast. Most systems require the end user to cut the seat mast to the correct height. The obvious concern here is cutting it too short or not

cutting it straight. The clamp usually has a small amount of height adjustment, sometimes with a fixing bolt and sometimes by means of shims, but it may not be enough to make up for a big cutting error. And of course, resale options for the bike are limited to people with legs no longer than allowed by the cut length of the seat mast.

Some integrated seat-mast frames do not require cutting; skip to §x-9c below.

a. Cutting a seat mast

LEVEL 3

Measure twice; cut once!

1. **Record your current seat height.** On your current bike, measure and record your saddle height from the bottom bracket (or from the bottom pedal if the new bike will have a different crank length).

2. **Set up your new bike.** Install the saddle on the clamp atop the uncut seat mast and measure and record the saddle height from the bottom bracket (or from the bottom pedal if this bike has a different crank length than your existing bike).

3. **Calculate how much to cut.** Subtract the step 1 measurement from the step 2 measurement. This is the amount you will cut from the top of the seat mast.

4. **Remove the seat clamp from atop the seat mast.**

5. **Measure from the top of the uncut seat mast the length you found in step 3.**

6. **Prepare the cut.** If you have a cutting guide for the frame, put that on the seat mast up against your mark. If not, wrap tape around the mast at your mark. Cut the seat mast along the cutting guide or tape, but don't cut all of the way through or the fibers will peel back when you come through the opposite side. Instead, cut halfway from one direction and halfway from the other, meeting in

the middle. You can use a standard hacksaw with a fine-tooth blade if you're careful, but a better option is the Effetto Mariposa CarboCut saw. It has a toothless, grit-edge tungsten-carbide blade for cutting hard materials, including ceramics, titanium, and steel, as well as for cutting carbon fiber (and Kevlar and boron fiber) without damaging the matrix surrounding the fibers. The blade cuts on both push and pull strokes and does not grab like a toothed blade, leaving a smooth cut edge that requires no sanding.

7. **Check the cut surface.** If your cut is not straight and/or smooth, carefully file or sand it smooth and flat.

8. **Create a height adjustment hole.** Some systems require you to also drill a hole in the seat mast for a bolt to allow some height adjustment and to hold the seat clamp at that height. If you have a cutting guide for your seat mast, it will have a guide hole for drilling through it in the right spot. If not, you will have to measure carefully using the guidelines in the owner's manual. If that is not available, measure from the seat clamp itself. Carefully drill through it, using a drill bit size specified by the manufacturer.

9. **Install the seat clamp, bottoming it out on the top of the seat mast.**

    a. Some systems have a cap with a pinch bolt that slides down over the seat mast. Make sure it is pushed on beyond the minimum insertion point, and tighten the bolt to torque spec.

    b. Some systems have a normal seat binder clamp surrounding the top of the seat mast, which is round in cross-section. The seat clamp is simply a short, little seatpost; insert it beyond the minimum insertion point and tighten the binder to torque spec.

    c. Some systems (Look, for example) have an elastomer that goes between the clamp and the seat mast, so insert that first. The Look seat clamp has an expander wedge inside that expands against the seat mast when you tighten a bolt atop the clamp.

10. **Install the saddle, and check that your seat position is correct.**

11. **Adjust saddle height.** If the seat is too high and you have no shims under the seat clamp, you will need to cut the seat mast a bit shorter. Again, measure twice and cut once!

b. If the seat mast is cut off too short

With some frames, this is not a problem. Certain Time integrated-seat-mast models allow you to cut the mast anywhere you want, slot it, and install a binder clamp and a 27.2mm seatpost. Similarly, Wilier Triestina's Cento 1 integrated seat mast has a Ritchey single-bolt seat-mast cap atop it, but you can cut the mast completely off where you wish, slot it, slap on a binder clamp, and stick in a 31.6mm seatpost.

With some systems, you can get a longer seatpost or seat-mast cap. If not, you may be able to insert more shims or elastomers, as long as you don't exceed the minimum insertion mark (for the seat mast itself, not for the shims) on the post or cap.

c. Seat masts that don't need to be cut

The BH Global Concept has a binder clamp atop the seat mast and a short seatpost; install it like a standard seatpost.

Installing the Trek seat-mast cap
The post-2007 Trek Madone (Fig. 10.13) mast is closed at the top, and a seat-mast cap slips over it and clamps onto it with two bolts. Two different cap lengths are available (120mm and

160mm), each in three different setback options (5mm or 20mm backward or 10mm forward). The cap has a ball-and-socket clamp: A horizontal clamp bolt pulls two ears against the saddle rails, which sit in grooves atop two hemispherical clamps (adjusting balls), into mating concave socket ends on the large, crosswise through-hole in the cap (Fig. 10.13).

1. **Lubricate the parts.** Grease the bolt and the concave and convex mating surfaces in the cap and on the adjusting balls.

2. **Assemble the saddle onto the clamp parts as in Figure 10.13.** Tighten the bolt only enough to hold everything together.

3. **Wipe excess grease from the clamp.**

4. **Loosen the clamp bolts on the seat-mast cap and slip it over the seat mast.** Trek recommends not greasing the cap interior or the mast exterior.

5. **Slide the cap up or down as necessary.** Do not tighten until step 7.

6. **Level the saddle, set the fore-aft adjustment by tapping on the nose or tail of the saddle, and tighten the saddle-clamp bolt.** If the clamp is already tight and the saddle won't move even with the bolt loose, you will have to knock the adjusting balls free. Loosen the bolt until the saddle-clamping ear will move aside enough that you can insert a 4mm hex key through the hole in the adjusting ball. Push on the hex key against the opposite adjusting ball to free it. Repeat from the other direction.

7. **Set the seat height.** Make sure the seat-mast cap covers the minimum insertion line.

8. **Tighten the clamp bolts.** Tighten them gradually in an alternating pattern to the torque specification embossed on the clamp —44–62 in-lbs (7 N-m).

9. **Fine-tune the adjustment.** If you cannot achieve the height or fore-aft adjustment you desire, get a different Trek seat-mast cap that will hold your saddle where you want it.

<hr>

x-10

SADDLES AND SEATPOSTS FOR CYCLOCROSS

In cyclocross, you are constantly jumping onto the saddle. Seatpost strength is imperative; imagine the consequences if the post were to break when you were jumping on the saddle with all of your weight.

Bending or breaking a seat rail or two while jumping on the bike is neither safe nor comfortable. If you keep riding on a saddle with a bent or broken seat rail, you obviously risk the saddle breaking off completely. But before that happens, you will screw up your pedaling mechanics by riding on a tilted saddle and potentially injure your back in the process.

Thus the first consideration in saddles and posts for cyclocross is strength. Unless you are a light person, opt for an aluminum seatpost of good quality, but not a superlight one, and get a saddle with chromoly steel rails. Of course, in cyclocross, you do want the bike to be as light as possible, because you are constantly hefting it up and running up hills and jumping over barriers with it. So don't overdo it. Get strong seatposts and saddles for your 'cross bikes that are also reasonably light.

Avoid saddles that are pointed at the tail. When you swing your leg over your saddle to jump up on it at speed, you want no long saddle tail (or spare-tire bag) to catch and deflect your leg. You can imagine what would happen.

Since you are leaping onto the saddle so often, it's not a bad idea to choose a saddle with some padding. You should land on the saddle with the inside of your thigh rather than on your crotch, but still, a superhard saddle may not be ideal. Although a more padded saddle does not necessarily equate to a more comfortable saddle, seek out a saddle you find comfortable. After all, you will be riding as fast as you can on bumpy surfaces without any suspension apart from the tires.

x-11

REMOVING A STUCK SEATPOST

LEVEL 3

You are having this difficulty because you did not follow the important Note in §x-8. This is a level 3 job because of the risk involved. It may be best to entrust this job to a shop because if you make a mistake, you run the risk of destroying your frame. If you're not 100 percent confident in your abilities, go to someone who is—or at least to someone who will be responsible if it gets screwed up.

1. **Remove the seat-lug binder bolt.**

2. **Squirt penetrating oil around the seatpost and let it sit overnight.** To get the most penetration, remove the bottom bracket (Chapter 8), turn the bike upside down, squirt more penetrating oil in from the bottom of the seat tube, and let it sit overnight.

3. **The next day, stand over the bike and twist the saddle.** No luck? For an aluminum post, repeat step 2 but use ammonia or Coca-Cola instead to dissolve the aluminum oxide.

4. **If step 3 does not free the seatpost, warm the seat-lug area with a hair dryer to expand it.** Discharge the entire contents of a tire inflator at the joint of the seatpost and the seat collar to freeze the post and shrink it. (Alternatively, ice the exposed seatpost with a plastic bag filled with crushed ice.) Now try twisting as in step 3.

5. **If step 4 does not free the seatpost, you will need to move into the difficult and risky part of this procedure.**

a. You will now sacrifice the seatpost. Remove the saddle and all of the clamps from the top of the seatpost. With the bike upside down, clamp the top of the seatpost into a large bench vise that is bolted to a very secure workbench.

b. Congratulations, you have just ruined the seatpost. Don't ever ride it again.

c. Perform the heat/ice or gas cartridge trick in step 4. Grab the frame at both ends and apply twisting pressure. You can easily apply enough force to bend or crack the frame, so be careful. If the seatpost releases, it can make such a large "pop" that you will think that you have broken many things!

6. **If step 5 does not work, you will need to cut the seatpost.** Cut off the seatpost a few inches above the seat lug and clamp the top of it in a vise. Warm up the seat-lug area with a hair dryer to expand it. Discharge the entire cartridge of a tire inflator down inside the seatpost to freeze it and shrink it. Now try twisting as in step 4.

7. **If step 5 or 6 does not work, you need to go to a machine shop and get the post reamed out of the seat tube.**

If, at this point, you still insist on getting the post out yourself, you should really sit down and think about it for a while. Will the guy at the machine shop really charge you so much money that it is worth the risk of completely destroying your frame yourself?

Still insist on going it alone? Okay, but don't say I didn't warn you.

Take a hacksaw and cut off the post a little more than an inch above the frame. Remove the blade from the saw and wrap a piece of tape around one end. Hold the taped end and slip the other end into the center of the post. Carefully—very carefully—make two outward cuts about

60 degrees apart. Your goal is to remove a pie-shaped wedge from the hunk of seatpost stuck in the frame. Be careful; this is where many people cut too far and go right through the seatpost into the frame. Of course, you wouldn't do that, would you?

Once you've made the cut, pry or pull this piece out with a large screwdriver or a pair of pliers. Be careful here too. A lot of overenthusiastic home mechanics have damaged their frames by prying too hard.

Once the wedge is out, work the remaining section of the post out by curling in the edges with the pliers to free more and more of it from the seatpost walls. It should eventually work its way out.

With the post out of the frame, clean the inside of the seat tube thoroughly. A flex hone, sold in auto parts stores (or loaned at rental stores) for reconditioning brake cylinders, is an excellent tool for the purpose. Turn the frame upside down, put the hone in an electric drill, and be sure to use plenty of honing fluid or cutting oil as you work. If you do not know how to use a hone, it may be best to take the frame to a bike shop to have the job done. An alternative is to use sandpaper wrapped around your fingers, although you will not be able to reach very far into the frame.

Inasmuch as removing a stuck post is so miserable that no one wants to do it twice, I'm certain that I do not need to remind you to grease any metal seatpost thoroughly before inserting it in the frame, and check it regularly thereafter as previously outlined. Carbon seatposts have a soft, clear-coated exterior and can mechanically lock into the frame or be held in by corrosion of the seat tube or seat-tube sleeve, so I recommend carbon assembly spray or paste to reduce these dangers (see the Pro Tip earlier in this chapter).

x-12

TROUBLESHOOTING PROBLEMS IN THE SEAT AND SEATPOST

a. Loose saddle

Check the clamp bolts. They are probably loose. Tighten the bolts and set the desired saddle tilt, after setting fore-and-aft saddle position (§x-2). Check for any damage to the clamping mechanism and replace the post if necessary. If parts of the saddle clamp are bent, they can bottom out on each other before clamping the saddle rail adequately.

b. Stuck seatpost

This can be a serious problem. Follow the instructions in §x-11 to avoid damaging the frame.

c. Saddle squeaks with each pedal stroke

This problem can come from the seat moving against metal parts or from grit in the points where the saddle rails enter the saddle base.

1. Contact from the leather overlapping the saddle shell with the seatpost clamp or rails is a likely culprit. Greasing the contact area will eliminate the noise. Also, roughing up the leather where it contacts metal will quiet it down. Or sprinkle the squeaky leather with talcum powder.

2. Also try squirting chain lube into the three points where the rails are inserted into the plastic shell of the saddle, in case some grit working at the rails is making the noise.

d. Creaking noises from the seatpost

A seatpost can creak from movement of the clamp holding the saddle. The shaft moving back and forth against the sides of the seat tube while you ride can also creak. Pull the post from the frame and regrease the post and seat tube, unless you have a carbon seatpost; carbon assembly paste is the ticket there (see the Pro Tip earlier in this chapter).

1. Some frames use a collar to adapt the seat tube to a certain seatpost diameter. Remember that the internal diameter of the seat tube is larger below the collar. I have seen bikes that creaked because the bottom of the seatpost rubbed against the sides of the seat tube below the extension of the collar. You can solve that problem by shortening the seatpost a bit with a hacksaw. If you do saw off the post, make sure that you still have at least 3 inches of seatpost inserted in the frame for security.

2. Similarly, movement between the frame, sizing shims, and the post can cause creaking. Grease all of these parts well.

3. If the creaking originates from the post head where the saddle is clamped, check the clamp bolts. Lubricate the bolt threads, and you will be able to tighten them a bit more.

4. The saddle rails can creak within the clamp areas. Loosen the clamp, oil or grease the rails and the clamp valleys, and retighten the parts. Wipe off any excess lubricant.

5. Shock-absorbing seatposts can squeak as they move up and down. Try greasing the sides of the inner shaft. Grease the elastomers inside too.

e. Seatpost slips down

Tighten the seat-lug binder bolt.

If the seat lug is pinched closed and the post still slips, you may be using a seatpost with an incorrect diameter, or the seat tube may be oversized or has stretched. Double-check the seat-tube diameter with calipers, or ask your local shop to do so. Try putting a larger seatpost in the frame, and replace it if you find one that fits better.

Try carbon assembly spray or paste on the post, even if it is not carbon (see the Pro Tip earlier in this chapter). The stuff expands against the inside of the seat tube and can increase clamping pressure at the same bolt torque.

If the next seatpost size up is too big and the assembly paste did not do the trick, you may need to shim the existing post. Cut a 1-by-3-inch piece of aluminum from a pop can. Pull the seatpost out, grease it and the pop-can shim (or put assembly paste on them), and insert both back into the frame. Bend the top lip of the shim over to prevent it from disappearing inside the frame. You may need to experiment with various shim dimensions until you find a piece that will go in with the seatpost and will also prevent slippage. Fortunately, they're cheap.

With a carbon-fiber seatpost, clean off any grease, and if you have carbon assembly paste or spray, put that on it (see the Pro Tip earlier in this chapter). Second, if you must tighten the clamp further, make sure it is not forcing the corners of the seat-tube slot into the seatpost, creating damage and the possibility of breakage. Use an offset-clamp binder, or turn the binder around so its slot does not line up with the seat tube's slot (see Fig. 10.6).

On a titanium frame or steel frame with an integral seat binder (one that is welded to the seat tube, as opposed to an external clamp), the seat tube can stretch if the binder is chronically overtightened. If the post is slipping because the binder slot has closed up, the shim method above may work. If not, contact the frame manufacturer for assistance. You may be able to remedy the situation by filing the binder slot wide enough to keep it from pinching closed. Plug the seat tube with a greasy rag to keep metal filings from falling into the bottom bracket, and suspend the frame upside down to encourage the filings to go elsewhere. This may not be a perfect solution, however, because while filing the slot wider will prevent the ears from hitting, the bolt will have to bend as the ears of the binder pull in. It may eventually break. By the way, don't file the frame until you speak to the frame builder, who may have a different solution or reasons not to do it; attacking the frame in this manner will usually void the warranty in the absence of explicit authorization. If filing isn't recommended, you will probably have to return the frame to the manufacturer for more comprehensive repair.

STEMS, HANDLEBARS, AND HEADSETS

I may not have gone where I intended to go, but I think I have ended up where I intended to be.
—Douglas Adams

On a bike, you maintain or change your direction by applying force to the handlebar. If everything works properly, variations in that pressure will result in your front wheel changing direction. Pretty basic, right? The interconnected parts between the handlebar and the wheel make that simple process possible. The parts of the steering system are illustrated in Figures 11.1 and 11.2. In this chapter, we'll cover most of that system by going over stems, handlebars, and headsets.

STEMS

The stem connects to the fork's steering tube (which is either 1 inch or 1-⅛ inches in diameter at its top) and clamps around the handlebar, which has one of two standard diameters: 26.0mm or 31.8mm (although Cinelli handlebars used to be 26.4mm, some 26.0mm handlebars call themselves 25.8mm, and many low-end handlebars have a 25.4mm clamp diameter). Stems come in one of two basic types: for thread-less fork steering tubes (Figs. 11.2–11.5) or for threaded ones (Figs. 11.1, 11.6–11.8).

Fork steering tubes on most high-end road bikes are 1-⅛ inch in diameter at the top, although many of them no longer maintain that diameter over the entire length of the steering tube; many forks now have a steering tube that tapers to 1-⅛ inch from a larger diameter at the base (i.e., at the top of the fork crown), where the stress is highest. In the 1990s, 1-inch-diameter threadless steering tubes were the norm on road forks, and prior to that, there was a century of road bikes with 1-inch-diameter threaded fork steering tubes.

Stems for unthreaded steering tubes (Fig. 11.3) have a clamping collar to grip the tube. Because the steering tube has no threads, the top headset cup merely slides on and off when the clamping collar is loosened. In this case, the stem plays a dual role. It clamps around the steering tube to connect the handlebar to the fork, and it also keeps the headset in proper adjustment by preventing the top headset cup from sliding up

11.1 The components of the steering system with a threaded fork

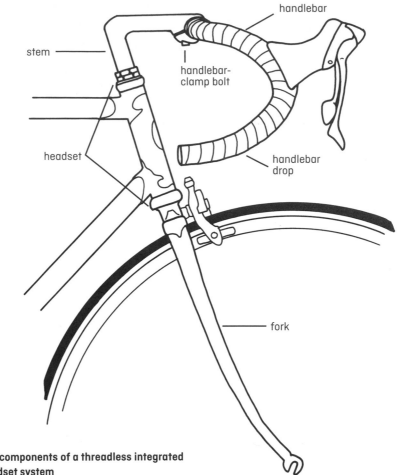

handlebar

stem

handlebar-clamp bolt

headset

handlebar drop

fork

11.2 The components of a threadless integrated headset system

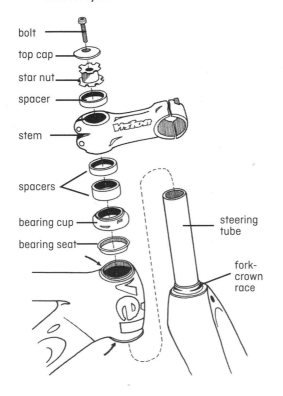

bolt

top cap

star nut

spacer

stem

spacers

bearing cup

bearing seat

steering tube

fork-crown race

11.3 Threadless stem

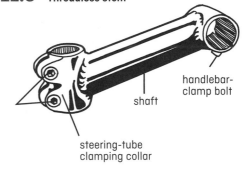

handlebar-clamp bolt

shaft

steering-tube clamping collar

the steering tube (Figs. 11.4, 11.5). If you have a 1-inch-diameter threadless steering tube (the old standard) and a stem for a 1-⅛-inch threadless steering tube (the current standard), you can get a slotted aluminum reduction bushing (normally supplied with a new stem) to allow the stem to be used with the 1-inch steering tube.

11.4 Threadless headset and stem cutaway

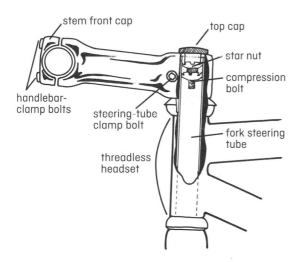

stem front cap

top cap

star nut

compression bolt

handlebar-clamp bolts

steering-tube clamp bolt

threadless headset

fork steering tube

On most bikes made before 1990, the steering tube on the fork has external threads at the top, and the headset screws onto it for attachment and adjustment. Stems for threaded steering tubes (Figs. 11.6–11.8) have a "quill" that extends into the steering tube of the fork and a shaft, or extension, that connects to the handlebar clamp. The stem binds to the inside of the steering tube by means of a conical plug (Fig. 11.6) or angularly truncated cylindrical wedge (Fig. 11.7) pulled up by a long stem-expander bolt that runs through the quill (Fig. 11.8).

11.5 Threadless headset cup held in place by stem

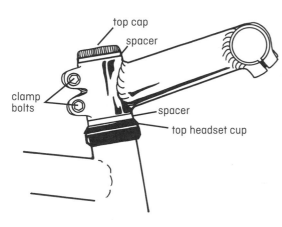

top cap

spacer

clamp bolts

spacer

top headset cup

11.7 Welded quill-type stem with expander wedge

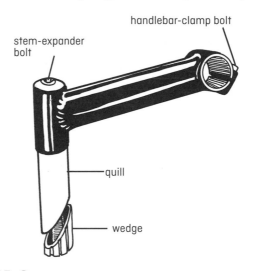

stem-expander bolt

handlebar-clamp bolt

quill

wedge

11.6 Forged aluminum quill road stem with expander plug

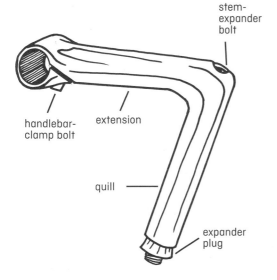

stem-expander bolt

handlebar-clamp bolt

extension

quill

expander plug

11.8 Threaded headset system cutaway: note the expander plug securing the stem inside the steering tube.

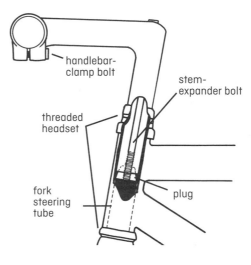

handlebar-clamp bolt

stem-expander bolt

threaded headset

fork steering tube

plug

CHAPTER 11

STEMS, HANDLEBARS, AND HEADSETS

11.9 Loosening and tightening the compression bolt on a threadless headset

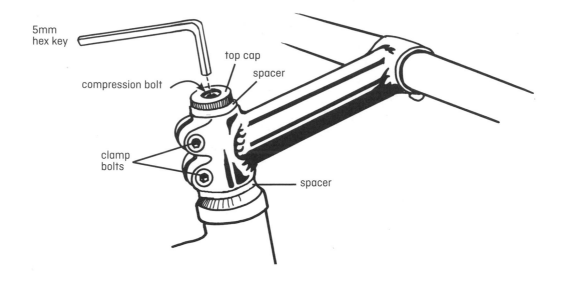

The shaft of a traditional road bike stem extends out at an angle of about 73 degrees from the fork steering tube so that, when installed on the bike, the shaft is horizontal out to the handlebar (Figs. 11.1, 11.8). Stems on track sprint bikes historically tended to be angled downward when mounted on the bike. Stems with 90-degree angles and greater, resulting in an upward angle on the assembled bicycle (Figs. 11.2–11.5, 11.7, 11.9), are becoming commonplace on road bikes and even track bikes.

xi-1

REMOVE CLAMP-TYPE STEM FROM THREADLESS STEERING TUBE

LEVEL 1

1. **Loosen the horizontal clamp bolt(s) (Fig. 11.5) securing the stem around the steering tube.**

2. **Unscrew the compression bolt.** With a 5mm (usually) hex key, unscrew and remove the compression bolt (or "adjusting bolt" because it compresses the headset into the proper bearing adjust-

---

| PRO TIP | Spacers with Carbon Steering Tubes |

f the fork has a carbon steering tube, always place one spacer above the stem (Figs. 11.5, 11.9). That way, the entire stem clamp is clamped onto the steerer, and there is no chance for the upper part of the clamp to pinch the end of the steerer. This is a good idea for a steel or aluminum steering tube as well.

If you want to raise the handlebar up high, be careful about using too many spacers below the

stem; consult the owner's manual for the fork for recommendations on maximum spacer stack height. From a strength and stiffness perspective, it's preferable to use an up-angled stem, rather than a level or down-angled one with a lot of spacers below it. And, of course, make sure the support plug inside the steering tube (which prevents the stem clamp from crushing the carbon steering tube) is supporting the area under the stem clamp.

ment) in the headset top cap (Fig. 11.9). The fork can now fall out, so hold the fork as you unscrew the bolt.

NOTE: *Some threadless headsets do not use a top cap. For instance, DiaTech threadless headsets have a collar beveled internally on the top and bottom to adjust headset compression. Without a top cap, as soon as you loosen the stem, the fork can slip out.*

3. **Remove the cap and stem.** With the bike standing on the floor, or while holding the fork to keep it from falling out, pull the cap and the stem off the steering tube. Leave the bike standing until you replace the stem, or slide the fork out of the frame, keeping track of all headset parts.

4. **If the stem is stuck to the steering tube and will not budge, see §xi-6a.**

---

xi-2

INSTALL AND ADJUST HEIGHT OF STEM ON THREADLESS STEERING TUBE

LEVEL 2

Installing and adjusting the height of a stem on a threadless fork are much more complicated than installing and adjusting the height of a standard stem in a threaded fork, because the stem is integral to the operation of the headset. As you can see from Figures 11.4 and 11.5, any change to the stem height would alter the headset adjustment. That's why this step is listed with a level 2 designation.

1. **Stand the bike on its wheels, so that the fork does not fall out.**

2. **Lubricate the parts.** Grease the top end of the steering tube if it is steel or aluminum, but leave it dry if it is carbon fiber (or apply carbon assembly paste or spray). Loosen the stem-clamp bolts and grease their threads. Slide the stem onto the steering tube.

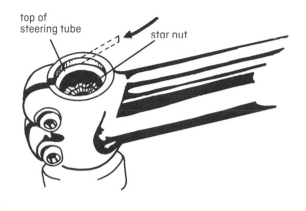
top of steering tube — star nut

3. **Set the stem height to the desired level.** If you want to place the stem in a position higher than directly on top of the headset, you must put some spacers between the bottom of the stem clamp and the top piece of the headset (Fig. 11.9). No matter what, there must be contact (either directly or through spacers) between the headset and the stem. Otherwise, the headset will be loose.

4. **Check the steering tube length.** In order to adjust the threadless headset, the top of the stem clamp (or, ideally, spacers placed above it; see the Pro Tip) should overlap the top of the steering tube by 3–5mm ($\frac{1}{8}$–$\frac{3}{16}$ inch) (Fig. 11.10). If it does, skip ahead to step 7.

NOTE ON 1-INCH STEERERS: *Most stems now have a 1-$\frac{1}{8}$-inch clamp size. Simple split shim sleeves (short pieces of tubing slotted down one side) are widely available to adapt a 1-$\frac{1}{8}$-inch clamp stem to a 1-inch steering tube. Slide the sleeve over the steering tube and slide the stem over it. With this type of stem and shim on a 1-inch steering tube, you can usually use spacers under the stem sized for a 1-inch steering tube, as long as they are wide enough to contact the entire bottom edge of the stem. However, above the stem, you may need to use a spacer and a headset top cap meant for a 1-$\frac{1}{8}$-inch steering tube, in order to* *push the stem down properly and to aesthetically match the top of the stem.*

5. **Check overlap.** If the top of the stem clamp overlaps the top of the steering tube by more than 5mm (³⁄₁₆ inch), the steering tube is too short to set the stem height where you have it. If you have spacers below the stem, remove some until the top edge of the stem clamp overlaps the top of the steering tube by a maximum of 5mm (Fig. 11.10). Ideally, have the steerer come all the way through the stem clamp, and put a spacer above it; see the Pro Tip. If you cannot or do not wish to lower the stem any farther, you will need a fork with a longer steering tube, a stem with a shorter clamp, or a stem that is angled upward to achieve the desired handlebar height. Stems for threadless steering tubes with clamps of differing lengths are available, as are stems of varying angles. Replacing the stem is a lot cheaper and easier than replacing the fork.

6. **If the steering tube is too long, there are several steps you can take.**

   a. If the top of the steering tube is less than 3mm (⅛ inch) below the top spacer or the top edge of the stem clamp, or if the steering tube sticks up above the top of the stem clamp by a small amount, put a headset spacer or two on top of the stem clamp until the top spacer overlaps the top edge of the steering tube by at least 3mm.

   b. If, on the other hand, you are sure you will never want the stem any higher, you can cut off the excess tube. First, mark the steering tube along the top edge of the spacer above the stem clamp (do not cut at the top of the stem clamp itself or lower; see the Pro Tip). Remove the fork from the bike. Wrap a piece of tape around the steering tube 3mm below the mark. Place the steering tube in a padded vise or bike-stand clamp. By using the edge of the tape as a guide for cutting straight, cut the excess steering tube off with a hacksaw.

   c. In steel and aluminum steering tubes that have already been installed in a bike, there is a star nut that is inserted inside the steering tube (Fig. 11.4). You screw the compression bolt through the top cap to adjust the headset bearings (but not to retain the headset; the stem-clamp bolts do that). If the star nut is already inside the steering tube and it looks like the saw is going to hit it, you must move the star nut down before cutting. See step 7 for instructions on pushing the star nut in deeper. (Carbon-fiber fork steering tubes have either a glue-in support insert with a star nut inside, or an expandable steering tube support insert with an integrated anchor for the top-cap bolt [Fig. 11.27]; in either case, the insert must be removed before cutting the steering tube.)

   d. Make your cut straight. Measure twice, cut once! Mark it straight by wrapping a piece of tape around the steering tube and cutting along it. If you are not sure the cut will be straight, start it a little higher and file it down flat to the tape line. If you really want to be safe, use a tool specifically designed to help you make a straight cut; Park Tool's "threadless saw guide" will do the trick (you need to put some spacers between the plates of this tool if you are using the fatter CarboCut saw blade). Remember that you can always shorten the steering tube, but you cannot make it longer! Use a round file on the inside of the tube and a flat file on the outside to remove any metal burrs left by the hacksaw or cutter.

e. When you have completed cutting and deburring, put the fork back in, replacing all headset parts the way they were originally installed (§xi-14). Return to step 1 in this section.

7. Check top cap clearance. Check that the top of the star-shaped nut or steerer support plug does not hit the bottom of the headset top cap once the adjusting bolt is tightened. Generally, you can fix this by putting another spacer (or a thicker one) above the stem. If the nut is not in deeply enough in a steel or aluminum steerer, you can drive it deeper into the steering tube after removing the stem. In the case of a carbon steering tube with an expander plug inside, you can move it down by loosening its bolt with a hex key, tapping it in deeper, and retightening it. An expander plug or glue-in support insert is a must to prevent crushing the carbon steering tube with the stem clamp.

Metal steering tubes

a. Driving the star nut deeper into a metal steering tube is best done with a star nut installation tool (Fig. 1.3). The tool threads into the nut, and you hit it with a hammer until it stops; the star nut will now be set 15mm deep in the steering tube. If you do not have this tool, go to a bike shop and have the nut set for you. If you insist on doing it yourself, read step b, below. Just remember that it is easy to mangle the star nut if you do not tap it in straight.

b. Pushing the star nut in deeper without a star nut installation tool requires three steps: (1) Put the adjusting bolt through the top cap and thread it six turns into the star nut. (2) Set the star nut over the end of the steering tube and tap the top of the bolt with a mallet; use the top cap as a guide to keep it going in straight. (3) Tap the bolt in until the star nut is 15mm below the top of the steering tube.

NOTE: *If the wall thickness of the steering tube is greater than standard, the stock headset star nut will not fit, and it will bend when you try to install it. Even pros sometimes ruin star nuts. It's not a big problem, because replacements can be purchased separately. If it goes in crooked, take a long punch or rod, set it on the star nut, and drive it to or all the way out of the bottom of the steering tube. Dispose of the star nut, and get another.*

If the internal diameter (ID) of the steering tube is undersized (standard ID is 22.2mm [7⁄8 inch] on a 1-inch steering tube; 25.4mm [1 inch] on a 1-1⁄8-inch steering tube; and 28.6mm [1-1⁄8 inch] on a 1-1⁄4-inch steering tube), you cannot use the stock star nut from the headset for that size. Get a correctly sized star nut at a bike shop or from the fork manufacturer. In a pinch, you can make a big stock star nut fit by bending each pair of opposite leaves of the star nut toward each other with a pair of slip-joint pliers to reduce the nut's width. Now you can insert the nut; be aware that it may not grip as well as a properly sized one.

8. **Install the headset top cap on the top of the stem clamp (or spacers you set above it).** Grease the threads of the top-cap compression bolt and screw it into the star nut inside the steering tube with a 5mm hex key (Fig. 11.9).

9. **Adjust the headset.** Tighten the top cap while keeping the stem lined up straight with the front wheel, and hold it in adjustment by

f you are cutting a carbon-fiber steering tube, cut three-quarters of the way through and then turn the steerer over and cut from the other side to meet your cut. This will prevent the peeling back of the last few layers of carbon at the bottom of a single cut.

You can use a standard hacksaw with a fine-tooth blade if you're careful, but a better option is the Effetto Mariposa CarboCut saw. It has a toothless, grit-edge tungsten-carbide blade for cutting hard materials, including ceramics, titanium, and steel, as well as for cutting carbon fiber (and Kevlar and boron fiber) without damaging the matrix surrounding the fibers. The CarboCut's tungsten-carbide blade cuts on both push and pull strokes and does not grab like a toothed blade. It leaves a smooth cut edge that requires no sanding. Note, however, that you still need to cut through partway from each side to avoid peeling back carbon fibers as the blade exits the tube.

tightening the stem-clamp bolts. The steps are outlined and possible complications are addressed in §xi-16.

---

xi-3

REMOVE QUILL-TYPE STEM FROM THREADED FORK

LEVEL 1

1. **Unscrew the stem-fixing bolt on the top of the stem about three turns or so.** Most stem bolts take a 6mm hex key. Some stems have a rubber plug on top that must be removed to get at the stem bolt.

2. **Tap the top of the bolt down with a mallet or hammer (Fig. 11.11).** This will disengage the plug or wedge from the bottom of the quill and will free the stem, as long as it's not rusted in place. If the head of the bolt is recessed down in the stem so that a hammer cannot get at it, leave the hex key in the bolt and tap the top of the hex key until the wedge is free.

3. **Pull the stem out of the steering tube.** If the stem will not budge, see §xi-6b.

11.11   Freeing the stem wedge

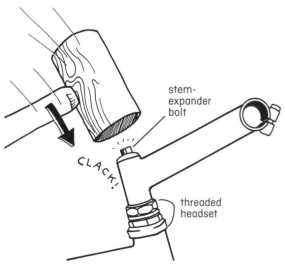

stem-expander bolt

CLACK!

threaded headset

---

xi-4

INSTALL AND ADJUST HEIGHT OF QUILL STEM IN THREADED FORK

LEVEL 1

1. **Lubricate the parts.** Generously grease the stem quill, the expander-bolt threads, the outside of the wedge or conical plug, and the inside of the steering tube. If this is the first time you've done this, I know what you're thinking: "Why put grease on something that I want to wedge together?" Don't worry; the grease won't prevent the wedge

from keeping the stem tight. Rather, it will prevent the parts from creaking, seizing, or rusting together.

2. **Assemble the parts.** Thread the expander bolt through the stem and into the wedge or plug until the bolt pulls the plug or wedge into place, but not so far as to prevent the stem from inserting into the steering tube.

3. **Install the stem.** Slip the stem quill into the steering tube (Fig. 11.8) to the depth you want. Make sure the stem is inserted beyond its height-limit line. Tighten the bolt until the stem is snug but can still be turned.

4. **Set the stem to the desired height, line it up with the front wheel, and tighten the bolt.** It needs to be tight, but don't tighten it so much that it bulges the steering tube.

---

xi-5

STEM MAINTENANCE AND REPLACEMENT SCHEDULE

A bike cannot be controlled if the stem breaks, so make sure yours doesn't break. Aluminum has no fatigue endurance limit (the point below which a material can be stressed indefinitely), which means that any aluminum part regularly stretched or flexed will eventually fail. Steel and titanium parts repeatedly stressed more than about one-half of their tensile strength will eventually fail as well. Carbon fiber has high fatigue resistance but is susceptible to breakage, particularly after an impact has damaged underlying fibers, even if that damage is invisible from the outside.

What this means is that stems made from any material may fail suddenly, causing a crash. Therefore, do not look at the stem on your bike as a permanent accessory. Replace it before it fails.

Clean the stem regularly. Whenever you clean it, look for corrosion, cracks, and bent or stressed areas. If you find any, replace the stem immediately. If you crash hard, especially hard enough to bend the handlebar, replace the stem and possibly the fork—and the bar, of course. Err on the side of caution.

Some stem makers recommend replacing stems every four years or less. If you rarely ride the bike, this is overkill. If you ride hard and ride often, every four years may not be frequent enough. Do what is appropriate for you, and be aware of the risks.

---

xi-6

REMOVING A STUCK STEM

LEVEL 3

A stem can get stuck onto (or into) the steering tube owing to poor maintenance. Regular maintenance involves periodically regreasing the stem and steering tube to enable the parts to slide freely when disassembled. The grease also forms a barrier to sweat and water.

If the stem is really stuck, be careful as you try to remove it; you can—quite easily—ruin the fork as well as the stem and the headset trying to get it out. In fact, you're better off having a shop work on it, unless you really know what you are doing and are willing to accept the risk of destroying a lot of expensive parts.

a. Removing a stuck stem from a threadless fork

1. **Remove the top cap (Fig. 11.9) and the bolts clamping the stem to the steering tube.**

2. **Thread the clamp bolts in from the other side.** Spread the stem clamp by inserting a coin into the slot between each bolt end and the opposing unthreaded half of the binder lug (Fig. 11.12). Tighten each bolt against each coin so that it spreads the clamp slot

11.12 Spreading the stem clamp to free a stuck stem

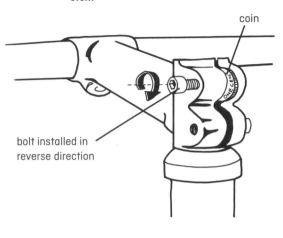

coin

bolt installed in reverse direction

11.13 Clamping the fork crown in vise

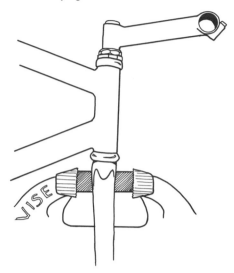

VISE

open wider. The stem should come right off the steering tube now.

NOTE: *If the stem is the type that comes with a single bolt in the side of the stem shaft ahead of the steering tube (Fig. 11.4), loosen the bolt a few turns and tap it in with a hammer to free the wedge. It might require some ammonia and perhaps some heat to expand it.*

If it still will not come free, you may have to use a vise (as long as it's not a carbon fork; see the Caution in the next section), following 6–7 in the following section on freeing a quill-type stem. Failing that, your last resort is to saw through the steering tube at the base of the stem clamp, and replace the stem and fork.

b. Removing a stuck stem from a threaded fork

1. **Unscrew the stem bolt on top of the stem three turns or more.** Smack the bolt (or the hex key in the bolt) with a mallet or hammer (Fig. 11.11) to disengage the wedge.

2. **Give it a twist.** Grasping the front wheel between your knees, make one last attempt to free the stem by twisting back and forth

on the bar. Don't use all of your strength because you can ruin a fork and front wheel this way.

3. **If the stem didn't budge, squirt ammonia or Coca-Cola around the stem where it enters the headset.** Let the bike sit for several hours and add more ammonia every hour or so.

4. **Turn the bike over and squirt ammonia into the bottom of the fork steering tube.** You want the ammonia to run down around the stem quill. Let the bike sit for several hours and add more ammonia every hour or so.

5. **Try step 2 again.** If still stuck, repeat steps 3 and 4 but try penetrating oil as a last resort. Ammonia or Coca-Cola generally will dissolve aluminum oxide, but if one of these hasn't worked, there is a slim chance that penetrating oil might work.

6. **Shrink the parts.** If the previous steps haven't worked, remove the stem-expander bolt and discharge a tire inflator inside the stem quill to shrink it with cold. Now try step 2 again.

7. **Use a vise.** If the stem does not come free this time and you don't have a carbon fork, you'll have to go to your workbench and use that heavy-duty vise. It's solidly mounted, isn't it? Good, because it will need to be.

8. **Remove the front wheel (Chapter 2) and the front brake (Chapter 7).** Put pieces of wood on each side of the vise. Clamp the fork crown into the vise (Fig. 11.13).

CAUTION: *Never clamp a carbon fork in a vise; you may damage it to the point that it could fail catastrophically while you are riding. Rather than risk that, get a new fork and stem if you can't remove this one (you can chop the stem off above the headset to get the fork out).*

9. **Grab both ends of the handlebar and twist back and forth.** Again, try discharging a tire inflator inside the stem quill to shrink it with cold. The stem will generally come free with a loud pop. If this doesn't work, you may have to saw off the stem just above the headset and have the bottom of the stem reamed out of the steering tube by a machine shop. In this case, unscrew the headset and remove the fork; don't take the bike to a machine shop as an assembly. I told you that you should have gone to a bike shop before getting to this point!

HANDLEBARS

LEVEL 1

I am generally referring here to standard road bike drop bars (Fig. 11.1), but most of these comments also apply to the "cowhorn" style of handlebar common on time trial and triathlon bikes (Figs. i.2, 11.16A–B). Handlebar work is straightforward; all of the procedures that follow are level 1 jobs.

HANDLEBAR REMOVAL

a. From a stem with a removable front stem cap

Stems with a removable front stem cap are shown in Figures 11.2 and 11.4.

1. **Completely remove the bolts holding the front stem cap.** There may be two (Figs. 11.2, 11.4), three, or four bolts, depending on model.

2. **Pull off the stem cap, and the handlebar will drop off the stem.** Makes it easy, eh, having a removable front cap?

b. From a stem with a single handlebar-clamp bolt

Stems with a single handlebar-clamp bolt are shown in Figures 11.1, 11.3, and 11.5–11.9.

1. **Remove the handlebar tape (Fig. 11.14), at least from one side.**

2. **Remove the brake levers (see Chapter 7).**

3. **Loosen the bolt on the stem clamp surrounding the bar.** This usually takes a 5mm hex key.

11.14 Removing handlebar tape

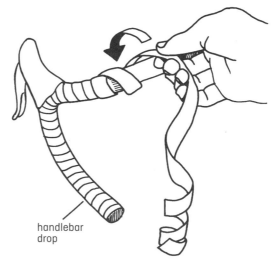

handlebar drop

STEMS, HANDLEBARS, AND HEADSETS

4. **Pull the bar out, working the bend around through the stem.** If the bar won't budge, if it will budge but it appears that you will tear up the bar's finish working it out through the stem, or if the bend in the bar will not pass through the stem clamp, you need to open the stem clamp a bit more. On many stems, you can do this by removing the clamp bolt, threading it back in from the opposite side with a coin inserted into the clamp slot, and tightening the bolt against the coin to spread the clamp. (Opening a stem clamp in this way—but in this case the steering tube clamp—is illustrated in Fig. 11.12.) Otherwise, you can (carefully!) pry the opening wider with a large screwdriver.

xi-8

HANDLEBAR INSTALLATION: DROP BAR

1. **Lubricate the parts.** Remove the handlebar stem's clamp bolt (or bolts), grease the threads, and replace it (or them). Grease the inside of the stem clamp and the clamping area in the center of the bar. Grease keeps the parts from seizing over time and prevents creaking noises from developing later. With a carbon-fiber handlebar, leave it dry or apply carbon assembly paste or spray (Fig. 10.6) on its clamping area and inside the stem clamp.

2. **Install the bar and rotate it to the position you find most comfortable.** The old-school way was to set a drop bar so that the bottom flat section (the "drop;" see Fig. 11.1) was horizontal. The style now tends to be with the drops aimed down and back toward the rear brake or the rear hub, but the setting you choose is entirely a matter of personal preference.

3. **Tighten the bolt or bolts that clamp the bar.** Tighten it or them to the recommended torque (see the torque table in Appendix E). This step is particularly important with expensive, lightweight stems and bars. You can pinch and thereby weaken a lightweight handlebar by overtightening, and the high-strength tubing will crack right next to the stem. Light stems come with small bolts with fine threads, and overtightening can strip the threads inside the aluminum (or magnesium, etc.) stem. If you don't have a torque wrench and you have a lightweight stem with small bolts (e.g., M5 or M6 bolts, which take 4mm and 5mm hex keys, respectively), use a short hex key so that you can't get much leverage. Proper torque is even more important with carbon-fiber handlebars.

Also, make sure that there is the same amount of space between the stem and the edge of the front plate on both the top and bottom of a front-opening stem. Any stem whose clamp gap or gaps get pinched nearly closed when tightened around the bar needs to be replaced, along with the handlebar.

xi-9

INSTALLING A CLIP-ON AERO BAR ONTO A DROP BAR OR COWHORN BAR

Open the clamps that will attach the aero bar to the handlebar by removing the bolts with a hex key. **NOTE:** *I will refer to the bike's handlebar when a clip-on is attached to it as the "base bar."*

Clip-ons (clip-on aero bars; Figs. 11.15, 11.16) generally mount on the bulge of the base bar, right next to the stem. If the clip-on you have chosen mounts on the thinner-diameter section of the base bar, you will have to peel back some handlebar tape from the section adjacent to the bulge (Fig. 11.14).

CAUTION: *Do not put a clip-on bar onto a carbon handlebar unless its manufacturer specifically*

11.15 Installing clip-on aero bars onto a drop bar

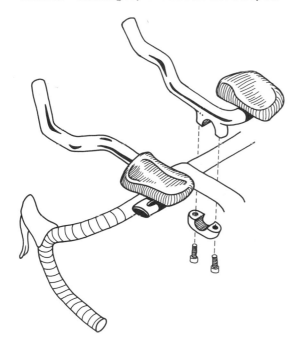

says that it is okay. Most carbon base bars are not rated for clip-on use; some can be downright dangerous if you attach a clip-on to them.

For starters, set the clip-on bar level or angled upward slightly. Bolt the clip-on clamps around the base bar as shown in Figures 11.15 and 11.16. Some clip-ons mount atop the base bar (Figs. 11.15, 11.16A); others mount either above or below the base bar and allow fore-aft adjustment of the extensions (Fig. 11.16B).

Tighten the bolts enough that the clip-on bars won't slip when you hit a bump or pull on them, but be careful not to pinch or crush the base bar. See the torque table in Appendix E.

Set the elbow pads in a medium-width position. The pad is often held onto the elbow support with Velcro; pulling off the pad will reveal the adjusting bolt (Figs. 11.16A–B). Ideally, you want the elbow pad positioned under your elbow or slightly forward of it, and you want the clip-on to be of such a length that your hands grasp the ends comfortably with the elbows on the pads.

11.16A–B Installing clip-on aerobars onto cowhown bars

11.16A Aerobar above the base bar

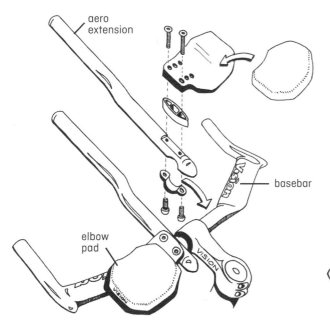

11.16B Aerobar with fore-aft adjustability below the base bar

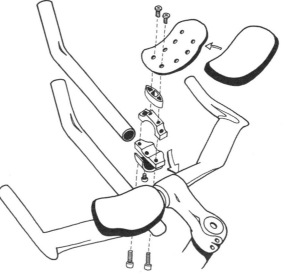

STEMS, HANDLEBARS, AND HEADSETS

INSTALLATION OF COMPLETE AERO BAR: BASE BAR, AERO EXTENSIONS, AND ELBOW PADS

1. **Assemble the parts.** If the aero bar has an integrated stem, clamp it onto the steering tube and adjust its height and the headset as in §xi-2 and §xi-16. If not, first clamp the handlebar into the stem, then clamp the stem onto the steering tube, and adjust its height and the headset as in §xi-2 or §xi-4 and §xi-16 or §xi-17.

2. **Set the angle.** Adjust the angle of the base bar (if you have a separate bar clamped into a stem) to the position you like, and tighten the stem clamp.

3. **Install the aero extensions and the elbow pads.** In many cases, the hardware holding the extensions is the same as that which holds the elbow pads (Figs. 11.16A–B). Some bars have hardware that allows you to run the extensions underneath the base bar (Fig. 11.16B) or on top of it; if you have the choice, try them both to see which you prefer. The elbow pads, of course, clamp above the base bar. You will also often have the choice of shape of the aero extensions, be they straight, single-bend, double-bend, S-bend, or the short, J-shaped bend of a Slam bar (Fig. 11.17).

4. **Adjust the positions.** Set the stem height; adjust the elbow pad fore-aft, twist, tilt, and width and the aero extension width, twist, and reach to your liking and tighten all of the clamp bolts. If you will be using end plugs in the tail ends of the aero extensions, insert them before you clamp the extensions in place, or you won't be able to get them in with some bars, once they are in place.

11.17A–E Bend variations of aero bar extensions

11.17A Straight extensions

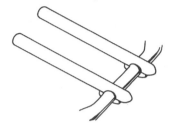

11.17B S-bend extensions

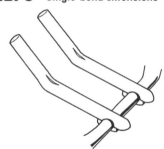

11.17C Single-bend extensions

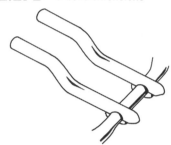

11.17D Double-bend extensions

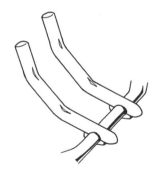

11.17E "Slam" bar extensions

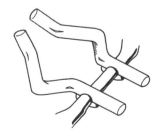

5. **Trim to length.** If you have excess length on the extensions, pull them back out and cut them down to the right length. If they are carbon fiber, saw in first from one side and then from the other and meet in the middle to avoid fraying and peeling the carbon layers (see the Pro Tip on cutting a carbon steering tube). Clamp the extensions back in place when you're done.

6. **Install the brake levers and shifters.** Unless the bar has integrated brake levers, clamp the brake levers onto the ends of the base bar and tighten the bar-end shifters into the ends of the aero extensions.

7. **Install the cables and housings.** Route them through or along the bars and frame and to the derailleurs and brakes (see Chapters 5 and 7). If you are running the shift cables straight out of the tail ends of the extensions, make sure the housing loops entering the frame or cable stops don't hit your knees; if the loops must be long due to frame or bar configuration, you may be able to restrain them with a zip tie that holds them together.

8. **Tape the handlebars (see §ix-12).**

9. **Check that all of the bolts are tight, and go ride your bike!**

xi-11

HANDLEBAR MAINTENANCE AND REPLACEMENT SCHEDULE

A bike cannot be controlled without a handlebar, so you never want one to break. Do not look at the bar as a permanent accessory on your bike. All handlebars will eventually fail. The trick is not to be riding them when they do.

Keep the bar clean, and check carbon bars for a sudden increase in flexibility. Regularly inspect the bar (yes, under the tape!) for cracks, crash-induced bends, corrosion, and stressed areas. If you find any sign of new flexibility, wear, bending, or cracking, replace the bar. Never straighten a bent handlebar! Replace it! Even though the bar was bent to shape in the first place, it was done when the aluminum was in an annealed (soft) state; the bar was then heat-treated for strength, making it more brittle.

If you crash hard, consider replacing the bar even if it looks fine. If the bar has taken an extremely hard hit, it's a good idea to replace it immediately rather than gamble on its integrity.

Some manufacturers recommend replacing stems and bars every four years or less. As with a stem, if you rarely ride the bike, this is overkill. If you ride hard and often, every four years may not be frequent enough. Do what is appropriate for you, and be aware of the risks.

xi-12

WRAPPING HANDLEBAR TAPE

You need both hands free and the bar rigidly held. Clamping the bike in a bike stand or holding it in a stationary trainer should do the trick, but you may need to stabilize the front wheel between your knees or with a strap around the down tube and rim or a bar-holder from the seatpost to the handlebar. Before wrapping, clean the bar and inspect it for cracks, crash-induced bends, corrosion, and stressed areas. If you find any sign of wear or cracking, replace the bar.

Tape down concealed brake and shift cables in a few places with electrical tape or strapping tape (Fig. 11.18). (Pre-1984 or so brake levers have no concealed cables; the brake cable comes out of the top of the lever.) Shimano STI levers up until 2009 always have concealed brake cables and exposed shift cables. Both the shift cables and brake cables are concealed on Campagnolo

11.18 Taping cables to the bar before installing bar tape

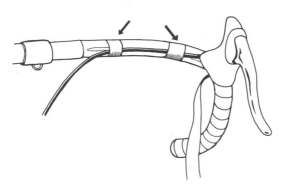

11.19 Wrapping handlebar tape

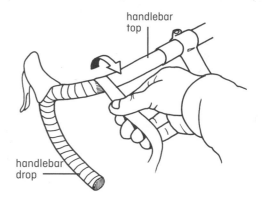

handlebar top

handlebar drop

Ergopower, SRAM DoubleTap, or post-2009 Shimano Dura-Ace STI levers.

Tape the cables down where they will be the most comfortable for your hands. Some handlebars have creases in them for the cables; tape the cables down so that they stay in the creases. Some levers allow cable housings to go either in front of or behind the handlebar. My preference is to route both the brake cable and the shift cable along the front of the handlebar.

If the handlebar tape does not have an adhesive back surface covered with a paper backing strip, smear a Glue Stick on the bar around the outside of all of its bends. These areas are where the handlebar tape tends to creep and separate; the glue will help keep that from happening.

Handlebar tape sets usually come with two short pieces to cover the brake-lever-clamp bands. Peel back the edges of the rubber hood on the brake lever, wrap the little tape piece around the clamp band, and insert each end under the hood. You may want to tape the ends down with some Scotch tape. Leave the hood peeled back so that you can wrap the bar tape up onto the edge of the lever body and then cover it with the skirt of the rubber hood.

Peel back the paper backing on the tape and start wrapping at the end of the bar from the inside out. Overlap the end of the bar by more than

about an inch, so that you can push the excess in with the end plug later. Lightweight bars tend to have thin walls and consequently a large inside diameter, and many end plugs will not fit tightly in them. In this case, the extra tape sticking out will fill the extra space. Alternatively, you can put the plugs in first and simply start wrapping right at the ends of the bar with no overlap; you'll need to wrap some tape around the insertion prongs of the plug until it fits tightly and won't rattle out.

To have a long-lasting tape job, you always want to wrap from the end of the bar so that each wrap holds down the inner edge of the prior one. The wrapping direction is important too. Wrapping from the center of the bar and finishing at the end plug is a mistake, because your hands will constantly peel back the edge of each tape wrap as you ride. The tape will look bad and get torn quickly. Wrap from the ends of the bar, working up to the stem.

Pull the tape tightly but don't break it. Overlap each wrap about one-quarter to one-half of its width (Fig. 11.19). Use as much overlap as you can to increase padding and decrease the chance of the tape slipping enough to reveal the handlebar. The amount of overlap will depend on the length of the tape, the width and drop depth of the bar, and the amount you stretch the tape as you wrap.

When you get to the bulged section of the bar that clamps into the stem, you should have just run out of tape. If you have more, you can rewrap part of the bar with more overlap, or you can cut off the excess. If the tape doesn't make it to the bulge, you can rewrap part of the bar with less overlap. If you want to end with only a narrow piece of sticky tape holding it down, trim the end of the bar tape to a point, and hold it down with a single width of electrical tape wrapped around a couple of times. You can follow with the decorative tape piece that came with the bar tape. Otherwise, just wrap around the bar a number of times with electrical tape, going wide enough with it to completely cover the square-cut end of the bar tape. Cut or break the electrical tape so that it ends under the bar.

Push the plugs into the ends of the bar, using them to push in the extra tape you left sticking off the ends of the bar. Most plugs are now simply that—cylindrical plastic plugs. Old-school end plugs have an expanding device in them; you tighten a screw on the end, and it pulls a wedge into its internally tapered inner end, expanding it out against the walls of the handlebar.

xi-13

SETTING STEM AND BAR POSITIONS

Setting handlebar height and reach is very personal. Much depends on your physique, your flexibility, your frame, your riding style, and a few other preferences. This subject is covered in depth in Appendix C. Here are some brief suggestions:

- I recommend setting a drop handlebar so that the flat section below the bend (the "drop") is horizontal or aimed slightly downward toward the rear hub (Fig. 11.1).
- If you stand a lot when you climb, you will want the bar low enough that you can use your arms efficiently when gripping the brake levers and pulling.

- A low, stretched-out position is better aerodynamically. A low position is one with the top of the handlebar more than 6cm (2 inches) lower than the top of the saddle. With your hands on the drops, a stretched-out position places your elbow at least 2cm (¾ inch) in front of your knee at the top of the pedal stroke.
- If you are using an aero (clip-on) bar, you want to find a position that maximizes both comfort and aerodynamic efficiency. The lower and more aerodynamic you are trying to be, the more forward you will want to position the saddle to open up the angle between your torso and your thigh. When setting the reach to the bar, a good rule of thumb is to position the elbow pads so that your ear is over the bend in your elbow. As for width, the narrower the elbow pads, the more aerodynamic you will be. Work on getting lower only after you have gotten comfortable and efficient with a narrow position.

HEADSETS

There are two main types of headsets: threadless and threaded. Nearly all modern bikes come with threadless headsets, of which there are three basic types: standard (i.e., external; Fig. 11.20), cupless internal (i.e., integrated; Fig. 11.21), and press-in internal with lipped cups (Fig. 11.22). Older bikes (and some current bikes that prefer a retro design) generally have threaded headsets (Fig. 11.23). A threaded headset requires a threaded steering tube.

Road headsets have traditionally come in the 1-inch-diameter size (originally only in threaded versions and, later, after a century, threadless), but now most road bikes take 1-⅛-inch threadless headsets. However, just as with cranksets, headset bearing standards are rapidly changing to systems that have a larger lower bearing than the 1-⅛-inch upper bearing (Fig. 11.26).

11.20 External threadless headset

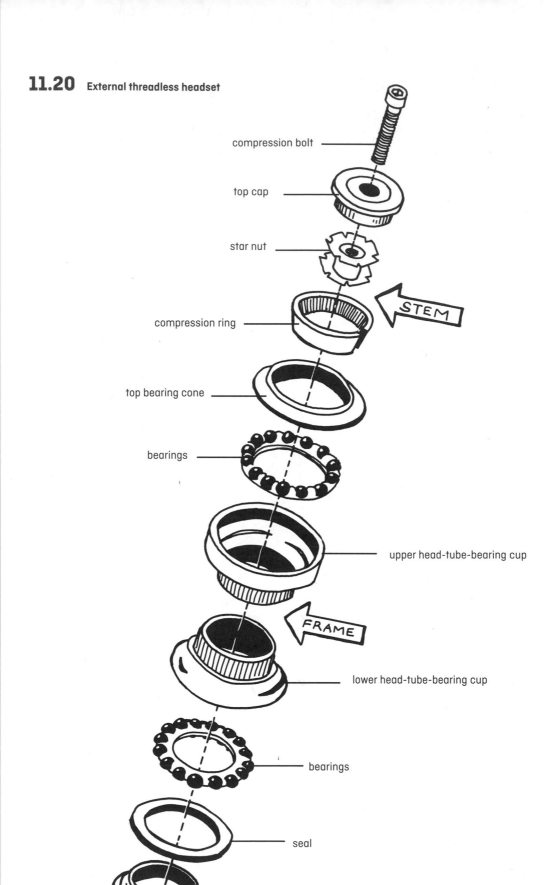

compression bolt

top cap

star nut

compression ring

STEM

top bearing cone

bearings

upper head-tube-bearing cup

FRAME

lower head-tube-bearing cup

bearings

seal

fork-crown race

11.21 Exploded cupless (drop-in) internal cartridge-bearing headset

11.22 Exploded inset (or zero stack) press-in internal headset with lipped cups

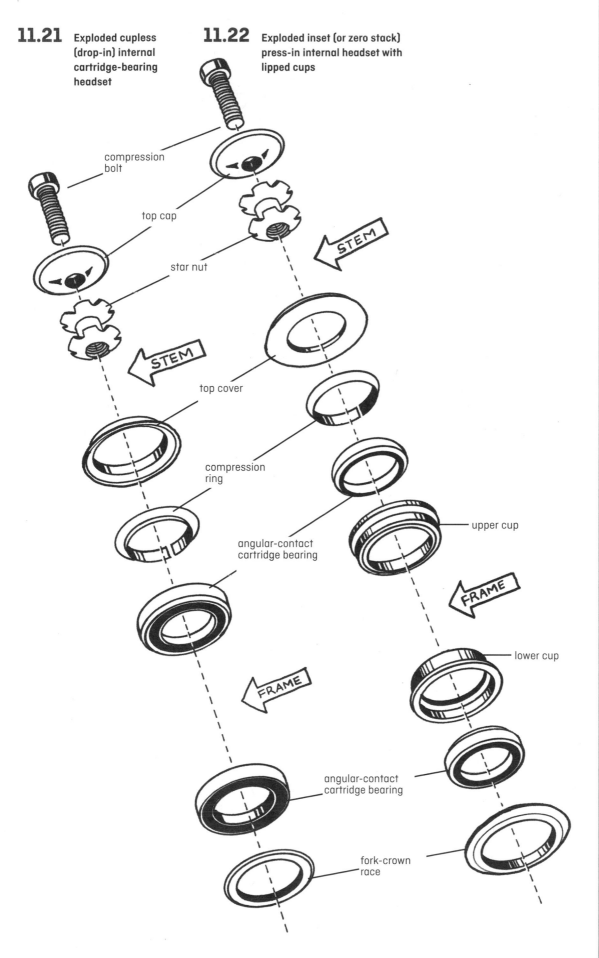

compression bolt

top cap

star nut

STEM

STEM

top cover

compression ring

angular-contact cartridge bearing

upper cup

FRAME

lower cup

FRAME

angular-contact cartridge bearing

fork-crown race

11.23 **Threaded headset**

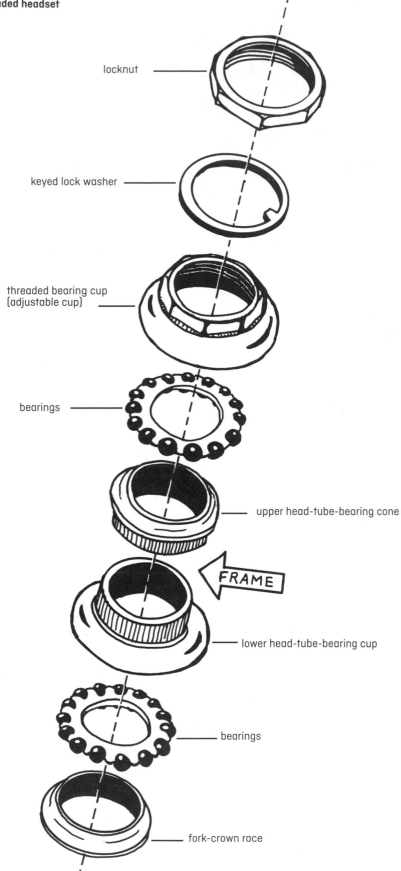

locknut

keyed lock washer

threaded bearing cup
(adjustable cup)

bearings

upper head-tube-bearing cone

FRAME

lower head-tube-bearing cup

bearings

fork-crown race

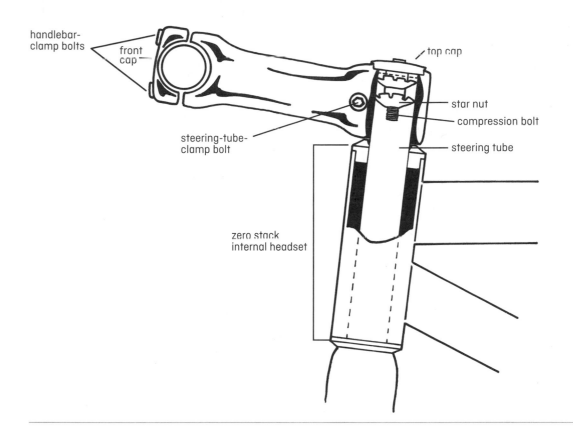

handlebar-clamp bolts

front cap

top cap

star nut

compression bolt

steering tube

steering-tube-clamp bolt

zero stack internal headset

---

xi-14

HEADSET ASSEMBLY

The Dia-Compe (now Cane Creek) AheadSet was the first threadless headset (Fig. 11.20), a lightweight system that eliminates the stem quill, bolt, and wedge of a threaded system. The threadless system's clamped connection between the handlebar and the stem saves weight and is more rigid, too.

On a threadless headset, the top cup or cone and a conical compression ring slide onto the steering tube (Figs. 11.20–11.22, 11.25, 11.26). The stem clamps around the top of the steering tube, above the compression ring and top cover. When its conical base is pressed into the beveled edges of the bore of the top bearing cup or cone, the compression ring keeps the top bearing cup or cone centered on the steering tube.

For forks with metal steering tubes, whether steel, aluminum, or titanium, a star nut—a nut with two layers of sharp, spring-steel teeth sticking out from it (originally dubbed the "Star Fangled Nut" by Dia-Compe)—fits into the steering tube and grabs its inner walls (Fig. 11.24). For steering tubes made of carbon fiber, an expandable insert (Fig. 11.27) or a glue-in insert with a threaded hole for the top-cap bolt replaces the standard star nut and serves the dual purpose of anchoring the top cap and protecting the steering tube from being crushed by the stem clamp.

The top cap pushes the stem clamp down to adjust the headset by means of the long compression bolt threaded into the star nut (Fig. 11.24) or into the crush-prevention insert in a carbon steering tube (Fig. 11.27). The stem clamp secured around the steering tube holds the headset in adjustment.

STEMS, HANDLEBARS, AND HEADSETS

11.25 Campagnolo Hiddenset drop-in-style (non-press-in) integrated headset

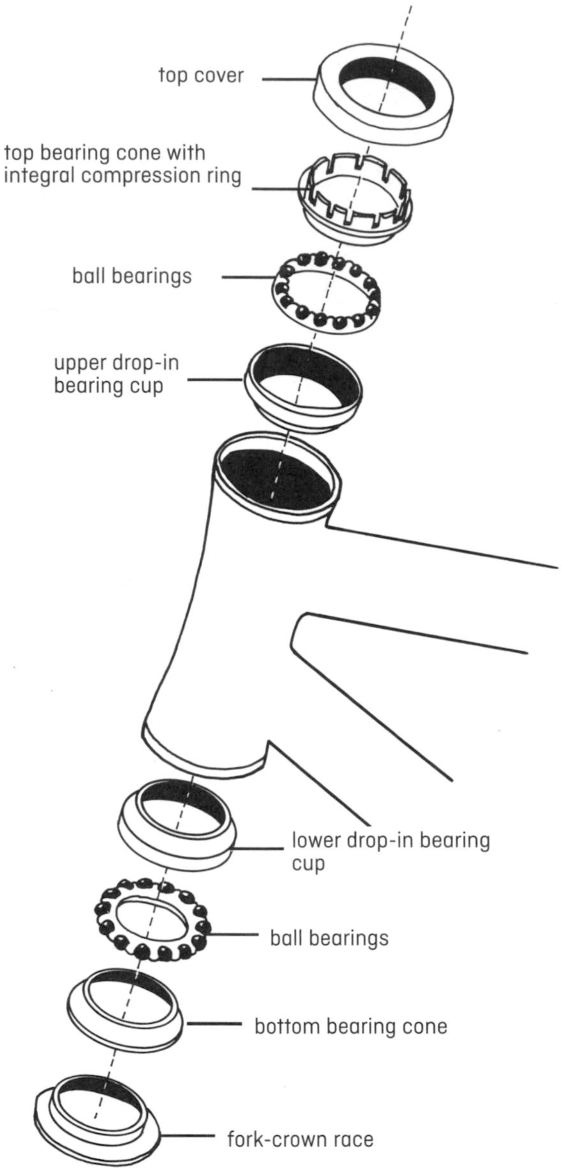

top cover

top bearing cone with integral compression ring

ball bearings

upper drop-in bearing cup

lower drop-in bearing cup

ball bearings

bottom bearing cone

fork-crown race

11.26 Trek E2 cupless integrated headset with tapered steering tube and differentially sized bearings

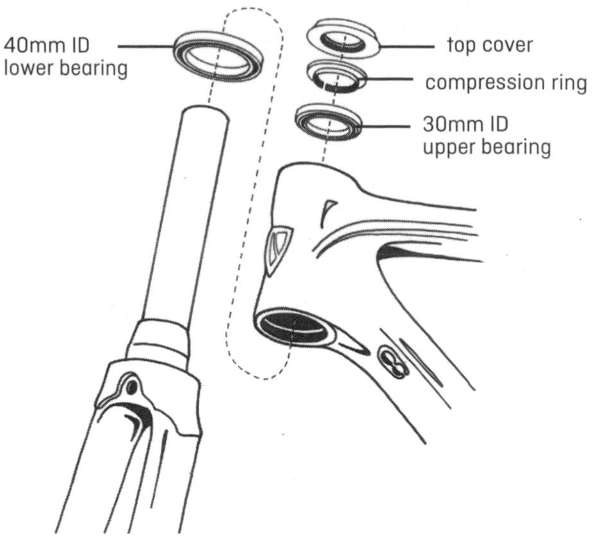

40mm ID lower bearing

top cover

compression ring

30mm ID upper bearing

11.27 Inserting an expandable support plug into a carbon-fiber fork steering tube

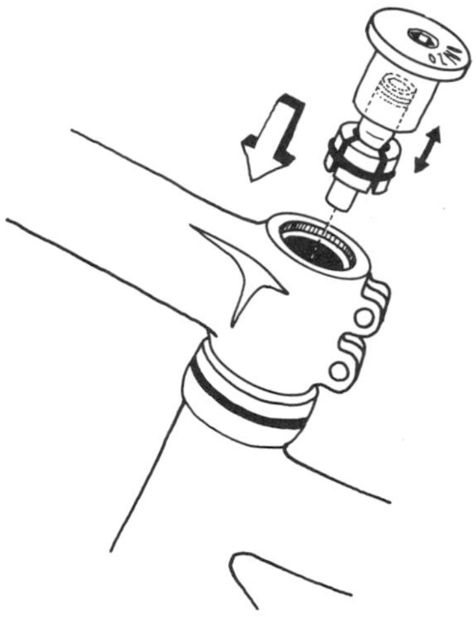

The latest generation of headset is the threadless internal type, or integrated headset, concealed inside the frame's head tube (Figs. 11.21, 11.22, 11.24–11.26). Whereas standard threadless and threaded headsets have bearing cups above and below the ends of the head tube (Figs. 11.20, 11.23), integrated headsets have bearings seated inside the head tube. Some types of integrated headsets have no press-in cups; either the bearings roll on bearing cups that drop into the flared head tube and rest on machined shelves within the head tube itself (Fig. 11.25), or the headset has angular-contact cartridge bearings that drop into the same style of flared head tube and rest without a cup on those machined or molded shelves within the head tube (Figs. 11.21, 11.26). Other types of internal headsets, called "zero stack" or "inset," have press-in cups with thin flanges that extend out to the edges of the head tube (Figs. 11.22, 11.24). Otherwise, integrated headsets are identical to, and are adjusted in the same way as, original threadless headsets.

Threaded headsets are different. The top bearing cup on a threaded headset has wrench flats, a keyed lock washer stacked on top of it, and a locknut that covers the top of the steering tube. That locknut tightens against the keyed lock washer and threaded cup (Fig. 11.23). Extra spacers may be included under the locknut.

Many headsets—threaded or threadless—use individual ball bearings held in some type of steel or plastic retainer or "cage" (Figs. 11.20, 11.23, 11.25) so that you are not chasing dozens of separate balls around when you work on the

bike. A variation on this has needle bearings held in conical plastic retainers (Fig. 11.28) riding on conical steel bearing surfaces.

Cartridge-bearing headsets usually employ "angular-contact" bearings (Figs. 11.21, 11.22, 11.26, 11.29, 11.35), since normal cylindrical cartridge bearings (Fig. 6.33) cannot take the side forces encountered by the lower bearing of a headset. Each angular-contact cartridge bearing is a separate, sealed, internally greased unit.

---

xi-15

CHECK HEADSET ADJUSTMENT

If the headset is too loose, it will rattle or clunk while you ride. You may even notice some play (back-and-forth movement) in the fork as you apply the front brake. If the headset is too tight, the fork will be difficult to turn or will feel rough to rotate.

1. **Check for headset looseness.** Hold the front brake and rock the bike forward and back. Try it with the front wheel pointed straight ahead and then with the wheel turned at 90 degrees to the bike. Feel for play at the lower head cup with your other hand. If there is play, you need to adjust the headset because it is too loose. If the headset is loose, skip to the appropriate adjustment section, §xi-16 or §xi-17.

2. **Check for headset tightness.** Turn the handlebar back and forth with the front wheel off the ground. Feel for any binding or stiffness of movement. Also, check for the chunk-chunk-chunk movement to fixed positions characterizing a pitted headset (if you feel this, you need a new headset; skip to §xi-20). Lean the bike to one side and then the other; the fork should turn as the bike is leaned (be aware that cable housings can resist the turning of the front wheel). Lift

11.28 Needle bearings

11.29 Lower parts of a cartridge-bearing headset

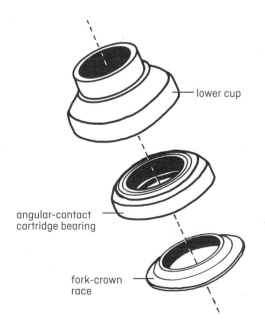

lower cup

angular-contact cartridge bearing

fork-crown race

the bike by the saddle so that it is tipped down at an angle with both wheels off the ground. Turn the handlebar one way and let go. See whether it returns to center quickly and smoothly on its own. If the headset does not turn easily on any of these steps, it is too tight, and you should skip to the appropriate adjustment section, §xi-16 or §xi-17.

3. **Check for loose parts on threaded headsets.** If the headset is a threaded model, try to turn the top nut and the threaded cup by hand. They should be so tight against each other that they can only be loosened with wrenches. If you can tighten or loosen either part by hand, even if it passed tests 1 and 2, you still need to adjust the headset; go to §xi-17.

xi-16

ADJUSTING A THREADLESS HEADSET

LEVEL 1

Adjusting a threadless headset—whether it is an internal (or "integrated") type (Figs. 11.21, 11.22, 11.24–11.26) or an external type (Figs. 11.4, 11.20)—is much easier than adjusting a threaded one. It's a level 1 procedure and usually only takes a hex key or two.

a. First steps

1. **Check the headset adjustment (§xi-15).** Determine whether the headset is too tight or too loose.
2. **Loosen the bolt or bolts that clamp the stem to the steering tube.**
3. **Adjust the headset by turning the top-cap compression bolt.** Be careful not to overtighten it, which will put too much pressure on the bearings and eventually pit the headset. If you're using a torque wrench, Dia-

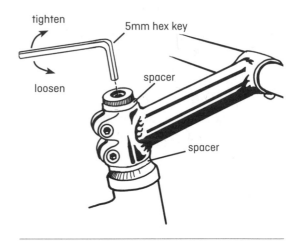

11.30 Loosening and tightening the compression bolt on a threadless headset

Compe recommends a tightening torque on this bolt of 22 in-lbs (2.5 N-m), which is a very low torque. This is a good place to start, but your headset may require a different torque for proper adjustment.

a. If the headset is too tight, loosen the compression bolt on the top cap about $\frac{1}{16}$th of a turn (Fig. 11.30). This step usually takes a 5mm hex key, but on many expander inserts for carbon-fiber steering tubes (Fig. 11.27), the top cap itself is turned with a 6mm hex key.

b. If the headset is too loose, tighten the compression bolt on the top cap about $\frac{1}{16}$th of a turn (Fig. 11.30) by using a 5mm hex key (sometimes 6mm).

NOTE: *Not all threadless stems are adjusted with the top-cap system. DiaTech threadless headsets have no top cap. Instead, a clamping collar below the stem adjusts headset tension. The stem is first clamped in place. The collar is beveled on the inside from both ends, and it slides down an externally beveled ring above it as you tighten the clamp screw to put pressure on the headset. As soon as you loosen the stem, the headset comes out of adjustment.*

Adjustment problems

If the cap does not move down and push the stem down, redo step 2, making sure the stem is not stuck to the steering tube.

Another hindrance occurs if the conical compression ring (Figs. 11.20–11.22, 11.25, 11.26) is stuck to the steering tube, preventing adjustment via the top-cap bolt. Remove the top cap, stem, spacers, and headset top cover first to address this problem.

With most (i.e., non-Campagnolo) compression rings, which are simply cone-shaped pieces split on one side (Figs. 11.20–11.22, 11.26), you need only tap the steering tube down with a mallet and then push the fork back up to free the compression ring. Grease the ring and the steering tube, and reassemble.

With a Campagnolo threadless headset (either an integrated Hiddenset [Fig. 11.25] or a standard external one [Fig. 11.31]), the compression ring is plastic and is conical on both ends. Its bottom end presses into the beveled hole in the top cone, but its turreted top end is also conical and presses into the bore of the headset top cover, which is beveled toward the bottom. Pushing down on the top cover (via the compression bolt pushing down on the stem) simply pinches the compression ring tighter in place, rather than pushing it down. Instead, you must flip the top cover upside down (Fig. 11.31) so that the nonbeveled end of its through-hole is against the turreted top edge of the compression ring. Now pushing down on it will push the compression ring down to preload the headset bearings by seating the top cone into them. Then flip the top cap back over (Fig. 11.32), put it back in place, and reassemble the spacers, stem, top cap, and compression bolt.

If neither the stem nor the compression ring is stuck, yet the cap still does not push the stem down, the steering tube may be so long that it is

11.31 Seating a Campagnolo threadless headset 1

11.32 Seating a Campagnolo threadless headset 2

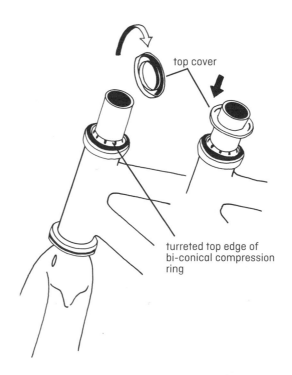

STEMS, HANDLEBARS, AND HEADSETS

hitting the lip of the top cap and preventing the cap from pushing the stem down. The steering tube's top should be either 3–5mm below the rim of the stem clamp (Fig. 11.10) or, ideally, 3–5mm below the rim of the spacer(s) placed above the stem (see the Pro Tip on spacers in carbon steering tubes). If the steering tube is too long, add a spacer above or below the stem, or use a flat file to make the steering tube shorter. Some top caps have thicker edge lips than others and require more space down to the top of the steering tube to avoid bottoming out on it.

Another thing that can thwart adjustment is the star nut not being installed deeply enough, so that the cap bottoms out on the star nut. The highest point of the star nut should be 12–15mm below the top of the steering tube. With metal steering tubes, tap the star nut deeper with a star nut installation tool, or put the bolt through the top cap, thread it five or six turns into the star nut, and gently tap it in with a soft hammer; the top cap is used to keep the star nut going in straight. Some top caps have taller center sections than others and require deeper insertion of the star nut to avoid bottoming out on it.

With a carbon steering tube, first loosen the aluminum expander with a 5mm hex key (Fig. 11.27). Next, unscrew its top cap a turn or two with a 6mm hex key. By hand, push the assembly farther into the steering tube until the top cap stops it, and reexpand the plug with a 5mm hex key. Finally, tighten the top cap down (22 in-lbs, or 2.5 N-m, of torque is standard) against the top of the stem to adjust the headset.

Once you have fixed the cause of the adjustment problem, return to step 1.

b. Final steps

4. **Tighten the stem's steering tube clamp bolt, or bolts.** Ideally, use a torque wrench to torque spec (see Appendix E).

5. **Recheck the headset adjustment.** Repeat steps 2–4 if necessary. With some integrated headsets, you may need a 1mm shim or two under the top bearing cover so that the edges of the cover do not drag and scrape on the top end of the head tube.

6. **Check alignment.** If the headset is adjusted properly, make sure the stem is aligned straight with the front wheel, and go ride.

xi-17

ADJUSTING A THREADED HEADSET

LEVEL 2

The secret to good adjustment is simultaneously controlling the steering tube, the adjustable cup, and the locknut as you tighten the latter two together.

NOTE: *Perform the adjustment with the stem installed. Not only does it give you something to hold on to that keeps the fork from turning during the process, but there are slight differences in adjustment when the stem is in place as opposed to when it is not. Tightening the stem bolt inside a threaded steering tube (Fig. 11.8) can sometimes bulge the walls of the steering tube slightly, just enough for it to shorten the steering tube and tighten a previously perfect headset adjustment.*

1. **Check for proper adjustment.** Following the steps outlined in §xi-15, determine whether the headset is too loose or too tight.

2. **Prepare your headset wrenches.** Put a pair of headset wrenches that fit the headset on the headset's top nut (the locknut) and top bearing cup (threaded cup or adjustable cup). Headset nuts come in a wide variety of sizes, so make sure you have purchased the proper wrench size. The standard wrench size for a road bike is 32mm. Place the wrenches so that the top one is slightly off-

11.33 Offsetting the headset wrenches to loosen the locknut

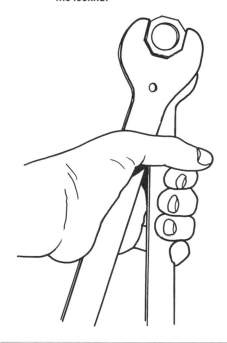

set to the left of the bottom wrench. That way you can squeeze them together to free the nut (Fig. 11.33).

NOTE: *People with small hands or weak grip will need to grab each wrench out at the end to get enough leverage.*

3. **Loosen the locknut (upper nut).** Hold the lower wrench in place and turn the top wrench counterclockwise about one-quarter turn to loosen the locknut. Breaking it loose may take considerable force, because it is generally tight to keep the headset from loosening.

4. **Adjust the headset.** If the headset was too loose, turn the lower (threaded) cup clockwise about 1/16 th of a turn while holding the stem with your other hand. Be careful not to overtighten the cup, which can ruin the headset by pressing the bearings into the bearing surfaces, making little indentations. The headset then stops at the indentations rather than turning smoothly, a condition known as a "pitted" or "brinelled" headset.

If the headset was too tight, loosen the threaded cup counterclockwise 1/16 th of a turn while holding the stem with your other hand. Loosen it until the bearings turn freely, but not to the point where play develops.

5. **Tighten the locknut.** Holding the stem, tighten the locknut clockwise with a single wrench. Make sure that the threaded cup does not turn while you tighten the locknut. If it does turn, either you are missing the keyed lock washer separating the cup and locknut (Fig. 11.23) or the washer you have is missing its key. In this case, remove the locknut (the stem has to come out first) and replace the keyed lock washer. Put the locknut on the steering tube so that the key engages the longitudinal groove in the steering tube. Thread on the locknut, install the stem, and redo the adjustment procedure.

NOTE: *You can adjust a headset without a keyed lock washer by working both wrenches simultaneously, but it is trickier, and the headset often will then come loose while you are riding.*

6. **Check the headset adjustment again.** Repeat steps 4 and 5 until the headset is properly adjusted.

7. **Tighten the locknut.** Once the headset is properly adjusted, place one wrench on the locknut and the other on the threaded cup. Tighten the locknut (clockwise) firmly against the washer(s) and threaded cup to hold the headset adjustment in place (Fig. 11.34).

8. **Check the headset adjustment again.** If it is off, follow steps 2–7 again. Once it is adjusted properly, make sure the stem is aligned with the front wheel before riding.

NOTE: *If you repeatedly get what you believe to be the proper adjustment and then find it to be too loose after you tighten the locknut and*

11.34 Offsetting the headset wrenches to tighten the locknut

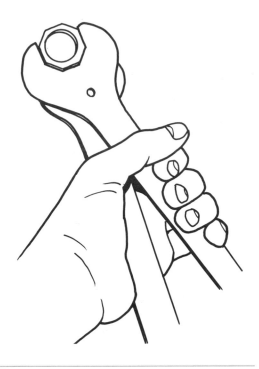

threaded cup against each other, the steering tube may be too long, causing the locknut to bottom out. Remove the stem and examine the inside of the steering tube. If the top end of the steering tube butts up against the top lip of the locknut, the steering tube is too long. Remove the locknut and add another spacer.

If you don't want to add another spacer, file 1–2mm from the steering tube. Be sure to deburr it inside and out after filing, and avoid leaving filings in the bearings or steering tube threads. Replace the locknut and return to step 5.

Wheels Manufacturing makes a headset locknut called the "Growler." It replaces the locknut and will not come loose, even on bumpy terrain. It threads on like a normal locknut and is adjusted the same way. The only difference between a Growler and a standard locknut is that the Growler is split on one side and has a pinch bolt bridging the split. Once the headset is adjusted, you tighten the pinch bolt to keep the locknut from unscrewing.

OVERHAUL THREADLESS HEADSET

LEVEL 2

These instructions apply to both internal (i.e., integrated) threadless headsets (Figs. 11.21, 11.22, 11.24–11.26) and external (Figs. 11.4, 11.20) threadless headsets.

Like any other bike part with bearings, headsets need periodic overhauls. If you use your bike regularly, you should probably overhaul a loose-bearing headset once a year. Headsets with cartridge bearings (Figs. 11.21, 11.22, 11.26, 11.29, 11.35) need less frequent overhaul due to the bearing seals on the cartridge. Some angular-contact bearings can be disassembled and cleaned, and some cannot. With those that cannot, if a bearing fails, you either replace the bearing or, if it has press-in bearings (like Chris King; Fig. 11.35), you replace the entire cup (§xi-20 and §xi-22).

Either place the bike upside down in the work stand or be ready to catch the fork when you remove the stem.

1. **Disconnect the front brake (Chapter 7).**
2. **Unscrew the top-cap compression bolt (Fig. 11.30) and the stem-clamp bolt(s).** Remove the top cap and the stem.
3. **Remove the top headset cup.** Slide the top cup or cover, conical compression ring (Fig. 11.20), and any spacers off the steering tube. Freeing the compression ring may require a

11.35 Chris King–style pressed-in cartridge bearing

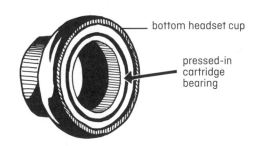

bottom headset cup

pressed-in cartridge bearing

tap with a mallet on the end of the steering tube, followed by pushing the fork back up and the top cup or cover back down.

4. **Pull the fork from the frame.**

5. **Remove any seals that surround the edges of the cups.** Remember the position and orientation of each.

6. **Remove the bearings from the cups.** Be careful not to lose any. Separate top and bottom sets if they are of different sizes.

7. **Check the bearings.** If the bearings are the type that will not come apart, check to see if they turn smoothly. If they do not, buy new ones and skip to step 8, or clean and regrease the bearings:

   a. With standard ball-bearing or needle-bearing headsets, put the bearings in a jar or old water bottle along with some citrus-based solvent. Shake. If the bearings from the top and bottom are of different sizes, keep them in separate containers to avoid confusion. Blot the bearings dry with a clean rag.

   b. Some cartridge bearings (Fig. 11.29) can be pulled apart and cleaned. Over a container to catch the balls, hold the bearing so that the beveled outer surface that fits into the cup faces down, and push up on the bearing's inner ring. The bearing should come apart—the inner ring will pop up and out with the bearings stuck to its outer surface. It may take a little rocking of the inner ring as you push up. If the bearing does not come apart, first pry off the plastic seal covering the bearings with a knife or razor blade, as in Figure 6.33, and then try again. Wipe the bearings and bearing rings and seals with a clean rag.

8. **Blot the bearings dry with a clean rag.** Plug the sink and wash the bearings in soap and water in your hands, just as if you were washing your palms by rubbing them together. Your hands will get clean for the assembly steps as well. Rinse the bearings thoroughly and blot them dry. Let them air-dry completely; an air compressor or hair dryer may come in handy here.

9. **Wipe all of the bearing surfaces with clean rags.** Wipe the steering tube clean.

10. **Inspect all bearing surfaces for wear and pitting.** If you see pits (separate indentations made by bearings in the bearing surfaces), you need to replace the headset. If so, skip to §xi-20.

11. **Apply fresh grease to all bearing surfaces.** If the headset has cartridge bearings, apply grease conservatively.

12. **Turn the bike upside down in the bike stand to begin assembly.**

    a. Place a set of bearings into the top cup and a set into the cup on the lower end of the head tube.

    b. With a Campagnolo or other integrated headset with drop-in bearing cups (Fig. 11.25), place a bearing cup into the seat in the bottom of the head tube. Place a greased set of ball bearings into the cup, with the bearing retainer oriented properly (see step 12d for tips on determining proper bearing orientation).

    c. With a cupless integrated headset (Figs. 11.21, 11.26), set a bearing into the seat in the bottom of the head tube itself. See step 12e regarding orientation.

    d. With loose-ball headsets, make sure you have the bearing retainer right side up so that only the bearings contact the bearing surfaces (note the different upper-cup styles and bearing orientations in Figs. 11.23, 11.20). If you have installed the retainer upside down, it will

STEMS, HANDLEBARS, AND HEADSETS

come in contact with one of the bearing surfaces, and the headset will not turn well. This is a bad thing, because assembling and riding it that way will turn the retainer into jagged chunks of broken metal. To be safe, double- and triple-check the retainer placement by turning each cup pair and bearing in your hand before proceeding. Most loose-ball headsets have the bearings set up identically top and bottom (Fig. 11.23). The top piece of each pair is a cup, and the bottom piece is a cone; the bearing retainer rides the same way in both sets. Some headsets, however, place both cups (and hence the bearing retainers) facing outward from the head tube (Fig. 11.20).

NOTE: *If the ball bearings are loose with no bearing retainer, stick the balls into the grease in the cups one at a time, making sure that you replace the same number you started with in each cup.*

    e. With angular-contact cartridge bearings, the beveled end faces into the cup (Fig. 11.29) or into the seat machined or molded inside of the head tube (Figs. 11.21, 11.26).

13. **Reinstall any seals that you removed from the headset parts.**

14. **Drop the fork into the head tube so that the lower headset bearing set seats properly (Fig. 11.36).**

15. **For Campagnolo headsets only:** With a Campagnolo or other integrated headset with drop-in cups (Fig. 11.25), place a bearing cup into the seat in the top of the head tube. Otherwise, skip this step.

16. **Install the upper bearing.** Slide first the bearing and then the top cup or cone (not required with a cartridge bearing) onto the steering tube. Keep the bike upside down at

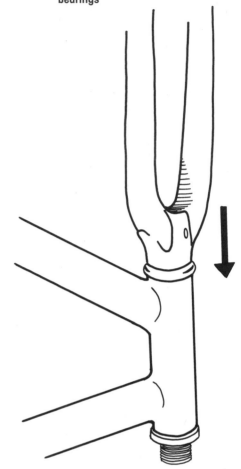

11.36 Setting the fork in the head tube to seat bearings

this point to keep the fork in place and prevent grit from falling into the bearings as you slide on the parts above it.

17. **Install the compression ring.** Grease the compression ring and slide it onto the (greased) steering tube, so that the narrower end slides into the conical space in the top of the top cup or cone or angular-contact cartridge bearing (Figs. 11.20–11.22, 11.25, 11.26).

NOTE: *On a Campagnolo threadless headset (integrated or external), there is a plastic biconical compression ring inserted into the top bearing cone (Fig. 11.25), and it acts like a normal split compression ring to center the top cone over the bearings. The upper edge of the plas-*

tic compression ring is notched like a turreted castle tower. Above this part comes the top bearing cover, whose inner edge is beveled for the turreted top conical edge of the plastic compression ring. To preload the bearings, you must first install the top bearing cover upside down (Fig. 11.31) and then push down on it. This preloads the bearings by pushing the top cone down. If you install the top bearing cover in its standard orientation before the top cone and plastic compression ring are slid down far enough to preload the bearings, the beveled inner edge of the top bearing cover will pinch the turreted upper conical edge of the plastic compression ring in place and not allow it to slide down farther. Once you have pushed the bearing cone down fully in this manner, flip the top bearing cover right side up and put it in place over the cone and compression ring (Fig. 11.32).

18. **Slide on any spacers you had under the stem.**

19. **Slide on the stem.** Tighten one stem-clamp bolt to hold it in place.

20. **Turn the bike over and inspect your work.** Check that the stem clamp or, ideally, the top spacer above the stem extends 3–5mm above the top of the steering tube (Fig. 11.10) and that the star nut is 12–15mm down in the steering tube. If they are, install the top cap on the top of the stem clamp and steering tube, and screw the compression bolt into the star nut (Fig. 11.30).

21. **If the steering tube is too long, remove the stem.** Add a spacer that extends 3–5mm above the top of the steering tube. If the steering tube is too short, remove spacers from below the stem, if there are any. If there are no spacers to remove, try a new stem with a shorter clamp.

22. **Adjust the headset (§xi-16).**

23. **Reconnect and adjust the front brake.**

OVERHAUL THREADED HEADSET

LEVEL 2

Like any other bike part with bearings, headsets need periodic overhauls. If you use your bike regularly, you should probably overhaul a loose-bearing headset once a year. Headsets with sealed cartridge bearings usually never need to be overhauled; if a bearing fails, you either replace the bearing (such as the standard type shown in Fig. 11.29) or, if the headset has pressed-in bearings (like Chris King; Fig. 11.35), you replace the entire cup. If you have a standard cartridge-bearing headset, continue with these instructions. If you are replacing a Chris King or other headset cup with a pressed-in bearing, move on to the instructions for headset removal and installation (§xi-20 and §xi-22).

A bike stand is highly recommended when overhauling a headset.

1. **Disconnect the front-brake cable (Chapter 7).**

2. **Remove the stem.** Loosen the stem bolt three turns, tapping the bolt down with a hammer to free the wedge (Fig. 11.11), and pulling it out.

3. **Either turn your bike upside down or be prepared to catch the fork as you remove the upper part of the headset.** To remove the top headset cup, unscrew the locknut and threaded cup with headset wrenches: Place one wrench on the locknut and one on the threaded cup. Loosen the locknut by turning it counterclockwise. It's easiest if the top wrench is angled just to the left of the lower wrench, and you squeeze them together (Fig. 11.33). Unscrew the locknut and the cup from the steering tube. The headset washer or washers will slide off the steering tube as you unscrew the threaded cup.

4. **Pull the fork out of the frame.**

5. **Remove any seals that surround the edges of the cups.** Make a point of remembering the position and orientation of each.

6. **Remove the bearings from the cups.** If the balls are loose, be especially careful not to lose any. Separate top and bottom sets if they are of different sizes.

7. **Clean or replace the bearings.**

   a. With standard ball-bearing (Fig. 11.23) or needle-bearing headsets (Fig. 11.28), put the bearings in a jar or old water bottle along with some citrus-based solvent. Shake. If the bearings from the top and bottom are of different sizes, keep them in separate containers to avoid confusion.

   b. With cartridge bearings (Fig. 11.29), check to see whether they turn smoothly. If they do not, buy new ones. Either way, skip to step 9.

8. **Blot the bearings dry with a clean rag.** Plug the sink and wash the bearings in soap and water in your hands, just as if you were washing your palms by rubbing them together. This helps keep your hands clean for the assembly steps as well. Rinse bearings thoroughly and blot them dry. Let them air-dry completely.

9. **Wipe all of the bearing surfaces with clean rags.** Wipe the steering tube clean, especially the threads, and wipe the inside of the head tube clean with a rag stuck to the end of a screwdriver.

10. **Inspect all bearing surfaces for wear and pitting.** If you see pits (separate indentations made by bearings in the bearing surfaces), you need to replace the headset. If that's the case, skip to §xi-20.

11. **Apply grease to all bearing surfaces.** A thin film will do, especially if you are using sealed cartridge bearings.

12. **Turn the bike upside down in the bike stand to begin assembly.** Place a set of bearings in the top cup and a set in the cup on the lower end of the head tube. Make sure you have the bearing retainer right side up so that only the bearing balls contact the bearing surfaces. If you have installed the retainer upside down, it will come in contact with one of the bearing surfaces, and the headset will not turn well. This is a bad thing, because assembling and riding it that way will turn the retainer into jagged chunks of broken metal. To be safe, double- and triple-check the retainer placement by turning each cup pair in your hand before proceeding.

   a. Most headsets have the bearings set up symmetrically top and bottom (Fig. 11.23). This way, the top piece of each pair is a cup, and the bottom piece is a cone; the bearing retainer rides the same way in both sets. Some headsets, however, place both cups facing outward from the head tube (Fig. 11.20), so that the bearing retainers are asymmetrical on either end of the head tube. Also, watch for asymmetry in ball size; some Ritchey and Campagnolo headsets have smaller balls on top than on the bottom.

NOTE: *Stronglight, Ritchey, and similar needle-bearing headsets come with two pairs of separate conical steel rings. These are the bearing surfaces that sit on either side of each needle bearing (Fig. 11.28). You will find that one conical ring of each set is smaller than the other ring. Place the smaller one on the lower surface supporting the bearing: For the bottom bearing, place the smaller ring on the fork-crown race; for the top bearing, place the smaller ring on the cup on top of the head tube.*

   b. If the ball bearings are loose with no bearing retainer, stick the balls into the grease in the cups one at a time, making sure that you replace the same number you started with in each cup.

13. **Reinstall any seals that you removed from the headset parts.**

14. **Drop the fork into the head tube so that the lower headset bearing set seats properly (Fig. 11.36).**

15. **Screw the top cup, with the bearings in it, onto the steering tube.** Keeping the bike upside down at this point keeps the fork in place and prevents grit from falling into the bearings as you thread the cup on.

16. **Turn the bike upright.** Slide on the keyed lock washer (Fig. 11.23). Align the key in the groove of the steering tube threads. Screw on the locknut with your hand.

17. **Grease the stem quill and insert it into the steering tube (Fig. 11.8).** Make certain that it is in at least as deep as the imprinted limit line, and preferably a bit deeper. Align the stem with the front wheel and tighten the stem bolt.

18. **Reconnect the front brake.**

19. **Adjust the headset as outlined in §xi-17.**

xi-20

REMOVING THE HEADSET

LEVEL 3

1. **Disconnect the front brake (Chapter 7).** If the bike has a standard caliper brake attached to the fork crown, remove the front brake as well. Disc brake calipers and cantilever brakes can be left in place

2. **Open the headset and remove the fork.** Follow steps 1–4 in either §xi-18 or §xi-19, depending on headset type.

3. **Remove the bearings.**

   a. If you have a cupless integrated headset (Figs. 11.21, 11.26) with bearings seated on steps machined or molded into the head tube itself, just pull the bearings out and skip to step 5. If the drop-in headset is a Campagnolo Hiddenset (Fig. 11.25) or any other non-press-in integrated headset with bearing cups, pull out both bearing cups as well as the bearings from either end of the head tube and skip to step 5.

   b. For a headset with cups pressed into the head tube (Figs. 11.20, 11.22, 11.23), just pull out the bearings, unless they are pressed into the cups as in Figure 11.35.

4. **On nonintegrated headsets, remove the cups.** For a headset with cups pressed into the head tube (Figs. 11.20, 11.22–11.24), slide the solid end of the headset-cup remover (sometimes called a headset "rocket," a wonderfully evocative name, as you'll see) through one end of the head tube (Fig. 11.37). As you pull the headset-cup remover through the head tube, the splayed-out tangs on the opposite end· of the tool will pull through the cup and spread out.

   a. Remove the first cup. Strike the solid end of the cup remover with a hammer, and drive the cup out (Fig. 11.38). Be careful as you do this, as the remover, or rocket, is liable to launch the cup across the room if hit with sufficient force.

   b. Remove the other cup. Place the cup-remover rocket into the opposite end of the head tube and repeat step 4a on the opposite end of the end tube.

5. **Remove the fork-crown race.**

   Some new integrated-headset forks have no crown race; the bearing just sits right atop the fork crown as in the Trek system in Figure 11.26; with one of these, just lift the bearing off if you did not already do so by pulling it out of the cup in step 3. Your headset removal is done. Easy peasy.

Old steel road bike fork crowns with 1-inch steering tubes in them are narrower than the diameter of the headset fork-crown race, so that you can elegantly remove the crown race with a U-shaped crown-race remover (step 5a) or an appropriately sized bench vise (step 5b). For forks whose crown race is not larger in diameter than the crown, skip to steps 5c and 5d.

a. To use an old-school U-shaped crown-race remover, stand the fork upside down on the steering tube. Place the U-shaped crown-race remover so that it straddles the underside of the fork crown and its ledges engage the front and back edges of the crown race. Smack the top of the crown-race remover with a hammer to knock the race off (Fig. 11.39).

b. To use a bench vise, slide the fork into the vise, straddling its center shaft. Tighten the vise so that its faces ever so lightly contact the front and back of the fork crown with the lower side of the crown race sitting on top of them. Put a block of wood on the top of the steering tube to pad it. Strike the block with a hammer to drive the fork down and knock the crown race off (Fig. 11.40).

c. If the fork crown is larger in diameter than the fork-crown race and you don't have the slick tool mentioned in step 5d, you will need to knock the race off with a screwdriver—preferably an old, cheap screwdriver that you no longer use to drive screws. Turn the fork upside down so that the top of the steering tube is sitting on the workbench, or clamp the steering tube horizontally in a bike stand or in a vise between a pair of V-blocks. If there are notches at the front and back

11.37 Inserting a headset-cup removal tool or "rocket"

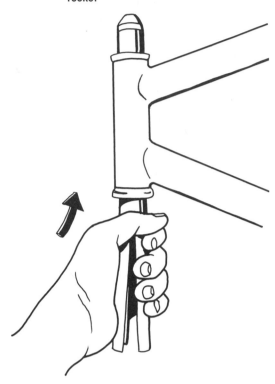

11.38 Removing a headset cup

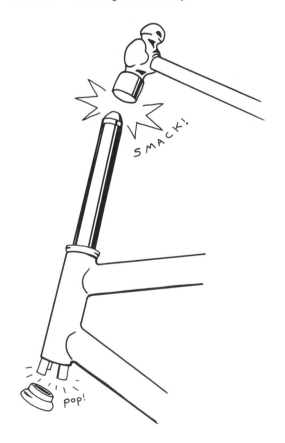

11.39 Removing the fork-crown race with a crown-race remover

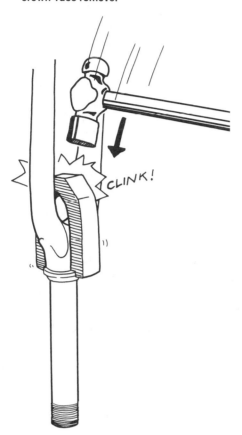

of the fork crown under the bearing race, place the blade of a large screwdriver into the notch on one side of the crown so that it butts against the bottom of the headset fork-crown race. If there is no notch, work the screwdriver blade under the race however you can; you may need to first drive a thin blade between the race and fork crown to open a gap. Tap the handle of the screwdriver with a hammer to drive the crown race up the steering tube a bit (Fig. 11.41). Move the screwdriver to the other side of the crown and tap it again to move that side of the crown race up a bit. Continue in this way, alternately tapping either side of the crown race up the steering tube, bit by bit, until it gets past the enlarged section of the steering tube and slides off.

d. If you are fortunate enough to have a Park Universal Crown-Race Remover

11.40 Removing the fork-crown race with a vise

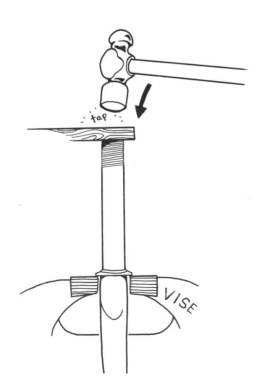

11.41 Removing the fork-crown race with a screwdriver

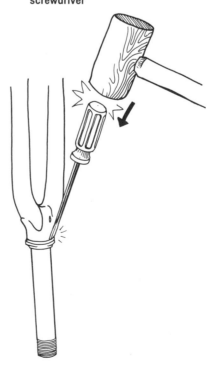

STEMS, HANDLEBARS, AND HEADSETS

(Fig. 1.4), use it! First back off the screw on the top enough that the tool will slide down over the steering tube until the blades are below the fork-crown race. Using the screws at its base, finger-tighten the blades in under the fork-crown race until they stop. Then tighten the handle of the long screw on top to pull the crown race off its seat.

xi-21

FRAME AND FORK PREPARATION PRIOR TO INSTALLATION OF HEADSET

LEVEL 3

The frame and fork need to be properly prepared for the headset prior to installation. If new frames and forks are not properly prepared prior to sale, the headset will bind up at some steering angles and be too loose at others. Proper frame and fork preparation requires tools that only some shops possess.

NOTE: *You can do nothing to prep the head tube on a carbon frame, unless it has pressed-in internal aluminum sleeves.*

1. **If this is a new frame (or one that has "eaten" headsets in the past):** Ream and face the head tube, if it is a frame for external-cup headsets (Figs. 11.1, 11.20, 11.23) or for an internal headset with cups (Fig. 11.24). If you do not have the tools for this, have a bike shop equipped with the proper tools do it for you. Reaming makes the head-tube ends perfectly round inside and of the correct diameter for the headset cups to press in. Facing makes the ends of the head tube parallel so that the bearings can turn smoothly and uniformly. The tool that simultaneously reams and faces the end of the head tube is pictured in Figure 1.4.

2. **If this is a metal bike frame for a cupless (non-press-in) integrated headset (Fig. 11.21), like a Campagnolo Hiddenset (Fig. 11.25):** These frames will eat bearings in a hurry if the bearing seats are so badly machined inside the head tube that the bearings are not parallel. Fortunately, many shops have a tool to recut the bearing seats so that they are parallel.

3. **If the fork is a metal one:** The base of the steering tube also needs to be turned down to the correct diameter for the crown race. And the crown-race seat on the fork crown must be faced in a way that places the crown race parallel to the head-tube cups and perpendicular to the steering tube.

NOTE: *With a carbon-fiber fork, do not run a cutter over the crown-race seat; doing so could cut the carbon fibers. You can be fairly confident that the crown race is perpendicular to the steering tube, whose base should also be the correct diameter. As carbon forks are molded rather than welded or brazed together, it is easier to control these dimensions during manufacturing than machining them later, as on metal forks. The same goes for any type of suspension fork, as their parts are generally machined before assembly. If the crown-race seat is oversized or untrue, many shops have a tool that simultaneously machines the outer dimension of the base of the steering tube and cuts the crown-race seat flat and perpendicular to the steering tube axis.*

4. **The fork steering tube (threaded or threadless) must also be cut to the proper length.** Remember, you can always go back and cut off more. You can't go back and add any, so be careful! You can wait until the headset (and stem and spacers, in the case of a threadless headset) is installed. Or you can figure out the length first.

Threadless headsets

a. The safest way to make sure you don't cut the steering tube too short is to install the headset, stem, and spacers onto the frame and fork first (§xi-22). Then cut the steerer to 3–5mm below the top of the spacer placed atop the stem (see the Pro Tip on cutting carbon steerers). With a steel or aluminum steerer, you can cut it to 3–5mm below the top edge of the stem (Fig. 11.10), but it's still preferable to have the steerer extend completely through the top of the stem clamp.

b. If you don't want to or can't install the headset yet, add the headset stack height (find it from the manufacturer or from Barnett's or Sutherland's manuals) to the length of the head tube, the spacers, and the stem clamp, and subtract 3mm from the total. This is the length the steering tube should be from fork crown to top. I recommend not cutting until the headset is assembled and the stem is installed so that you can see if you want some more spacers under the stem to raise the bar higher.

c. Cut off the steerer, and smooth and straighten its end as instructed in §xi-2, steps 6b–e.

Threaded headsets

a. The safest way to make sure you don't cut the steering tube too short is to install the headset first (§xi-22). Once a threaded headset is assembled, you can measure the amount of excess length as in Figure 11.42, remove the top nut, and add keyed lock washers (Fig. 11.23), adding up to 2mm taller than that gap in total. Or you can trim that much length from the top of the steering tube,

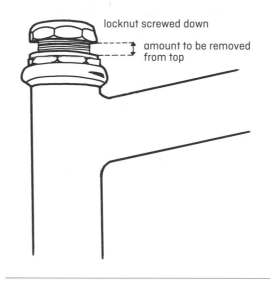

locknut screwed down

amount to be removed from top

deburring it inside and out afterward. Determining the steering tube length for an already installed threadless headset is detailed in §xi-2.

b. If you choose to cut the steering tube before installing the headset and are using a threaded headset, you need to know the headset's stack height. It is often listed in the headset owner's manual, or a bike shop can look it up in Barnett's manual or Sutherland's manual. Armed with this number, measure the length of the frame's head tube and add the headset stack height to this length. If you are adding extra spacers or brake-cable hangers between the headset nuts, add their thickness in as well. The resulting value represents the length that the steering tube must be. If the steering tube is already more than 5mm shorter than this sum, you need to find another headset with a shorter stack height (or, if you have included spacers, remove as many as needed).

c. If the steering tube is longer than this sum, you can cut the tube down to

STEMS, HANDLEBARS, AND HEADSETS

size. Measure twice and mark the cut line well, so you only have to cut once. Thread the headset adjustable cup onto the steering tube well below the cut point, and then cut the steering tube to the correct length with a hacksaw, following a thread for straightness. Use a flat file to square off the cut, and a round file to remove the burrs the hacksaw left on the inside and outside edges of the steering tube end. Then unscrew the adjustable cup, which, as it comes off the steering tube, will dress the threads.

11.43 Setting the fork-crown race

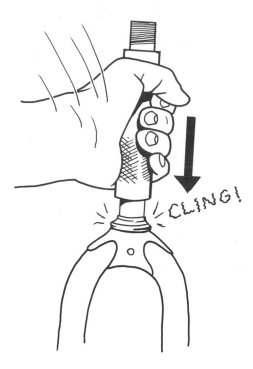

xi-22

INSTALL HEADSET

LEVEL 3

With the exception of the super-simple assembly of a frame like the Trek Madone (Fig. 11.26), there is really no good way to install a headset without at least a fork-crown-race punch (Fig. 11.43) and, for pressed-in cup frames, a headset cup press (Fig. 11.44). For most integrated headsets (Figs. 11.21, 11.25), you need only the former tool. If you do not have the necessary tools, it is better to take the parts to a bike shop for installation.

11.44 Pressing in headset cups with a headset press

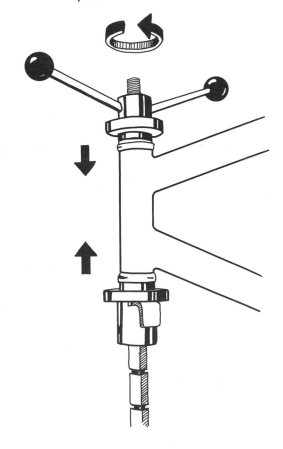

a. Headset installation in a Trek Madone (post-2006) and other frames with drop-in bearings and no races to press in the frame or on the fork

1. **Clean the parts.** Clean inside the ends of the head tube and around the base of the steering tube atop the fork crown; apply a thin layer of grease to those surfaces.

2. **Install the lower bearing.** Slide the bigger bearing down the (tapered) steering tube

onto the top of the fork crown (Fig. 11.26). On a Trek, the bearing is symmetrical; either side can face up.

3. **Install the fork.** Insert the steering tube up into the head tube from the bottom.

4. **Install the upper bearing.** Slide the smaller bearing down the steering tube into the bearing surface in the top end of the head tube. On a Trek, the bearing is symmetrical; either side can face up.

5. **Install the compression ring.** Slide the compression ring down the steering tube, narrow end first, and push it into the bore of the bearing.

6. **Install shims, if present.** Some frames will require 1mm shims between the compression ring and the bearing cover to prevent the edge of the bearing cover from rubbing on the edge of the head tube as the fork turns. If yours has the shims, install them.

7. **Install the bearing cover.** Slide the bearing cover down the steering tube against the compression ring or shim.

8. **Check clearances.** If the edges of the bearing cover rub on the edges of the head tube, pull the cover off and put in a 1mm shim. If the edge of the bearing cover is more than 1mm, remove a shim. The gap between the top edge of the head tube and the bottom edge of the bearing cover should be 0.5mm.

9. **Install the preload adjuster.** Install a steering tube support plug (Fig. 11.27) if the fork has a carbon steering tube. Install a star nut (Figs. 11.20, 11.24) if the fork has a metal steering tube.

10. **Install the headset spacers, stem, top cap, and compression bolt.**

11. **Adjust the headset (§xi-16).** Line the stem up with the front wheel, and tighten the stem.

b. Installation in a frame with a press-on fork-crown race, with or without pressed-in headset cups (external or internal)

1. **Lubricate the parts.** Put a thin layer of grease on the ends of the headset cups that will be pressed into the head tube, in the fork-crown-race bore, inside the ends of the head tube itself, and on the base of the steering tube.

2. **Install the crown race.** Slide the fork-crown race down on the fork steering tube until it hits the enlarged section at the bottom. Slide the crown-race punch up and down the steering tube, pounding the crown race down until it sits flat on top of its seat on the fork crown (Fig. 11.43). Some crown-race punches are longer and closed on the top and are meant to be hit with a hammer rather than slid up and down by hand. Hold the fork up against the light to see if there are any gaps between the crown race and the crown.

NOTE: *Thin crown races can be bent or broken by the crown-race punch. Chris King, Park Tool, and Shimano all offer support tools that sit over the race and distribute the impact from the punch. The Park punch, for instance, has three interchangeable ends (for each steering tube diameter). Hold the crown race against each of the three to see which one will best support the race while you strike the punch with a hammer.*

NOTE ON INTEGRATED HEADSETS: *For integrated-headset frames with a press-on fork-crown race, there are no bearing cups requiring installation in the frame, so there is no sense in continuing with these instructions. Instead, continue with the assembly following the instructions in §xi-22a, above, except note that the bearings will probably require a specific side to be up, since they won't be beveled on both ends like the Trek bearing. Make sure you install them right side up; the*

STEMS, HANDLEBARS, AND HEADSETS

beveled edge of the bearing must sit in the beveled seat in the frame. You can tell by looking at them and also by the way the headset turns.

3. **Install the headset cups.** By hand, place the headset cups into the ends of the head tube. Slide the headset press shaft through the head tube. Press the button on the detachable end of the tool and slide it onto the shaft until it bumps into one of the cups (Fig. 11.44). Or, with the press shown in Figures 8.25 and 8.27, screw the arms on as far as they need to go. This same method, and often the same press, can be used for internal (Fig. 11.22) and external (Figs. 11.20, 11.23) headsets with cups. You must make sure with internal cups that the press makes contact only with the outer cup flange and not the bearing seat. Some headset presses use a system of spacers and cones on both ends of the cups. Follow the instructions to set yours up properly. Whatever you do, be certain that the parts that make contact with the cups are not touching the precision surfaces the bearings roll in.

NOTE: *Chris King headsets have bearings that are pressed into the cups and cannot be removed (Fig. 11.35). If you use a headset press that pushes on the center of the cups, you will ruin the bearings. You need a press that pushes the outer part of the cup and does not touch the bearings. Chris King makes tool inserts that fit most headset presses, and Park has a headset press with large, flat ends for the purpose. On the other hand, some thin aluminum headset cups can be mashed by pushing on the outside of the cup with the flat surface of a headset press; stop pressing as soon as they reach the ends of the head tube. Otherwise, these cups need press inserts pushing on the edges of the bearings to support them under high loads.*

4. **Press the headset cups fully into place.** Hold the lower end of the cup press shaft with a wrench. That will keep the tool from turning as you press in the cups. Tighten the press by turning the top handle clockwise (Fig. 11.44). Keep tightening the tool until the cups are fully pressed into the ends of the head tube. Examine them carefully to make sure there are no gaps between the cups and the ends of the head tube.

NOTE: *You can easily crush thin headset cups with a flat-surface headset press, so be careful and stop when the cups reach the head tube.*

5. **Liberally apply grease to all bearing surfaces.** If you are using sealed cartridge bearings, a thin film will do.

6. **Assemble and adjust the headset.** Follow the directions in §xi-18 and §xi-16 for a threadless headset and those in §xi-19 and §xi-17 for a threaded headset.

xi-23

HEADSETS, STEMS, AND BARS FOR CYCLOCROSS

Given the mud bath a 'cross bike gets, the headset must be well sealed. The front tire is constantly flinging mud straight up at the bottom headset bearing, so the seal there has to be particularly good. The headset is no place to scrimp on a 'cross bike.

If the bike has cantilever brakes, you'll need a front-brake cable stop somewhere in the steering system. Although there are other ways to stop the front-brake cable housing before the bare cable runs to the straddle cable yoke (Figs. 7.27–7.36), the most common way is with a headset spacer that has a cable hanger on it (Fig. 7.8).

Regarding stem choice, your position on your 'cross bike will be similar to that on your road bike, so select a stem length and angle that give you a similar fit, at least to start with. You can adjust from there.

Regarding handlebar choice, the bar should be similar to the bar on your road bike. If your 'cross bar differs at all, it should be wider and have a shallower drop, so the height of your hands in the drops is closer to their height when riding on the lever hoods. The bar should have a round cross-section on the tops in case you decide to mount bar-top levers (Fig. 7.39).

xi-24

TROUBLESHOOTING STEM, HANDLEBAR, AND HEADSET PROBLEMS

a. Bar slips

Tighten the pinch bolt on the stem that holds the bar, but not beyond the maximum allowable torque (see Appendix E). With a front-opening stem, make sure that there is the same amount of space between the stem and the front plate on both edges of the front plate. With any stem, if the clamp closes on itself without holding the bar securely, check to see if the bar is deformed or of a smaller diameter than the stem was made to fit and if the stem clamp is cracked or stretched. Replace any questionable parts.

Especially with a carbon handlebar, smear or spray carbon assembly compound on the bar and inside the stem clamp (this often works to increase clamping force with an aluminum bar as well). Whether it's a paste or a spray, it expands against the clamp and holds the bar tighter.

Failing that, you can slide a shim made from a beer or soda can between the stem and bar to hold it better, but never do this on a carbon or superlight aluminum handlebar; even with a heavy bar, replacing parts is a safer option. There is always a reason why parts that are meant to fit together no longer do! With superlight stems and bars, you cannot just keep tightening the small clamp bolts as you can the larger bolts on heavy stems because you will strip threads and/or cause bar and stem failures.

b. Bar makes creaking noise while you are riding

Loosen the stem clamp, grease the area of the bar that is clamped in the stem, slide the bar back in place, and tighten the stem bolt. Or, better yet, use carbon assembly paste or spray as recommended in §xi-24a, above. Creaks are caused by two parts moving relative to each other, so filling those spaces with grease or assembly compound will quiet them down.

Sanding the hard anodized surface inside the stem clamp and on the clamping area of the bar can sometimes eliminate creaking.

If the bar has a sleeved center section rather than a bulged section, the bar could be creaking inside the sleeve. There's no cure for this; replace the bar.

Less commonly, creaking can also emanate from between the steering tube and the rear stem clamp. Apply grease (or, with carbon parts, carbon assembly paste or spray) inside the stem clamp and on the steerer.

c. Clip-on bar slips

Tighten the clip-on's clamp bolts.

d. Stem not pointed straight ahead

Loosen the bolt (or bolts) securing the stem to the fork steering tube, align the stem with the front wheel, and tighten the stem bolt (or bolts) again. With a threaded headset, the bolt you are interested in is a single vertical bolt on top of the stem; loosen it about two turns, and tap the top of the bolt with a hammer to disengage the wedge on the other end from the bottom of the stem (Fig. 11.11). With a threadless headset, there are one (Fig. 11.4), two (Fig. 11.5), or, rarely, three horizontal bolts pinching the stem around the steering tube that need to be loosened to turn the stem on the steering tube. Do not loosen the bolt on the top of the stem cap (Fig. 11.30); you'll have to readjust the headset if you do.

Line up the stem by eyeballing it with the front wheel, and tighten the stem bolt(s).

e. Fork and headset rattle or clunk when you are riding

The headset is too loose. Adjust the headset (see §xi-16 or §xi-17).

f. Stem-bar-fork assembly does not turn smoothly but instead stops in certain fixed positions

The headset is pitted and needs to be replaced (see §xi-20–§xi-22).

g. Stem-bar-fork assembly does not turn freely

The headset is too tight. The front wheel should swing easily from side to side when you lean the bike or lift the front end. Adjust the headset (see §xi-16 or §xi-17, depending on type).

h. Stem is stuck in or on fork steering tube

See §xi-6.

i. Turning the fork, you hit a tight spot; it turns freely through some of the range and is too tight at other points

The bearings are not running parallel to each other and perpendicular to the axis of the steering tube and head tube. It is possible that the fork-crown race and/or headset cup(s) are not pressed in fully against their seats. If you see gaps under any of these, try pressing them in again (see §xi-22). More likely, however, the surfaces on the frame and/or fork onto which the bearing cups and/or bearings sit are not cut parallel and concentric with the fork steerer and head tube. The fork and/or frame needs to be faced (see §xi-21). This only works with metal frames and forks, however. If you have these symptoms with a carbon frame and fork, there is nothing you can do to correct it. In that case, take the frame and fork to a bike shop or send them back to the manufacturer.

WHEEL BUILDING

*If you think you can or
think you can't, you're right.*
—Henry Ford

Congratulations! You have arrived at the task most often used to gauge the talent of a bike mechanic. Next to building a frame or fork, building a good set of wheels is a mechanic's most critical and creative task. Despite the air of mystery surrounding the art of wheel building, the construction of a good set of bicycle wheels is actually straightforward. I have not labeled any of the procedures in this chapter as level 1, 2, or 3 tasks, because apart from a few special tools, the art of wheel building isn't terribly difficult. It only requires concentration, patience, and a love of mechanical objects.

Wheels are the central component of a bike. For any bike to perform well, its wheels must be well made and properly tensioned. Turning a pile of small parts into a set of strong, light wheels on which you can corner and descend with confidence is quite rewarding, once you learn how. You will be amazed at what they can withstand, and you will no longer go through life thinking that building wheels is something only the "experts" do. With practice and patience, you can build wheels at your house that are as good as any custom-made set, and far superior to those built by machine.

This is not meant to be an exhaustive description of how to build all types of wheel spoking patterns. Entire books are devoted to the subject—justifiably so, because the bicycle wheel is an artful engineering miracle that deserves thoughtful exegesis. (If you are interested in a more comprehensive treatment of the subject of wheel building, I recommend *Barnett's Manual* by John Barnett, *The Art of Wheelbuilding* by Gerd Schraner, or *The Bicycle Wheel* by Jobst Brandt.)

You can, however, build great wheels following the methods presented here. The first section describes how to build a wheel laced in the classic "three-cross" spoking pattern, in which each spoke crosses three other spokes (Fig. 12.1). A later section (§xii-7) details how to build a radially spoked front wheel or a rear wheel spoked radially on one side and three-cross on the other side. So let's get started.

12.1   **The complete wheel with a three-cross spoke pattern**

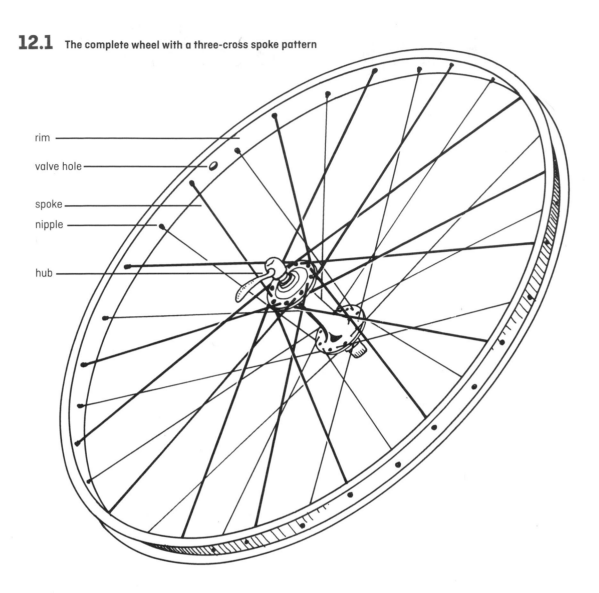

rim

valve hole

spoke

nipple

hub

12.2   **Spoke and nipple**

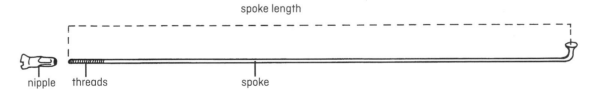

spoke length

nipple   threads   spoke

---

xii-1

PARTS AND TOOLS

Gather the parts you need: a rim, a hub (make sure that the hub has the same number of holes as the rim), and properly sized spokes and nip-

ples to match. Make sure you have the right-size spoke wrench for those nipples as well.

a. Spokes and nipples

I suggest getting the spokes from your local bike shop. That way, a mechanic can help make sure you get the right spoke lengths (Fig. 12.2) and can counsel you on which gauge (thickness) of spoke to select, as well as which rim makes sense for your weight, budget, and the kind of riding you do. If you will not be getting the spokes from a local shop, you can find the spoke lengths you need by using a number of online spoke calculators. The one I always use is at dtswiss.com. Remember when you calculate spoke length to specify that you will be using a three-cross spoking pattern (unless you are building a radial wheel [§xii-7] or other spoke pattern).

NOTE ON USING OLD SPOKES: *If you are replacing a rim on an old wheel, do not use the old spokes unless the wheel had limited mileage before you trashed the rim, and never reuse the nipples. Saving money by reusing the old parts is a false economy. Once the nipples get rounded out, your spoke wrench can no longer turn them as you're building the wheel, and the weakened spokes will start to fail when you're riding.*

b. Tensioning tools

You only need a spoke wrench. If you are building lots of wheels, though, a bent-handle nipple screwdriver (Fig. 12.3A) is a must to speed up tensioning.

c. Tools for aero (bladed) spokes

If you will be using bladed spokes, you will need a slotted tool to grab the flat of the spoke to keep it from twisting. DT Swiss makes a nice nesting pair of tools for this: a spoke wrench with a cone-shaped longitudinal groove that mates with the cone-shaped end of a slotted, L-shaped tool (Fig. 12.3B). With these tools, you can hold the spoke way down at the end of its flat section, close to the nipple, as you turn the spoke; with other slotted tools you will be grabbing the spoke above the spoke wrench, far from the nipple, and, with a thin spoke, you can easily leave a permanent kink—a twist in the middle of the flat section of the spoke.

d. Tools for deep rims

If you will be building onto a deep-section rim, you will need another special tool. Which tool that is will depend on whether the rim has standard-size spoke holes so the nipples extend out of the rim in the normal way, or the rim has tiny spoke holes so the nipples will be internal to the rim. In the former case, you need a way to hold the nipple as you extend it through the large hole in the rim bed to the hole in the inner wall without losing it in the open cavity of the rim. Alchemy Bicycle has a special tool for this, but for building a few deep-section wheels, an extra spoke with another nipple threaded on it will do the trick. Spin the nipple on to leave about 6mm of thread exposed, and then fix it in place by crimping it onto the spoke. You'll thread this "tool" into the top of a nipple until it stops

12.3A Bent-handle nipple screwdriver

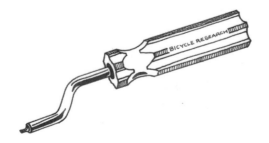

12.3B DT Swiss spoke wrench and antitwist tool for aero spokes

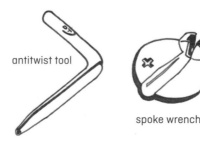

antitwist tool

spoke wrench

382

12.3C Three-way spoke wrench for internal nipples

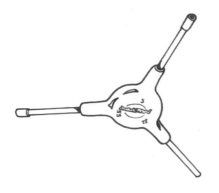

against the crimped nipple; reach through the rim with the tool and thread the nipple a few turns onto a spoke coming from the hub. This tool will also speed tensioning later, because the crimped-on nipple will only allow each nipple to thread onto its spoke a set number of turns before it stops when it hits the end of the tool spoke. Each nipple will be threaded onto each spoke the same amount, eliminating any disparities as you begin the tensioning process (you'll understand the importance of this when we reach that section).

If the deep rim has only small holes that will not let a nipple through, you will need a deep-wall socket with which to turn the internal nipples. Park makes a three-way square/5mm/5.5mm specialty spoke wrench for this purpose (Fig. 12.3C); the square drive is for using standard nipples upside down in the rim, and the 5mm and 5.5mm deep-wall sockets are for turning long hex nuts, including ³⁄₁₆-inch ones (equaling 4.7mm, which is close enough to 5mm to work fine in this tool).

e. Spoke prep

For the sake of brevity and clarity, I do not mention using spoke prep compound with every instruction to thread a nipple onto a spoke. Although the use of thread compound is not mandatory, I think that the wheel is improved: It

encourages the nipples to thread on smoothly, it takes up some of the slop between the spoke and nipple threads, and its thread-locking ability discourages the nipples from vibrating loose. Better yet, use DT Pro Lock nipples, which contain a two-component adhesive in the nipple thread to prevent the spoke-nipple connection from loosening under the effect of operating loads (loading and unloading of the wheel during riding), thus ensuring constant spoke tension.

If you use spoke prep, apply it to the spoke threads before putting on the nipples. You do not want too much, as it will be hard to adjust the nipples months and years down the road; you just want the spoke prep in the valleys of the threads. You can get the right amount if you dip the threads of a pair of spokes into the prep compound, and then take two more dry spokes and roll the threads of all four spokes together with your fingers.

With DT Pro Lock nipples, you don't have to do any of this; just thread them onto the spoke. However, you will want to complete the wheel in one sitting. As you thread the nipples, you will be bursting little beads of the two glue components inside the nipple, like epoxy glue. If you finish the wheel while the glue is viscous, the nipples will hold better than if you let them harden and then turn them again in ensuing days. The nipples still offer benefits upon later wheel truing, since not all of the spheres will burst during initial wheel building, but the efficacy of the thread-locking will be reduced each time.

In the absence of spoke prep, at least dip the threads of each spoke in grease. Grease accomplishes everything spoke prep does, save for locking the threads.

A little linseed oil around the head of a nipple where it contacts the rim makes turning it easier as tension increases.

LACING THE WHEEL

1. **Divide the spokes into two separate groups, one set for each side of the hub flange, and rubber-band each set together.** If you are building a rear wheel, you should be working with two different spoke lengths, because spokes on the right-hand side, or drive side, are almost always shorter. For a radial front wheel, skip to §xii-7.

2. **Hold the rim on your lap with the valve hole away from you.** Note that the holes may alternate being offset upward or downward from the rim centerline.

NOTE: *If you are building a rear wheel onto a rim with spoke holes drilled asymmetrically off center (e.g., Ritchey OCR [Off-Center Rear], Bontrager ASYM, Campagnolo asymmetrical), make sure that you orient the rim so that the spoke holes are offset to the left (non-drive) side (Fig. 12.4). The asymmetrical rim is meant to reduce wheel dish, so that offsetting the nipples to the left reduces the otherwise very steep angle at which drive-side spokes normally hit the rim. The balanced left-to-right spoke tension should increase the lifetime of the wheel, and the lower spoke angle moves the drive-side spokes away from the rear derailleur. So with an asymmetrical rim (Fig. 12.4), have the spoke holes offset downward, toward your lap.*

3. **Hold the hub in the center of the rim, with the right side of the hub pointing up.** On a rear hub, the right side is the drive side. Front hubs are symmetrical; pick a side to be the right side. In the illustrations, the right side has the nut end of the quick-release.

a. First set of spokes

4. **Drop a spoke down into every other hole in the top (right-side) hub flange, so that the spoke heads are facing up (Fig. 12.5).**

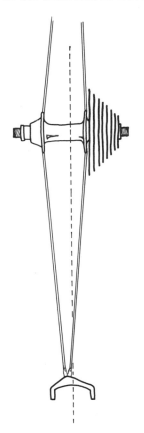

12.5 First half of right-side spokes placed in a hub

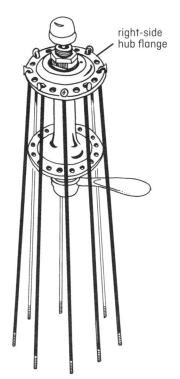

right-side hub flange

12.6 First spoke, right-side up

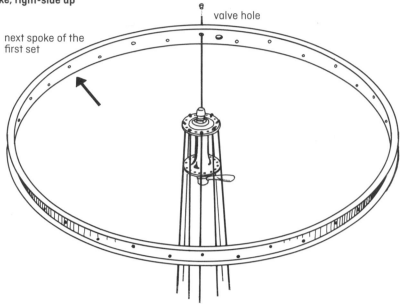

Make sure if it's a rear wheel that you put the shorter spokes on the right (drive) side. On some (older) hubs, half of the holes you are looking at will be countersunk deeper into the hub flange to provide a radius less stressful on the spoke elbow, so don't use those holes—use their neighbors. That said, most hubs these days have the same countersinking on all holes to prepare for the eventuality of building a completely symmetrical, radially spoked wheel (§xii-7).

5. **Put a spoke into the first hole counterclockwise from the valve hole, and screw the nipple on three turns (Fig. 12.6).** Notice that this hole is offset upward. On an asymmetrically drilled rim (Fig. 12.4), this means that the hole is offset upward from the centerline of the spoke holes, not the centerline of the rim. If the first hole counterclockwise from the valve hole isn't offset upward, you have a misdrilled rim, and you must offset all instructions one hole.

6. **Working counterclockwise, put the next spoke on the hub into the hole in the rim four holes away from the first spoke, and**

screw a nipple on three turns. There should be three open rim holes between these spokes, and the hole you put the second spoke into should also be offset upward.

7. **Continue counterclockwise around the wheel in the same manner.** You should now have used half of the rim holes that are offset upward, and there should be three open holes between the spokes (Fig. 12.7).

8. **Flip the wheel over.**

12.7 First set of spokes laced

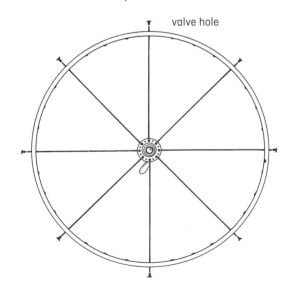

b. Second set of spokes

9. **Sight across the hub from one hub flange to the other.** Notice that the holes in one flange do not line up with the holes in the other; each hole lines up between two holes on the opposite flange (Fig. 12.8).

12.8 Spoke-hole offset

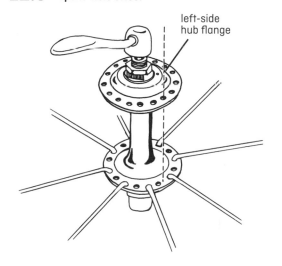

left-side
hub flange

10. **Drop a spoke down through the hole in the top flange that is immediately clockwise from the first spoke you installed (the spoke that is just clockwise from the valve hole).**

11. **Put this new spoke into the second hole clockwise from the valve hole, next to the first spoke you installed (Figs. 12.9, 12.10).** This hole will be offset upward from the rim centerline.

12. **Thread the nipple on three turns.**

13. **Double-check your work.** Make sure that the spoke you just installed starts at a hole in the hub's top (left-side) flange that is a half-hole space clockwise from the hole in the lower flange where the first spoke you installed started. When you look at the wheel from the side, these two spokes (your first spoke and the one you just installed) should not cross each other and should look like they are trending slightly away from each other (Fig. 12.10). In wheel-building parlance, these two spokes are called "diverging parallel" spokes.

12.9 Lacing second set

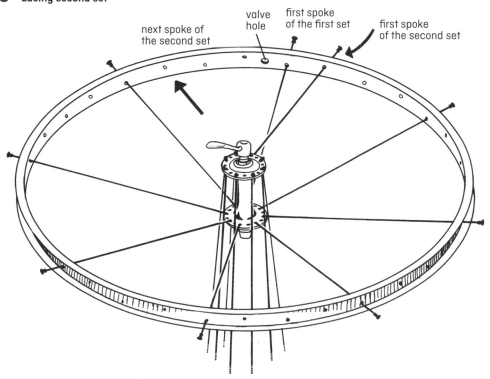

next spoke of
the second set

valve
hole

first spoke
of the first set

first spoke
of the second set

12.10   "Diverging parallel" spokes

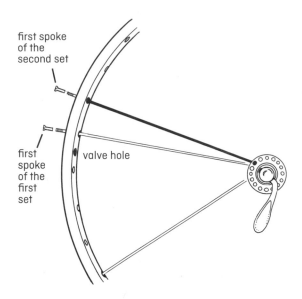

first spoke
of the
second set

first
spoke
of the
first
set

valve hole

12.11   Second set of spokes laced

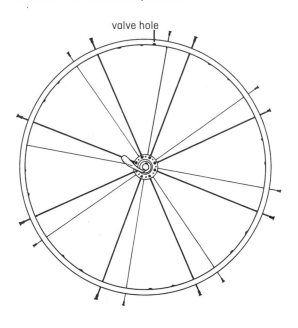

valve hole

14. **Drop a spoke down through the hole in the top (left-side) hub flange two holes away in either direction.** Continue around until every other hole has a spoke hanging down through it (Fig. 12.9).

15. **Working counterclockwise, take the next spoke from the hub and put it in the rim hole that is three holes counterclockwise**

from the valve hole. This hole should be off-set upward and four holes to the left of the spoke you just installed. Thread the nipple on three turns.

16. **Follow this pattern counterclockwise around the wheel (Fig. 12.11).** You should have now used half of the rim holes that are offset upward, as well as half of the total rim holes. The second set of spokes should all be in upwardly offset holes, one hole clockwise from each spoke of the first set.

c. Third set of spokes

17. **Drop spokes through the remaining holes on the right side of the hub, from the inside out (Fig. 12.12).** Remember, if it's a rear wheel, these spokes should be shorter than the spokes used on the left side.

18. **Flip the wheel over, grabbing the spokes you've just dropped through to keep them from falling out.**

12.12   Placing the third set of spokes in hub

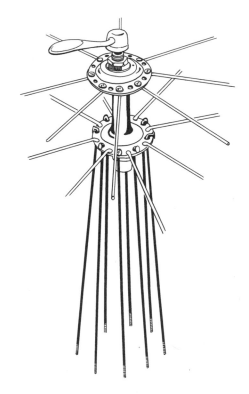

19. **Fan the spokes out.** Now they cannot fall back down through the hub holes.

20. **Grab the hub shell and rotate it counterclockwise as far as you can (Fig. 12.13).**

21. **Pick any spoke on the top (right-hand) hub flange that is already laced to the rim.**

12.13 Rotating the hub counterclockwise

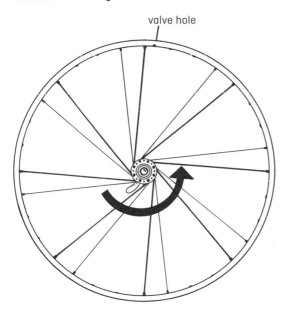

12.14 Lacing the third set of spokes

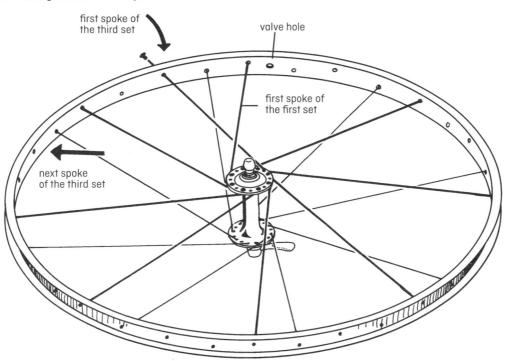

Now find the spoke five hub holes away in a clockwise direction.

22. **Take this new spoke, cross it under the spoke you counted from (the one five holes away), and stick it into the rim hole two holes counterclockwise from that spoke (Fig. 12.14).** Thread a nipple on three turns.

23. **Continue around the wheel, doing the same thing (Fig. 12.15).** You may find a spoke or two that don't reach quite far enough. If that's the case, at a point about an inch from the spoke elbow, push down on the spoke to help it reach.

24. **Make sure that every spoke coming out of the upper side of the top flange (the spokes that come out toward you with their spoke heads hidden from view) crosses over two spokes and under a third.** All three of these crossing spokes come from the underside of the same flange and have their spoke heads facing toward you. These crossing spokes begin one, three, and five hub holes counterclockwise from the spoke that you just

inserted into the rim (Fig. 12.15). This is called a "three-cross" pattern because every spoke crosses three others on its way to the rim (over, over, under). Every upwardly offset hole should now be occupied on the rim.

12.15 Third set of spokes laced

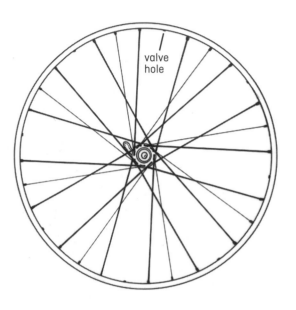

d. Fourth set of spokes

25. **Drop spokes down through the remaining hub holes in the bottom flange from the inside out.** (They should look like Figure 12.12, but with the other side of the hub up.)

26. **Flip the wheel over.** Grab the spokes to keep them from falling back down through the holes.

27. **Fan the spokes out.**

28. **Pick any spoke on the top (left-hand) hub flange that is already laced to the rim.** Now find the spoke five hub holes away in a counterclockwise direction.

29. **Take that spoke, and cross it over two spokes and under the spoke you counted from.** Stick the spoke into the rim hole two holes clockwise from the spoke it crosses under (Fig. 12.16). Thread a nipple on three turns.

30. **Continue around the wheel, doing the same thing until the wheel is laced (Fig.**

12.16 Lacing the fourth set of spokes

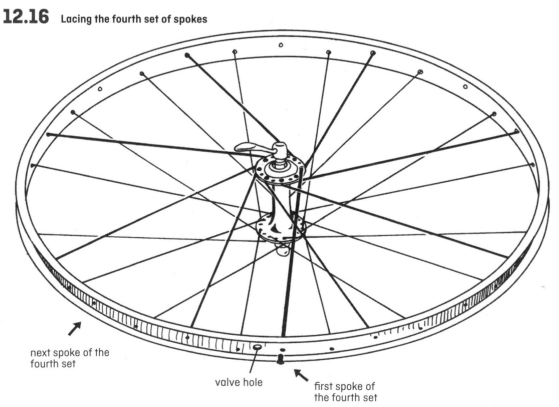

next spoke of the fourth set

valve hole

first spoke of the fourth set

12.1). You may find that some spokes don't reach far enough. In that case, at a point about an inch from the spoke elbow, push down on the spoke to help it reach.

31. **Make sure that every spoke coming out from the upper side of the top flange (the spokes that come out toward you with their spoke heads hidden from view) crosses over two spokes and under a third (Fig. 12.1).** All three of these crossing spokes come from the underside of the same hub flange and have their spoke heads facing you. The crossing spokes begin one, three, and five hub holes clockwise from each spoke emerging from the top of the upper (left) hub flange (Fig. 12.1). Every hole should now be occupied on the rim. When you look at the wheel from the side, the valve hole should be between two spokes (your first spoke and the first spoke of the fourth set) that do not cross each other but whose trajectories look like they are trending slightly toward each other. In other words, if these spokes were to continue infinitely outward, their trajectories would eventually cross far beyond the rim (Fig. 12.17). In wheel-builder speak, these two spokes are called "converging parallel" spokes. Lacing the spokes this way around the valve hole will provide the maximum possible space between the spokes for the pump head when inflating the tire.

NOTE: *If this is a rear wheel, the spokes coming out of the outside of the hub flange on both sides oppose the clockwise twist the chain applies on the cogs. See §xii-6 for more on this subject.*

xii-3

TENSIONING THE WHEEL

1. **Put the wheel in the truing stand.**
2. **Tighten each nipple first with a screwdriver and then with a spoke wrench until only three threads are visible beyond the bottom of the nipple.** See Figure 12.18 for tighten rotation direction. The bent-shaft nipple screwdriver shown in Figure 12.3A speeds this process up immeasurably. The shaft spins in the handle, which you just turn like a crank; it's much faster than twisting a screwdriver.

   From now on, every time you tighten or loosen a spoke nipple, turn it back the opposite direction one-eighth turn afterward. This unwinds the twist in the spoke that your tightening or loosening just caused. If you are using aero spokes, keep them from twisting with the tool shown in Figure 12.3B.
3. **Using your thumb, press the spokes coming outward from the outer side of the hub flanges down at the elbow to straighten their line to the rim.** Spokes coming out of the inner side of the flange do not need this.
4. **Go around the wheel, tightening each nipple a half turn.** Do this uniformly, and only a half turn, so that the wheel is not thrown out of true.

12.17 "Converging parallel" spokes

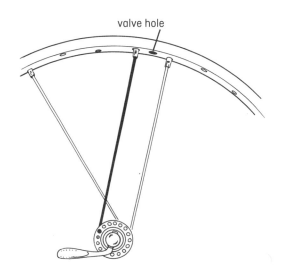

valve hole

WHEEL BUILDING

5. **Check to see if the spokes are tight enough to give a tone when plucked.** Squeeze pairs of spokes together and compare with a good wheel with spokes of the same gauge; your new wheel should have considerably less tension at this point.

6. **Repeat steps 4 and 5 until the spokes all make a tone but are under less tension than an existing, good wheel.** Final tensioning will come with the remainder of the truing process.

NOTE ON BLADED SPOKES: *If you are using flat spokes, you will need to hold the spoke flats (§xii-1, Fig. 12.3B) to keep them from twisting.*

---

xii-4

TRUING THE WHEEL

a. Lateral true

Side-to-side trueness is the most obvious wheel parameter when you spin a wheel.

1. **Make sure the hub axle has no end play.** If play is present, adjust the hub (see hub adjustment in §vi-19d).

2. **Optionally, put a drop of linseed oil around the top of each nipple where it seats in the rim.** The oil will lubricate the contact area between it and the inside of the rim hole.

3. **Set the truing stand feelers so that one of them scrapes the side of the rim at the worst lateral wobble (Figs. 12.18, 12.19).**

4. **Ending a few spokes on either side of where the rim scrapes, tighten the spokes coming from the opposite flange of the hub, and loosen the spokes coming from the same-side flange of the hub (Figs. 12.18, 12.19).** Start with a one-quarter turn on nipples at the center of the scraping area, and decrease the amount you turn each nipple as you move away in either direction. This step pulls the rim away from the feeler. If it does the opposite, you are turning the nipples in the wrong direction. Remember, you normally turn something to the right to tighten and to the left to loosen, but tightening and loosening spoke nipples at the bottom of the wheel are the opposite of what you would normally do (Figs. 12.18–12.21). This is because the nipple head is underneath your spoke wrench. Try opening a jar that is upside down, and you will immediately understand the principle involved.

12.18 Adjusting spokes to pull the rim to the right

loosen

tighten

scrapes here . . .

pull rim to right

12.19 Adjusting spokes to pull the rim to the left

tighten

loosen

scrapes here . . .

lateral truing

pull rim to left

truing stand feelers

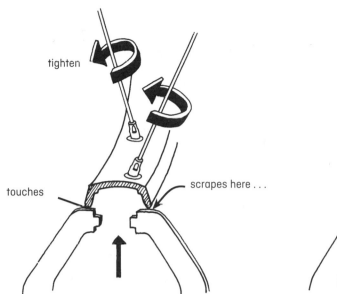

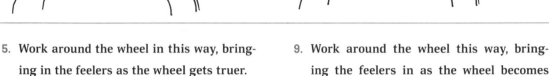

5. Work around the wheel in this way, bringing in the feelers as the wheel gets truer.

b. Radial true

While not as obvious visually as side-to-side trueness, out-of-roundness is more noticeable when riding, and it is more important to the longevity of the wheel, because a wheel with uniform tension lasts longer. Radial truing, however, can be somewhat slow and frustrating work. If you find yourself running out of patience for this job, step away for a while and then start again when you feel fresh and ready.

6. **Set the truing-stand feelers so that they now contact the circumference of the rim, rather than the sides.**

7. **Bring the feelers in until they scrape against the highest spot on the rim (Fig. 12.20).**

8. **Tighten the spokes a one-quarter turn where the rim scrapes.** This will pull the rim inward. Decrease the amount of each turn (to a one-eighth turn and less) as you move away from the center of the scraping area.

9. Work around the wheel this way, bringing the feelers in as the wheel becomes rounder.

10. **Wherever there is a dip in the rim, loosen the spokes (Fig. 12.21).** If the spokes are too tight at this point, they will be hard to turn and will creak and groan as you do. When the spokes become hard to turn (i.e., the nipples feel on the verge of rounding off), loosen all of the spokes in the wheel a one-quarter turn before continuing. Compare tension with a good wheel with the spokes of the same gauge; tension at this point should still be lower in the wheel you are building.

---

xii-5

DISHING (CENTERING) THE WHEEL

1. **Place the dishing tool across the right side of the wheel, bisecting the center (Fig. 12.22).**

2. **Tighten or loosen the dishing gauge screw until the gauge contacts the outer face of the axle end nut (Fig. 12.22).**

12.22 Using the dishing tool to check the center-ing of the rim relative to the axle ends

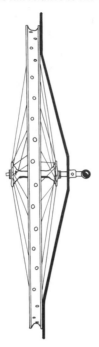

12.23 Checking the wheel dish on the other side of the hub

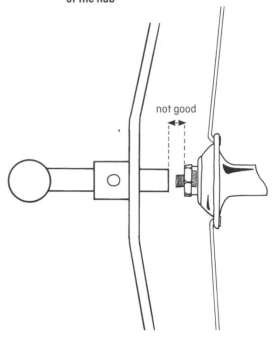

not good

3. **Flip the wheel over.**

4. **Place the dishing tool across the other side of the wheel.**

5. **Check the gap of the dishing gauge with this axle end nut face (Fig. 12.23).** Any gap between the dishing gauge and the axle end nut face indicates the amount the rim is off-set from the centerline of the wheel. If there is no gap but an overlap instead, reset the dishing gauge on this side (the previously overlapped side). Then flip it over and check the other side (i.e., repeat steps 3–5 on the opposite side).

6. **Put the wheel back in the truing stand.**

7. **Pull the rim toward the center (reducing the gap between the dishing tool and the axle end face) by tightening the spokes on the opposite side of the wheel from the axle end that had the gap between it and the dishing gauge.** Tighten a half turn each—no more. If the spokes are getting really tight (they will creak a lot when tight-

ening, the nipples will start rounding off, and the spokes will feel much tighter than the spokes in a comparable wheel), then loosen the spokes uniformly on the opposite side of the wheel.

NOTE ON BLADED SPOKES: *You will need to hold the flats of bladed spokes with a slotted tool (Fig. 12.3B), as explained in §xii-1, to keep them from twisting. Turning back one-eighth after each nipple tightening or loosening (§xii-3, step 2, above) may reduce the twist somewhat, but a bladed spoke has so much less torsional stiffness than a round spoke (twist a round vs. flattened paper towel tube to see what I mean) that it may just twist back and forth without actually turn-ing in the nipple if you don't prevent the spoke from twisting.*

8. **Recheck the wheel with the dishing gauge by repeating steps 1–5.**

9. **If the dish is still off (there is still a gap between the dishing gauge and the end nut when you flip it over), repeat steps 6–8.**

Continue until the dish is correct (the gap is zero).

10. **Stress the spokes by squeezing each pair together with your hands (Fig. 12.24).** They will make a "ping" noise as they unwind. If you followed my recommendation in §xii-3, step 2, to turn the nipple back the opposite direction one-eighth turn after each time you tighten or loosen it, the spokes should not be wound up much, and prestressing the wheel will be unnecessary (you'll know because the spokes won't ping when you stress them).

    a. Leaning on the wheel is a quick way to prestress it, but you can wreck the wheel if you are not careful. To proceed, set the axle end on the workbench and carefully press down on the rim with your hands at the nine o'clock and three o'clock positions. This pressure will affect an area of about three spokes on each side, so rotate the wheel three spokes, press down again, rotate three more spokes in the same direction, press down again, and so on. After you finish one side, flip the wheel over and do the other side. Do not press down with all your might; too much pressure can destroy your work.

    b. If prestressing throws the wheel way out of true, the spokes are probably too tight. Loosen them all one-eighth turn. Note, though, that some loss of wheel "trueness" is normal. If the loss is minor, you can overlook it and continue with step 11.

11. **Repeat the process.** Repeat truing the wheel (§xii-4), followed by dishing the wheel (§xii-5), prestressing the spokes (and turning the nipples back a one-eighth turn from the rotation direction on each adjustment of one) frequently as you go. Keep improving the accuracy of the build this way.

12. **Bring up the tension to that of a comparable wheel by making small tightening adjustments to every nipple.** Adjust dish and true after each time around, until the wheel is as you want it.

13. **If the rim is oily, wipe it down with a citrus-based biodegradable solvent.**

14. **Congratulate yourself on building your wheel, and show it off to your friends.**

12.24 Relieving tension

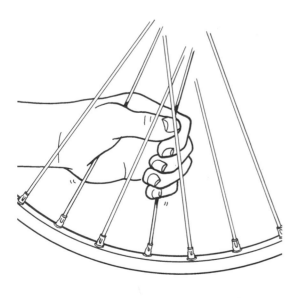

---

xii-6

COMMENTS ON WHEEL BUILDING

Your wheel has some features that you won't find on machine-built wheels. Most significantly, on your rear wheel, the "pulling spokes" are to the outside. This means that you have a spoking pattern that best resists the twisting force on the hub produced by pedaling forces on the chain.

In the wheel you've built, half of the spokes are called "pulling" or "dynamic" spokes, and the other half are called "static" spokes (this is true of any spoking pattern except radial). The pulling spokes are the ones directed in such a way that a clockwise twist on the hub increases the tension in them. If you look at the wheel from the drive side, you will see what I am talking about.

You will also see that the static spokes do not oppose a clockwise twist on the hub. In fact, their tension decreases when you stomp on the pedals.

By placing all of the pulling spokes so that they come out to the outside of the hub flanges (i.e., the spoke heads are on the inward side of the flanges), we have attached the spokes doing the most work the farthest outward on the hub, reducing the fatigue on them and increasing their ability to oppose forces acting on the rim. The reasoning is that the spokes whose tension changes the most during the working of the wheel should be the ones that are lying across the hub flange with the heads on the inside of the flange. Tension changes lead to spoke breakage due to fatigue, and the weakest part of a spoke is the elbow. If there is more contact between the spoke elbow and the flange, there is less stress on the spoke elbow. Also, the spokes under the most stress should have the widest "stance" (if you want to resist being knocked over, you plant your feet farther apart), because they come from the outside of the flanges and are thus farthest apart at their elbows.

If you choose the appropriate parts for your weight and riding style, and have the proper spoke tension, you should have a strong wheel that will last a long time. Congratulations!

xii-7

BUILDING RADIALLY SPOKED WHEELS

With the advent of stronger rim materials and stiffer, deep-section rim cross-sections, radially spoked wheels (Fig. 12.25) have become popular. They are simple to build, and radial spoking offers a number of advantages.

12.25 Radially spoked front wheel

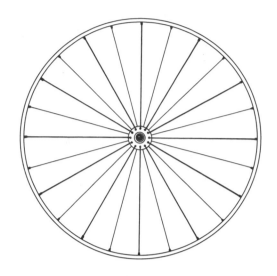

A radially spoked wheel is vertically stiffer than a crossed one, because radial spokes allow little opportunity for spokes to absorb energy in the spoking pattern. The radial wheel can be stiffer laterally too, because the spoke length is shorter, increasing their pulling angle to the rim.

A radial wheel is lighter because the spokes are shorter. Further weight can be removed with fewer spokes (made possible by deep, stiff rims), and radial spoking allows any even spoke count to be used (with nonradial patterns, the spoke count must be a multiple of four). And radial spoking allows the use of direct-pull hubs and nail-head spokes (straight spokes without elbows), eliminating a potential weak spot in the spokes.

Radially laced spokes line up behind each other and thus improve the aerodynamics of the wheel. Aero-shaped spokes can improve the aerodynamics even further, but using wide aero-shaped spokes in a standard hub often requires slotting the hub holes with a jeweler's file to get the spoke through. If you do this yourself, make sure you only file downward from the hole, toward the meat of the flange. Slotting upward toward the edge greatly weakens the hub and invites the spoke to rip through.

Speaking of torn hub flanges, the warranty of some hubs is voided when they are spoked radially; Shimano, for one, has this stipulation. The stress is greater on hub holes with radial spoking because the spoke tension in a radial wheel is often higher and because there is less material resisting the hub's tearing out when the spoke is pulling straight outward than when it is pulling at an angle along the hub flange.

A completely radial wheel can only be used on the front. On the rear, the drive side (or the non-drive side, if the hub shell is oversized and stiff) must still have a crossing pattern to oppose the twist on the hub caused by the chain (Fig. 12.26).

a. How to lace a radial front wheel

Drop all of the spokes from the inside of each flange outward, or from the outside of the flange inward, and lace them straight to the rim.

12.26 Radial/three-cross rear wheel

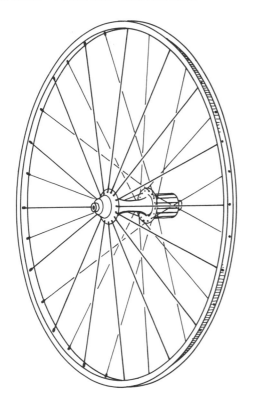

b. How to lace a rear wheel with a radial left side and a three-cross drive side

First lace the drive side following the instructions in §xii-2a, steps 4–7, and §xii-2c, steps 17–24. Now lace the left-side spokes outward through the hub flange (inward through the hub flange is okay too, but slightly less laterally stiff) and straight to the rim.

The tensioning and truing steps are the same as for standard three-cross wheels, but radial-spoke tension must be high to help prevent the spokes from vibrating loose.

c. How to lace a rear wheel with a radial drive side and a three-cross left side
Advantages

If the hub is stiff enough not to twist when the only thing opposing the twist created by power applied on the drive side via the chain and cogs will be crossed spokes on the opposite end of the hub, then this method has advantages over the pattern in step b, above, as well as over three-cross and two-cross patterns on both sides.

As in the pattern in step b, the radial spokes will improve the aerodynamics and reduce the weight of the wheel. And, as in the step b pattern, the chain winding up the hub always tightens all of the spokes on the radial side, rather than loosening half of them while tightening the other half as happens with a crossing pattern.

But there is another benefit in terms of spoke tension. The Achilles' heel of most rear wheels is the difference in tension on the two sides, due to the greater width from hub flange to axle end on the drive side to make space for the cogs. If you have radial spokes on the drive side that come out to the outside of the hub flange (i.e., the spoke heads are on the inboard side of the hub flange), you have made the side-side angle from the spoke elbow to the rim the widest possible. Even more important, since these spokes are so much shorter than the crossed spokes on the non-drive side, the relative angle to the rim of the spokes on the two opposing sides is lower than in a symmetrically crossed wheel, and lower yet than in the wheel in step b, above. That is because the spokes on the left side in this arrangement travel a longer distance to move the same distance laterally inward to their attachment point on the rim, making their angle to the rim steeper, and vice versa on the drive side. So, if the angle to the rim of the spokes on the left is steeper than normal, and that of the spokes on the right is shallower than normal, then the angles are closer to being the same on both sides, making the spoke tension more even. This makes for a stiffer, longer-lasting wheel.

Method

First lace the non-drive side following the instructions in §xii-2b, steps 9–16, and §xii-2d, steps 25–30. Now lace the drive-side spokes outward through the hub flange and straight to the rim.

xii-8

BUILDING TWO-CROSS WHEELS

Two-cross wheels are stiffer vertically and slightly lighter than three-cross wheels. And two-cross (or radial) may be the only good way to go with deep-section rims with internal spoke nipples, because three-cross will probably not be possible to build. That is because the spoke-nipple access holes in the rim bed will not be wide enough to allow you to get at the nipple with the long nipple-driver socket (see tool in Fig. 12.3C), since the spoke will be coming in at such an angle from the hub flange. The straighter fore-aft spoke angle from flange to rim hole will allow you to get the nipple on the end of the spoke and turn it.

To build a two-cross pattern, follow the lacing instructions in §xii-2 exactly, with the following changes, starting at step 21:

21. **Pick any spoke on the top (right-hand) hub flange that is already laced to the rim. Now find the spoke three hub holes away in a clockwise direction.**

22. **Take this new spoke, cross it under the spoke you counted from (the one three holes away), and stick it into the rim hole two holes counterclockwise from that spoke.** Thread a nipple on three turns.

23. **Continue around the wheel, repeating the pattern.** You may find a spoke or two that doesn't reach quite far enough. If that's the case, at a point about an inch from the spoke elbow, push down on the spoke to help it reach.

24. **Make sure that every spoke coming out of the upper side of the top flange (the spokes that come out toward you with their spoke heads hidden from view) crosses over one spoke and under a second.** Both of these crossing spokes come from the underside of the same flange and have their spoke heads facing toward you. These crossing spokes begin one and three hub holes counterclockwise from the spoke that you just inserted into the rim. This is called a "two-cross" pattern because every spoke crosses two others on its way to the rim (over, under). Every upwardly offset hole should now be occupied on the rim. Follow steps 25–27 as in §xii-2.

28. **Pick any spoke on the top (left-hand) hub flange that is already laced to the rim. Now find the spoke three hub holes away in a counterclockwise direction.**

29. **Take that spoke, and cross it over one spoke and under the spoke you counted from.** Stick the spoke into the rim hole two

12.27 Two-cross wheel

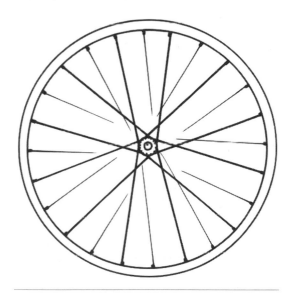

holes clockwise from the spoke it crosses under. Thread a nipple on three turns.

30. **Continue around the wheel, doing the same thing until the wheel is laced as in Figure 12.27.** You may find that some spokes don't reach far enough. If that's the case, at a point about an inch from the spoke elbow, push down on the spoke to help it reach.

31. **Make sure that every spoke coming out from the upper side of the top flange (the spokes that come out toward you with their spoke heads hidden from view) crosses two spokes (Fig. 12.27).** Both of these crossing spokes come from the underside of the same hub flange and have their spoke heads facing you. The crossing spokes begin one and three hub holes clockwise from each spoke emerging from the top of the upper (left) hub flange. Every hole in the rim should now be occupied. When you look at the wheel from the side, the valve hole should be between two spokes (your first spoke and the first spoke of the fourth set) that do not cross each other but whose trajectories look like they are trending slightly toward each other. In other words, if these spokes were to con-

tinue infinitely outward, their trajectories would eventually cross far beyond the rim (Fig. 12.17). In wheel-builder speak, these two spokes are called "converging parallel" spokes. Lacing the spokes this way around the valve hole will provide the maximum possible space between the spokes for the pump head when inflating the tire.

NOTE: *If this is a rear wheel, the spokes coming out of the outside of the hub flange on both sides oppose the clockwise twist the chain applies on the cogs. See §xii-6 for more on this subject.*

xii-9

LACING REAR THREE-CROSS DISC-BRAKE WHEELS

Disc-brake wheels need to have crossed (non-radial) spokes to oppose the twist applied to the hub by the brake pads grabbing the rotor. And as explained in §xii-6 regarding the chain force on a rear wheel, the spokes coming out of the outside of the hub flange should ideally be oriented to oppose the twist the rotor being grabbed by the brake pads applies on the hub. This pattern makes for a stronger wheel, by having the wider-angle spokes doing more of the work. On the front, you would set the spokes coming from the inside of the hub flange out on both sides to head counterclockwise toward the rim when viewed from the brake (non-drive) side (Fig. 12.28) to oppose a clockwise twist on the hub by the rotor.

However, on the rear wheel, while the brake applies a clockwise twist on the hub viewed from the brake side, the chain still applies a clockwise twist on the hub viewed from the drive side. So, if you are building a rear disc-brake wheel (Fig. 12.30), you want the drive-side outer spokes opposing the chain force on the cogs, but you still want the left-side outer spokes opposing the braking force on the rotor. And with all disc-brake wheels, I recommend 14/15-gauge double-butted spokes and brass nipples (see §xii-10a and §xii-10b for more on this).

The drive side will be laced in just the same way as described in the lacing instructions in §xii-2 above, but the non-drive side will be laced in the opposite way that the left side turns would be laced in §xii-2.

a. First set of spokes

1. Follow steps 1–9 from §xii-2.

b. Second set of spokes

2. **Push a spoke up through the hole in the top flange that is immediately clockwise from the first spoke you installed (the spoke that is just clockwise from the valve hole).**

3. **Follow steps 11, 12, and 13 from §xii-2 and then step 4 below.**

4. **Drop one spoke down through each of the adjacent hub holes on either side of the newly laced spoke.** Skip a hole and continue around the hub flange, dropping a spoke down into every other hole.

5. **Rotate the hub shell clockwise as far as you can.**

6. **Find the spoke that is five hub holes counterclockwise from the single spoke coming up out of the flange that you installed in steps 2 and 3.**

7. **Take this new spoke, cross it over the spoke you counted from (the one five holes away), and stick it into the rim hole two holes clockwise from that spoke.** Thread the nipple onto the spoke three turns.

8. **Find the next spoke counterclockwise on the hub flange.** Put it in the rim hole four holes counterclockwise from the spoke you just installed in step 7. Thread the nipple onto the spoke three turns.

12.28 **Completed front disc-brake wheel**

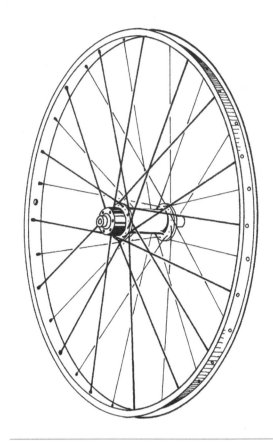

9. **Continue counterclockwise around the top (brake-side) hub flange until all spokes whose heads stick out of the top flange are one rim hole counterclockwise from the first set of spokes installed in the rim.**

c. Third set of spokes

10. **Follow steps 17–27 in §xii-2.** After you complete step 22, the wheel should look like the wheel shown in Figure 12.29 (except the other fanned-out, unlaced spokes coming out of the top flange are not shown).

d. Fourth (and final) set of spokes

11. **Pick any spoke on the top (rotor-side) flange whose head is facing up and is already laced to the rim. Now find the spoke five clockwise hub holes away.**

12. **Follow steps 22–24 in §xii-2.**

12.29 Rear disc-brake wheel: first two sets of spokes completed, first spoke of third set installed

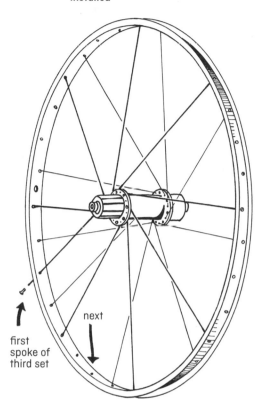

next

first spoke of third set

12.30 Completed rear disc-brake wheel

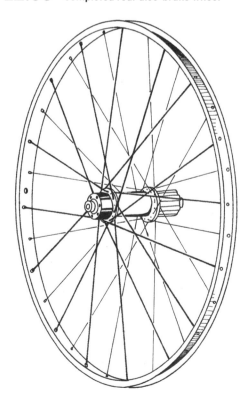

13. **Your wheel is now laced.** Note that the drive-side outer spokes oppose the chain pull, and the rotor-side outer spokes oppose the braking force on the rotor (Fig. 12.30). Give yourself a big pat on the back and then begin tensioning and truing your wheel, starting with §xii-3.

xii-10

BUILDING WHEELS FOR BIG RIDERS

Building wheels for heavy and tall riders requires greater lateral and vertical stiffness. The weight of the rider can bend and flex the rim, but it creates another problem as well. The heavier rider reduces the tension of the spokes at the bottom of the wheel more by making the rim more D-shaped at the bottom as it rolls. If the tension drops to the point that the nipple flanges periodically lose contact with the bases of the rim holes, the nipples can unscrew, and the wheel will fall apart. To achieve the higher strength required, you can add the following characteristics.

a. Spoke count and thickness

The spoke count needs to be high: Thirty-six or more spokes is highly preferable for riders over 190 pounds. The spokes need to be heavier, as thicker spokes are less prone to breakage. Although 14/15-gauge (2.0mm, or 14-gauge, on each end, and 1.8 mm, or 15-gauge, throughout the center section) double-butted spokes are thinner than straight 14-gauge spokes, DT Swiss testing has shown that the wheel will probably last longer with them. Because most breakage occurs at the nipple or the elbow, and butted spokes are the same thickness there, spoke breakage will not increase. But butted spokes will stretch more, allowing the spoke nipples to stay in contact with the rim better as the rim changes shape while rolling.

WHEEL BUILDING

b. Nipple type

Brass nipples are preferable to aluminum ones, due to the extra stress a big rider puts on the wheel. And ones with threadlock compound inside them, like DT Pro Lock nipples, will be far less likely to loosen up over time.

c. Rim section and drilling

The deeper the rim, the higher its hoop strength (vertical stiffness and strength). Very deep V-section rims work with low spoke counts because of this high hoop strength. The strongest wheel would be from a deep-section rim drilled for more spokes. Unfortunately for heavy riders, many deep V-section rims are also thinner to reduce weight and hence lose some strength.

d. Spoking pattern

With 8-, 9-, 10-, and 11-speed rear wheels, dish is high (one side of the wheel is flatter than the other), meaning that there is a great tension difference between spokes on the two sides. The loose spokes on the left can unscrew, especially under high pedaling forces, and the tight spokes on the right can break. As the chain twists the cogs clockwise, the spokes opposing the twist (the "pulling spokes") get tighter, while the "static spokes" are under reduced tension and can unscrew (especially without locked nipples).

An off-center rim can help by reducing the wheel dish. The rim holes are offset to the left side (Fig. 12.4), so that the drive-side spokes come to the rim at a lower angle and can work with lower tension and more even tension between the two sides. The left-side spokes come to the rim at a higher angle and can be under higher tension without forcing the use of dangerously high tensions on the drive side. Before lacing an off-center rim, make sure you read the Note in step 2 of §xii-2 above.

Using radial spokes on the left side (see §xii-7b above) can counteract the problem of grossly uneven tension. With a radial left side, the chain twisting the hub forward always tightens all of the left-side spokes, rather than loosening half of them as it would with a crossing pattern.

There is also an argument that you want the radial spokes on the drive side and the crossing spokes on the left side (Mavic wheels use this philosophy). The idea is that the shorter drive-side spokes, by taking a shorter distance to the rim, increase the effective spoke bracing angle. Similarly, the longer crossed spokes on the left, which would normally have a much bigger bracing angle than the drive-side spokes, will have the bracing angle reduced due to their increased length. Thus, spoke tension on each side will be more balanced. However, the hub shell must be stiff enough to carry the drive-force twist from the cog side to the non-drive side.

xii-11

BUILDING WHEELS FOR CYCLOCROSS

a. Firm courses

Wheels for cyclocross races on hard ground need to be light (since you're carrying the bike so much as well as repeatedly accelerating it), strong (due to the abuse they receive), and vertically compliant (due to the harsh ride on the firm, bumpy surface without any suspension apart from the tires). A strong, light rim with a shallow cross-section built up three-cross with double-butted spokes (thin in the middle, thick on the ends) will make for a great hard-course wheel. Choose one that has some curvature to the nipple side (Fig. 12.31); a domed or teardrop shape will help shed mud. If you are using disc brakes, be sure to build the wheel with brass nipples. Disc brakes place more stress on the spokes and nipples because the braking force

12.31 Shallow-section clincher rim cross-section (with a bit of a domed shape)

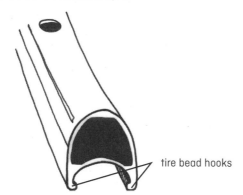

tire bead hooks

12.32 Deep-section clincher rim cross-section

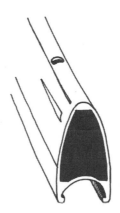

must be transmitted through them to reach the rim and tire.

b. Soft courses

Wheels for muddy and/or sandy courses need to be light, but, most important, they must steer well through the mud or sand. They can be stiff vertically because the soft ground absorbs much of the impact.

A deep-section rim (Fig. 12.32) will steer straighter through mud and deep sand than will a shallow-section one. It will also shed mud better, so you won't be lifting or accelerating as much weight or pedaling as much glop into the brakes and into the junctions of the fork, chainstays, and seatstays.

Deep aluminum rims are heavy; deep carbon tubular rims are a better choice (Fig. 6.48B), and be sure to use carbon-specific brake pads as well.

Get a rim with full-size holes for the nipples so that you can use external nipples rather than nipples hidden inside the rim. You can end up truing 'cross wheels frequently, and removing the tire to do so is a pain, particularly with a tubular tire—which is what you will choose if you want to minimize rim and tire weight.

A two-cross (§xii-8) or three-cross (§xii-2) pattern will give the wheel a bit more vertical compliance, but on soft ground you may prefer

radial spokes (§xii-7a); if so, go with three-cross on the non-drive side of the rear wheel (§xii-7c) and radial front (§xii-7a).

c. Tire choice determines rim type

If you're using tubular tires, you will be able to choose among lighter rims than for clinchers or tubeless clinchers, because tubular rims don't have the extra rim wall needed for the clincher bead hook (Fig. 12.31).

d. Build lots of wheels

To be competitive in cyclocross on muddy courses, you need multiple sets of wheels for racing. The reason, of course, is that on muddy courses, you need a second bike that your mechanic buddy cleans for you and exchanges with you every lap or so. That bike needs to have similar wheels to the bike you start on, for the reasons listed above, and you will want to bring extra wheels in case you get flat tires. It makes sense, therefore, to have a number of lightweight wheelsets for different race conditions and bikes. You will also want to have at least one set of sturdy clincher wheels for training.

Unless you are running disc brakes, be sure to select rims that have the same width for all of your 'cross wheelsets. Doing so will eliminate the hassle of adjusting brakes when changing wheels.

FORKS 13

TOOLS

2mm, 2.5mm, 5mm,
 8mm hex keys

8mm open-end
 wrench

Small screwdriver

Optional

Ruler

True front wheel

Dropout alignment
 tools

V-blocks

Vise

Threadlock compound

The fork serves a number of purposes. It connects the front wheel to the handlebar, allows the bike to be steered, and supports the front brake. The fork also offsets the front hub some distance forward of the steering axis (Fig. 13.1). This offset distance (fork rake, R in Fig. 13.1), combined with the steering axis (the head angle, Ø in Fig. 13.1) and the wheel size (the radius, r in Fig. 13.1), determines the fork trail (T in Fig. 13.1), which largely dictates how your bike is going to handle and steer.

All forks—even rigid road forks (Fig. 13.2)—provide at least a minimum amount of suspension by allowing the front wheel to move up and down. The steering axis angles the fork forward from vertical, while the front hub is offset farther forward yet, and these things allow for a fork to flex along its length and absorb vertical shocks.

Virtually every road bike fork is made of the components illustrated in Figure 13.2: the steering tube, the fork crown, the fork legs (sometimes called "blades"), and the fork ends (also called "dropouts" or "fork tips"). Forks designed for larger tires—as on cyclocross bikes and some touring bikes—also have cantilever or V-brake posts (Fig. 13.3) or disc-brake mounts (Fig. 13.4), none of which have brake arms above the tire that would limit its diameter. Older forks are threaded (Fig. 13.2); newer forks are not.

Road bike forks are manufactured from carbon fiber, steel, aluminum, or titanium, as well as countless mixes of these materials. Carbon forks are now standard on all but the least expensive road bikes. These generally have threadless steering tubes with a diameter of 1-⅛ inch (threaded steering tubes and early threadless ones are 1-inch diameter). Many newer high-end bikes have a larger lower headset bearing than an upper one (Chapter 11), so that the steering tube tapers from a larger diameter at its base up to the standard 1-⅛-inch diameter at the top (Figs. 13.4, 13.5). Disc brakes are now becoming common on road bikes (as on the bike on the cover), so disc-brake forks (Fig. 13.4) are ever more prevalent.

13.1 Front-end geometry of a bicycle

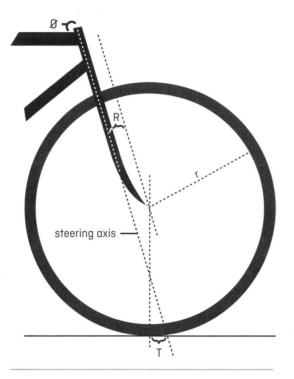

steering axis

xiii-1

FORK INSPECTION

Forks are pretty durable, but they do break occasionally. A fork failure can ruin your day, since it means you can't control the bike. Such loss of control usually precedes the rapid acceleration of your body downward onto the road, resulting in substantial pain.

Ever since I first opened my frame-building shop, people have regularly brought in broken forks of all types to show me, sometimes in the hope that I can repair them. Some forks had broken with catastrophic consequences. Some had steering tubes broken at the fork crown or in the threads. Others had fork crowns that broke or separated (releasing a fork leg or two), fork legs that folded, cantilever posts that snapped, and front dropouts that bent over, pulled out, or broke off. You can go a long way toward preventing problems like these by regularly inspecting your bike's fork.

13.2 Threaded steel road fork

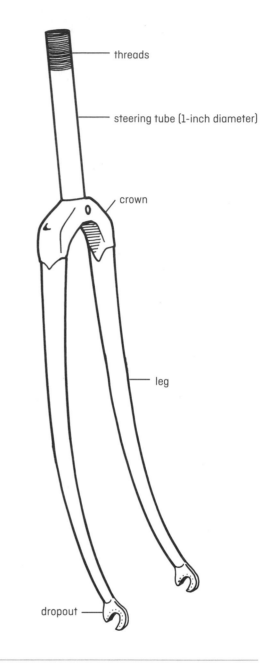

threads

steering tube (1-inch diameter)

crown

leg

dropout

With that in mind, get into the habit of checking the fork regularly for signs of impending failure. If you find something amiss, read the next section (§xiii-2) to see whether there is a remedy.

Obvious things to look for include bends, cracks, and stressed paint. On carbon forks, look for cut or torn fibers on the legs and crown, or

13.3 Threadless cyclocross fork

13.4 Carbon-fiber road fork with disc-brake mounts and tapered steering tube

13.5 Trek Madone carbon road fork with tapered steering tube

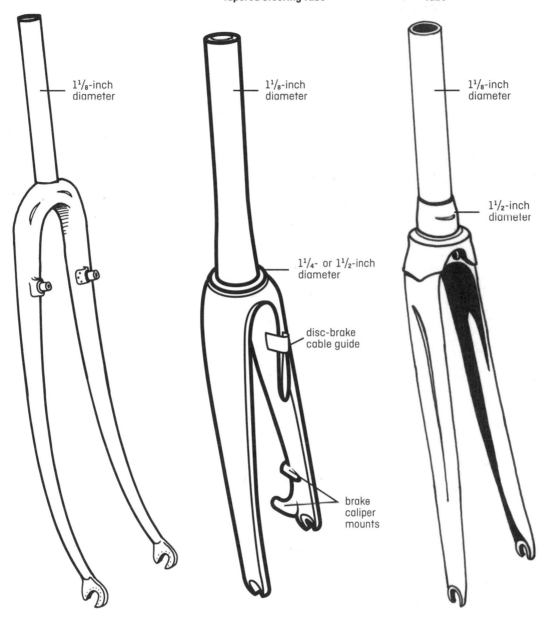

1¹⁄₈-inch diameter

1¹⁄₈-inch diameter

1¹⁄₄- or 1¹⁄₂-inch diameter

disc-brake cable guide

brake caliper mounts

1¹⁄₈-inch diameter

1¹⁄₂-inch diameter

loose glue bonds on the dropouts, fork crown, or steering tube. Feel for a change in stiffness and listen for strange noises. Try tapping on the fork legs with a coin over their length, listening for a change in sound from point to point and comparing it with the other side; this is a way to discover delamination or cracking in underlying carbon layers that is not visible from the outside.

If you have crashed your bike, give the fork an especially thorough inspection. If you find any indication that the fork has been damaged, replace it. A new fork is cheaper than emergency room charges, brain surgery, or an electric wheelchair.

When you inspect a fork, remove the front wheel, wipe any dirt off the legs and crown, and look under the crown and between the fork legs.

Carefully examine all of the outside areas. Look for any areas where the paint or finish looks cracked or stretched. Look for bent parts, from little ripples in fork legs to bent dropouts (Fig. 13.6). Skewed or broken cantilever posts are something to look for on cyclocross and touring forks (Fig. 13.3).

Put the wheel back in and watch to see if the fork legs twist when you tighten the hub into the dropouts. Check to make sure that a true wheel centers under the fork crown. If it doesn't, turn the wheel around and put it back in the fork to determine whether the misalignment is in the fork or the supposedly true wheel. If the wheel lines up off to one side when it is in one way, and off the same amount to the other side when it is in the other way, the wheel is off and the fork is straight. If the wheel is skewed off to the same side in the fork no matter which way you install the wheel, the fork is misaligned. A misaligned fork can cause problems like front-end shimmy, especially at high speed; uneven tire wear; and inconsistent steering.

I recommend overhauling the headset annually (§xi-18 and §xi-19); when you do, carefully examine the steering tube for any signs of stress or damage. Check for bent, cracked, or stretched areas, stripped threads (Fig. 13.6), a bulging threaded steering tube where the stem expands inside (on an older-style threaded steerer), or a crimped threadless steering tube where the stem clamps around its top. Look for cracks on a carbon steering tube where the stem is clamped on, and make sure that there is an expandable or glue-in support inside the steering tube under the stem clamp. Check also to see that the steering tube shows no signs of pulling up out of the fork crown.

With a threaded fork, hold the stem up next to the steering tube to make sure that, when the stem is inserted to the depth you have been using it, the bottom of the stem is always more than an inch below the bottom of the steering tube threads. If the stem is expanded in the threaded region, you are asking for trouble; the threads cut the steering tube wall thickness down by about 50 percent, and each thread offers a sharp breakage plane along which the tube can cleave.

xiii-2

FORK DAMAGE

If your inspection uncovers damage that does not automatically require fork replacement, here are some guidelines to help you.

a. Dents
Not all fork dents threaten the integrity of the fork. A small dent in a steel fork usually poses little risk; a large dent (Fig. 13.6) demands attention (replace the fork). Carbon forks don't tend to dent. If yours has a dent, that is a cause for immediate replacement, especially if you see cracking in the clear coat and/or separated fibers in the same area. In a carbon fork, a dent that holds its shape can indicate delaminated (separated) carbon layers underneath. Tap on the fork leg with a coin at that spot and compare it with the sound in surrounding areas and the other side; you'll be able to hear how the delamination or cracking in underlying carbon layers deadens the nice "clack" noise you should hear.

b. Fork misalignment
Within limits, a rigid steel fork can be realigned if it is slightly off-center (§xiii-3b). Aluminum, carbon-fiber, and titanium forks cannot be realigned. Don't try it!

c. Stripped steering tube threads
If the threads on the steering tube are damaged (Fig. 13.6) so that the headset slips when you try

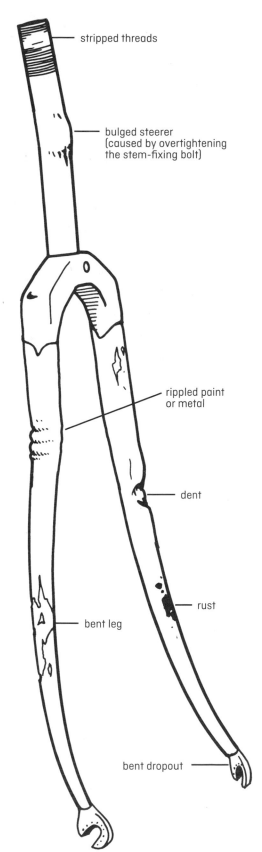

stripped threads

bulged steerer
(caused by overtightening
the stem-fixing bolt)

rippled paint
or metal

dent

rust

bent leg

bent dropout

to tighten it, you need to replace the fork. Same story if the steering tube is bulged; replace the fork, because it can split.

You can have a frame builder replace the steering tube on a steel fork, but getting a new fork makes more economic and safety sense.

d. Obvious bend, ripple, or crease in fork legs

Replace the fork if ripples and bends are obvious (Fig. 13.6). The poor handling and potential breakage threaten your safety. Save a few bucks on something else.

e. Bent or stripped cantilever bosses

The pivot studs on some cantilever bosses (Fig. 13.3) thread into the boss and can be unscrewed with an 8mm open-end wrench and replaced. It is a good idea to use a thread-locking compound on the threads of the new stud.

On many touring and cyclocross forks, the entire cantilever boss is welded on (Fig. 13.3). Bent or stripped cantilever bosses on such forks usually mean that you have to buy a new fork. If you have a frame builder in your area, he or she may be able to weld or braze a new one on a steel, titanium, or aluminum fork. If it's steel, you will also need to repaint the fork; all that work may cost more than a new fork, by the way.

xiii-3

MAINTAINING ROAD AND CYCLOCROSS FORKS

LEVEL 3

Beyond touching up the paint on steel forks and performing regular inspections, the only maintenance procedure for a road or cyclo-cross fork is to check the alignment (§xiii-3a) if your bike is handling badly or has a shimmy at high speeds or with your hands off. You can perform minor realignment on a steel fork if you find that it is off-center, but note that it is risky enough to qualify as a level 3 job. Do not try to realign titanium, carbon-fiber, or aluminum forks. If the alignment is correct and the headset is correctly adjusted but shimmy is a problem, a fork with more rake can sometimes reduce shimmy problems.

a. Check fork alignment

You will need a ruler, a true front wheel, and dropout-alignment tools (Fig. 1.4). If you have an aluminum, titanium, or carbon-fiber fork, this procedure is diagnostic only, because you should not try to realign any of these forks. Checking the alignment may help explain bike-handling problems and may indicate that a different fork could reduce or solve them.

If you find the alignment to be off more than a couple of millimeters in any direction with any fork other than a steel unsuspended one, you will need a new fork. If the fork is new, misalignment should be covered by the warranty.

If a steel fork is more than 8mm off in any direction, you ought to get a new fork. If the dropouts of a steel fork are slightly bent, you can realign them. You can also take a moderately bent (less than 8mm off) steel fork to a frame builder or a bike shop for realignment. Make sure that whoever you take it to is properly equipped with a fork jig or alignment table and is well versed in the art of "cold setting" (a fancy term for bending) steel forks.

1. **Remove the fork from the bike (§xi-18 and §xi-19).**

2. **With the front wheel out, measure the spacing between the faces of the dropouts (Fig. 13.7).** Adult bikes should have a spacing of 100mm between the inner surfaces of the dropouts. (Some low-end kids' bikes have narrower spacing—about 90mm or so.

But if that's the type of bike you are working with, don't bother checking alignment; it isn't worth the trouble.) Remember that you are measuring the distance between the flat surfaces that meet the hub-axle faces (and not between wheel-retaining nubs that protrude inward from the dropouts on some forks). Dropout spacing as wide as 102mm and as narrow as 99mm is acceptable. Beyond that in either direction means a trip to the bike shop for a new fork. If you have a steel fork, you can take it to a bike shop or frame builder for alignment.

3. **Clamp the steering tube of the fork in a bike stand or between V-blocks in a vise.** Install the dropout-alignment tools (Fig. 13.8). They can be used on either the fork or the rear triangle of the bike, and thus they have two axle diameters and spacers for use in the wider rear dropouts. Move all of the spacers to the outside of the dropouts so that only the cups of the tools are placed inboard of the dropouts. Install the tools so that the shafts are seated up against the tops of the dropout slots. Tighten the handles.

13.7 Measuring dropout spacing

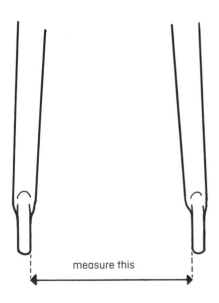

measure this

4. **Check the positions of the alignment tool cups.** Ideally, the ends of the cups on the dropout-alignment tools should be parallel and lined up with each other (Fig. 13.9). The cups of Campagnolo dropout-alignment tools are nonadjustable and are nominally 50mm in length; the ideal space between their ends is 0.1–0.5mm. The cups on Park dropout-alignment tools (illustrated in Figs. 13.8–13.10) are adjustable in length, so that you can bring the faces up close to each other no matter what the dropout spacing. If they are lined up with each other and the dropouts are spaced between 99mm and 102mm apart, continue to step 5. If a steel rigid fork's dropouts are not lined up straight across with each other (Fig. 13.10) and the dropouts are within the 99–102mm spacing range, skip to §xiii-3b to align them before returning to this point for the next steps.

NOTE: *The dropout faces must be parallel before you continue with step 5, or the rest of the alignment procedures will be a waste of time. Clamping the hub into misaligned dropouts will force the fork legs to twist. If the dropouts are*

13.8 Installing a dropout-alignment tool and bending the dropout with it

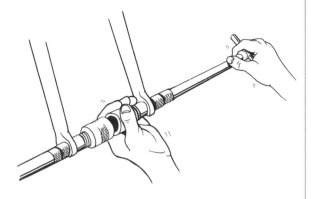

13.9 Correct dropout alignment

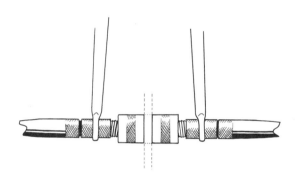

13.10 Incorrect dropout alignment (dropout is twisted or right fork leg is bent back)

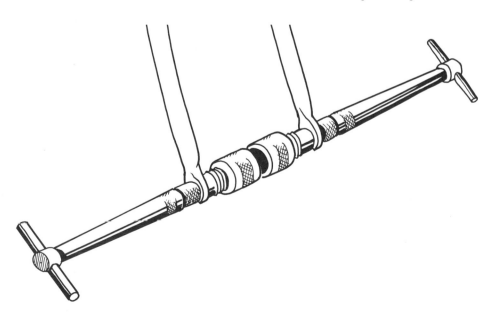

FORKS

misaligned, any measurement of the side-to-side and fore-and-aft alignment of the fork legs will not be accurate.

5. **Remove the tire from the front wheel.** Make sure the wheel is true and properly dished (§xii-4 and §xii-5).

6. **Install the wheel in the fork.** Make sure the axle is seated against the top of the dropout slot on either side, and make sure the quick-release skewer is tight. Lightly push the rim from side to side to make certain that there is no play in the front hub. If there is play, you first must adjust the hub (Chapter 6).

7. **Look down the steering tube and through the valve hole to the bottom side of the rim (Fig. 13.11).** The steering tube should be lined up with this line of sight through the wheel (Fig. 13.12).

NOTE ON CARBON FORKS: *Carbon forks generally are closed under the fork crown, so you cannot*

sight down through them. In that case, the best you can do is compare the rim's position (flip the wheel around and install it the other way as well) with the brake hole and with the fork legs on either side of the rim to determine if it is centered in the fork. This will tell you if the fork legs are symmetrical but not if the steering tube is in alignment with them.

a. When you are sighting through the steering tube and the valve hole, you should see the same amount of space between either side of the rim and the sides of the steering tube. You should also see the center of the bottom side of the rim through the valve hole.

b. Turn the wheel around and install it again so that what was the right end of the axle is now the left and vice versa. Sight through the steering tube and the wheel valve hole again.

13.11 **Correct alignment of the wheel valve hole in a straight fork**

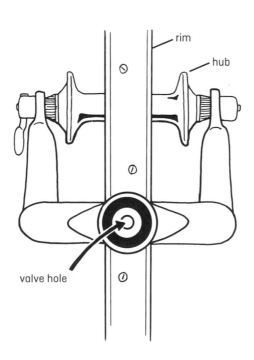

13.12 **Sighting through the steering tube to check fork alignment**

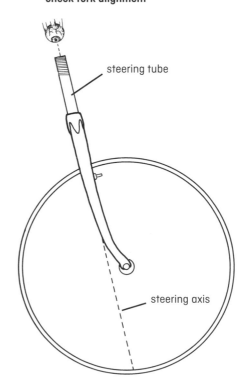

c. Placing the wheel in the fork both ways corrects for deformation in the axle or any wobble in the wheel. If the wheel is true and dished properly, and the axle is in good shape, the wheel should line up exactly as it did before. If it does not line up but is off by the same amount to one side as it is to the opposite side, when the wheel is turned around, the wheel is off and the fork is fine side to side.

d. If this test indicates that the fork is as much as 2–3mm off to the side, that is close enough; continue on. If it is off by more than 3mm, get a new fork or have it aligned by a frame builder (if it is steel, that is; do not try to realign suspension, titanium, carbon-fiber, or aluminum forks).

NOTE: *If you are sighting through the wheel in this way and you cannot see the bottom side of the rim through the valve hole because the hub is in the way, the fork has big problems. In order for the bike to handle properly, the fork must have some forward offset of the front hub from the steering axis. This offset, or "rake," is usually around 4–5cm. If you sight through the steering tube and see the front hub, the fork is bent backward so much that it has little or no offset! If this is the case, you need a new fork.*

8. **With the wheel still in the fork, place a ruler on edge across the fork blades with its flat side resting on the rim (Fig. 13.13) and its length perpendicular to the steering tube.**

9. **Holding the ruler in place, lift the fork toward a light source so that you are sighting across the ruler and the front hub toward the light.** The ruler's edge should line up parallel with the fronts of the dropouts (or with the axle ends sticking out of

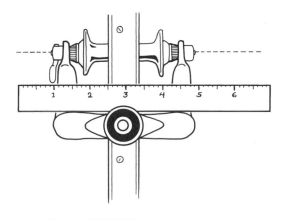

either end of the hub; Fig. 13.13). This test will tell you whether one fork leg is bent back relative to the other one. If the two line up parallel or very close to that, the fork alignment has checked out completely, and you can put the fork back in the bike. If one fork leg is considerably behind the other, you need to get a new fork or have this one aligned (only possible if it is a steel fork). If the dropout-alignment tools also indicated that one dropout was ahead of the other (Fig. 13.10), then the fork legs alone could be bent, and not the dropouts.

b. Align dropouts on steel fork

Dropouts are easy to tweak out of alignment; simply pulling the bike off a roof rack and failing to lift it high enough to clear the rack skewer will do it. Forks can also come with misaligned dropouts to start with. Dropouts can be aligned, but only on a steel, nonsuspension fork.

If the dropout is bent more than 7 degrees or so, or if the paint is cracked at the dropout where it is bent, bending it back may be dangerous. Replace the fork.

1. **Install dropout-alignment tools and check alignment as described in steps 3 and 4 of §xiii-3a.** If one alignment tool is ahead of the

other (Fig. 13.10), it could indicate (a) that the dropouts are bent, (b) that one fork leg is ahead of the other (which you checked for in §xiii-3a, steps 8 and 9), or (c) a combination of both problems.

2. **If the dropouts are not aligned and the fork spacing is between 99mm and 102mm, and step 9 of §xiii-3a indicated that both fork legs are parallel, then you can align the dropouts.** (You'll have to go through all of the steps in §xiii-3a again to check the fork alignment again after you align the dropouts, because that will change how the wheel sits in the fork.) If the fork spacing is wider than 102mm or less than 99mm, there is no point in aligning the dropout faces, because you must bend the fork legs as well to correct the spacing. Without an alignment table or fork jig, you cannot do this accurately. You should get a new fork or have a qualified mechanic or frame builder align the steel fork. If the fork spacing is between 99mm and 102mm, clamp the crown or unicrown of the fork very tightly between two wood blocks in a well-anchored vise.

3. **Grab the end of the dropout-alignment tool handle with one hand and the cup of the tool with the other (Fig. 13.8).** Bend each dropout until the open faces of the dropout-alignment tools are parallel and the edges align with each other (Fig. 13.9).

4. **Remove the tools and continue with §xiii-3a, step 5.**

xiii-4

FORK UPGRADES

You may be able to improve the ride of your bike by replacing the fork. There are a number of reasons to do this. To lighten the bike and add gee-whiz value, you could get a carbon-fiber fork. To stiffen the ride, you could get a steel fork or a beefier carbon fork. To lighten the bike and get a more rigid fork-to-bar connection on your old bike with a gooseneck stem and threaded fork (Fig. 11.1), you could switch to a threadless system (see Chapter 11 on headsets for the difference between threaded and threadless systems). To switch to a disc brake, you could get a disc-brake-specific fork (Fig. 13.4). And to reduce aerodynamic drag, you could get an aero fork.

Make sure you get a fork with a steering tube of the same diameter and length as your old fork, unless you are also switching from a threaded to a threadless system, in which case you will just get a long, unthreaded steering tube that must be considerably longer than your threaded steerer was. Chapter 11 covers the installation of the headset.

The crowns on many carbon forks are so deep that they require an extra-long brake nut to reach the brake bolt. The longer nut should be supplied with the fork.

For cyclocross, weight is as much or more of an issue than it is for a road bike, because you throw the bike onto your shoulder and carry it so much. So a carbon cyclocross fork with a carbon steering tube will be a benefit. It of course needs to have cantilever brake bosses or disc-brake mounts on it (Figs. 13.3, 13.4) so it can handle tires at least up to 700×33mm. It also must have extra room under the crown and between the fork legs for good mud clearance around the tire.

With road bikes and particularly with cyclocross bikes, given the regular bashing they take, replacing the fork after a few years is prudent for safety reasons, and you may as well upgrade it and get more performance out of your bike while you're at it.

FRAMES 14

Duct tape is like The Force. It has a light side, a dark side, and it holds the universe together.
—Carl Zwanzig

TOOLS

2.5mm, 3mm, 4mm, 5mm hex keys
A true rear wheel
Oil
Grease

Optional

Derailleur-hanger-alignment tool
String
Ruler
Dropout-alignment tools
Metric taps
Bottom bracket tap set
Electric drill
Drill-bit set
16mm wrench
8mm open-end wrench

Pay close attention to the frame because it holds your entire bike together. It is nearly impossible to fix on the road, and if it fails, the consequences can be serious.

xiv-1

FRAME DESIGN

Road

The traditional "double-diamond" design of a road bike frame relies on a "front triangle" and a "rear triangle" (Fig. 14.1); never mind that the front triangle is not actually a triangle—or much of a diamond, for that matter.

Referring to Figure 14.2, the angle of the seat tube relative to the horizontal (the "seat angle") determines the fore-and-aft position of the rider relative to the pedals. It also plays a role in determining the weight distribution on the wheels. And seat angle partially dictates the length of the chainstays, because the more tipped back the seat tube is, the farther back the rear wheel will have to be to avoid hitting it.

For a given top-tube length and front-end geometry, the seat angle also dictates whether or not your feet hit the front wheel when pedaling around a tight, low-speed turn (the interference is called, quaintly these days, "toeclip overlap"). And unless the frame tubing is altered to compensate, the vertical and lateral compliance of the rear of the bike will increase with decreasing seat angles and correspondingly longer chainstays.

The angle of the head tube relative to the horizontal (the head angle)—in combination with the fork offset, or "rake" (explained at the beginning of Chapter 13), and wheel diameter—determines much of the steering and handling characteristics of the bike. The head angle and fork rake also dictate in large part how much shock is absorbed by the fork; the shallower the head angle and/or greater the fork offset, the more suspension the bike will offer. Most road frames will have seat angles and head angles in the 72.5- to 75-degree range.

The height of the bottom bracket above the ground determines how much clearance you will

14.1 The frame and its parts

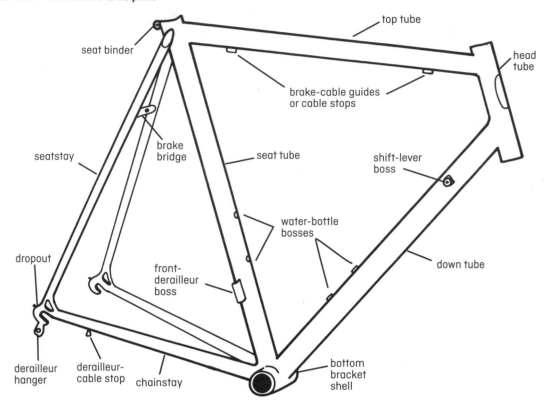

seat binder

top tube

head tube

brake-cable guides
or cable stops

seatstay

brake
bridge

seat tube

shift-lever
boss

water-bottle
bosses

dropout

front-
derailleur
boss

down tube

derailleur
hanger

derailleur-
cable stop

chainstay

bottom
bracket
shell

14.2 Frame dimensions

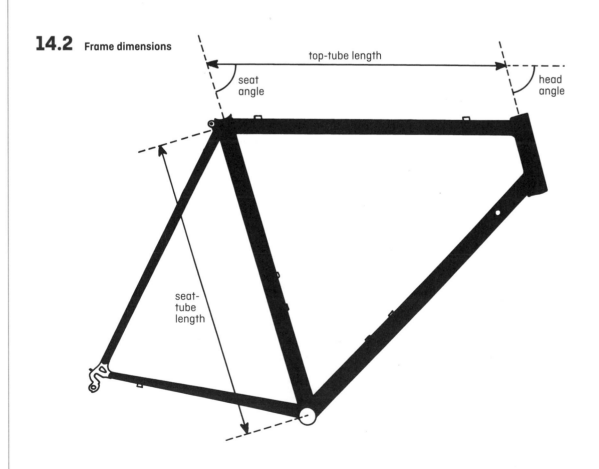

top-tube length

seat
angle

head
angle

seat-
tube
length

seat angle

have for the pedals when rounding a turn. Low bottom brackets lower the center of gravity of the rider and impart a feeling of stability. Frame builders often make compromises between cornering clearance and stability, especially in pro-level bikes where the rider is assumed to have sufficient experience to always corner with the inner crank up. Along with the seat-tube length and angle, the bottom bracket height also helps determine the standover clearance your crotch has over the top tube. A typical bottom bracket height for a road bike is around 265mm.

The top-tube length—along with the stem length, seat angle, and seat fore-aft position on the seatpost—determines your reach to the handlebar.

The seat-tube length (or frame size) determines the amount of seatpost extension you will require to attain a given seat height, as well as the minimum seat height possible on the bike. It also is one of the variables determining standover height.

The wheelbase is the distance between the wheel axles. It determines the minimum possible turning radius.

On modern road bike frames, the shift-lever boss on the down tube shown in Figure 14.1 is generally replaced by a threaded shift-cable stop to accept a barrel adjuster, and this is usually located either on the head tube or on the down tube near the intersection of these two tubes.

Cyclocross

Cyclocross frames have either disc-brake mounts (Fig. 14.3) or cantilever-brake posts and a slotted cable hanger attached to the seatstays (Fig. 14.4); the cable hanger may even have a threaded barrel adjuster on it for adjusting the tension on the rear brake cable. Many 'cross frames have slotted cable guides on the top tube not only for the rear brake cable, but also for both shift cables to keep them up out of the muck they would encounter with standard routing under the bottom bracket. Cyclocross

14.3 Carbon-fiber road or cyclocross frame and fork with disc-brake mounts and tapered head tube and steering tube

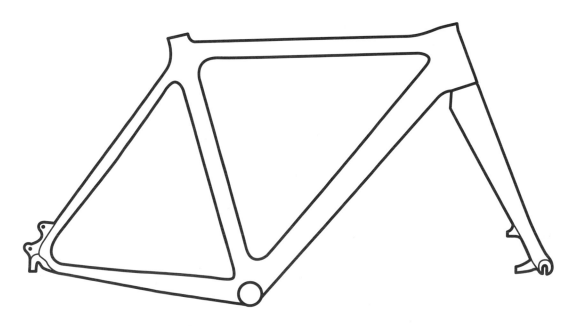

FRAMES

14.4 Carbon-fiber cyclocross frame and fork with cantilever brake mounts

cable hanger

cantilever
brake boss

cantilever
brake boss

frames will generally also have a threaded hole on the back of the seat tube about an inch up from the bottom bracket. This is to screw on a cable roller (Fig. 5.47) if the frame has over-the-top cable routing and the rider will be using a front derailleur. 'Cross frames may or may not have bottle mounts.

To achieve greater stability and slower steering, thanks to increased fork trail (Fig. 13.1), cyclocross frames have shallower head angles than road frames, generally in the 72- to 72.5-degree range. The seat angle on a 'cross frame will usually be a degree or so shallower as well; 72–73 degrees is pretty common. The bottom bracket height will be 15–25mm higher than a road frame. A 280mm+ bottom bracket height will provide better pedaling clearance than a 265mm one, allowing the rider to keep pedaling hard over hummocks and other localized topography variations. The rear end will be longer, and the

chainstays and seatstays will generally be bent in the area near the tire; all of this will be done to improve mud-clearing ability.

Frame materials for cyclocross are the same as for road bikes, but some of the reasons for them and ways that they are employed are different. Aluminum or superthin steel frames were de rigueur until the turn of the millennium because they offered low weight and sufficient strength, durability, and compliance. A problem with both of those designs is that when the rider crashed, the handlebar could easily dent the top tube. Carbon, titanium, and magnesium 'cross frames offer the low weight, strength, and toughness required for the sport, and they can resist denting without being any heavier than a superlight steel or aluminum frame. Carbon and titanium frames will not rust or otherwise oxidize in the horrendous environmental conditions to which they can be exposed.

Time trial/triathlon

Some frames designed for time trials and triathlons are designed for improved aerodynamic
performance and have wing-shaped tubes and
a low-profile design to reduce air drag (Fig. i.2).
They generally have much steeper seat angles than
standard road frames; 78 degrees is common.

Touring

The single most distinguishing feature of touring
frames is the presence of mounts for front and
rear racks. Touring frames are also sturdier—
meaning heavier—in order to carry high loads.
Compared with road bikes, they have longer rear
ends for more vertical compliance and to make
room for fenders and fatter tires; the clearance
under the brake bridge and fork crown is also
higher to accommodate fenders. They may be
built with disc-brake mounts (Fig. 14.3), cantilever brake mounts (Fig. 14.4), or standard brake
holes, but if the latter, the holes will be higher
to fit fenders and larger tires, so longer-reach
brakes will be required. The head and seat angles
are shallower, as described for a cyclocross
frame, for many of the same reasons.

xiv-2

FRAME MATERIALS

Bicycle materials have evolved continually over
time. Wood was the material of choice for the
first bikes but was soon replaced by steel, aluminum, and even bamboo. Carbon-fiber composites,
aluminum, and steel are the materials most commonly used to build frames today, but titanium,
magnesium, and metal matrix composites account
for a significant share at the more expensive end.

Carbon fiber, boron fiber, and similar composite frame materials consist of fibers embedded in a resin (plastic) matrix. These materials

can be very light, very strong, and very stiff.
Bikes can be built by gluing carbon-fiber tubes
into lugs (usually made of carbon fiber or aluminum); by gluing several large, molded sub-
assemblies together; or by molding the frame in
a single piece (monocoque construction).

The big advantage of carbon composites is
that extra composite fabric can be added into
sections of the mold to add thickness precisely
where extra strength is needed. The tricky part is
holding the composite parts together in a frame
that won't come apart.

Metals used in road bike frames come in a
variety of grades with varying costs and physical properties, but in the following discussion
I am talking about the highest grades used in
bicycles. For example, the aluminum used in pop
cans and window frames is much weaker than
the 6061 and 7000 series aluminum used in high-
end bicycle frames.

Steel has the highest modulus of elasticity
(a principal determinant of stiffness) as well as
the highest density and tensile strength of any of
the metals commonly used in frames. Aluminum
has a much lower modulus, density, and tensile
strength than steel; titanium has a modulus, density, and tensile strength between the two. With
good frame design and construction combined
with intelligent selection of tube properties, diameters, shapes, and wall thicknesses, long-lasting
frames with comparable stiffness-to-weight and/
or strength-to-weight ratios can be built from
any of these metals.

Butting of metal tubing reduces weight by
putting thicker material at the tube ends and
thinning the center sections. "Double-butted"
means that both ends are thicker than the center section, whereas "triple-butting" and "quad-
butting" refer to gradation steps in the thickness
at the ends.

The tensile strength of most metals used for bikes is boosted by the addition of alloys into the pure base metal, by heat treatments, or both. Low-carbon steel (like gas pipe) is soft and easy to bend and break. High-carbon steels alloyed with chromium, molybdenum, and other materials are far stronger; heat treating makes them stronger yet. The same goes for aluminum. One improvement in aluminum for bicycles is alloying it with the element scandium, which raises aluminum's strength considerably. Most aluminum frames require a postweld heat-treatment step or they will be soft and breakable.

Titanium alloyed with 3 percent aluminum and 2.5 percent vanadium (3Al/2.5V) is far stronger than commercially pure (CP) titanium, which is 98 percent titanium. Titanium alloyed with 6 percent aluminum and 4 percent vanadium (6Al/4V) is stronger yet but is rarely drawn into tubing, so 6/4 bike tubes are generally made from rolled and welded sheet, which can reduce ultimate strength somewhat. Titanium, like steel, requires no postweld heat treatment, but it must be welded in an inert-gas atmosphere or it will oxidize and become extremely brittle.

Advertising claims touting one frame-tubing material over another can be misleading, because you may not know whether a manufacturer is comparing its material with the high-strength alloyed forms of competitors' materials. If scandium-alloyed aluminum is compared with commercially pure titanium, for example, it comes off looking much better than if it were compared with hardened 6/4 or 3/2.5 titanium, but the consumer just sees "titanium" listed in the advertisement.

Metal-matrix composite frame materials contain added ingredients that improve mechanical properties (usually tensile strength). These additions are not alloying materials (i.e., they are not melted together with the metal), because that would generally contaminate the metal. Rather, particles of sand-like materials (aluminum oxide, silicon oxide, etc.) are worked into the metal (usually aluminum) without melting the particles. The trick with metal-matrix composites is making them weldable without weakening the frame at the joints.

Frame builders endlessly experiment with all sorts of exotic materials that offer mechanical advantages. Beryllium, for example, is a rare and expensive metal used in the defense industry. Its light weight and low density, coupled with high strength and stiffness, made it an ideal material to use on the nose cones of nuclear missiles. Since they're not making many of those anymore, a few folks have tried building bikes out of the stuff. It works great but is poisonous if ingested or inhaled. It is also so expensive that it makes titanium and carbon fiber look like a bargain.

xiv-3

FRAME INSPECTION

You can avoid potentially dangerous frame failures by inspecting your frame frequently. If you find damage and you are not sure if the bike may be dangerous to ride, take it to a bike shop for advice.

1. **Clean the frame every few rides or when it gets dirty.** It's easier to spot problems on a clean frame.

2. **Inspect all tubes for cracks, bends, buckles, dents, and paint stretching or cracking, especially near the joints where stress is highest.** With a carbon frame, use the "coin test" to check for underlying damage. Tap on the tube with a coin in questionable areas and compare it with the sound on other tubes, in surrounding areas, and on the opposite side. If delamination or cracking

exists in underlying carbon layers, especially in central areas away from the joints, you'll be able to hear the difference; the damaged fibers deaden the nice "clack" sound you hear when tapping on an undamaged tube. If in doubt, take it to an expert for advice.

Tubes in metal frames can be rewelded or rebrazed in. Some types of damage in carbon frames can be repaired by specialists such as Calfee Design (www.calfeedesign.com). Otherwise, carbon frames must be replaced if they have large dents, buckles, cracks, bends (sometimes indicated by stretched or fractured paint), or delamination.

3. **Inspect the rear dropouts.** Check the welds or glue joints around them and around the brake bridge and chainstay bridge (the little cross-tube between the chainstays just behind the bottom bracket on some frames) for cracks (see Fig. 14.1 for names and locations of frame parts). Check to be sure the dropouts (and brake posts and cable hangers on cyclocross and touring frames) are not bent. Some dropouts and brake posts bolt on and are replaceable, and some cable hangers are glued in and replaceable. Otherwise, badly bent or broken dropouts, brake posts, and cable hangers need to be replaced; a frame builder may be able to do the job.

4. **Remove the seatpost every few months and invert the bike to remove any water that has collected in the seat tube and let it dry out.** On steel frames, look for deeply rusted areas. Look and feel for rust inside or for rust falling out. I recommend squirting oil or a rust-preventive spray for bicycle frames (like Frame Saver) inside the tubes periodically. With thin-walled steel tubing, the time from when the rust starts until the frame rusts through can be short. Often you

will see bubbles in the paint, for example, around the bottom bracket joints or on the back of the seat tube. Although bubbles can indicate paint problems, they often indicate that the seat tube has pinholes rusted through it under the paint and needs to be replaced.

Also on steel frames, remember to grease both the seatpost and the inside of the seat tube when you reinsert the seatpost. After sanding off the rust, touch up any external areas where the paint has come off with touch-up paint or nail polish (hey, it's available in lots of cool colors).

5. **Check that a true and properly dished rear wheel sits straight in the frame.** It should be centered between the chainstays and seatstays and lined up in the same plane as the front triangle. Check that tightening the hub skewer does not result in bowing or twisting of either the chainstays or the seatstays.

xiv-4

CHECK AND STRAIGHTEN REAR-DERAILLEUR HANGER

LEVEL 3

1. If you have a derailleur-hanger-alignment tool (Fig. 1.4), thread it into the derailleur hanger on the right dropout (Fig. 14.5).

2. Install a true rear wheel in the rear dropouts.

3. **Swing the tool around, measuring the spacing between its arm and the rim all the way around.** The arm of the tool should be the same distance from the rim at all points. Some tools, like the one shown in Figure 14.5, have an indicator rod extending from the arm that you can adjust to check

14.5 Checking derailleur-hanger alignment

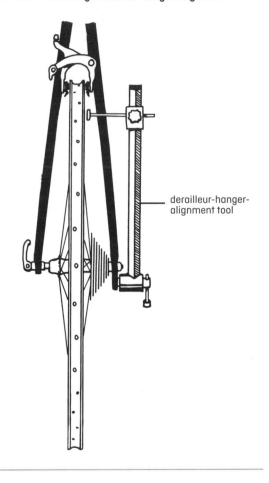

derailleur-hanger-alignment tool

the spacing; others require you to measure the gap with a ruler or caliper.

4. **If the tool has play in it, keep it pushed inward lightly as you perform all of the measurements, or you will get inconsistent data.**

5. **If the spacing between the tool arm and the rim is not consistent (within a millimeter or two all the way around), carefully bend the hanger by pulling outward lightly on the arm of the tool where it is closest to the rim.** You can do this on replaceable aluminum derailleur hangers as well as on steel, aluminum, or titanium ones that are a single piece with the dropout. A titanium hanger may require considerable force to align; if you are not confident about rebend-

ing it correctly, take the frame to a shop or frame builder. Do not heat the hanger with a torch to soften it for alignment; heating will weaken the metal.

6. **If the derailleur hanger is severely bent, you may not be able to align it without breaking it.** You may even have trouble threading the tool in, because the threaded hole will be ovalized. If the dropout bolts to the frame, remove it and take it to your dealer to get an exact replacement.

7. **If the threads or the hanger itself is really screwed up and you do not have a replaceable dropout, see §xiv-7b for other derailleur-hanger options.**

xiv-5

CHECK FRAME ALIGNMENT AND ADJUST DROPOUT ALIGNMENT

LEVEL 3

Exacting alignment checks require a precision surface plate, an uncommon tool in the home workshop. Thus the following methods for determining frame alignment are inexact, but sufficient for determining gross alignment woes.

If you find problems more severe than moderately bent dropouts or a misaligned derailleur hanger, do not attempt to correct them. Adjusting frame alignment, if it can be done at all, should only be performed with an accurate frame-alignment table by someone who is practiced in its use.

1. **With the frame clamped in a bike stand, tie the end of a string to one rear dropout.** Stretch it tightly around the head tube, and tie it symmetrically to the other dropout (Fig. 14.6).

2. **Measure from the string to the seat tube on each side (Fig. 14.6). The measurement should be the same within 1mm.**

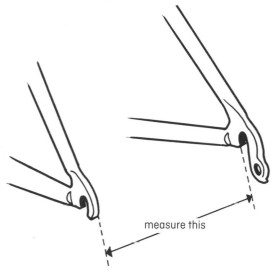

measure this

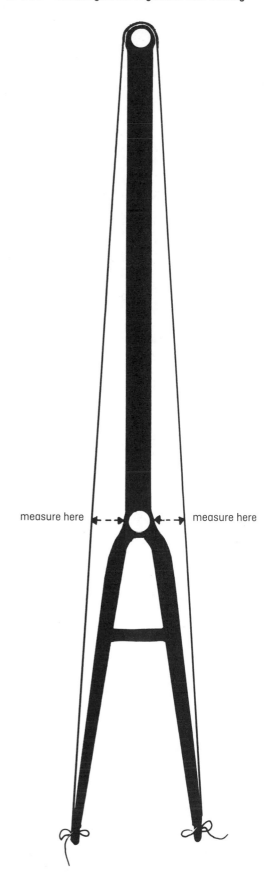

measure here ◄--►◄--► measure here

3. **Put a true and properly dished rear wheel in the frame and check that it lines up in the same plane as the front triangle.** Make certain that the wheel is centered between the seatstays and chainstays. If you have an old steel frame with dropouts with tip screws that thread in from the back of the dropout, turn one or the other of them so that the true wheel lines up straight behind the seat tube (centered between the chainstays).

   The hub should slide easily into the dropouts without requiring you to pull outward or push inward on the dropouts. Tightening the hub quick-release should not result in bowing or twisting of frame members.

4. **Remove the wheel and measure the spacing between the dropouts (Fig. 14.7).** For 8-, 9-, 10-, or 11-speed rear hubs, this spacing should be 130mm; it should be 126mm for 5-, 6-, or 7-speed rear hubs. Measure the width of the rear hub with a caliper to see what the rear-end spacing of the frame should be. If the spacing on the frame is 1mm less or 1.5mm more than nominal, it is acceptable. For instance, if you have a frame whose rear

14.8 Using dropout-alignment tools on rear dropouts

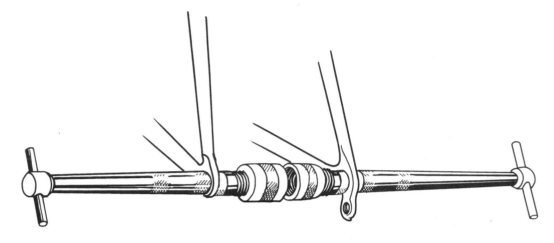

spacing should be 130mm, acceptable spacing is 129–131.5mm.

5. **If you have dropout-alignment tools, put them in the dropouts so that their shafts are fully seated into the dropouts (Fig. 14.8).**

If you have an old steel frame with dropouts with tip screws that thread in from the back of the dropout, you can remove them and seat the dropout-alignment tools all the way to the rear of the dropout slots. Alternatively, you can leave the tip screws installed, and before installing the dropout-alignment tools, turn one or the other of them until a true wheel lines up straight behind the seat tube.

Arrange the tool spacers (and the cups, if they are adjustable) so that the faces of the cups are within a millimeter of each other. Tighten the handles on the tools. The tool cups should line up straight across from each other, with their faces exactly parallel. If the tools do not align, one or both dropouts are bent. If the frame has replaceable dropouts, go ahead and replace one or both of them. If the frame has a composite (i.e., carbon) or bonded rear triangle of any kind, there is nothing you can do about the problem if the bike is not equipped with replaceable dropouts. If the bike has a steel rear triangle, you can align the dropouts by bending them carefully with the dropout-alignment tools. Hold the cup of the tool with one hand and push or pull on the handle with the other. Aluminum or titanium rear dropouts can sometimes be aligned, but it is something you should have a shop do unless the misalignment is slight. Titanium is hard to bend because it keeps springing back, and you run a great risk of breaking aluminum by bending.

CAUTION: *Never heat the dropouts (or any part of the frame) for alignment purposes. Doing so could irreparably change the strength, temper, or hardness of the part and lead to failure.*

xiv-6

CORRECTING FRAME DAMAGE

Apart from the alignment items already covered in this chapter, the only frame problems you can correct are damaged threads, chipped paint, and small dents. Broken braze-ons and bent, broken, or deeply dented tubes call for a new frame or require a frame builder to perform the repair.

FIXING DAMAGED THREADS

a. Retapping and using a new bolt

LEVEL 3

A road bike frame has threads in the bottom bracket shell, the water bottle bosses, and the rear-derailleur hanger, and it usually will have a small threaded hole in the bottom of the bottom bracket shell to which a derailleur-cable guide is bolted. In addition, some bikes have a threaded seat binder rather than a replaceable seatpost binder clamp. Cyclocross frames (and some road touring frames) have cantilever brake posts (Fig. 14.4), and many 'cross frames also have a threaded hole for a front-derailleur cable roller on the back of the seat tube, near its base (Fig. 5.47). Cyclocross and road frames with disc-brake mounts generally have threaded post mounts on the front (Fig. 13.4) and unthreaded transversely drilled International Standard (IS) mounts on the rear (Fig. 14.3), but they can also have post mounts on the rear.

1. **If any threads on the frame are stripped or cross-threaded, try chasing the threads with the appropriate thread tap.** Then replace the bolt or bottom bracket cup with a new one. Whenever you retap any threads, use oil on the tap (use canola vegetable oil on titanium threads). Specific thread-cutting oil is not necessary on old threads because they are already cut. The following tap sizes are commonly found on most road bikes:

Water bottle bosses and the hole for a plastic shift-cable guide:	M5 (5mm × 0.8)
Hole under bottom bracket shell for derailleur-cable guide:	M5 (5mm × 0.8)
Cyclocross front-derailleur roller:	M5 (5mm × 0.8)
Seat binders, disc-brake mounts, and cantilever brake posts:	M6 (6mm × 1)
Derailleur hanger:	M10 (10mm × 1)
Bottom bracket shells, English thread:	1.37 inches × 24 tpi (threads per inch)
Bottom bracket shells, Italian thread:	36mm × 24 tpi

NOTE: *(1) The drive-side (right-side) English bottom bracket threads are left-hand threaded; the other side is right-hand threaded; (2) Italian bottom bracket shells are right-hand threaded on both ends.*

2. **Turn the tap forward (clockwise) a bit, then turn it back, then forward (two steps forward and one back), and so on, to prevent the tap from binding and possibly breaking.** Taps are made of hard, brittle steel. If you put any side or twisting force on small taps, they can easily break. If the tap breaks, you'll have a real mess; the broken tap in the hole is harder than the frame, and it's impossible to drill the broken tap out. If you break off a tap in the frame, do not try to get it out yourself. Take it to a bike shop, a machine shop, or a frame builder before you break off what little is left sticking out. Unless you put the tap in crooked, breaking one should not be a problem when retapping damaged frame threads because these threads will be so worn; getting the tap to find any metal to bite into will probably instead be your biggest problem.

IMPORTANT NOTE: *Tapping a bottom bracket shell requires expertise. If you have never done it before and want to do it yourself, get some expert supervision. In addition to making sure that you place the correct tap in the correct end of the shell, you must be certain that the taps go in straight. Most bottom bracket taps have a shaft between the two taps to keep them parallel* *to each other (Fig. 1.4). They must both be started at the same time from both ends. If you mess up the threads, you can ruin the frame. So if in doubt, ask an expert.*

b. Other specific remedies

1. Damaged water bottle bosses or threaded cyclocross seat-tube front-derailleur roller bosses (Fig. 5.47): Some bike shops have a tool that rivets bottle bosses into the frame. Check for this possibility first, since you can avoid a new paint job that way. But note that these riveted bosses tend to loosen up over time, especially if the bottle-cage bolts are overtightened. Otherwise, take the bike to a frame builder to get a new boss welded or brazed in.

2. Damaged threads in rear-derailleur hanger: The threads can be so stripped or cross-threaded that a tap (§xiv-7a, above) will not rethread it properly, or the hanger can be so bent or twisted that the threads will not work, even if the hanger is bent back straight. Some bikes have replaceable rear dropouts or derailleur hangers that bolt onto the frame. If your bike doesn't, one option is to use a Dropout Saver derailleur-hanger backing nut (Fig. 14.9), made by Wheels Manufacturing and available at bike shops. The Dropout Saver is simply a sleeve threaded the same as the dropout, with 16mm wrench flats. You drill out the hole in the damaged derailleur hanger with a ¹⁴⁄₃₂-inch drill bit, push the Dropout Saver in from the backside, and screw in the derailleur. Dropout Savers come in two lengths, depending on the thickness of the dropout. After installing it, realign it as in §xiv-4, Figure 14.5.

   Another option is to saw off the derailleur hanger with a hacksaw and use a separate

14.9 Inserting Dropout Saver in damaged derailleur hanger

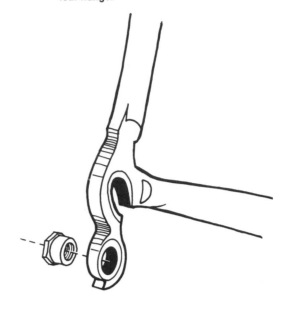

derailleur hanger from a cheap bike that fits flat against the outside of the dropout and is held in by the hub-axle bolts or quick-release. Or, for a metal frame, you could have the dropout replaced by a frame builder (i.e., have a new one welded or brazed on). As a final option, you may have to get a new frame.

3. Damaged seat binders: Drill out the threads and install a quick-release or a bolt and nut. Seat-binder threads rarely get stripped, however; it is usually the bolt that is the problem, and that's easy to replace.

4. Damaged bottom bracket shell threads: If you are using old-school square-taper cranks, you can use an old-style Mavic or Stronglight bottom bracket (§viii-12b, Fig. 8.26), if you can still find one, because it does not depend on the threads in the shell to anchor it. Mavic stopped producing these bottom brackets in 1995, but Stronglight took up making them. You must have a shop bevel the ends of the bottom bracket shell with a special cutting tool. If the shop has

the cutting tool, it likely will have the tools to install the bottom bracket as well.

5. Damaged bottom bracket cable-guide threads: A new hole in the bottom of the bottom bracket can be drilled and tapped, or the stripped hole can be tapped out with larger threads for a larger screw. Make sure the screw you use is short enough that it does not protrude into the inside of the bottom bracket shell.

6. Damaged cantilever brake post on cyclo-cross (or touring) frame (Fig. 14.4): Some brake posts are replaceable; they have wrench flats (usually 8mm) at the base, and they thread into a boss welded onto or molded into the frame. If the brake posts are not of this type, you will have to ask a frame builder to install a new boss, if it's a metal frame. With a carbon frame, if Craig Calfee can't fix it, it's toast.

xiv-8
REPAIR CHIPPED PAINT AND SMALL DENTS

Fixing paint chips is simply a matter of cleaning the area and applying a bit of touch-up paint. Sand any chipped paint or rust completely away before repainting. Use a touch-up paint made for your bike, model paint of a similar color, or fingernail polish.

Small dents can be filled with automotive body putty, but there is little point to filling them if you are only doing a paint touch-up, because the repaired area probably won't look that great anyway.

There are plenty of frame painters around the country who can fill dents, repaint frames, and even match original decals. Many of them advertise in bike magazines or can be found on the Internet.

xiv-9
HIGH-SPEED SHIMMY

More typical with tall frames and heavy riders, the bike developing a shake that builds rapidly in amplitude at high speed or when riding with the hands off the handlebars is an alarming and dangerous occurrence. If it happens to you, immediately clamp your knees against the top tube to damp it and slow down. Another method that usually stops the shimmy but that takes a larger leap of faith is to push your butt far off the back of the saddle (as when going off a steep drop on a mountain bike) to concentrate as much weight as possible on the rear wheel and as little as possible on the front wheel and thus reduce the vibrational feedback between them; it's like letting the string go slack between tin-can telephones. When you get home, do something about the bike; you don't want that to happen again! You can imagine the horror stories of when it becomes uncontrollable.

As I discussed in Chapter 13, replacing a misaligned fork with an aligned one can help a lot. Sometimes a fork with more rake can help, too. So can a stiffer frame and stiffer wheels. A loose headset or loose wheel bearings can also cause shimmy.

xiv-10
COUPLED TRAVEL FRAMES

Due to the rising cost of traveling by air with a bike, travel frames are becoming more common. The bikes are full-size road bikes with standard 700C wheels that can be broken down to fit into a suitcase, thus avoiding oversize baggage charges.

These frames generally have one of two types of connection systems. One consists of screw-together couplers on the top tube and down tube;

the couplers have a toothed Hirth joint inside and are tightened with a special wrench. These couplers are usually made by S and S Machine. The other system, made by Ritchey, uses a seatpost binder in the seat tube as well as on the top tube, so that the seatpost holds the upper part of the frame together, and a small ringlike coupler with a pinch bolt connects the down tube to the bottom bracket.

If you are using a bike with one of these systems, check the couplers frequently to ensure that they are tight and that there is no cracking in the tubes surrounding them. You don't want your frame coming apart while you're riding it.

APPENDIX A
TROUBLESHOOTING INDEX

This index is intended to assist you in finding and fixing problems. If you already know wherein the problem lies, consult the table of contents for the chapter covering that part of the bike. If you are not sure which part of the bike is affected, this index can be of assistance. It is organized alphabetically but, because people's descriptions of the same problem vary, you may need to look through the entire list to find your symptom.

This index can assist you with a diagnosis and can recommend a course of action. Following each recommended action are listed chapter numbers to which you can refer for the repair procedure.

TABLE A.1	Troubleshooting Bike Problems		
SYMPTOM	**LIKELY CAUSES**	**ACTION**	**CHAPTER**
bent wheel	1. maladjusted spokes	true wheel	6
	2. broken spoke	replace spoke	6
	3. bent rim	replace rim	12
bike pulls to one side	1. wheels not true	true wheels	6
	2. tight headset	adjust headset	11
	3. pitted headset	replace headset	11
	4. bent frame	replace or straighten	14
	5. bent fork	replace or straighten	13
	6. loose hub bearings	adjust hubs	6
	7. low tire pressure	inflate tires	2, 6
bike shimmies at high speed or when hands off of handlebars	1. frame cracked	replace frame	14
	2. frame bent	replace or straighten	14
	3. wheels way out of true	true wheels	6
	4. loose hub bearings	adjust hubs	6
	5. wheels too flexible	build stiffer wheels	12
	6. headset too loose	tighten headset	11
	7. misaligned fork	replace fork	13
	8. soft frame/heavy rider	replace frame	14
	9. poor frame design	replace frame	14
bike vibrates when braking	see "chattering and vibration when braking" under "STRANGE NOISES"		
brake doesn't stop bike	1. maladjusted brake	adjust brake	7
	2. worn brake pads	replace pads	7
	3. wet rims	keep braking	7
	4. greasy rims	clean rims	7

Continues >>

TABLE A.1	Troubleshooting Bike Problems, *continued*		
SYMPTOM	**LIKELY CAUSES**	**ACTION**	**CHAPTER**
brake doesn't stop bike (cont.)	5. sticky brake cable	lube or replace cable	7
	6. steel rims in wet weather	use aluminum rims	12
	7. brake damaged	replace brake	7
	8. sticky or bent brake lever	lube or replace lever	7
	9. wrong pads for rim	get correct pads	7
brake pad rubs on rim	1. brake misaligned	adjust brake	7
	2. untrue wheel	true wheel	6, 12
	3. cable pull insufficient for V-brake	get V-brake lever	7
chain falls off in front	1. maladjusted front derailleur	adjust front derailleur	5
	2. chainline off	adjust chainline	5
	3. chainring bent or loose	replace or tighten	8
chain jams in front between chainring and chainstay (called chain suck)	1. dirty chain	clean chain	4
	2. bent chainring teeth	replace chainring	8
	3. chain too narrow	replace chain	4
	4. chainline off	adjust chainline	5
	5. stiff links in chain	free links, lube chain	4
chain jams in rear	1. maladjusted rear derailleur	adjust derailleur	5
	2. chain too wide	replace chain	4
	3. small cog not on spline	reseat cogs	6
	4. poor frame clearance	return to dealer	14
chain skips	1. tight chain link	loosen tight link	4
	2. elongated (worn) chain	replace chain	4
	3. maladjusted derailleur	adjust derailleur	5
	4. worn rear cogs	replace cogs and chain	4, 6
	5. dirty or rusted chain	clean or replace chain	4
	6. bent rear derailleur	replace derailleur	5
	7. bent derailleur hanger	straighten hanger	14
	8. loose derailleur jockey wheel	tighten jockey wheel	5
	9. bent chain link	replace chain	4
	10. sticky rear shift cable	replace shift cable	5
	11. upside-down master link	reset link	4
chain slaps chainstay	1. chain too long	shorten chain	4
	2. weak rear-derailleur spring	replace spring or derailleur	5
	3. terrain very bumpy	use large chainring	n/a
derailleur hits spokes	1. maladjusted rear derailleur	adjust derailleur	5
	2. broken spoke	replace spoke	6
	3. bent rear derailleur	replace derailleur	5
	4. bent derailleur hanger	straighten or replace	14
knee pain	1. poor shoe cleat position	reposition cleat	9
	2. saddle too low or high	adjust saddle	10
	3. clip-in pedal has no float	get floating pedal	9
	4. foot rolled in or out	replace shoes or get orthotics	n/a

TABLE A.1	Troubleshooting Bike Problems, *continued*		
SYMPTOM	**LIKELY CAUSES**	**ACTION**	**CHAPTER**
pain or fatigue when riding, particularly in the back, neck, and arms	1. incorrect seat position	adjust seat position	App. C
	2. stem too low	raise stem	App. C
	3. too much riding	build up miles gradually	n/a
	4. incorrect stem length	replace stem	App. C
	5. poor frame fit	replace frame	App. C
pedal entry difficult (with clip-in pedals)	1. spring tension set high	reduce spring tension	9
	2. cleat guide loose or gone	tighten or replace	9
pedal release difficult (with clip-in pedals)	1. spring tension set high	reduce spring tension	9
	2. loose cleat on shoe	tighten cleat	9
	3. dry pedal spring pivot	oil spring pivots	9
	4. dirty pedals	clean and lube pedals	9
	5. bent pedal clips	replace pedals or clips	9
	6. dirty cleats	clean lube cleats	9
pedal release too easy (with clip-in pedals)	1. release tension too low	increase release tension	9
	2. cleats worn-out	replace cleats	9
pedal(s) move laterally or clunk, click, or twist while pedaling	1. loose crankarm	tighten crank bolt	8
	2. pedal loose in crank	tighten pedal to crank	9
	3. bent pedal axle	replace pedal or axle	9
	4. loose bottom bracket	adjust bottom bracket	8
	5. bent bottom bracket axle	replace bottom bracket or axle	8
	6. bent crankarm	replace crankarm	8
	7. loose pedal bearings	adjust pedal bearings	9
rear shifting working poorly	1. maladjusted derailleur	adjust derailleur	5
	2. sticky or damaged cable	replace cable	5
	3. loose rear cogs	reseat and tighten cogs	6
	4. worn rear cogs	replace cogs and chain	4, 6
	5. worn/damaged chain	replace chain	4
	6. see also "chain jams in rear" and "chain skips," above		
resistance while coasting or pedaling	1. tire rubs frame or fork	adjust axle; true wheel	2, 6
	2. brake pad drags on rim	adjust brake	7
	3. tire pressure too low	inflate tire	2, 6
	4. hub bearings too tight	adjust hubs	6
	5. hub bearings dirty/worn	overhaul hubs	6
	6. mud packed around tires	clean bike	2
resistance while pedaling only	1. bottom bracket too tight	adjust bottom bracket	8
	2. bottom bracket dirty/worn	overhaul bottom bracket	8
	3. chain dry/dirty/rusted	clean/lube or replace	4
	4. pedal bearings too tight	adjust pedal bearings	9
	5. pedal bearings dirty/worn	overhaul pedals	9
	6. bent chainring rubs frame	straighten or replace	8
	7. true chainring rubs frame	adjust chainline	5

Continues >>

TABLE A.1	Troubleshooting Bike Problems, continued		
SYMPTOM	**LIKELY CAUSES**	**ACTION**	**CHAPTER**
stiff steering	tight headset	adjust headset	11
tire bulged	1. broken casing threads	replace tire	6
	2. slipped tubular tire	reglue tire and line up valve stem	6
tire pinch flats	1. insufficient pressure	pump tire higher	6
	2. tire diameter too small	replace with larger tire	6
tire valve stem angled sharply	1. tube slipped in tire	deflate and slide tire around rim	6
	2. slipped tubular tire	reglue tire and line up valve stem	6

STRANGE NOISES			

Weird noises can be hard to locate; use this to assist in locating them.

SYMPTOM	**LIKELY CAUSES**	**ACTION**	**CHAPTER**
chattering and vibration when braking; fork shudder when braking	1. bent or dented rim	replace rim	12
	2. loose headset	adjust headset	11
	3. brake pads toed out	adjust brake pads	7
	4. wheel way out of round	true wheel	6
	5. standard pads on carbon rim	get correct brake pads	7
	6 greasy sections of rim	clean rim	6
	7. loose brake pivot bolts	tighten brake bolts	7
	8. rim worn through and ready to collapse	replace rim ASAP!	12
	9. steering tube flex with cantilever brake	fork-crown cable hanger, stiffer fork, mini V-brake instead of cantilever	7
clicking noise	1. cracked shoe cleats	replace cleats	9
	2. cracked shoe sole	replace shoes	9
	3. loose bottom bracket	tighten BB	8
	4. loose crankarm	tighten crankarm	8
	5. loose pedal	tighten pedal	9
clunking from fork	headset loose	adjust headset	11
creaking noise	1. dry handlebar/stem joint	grease inside stem clamp	11
	2. loose seatpost	tighten seatpost	10
	3. loose shoe cleats	tighten cleats	9
	4. loose crankarm	tighten crankarm bolt	8
	5. cracked frame	replace frame	14
	6. dry, rusty seatpost	grease seatpost	10
	7. see "squeaking noise," below		
rubbing or scraping noise when pedaling	1. crossed chain	avoid extreme gears	5
	2. front derailleur rubbing	adjust front derailleur	5
	3. chainring rubs frame	install longer BB or move BB over	8

TABLE A.1	Troubleshooting Bike Problems, continued		
SYMPTOM	**LIKELY CAUSES**	**ACTION**	**CHAPTER**
rubbing, squealing, or scraping noise when coasting or pedaling	1. tire dragging on frame	straighten wheel	2, 6
	2. tire dragging on fork	straighten wheel	2, 6
	3. brake dragging on rim	adjust brake	7
	4. dry hub dust seals	clean and lube dust seals	6
squeaking noise	1. dry hub or BB bearings	overhaul hubs or BB	6, 8
	2. dry pedal bushings	overhaul pedals	9
	3. squeaky saddle	grease edge of leather	10
	4. rusted or dry chain	lube or replace chain	4
	5. squeaky seatpost clamps	tighten seatpost clamp	10
	6. seatpost squeaking inside seat tube	shim or shorten seatpost	10
squealing noise when braking	1. brake pads toed out	adjust brake pads	7
	2. greasy rims	clean rims and pads	7
	3. loose brake arms	tighten brake pivot bolt(s)	7
	4. improper pads on carbon rim	get correct pads	7
ticking noise when braking	1. glue on rim sidewall	clean rim with solvent	6
	2. gouge in rim sidewall	sand rough spot	6
	3. high rim seam junction	ignore, or sand seam	6
ticking noise when coasting	1. wheel magnet hits sensor	move computer sensor	n/a
	2. badly glued tubular	reglue tire	6

APPENDIX B
GEAR CHART

The following gear table is based on a 700C × 23mm tire (671mm diameter). Your gear-development numbers may be slightly different if the diameter of the fully inflated rear tire, with your weight on it, is not 671mm. Unless your bike has 650C, 24-inch, or some other nonstandard-size wheels, these numbers will be very close.

To obtain accurate gear-development numbers for the tire you happen to have on at the time, at a certain inflation pressure, measure the tire diameter very precisely using the following procedure. You can come up with your own gear chart by plugging your tire diameter into the gear-development formula below the chart on the following pages or by multiplying each number in this chart by the ratio of the tire diameter divided by 671mm (the tire diameter I used). Even easier, go to Tom Compton's interactive gear chart at www.analyticcycling.com/GearChart_Page.html.

MEASURING TIRE DIAMETER

1. Sit on the bike with the tire pumped to your desired pressure.
2. Mark the spot on the rear rim that is at the bottom, and mark the floor adjacent to that spot.
3. Roll forward one wheel revolution, and mark the floor again where the mark on the rim is again at the bottom.
4. Measure the distance between the marks on the floor; this is the tire circumference at pressure with your weight on it.
5. Divide this number by π (π = 3.14159) to get the diameter.

NOTE: *This rollout procedure is also the method for measuring the wheel size with which to calibrate your bike computer, except that the procedure will be done on the front wheel for most computers.*

TABLE B.1 — Gear Chart

		NUMBER OF TEETH ON FRONT CHAINRING												
	27	**28**	**29**	**30**	**31**	**32**	**33**	**34**	**35**	**36**	**37**	**38**	**39**	**40**
11	65	67	70	72	74	77	79	82	84	86	89	91	94	96
12	59	62	64	66	68	70	73	75	77	79	81	84	86	88
13	55	57	59	61	63	65	67	69	71	73	75	77	79	81
14	51	53	55	57	58	60	62	64	66	68	70	72	73	75
15	47	49	51	53	55	56	58	60	62	63	65	67	69	70
16	45	46	48	49	51	53	54	56	58	59	61	63	64	66
17	42	43	45	47	48	50	51	53	54	56	57	59	61	62
18	40	41	42	44	45	47	48	50	51	53	54	56	57	59
19	37	39	40	42	43	44	46	47	49	50	51	53	54	56
20	36	37	38	40	41	42	44	45	46	47	49	50	51	53
21	34	35	36	38	39	40	41	43	44	45	46	48	49	50
22	32	34	35	36	37	38	40	41	42	43	44	46	47	48
23	31	32	33	34	36	37	38	39	40	41	42	44	45	46
24	30	31	32	33	34	35	36	37	38	40	41	42	43	44
25	28	30	31	32	33	34	35	36	37	38	39	40	41	42
26	27	28	29	30	31	32	33	34	36	37	38	39	40	41
27	26	27	28	29	30	31	32	33	34	35	36	37	38	39
28	25	26	27	28	29	30	31	32	33	34	35	36	37	38
29	25	25	26	27	28	29	30	31	32	33	34	35	35	36
30	24	25	25	26	27	28	29	30	31	32	33	33	34	35
31	23	24	25	26	26	27	28	29	30	31	31	32	33	34
32	22	23	24	25	26	26	27	28	29	30	30	31	32	33

(Left axis label: NUMBER OF TEETH ON REAR COG)

GEAR FORMULA

Gear = (number of chainring teeth) x (tire diameter) ÷ (number of cog teeth)

If you want the gear in inches, put in the tire diameter in inches.

To find out how far you get with each pedal stroke (gear rollout), multiply the gear by π (3.14159).

TABLE B.1 — Gear Chart, continued

NUMBER OF TEETH ON FRONT CHAINRING															
41	42	43	44	45	46	47	48	49	50	51	52	53	54	55	56
98	101	103	106	108	110	113	115	118	120	122	125	127	129	132	134
90	92	95	97	99	101	103	106	108	110	112	114	117	119	121	123
83	85	87	89	91	93	95	97	99	101	103	106	108	110	112	114
77	79	81	83	85	87	89	90	92	94	96	98	100	102	23	106
72	74	76	77	79	81	83	84	86	88	90	91	93	95	97	98
68	69	71	73	74	76	77	79	81	82	84	86	87	89	91	92
64	65	67	68	70	71	73	74	76	78	79	81	82	84	85	87
60	62	63	64	66	67	69	70	72	73	75	76	78	79	81	82
57	58	60	61	62	64	65	67	68	69	71	32	74	75	76	78
54	55	57	58	59	61	62	63	65	66	67	69	70	71	73	74
51	53	54	55	57	58	59	60	62	63	64	65	67	68	69	70
49	50	52	53	54	55	56	58	59	60	61	62	64	65	66	67
47	48	49	50	52	53	54	55	56	57	58	60	61	62	63	64
45	46	47	48	49	51	52	53	54	55	56	57	58	59	60	62
43	44	45	46	47	49	50	51	52	53	54	55	56	57	58	59
42	43	44	45	46	47	48	49	50	51	52	53	41	55	56	57
40	41	42	43	44	45	46	47	48	49	50	51	43	53	54	55
39	40	41	41	42	43	44	45	46	47	48	49	50	51	52	53
37	38	39	40	41	42	43	0	45	45	46	47	48	49	50	51
36	37	38	39	40	40	41	42	43	44	45	46	47	47	48	49
35	36	37	37	38	39	40	41	42	43	43	44	45	46	47	48
34	35	35	36	37	38	39	40	40	41	42	43	44	45	45	46

APPENDIX C
ROAD BIKE FITTING

If you are getting a new bike, get one that fits you properly. Fit should be the primary consideration when selecting a bike; you can adapt to heavier bikes and bikes not painted your favorite color, but your body will soon protest on one that doesn't fit. The simple need to protect your most sensitive parts should keep you away from a bike without sufficient standover clearance (Fig. C.1), but there are a lot of other factors to consider as well, including top tube length, handlebar width and drop, stem length, crank length, and toe overlap with the front wheel. An improperly sized bike will cause you to ride with less efficiency and more discomfort. Finding a bike with the right fit isn't difficult; just follow the guidelines in this appendix.

I've outlined two methods for finding your frame size. The first is a simple method of checking your fit on fully assembled bikes at a bike shop. The second method is a bit more elaborate, since it involves taking body measurements. This more detailed approach will allow you to calculate the proper frame dimensions whether the bike is assembled or not.

One other thing: If you are racing triathlon or time trials, aerodynamics and efficient positioning on aero handlebars will be important, as will compliance with technical rules in UCI-sanctioned time trials. See the following sections for more information on those topics.

C-1

SELECTING THE SIZE OF AN ASSEMBLED BIKE

1. Standover height

Stand over the bike's top tube and lift the bike straight up until the top tube hits your crotch. The wheels should be at least 1 inch off the ground to ensure that you can jump off of the bike safely without hitting your crotch. On a bike with sloping top tube, there is no maximum measurement. On a bike with a level top tube, unless the frame has been built with a head tube with extra extension above the top tube to lift the stem higher, you probably don't want any more than 3 or 4 inches of standover.

NOTE: *If you have 2 inches of standover clearance on a bike, do not assume that another bike with the same listed frame size will offer the same standover clearance. Manufacturers use different methods to measure frame size. They also slope their top tubes differently and use different bottom bracket heights (Fig. C.1), all of which affect the final standover height.*

All manufacturers measure the frame size up the seat tube from the center of the bottom bracket, but the top of the measurement varies. Some manufacturers measure to the center of the top tube ("center-to-center" measurement), some measure to the top of the top tube ("center-to-

C.1 Standover clearance and bottom bracket height

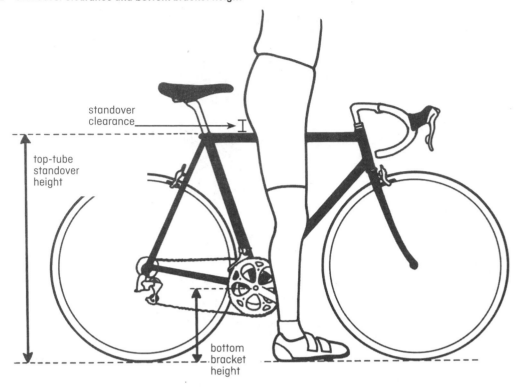

top"), and others measure to the top of the seat tube (also called "center-to-top"), even though there is wide variation in the length of the seatpost collar above the top tube. And some sloping-top-tube bikes (often called "compact geometry"), which may come sized in S, M, L, etc., may list an "effective" frame size or seat tube length, which would correspond to the size of the frame if the top tube were horizontal rather than sloped. Obviously, each of these methods will have a different "frame size" for the same frame.

No matter how the frame size is measured, the standover height of a bike depends on the slope of the top tube. Nowadays, most road bikes have sloping top tubes that slant up to the front, and standover clearance above a sloping tube is obviously a function of where you are standing. With an up-angled top tube, stand over it an inch or two forward of the nose of the saddle, and then lift the bike up into your crotch to measure standover clearance.

Standover height is also a function of bottom bracket height above the ground, but there is normally not substantial variation between sizes and brands of standard road bikes.

NOTE: *Unless the manufacturer lists the standover height in its brochure and you know your inseam length, you need to stand over the actual bike.*

ANOTHER NOTE: *If you are short and cannot find a frame size small enough to get at least one inch of standover clearance, consider a bike with 650C (26-inch) wheels rather than 700C.*

2. Knee-to-handlebar clearance

Make sure your knee cannot hit the handlebar (Fig. C.2). Do this standing out of the saddle as well as seated and with the front wheel turned slightly, to make sure that the knee will not hit when you are in the most awkward pedaling position you might use. If your knee hits, you need a longer stem or a frame with a longer top tube.

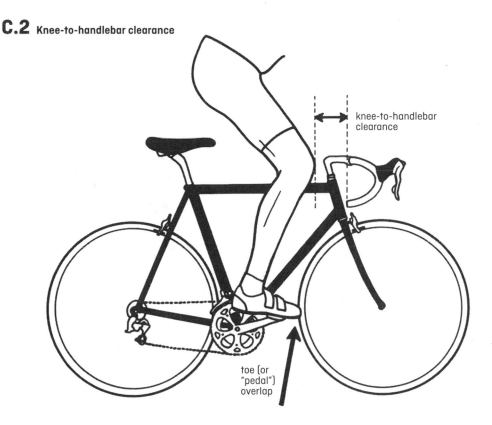

knee-to-handlebar
clearance

toe (or
"pedal")
overlap

3. Handlebar reach and drop

Ride the bike. See if the reach feels comfortable to you when holding the bars on the flat section adjacent to the stem clamp, on top of the brake hoods, and in the drops. Make sure it is easy to grab the brake levers. Make sure your knees do not hit your elbows as you pedal (Fig. C.6). Make sure that the stem can be raised or lowered enough to achieve a comfortable handlebar height.

NOTE: *Threadless headsets (the standard on all bikes today) allow very limited adjustment of stem height (§xi-2). Large changes in height require a change in stems.*

4. Toe overlap

In bike shops, this measurement is often called "pedal overlap;" that's a misnomer, since you are actually interested in whether your toes, not the pedals, can hit the front tire when turning sharply at low speeds. Sitting on the bike with the crankarms horizontal and your foot on the pedal, turn the handlebars and check that your toe does not hit the front tire (Fig. C.2). Toe overlap is to be avoided for any kind of slow-speed riding, since making a slow, tight turn in a parking lot can put you on your nose. Toe overlap is not an issue for most other riding, since the speeds are high enough on the road that turning the bike does not require turning the front wheel at enough of an angle to hit the foot.

C-2

CHOOSING A FRAME SIZE FROM BODY MEASUREMENTS

By taking three easy measurements (Fig. C.3), most people can get a very good frame fit (you will need someone to assist you in taking the measurements). When designing a custom frame, I go through a more complex procedure than this, involving more measurements. For

C.3 Body measurements

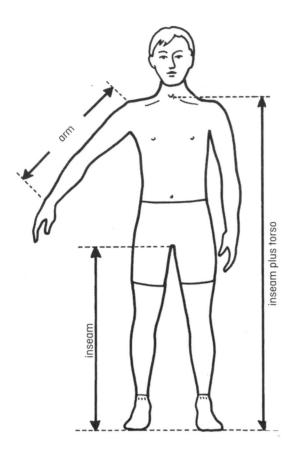

C.4 Measuring inseam using a bubble level on a dowel

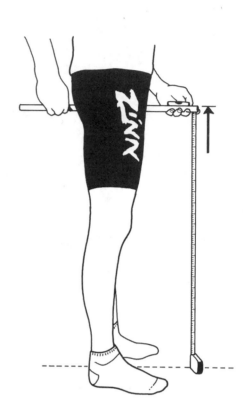

picking an off-the-shelf bike, though, the following method works well. To avoid the trouble of making these calculations yourself, you can go to the free FIT page at www.zinncycles.com and it will automatically calculate your frame size from these measurements.

1. Measure your inseam

Spread your stocking feet about 2 inches apart, and measure from the floor up to a broomstick or dowel held level and lifted firmly up into your crotch (Fig. C.4). You can also use a large book and slide it up a wall to keep the top edge horizontal—as you pull it up as hard as you can—into your crotch. You can mark the top of the book on the wall and measure up from the floor to the mark.

2. Measure your inseam-plus-torso length

Hold a pencil horizontally in your sternal notch, the U-shaped bone depression just below your Adam's apple. Standing up straight in front of a wall, mark the wall with the horizontal pencil. Measure up from the floor to the mark.

3. Measure your arm length

Hold your arm out from your side at a 45-degree angle with your elbow straight. Measure from the sharp bone point directly behind and above your shoulder joint (the lateral tip of the acromion) to the wrist bone on your little finger side.

4. Find your frame size

Subtract 27.5 to 32cm (10.8 to 12.6 inches) from your inseam length. This length is your frame

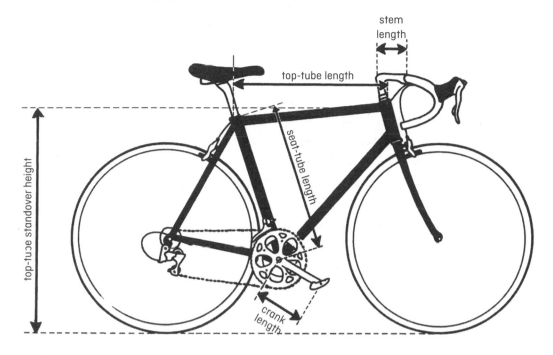

size (also known as seat-tube length) measured along the seat tube from the center of the bottom bracket to the top of the top tube (Fig. C.5). If the frame you are interested in has a sloping top tube, you need a bike with a shorter seat tube. In the case of a sloping top tube, project a horizontal line back to the seat tube (or seatpost) from the top of the top tube at the center of its length (Fig. C.5). Mark the seat tube or seat post at this line. Measure from the center of the bottom bracket to this mark; this length should be 27.5–32cm less than your inseam measurement.

Also, if the bike has a bottom bracket higher than 27cm (10.6 inches), subtract the additional bottom-bracket height from the seat-tube length as well.

Generally, smaller riders will want to subtract close to 27.5cm from their inseam measurement, while taller riders will subtract closer to 32cm. Since an average bottom-bracket height on a road bike is 26.5cm, subtracting any less than 27.5cm could result in less than one inch (2.5cm)

of standover clearance on a bike with a level top tube. But there is considerable range here. The top-tube length is more important than the frame size, and, if you have short torso and arms, you can use a small frame to get the right top-tube length, as long as you can raise your bars as high as you need them.

If you are short and cannot find a bike small enough for you to get at least an inch of standover clearance, consider one with 650C (26 inches) or even 24-inch wheels rather than 700C.

NOTE: *A step-through frame (i.e., "women's" frame, "mixte frame," or "girl's bike") having a steeply up-angled top tube meeting near the bottom bracket shell makes seat-tube length irrelevant for determining standover clearance. With a step-through bike, the only considerations will be horizontal and vertical reach to the bars.*

5. Find your top-tube length

To find your torso length, subtract your inseam measurement (found in step 1) from your inseam-plus-torso measurement (found in step 2). Add this torso length to your arm length measurement (found in step 3). To find the top-tube length, multiply this arm-plus-torso measurement by a factor in the range between 0.47 and 0.485. If you are a casual rider, use 0.47; if you are a very aggressive rider, use 0.485; and, if you are in between, use a factor in between. This top-tube length is measured horizontally from the center of the seat tube to the center of the head tube (Fig. C.5).

If this is a bike you plan to set up exclusively with aero handlebars and race in time trials or drafting-prohibited triathlons, you will generally want a longer top tube. Use 0.495 as the multiplier to find the top tube in this case. If the seat angle on the bike you will be using for this purpose is not very steep—less than 75 degrees—you will likely need to add more length yet to the top tube. This would occur if you will be pushing your saddle all of the way forward or using a forward-offset seatpost to position yourself in a forward position. The forward-set saddle will consume much of your reach to the bars, so you will need more top-tube length to stretch out properly. The longer top tube will also ensure a more even weight distribution over the wheels and prevent you from using such a long stem and bar that you will be hanging way out over the front of the bike with too much weight on the front wheel.

Use 0.49–0.5 as the multiplier if you're using a straight (mountain bike–style) handlebar.

NOTE: *On a sloping-top-tube bike, the actual horizontal top-tube length is less than the length found by measuring along the top tube.*

6. Find your stem length

Multiply the arm-plus-torso length you found in step 5 by 0.09 to 0.11 to find the stem length. Again, a casual rider will multiply by 0.09 or so,

while an aggressive rider will multiply by closer to 0.11. This is a starting stem length and is dependent on the top tube being the length you figured above; the stem length needs to increase or decrease accordingly if the top tube is shorter or longer than your calculation. Finalize the stem length (Fig. C.5) once you are sitting on the bike and see what feels best.

7. Determine crankarm length

Generally, road crankarms come in 2.5mm length increments (Fig. C.5) from 165mm to 180mm (although 167.5mm is often hard to find). Longer than 175mm can usually only be found on high-end cranks, if even then. It is possible to find 185–220mm as well as 130–160mm from Zinn Cycles and a few other custom crank manufacturers.

There is no general consensus on ideal crank length. Here is a simple selection method that works reasonably well. If the frame size you determined in step four is less than 45cm, use 165mm cranks; if your frame is between 46 and 49cm, use 167.5mm; 50–53, use 170mm; 54–57, use 172.5mm; 58–61, use 175mm; 61–64, use 177.5mm, and if your frame size is 65cm or bigger use 180mm or longer. If your riding is focused on time trialing, triathlon, or hill climbing, try 2.5mm longer than the recommendations above.

Another way to look at this is to use a factor multiplied by your leg or thigh length, like leg length times 0.21 to 0.216. I think this and similar multiplication methods make more sense and result in more efficient pedaling than the almost one-size-fits-all approach by most bike and crank manufacturers. That said, I must warn you that for short-legged and long-legged people, the formulas will result in crank lengths considerably shorter or longer than are generally available. But tall riders will often be better off with custom cranks longer than 175mm or 180mm and short riders with custom cranks shorter than 165mm or 170mm. See zinncycles.com for formulas and custom crank availability.

8. Choosing handlebar width and drop

Road drop handlebars should be the same width or slightly wider than the distance from the center of the top of one upper-arm bone—humerus—to the other. You can hold the front of the bar up to your shoulders and see if each side meets in the center of the top of each humcrus or slightly overlaps the outside of your arms. That way, your arms will support your shoulders straight in line, and your chest will be able to open for efficient breathing.

If you are a small person, you will want a handlebar with a shallow drop, while a big person will want a deep drop.

If you have small hands, look for a bar with a bend specifically made to reduce the reach to an STI or Ergopower brake lever.

C-3

POSITIONING OF SADDLE AND HANDLEBARS

The frame fit is only part of the equation. Except for the standover clearance, a good frame fit is relatively meaningless if the seat setback, seat height, handlebar height, and handlebar reach are not set correctly for you.

1. Saddle height

When your foot is at the bottom of the stroke and clipped into the pedal, lock your knee without rocking your hips. Do this sitting on your bike on a trainer with someone else observing. Your foot should be level, or the heel should be slightly higher than the ball of the foot. Another way to determine seat height is to take your inseam measurement (found in step 1 under "Choosing a frame size from body measurements" above) and multiply it by 1.09; this is the length from the center of the pedal spindle (when the pedal is down) to level with the top of the saddle where your butt bones (ischial tuberosities) contact it. Adjust the seat height (Chapter 10) until you get the proper height.

NOTE: *These two methods yield similar results, although the measurement-multiplying method is dependent on the thickness of your shoe sole and the pedal. Either method yields a biomechanically efficient pedaling position.*

2. Saddle setback

Sit on your bike on a stationary trainer with cranks horizontal and forward foot at the angle it normally assumes at that point when pedaling. An easy way to check that the center of rotation of the knee is over the center of rotation of the pedal is to drop a plumb line from the front of the kneecap (Fig. C.6). It should drop right over the front end of the crankarm. A saddle positioned fore-aft in this manner encourages smooth pedaling at high rpm, while 2cm farther back encourages powerful seated climbing.

You also will want to make sure that your cleat position (§ix-2) is set properly. Generally, you will want your foot deep enough into the pedal that the ball of the foot is right over the pedal spindle or up to 2cm ahead of it; riders with big feet will want their cleats further back, and vice versa.

Slide the saddle back and forth on the seatpost (Chapter 10) until you achieve the desired fore-aft saddle position. Set the saddle level or very slightly tipped down. Re-check the seat height in step 1 above, since fore-aft saddle movements affect seat-to-pedal distance as well.

For time trial and draft-prohibited-triathlon purposes, most riders using aero bars will want to position their saddle considerably farther forward. Being forward will allow the shoulders to drop low and out of the wind without constraining the hips and having the knees hit the chest— or forcing the knees to swing outward to avoid contact. If it is a frame built for triathlon or time trials, it will generally have a steep seat angle (76 to 78 degrees), making the forward seat position easy to accomplish. If not, you may need to get a forward-position seatpost, being careful that such a post does not make your reach to the bars too short or require such a long stem that you will be hanging dangerously far out over the front wheel. Set the fore-aft seat position so that you are not constricted at the hips when your shoulder joint is the same level as your hip joint. You may need to tip the saddle very slightly downward and even perhaps turn it a few degrees from straight ahead to find some more crotch comfort. Speed can be painful.

If you are competing in UCI-sanctioned time trials, your bike will be subject to the UCI's technical rules and will most likely be checked by a race official for compliance. The UCI rules limit how far forward the saddle and handlebars can be positioned, among other things. See section C-4 below for how to ensure that your bike is UCI-compliant.

3. Handlebar height

Measure the handlebar height relative to the saddle height by measuring the vertical distance of the saddle and bar up from the floor (Fig. C.6). How much higher the saddle is than your bar, or vice versa, depends on flexibility, riding style, overall size, and type of riding you prefer.

Aggressive and/or tall riders will prefer to have their saddle 10cm or more higher than the bars. Shorter riders will want proportionately less drop, as will less aggressive riders. Generally,

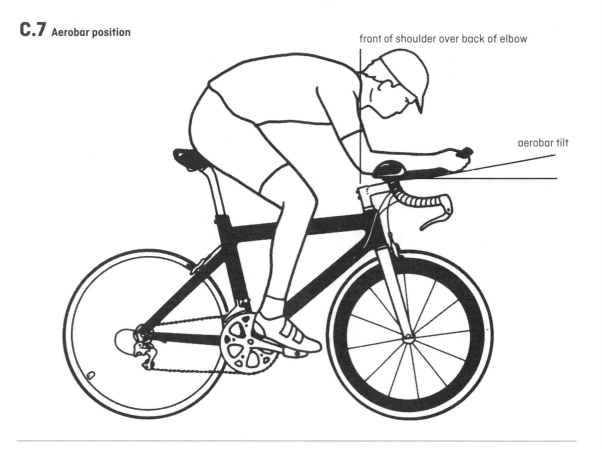

front of shoulder over back of elbow

aerobar tilt

people beginning at road riding will like their bars high and can lower them as they gain flexibility and become more comfortable with the bike.

If in doubt, start with 4cm of drop and vary it from there. The higher the bar, the more weight is carried on your butt, and the more wind resistance you can expect. Change the bar height by raising or lowering the stem (Chapter 11), or by switching stems and/or bars.

Again, threadless headsets allow only limited stem-height adjustment without substitution of a differently angled stem.

For optimal aerodynamic positioning for time trials and draft-prohibited triathlons on flat or rolling terrain, you will want your aerobar elbow pads low enough to get your back close to parallel with the ground (Fig. C.7). This will make significant aerodynamic difference, but it may take a while to get used to it, so you should work the handlebar height down gradually. Also, you

may find such a low position impossible to maintain for an Ironman distance or other long event.

4. Setting handlebar reach

The reach from the saddle to the handlebar is also dependent on personal preference. Aggressive riders will want a more stretched position than will casual riders. This length is subjective, and I usually need to look at the rider on the bike to get a feel for how to make him or her comfortable and efficient.

A useful starting place is to drop a plumb line from the back of your elbow with your arms bent in a comfortable riding position. This plane determined by your elbows and the plumb line should be 2 to 4cm horizontally ahead of each knee at the point in the pedal stroke when the crankarm is horizontal and forward (Fig. C.6). The idea is to select a position you find comfortable and efficient; listen to what your body wants.

C.8 UCI technical rules diagram

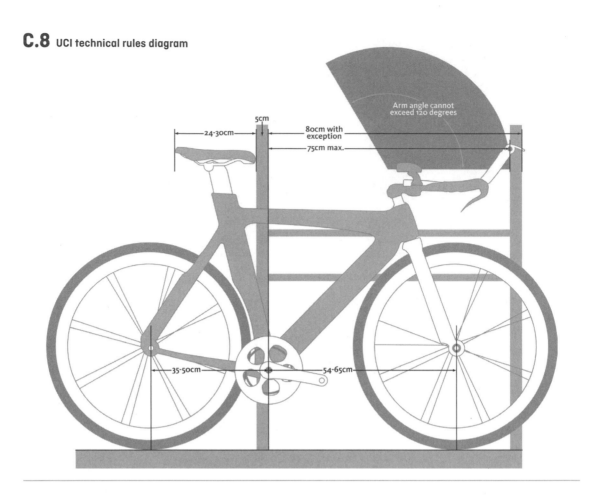

Vary the saddle-to-bar distance by changing stem length (Chapter 11), not by changing the seat fore-aft position, which is based on pedaling efficiency (step 2 above).

On aerobars, set the reach so that a plumb bob from your ear comes out over the crook of your elbow (Fig. C.7), or with the front of your shoulder over the back of your elbow. This will position your upper arms to be angled slightly forward. Again, consult section C-4 below if you will be racing this bike in UCI-sanctioned time trials.

NOTE: *There is no single formula for determining handlebar reach and height. Using the all-too-common method of placing your elbow against the saddle and seeing if your fingertips reach the handlebar is close to useless. Similarly, the oft-suggested method of seeing whether the handlebar obscures your vision of the front hub is not worth the brief time it takes to look, since it is so dependent on elbow bend and front end geometry. Another method involving dropping a plumb bob from the rider's nose is dependent on the handlebar height and elbow bend and thus does not lend itself to a proscribed relationship for all riders.*

5. Other settings for aero handlebars

The elbow pads should be positioned for comfort, except in the case of racing in time trials and draft-prohibited triathlons on flat or rolling terrain, in which case they should be placed close to each other—no more than knee-width apart.

The farther forward the pads are from your elbows, the more leverage you will have smashing the pads against your forearms. You will be more comfortable with the pads farther back, but many riders feel that more power is attained with the pads midway between the elbow and the wrist.

Narrow elbows can make a big difference in aerodynamic efficiency. Wind tunnels often show that having the elbows as narrow as possible is most efficient, but not always; sometimes knee-width apart is fastest. But if you find it hard to breathe well, to pull hard, or to handle the bike well with narrowly spaced elbow pads, move them out until you can.

The tilt of the aerobar is a matter of personal preference. Wind tunnel tests have shown that many different angles appear to be equally efficient aerodynamically. Start with a moderate up-angle to the bar, perhaps 5 or 10 degrees (Fig. C.7).

C-4

POSITIONING A TIME TRIAL BIKE FOR UCI RULE COMPLIANCE

Figure C.8 is a visual representation of the UCI technical rules that must be followed when setting up a bike for a UCI-sanctioned time trial. UCI commissaires at a UCI race inspect every rider's bike before each time trial for saddle and handlebar position. After weighing the bike to ensure compliance with the UCI-mandated minimum bike weight of 6.8 kilograms (15 pounds), a commissaire sets the bike against a jig that has two vertical, 5cm-wide standards whose adjacent edges are 75cm apart, as in Figure C.8. The commissaire lines up the center of the bottom bracket with the forward leading edge of the rear vertical standard.

UCI rule 1.3.013 states that "the peak of the saddle shall be a minimum of 5cm to the rear of a vertical plane passing through the bottom bracket spindle." So, if the nose of the saddle overlaps the trailing edge of the rear vertical member shown in Figure C.8, the bike violates UCI rule 1.3.013 (see rules sidebar). If the tip of the

handlebar (often defined as the center of rotation of the bar-end shift lever) overlaps the trailing edge of the forward vertical member shown in Figure C.8, indicating that it is over 75cm forward of the center of the bottom bracket, it violates UCI rule 1.3.023 (see rules sidebar). And if the distance from the bottom bracket to the plane of the front hub (a.k.a. the "front center dimension;" it is shown in Fig. C.8) exceeds 65cm (this would generally only be an issue with a very large bike), the bike is out of compliance with rule 1.3.016 (see rules sidebar).

If the tip of your saddle is ahead of the bottom bracket, you cannot race the bike unless you move it back or get a shorter saddle (at least 24mm long). However, if the tip of your saddle is between zero and 5cm behind the center of the bottom bracket (it comes out over the rear vertical member of the jig shown in Fig. C.8), you may be able to qualify for the morphological exception permitting you to ride with this setup. To do so, you must demonstrate while sitting on the bike in front of the commissaires who just rejected your bike for non-compliance that a plumb bob dropped from the front of your knee does not come out ahead of the pedal spindle.

It is worth establishing this ahead of time if you know your saddle falls within this 5cm range. Notice that the plumb bob moves back if you drop your heel. Also check whether one knee is farther back than the other and see to it that the commissaire checks with the plumb bob on that knee.

If the tip of your aerobars (or the center of the pivot of your shift lever; the interpretation of "the extremity of the handlebar" varies from country to country and commissaire to commissaire) is more than 80cm forward horizontally from the center of your bottom bracket, you cannot race the bike without shortening the bar. However, if that distance is between 75 and 80cm

Below is an excerpt of the UCI technical rules. I have listed here the most problematic rules. The full rules can be found at www.uci.ch.

1.3.007 Bicycles and their accessories shall be of a type that is or could be sold for use by anyone practicing cycling as a sport. The use of equipment designed especially for the attainment of a particular performance (record or other) shall be not authorized.

1.3.013 The peak of the saddle shall be a minimum of 5cm to the rear of a vertical plane passing through the bottom bracket spindle (1).

(1) The distances mentioned in footnote (1) to articles 1.3.013 and 1.3.016 above may be reduced where that is necessary for morphological reasons. By morphological reasons should be understood everything to do with the size and limb length of the rider.

Any rider who, for these reasons, considers that he needs to use a bicycle of lesser dimensions than those given shall inform the commissaires' panel to that effect when presenting his license. In that case, the panel may conduct the following test. Using a plumb-line, they shall check to see whether, when pedaling, the point of the rider's knee when at its foremost position passes beyond a vertical line passing through the pedal spindle [see Fig. C.6; the line touching the front of the knee must pass through the center of the pedal spindle or behind it].

1.3.014 The saddle support shall be horizontal. The length of the saddle shall be 24cm minimum and 30cm maximum.

1.3.016 The distance between the vertical passing through the bottom bracket spindle and the front wheel spindle shall be between 54cm minimum and 65cm maximum [see Fig. C.8].

1.3.018 In order to be granted approval wheels must have passed a rupture test as prescribed by the UCI in a laboratory approved by the UCI.

1.3.019 b) Weight The weight of the bicycle cannot be less than 6.8 kilograms.

1.3.020 c) Configuration For road competitions other than time trials and for cyclo-cross competitions, the frame of the bicycle shall be of a traditional pattern, i.e. built around a main triangle. It shall be constructed of straight or tapered tubular elements.

1.3.021 For road time trials and for track competitions, the elements of the bicycle frame, including the bottom bracket shell, shall fit within a template of the "triangular form" defined in article 1.3.020.

1.3.023 For road time trial competitions and for the following track competitions: individual and team pursuit, kilometer and 500m, an extension may be added to the steering system. The distance between the vertical line passing through the bottom bracket axle and the extremity of the handlebar may not exceed 75cm [see Fig. C.8], with the other limits set in article 1.3.022 (b, c, d) remaining unchanged. A support for the elbows or forearms is permitted (see diagram "Structure (1B)").

For road time trial competitions, controls or levers fixed to the handlebar extension may extend beyond the 75cm limit as long as they do not constitute a change of use, particularly that of providing an alternative hand position beyond the 75cm mark.

For the track and road competitions covered by the first paragraph, the distance of 75cm may be increased to 80cm to the extent that this is required for morphological reasons; "morphological reasons" should be taken as meaning anything regarding the size or length of the rider's body parts. A rider who, for this reason, considers that he needs to make use of a distance between 75 and 80cm must inform the commissaires' panel at the moment that he presents his license. In such cases the commissaires' panel may carry out the following test: ensuring that the angle between the forearm and upper arm does not exceed 120° when the rider is in a racing position.

[Ed. note: The UCI's accompanying "Structure 1B" diagram also indicates that the entire handlebar must be below the top of the saddle.]

1.3.024 Any device, added or blended into the structure, that is destined to decrease, or which has the effect of decreasing, resistance to air penetration or artificially to accelerate propulsion, such as a protective screen, fuselage form of fairing or the like, shall be prohibited.

A fuselage form shall be defined as an extension or streamlining of a section. This shall be tolerated as long as the ratio between the length L and the diameter D does not exceed 3.

A fairing shall be defined as the use or adaptation of a component of the bicycle in such a fashion that it encloses a moving part of the bicycle such as the wheels or the chainset. Therefore it should be possible to pass a rigid card (like a credit card) between the fixed structure and the moving part.

(it comes out over the forward vertical member of the jig shown in Fig. C.8), you may be able to race the bike as is if you qualify for the morphological exception. To qualify, you must demonstrate in front of the commissaires that when you are sitting on it in your riding position that the bend in your elbows is not more open than 120 degrees. This should also be checked ahead of time, if you know that your shifter pivot comes out between 75 and 80cm forward of the bottom bracket. Notice that you can reduce your elbow angle if you slide forward on the saddle and/or rotate your pelvis forward and flatten your back.

If the commissaires check your bike's front center dimension (which they seldom do) and you know it is a bit over 65cm, practice turning the front wheel slightly while holding the bike so that it measures 65cm without the commissaires noticing the slight twist you're giving the front wheel.

The commissaires generally are interested in you being able to race in the event and are not wishing to create trauma and hassles. They want you to pass the inspection, so make their job easier by understanding the rules and what you need to do for you and your bike to comply with the measurement standards. Remember that the rules can dictate the structure of the bike, but they cannot dictate how you have to sit on the bike, so if you know how to sit on it to pass, then do that if asked to.

adjustable cup the non-drive-side cup in the bottom bracket. This cup is removed for maintenance of the bottom bracket spindle and bearings, and it adjusts the bearings. The term is sometimes applied to the top headset cup as well.

Aheadset a style of headset that allows the use of a fork with a threadless steering tube. Also called a "threadless headset." The name is a trademark of Dia-Compe and Cane Creek.

Allen key (or Allen wrench or hex key) a hexagonal wrench that fits inside a hexagonal hole in the head of a bolt.

anchor bolt (cable anchor bolt, cable-fixing bolt) a bolt securing a cable to a component.

axle the shaft about which a part turns, usually on bearings or bushings.

axle overlock dimension the length of a hub axle from dropout to dropout, referring to the distance from locknut face to locknut face.

ball bearings a set of balls, generally made out of steel or ceramic, rolling in a track to allow a shaft to spin inside a cylindrical part. May also refer to the individual balls.

barrel adjuster a threaded cable stop that allows for fine adjustment of cable tension. Barrel adjusters are commonly found on rear derailleurs, shifters, and brake levers.

BB (see "bottom bracket").

bearing (see "ball bearing").

bearing cone a conical part with a bearing race around its circumference. The cone presses the ball bearings against the bearing race inside the bearing cup.

bearing cup a polished, dish-shaped surface inside of which ball bearings roll. The bearings roll on the outside of a bearing cone that presses them into their track inside the bearing cup.

bearing race the track or surface the bearings roll on. It can be inside a cup, on the outside of a cone, or inside a cartridge bearing.

binder bolt a bolt clamping a seatpost in a frame, a bar end to a handlebar, a handlebar inside a stem, or a threadless steering tube inside a stem clamp.

bonk (1) v. to run out of fuel for the (human) body so that the ability to continue further strenuous activity is impaired. (2) n. the state of having such low blood sugar from insufficient intake of calories that the ability to perform vigorous activity is impaired.

bottom bracket (or BB) the assembly that allows the crank to rotate. Generally the traditional bottom bracket assembly includes bearings, an axle (or spindle), a fixed cup, an adjustable cup, and a lockring.

bottom bracket drop the vertical distance between the center of the bottom bracket and a horizontal line passing through the wheel-hub centers. Drop is equal to the wheel radius minus the bottom bracket height.

bottom bracket shell the cylindrical housing at the bottom of a bicycle frame through which the bottom bracket axle passes.

brake the mechanical device that decelerates or stops the motion of the wheel (and hence of the bicycle and rider) through friction.

451

452

brake boss (or brake post or pivot; or cantilever boss, post, or pivot) a fork- or frame-mounted pivot for a brake arm.

brake bridge the cross-tube between the seatstays to which a rear road brake is bolted.

brake caliper brake part fixed to the frame or fork containing moving parts attached to brake pads that stop or decelerate a wheel.

brake pad (or brake block) a block of rubber or similar material used to slow the bike by creating friction on the rim, hub-mounted disc, or other braking surface.

brake post (see "brake boss").

brake shoe the metal pad holder that holds the brake pad to the brake arm.

braze-on boss a generic term for most metal frame attachments, even those welded or glued on.

brazing a method commonly used to construct steel bicycle frames. Brazing involves the use of brass or silver solder to connect frame tubes and attach various "braze-on" items, including brake bosses, cable guides, bottle bosses, and rack mounts, to the frame.

bushing a metal or plastic sleeve that acts as a simple bearing on pedals, suspension forks, suspension swing arms, and jockey wheels.

butted tubing a common type of frame tubing with varying wall thicknesses. Butted tubing is designed to accommodate high-stress points at the ends of the tube by being thicker there.

cable (or inner wire) wound or braided wire strands used to operate brakes and derailleurs.

cable anchor (see "anchor bolt").

cable anchor bolt (see "anchor bolt").

cable end a cap on the end of a cable to keep it from fraying.

cable-fixing bolt an anchor bolt that attaches cables to brakes or derailleurs.

cable hanger cable stop on a stem, headset, fork, seat binder, or seatstay used to stop the brake-cable housing for a cantilever brake.

cable housing a metal-reinforced exterior sheath through which a cable passes.

cable stop (or cable-housing stop) a fitting on the frame, fork, or stem at which a cable-housing segment terminates.

cage two guiding plates through which the chain travels. Both the front and rear derailleurs have cages. The cage on the rear also holds the jockey pulleys. Also, a water bottle holder.

caliper (see "brake caliper" and "measuring caliper").

Campagnolo Italian bicycle-component company.

Cane Creek American bicycle-component company and originator of the threadless headset. Originally known as Dia-Compe USA.

cantilever boss (see "brake boss").

cantilever brake a cable-operated rim brake consisting of two opposing arms, pivoting on frame- or fork-mounted posts. Pads mounted to each brake arm are pressed against the braking surface of the rim via cable tension from the brake lever.

cantilever pivot (see "brake boss").

cantilever post (see "brake boss").

carbon pad brake pad intended for use on carbon-fiber wheel rims.

cartridge bearings ball bearings encased in a cartridge consisting of steel inner and outer rings, ball retainers, and, sometimes, bearing covers.

cassette the group of cogs that mounts on a freehub.

cassette hub (or freehub) (see "freehub").

chain a series of metal links held together by pins and used to transmit energy from the crank to the rear wheel.

chainline the imaginary line connecting the center of the middle chainring with the middle of the cogset. This line should, in theory, be straight and parallel with the vertical plane passing through the center of the bicycle. The chainline is measured as the distance from the center of the seat tube to the center of the middle chainring of a triple crank or, in the case of a double crank, to the center plane midway between the two chainrings.

chain link a single unit of bicycle chain consisting of four plates with a roller on each end and in the center.

chainring a multiple-tooth sprocket attached to the right crankarm.

chainring-nut tool (or chainring-nut spanner) a tool used to secure the chainring nuts while tightening the chainring bolts.

chainstays frame tube on a bicycle connecting the bottom bracket shell to the rear dropout (and hence to the rear-hub axle).

chain suck the dragging of the chain by the chainring past the release point at the bottom of the chainring. The chain can be dragged upward until it is jammed between the chainring and the chainstay.

chain whip (or chain wrench) a flat piece of steel usually attached to two lengths of chain. This tool is used to remove the rear cogs on a freehub or freewheel.

chase, wild goose (see "goose chase, wild").

Chris King American bicycle component manufacturer.

circlip (or snapring or Jesus clip) a C-shaped snapring that fits in a groove to hold parts together.

clincher rim a rim with a high sidewall and a "hook" facing inward to constrain the bead of a clincher tire.

clincher tire a tire with a "bead" to hook into the rim sides. A separate inner tube is inserted inside the tire.

clip-in pedal (or clipless pedal) a pedal that relies on spring-loaded clips to grip a cleat attached to the bottom of the rider's shoe, without the use of toeclips and straps.

clipless pedal (see "clip-in pedal").

cog a sprocket located on the drive side of the rear hub.

cogset (see "cassette").

cone a threaded conical nut that serves to hold a set of bearings in place and also provides a smooth surface upon which those bearings can roll. Can refer to the conical (or male) member of any cup-and-cone ball-bearing system (see also "bearing cone").

crankarm the lever attached at the bottom bracket spindle and to the pedal used to transmit a rider's energy to the chain.

crankarm anchor bolt (or crank bolt or crankarm-fixing bolt) the bolt attaching the crank to the bottom bracket spindle on a cotterless drive train.

crank bolt (see "crankarm anchor bolt").

crank length the distance measured along the crank between the centerline of the bottom bracket spindle and the centerline of the pedal axle.

crankset the assembly that includes a bottom bracket, two crankarms, chainring set, and accompanying nuts and bolts.

cross three (see "three-cross").

cup a cup-shaped bearing surface that surrounds the bearings in a bottom bracket, headset, or hub (see "bearing cup").

derailleur a gear-changing device that allows a rider to move the chain from one cog or chainring to another while the chain is in motion.

derailleur hanger a metal extension of the right rear dropout through which the rear derailleur is mounted to the frame.

diamond frame the traditional bicycle frame.

disc brake a brake that stops the bike by squeezing brake pads attached to a caliper mounted to the frame or fork against a circular disc attached to the wheel.

dish a difference in spoke tension on the two sides of the rear wheel adjusted such that the rim is centered in the frame or fork.

dishing centering the rim by adjusting spoke tension in a wheel.

dishing tool a tool to check the centering of a rim on a wheel.

double a two-chainring drivetrain setup (as opposed to a three-chainring, or "triple," one).

Double Tap an integrated road brake/shift lever manufactured by SRAM.

down tube the frame tube that connects the head tube and bottom bracket shell together.

drivetrain the crankarms, chainrings, bottom bracket, front derailleur, chain, rear derailleur, and freewheel (or cassette).

drop (1) the vertical distance between the center of the bottom bracket and a horizontal line passing through the wheel-hub centers (see also "bottom bracket drop"). (2) the difference in height between two parts. (3) a terrain discontinuity you may or may not want to ride off of. (4) something not to do with your tools.

dropouts the slots in the fork and rear triangle where the wheel axles attach.

DT (a.k.a. DT Swiss) manufacturer of spokes, other bicycle components, and tools.

dual-pivot sidepull brake a sidepull brake whose arms pivot at two points rather than one.

dust cap a protective cap keeping dirt out of a part.

elastomer a urethane spring sometimes used in suspension forks and rear shocks. Also called an "MCU."

Ergopower an integrated road brake/shift lever manufactured by Campagnolo.

expander bolt a bolt that, when tightened, pulls a wedge up inside or alongside the part into which the bolt is anchored to provide outward pressure and secure said part inside a hollow surface. Expander bolts are found inside quill stems and some handlebar-end plugs and handlebar-end shifters.

expander wedge a part threaded onto an expander bolt and usually used to secure a quill stem inside the fork steering tube or handlebar-end plugs or handlebar-end shifter inside a handlebar. An expander wedge is threaded down its center axis to accept the expander bolt and is either cylindrical in shape and truncated along an inclined plane or conical in shape and truncated parallel to its base.

ferrule a cap for the end of cable housing.

fixed cup the nonadjustable cup of the bottom bracket located on the drive side of the bottom bracket.

flange the largest diameter of the hub where the spoke heads are anchored.

fork the part that attaches the front wheel to the frame.

fork crown the cross-piece connecting the fork legs to the steering tube.

fork ends (see "dropouts").

fork rake (or rake) the perpendicular offset distance of the front axle from an imaginary extension of the steering-tube centerline (see "steering axis"). Also called "wheel offset" or simply "offset."

fork tips (see "dropouts").

frame the central structure of a bicycle to which all of the parts are attached.

freehub a rear hub that has a built-in freewheel mechanism to which the rear cogs are attached.

freewheel the mechanism through which the rear cogs are attached to the rear wheel on a derailleur bicycle. The freewheel is locked to the hub when turned in the forward direction, but it is free to spin backward independently of the hub's movement, thus allowing a rider to stop pedaling and coast as the bicycle is moving forward.

friction shifter a traditional (nonindexed) shifter attached to the frame or handlebar. Cable tension is maintained by a combination of friction washers and bolts.

front triangle (or main triangle) the head tube, top tube, down tube, and seat tube of a bike frame.

FSA acronym for Full Speed Ahead, a component manufacturer.

girl's bike (see "step-through frame").

goose chase, wild (see "wild goose chase").

granny ring the lowest gear on the bike in which the chain is on the inner (of three) front chainring and the largest rear cog.

Grip Shift a trademarked twist shifter from the SRAM Corporation that is integrated with the handlebar grip of a bike. The rider shifts gears by twisting the grip (see also "twist shifter").

handlebar the curved tube, connected to the fork through the stem, that the rider grips in order to turn the fork and thus steer the bicycle. The brake levers and shift levers are attached to it.

head angle the acute angle formed by the centerline of the head tube and the horizontal.

headset the bearing system consisting of a number of separate cylindrical parts installed into the head tube and onto the fork steering tube that secure the fork and allow it to spin and swivel in the frame.

headset cup (see "bearing cup").

headset top cap (see "top cap").

head tube the front tube of the frame through which the steering tube of the fork passes. The head tube is attached to the top tube and down tube and contains the headset.

hex key (see "Allen key").

hub the central part of a wheel to which the spokes are anchored and through which the wheel axle passes.

hub brake a disc, drum, or coaster brake that stops the wheel with friction applied to a braking surface attached to the hub.

hydraulic brake a type of brake that uses oil pressure to move the brake pads against the braking surface.

index shifter a shifter that clicks into fixed positions as it moves the derailleur from gear to gear.

inner wire (see "cable").

integrated headset a headset in which the bearing seats are integrated into the head tube (rather than requiring separate headset cups) and the bearings are completely concealed inside of the head tube.

Jesus clip (see "circlip").

jockey wheel (or jockey pulley) a circular, cog-shaped pulley attached to the rear derailleur that is used to guide, apply tension to, and laterally move the chain from rear cog to rear cog.

link a pivoting steel hook on a V-brake arm that the cable-guide "noodle" hooks into (see also "chain link").

locknut a nut that serves to hold the bearing adjustment in a headset, hub, or pedal, usually by jamming against another nut.

lockring a large, thin, circular locknut. On a bottom bracket, the outer ring that tightens the adjustable cup against the face of the bottom bracket shell. On a freehub, the lockring holds the cogs on.

lock washer a notched or toothed washer that serves to hold surrounding nuts and washers in position.

master link a detachable link that holds the chain together. The master link can be opened by hand without a chain tool.

Mavic French bicycle-component company.

measuring caliper tool for measuring the outside dimensions of an object or the inside dimensions of a tube or hollow object by means of movable jaws.

Mektronic Mavic electronic rear-derailleur system.

mixte frame (see "step-through frame").

mounting bolt a bolt that mounts a part to a frame, fork, or component (see also "pivot bolt").

needle bearing steel cylindrical cartridge with rod-shaped rollers arranged coaxially around the inside walls.

nipple a thin nut designed to receive the end of a spoke and seat it in a hole in a rim.

noodle curved cable-guide pipe on a V-brake arm that stops the cable housing and directs the cable to the cable anchor bolt on the opposite arm.

outer wire (see "cable housing").

outer wire stop (see "cable stop").

Park Tool bicycle tool manufacturer.

pedal platform the foot pushes on to propel the bicycle.

pedal overlap the overlapping of the toe with the front wheel while pedaling.

Pedro's bicycle tool and lubricant company.

pin spanner a V-shaped wrench with two tip-end pins to fit into holes in a lockring; often used for tightening the adjustable cup of the bottom bracket or other lockrings.

pivot a pin about which a part rotates through a bearing or bushing. Found on brakes and derailleurs.

pivot bolt a bolt on which a brake or derailleur part pivots.

preload (bearings) to adjust the bearings to rotated freely without end play in the axle. This allows them to turn most freely once loaded.

Presta valve thin, metal tire valve that uses a locking nut to prevent air from escaping out of the inner tube or tire.

quick-release (1) the tightening lever and shaft used to attach a wheel to the fork or rear dropouts without using axle nuts. (2) a quick-opening lever and shaft pinching the seatpost inside the seat tube, in lieu of a wrench-operated bolt. (3) a quick cable release on a brake. (4) a fixing mechanism that can be quickly opened and closed, as on a brake cable or wheel axle. (5) any anchor bolt that can be quickly opened and closed by a lever.

quill the vertical tube of a stem for a threaded headset system that inserts into the fork steering tube. It has an expander wedge and bolt inside to secure the stem to the steering tube.

quill pedal a pedal with a cage supporting the foot on only the top side, and whose cage plate is a single continuous piece that curves up to a point at the outboard end of the pedal to protect the side of the foot from being scraped on the road (Fig. 9.1). This type of pedal is meant to be used with a toeclip. The cage offset toward the top and curved upward at the outer end also serves to increase pedaling clearance when the rider leans the bike over when riding around a corner, as well as eliminating the excess weight of cage plates extending downward where they would never be used because of the toeclip on the top. A quill pedal will generally also have a tab on its trailing cage plate so that the rider can flip the pedal upright with the toe of the shoe in order to slide the foot into the toeclip.

race a circular track on which bearings roll freely.

rear triangle the rear part of the bicycle frame, including the seatstays, the chainstays, and the seat tube.

rebound damping the diminishing of speed of return of a spring by hydraulic or mechanical means.

rim the outer hoop of a wheel to which the tire is attached.

Ritchey an American bicycle-component and bicycle company.

rotor the brake disc attached to a wheel hub for a disc brake system.

Rotor a bicycle-component company.

saddle (or seat) a platform made of leather and/or plastic upon which the rider sits.

saddle rails the two metal rods supporting the saddle; the seatpost is clamped to these rods.

Schrader valve a high-pressure air valve with a spring-loaded air-release pin inside. Schrader valves are found on some bicycle inner tubes and air-sprung suspension forks as well as on adjustable rear shocks and automobile tires and tubes.

sealed bearing a bearing enclosed in an attempt to keep contaminants out (see also "cartridge bearings").

seat (see "saddle").

seat angle the acute angle formed by the centerline of the seat tube and the horizontal.

seatpost the tube (inserted into the frame) that supports and secures the saddle.

seatstay a frame tube on a bicycle connecting the seat tube or the rear shock to the rear dropout (and hence to the rear-hub axle).

seat tube the frame tube to which the seatpost (and, usually, the cranks) are attached.

sew-up tire (see "tubular tire").

shim a thin element inserted between two parts to ensure that they are the proper distance apart. On bicycles, a shim is usually a thin washer and can be used to space a disc-brake caliper away from the frame or fork or to space a bottom bracket cup away from the frame's bottom bracket shell.

Shimano Japanese bicycle-component company and maker of Dura-Ace and Ultegra component lines as well as SPD (pedals) and STI (shifting system).

sidepull cantilever brake (see "V-brake").

skewer (1) a long rod. (2) a hub quick-release. (3) a shaft passing through a stack of elastomer bumpers in a suspension fork.

Slime tire sealant consisting of chopped fibers in a liquid medium that can be injected inside a tire or inner tube to flow to and fill small air leaks.

snapring (see "circlip").

socket a cylindrical tool with a square hole in one end to mount onto a socket-wrench handle and with hexagonal walls inside the opposing end to grip a bolt head or nut to turn it.

socket wrench a cylindrical wrench handle with a ratcheting square head extending at right angles to the handle onto which sockets or other wrench bits for turning bolts or nuts are installed. Also called "socket-wrench handle" or simply "wrench handle."

spacer on a bicycle, generally a thick washer, cylindrical in shape, intended to space two parts farther apart. Spacers can be found between the headset and the stem and between the stem and the top cap on a threadless steering tube, or between the upper bearing cup and the top nut on a threaded steering tube. Spacers may also be used to space a bottom bracket cup away from the frame's bottom bracket shell.

spanner a wrench, in primarily British parlance.

spider a star-shaped piece of metal that connects the right crankarm to the chainrings.

spline one of a set of longitudinal grooves and ridges designed to interlock two mechanical parts together.

spokes metal rods that connect the hub to the rim of a wheel.

spring an elastic contrivance that, when compressed, returns to its original shape by virtue of its elasticity. In bicycle-suspension applications, the spring used is normally either an elastic polymer cylinder, a coil of steel or titanium wire, or compressed air.

spring preload the initial loading of a spring so that part of its compression range is taken up prior to impact.

sprocket a circular, multiple-toothed piece of metal that engages a chain (see also "cog" and "chainring").

SRAM American bicycle-component company. Owner of Sachs, Avid, and Truvativ bicycle-component companies.

standover clearance (or standover height) the distance between the top tube of the bike and the rider's crotch when standing over the bicycle.

star nut (or star-fangled nut) a pronged nut that is forced down into the steering tube and that anchors the headset top-cap bolt to adjust a threadless headset.

steering axis the imaginary line about which the fork rotates.

steering tube the vertical tube on a fork that is attached to the fork crown and that fits inside the head tube and swivels within it by means of the headset bearings. A steering tube can be threaded or threadless, meaning that the top headset cup can either screw onto the steering tube or slide onto it, and the stem can either (1) insert inside the steering tube and clamp with an expander wedge (threaded) or (2) clamp around the steering tube (threadless). Also called "steerer" or "fork steerer."

stem connection element between the fork steering tube and the handlebar. An archaic word for stem is "gooseneck."

stem length the distance between the center of the steering tube and the center of the handlebar measured along the top of the stem.

step-through frame (or women's frame or girl's bike or mixte frame) a bicycle frame with a steeply up-angled top tube connecting the bottom of the seat tube to the top of the head tube. The frame design is intended to provide ease of stepping over the frame and ample standover clearance.

STI (Shimano Total Integration) an integrated brake/shift lever manufactured by Shimano.

straddle cable short segment of cable connecting two brake arms together.

straddle-cable holder (see "yoke").

threaded headset a headset whose top bearing cup and top nut above it screw onto a threaded steering tube.

threadless headset (see "Aheadset").

three-cross a pattern used by wheel builders that calls for each spoke to cross three others in its path from the hub to the rim.

thumb shifter a thumb-operated shift lever attached on top of the handlebars.

tire bead the edge of the tire that seats down inside the rim. The bead's diameter is held fixed to established standards by means of a strong, stretch- and tear-resistant material—usually either steel or Kevlar. These strands alone are also referred to as the "bead."

tire lever a tool to pry a tire off the rim.

tire sealant (see "Slime").

toe overlap (or toeclip overlap) (see "pedal overlap").

top cap the round top part of a headset that has a bolt passing through it that screws into the star nut to apply downward pressure on the stem to properly load and adjust the headset bearings on a threadless steering tube.

top tube the frame tube that connects the seat tube to the head tube.

torque the rotational analogue of force. Torque is a vector quantity whose magnitude is the length of the radius from the center of rotation out to the point at which the force is applied, multiplied by the magnitude of the force directed perpendicular to the radius. On bicycles, we are primarily interested in (1) the tightening torque applied to a fastener (this value can be measured with a torque wrench—see Appendix E) and (2) the torque applied by the rider on the pedals to propel the rear wheel and hence the bicycle.

torque wrench a socket-wrench handle with a graduated scale and an indicator to show how much torque is being applied as a bolt is being tightened.

Torx wrench a tool with a star-shaped end that fits in the star-shaped hole in the head of a Torx bolt.

triple a term used to describe the three-chainring combination attached to the right crankarm.

Truvativ a bicycle-component manufacturer. Subsidiary of SRAM.

tub, tubular (see "tubular tire").

tubular rim a rim for a tubular tire. A tubular rim is generally double-walled and concave on top. It is devoid of hook sides that constrain the beads of a clincher tire.

tubular tire a tire without a bead. The tube is surrounded by the tire casing, which is sewed together on the bottom. A layer of cotton tape is usually glued over the stitching, and rim cement is applied to the base tape and the rim to bond the tire to the rim (also called "tubular," "sew-up," and in British parlance, "tub").

twist shifter a cable-pulling derailleur control handle surrounding the handlebar adjacent to the hand grip; it is twisted forward or back to cause the derailleur to shift (see also "Grip Shift").

V-brake (sidepull cantilever brake) a cable-operated cantilever rim brake consisting of two vertical brake arms that can pivot on frame- or fork-mounted bolts when pulled together by a horizontal cable. A brake pad is affixed to each arm, and there is a cable link and cable-guide pipe on one arm and a cable anchor on the opposite arm.

vise a device, usually mounted on a workbench, with opposed jaws operated by a screw to hold objects.

Visc Grip brand name for adjustable clamping pliers.

Vise Whip an adjustable tool made by Pedro's for holding a cog when removing a casette; replaces a chain whip. Designed by the author of this book.

welding the process of melting two metal surfaces in order to join them.

wheel base the horizontal distance between the two wheel axles.

wheel dish (or wheel dishing) (see "dish" or "dishing").

wheel-dishing tool (see "dishing tool").

wheel-retention tabs integral or separate fixtures at the fork ends designed to prevent the front wheel from falling out if the hub quick-release lever of axle and nuts are loose.

wheelset a pair of wheels for the front and rear of the bicycle.

wild goose chase (see "chase, wild goose").

women's frame (see "step-through frame").

wrench a tool having jaws, a shaped insert, or a socket to grip the head of a bolt or a nut to turn it. In British parlance, a "spanner."

yoke the part on a cantilever or V-brake attaching the brake cable to the straddle cable.

Zinn author of this book; not to be confused with Zen.

APPENDIX E
TORQUE TABLE

One of the single biggest sources of mechanical problems (and breakage) is the overtightening or undertightening of fasteners, particularly on lightweight equipment. It is great to have a "feel" for what is tight enough, but many people either do not have this sense or overestimate their sensitivity to it; "feel" should only supplement torque measurement. With some parts, particularly today's superlight stems and handlebars, it is important to tighten them to their exact torque specification to prevent them from breaking while riding, which would result in an immediate and terrifying loss of control. Even experienced mechanics, with their sense of feel well developed from years of practice, sometimes overtighten the small bolts on lightweight stems.

That said, I do recommend that you try to develop that feel for bolt tightness. For small bolts, choke up on the wrench or hex key so you can tell more easily how hard you are twisting it. (Torque = Force × Radius; when you choke up on the wrench you reduce the radius at which you apply force, so that you have to apply more force to get the same torque on the bolt. That in turn makes you aware of the effort it takes.) When you think the bolt is tight enough, check the tightness with a torque wrench to calibrate your sense of feel.

There is also a danger in undertightening fasteners. The handlebar in an undertightened stem clamp can come loose and twist, or an undertightened brake cable can pull free when you yank hard on the brakes. Also, an undertightened bolt suffers more fatigue during use than one that is preloaded.

The standard method for calculating a torque specification is to load the fastener to 80 percent of its yield strength. This method works on rigid joints. High bolt preload ensures that the fastener is always in tension to prevent metal fatigue in the fastener. However, many bike parts are not rigid, and high torques can overcompress or crush components. This is especially important when you are using parts of different brands, eras, or materials together, since a stem manufacturer's torque specification for a handlebar clamp may not have anticipated that a carbon handlebar would be used; what works for an aluminum bar can crush the carbon one. There is no springback in a rigid joint, but if parts flex under tightening (a handlebar is a good example), that flex may provide the preload that the bolt needs at a considerably lower torque setting than if it were bolted through solid steel parts.

Modern torque wrenches usually have a knob at the base of the handle to pull tension on an internal spring. You set the desired torque by twisting the knob and reading the torque setting on a vernier scale or against a line in an indicator window. When the set torque is reached, the head of the wrench snaps over to the side. An older style of torque wrench, called a beam wrench, has a needle arm parallel to the wrench shaft that moves across a scale. When using either type of torque wrench, hold it at the handle and pull smoothly.

You actually need two torque wrenches for working on bikes. Big ones cannot measure torques accurately for small bolts. Small ones

461

have a limited capacity and cannot tighten a bottom bracket or crank bolt sufficiently.

Using a torque wrench is not a guarantee against a screwup; it simply reduces the chances of one. First, you must make sure that the torque setting you use is the one recommended for the bolt you are tightening. The torque table in this appendix includes a lot of bolts, but it obviously cannot include all bolts from all manufacturers, so if you can consult an owner's manual or find the correct torque on the manufacturer's website, do so. Also, manufacturers often adjust torque specifications following changes in design or materials, so always check the instruction manual for torque settings when possible, even if the bolt is listed in this chart.

Second, lubrication of the bolt, temperature, and a variety of other variables will affect torque readings as well. Bicycle specifications generally assume that the bolt threads have received lubrication or threadlock compound (which provides lubrication before it dries), but that the underside of the bolt head is dry. Lubricating under the bolt head allows the bolt to turn farther at the same torque setting than the same bolt without lubrication under the head, and it thus increases the tension on the bolt.

Third, the torque reading will depend on whether the bolt is turning or you are starting a stationary bolt into motion, since its coefficient of static friction will be higher than its coefficient of dynamic (sliding) friction. If you try to determine the torque of a bolt by checking the torque required to unscrew the bolt, you will have estimated a higher torque than the actual one, particularly if the bolt has been in place for some time and has corrosion or dirt around it. This may be the best you can do in some circumstances, but proceed with caution.

Fourth, the reading on the torque wrench assumes that the head is centered over the bolt;

the torque reading will be low if you have a radius multiplying the torque. For example, measuring tightening torque on a pedal axle (if not using a 6mm hex key in the hex hole in the axle end) requires a "crow's foot" 15mm open-end wrench attachment on a torque wrench. If extending straight out, the crow's foot creates an offset between the axle centerline and the tool head centerline, which multiplies the torque setting displayed on the wrench handle (i.e., it will make the wrench—the radius—effectively longer). The decimal by which you must multiply the torque reading on the wrench to determine the actual torque applied to the bolt will usually be imprinted on the crow's foot. You must use this torque multiplication factor if you have the crow's foot extending straight out from the torque wrench. If you keep the crow's foot at 90 degrees from the torque wrench, provided the crow's foot is short relative to the length of the torque wrench, you can use the torque settings as is on the wrench (since the hypotenuse and the long side of the right triangle will be close to the same length).

Finally, torque wrenches are not 100 percent accurate, and their accuracy changes over time. Most torque wrenches can be calibrated; automotive parts stores and some hardware stores can do this for you. Ultimately, your feel and common sense are also necessary to ensure safety.

It will be worth your while to review §ii-19 (in Chapter 2) to help you develop a feel for bolt tightness. Whether or not you have "the touch," a torque wrench is a wonderful thing, as long as you know how tight the bolt is supposed to be.

Listed below are tightening torque recommendations from many component manufacturers. Where there is only a maximum torque listed, you can assume the minimum torque should be about 80 to 90 percent of that number.

Most torques are for steel bolts; where possible, aluminum and titanium bolts are described as such in the table. Note that it is particularly important to use a copper-filled lubricant like Finish Line Ti-Prep on titanium bolts to prevent them from binding and galling; the same goes for installing any bolt into threads in a titanium component or bike frame.

CONVERSION BETWEEN UNITS

Table E.1 is in inch-pounds (in-lbs), foot-pounds (ft-lbs), and Newton-meters (N-m) (the latter being the one I find easiest to use, since the numbers tend to be nice, round one- or two-digit numbers). Divide in-lbs settings by 12 to convert to foot-pounds (ft-lbs). Multiply in-lbs settings by 0.113 to convert to Newton-meters (N-m). Multiply kilogram force-centimeter (kgf-cm) settings by 0.098 to convert to Newton-meters (N-m).

BOLT SIZES

- **M5 bolts** are 5mm in diameter and take a 3mm or 4mm hex key (except on derailleurs, which often take a 5mm hex key or an 8mm box wrench).
- **M6 bolts** are 6mm in diameter and generally take a 5mm hex key.
- **M7 bolts** are 7mm in diameter and generally take a 6mm hex key.
- **M8 bolts** are 8mm in diameter and generally take a 6mm hex key.
- **M10 bolts** are 10mm in diameter and on bikes will likely take a 5mm or 6mm hex key (rear derailleur mounting bolt).

The designation M in front of the bolt size number means millimeters and refers to the bolt shaft size, not to the hex key that turns it; an M5 bolt is 5mm in diameter, an M6 is 6mm, and so on, but there may be no relation to the wrench size. For example, an M5 bolt usually takes a 4mm hex key (or in the case of a hex-head style, an 8mm box-end or socket wrench), but M5 bolts on bicycles often accept non standard wrench sizes. M5 bolts attach bottle cages to the frame, and while some accept a 4mm hex key, many have a rounded "cap" head and take a 3mm hex key or sometimes a 5mm hex key. The M5 bolts that clamp a front derailleur around the seat tube or that anchor the cable on a front or rear derailleur also take a nonstandard hex key size, namely a 5mm. And M5 disc-brake rotor bolts often take a Torx T25 key. Conversely, the big single pinch bolts found on old stems usually take only a 6mm hex key, but they may be M6, M7, or even M8 bolts.

Generally, tightness can be classified in four levels:

1. Snug (10–30 in-lbs, or 1–3 N-m): small setscrews, bearing preload bolts (as on threadless headset top caps) and screws going into plastic parts need to be snug.

2. Firmly tightened (30–80 in-lbs, or 3–9 N-m): this refers to small M5 bolts, like shoe cleat bolts, brake- and derailleur-cable anchor bolts, derailleur band clamp bolts, small stem faceplate, or stem steerer clamp bolts. Some M5 and M6 seatpost clamp bolts need to be firmly tightened.

3. Tight (80–240 in-lbs, or 9–27 N-m): wheel axle nuts, old-style single-bolt stem bolts (M6, M7, M8), and some seatpost binder bolts and seatpost saddle clamp bolts need to be tight.

4. Really tight (280–600 in-lbs, or 31–68 N-m): crankarm bolts, pedal axles, cassette lockring bolts, and bottom bracket cups are large parts that need to be really tight. The load on them is so high that they will creak or loosen if they are not tight enough.

TABLE E.1 — Road Bike Fastener Torque Table*

*Unit conversion factors are at end of table

GENERAL TORQUE SPEC FOR STEEL BOLT THREADED INTO AN ALUMINUM PART	IN-LBS	N-M	FT-LBS
M5 bolt	60	7	5
M6 bolt	120	14	10
M6 bolt clamping a carbon part	100	11	8
M7 bolt	180	20	15
M8 bolt	220	25	18

BOTTOM BRACKETS AND CRANKS	IN-LBS		N-M		FT-LBS	
	MIN	MAX	MIN	MAX	MIN	MAX
Bontrager square-taper (Sport) crankarm fixing bolts, M8	320	372	36	42	27	31
Bontrager ISIS (Select, Race) crankarm fixing bolts, M15		480		55		40
Bontrager GXP (Race Lite, Race X Lite) crankarm fixing bolt		480		55		40
Bontrager chainring fixing bolt, steel	70	95	8	11	6	8
Bontrager chainring fixing bolt, aluminum	50	70	6	8	4	6
Campagnolo/Fulcrum Power Torque and Ultra-Torque crank fixing bolt	372	531	42	60	31	44
Campagnolo/Fulcrum Power Torque and Ultra-Torque external bearing cups		310		35		26
Campagnolo square-taper crankarm fixing bolt (M8 steel)	283	336	32	38	24	28
Campagnolo square-taper cartridge bottom bracket cups		619		70	0	52
Campagnolo chainring fixing bolt		71		8		6
Easton external bearing cups	301	363	34	41	25	30
Easton left crankarm fixing pinch bolts (M5)		105		12		9
Easton chainring fixing bolt		40		4.5		3.3
FSA M8 steel crankarm fixing bolt	304	347	34	39	25	29
FSA M12 steel crankarm fixing bolt	434	521	49	59	36	43
FSA M14 steel crankarm fixing bolt	434	521	49	59	36	43
FSA M14 aluminum crankarm fixing bolt	391	434	44	49	33	36
FSA M15 steel crankarm fixing bolt	434	521	49	59	36	43
FSA M15 aluminum crankarm fixing bolt	434	521	49	59	36	51
FSA M18 bearing preload bolt, MegaExo	4	6	0.4	0.7	0.3	0.5
FSA M18 bearing preload bolt, BB90, BB86	6	13	0.7	1.5	0.5	1.1
FSA M5 pinch bolt, split aluminum crankarm, MegaExo	106	115	12	13	9	10
FSA M5 pinch bolt, split aluminum crankarm, BB90, BB86	97	133	11	15	8	11
FSA M17 crankarm fixing bolt, carbon crank, BB90, BB86	398	487	45	55	33	41
FSA M18 crankarm fixing bolt, carbon crank, MegaExo	398	487	45	55	33	41

TABLE E.1	Road Bike Fastener Torque Table, continued					
BOTTOM BRACKETS AND CRANKS, CONT.	**IN-LBS**		**N-M**		**FT-LBS**	
	MIN	**MAX**	**MIN**	**MAX**	**MIN**	**MAX**
FSA BB30 crankarm fixing bolt	345	434	39	49	29	36
FSA steel Allen chainring fixing bolt	80	106	9	12	7	9
FSA aluminum Allen chainring fixing bolt		87		10	0	7
FSA aluminum Torx chainring fixing bolt		104		11	0	9
FSA aluminum cartridge bottom bracket cups	347	434	39	49	29	36
FSA MegaExo bottom bracket cups	345	434	39	49	29	36
Race Face X-Type crankarm fixing bolt	363	602	41	68	30	50
Shimano square-taper crankarm fixing bolt (M8 steel)	305	391	34	44	25	33
Shimano crankarm fixing bolt (OctaLink/Hollowtech)	305	435	35	50	25	36
Shimano left crankarm bearing preload cap (Hollowtech 2)	4	6	0.5	0.7	0.3	0.5
Shimano Hollowtech 2 left crankarm fixing pinch bolts (M5)	88	132	12	14	7	11
Shimano chainring fixing bolt, steel	70	95	8	11	6	8
Shimano square/OctaLink cartridge bottom bracket cups	435	608	50	70	36	51
Shimano integrated-spindle (Hollowtech 2) bearing cups	305	435	35	50	25	36
Shimano loose-ball-bearing bottom bracket fixed cup	609	695	69	79	51	58
Shimano loose-ball-bearing bottom bracket lockring	609	695	69	79	51	58
SRAM/Truvativ steel chainring bolts	106	124	12	14	9	10
SRAM/Truvativ aluminum chainring bolts	71	80	8	9	6	7
SRAM/Truvativ GXP left crank bolt	416	478	47	54	35	40
SRAM/Truvativ GXP self extractor cup (16mm hex key)	106	133	12	15	9	11
SRAM/Truvativ GXP external bearing cups	301	363	34	41	25	30
SRAM/Truvativ Howitzer ISIS external bearing cups	301	363	34	41	25	30
Trek tandem eccentric	75	100	8	11	6	8
Truvativ ISIS cartridge bearing cups	301	363	34	41	25	30
Truvativ M8 crank bolts, square taper	336	372	38	42	28	31
Truvativ M12 crank bolts, ISIS	381	425	43	48	32	35
Truvativ M15 crank bolts, ISIS	381	425	43	48	32	35
Truvativ self-extractor cup, ISIS or square taper (10mm hex key)	106	133	12	15	9	11
Zinn Zinn-tegrated left crank bolt	400	450	45	51	33	38
Zinn Zinn-tegrated self extractor cup (10mm hex key)	106	133	12	15	9	11
Zinn Zinn-tegrated external bearing cups	301	363	34	41	25	30

Continues >>

TABLE E.1   Road Bike Fastener Torque Table, continued

BRAKES	IN-LBS		N-M		FT-LBS	
	MIN	MAX	MIN	MAX	MIN	MAX
SIDEPULL CALIPERS						
Caliper fixing bolt onto Trek, LeMond, or Klein carbon seatstays	55	60	6	7	5	5
Campagnolo caliper fixing bolt (to frame or fork)		88		10		7
Campagnolo cable-fixing bolt		44		5		4
Campagnolo brake-shoe fixing bolt		71		8		6
FSA caliper fixing bolt (to frame or fork)	70	86	8	10	6	7
FSA cable-fixing bolt	53	69	6	8	4	6
FSA brake-shoe fixing bolt	44	60	5	7	4	5
Shimano caliper fixing bolt (to frame or fork)	70	86	8	10	6	7
Shimano cable-fixing bolt	53	69	6	8	4	6
Shimano brake-shoe fixing bolt	44	60	5	7	4	5
SRAM caliper fixing bolt (to frame or fork)	70	86	8	10	6	7
SRAM cable-fixing bolt	53	69	6	8	4	6
SRAM brake-shoe fixing bolt	44	60	5	7	4	5
CANTILEVERS AND V-BRAKES						
Avid brake shoe fixing bolt	26	44	3	5	2.2	3.7
Avid cantilever brake mounting bolt	44	61	5	7	3.7	5.1
Avid straddle wire carrier cable pinch bolts	26	44	3	5	2.2	3.7
Avid split-clamp flat handlebar lever dual mounting bolts	28	36	3	4	2	3
brake arm mounting bolt, M6	40	60	5	7	3	5
brake cable fixing bolt, M5	50	70	6	8	4	6
cantilever brake pad fixing bolt	70	78	8	9	6	7
flat handlebar brake lever clamp bolt, M6	50	70	6	8	4	6
flat handlebar brake lever clamp — slotted screw	22	26	2.5	2.9	1.8	2.2
Shimano V-brake leverage adjuster bolt	9	13	1.0	1.5	0.8	1.1
straddle cable yoke fixing nut	35	43	4	5	3	4
Trek, Fisher, Klein spec for brake arm mounting bolt, M6	70	85	8	10	6	7
V-brake pad fixing nut	50	70	6	8	4	6
DISC BRAKES						
TRP cable anchor bolt	44	61	5	7	3.7	5.1
TRP caliper bolts	53	69	6	8	4.4	5.9
TRP disc-brake adapters	53	69	6	8	4.4	5.9
TRP hydraulic hose compression nut	35	53	4	6	2.9	4.4
TRP rotor bolts	35	53	4	6	2.9	4.4
TRP straddle cable yoke pinch bolt	22	26	2.5	3	1.8	2.2
TRP Parabox hydraulic master cylinder clamp	53	69	6	8	4.4	5.9
TRP Parabox master cylinder setup pin	7	8	0.8	1	0.6	0.7

TABLE E.1	Road Bike Fastener Torque Table, continued					
DERAILLEURS AND SHIFTERS	**IN-LBS**		**N-M**		**FT-LBS**	
	MIN	**MAX**	**MIN**	**MAX**	**MIN**	**MAX**
barrel adjuster mounting screw to frame down tube shifter boss	13	18	1.5	2.0	1.1	1.5
Campagnolo braze-on type front-derailleur mounting bolt, M5		62		7		5
Campagnolo front-derailleur band clamp bolt, M5		44		5		4
Campagnolo front-derailleur cable fixing bolt, M5		44		5		4
Campagnolo rear-derailleur cable fixing bolt, M5		53		6		4
Campagnolo rear-derailleur mounting bolt, M10		133		15		11
Shimano front-derailleur cable fixing bolt, M5	44	60	5	7	4	5
Shimano front-derailleur band clamp bolt, M5	44	60	5	7	4	5
Shimano braze-on type front-derailleur mounting bolt, M5	44	60	5	7	4	5
Shimano rear-derailleur cable fixing bolt, M5	35	52	4	6	3	4
Shimano rear-derailleur mounting bolt, M10	70	86	8	10	6	7
Shimano rear-derailleur pulley center bolts, M5	27	34	3	4	2	3
SRAM front-derailleur cable fixing bolt, M5	35	45	4	5	3	4
SRAM braze-on type front-derailleur mounting bolt, M5	35	44	4	5	3	4
SRAM bolt-on front-derailleur adaptor band for braze-on type, M5	27	35	3	4	2	3
SRAM front-derailleur band clamp bolt, M5	44	62	5	7	4	5
SRAM rear-derailleur cable fixing bolt, M5	35	45	4	5	3	4
SRAM rear-derailleur mounting bolt, M10	70	85	8	10	6	7
SRAM rear-derailleur pulley center bolts, M5		22		3		2
Trek spec for front-derailleur clamp bolt, M5	25	35	3	4	2	3
DUAL CONTROL LEVER						
Campagnolo Ergopower fixing bolt (to handlebar)		88		10		7
Shimano STI fixing bolt (to handlebar)	35	43	4	5	3	4
Shimano Dura-Ace 7900 STI lever fixing bolt (to handlebar)	53	71	6	8	4	6
Shimano Dura-Ace 7900 lever nameplate screw		2		0.2		0.1
SRAM DoubleTap fixing bolt (to handlebar)	53	70	6	8	4	6
HUBS, CASSETTES, AND QUICK-RELEASE SKEWERS	**IN-LBS**		**N-M**		**FT-LBS**	
	MIN	**MAX**	**MIN**	**MAX**	**MIN**	**MAX**
bolt-on steel skewer		65		7		5
bolt-on titanium skewer		85		10		7

Continues >>

TABLE E.1   Road Bike Fastener Torque Table, continued

HUBS, CASSETTES, AND QUICK-RELEASE SKEWERS, CONT.	IN-LBS		N-M		FT-LBS	
	MIN	MAX	MIN	MAX	MIN	MAX
Campagnolo cassette cog lock ring, steel		442		50		37
Campagnolo cassette cog lock ring, aluminum, for 11-speed cogs		354		40		29
locknut on quick-release axle	87	217	10	25	7	18
Mavic cassette cog lock ring		354		40		30
nutted front hub		180		20		15
nutted rear hub		300		34		25
Shimano freehub cassette body fixing bolt	305	434	35	50	25	36
Shimano cassette cog lock ring	261	434	30	50	22	36
Shimano hub quick-release lever closing	79	104	8.8	11.8	7	9
Shimano fixed-gear locknut	250	300	28	34	21	25
Shimano single-speed freewheel	250	300	28	34	21	25
Trek spec for front axle nuts (bolt-on hubs)	180	240	20	27	15	20
Trek spec for rear axle nuts (bolt-on hubs)	240	300	27	34	20	25

MISCELLANEOUS	IN-LBS		N-M		FT-LBS	
	MIN	MAX	MIN	MAX	MIN	MAX
Aheadset bearing preload, M6 top cap bolt		22		2		2
fender to frame bolts, M5	50	60	6	7	4	5
Trek spec for rack or fender strut bolts to frame or fork	20	25	2	3	2	2
Trek spec for rear-derailleur hanger bolt	50	70	6	8	4	6
Trek spec for water bottle cage bolts, M5	20	25	2	3	2	2
water bottle cage bolts, M5	25	35	3	4	2	3

PEDALS AND SHOES	IN-LBS		N-M		FT-LBS	
	MIN	MAX	MIN	MAX	MIN	MAX
Campagnolo pedal axle to crankarm		354		40		29
Crank Bros. pedal axle to crankarm	301	363	34	41	25	30
Crank Bros. shoe cleat fixing bolt, M5	35	44	4	5	3	4
pedal axle into FSA carbon crankarm	257	301	29	34	21	25
pedal axle into Truvativ ISIS or square taper crankarm	186	301	21	34	15	25
pedal axle into Truvativ GXP crankarm	416	478	47	54	35	40
Shimano pedal axle to crankarm	307		35		26	
Shimano shoe cleat fixing bolt, M5	44	51	5	6	4	4
Shimano shoe spike, M5		34		4		3
Speedplay Frog spindle nut	35	40	4	5	3	3
Time pedal axle to crankarm		310		35		26
toeclips to pedals, M5	25	45	3	5	2	4
Trek spec for pedal axle to crankarm	350	380	40	43	29	32

TABLE E.1	Road Bike Fastener Torque Table, continued					
SEATPOSTS AND SEAT BINDERS	IN-LBS		N-M		FT-LBS	
	MIN	**MAX**	**MIN**	**MAX**	**MIN**	**MAX**
Bontrager seatpost with bolt across seat-post head	120	130	14	15	10	11
Bontrager Select seatpost, M6 bolt		120		14		10
Bontrager Race, Race Lite, Race X Lite, Race XXX Lite, M6 bolt		150		17		13
Campagnolo seatpost single saddle rail clamp bolt	159	195	18	22	13	16
Campagnolo seatpost binder pinch bolt, carbon seatpost		88		10		7
Deda saddle rail clamp bolt		195		22		16
Easton EC90, EC70, EA70 saddle rail clamp bolts		100		11		8
Easton EC90 Zero, EC70 Zero saddle rail clamp bolts		55		6		5
FSA M5 seatpost rail clamp bolts (steel)		78		9		6
FSA M6 seatpost rail clamp bolts (steel)		106		12		9
FSA M7 seatpost rail clamp bolts (steel)		146		17		12
ITM K-Sword M6 (for GWS system)	88	97	10	11	7	8
ITM K-Sword Special Bolts (saddle clamp bolt)	88	97	10	11	7	8
ITM Forged Lite All series (alu, alu-carbon, carbon) M7	62	71	7	8	5	6
Oval Concepts M6 saddle rail clamp bolts		133		15		11
Ritchey single saddle rail clamp bolt: Comp, Old Pro, M8		400		45		33
Ritchey dual saddle rail clamp bolt: WCS, New Pro, M6		165		19		14
seat collar bolt, M5	40	60	5	7	3	5
seat collar bolt, M6	60	80	7	9	5	7
seatpost saddle rail clamp bolt, M8	175	345	20	39	15	29
seat-tube clamp binder bolt, M6	105	140	12	16	9	12
Selcof saddle rail clamp bolt, M6		71		8		6
Selcof saddle rail clamp bolt, M8		177		20		15
Thomson saddle rail clamp bolt, M6		60		7		5
Trek Madone seat mast cap clamp bolt	44	62	5	7	4	5
Trek Madone saddle rail clamp bolt on seat mast cap	124	142	14	16	10	12
Trek spec for single bolt using 6mm hex key	150	250	17	28	13	21
Trek spec for single bolt using 5mm hex key	80	125	10	14	7	10

Continues >>

TABLE E.1 Road Bike Fastener Torque Table, continued

SEATPOSTS AND SEAT BINDERS, CONT.	IN-LBS		N-M		FT-LBS	
	MIN	MAX	MIN	MAX	MIN	MAX
Trek spec for double bolt using 4mm hex key	45	60	5	7	4	5
Trek spec for binder bolt for aluminum seatpost	85	125	10	14	7	10
Trek spec for binder bolt for carbon-fiber seatpost	65	80	7	9	5	7
Truvativ M6 two-bolt	53	62	6	7	4	5
Truvativ M8 single bolt	195	212	22	24	16	18
two-piece steel seatpost saddle rail clamp bolt	175	345	20	39	15	29
two-piece seat binder bolt, M6	35	60	4	7	3	5

STEMS	IN-LBS		N-M		FT-LBS	
	MIN	MAX	MIN	MAX	MIN	MAX
3T M5 bolts (front clamp, steerer clamp)		44		5		4
3T M6 bolts (single steerer clamp)		130		15		11
3T M6 bolts (two-bolt front clamp plate)		130		15		11
3T M8 bolts (single handlebar clamp)		220		25		18
NOTE: 3T specs also apply to Cinelli stems through 2006						
bar end for flat handlebar M6 clamp bolt	120	140	14	16	10	12
Bontrager M8 steerer tube clamp bolts		200		23		17
Bontrager M7 stem bolts (6mm hex key)		150		17		13
Bontrager M6 stem bolts (5mm hex key)		120		14		10
Bontrager M5 stem bolts (4mm hex key)	46	60	5	7	4	5
Cinelli M5 steel bolts (4mm hex key)		62		7		5
Cinelli M6 steel bolts (5mm hex key)		80		9		7
Deda M5 steel bolts (bar clamp, steerer clamp)		71		8		6
Deda M5 titanium bolts (bar clamp, steerer clamp)		70		8		6
Deda M6 bolts (bar clamp, steerer clamp)		85		10		7
Deda M6 old-model hidden steerer clamp bolt		130		15		11
Deda M8 bolts (quill expander)		85		10		7
Dimension two-bolt face plate bar clamp, M6	80	90	9	10	7	8
Dimension two-bolt steerer tube clamp, M6	80	90	9	10	7	8
Dimension one-bolt handlebar clamp, M8 bolt	205	240	23	27	17	20
Easton M5 bar & steerer clamp bolts	44	70	5	8	4	6
FSA M5 titanium bolts (use Ti prep!)		68		8		6
FSA M5 steel steerer clamp bolts (4mm hex key)		53		6		4
FSA M6 steel bolts		104		12		9
FSA M8 steel bolts		156		18		13

TABLE E.1	**Road Bike Fastener Torque Table, continued**					
	IN-LBS		N-M		FT-LBS	
STEMS, CONT.	MIN	MAX	MIN	MAX	MIN	MAX
ITM M8 bolts (single-bolt clamp or expander)	150	160	17	18	13	13
ITM M7 bolts	106	120	12	14	9	10
ITM M6 bolts (bar clamp, steerer clamp)	88	105	10	12	7	9
ITM M5 bolts (bar clamp, steerer clamp) 2 front bolts	62	70	7	8	5	6
ITM M5 bolts (bar clamp) 4 front bolts	35	44	4	5	3	4
ITM aluminum M6 bolts in magnesium stem	44	53	5	6	4	4
LOOK stems, all bolts		44		5		4
Modolo M5 handlebar clamp bolt (4mm hex key)		62		7		5
Modolo M5 steerer clamp bolt (4mm hex key)		71		8		6
Oval Concepts titanium M5 faceplate bolts for alloy bars		84		10		7
Oval Concepts titanium M5 faceplate bolts for carbon bars		49		6		4
Oval Concepts M6 faceplate bolts for carbon bars		53		6		4
Oval Concepts titanium M6 clamp bolts for alloy steerers		84		10		7
Oval Concepts titanium M6 clamp bolts for carbon steerers		53		6		4
Oval Concepts M6 clamp bolts for alloy steerers		93		11		8
Oval Concepts M6 clamp bolts for carbon steerers		58		7		5
PRO M5 handlebar clamp bolt (4mm hex key)		35		4		3
PRO M5 steerer clamp bolt (4mm hex key)		44		5		4
Profile M6 steel bolts (5mm hex key)		80		9		7
RaceFace M5 steel bolts (4mm hex key)	61	79	7	9	5	7
Ritchey WCS M5 faceplate bolts for alloy bars	26	44	3	5	2	4
Ritchey WCS M5 faceplate bolts for carbon bars		35		4		3
Ritchey M5 steerer clamp bolts (4mm hex key)		44		5		4
Ritchey WCS M6 clamp bolts for alloy steerers	52	86	6	10	4	7
Ritchey WCS M6 clamp bolts for carbon steerers		78		9		7
Salsa SUL two-bolt face plate bar clamp, M6	120	130	14	15	10	11
Salsa one-bolt handlebar clamp, M6 bolt		140		16		12
Salsa one-bolt steerer tube clamp, M6 bolt	100	110	11	12	8	9

Continues >>

TABLE E.1	Road Bike Fastener Torque Table, continued					
STEMS, CONT.	**IN-LBS**		**N-M**		**FT-LBS**	
	MIN	**MAX**	**MIN**	**MAX**	**MIN**	**MAX**
single stem handlebar clamping bolt, M8	145	220	16	25	12	18
Syntace M5 steel bolts (4mm hex key)		53		6		4
Thomson Elite, X2, X4 steerer clamp bolts, M5		48		5		4
Thomson Elite handlebar clamp bolts, M5		48		5		4
Thomson X4 handlebar clamp bolts, M5		35		4		3
Trek spec for handlebar clamp bolts on forged stems	150	180	17	20	13	15
Trek spec for handlebar clamp bolts on welded stems	100	120	11	14	8	10
Trek spec for handlebar clamp bolts with carbon handlebar		100		11		8
Trek spec for stem angle adjustment bolt	150	170	17	20	13	14
Trek spec for stem expander bolt	175	260	20	29	15	22
Trek spec for stem steerer clamp bolts	100	120	11	14	8	10
Trek spec for tandem stoker stem extension adjustment bolt	120	140	14	16	10	12
Trek spec for tandem stoker stem seatpost clamp bolt	100	120	11	14	8	10
Truvativ M5 bolts-handlebar	40	50	5	6	3	4
Truvativ M6 bolts-handlebar	50	60	6	7	4	5
Truvativ M6 bolts-steerer	70	80	8	9	6	7
Truvativ M7 bolts-steerer	110	120	12	14	9	10
wedge expander bolt for quill stems, M8	140	175	16	20	12	15
HANDLEBARS						
Bontrager aluminum handlebar, M7 stem face plate bolt		150		17		13
Bontrager aluminum handlebar, M6 stem face plate bolt		120		14		10
Bontrager aluminum or carbon handlebar, M5 stem face plate bolt		60		7		5
Bontrager carbon handlebar, M6 stem face plate bolt		100		11		8
AERO HANDLEBARS						
3T Bio Arms handlebar clamp/armrest bolts, M8		177		20		15
3T extension clamp bolts, all models, M6		133		15		11
3T New Ahero armrest offset arm mounting bolt, M5		80		9		7
3T New Ahero armrest bolts, M6		106		12		9
3T Sub-8 and Mini Sub-8 armrest bolts, with riser, M5		71		8		6
3T Sub-8 and Mini Sub-8 armrest bolts, without riser, M5		44		5		4

TABLE E.1	Road Bike Fastener Torque Table, continued					
AERO HANDLEBARS, CONT.	**IN-LBS**		**N-M**		**FT-LBS**	
	MIN	MAX	MIN	MAX	MIN	MAX
Oval Concepts A900 extension clamp bolts, M5		51		6		4
Oval Concepts A900 base bar clamp bolts, M5		51		6		4
Oval Concepts A700 extension clamp bolts, M6		84		10		7
Oval Concepts SLAM extension clamp bolts, M5		71		8		6
Oval Concepts SLAM handlebar clamp bolts, M5		71		8		6
Oval Concepts armrest bolts, carbon bars, M5		62		7		5
Oval Concepts armrest bolts, aluminum bars, M5		88		10		7
VisionTech armrest bolts, M5		70		8		6
VisionTech extension clamp bolts, M6		88		10		7
Trek spec for armrest bolts, M5		45		5		4
Trek spec for extension clamp bolts, M6		60		7		5

CONVERSION BETWEEN UNITS

- Divide in-lb settings by 12 to convert to foot-pounds (ft-lbs).
- Multiply in-lb settings by 0.113 to convert to Newton-meters (N-m).
- Multiply kgf-cm settings by 0.098 to convert to Newton-meters (N-m).

BIBLIOGRAPHY

Barnett, John. *Barnett's Manual: Analysis and Procedures for Bicycle Mechanics.* Brattleboro, VT: Vitesse Press, 1989, VeloPress, 1996.

Brandt, Jobst. *The Bicycle Wheel.* Menlo Park, CA: Avocet, 1988.

Compton, Tom. www.analyticcycling.com, 1998.

Dushan, Allan. *Surviving the Trail.* Tumbleweed Films, 1993.

Editors of Bicycling and Mountain Bike magazines. *Bicycling Magazine's Complete Guide to Bicycle Maintenance and Repair.* Emmaus, PA: Rodale Press, 1994.

Muir, John and Gregg, Tosh. *How to Keep Your Volkswagen Alive: A Manual of Step-by-Step Procedures for the Complete Idiot.* Santa Fe, NM: John Muir Publications, 1969, 1994.

Pirsig, Robert. *Zen and the Art of Motorcycle Maintenance.* New York, NY: William Morrow & Co., 1974.

Schraner, Gerd. *The Art of Wheelbuilding.* Denver, CO: Buonpane, 1999.

Taylor, Garrett. *Bicycle Wheelbuilding 101, a Video Lesson in the Art of Wheelbuilding.* Westwood, MA: Rexadog, 1994.

Van der Plas, Robert. *The Bicycle Repair Book.* Mill Valley, CA: Bicycle Books, 1993.

Zinn, Lennard. *Zinn & the Art of Mountain Bike Maintenance, 5th Edition.* Boulder, CO: VeloPress, 2010.

Zinn, Lennard. *Zinn & the Art of Triathlon Bikes.* Boulder, CO: VeloPress, 2007.

Zinn, Lennard. *Mountain Bike Performance Handbook.* Osceola, WI: MBI, 1998.

INDEX

477

ILLUSTRATION INDEX

487

ABOUT THE AUTHOR

Lennard Zinn is a bike racer, frame builder, and technical writer. He grew up cycling, skiing, whitewater rafting, and kayaking as well as tinkering with mechanical devices in Los Alamos, New Mexico. After receiving his physics degree from Colorado College, he became a member of the U.S. Olympic Development (road) Cycling Team. He went on to work in Tom Ritchey's frame-building shop and has been producing custom road, triathlon, and mountain frames, as well as custom cranks and stems, at Zinn Cycles since 1982.

Zinn began writing for *VeloNews* in 1989 and is the now the senior technical writer for *Velo* magazine and a columnist for velonews.com. Other books by Zinn are *Zinn & the Art of Mountain Bike Maintenance* (VeloPress, 5th ed. 2010), *Zinn & the Art of Triathlon Bikes* (VeloPress, 2007), *Zinn's Cycling Primer* (VeloPress, 2004), *Mountain Bike Performance Handbook* (MBI, 1998), and *Mountain Bike Owner's Manual* (VeloPress, 1998).

ABOUT THE ILLUSTRATORS

A former mechanic and bike racer, **Todd Telander** devotes most of his time these days to artistic endeavors. In addition to drawing bike parts, he paints and draws wildlife and landscapes for publishers, museums, design companies, and individuals. You can see more examples of his work on his web site, www.toddtelander.com.

Mike Reisel is a graphic designer who spends most of his time art directing magazines, riding his bike, and ignoring the pleas to lubricate his drivetrain.